PRACTICAL EXPORT TRADE FINANCE

PRACTICAL EXPORT TRADE FINANCE

Eugene W. Perry

Dow Jones-Irwin
Homewood, Illinois 60430

Dow Jones-Irwin is a trademark of Dow Jones & Company, Inc.
All rights reserved. No part of this publication may be
reproduced, stored in a retrieval system, or transmitted,
in any form or by any means, electronic, mechanical,
photocopying, recording, or otherwise, without the prior
written permission of the publisher.

This publication is designed to provide accurate and
authoritative information in regard to the subject matter
covered. It is sold with the understanding that the
publisher is not engaged in rendering legal, accounting, or
other professional service. If legal advice or other expert
assistance is required, the services of a competent
professional person should be sought.

*From a Declaration of Principles jointly adopted by a Committee
of the American Bar Association and a Committee of Publishers.*

Project editor: *Ethel Shiell*
Production manager: *Ann Cassady*
Compositor: *TCSystems, Inc.*
Typeface: *11/13 Times Roman*
Printer: *Arcata Graphics/Kingsport*

Library of Congress Cataloging-in-Publication Data
Perry Eugene W.
    Practical export trade finance / Eugene W. Perry.
      p.   cm.
    Includes index.
    ISBN 1-55623-018-4
    1. Export credit—United States. 2. United States—Manufacturers.
3. Foreign trade promotion—United States. 4. Competition,
International. I. Title.
HG3754.5.U6P47   1989
658.8'48—dc19   88–34264
                                      CIP

Printed in the United States of America

1 2 3 4 5 6 7 8 9 0 K 6 5 4 3 2 1 0 9

To my lovely bride, Carol Ann, . . .
for your patience, love, and understanding
during this project.

PREFACE

Competitiveness has become the trendiest worry around. A number of schemes are floating through Capital Hill: schemes that range from critizing trading partners for unfair trade practices to implementing trade barriers on U.S. imports.

The huge merchandise trade deficit for 1987 was a negative U.S. $171.2 billion (U.S. $156.2 billion in 1986). It is serious and the United States must regain its competitiveness or "Yankee trading" prowess early in the next decade. It is critical to our future.

The cure for this problem can be effected by manufacturers of goods and services. The answer does not lie in the dollar's fall, trade barriers, or relocating plants overseas at the expense of U.S. jobs and standards of living. It lies in good old-fashioned American industrial competitiveness: goods made more efficiently and sold aggressively at the best trade financing package possible. It means getting back to basics by emphasizing competitiveness at the heart of our educational system, and our manufacturers, businesses, and financial institutions. It means taking exports seriously as an integral part of the whole of each company by preparing and organizing oneself for the new world economy. U.S. companies can no longer be dependent on domestic business alone in order to survive to their fullest capabilities.

By way of background, it is important to note that during the 1950s and 1960s, the growth of U.S. companies internationally was staggering in the form of trading goods and services and investing within the international marketplace. A number of factors that favored U.S. economic development converged during the post-World War II period.

- The United States had the capacity to meet a large and growing demand for its products and investments. With the

U.S. dollar being the strongest currency, U.S. investment was not only welcome—it was sought.
- U.S. management skills, technology, and manufacturing efficiency enjoyed a perception of leadership status.
- Conditions were generally stable around the globe. Foreign exchange rates were fixed and inflation was negligible. Markets developed along predictable courses. Government surprises were few.
- Country risks were benign—fostering and encouraging foreign investment.

U.S. company growth overseas was not only inevitable, but seemed unstoppable during this period. However, the seeds of future deterioration had been sown. Many U.S. companies invested abroad and exported to countries haphazardly, without regard to some logical and applicable controls and sufficient thought to long-term strategic objectives and country risks. As a result, their market positions were often tenuous, without sufficient support of efficient manufacturing, selling, credit control, finance, or technical activities, especially as it pertained to country risk analysis.

The events in the 1970s led to a series of major disruptions worldwide that carried into the 1980s. Most notably are the breakdown of the Bretton Woods Agreement and OPEC's arbitrary actions. These set in motion rampant inflation, gyrating exchange rates, high interest rates, and the decline of the value of the U.S. dollar. As a result, social and political pressures in one host country after another began to increase their involvement in the affairs of industry, through nationalization, regulation, and greater direct interaction in commercial activities. These changes were generally unfavorable to all businesses involved in international trade and a number of them clearly put U.S. companies at a particular disadvantage. Our lack of a clear-cut government policy for export trade business and finance did not keep pace with the policies of other nations, especially industrialized nations.

From the post-World War II era, foreign competitors emerged who have successfully challenged America's supremacy in international trade. They have reversed the flow not only in technology, but in trade finance, management techniques, and manufacturing efficiency. These foreign competitors enjoy a level of support from their governments that far exceeds that of U.S. business. Most notable is Japan, with its three-way partnership with government, business, and labor in addition to the structure and role of the Japanese export trade company called the Sogo Shosho.

U.S. industry must be aware of the unceasing competition among nations, the political influences affecting their ability to trade among nations, and the increase of nationalism and its inevitable repercussions. Also, American business should keep up with the effects of fluctuating exchange rates, the International Monetary Fund's (IMF) painstaking negotiations with countries who are unable to pay their interest or principal on debts to other creditors, Organization of Petroleum Exporting Countries (OPEC), export credit insurance availability, and General Agreement on Tariffs and Trade (GATT) with its fragile agreements among trading nations.

Competition is more fierce than ever, but the U.S. can still regain the competitive advantages it once held by instituting or reinstituting a renewed faith in international trade. Choosing the best possible credit terms and trade finance package while assuming a reasonable amount of risk is one sure way of becoming competitive.

Companies in overseas ventures that sell their products domestically and around the world must eliminate specific operations and techniques that limit their competitiveness. For example:

1. Some companies will make sales to certain countries and not to others.
2. A company may differ in the currencies with which it will accept payment.
3. Credit terms may vary from open account to letter of credit to some sort of specialized financing technique, such as forfaiting or countertrade.
4. Some companies will ship direct to foreign customers while others will deal through foreign-based subsidiaries or related companies, purchasing agents, or distributors or a combination of several.

This disparity undermines the effectiveness of their business practices. It is important to realize a common goal—productive and profitable export credit sales. This is accomplished by the way each company organizes and implements its plans and strategies to achieve worldwide profit, cash flow, and market share. Many companies have learned that their ability to offer the best possible competitive export trade finance scheme and credit terms contributes to their success in selling goods and services overseas.

This book is specifically written to provide practical non-theoretical material on export trade financing for the following:

1. Small- to medium-size companies. Exporting is not just for the large multinational corporations. It is also for the small- and medium-size companies with limited resources.
2. Undergraduate and graduate students of international finance.
3. Larger companies and financial institutions with training programs and reference libraries.

This book is intended to give the academic and business community a better understanding of the details and technical aspects pertaining to export trade finance. It deals with many of the complexities and problems of export trade finance. Throughout the book, examples and solutions to problems based on actual business experience are explained and illustrated.

Business people want and need to know more about the detailed practical aspects and procedures of export trade finance. Students need to study it as part of their general business education or to make it their field of specialization.

As you go through each chapter, you will have a better understanding of the different types of export credit terms, the various export trade finance schemes, and how to promote exports while minimizing the risks inherent when selling goods and services to foreign customers.

ACKNOWLEDGMENTS

I have learned writing a book is a stressful, time consuming, and complex process, especially since it was done entirely around my full-time job.

The book would be incomplete without thanking a few people. First and foremost is my good friend Dr. Alan N. Cook, Director of

Special Projects, Hankamer School of Business, Baylor University, Waco, Texas. His persistence and inspiration made this book possible. Alan had the foresight to know that a book of this context would fill a long-standing and large gap in our educational and business community regarding international trade.

I would be remiss without a sincere thanks to Gerd-Peter Lota, Executive Vice President, Finance Credit and International Business (FCIB), the international subsidiary of the National Association of Credit Management (NACM) Corporation, New York, for his friendship, encouragement, and support with this book.

Special thanks go to the following individuals and their organizations for their invaluable aid and support in editing, correcting, and supplying pertinent information for this book. These individuals and the products and services their firms offer to the international business community are truly professional.

- Francis N. McWilliams, President, The Credit International Associates, Inc., New York.
- Neil Leary, The Philadelphia National Bank, Philadelphia, Pennsylvania.
- Peg Weiland, formerly of the Chase Trade Information Corporation, The Chase Manhattan Bank, N.A., New York.
- Carol R. Cline, President, Global Business Communcations, Inc., Gillette, New Jersey.
- Dr. Hans P. Belcsak, President, S.J. Rundt's & Associates, New York.
- William Redway, Foreign Credit Insurance Association, New York.

I am also grateful to many of my friends who are members of the FCIB and International Credit Executives (ICE) groups. These people are always ready and more than willing to exchange their experiences and offer new ideas regarding international trade.

Last, but not least, Dow Jones-Irwin, who was gracious enough to support and publish this book. I greatly appreciate their cooperation and guidance.

Eugene W. Perry

CONTENTS

CHAPTER 1

CREDIT AND ACCOUNTS RECEIVABLE MANAGEMENT

In a small company, the proprietor or manager usually approves or rejects credit and collects from slow-paying domestic or foreign customers. As the company grows, this function is delegated to a management employee, usually an accountant, but sometimes an office manager. At some point during the growth of the company, the exclusive services of one person (specifically, a credit manager) might be required to manage credit and collections. The bigger and more complex the company, the more employees are needed to assist the credit manager with credit investigations, credit analysis, and collections.

The functions of credit and accounts receivable management have changed dramatically since the 1940s. Then, there was very little concern over the condition of accounts and delinquencies because bankruptcies and past dues were low and accounts receivable turnover was high. Extended credit to companies was not the norm. Therefore, trade accounts receivable (credit sales to nonaffiliated companies) as an asset on the balance sheet was small as a percent in relation to other company assets. It was not until the 1950s that important changes occurred bringing about a period of slower turnover in receivables and a rise in bad debts. According to a March 1985 Credit Research Foundation (CRF) Staff Report, "the seven years from 1955 to 1962, receivables gained $60 billion, or 75 percent, as a result of heavy emphasis on sales/marketing." The trend still continues today.

In the 1960s, credit departments and credit personnel grew. Improved collection techniques reduced the type of results obtained in the 1950s and early 1960s. Credit department functions became more complex and one of their main objectives was to minimize bad debt losses.

In the 1970s, management took a different approach towards the credit management of receivables. They justified increasing trade receivable turnover, known as *days sales outstanding (DSO),* through the credit-risk/sales-reward concept. In order to obtain larger pieces of market share, companies accepted the cost of slower receivable turnover and increased bad debts even though receivables would represent a larger percentage of current assets or more working capital tied up in receivables. However, as companies grew internationally, so did their investment in international trade accounts receivable.

Many U.S. companies simply treated the credit management of foreign receivables as something "foreign" to them during these periods despite their growth internationally. Foreign receivables only represented a small percentage of total receivables and sales for most companies and there was a lack of understanding international credit management principles and practices. If insufficient credit information could not be obtained on overseas accounts or if there was a lack of trust or the risks of uncertainty were too high with the foreign customer and/or its country, then the credit decision or "out" was to request confirmed irrevocable sight letter of credit payment terms. In a seller's market many U.S. exporters could demand these stringent payment terms. In the final analysis, U.S. companies, sales, and especially credit people felt more comfortable requesting letter of credit payment terms than offering extended credit terms to match the needs of the foreign customer or competition. They could not analyze financially the risk of getting paid slow from foreign customers, or worse, risk the possibility of a bad debt write-off. In the United States the Uniform Commercial Code (UCC) gives creditors a security interest in property of debtors. There is no international code between nations for the trading of goods and services. The closest to the UCC, for example, in some countries are Retention of Title clauses exercised in some Western European countries, and the recognition of certain conditions in sales contracts when properly registered with appropriate local government entities overseas. Without a collateralized position, many credit managers felt more comfortable requesting letter of credit payment terms from a foreign customer. Many foreign competitors will not ask for such restrictive payment terms unless the country risks are too high.

Credit people must continually consider their company's overall policies designed to achieve the objectives of the marketing/sales and treasury departments. The credit manager must constantly manage accounts receivable to balance the department between meeting the cash flow needs of the treasury department and the needs of the marketing/sales department. Cash flow isn't generated until the foreign customer's orders are approved, invoiced, and collected. The policies and objectives of each department must be integrated, understood, and set forth in the financial planning process to meet the short-, medium-, and long-term policies and strategies of their company. In addition, how will the credit department be organized to meet the cash flow and sales needs of their companies? Will they be organized to create efficiency in the processing and expediting of customer orders, interacting with marketing/sales, traffic, and accounting personnel? Will the credit department be centralized or decentralized by region, segments, groups, or product lines?

ACCOUNTS RECEIVABLE

Accounts receivable is usually the third classification down on the current asset side of a company's balance sheet, after cash and marketable securities. It can be found on the balance sheet of financial statements as current and noncurrent assets. It represents amounts owed to a company by its customers, arising from the sale of goods and services to them on such credit or payment terms as open account, cash against documents, cash against goods, promissory notes or drafts or bills of exchange, letters of credit, or other payment term arrangements. These sales and credit terms are practically all transacted between companies, domestically and internationally, on a credit or credit sale basis. It is estimated that 90 to 95 percent of all business transactions are completed on some sort of credit terms. That is, credit terms are granted to purchasers of goods and services on such payment terms as 30, 60, or 90 days.

The amount of time foreign customers (foreign debtors or simply customers) have to pay for each shipment or service provided by the exporter (creditor or supplier) varies from one company and industry to the next. The amount of time can range from discount payment terms of 1 percent 10 days, net 30 days, up to 180 days to one year—even longer for capital good suppliers.

The Importance of Managing Receivables

The management of accounts receivables consists of two separate functions—credit management and accounts receivable management. Most companies split these functions into two separate departments to avoid conflicts of interest (depending on the size of the company). A company's external auditors also prefer splitting these into two separate and distinct departments. The credit management function is normally the responsibility of credit personnel. These people are responsible for extending credit and collecting money from customers. Accounts receivable management, normally the responsibility of accounting, is responsible for applying cash received from customers to outstanding invoices or promissory note accounts, making any necessary journal entries, and reconciling accounts.

Trade notes and accounts receivable (explained later) from the credit sale of goods or services made to customers (buyers) are one of the largest assets on the balance sheets of most companies. Tables 1–1 to 1–3 represent a random selection of company receivables in terms of dollars and percentages. It is broken down by:

- Percentage of accounts receivable to current assets and total assets.
- Percentage of inventory to current assets and total assets.
- Percentage of accounts receivable to net sales.

The net accounts receivable and inventory balances vary from one industry or company to the next and/or are effected by economic conditions, company goals, policies, and strategies. The intent in this book is to give the reader an idea of what accounts receivable represents in relationship to other major current assets.

According to a March 1985 staff report from the Credit Research Foundation (CRF), accounts receivable has become the second largest asset on most company balance sheets. This is

TABLE 1–1
Random Selection of Company Receivables, 1985

Company	Net Accounts Receivable			Inventory		
	Percent of Net Sales	Percent of Total Current Assets	Percent of Total Assets	Percent of Net Sales	Percent of Total Current Assets	Percent of Total Assets
Pennzoil	15.0%	58.5%	10.2%	8.2%	31.9%	5.5%
Motorola	14.9	38.5	18.6	14.7	38.0	18.3
GAF	15.0	25.6	12.5	12.8	21.9	10.7
Johnson & Johnson	14.9	33.1	18.8	14.9	33.0	18.7
Exxon	8.2	43.4	10.9	5.2	27.6	6.9
Black & Decker	19.2	38.5	22.9	26.5	53.0	31.6
Gillette	20.7	32.5	20.5	19.5	30.6	19.3
Compaq Computer	16.6	34.9	26.8	15.0	31.6	24.3
Baxter Travenol	39.6	39.5	13.6	44.0	43.8	15.2
Dana	13.4	38.8	20.8	18.8	54.4	29.2
Pfizer	20.2	37.7	18.2	19.9	37.1	18.0

TABLE 1–2
Random Selection of Company Receivables, 1986

Company	Net Accounts Receivable			Inventory		
	Percent of Net Sales	Percent of Total Current Assets	Percent of Total Assets	Percent of Net Sales	Percent of Total Current Assets	Percent of Total Assets
Cooper Industries	16.8%	37.2%	16.9%	25.2%	56.1%	25.5%
Johnson & Johnson	12.2	26.8	14.6	14.4	31.6	17.2
Pennzoil	13.7	28.6	7.2	10.1	21.1	5.3
Gillette	21.6	40.9	24.0	21.4	40.5	23.7
Compaq Computer	18.6	44.8	30.8	13.0	31.3	21.5
Baxter Travenol	20.4	48.3	16.0	19.6	46.3	15.4
SmithKline Beckman	20.5	40.5	18.2	14.2	28.2	12.6
Pfizer	21.5	41.1	18.6	19.9	38.0	17.2
Colgate-Palmolive	11.1	37.3	19.4	12.8	42.9	22.4
AMP	18.4	37.0	19.9	18.2	36.7	19.7
Union Camp	11.5	41.5	8.6	12.9	42.2	9.6

TABLE 1–3
Random Selection of Company Receivables, 1987

Company	Net Accounts Receivable			Inventory		
	Percent of Net Sales	Percent of Total Current Assets	Percent of Total Assets	Percent of Net Sales	Percent of Total Current Assets	Percent of Total Assets
American Brands	11.9%	32.1%	14.8%	18.5%	49.9%	23.1%
Squibb	22.4	27.7	17.4	14.6	18.1	11.3
Motorola	16.4	40.7	20.7	13.6	33.6	17.1
International Paper	12.9	46.1	11.5	11.0	39.4	9.8
Dana	16.6	45.4	24.6	17.5	47.9	25.9
Phillips Petroleum	11.8	44.0	10.5	5.1	18.8	4.5
Pfizer	24.1	28.9	17.1	20.9	25.1	14.9
Parker Hannifin	14.7	36.7	19.4	21.9	54.5	28.8
General Signal	20.6	38.1	23.7	21.4	39.5	24.6
Armco	12.2	30.8	12.9	9.9	24.8	10.4
Pennzoil	17.2	37.3	9.5	9.4	20.4	5.2

because of the expanding use of trade credit, and means that more customer sales are made on credit terms. Because this asset represents a company's investment in the future, senior executives or principals of companies must realize that the receivable investment should be managed by the best qualified and experienced credit people available. This is especially true for those companies that intend to enter the international marketplace, anticipate increased growth from overseas business credit sales, and have a large percentage of their sales in the international marketplace. Also, it is especially applicable when the company has risks and/or slow receivable turnover from international trade credit sales and is still willing to accept risks to maintain or increase market share, profitability, and/or productivity.

Every time a company extends credit to another company, certain risk factors must be taken into account when the investment in receivables is evaluated: the added cost of collection from accounts that will pay slow; bad debt losses on accounts that will never pay; and the cost of carrying accounts receivable and the financial implication of that cost on a company's profitability. The latter can be measured by using the financial concepts of cost of capital and time value of money.

Time is money and the amount of money invested in receivables and the length of time it is invested represent a cost of capital to the company. Money tied up in receivables cannot be used in any other company activity until it is collected. Also, the longer any particular invoice or installment note payment remains uncollected, the more expensive the investment in receivables is and the potential of a bad debt write-off increases.

Domestically, creditors use a number of proven methods to protect themselves against the possibility of a bad debt loss. For example, the creditor can take a collateralized position in personal or business real estate, buildings, or equipment. Each piece of collateral is a lien on certain real property and can be protected under the auspices of the U.S. Uniform Commercial Code within each state. However, no similar law to protect international creditors exists internationally. There can be no assurances a creditor has a valid and enforceable lien on certain property of a debtor because of the lack of such a law among nations. Therefore, without sufficient collateral and evidence the collateral is not encumbered by other creditors, the element of risk widens.

What about country risk? Does it complicate the sale on extended credit terms with no real hard collateral to protect the creditor in the event of default or bankruptcy of the debtor? How does a company protect its receivables against such things as unexpected or unanticipated war, riot, revolution, or foreign exchange fluctuations? How does a company finance the sale of goods to foreign customers when it must extend payment terms beyond 30, 60, or even 90 days to compete or abide by a country's import or foreign exchange regulations? If a company does not use the right credit terms in their international trade, export trade financing program, collection procedures, or export credit insurance protection, that company runs the risk of poor collections or worse, the potential of bad debt write-offs. Each one is vitally important to the success or failure of the exporting company as it pertains to protecting the investment in accounts receivable, sales, and profitability.

Types of Accounts Receivable

Companies, especially multinational organizations, can create two separate types of accounts receivable. One represents credit sales to unaffiliated or independent buyers (third party customers) who have no ownership relationship with the selling company and is often referred to as *trade accounts receivable*. The other represents credit sales to related subsidiaries, joint ventures, branches, or affiliates and is commonly referred to as *intercompany accounts receivable* (intercompany sales). Both must be considered separately because of varying degrees of economic risk.

Trade Accounts Receivable
This documentary evidence of given transactions may be in the form of purchase orders or sales slips signed by the customer, telex or cable orders from customers, shipping documents and/or receipts of goods delivered (proof of delivery—POD) or services provided, and internal invoices by which the amounts involved

were charged. Trade receivables are normally due within one year. On the balance sheet they are classified as a current asset.

Intercompany Accounts Receivable
Represents amounts owed to the company from within its own organization or from companies in which it holds a majority interest (50 percent or more). This would include the sale of goods and services between divisions, segments, branches, wholly owned domestic or foreign companies or subsidiaries/affiliates, and joint ventures. International intercompany accounts receivable are usually managed by a Director or Manager of International Finance, Foreign Exchange Manager, or other treasury service type personnel. Again, intercompany receivables are classified as current or noncurrent assets, depending on their term.

Notes Receivable
This type of accounts receivable is the debts of customers or borrowers acknowledged by them in signed written statements (promissory notes) in which they have agreed to pay certain sums of money under terms and conditions mutually agreed on. Notes receivable can be shown separately from trade accounts receivable when there are a significant portion of them. The reason for this is that in the case of notes connected with installment sales, the maturity of the note is usually longer (one year or more) than it would be for trade accounts receivable. Notes receivable on the balance sheet are classified as a current asset for any installments due within a company's calendar year. Installments due longer than one year are classified as noncurrent assets.

Credit sales to foreign customers can either be denominated in the currency of the exporting host country (local currency billings), the currency of the foreign customer, or a third-country currency.

Accounts Receivable—Other
Other types of receivables in significant amounts are shown separately or by separate specific classifications, in keeping with the accounting convention of making full disclosure of material facts.[1]

For example, loans to officers or employees could be classified as current or noncurrent assets on the balance sheet, depending on their term. Under a rule adopted in 1934 by the membership of the American Institute of Certified Public Accountants: "Notes or accounts receivable due from officers, employees, or affiliated companies must be shown separately and not included under a general heading such as notes receivable or trade accounts receivable."[2]

Accounts Receivable Management

Depending on the organizational structure and reporting lines of companies, the administration of accounts receivable can be an additional function of the credit department. This administration includes cash application, the handling of adjustments and claims, and the policing of cash discounts. Many are responsible for the issuance of credit management reports.

However, as already previously mentioned, most internal auditors of larger companies prefer that some of these functions be delegated to the accounting department rather than the credit department. This is mainly done in order to minimize conflicts of interest between how and when payments from customers are applied to customer accounts and the effect these conflicts could have on customer historical data records, audit trails, and company records. Accounting departments normally prefer control over the function of accounts receivable to minimize problems with monthly reconciliations between accounts receivable and general ledger records. The functions of adjustments, claims, and the policing of cash discounts at specified periods in time do involve the credit function. At this point it is important to mention that the impact of advanced data-processing systems (available in software packages) has greatly improved not only the efficiency and accuracy of cash application and record keeping, but the overall performance of credit management, its personnel, and accounts receivable turnover.

Cash application is a key procedure in the control of accounts receivable. It is the application of customer's remittances (checks/payments) to specific items (invoices, adjustments, credit memos) being paid. Efficient cash application procedures simplify the processing of remittances, the updating of customers' files or records, and provide information to expedite credit decisions. In most small- and some medium-size companies, the credit department is normally responsible for cash application.

CREDIT MANAGEMENT

Ideally, every company would like to sell its goods or services at the best price, on the shortest credit terms, to the best customer risks, and to the best countries resulting in no bad debt losses (account write-offs). In reality, companies do accept risks. Some accept more risk than others because the seller accepts risks in return for the opportunity to earn additional profit, and maintain or increase productivity and market share.

The person(s) or department(s) delegated and charged with the responsibility of extending credit to and collecting from customers on credit is the credit department. This department is usually headed by a credit manager. In actuality, extending credit to foreign customers is, in effect, making a loan to a customer. Goods sold to a customer cost the seller money (time value of money), since valuable working capital, carried at an interest expense, is tied up until each credit sale is collected and turned into cash. The receivable resulting from credit sales also includes an amount of profit on the sale, unless the product is being sold at a loss.

In order to compete in this complex and competitive world of international trade, the credit person delegated the responsibility for international credit must play a role in their company very much different from the role they performed in domestic credit, despite some basic similarities.

A company's credit department can be considered a "policing agency," because it acts as a guardian or protector of a company's investment in accounts receivable. It is the department that sees the end result of the business cycle. That is, from the time an order is placed, processed, manufactured, and delivered to the customer, a whole process transpires. The result is an invoice sent to the customer with other important documents needed by the foreign customer to import the goods which represent the goods ordered.

The international credit department makes credit decisions on customers who request credit by gathering credit, financial, and country information, analyzing it, and setting credit lines or limits on customers to justify and control its extension of credit to customers, and collecting invoices or installment notes at agreed-on maturity dates. Lastly, they coordinate their decisions, goals, and activities with marketing/sales and other departments, enhance customer good will, and formulate and integrate credit policies and procedures with company strategy and the objectives of marketing/sales.

Like domestic credit management, effective and efficient management of international credit sales can play a critical role in the overall international competitive performance of companies. There is little doubt that what really makes or breaks international credit sales to foreign customers are credit terms and the trade financing supporting each sale (with or without government or private support). It only stands to reason that those individuals in the credit department delegated the responsibility for making credit decisions and collecting from foreign accounts can play a critical role in the success or failure of their companies selling goods and services internationally.

Therefore, it is important to properly manage trade accounts receivable, no matter where domiciled in the world. By stating the credit department's mission or "mission statement," a company can:

Develop or create ideas, procedures, and actions; analyze, recommend and execute these ideas, procedures, and actions in a timely manner (after they have been approved by senior management).

Incorporate these ideas, procedures, and actions to improve the company's cash flow value and its financial flexibility over the long term. This will improve the rate of return on the company's investment in accounts receivable.

Specifically, credit department goals should include the following:

1. Past due credit sales (delinquencies) from customers should be minimized.
2. In order to minimize delinquencies and excessive (extended) credit terms (credit terms extended beyond published credit terms), correct credit decisions must be made. Major considerations should be who should get credit in the first place, how much, and under what conditions.

3. There must be a proper assessment of country risk (political, economic, and foreign exchange). Even though credit sales might be to first class or highly rated foreign customers, country conditions might determine whether or not payment is received on due date (maturity). This is especially true when there is unavailability of your billing currency which creates foreign exchange delays.

4. If good credit decisions are made, monthly reserves for bad debts and write-offs will be minimized, thereby reducing charges to operating profit and loss (P&L) statements, thus increasing profit margins.

5. Credit risks can result in slow payments from customers. The added cost of collections and its administrative costs to manage credit risks, must be taken into consideration.

6. Companies should strive to improve or maintain financial ratios, such as receivable turnover, current ratio, quick (acid-test) ratio, and receivable to net sales.

7. It is important to minimize the cost of carrying (cost of capital) accounts receivable and the financial implications of that cost on profitability (time value of money).

8. Small- to medium-size companies who do not have the financial capacity of large companies, may have about as much money tied up in delinquent accounts as it wants to borrow. Receivables can be used for so-called asset-based lending. If a company is highly leveraged, has a high ratio of debt to net worth, and is having difficulty raising funds, a bank may suggest a line of credit against receivables. The bank may lend money on the basis of 75 percent of receivables less than 90 days old, with a deeper discount on older bills (receivables). Point 1 mentioned above is important under these conditions.

9. Under a divestiture of assets, the selling price can be affected by the quality of the accounts receivable and the customer base. Specifically, buyers will want to know what is the overall financial condition of the customer base (especially large purchasers), and the historical trends of receivable turnover and bad debt write-offs.

It is important to understand the flow of international credit as it relates to the sale of goods and services and cash flow. During the flow process, the more input the credit department has over the sale of goods and services to foreign customers, the more efficient is its control over the credit management of accounts receivable. This is especially true when discussions are held between marketing/sales and new/old foreign customers for the sale of goods and services. Credit policies and procedures can assist in minimizing the need for input from the credit department. However, problems can arise each and every time discussions are held with foreign customers. This can be due to country condition changes (which are frequent) and/or change in the foreign customers' financial condition.

To minimize potential problems, there must be a constant flow of information and interchange (feedback) during the flow of the international credit process between all those interrelated with the process. The objective is to communicate!

Figure 1–1 outlines and explains the flow process that normally occurs inside and outside a company.

But what are the principle responsibilities of a credit department for the management of international receivables? One responsibility is to expedite the flow of credit to foreign customers as efficiently as possible. The credit department also should be prepared to approve sales as expeditiously as possible, and implement and maintain adequate controls for the effective credit management of international trade accounts receivable. By keeping delinquent customers at a minimum, the department will place itself in a position to approve new orders (provided they do not exceed a customer or country credit limit). It doesn't make much sense to approve and ship another order if the customer didn't pay or accept a draft or invoice for a previous sale when it came due for payment or acceptance.

Obtaining and updating current factual credit and financial information on all active accounts is very important and it is efficient to obtain this information before the sales department accepts orders from foreign customers. It takes longer to obtain information on foreign accounts than it does in domestic credit. Normally, information on active accounts older than one year should be updated. New orders should not be held up because a credit person didn't update credit and financial information on an existing customer who continually purchases goods. It is important to obtain sufficient information to properly assess country risk on

FIGURE 1–1
Flow of International Credit Outline

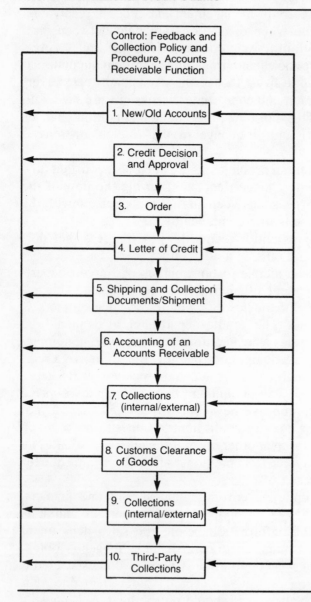

Legend

1. New accounts are reviewed by the credit department before orders are received
   and/or delivery takes place. The same occurs with old accounts that have not
   purchased in over a year because the credit and financial information on the foreign

the countries to be marketed. Maintaining up-to-date information on countries should be a continuous process.

The credit department must expedite the processing of customer orders that require credit approval. Customer orders must take priority over all other department business, and foreign customers should be served first. To minimize delinquencies, a systematic collection follow-up sequence should be established for all of the different types of export payment terms extended to foreign customers. It is important to determine credit limits or lines of credit on each foreign customer (sometimes referred to as credit limit guides) for proper credit control purposes. The department should assist foreign customers in solving financial problems. Credit personnel shouldn't complain or shouldn't point out a

---

customer usually needs updating and the customer's country needs review to determine any country risk changes, pro or con, since business was last transacted.

2. On receipt of sufficient amounts of information, a decision is made on credit terms, order/credit limits, and other terms and conditions. When applicable, the country credit limit is reviewed.

3. Orders are reviewed based on parameters established by the credit department.

4. If letter of credit (L/C) payment terms are established, the L/C needs to be received and reviewed before orders are placed on manufacturing or sourcing locations and/or goods are shipped to ensure the terms and conditions of each L/C can be complied with.

5. Shipping and collection documents are prepared based on customer purchase orders, country import regulations, and/or the terms and conditions of the L/C.

6. Depending on title transfer, commercial invoices are booked to trade accounts receivable or as inventory intransit by the exporter's accounting department; the foreign customer either books the purchase as goods intransit or as a trade accounts payable.

7. Shipping documents, drafts (bills of exchange), promissory notes, and other financial instruments of payment evidencing indebtedness are submitted to domestic or foreign international commercial banks for acceptance and/or collection from a foreign customer. Letters of credit are followed up for payment or acceptance.

8. Customs clearance takes place on arrival of the goods at the foreign port of destination.

9. The banks and/or the credit department of the exporter follow-up for acceptance or payment of financial instruments in accordance with the terms and conditions mutually agreed on between both parties to the export transaction. On payment, the foreign customer's account will be debited and the exporter's account will be credited.

10. Foreign accounts are referred to outside collection agencies or attorneys (solicitor/ lawyer) when payment is not received or an acceptance is not created within a specified period of time designated by the credit department, or claims are filed with appropriate export credit insurance agencies in accordance with their stated commercial or political risk terms and conditions.

customer's financial weaknesses, but instead could do something about them by suggesting methods to improve these weaknesses to the customer. It is also important to point out their strengths.

The credit department coordinates many of the above mentioned responsibilities with the marketing/sales department and, when appropriate, the order processing and traffic/distribution departments. The idea is to keep everyone advised of problems—to communicate.

The credit department can provide a number of other services to its company. For example, the department can make credit decisions or recommendations on foreign suppliers for its purchasing department; offer credit and collection training programs, seminars, or workshops to its foreign customers; or assist the marketing/sales or financial planning departments with credit/financial information for market surveys or potential acquisitions.

How each credit department manages and performs its credit management of accounts receivable is determined and affected by senior management's foreign business credit philosophy. It is also determined by the policies of management toward recognition of the credit and accounts receivable management functions as a vital and integral part of their company, and organizational structure. The authority levels of each credit person within the organization, strict or lenient credit and collection policies, and the company's overall financial condition and financial commitment to foreign credit and accounts receivable management is important. For example, will the company spend money to automate, or for sufficient travel budgets? What is its commitment to sell or invest overseas? How are intra and interdepartmental relations, especially with the marketing/sales department? A coordinated cohesive team effort is absolutely essential between both departments. If continuous conflicts of interest exist between selling, collecting, or extending credit to foreign customers neither department can function properly. The element of risk in the trading of goods and services overseas is too high and the competition too severe. Salespeople often think of credit people as advisorial or people who can restrict sales. Credit people feel salespeople are more interested in selling than collecting from past due customers and think they do not consider the risks of selling to customers in poor financial condition. It is vitally important that the credit department has a clear understanding of the company's overall strategy, objectives, and financial capacity. The credit department must integrate and coordinate its policies and procedures within company strategy, objectives, and financial capacity, and with the marketing/sales department.

If the company's objectives are clear and communicated through the credit manager to each individual employee in the credit department, then everyone will know what is expected. It will basically answer: how, what, where, when, and why! Appendix 1–A contains a detailed listing of the duties and responsibilities of an international credit department.

The Role of the Credit Manager

The credit manager in large organizations is more of an administrator, but is still involved in large-risk-type account situations and planning. In large organizations, work is usually divided among a number of job classifications and descriptions which range from clerical to chief credit executive levels. In large companies, the responsibility for the administration of foreign credit can be delegated to an existing domestic credit manager, or a separate and distinct position and department that is totally responsible for international credit can be created. The person's title might be Export or International Credit Manager—and the duties and responsibilities can vary from company to company. How a company is organized, its annual amount of nonintercompany international credit sales, the risks involved, where products are sourced and manufactured from, and other factors determine whether the responsibility will require a full- or part-time management person. Because of the differences between domestic and international credit approval, collection techniques, and the type of risks inherent by selling goods or services overseas, delegating the responsibility of managing international credit sales to an existing domestic credit manager may not be in the best interests of the company.

Domestic and/or international credit management do share many similar managerial techniques. The credit manager with international responsibility is responsible for the successful operation of the department by ensuring department objectives and responsibilities are controlled and administered properly. The principle objective is to protect the company's investment in international accounts receivable. The manager formulates operations and procedures to ensure that orders are approved timely, credit information is gathered and analyzed promptly, credit files are established and maintained, and delinquent accounts receive timely follow-up.

Management of international receivables does require that the manager has a working knowledge of international cash management and, in some circumstances, a thorough understanding of the function. Historically, most companies equate international cash management with the management of foreign exchange exposures and international banking. It does not relate to the international cash management of receipts from foreign customers. Remember, there is no federal reserve system for clearing international payments. The credit manager will expeditiously credit funds to a customer's account only if his or her bank or banks maintains an account with the foreign bank who issued the remittance. In addition, a credit manager's flow of funds from the sale of goods and services to foreign customers is affected by the export shipping, financial documentation, and bank collection documents prepared for each export sale transaction. Many times, these valuable and important documents are prepared both internally and externally by noncredit-related people. Payment is affected by the accuracy and timely preparation of these documents.

In the case of letters of credit (L/C), the smallest documentation error can affect payment of the L/C until the error is corrected. In the case of sales made on a documentary collection basis, if the documents are not sent timely, a draft may not be accepted timely which is needed for discounting or a sight draft will not get paid as quickly. Payments terms can extend all the way out to 180 days—even longer in the case of raw materials or consumer goods. In the case of capital equipment, the terms could go up to (or even beyond) five years. Unlike domestic payment terms which are usually payable in 30 days from invoice date or a discount for payment within 10 or 15 days, international cash flows vary substantially. Payment instructions are important because the mailing time from some countries can take up to one week or even longer. Therefore, the payment instructions on invoices and bank collection items over a specified amount should specify a wire transfer of funds to a designated location of the exporter. Again, this is usually done by noncredit people.

The terms of sale quoted to the foreign customer can affect title transfer and payment. Irrespective of the payment terms, many foreign customers refuse to pay until they have the original bill of lading and other important original documents in hand. In many instances, they calculate the due date from the date of the on-board ocean bill of lading which evidences the goods are actually on board the steamship carrier.

To assist credit managers, credit and accounts receivable management systems can provide up-to-date information on the status of customer accounts. These systems can provide such information as when are invoices due for payment? How long has the account been a customer? How does the customer pay (i.e., 30 or 60 slow)? Does your system have the latest technology? Is it on-line or a batch mode system with respect to cash application of customer accounts? Are you still using antiquated ledger cards with balance carried forward accounting? Do you have an order entry system and is it tied into your credit and accounts receivable management system to update each customer account with timely invoice information? How quickly are customer orders processed and how is the credit department informed if orders exceed parameters (order limits or payment terms) established by the credit department?

The international commercial banks used in the collection-of-receipts process is an important piece of cash mobilization. Do the U.S. collection banks used by the credit department have sufficient correspondent relationships that closely match up with the banks of your foreign customers? The credit manager's systematic collection follow-up sequence should provide for the follow-up on a timely basis for acceptance of drafts or payment at maturity of each export transaction. This will ensure a timely funds flow.

In most small- to medium-sized companies, the cash management function is usually concerned with domestic funds flow management as it relates to domestic bank lockboxes, investments, cash receipts, and disbursements. International cash management is too small for most domestic cash managers to be concerned about. Therefore, the credit manager, in order to improve his or her performance, is forced to assume some of these responsibilities, which means setting up bank accounts and the movement of bank deposits.

Functions and Goals of the Credit Manager

Every department needs a philosophy of management that enhances individual responsibility and strength, but creates a cohesive direction of effort, maintains teamwork, and harmonizes the goals of the individual and business firms.[3] This responsibility belongs to the credit manager.

The function and goals of credit management may be divided into four main areas: setting objectives, planning, organizing, and controlling.[4]

Setting Objectives.   The objectives of the credit department should be short, medium, and long term in nature. Each objective should be formulated to take into consideration broad company strategy, marketing/sales objectives, the financial capacity of the company, and any external factors.

Planning.   There is no substitute for good planning. It is essential in order to meet the objectives of both the department and the company. Without a well thought-out plan, the department might try to accomplish too much in a short period of time or vice versa. Good planning establishes expectations for each person to accomplish personal and departmental objectives. All personnel concerned should make a coordinated effort to eliminate duplications or omissions.

Organizing.   Good organization requires structure, staffing, and training in order to achieve results. Without good organization, the efficiency, performance, and effectiveness of individuals and the department will be adversely affected.

Structure means making sure everyone in the department understands the objectives, formulates activities to accomplish the objectives, and coordinates functions when and where necessary.

Staffing is one of the most important responsibilities of department managers. Without a well-qualified, well-educated *and* well-compensated staff, the objectives and results of the department and the performance of the manager will be poor. Like any other managerial position in a company, the credit manager is only as good as the people in the department.

Training and education are essential to obtain optimum performance from individual employees and to improve department results. The credit manager must continually offer in-house training programs, as well as external ones. An adequate budget should be provided each year and department employees should be encouraged to attend and actively participate in internal/external training programs, seminars, courses, workshops, or special degree-type programs.

Controlling. In a larger company, the individual international credit manager dedicates more time to maintaining adequate controls over more employees, customers, invoices, documents, export credit instruments of payment, larger receivable investments, and larger intradepartmental communications and relationships.

To obtain desired results from each individual employee, it is necessary to exercise and maintain certain controls. For example, if not properly planned, too many employees might be out of the office on vacation or on overseas business travel at the same time. Also, too much managerial control over department employees might cause frustration and/or discouragement. This could hamper the individual ability of the employee. Therefore, the manager must provide a flexible atmosphere that encourages top performance from each and every employee. In order to obtain planned objectives and goals, the manager should establish a review and appraisal process/program. This program would allow management to consult with employees on ways to improve or attain results, and would use this feedback to change policies and procedures when necessary.

Goals of Dynamic Credit Management. In summary, it is the responsibility of the manager of the credit department to plan and direct the activities of the credit function in keeping with company policy and with the following ends in mind:[5]

1. Increased sales and profits, resulting from a better understanding and more skillful handling of all credit functions.
2. Improved quality of work performed within the department, due to greater accuracy, thoroughness, and care exercised by every member of the staff.
3. Increased volume of credit workload handled with less effort and expense, and with greater promptness; the most effective utilization of the abilities, skills, and interests of the individual members of the staff and the total work force.
4. Decreased cost per unit of work performed, resulting from improved planning, direction, and supervision.
5. Greater satisfaction to all concerned, resulting from a clarification of the results that are expected.

Dynamic credit management requires, in addition to expertness in all the technical phases of credit, the ability to:

1. Analyze, plan, and develop objectives, policies, and programs.
2. Build an organization.
3. Assign responsibility, delegate commensurate authority, and maintain accountability for results.
4. Review and appraise operations for conformity with objectives, policies, standards, and practices; take remedial action wherever and whenever required.
5. Inspire confidence, motivate teamwork, and maintain growth.

CREDIT POLICY

Before a company considers a foreign customer's order or offer, it should have formulated a credit policy that defines in broad terms the degree of risk it is willing to assume and the preferred payment terms it is willing to accept. The exporter's primary concern is to assure itself of a reasonable expectation for repayment for the goods shipped.

All businesses need a credit policy that is issued by its senior management. The policy for international credit can either be integrated with domestic credit policy or issued separately. Most experienced companies prefer to issue it separately. The policy should be formulated in very broad terms, but simple in essence. It is senior management's responsibility to set forth the tone of business conduct for the current and ensuing years. Policy guides action and the credit policy should set forth the framework that each functional department operates within. It is the basis on which plans are formulated and decisions are made to reach the short-, medium-, or long-term strategies, goals, and objectives set by senior management. Senior management must communicate the company's broad strategies, goals, and objectives through to functional department heads (i.e., the credit manager) so that department heads know the overall game plan. It helps answer the perplexing question, "Where are we going and how do we plan on getting there?"

Senior management should consult and/or involve the credit manager in the formulation of the credit policy. The credit manager has practical day-to-day experiences in managing the company's investment in accounts receivable. These experiences could include country risk conditions (from both its own experiences and from outside sources of information), the financial condition of certain country industries as evidenced by payment conditions and customer financial statement information, and, competitive terms and conditions. The idea is to make a realistic credit policy that allows for flexibility, entrepreneurial development, creativity, and less rigidity.

Often, a business and its people confuse policy with objectives, procedures, or practices. They are all interrelated in the process that leads to fulfillment of the strategies and goals of the business. However, it is important to distinguish them in order to avoid confusion or conflicts.

Policy and Objectives. These policies, stated by senior management, define in broad terms the objectives of the business. However, the broad policies and objectives should cover stated periods of time. They may involve sales volumes, return on investment, profit levels, bad debt losses, or market share. To help the business achieve these overall policies and objectives, each functional department within the organization, including the credit department, must establish its own policies and objectives. For the credit department, these might be stated in terms of sales volume by customer and country in various risk classifications, authority levels, relationships to marketing/sales, establishing and developing training programs for company personnel (including credit personnel), and the amount of capital committed to accounts receivable.

Policy and Procedures.   Since the credit policy does not offer definitive solutions for certain types of credit situations, the credit manager establishes procedures. The procedures guide the actions of subordinates in specific situations and by reducing doubt or confusion gives them an idea of what is expected from them.

Policy and Practice.   Although credit policies are broad and allow wide latitude, practice reduces the range of possible decisions confronting subordinates. It is important to note that business practices vary from one business to the next. This is especially true for a person coming from a financial institution to an industrial business. At a bank, the procedures are rigid and everyone's actions are usually well documented. In industry, almost the direct opposite occurs.

How best to accomplish these strategies and objectives depends on the application of the good business sense of all concerned and a combination of factors peculiar to the business. Among the alternative types of credit policy that can be chosen are:

- A liberal credit policy with a liberal collection policy.
- A liberal credit policy with collection strictly enforced.
- A strict credit policy with a flexible collection policy (collections adjusted to individual circumstances, while avoiding a rigid collection procedure).
- Strict credit policy with a strict collection policy.

A liberal credit policy provides wide latitude in the margin of risks to be accepted. While it may stimulate credit sales, such a policy may result in increased collection efforts and costs, slow turnover of receivables, and susceptibility to greater bad debt losses. Such a policy might be used to gain market share. Under this type of credit policy, senior management might issue the following written guidelines:

- To obtain market share in the next three years in the Far East, credit will institute liberal credit and collection procedures.
- Offer extended credit terms where and when necessary.

A strict or conservative credit policy usually requires less collection effort, improves receivable turnover, and minimizes bad debt loss; but credit sales to marginal accounts are curtailed and potentially profitable business may be lost. To accomplish this type of credit policy, senior management might issue the following written guideline: The credit and sales departments will endeavor to maximize return on investment in accounts receivable by achieving the lowest possible days sales outstanding (DSO) to optimize cash receipts by collecting accounts at agreed on credit terms.

A collection policy that is too liberal, with lax enforcement of credit terms, can play havoc with accounts receivable and seriously hamper the liquidity of a business. On the other hand, too conservative a collection policy can impair customer goodwill.

Careful consideration of the advantages and disadvantages of each type of policy, in light of factors mentioned previously, should help in choosing a good working credit policy for a particular business. Any policy must be somewhat flexible but a firm, businesslike attitude should be maintained in the relationship with both sales and foreign customers. The payment terms should be sound, practical, competitive, and clearly expressed or defined; the credit period should be clearly stated and adhered to as closely as possible.[6] A written credit policy, issued in broad and simplistic terms, can help bridge the communication and relationship gap with many other departments. It can minimize disputes over responsibility, eliminate costly errors, and create efficiency. Most of all, a written credit policy can clearly define exactly what is expected of credit department personnel, no matter what the organizational structure.

Establishing and Implementing Credit Policy

Each credit manager should take the steps necessary to translate broad, flexible policy statements issued by senior management into guides that can be used by credit personnel in the daily operation of their respective departments. In international trade, it is advisable to implement credit policies by regions or areas of the world—Latin America, the Far East, the Middle East, North Africa, Africa, Western Europe, and Eastern Europe. This allows greater latitude and flexibility for the credit manager to implement detailed policies and procedures without inhibiting sales or cash flow.

The implementation of credit policy also involves assigning duties and responsibilities, delegating authority, establishing procedures and controls, and providing for periodic progress reports and evaluations. Once established, it should be communicated to all concerned, both inside and outside the credit department. Whether it is disseminated orally or in writing, there must be a clear and mutual understanding as to exactly what the policy is and how it is to be applied. This is especially true for the sales and distribution departments as it will minimize confusion and enhance relations.

To achieve a competitive stance in today's highly competitive and complex world of international trade, credit people must be dynamic, creative, flexible, and better integrated with the company's strategies and objectives—especially those of the marketing/sales department. The risks in international trade are high and it is necessary to respond properly, effectively, and efficiently to the needs of the company overall and those of marketing/sales. When integrated, the credit manager's task of accomplishing the strategies and objectives of each is made easier. The credit manager must have a thorough understanding and be knowledgeable in four major elements: (1) the company's business strategy or goals, (2) the objectives of marketing/sales, (3) the financial capacity and condition of the company, and (4) the external factors that can have positive or negative effects on all of the aforementioned and credit policy. In actuality, credit policy is a function of complex interrelationships between these four major elements.

Business Strategy. Strategy contemplates "where are we," "where are we going," and "how do we plan on getting there." Many times it is dictated by the legal structure of the business. For example, publicly traded businesses in the United States historically have concentrated on short-term strategies in an effort to maximize shareholder investment or earnings per share (EPS). Private businesses only have to satisfy private shareholders and not worry about public concerns or criticism. These strategies can be short, medium or long term in nature. In Japan, businesses historically have concentrated on long-term strategies that aim at sacrificing short-term profits for long-term goals—for example, market share in the United States and the Far East. A long-term goal of a business might be to manufacture in a country, say within 8 or 10 years.

Sales/Profits. Is the business trying to increase sales and profits in certain countries or simply sacrificing profit margins for the sake of getting sales? If sales increase by large percentages, the credit manager might not have the staff to handle the additional sales volume. Being understaffed will create inefficiency and poor service to the sales department which ultimately affects the customer.

Markets. Where exactly is the business interested in selling its goods and services? Is it to countries in the Far East, China, Western Europe, or the Middle East? If so, the credit manager can update country information in advance of selling to these countries or areas of the world and be prepared in advance to service the needs of marketing/sales. He or she can inform the marketing/sales personnel in advance of country credit and collection conditions (i.e., the information provided by the FCIB's Credit and Collection Survey, or S. J. Rundt's Weekly Intelligence Reports).

Market Share. Is your company attempting to gain or hold a market share in certain markets? What products will be sold and when? How will your company market its goods and services to gain market share? Will it sell directly or indirectly (foreign agents, distributors, or export trading companies)? If informed in advance and given alternatives for extending credit, the credit manager can inform the marketing/sales department before selling to foreign customers. This helps minimize frustration for all concerned, especially the individual salesperson who was hoping to sell product or products to a particular buyer or buyers, only to find out they are not creditworthy for the volume or the credit terms. Advance planning is required so the credit department can tell the marketing/sales department which foreign buyers are financially sound. Why sell to financially weak buyers? They may not have the cash flow or capability to buy a lot of product! What about spreading the risks around by selling to a combination of both financially weak and strong customers if the ultimate goal is to obtain market share at the risk of smaller profits?

Production. Is the company's goal to get a larger market share by making a direct investment in a country? Will this be accomplished by setting up a joint venture or manufacturing plant to service the local market place and export to surrounding countries? If so, the credit manager may be losing part of his customer base. Will one or more people have to be laid off? Who will be responsible for credit administration at the new overseas facility? Will it be an experienced credit person, consultant, internal or external accountant, or the general manager of the facility? Will the credit manager be permitted to help establish a credit and accounts receivable department with adequate credit controls and systems? Who will credit report to at the new venture?

Investment. What will it cost the business to sell to certain countries or areas of the world, to get market share, and to produce goods overseas? How much capital will be tied up? Where will the funds come from? Are there any tax advantages?

Marketing/Sales Objectives. These objectives are based on many factors, such as product life cycles, productive capacity, market share, and competition. If the strategy is to manufacture in a country, the marketing department might study several alternatives: a distributor or distributors to boost market share; potential manufacturers to acquire; setting up a joint venture with a business inside or outside the country; or, building a plant in a foreign country to increase market share.

Planning. When does the marketing department plan to market goods into certain countries? How will the goods be marketed? Will a foreign marketing/sales office be established? Where will the credit, accounting, and finance be handled?

Organization—Structure and Staffing. How will the marketing/sales department want to organize itself to accomplish the strategies of the business and its own objectives. Corporate senior management sometimes makes this decision or makes a recommendation for this organization. Will they be organized by an international division, worldwide product division, worldwide regional or area structure, worldwide functional structure, or national subsidiary structure? How will the credit department be organized and how many credit people will it require to accomplish and accommodate the strategies and goals of the company, the objectives of marketing/sales, and to accommodate the structure? Should the credit department structure be aligned with that of the marketing/sales function? What credit department structure will create the greatest efficiency, communications, and cash flow?

Controls and Systems. What types of credit and accounts receivable systems will be required to accomplish these strategies and objectives? Will the systems provide adequate controls over such things as, credit limits, order approval controls, sales volume information, customer and business summary aging reports, and management-by-exception reporting? What about customer payment and credit history information? Will the computer expertise to implement the systems come from parent or local country personnel?

Personnel and Training. Where will the credit people come from? How many will be needed to accomplish all of the aforementioned? Will they require a lot of training or just a minimal amount of training?

Financial Capacity. The ability of a business to offer competitive pricing and financing for its foreign customers is determined by its financial capacity. This includes product profit margins and balance sheet capacity to raise the necessary financing from financial institutions, export credit insurers, and investment bankers. Each business can analyze its own position for its products and evolve an internal credit policy by setting terms of sale and credit terms for each product and country.

Commercial and Investment Bankers. Does the company have adequate financing to accomplish its strategies and goals? Will the business have to leverage itself? How will all of the aforementioned affect its ratings (S&P and Moody's)? Is the financial community willing and able to accommodate these strategies and goals?

Financial Condition. What is the present financial condition of the company? Is it already highly leveraged? What about it's debt-to-equity and debt-to-total capitalizations ratios? Are they high?

Profitability. Is the company profitable or unprofitable? In which product lines? What about earnings per share? How has it stacked up? How has its product line profitability stacked up versus the industry? Will the strategies and goals of the company increase profits in the short, medium, or long term?

Asset Quality. What about its assets? How have they been turning? Are the company's plants old and in need of repair or replacement? At what cost to the company? What about inventory and accounts receivable turnovers? How do they compare to the industry?

External Factors. It is difficult to superimpose the external factors to consider in the real world of fierce competition. These factors include a sharp rise in country risk perception, a trend to protectionism, and financial constituencies (like commercial and investment bankers, institutional investors). Also, you might perceive that you are too highly leveraged, with low profit margins, and poor-quality assets because certain assets are located in countries that are considered large risks. If nonfinancial constituencies (politicians, regulators) are not fully cognizant of the problems of dealing in international trade, it can constitute another problem. Your competition now includes businesses in Brazil, South Korea, and Taiwan—not just Europe and Japan. Your government export credit insurance schemes and financing programs have not always been competitive with those of your competition.

As if these problems are not enough to deal with, you also have to face a change in the banking environment for financing export sales. Banks have large country risk exposures, some of which are being rescheduled and/or are on a noninterest accrual basis.

What do these external factors mean to export credit policy? Banks will be reluctant to increase their country risk positions, and when they do, they are looking for shorter maturity dates which are tied to specific export transactions. Businesses are going to have to carry a greater proportion of export receivables on their own books and/or move to taking more risks directly thereby sharing the risks with their banks. The structuring and management of export financing positions is going to become more complex. Creative and imaginative approaches to risk taking and export financing are necessary to achieve sales objectives.

Country Conditions. What have the historical risk conditions been of the countries targeted for growth? What about future country risk trends? How have external payments been to creditors, including trade credit suppliers? In other words, are the countries targeted for growth short, medium, or long term as far as business strategy is concerned? Is your company willing to sacrifice short-term risks for long-term goals?

Billing Practices. In order to gain or hold market share in certain countries is it necessary to switch to alternative billing currencies (a break from billing in traditional U.S. dollars)? Which currencies? Will the business inherit a foreign exchange risk exposure?

Competition. What is competition doing in the market places targeted for growth? What are their credit terms? Are they willing to take more risks (i.e., selling to financially weak customers to gain or hold market share)? Are they getting subsidized financial support from their private or government sectors? Are they export credit insured? If so, are the insurers willing to take risks and grant creative financing?

Credit Insurance. Will the business strategies and goals require export credit insurance? Are the insurers willing or able to insure goods sold to certain countries? Do they have any restrictive country limitations imposed on your countries targeted for growth? Are their insurance schemes competitive? What is the cost of getting credit insurance coverage?

Commercial Bank Financing.   Extending longer credit terms to certain customers and countries to get or hold market share can create balance sheet risk exposures. Can the credit manager get export trade financing from commercial financial institutions to offset some of these balance sheet risk exposures? Are they willing to confirm letters of credit to the countries targeted for growth, if applicable?

Export Credit Guidelines

The credit department's export credit and collection policies and procedures are best stated in general broad guidelines to allow sufficient flexibility and are often referred to simply as credit guidelines. They should always be issued to all appropriate sales and marketing personnel, including traffic/distribution, accounting, and internal audit. It helps minimize confusion over who is responsible for which function. It is never to be conceived as an absolute. Export credit guidelines could conceivably consist of the following topics:

1. Purpose.
2. Objectives
3. Credit policy.
   a. Payment terms.
   b. Credit limits.
   c. Coordination with other departments.
4. Procedures.
   a. Payment terms.
   b. Establishing customer credit.
   c. Credit controls.
   d. Collection activity.
   e. Accruals and write-offs to bad debts.

Appendix 1–B is an example of export credit and collection guidelines.

The credit manager may have administrative responsibility for coordinating the credit functions located at foreign subsidiaries or other foreign-related operations. The manager may be responsible for issuing a foreign subsidiary credit and collection guideline. The purpose of this outline is to set forth the minimum requirements of the parent company regarding the administration of the credit function at these respective overseas locations. Appendix 1–C is an example of a foreign subsidiary credit and collection guideline.

In any case, some written guidelines regarding negotiation of specific payment terms with a foreign customer must be based on an overall credit policy that defines the degree of risk the exporter is willing to assume and his preferred selling terms for international trade. Determination of such a credit policy rests on the following questions:

1. What is the payment term, and how much protection does it require?
2. What terms are offered by the competition?
3. What are the industry practices?
4. What is my financing capacity in relation to the importer's credit capacity?
5. How strong is my trading partner's negotiation position?

Example

Exporter A has a firmly established market position and a reliable distribution network. He is therefore in a stronger position to establish price and selling terms. Exporter B is just breaking into the market and has not yet created a solid distribution network. Consequently, he must be more willing to compete on price and selling terms to increase his market share. Exporter B's credit policy will permit more risks than Exporter A's, and his selling terms will have to be more liberal than those of his well-entrenched competitor.

A financial executive at an electronics firm outlined his firm's strategy in courting new customers: "We very often start out a new customer on a letter of credit or on cash in advance. Then, if his sales pick up or we think that he's fairly good, we might put him on a time draft or sight draft basis, depending on their terms. And then, if he does really well, we might even sell to him on open account. So, in effect, we use generous terms as a selling incentive.''

There are no absolutes in credit policy decisions or written guidelines. There are often different perspectives on the right policy, and there are usually departmental differences of opinion. The sales department has the goal of increasing sales and profits and of diversifying and expanding markets. Therefore, salespeople will lobby for taking credit risks and extending liberal credit terms. Meanwhile, credit department goals are to minimize risk and to obtain prompt payment. Credit people consequently will strive to sell selectively and to take only high-quality risks.

One way to reconcile the conflicting objectives of the sales and finance units is to give salespeople a stake in the credit/collection game. For example, a consumer products manufacturer that exports to Asia was distressed by slow collections for that region. It decided to remedy the situation by linking its salespeople's commission to collections, thus giving them the incentive to reduce DSOs. The company paid its sales staff 50 percent of the commission when the sale was made and the other 50 percent after payment was received.

Companies must adopt credit policies and procedures that fit their financial capacity and assure quality and liquidity management of receivables. They must also offer competitive market credit terms and export trade financing. The importance of credit policy cannot be overstated or underestimated. It can provide the exporter with guidelines for negotiating with foreign customers. It gives the credit manager an indication of his or her own strengths and weaknesses, and of how many and what types of concessions he or she can make.

ORGANIZATIONAL STRUCTURE

Business people agree that the subject of organizing a business both domestically and internationally is most controversial and complex. But why worry about organizational structure when the obvious, urgent, and crucial problem is how to get the job done.

How is it possible to protect assets and currencies, minimize costs, battle inflation in highly inflationary countries, and maximize profits in today's risky, complicated international environment? It is difficult to get a consensus of opinion when business people get together to discuss and agree on what is the best organizational structure. The ideal organizational structure of the credit function is an issue that arises periodically in almost every business that is of medium size or larger. Credit is seen either as a function that should be attached to a headquarter's location, fine-tuned to the macroeconomic strategies of senior management and the fluctuations of the economy, or as a function that should be attached to a regional office and subservient to accounting or marketing. The former view could be called the centralized approach, and the latter the decentralized approach. Within these complex issues is the question of where the management of U.S. exports fits within the overall scheme of things. How a business organizes itself domestically will have a profound affect on the handling of its exports. Many will say, "people can make any organization work. Good people can make a bad organization work, bad people cannot make the best organization work. We stay in constant communication. Whenever there's a problem, we just pick up the telephone or telex someone and set to work solving it. . . ." They are right: people do count. It is people who make the organization work in the real world.

In effect, organization charts are only an abstract pattern (and hardly comprehensive at that) of relationships among people. Job descriptions are often filed and people are given or assume responsibility above and beyond the original job description or are completely forgotten. Reporting relationships—up, down, and sideways—in a person's actual job defy conventional organizational descriptions in number, variety, frequency, timing, content, and manner.

In reality, the vast majority of credit operations fall between the two extremes of centralization and decentralization. Elements from both organizational models are extracted to fit the perceived needs of the business at any particular time. Yet, most export credit operations can be characterized as primarily centralized or decentralized in nature.

Many large firms maintain a centralized domestic and U.S.

export (nonaffiliated foreign customers) credit function whereby credit is controlled and administered from one central point (i.e., a headquarters location or at an operating unit). This would include all product lines or lines within segments, groups, divisions, regions, or areas. One very significant feature of the centralized approach to credit management is that the "reporting lines" are concentrated with one chief credit executive or financial person. That is, all credit managerial personnel report on a straight line to one central person, no matter where they are located domestically. In addition, the centralized approach can take into consideration those credit staffs domiciled at different locations throughout the United States. These staffs are located at regional or divisional offices, but ultimately they report on a straight line basis to a chief credit executive. Depending on the international organizational structure of the business, U.S. exports to nonaffiliated foreign companies could be either centralized at headquarters and con-trolled by an export credit manager for all product lines or dispersed among domestic credit people. In decentralized opera-tions, domestic and U.S. export (nonaffiliated foreign customers) credit is controlled and administered at operating units spread throughout a number of locations. Credit management people do not report to one single chief credit executive or financial person in the business. Instead, these people report to individuals—usually a financial person, but possibly the chief operating executive within their operating units.

Businesses with centralized U.S. export credit operations are best able to maximize cash inflows and utilize human resources efficiently. The minority of businesses that could be described as having decentralized U.S. export credit operations vis-à-vis the credit function report increased responsiveness to accounting or sales, improved customer contact, and improved receivable per-formances.

**Export Credit Function: Centralized
versus Decentralized**

A comparative listing of the benefits of each structure might be drawn as follows, with rank indicating maximized benefits. It is important to note that such variables as industry peculiarities, economic fluctuations, and personnel idiosyncracies introduce varying degrees of subjectivity to any such comparison.

Centralized	*Decentralized*
1. Accounts receivable performance improves.	1. Responsiveness to sales and marketing increases.
2. Internal credit communication improves.	2. Accounts receivable performance improves.
3. Responsiveness to sales and marketing increases.	3. Flexibility in marketplace increases.
4. Greater cost savings realized.	4. Customer contact improves.
5. Manpower efficiency improves.	5. Bad debt control improves.
6. Bad debt control improves.	6. Intracredit communication improves.
7. Improved control over product groups who sell to the same foreign customers.	
8. Country risk exposures are better controlled by product line structures who sell to the same countries.	

The increasing responsiveness to marketing and sales is self-evident. However, of even more importance to senior management is the management of accounts receivable. With more businesses having anywhere from 15 to 20 percent of total assets tied up in accounts receivable, modern cash management theories demand more from credit managers since receivables are a cost of doing business.

It might be said that the more credit is decentralized, the closer it comes to marketing and sales and the more it is centralized, the more objectively it functions as a risk analyst and collections specialist.

The independent stance of the credit function is, in the long run, in the best interests of the business. The purpose of credit is not to eliminate all losses, but rather to control those losses by establishing the risk level that allows for heaviest volume of sales, including sales to marginal customers. The ability of credit to provide this service implies that the credit manager is not functioning in an ivory tower, far removed from the day-to-day realities of the marketplace. When that is the case, the tendency is to become overly risk-aversive in an effort to eliminate all losses. That represents an extreme, and is not justifiable. Too many profitable sales are lost by this ultraconservative approach. It is uniformly true that the marginal customer is an unacceptable customer. Market consideration must be taken into account. Credit must exist autonomous of marketing, but not isolated from it.

This savvy interpretation of the marketing role is crucial to the successful functioning of credit as a commercial and country risk analyst (and thus as a valuable staff function). The credit manager must be cognizant of such considerations as market penetration and market share. Payment terms and pricing are responsibilities rightly charged to marketing. Credit is charged with coordinating the committed economic exposure.

However, it is wrong to think that the organizational structure of the credit function is unneeded. All work must be organized if it is to be accomplished effectively and economically. An individual must organize his or her work to do it effectively and efficiently. So must a group of individuals who divide up the total tasks to be accomplished when working toward a common goal.

The conceptual problem of organization of the credit function, like any other function, revolves around two central processes: the structuring (organizing) of work, and the reporting lines (reporting). Work presupposes strategies (the major plans for accomplishing the results desired) and strategies presuppose objectives (the fundamental goals to be achieved).

The organization of a business, like a house or building, is made up of parts or building blocks. The blocks are fitted together and one feeds into the other. For example: Sales get orders from customers; the credit department approves the order; the order is given to the distribution/traffic department; they give the order to a plant for manufacture or warehouse with inventory for processing; the traffic department arranges shipment of the goods to the customer. In between this process are the functions of purchasing, labor, research and development, accounting, cash management, and human resources.

The Organizational Entities

What will be the dimension of the organizational structure itself? Each of the finance functions and subfunctions for which the business determines a need must be organized at various levels of the corporate pyramid or structure. The major segments or entities of the credit function typically found in most businesses include the corporate level, product divisions, the international division, regional or area organizations, country wholly-owned subsidiaries, and joint ventures and minority affiliates.

The Corporate Level.   This is usually a staff function which houses the top credit person and department or unit. Typically it is primarily responsible for broad companywide policies and procedures; decisions of a companywide nature, and major decisions on projects of sufficient size to affect the welfare of the business as a whole.

Product Divisions.   Most businesses organize themselves at least partially around product divisions, which usually have worldwide responsibility for their sales and profits. As domestic divisions, their financial activities regarding such things as foreign exchange management, intercompany payables and receivables, and credit and banking relations are usually tightly controlled by corporate finance. Even as domestic divisions, their financial affairs may have an international aspect through exports direct to third parties and foreign subsidiaries which are marketing/sales offices. If they have worldwide responsibilities, they will, of course, have financial transactions involving the international sphere. This may considerably complicate the organization of the credit and finance functions by spreading the international dimension across many divisions. Divisions selling to the same high-risk markets and customers lend themselves to over-exposed commercial and country exposures.

International Division.   This division, where it exists, is a natural vehicle for focusing expertise and coordinating communications for international credit and financial decision making. The division itself may have considerable authority and autonomy or, as is increasingly common, it may primarily assist the corporate level.

Regional or Area Organizations.   Where they exist, these are natural vehicles for focusing expertise in their geographic domains. As with product divisions, however, the needs and levels of expertise of the regions may differ widely. For example, although European and U.S. credit and financial managerial personnel may vie with each other in sophistication, the expertise and personnel available in Latin America or Asia is equally high or sophisticated. The special requirements of doing business in Latin America with its many import and foreign exchange regulations may give rise to an expertise in that field that is unparalleled elsewhere.

Country Wholly Owned Subsidiaries.   Foreign subsidiaries must have some sort of credit organization or level of responsibility for credit and collections. This depends on a great many factors such as size, business revenues, exposures, and degree of delegated authority.

Joint Ventures and Minority Affiliates.   These units also could justify having their own credit function, depending on the elements previously mentioned. Organizationally, they are a variation of the wholly owned country subsidiary because of the less degree of ownership.

Export Credit Concerns
There are basically four areas of concern for the finance and credit functions of a business. All four of these determinants, broadly speaking, either push towards or facilitate increasing centralization of the financial organization. Either they tend to require a decision-making perspective that is regional or corporate wide in scope, transcending individual operations, or they permit, in a mechanical sense, such a perspective to be established and to be made operative. These are not the only determinants of financial organization; there are many others, some of which go directly to a centralizing tendency.

Increased Risk of Doing Business Abroad.   The stakes in selling goods and services overseas have risen dramatically since August 1982 when Mexico announced it would be unable to pay its external debts. For many businesses, the risks and costs have risen faster and higher than potential returns. The risks and uncertainties since that time are by no means new to those businesses with histories of selling goods around the globe. This especially holds true for those caught in Cuba during the revolution of 1958–1959 and the overthrow of the Allende regime in Chile in 1973. Of course, the Third World debt crisis of today has created more uncertainty with respect to adverse political, social, and economic risks than in the past. This includes increased terrorism, violence, and access to vital raw materials from abroad (i.e., the disruptions the oil embargo caused in the 1970s). The effect of these risks and disruptions increases inflation, the cost of capital, the costs of key raw materials, the social costs of doing business, and, to credit managers, the increased probability of foreign bankruptcies from businesses unable to cope with higher inflation and increased prices for imported goods. All of these risks and costs must be assessed by the credit manager for potential impact on the management of foreign receivables and future export credit sales.

Exchange Rates.   Prior to 1941, the world formally recognized a system of fixed exchange rates. In that year, the Bretton Woods agreement was completed and it was necessary to switch to a system of floating exchange rates. As a result, businesses must now operate in a world of fluctuating exchange rates. Some of these rates are rather severe, as some central bankers repeatedly intervene to maintain stability while others simply devalue their currencies to cope with economies running in adverse directions (i.e., Third World countries such as Mexico, Brazil, and Argentina). This means the credit manager has to reevaluate overall country credit exposures and the creditworthiness of foreign buyers. Certain buyers may have to put up more of their local currency when their government decides to devalue its currency against that of another nation (foreign supplier).

Regulations.   The uncertainties and risks of the international marketplace have encouraged various standard-setting and regulatory agencies to implement new financial reporting, accounting, and disclosure requirements for businesses around the globe. In the United States, the Financial Accounting Standards Board (FASB), the Securities and Exchange Commission (SEC), and others have implemented changes. And, more will come. In the United Kingdom, Australia, and Canada, particular attention is being paid to inflation accounting. These additional requirements put considerable strain on the financial organization of a business, especially overseas accountants who already have to maintain two sets of accounting records—one for the parent company and one for the local company—and who might also be responsible for credit administration and cash application.

Many foreign countries, especially Third World debtor nations, have implemented import and foreign exchange regulations to discourage certain imports and the allocation of hard currency to pay for such imports. These regulations can create paper nightmares for exporters as well as problems for financial people at both ends of the export transaction who have to account, control, monitor, and properly manage the business.

Specialization. The need for specialized knowledge has proliferated throughout many businesses, especially those that expanded internationally prior to 1982 and depend on international trade. There is a great need for specialization in finance because of financial risks of movements in foreign exchange and the management of foreign-trade-related receivables. The need for specialization is produced by the major areas enumerated above. Therefore, the increasing need for specialization places a strain on the organizational structure. It tends to flatten out the organizational hierarchy or pyramid because specialized experts are not mere subordinates and may have greater knowledge in their particular areas than their superiors. In addition, the specialized person (or lack thereof) is frustrated by a decentralized organizational structure that does not give the individual direct control over areas he or she should be responsible for (i.e., without direct control over foreign-trade-related receivables and/or direct reporting lines, direct management cannot be exercised and lines of communications are poor). Lack of direct control over people creates a loss of effectiveness and control.

Structuring

In terms of overall corporate organization, there are basically five structures, plus various blends and combinations, that businesses have devised to operate successfully. They are:

1. International division structure.
2. Worldwide product division structure.
3. Worldwide regional structure.
4. Worldwide functional structure.
5. National subsidiary structure.

The basic organization problem common to all firms operating internationally can be summed up in three questions:[7]

1. Should the corporation be divided into domestic and international divisions?
2. Should line responsibility be subdivided for management purposes according to major functions, major product lines, or major geographic areas?
3. What is the best way to provide for needed specialization and coordination according to the other two variables, or how should the three necessary inputs—functional, product, and geographic—be meshed?

Within the business, there are two significant variations from the overall corporation organization picture when it concerns the finance function of the business. One is structural and the other is qualitative.

The structural variation deals with the finance function as a staff function, headed by a corporate department. In this case, the corporate finance department heads all of the basic international organizational structures and has ultimate financial responsibility. Therefore, no matter what the structure, this function cuts across the major structural lines of the organization.

The qualitative variation deals with two important dimensions, functional and geographic. These two dimensions encompass the knowledge or expertise primarily needed in financial decision making. As a result, the business needs to determine how to blend the functional and geographic dimensions of financial organization in its overall structure. This determination will vary from business to business.

Organizationally, the corporate response to these two dimensions is fundamentally different despite what the organization charts and broad position charters may show or specify. The organization charts may show that finance is "staff" to the "line" organization—yet in reality, certain financial matters report outside that line organization. In this case, the position of the line manager may be seriously compromised because of a lack of proper communications. Moreover, the organization charts do not tell the organization truths, and can give rise to major confusion as to who is responsible for what.

Corporate Finance. The basic question at the corporate finance level is what will be the degree of centralization versus decentralization in the international financial operation within the corporate finance department. Corporate practice offers no meaningful alternative to having a corporate finance department. All businesses have them, but there is a great difference in the scope of that department's operations.

Centralization: Advantages versus Disadvantages

Advantages

1. Financial control: Decisions are made by the top level of the organization and are dealt with by or under the immediate direction of senior corporate management. Senior management is in a position to have a continuous, up-to-date and worldwide perspective of the implication of any decision.
2. Maximizes corporate perspective: Decisions can be integrated with domestic financial and nonfinancial matters and treated in a global context.
3. Minimizes risks: From a conservative context, centralization reduces risk. It assumes all important critical facts and problems are brought to the attention of corporate and that corporate takes the correct appropriate action, if any at all.

Disadvantages

1. Weakened line management: Line management at all levels has less authority and leeway in taking appropriate actions and making certain decisions. They have less ability to take advantage of certain opportunities specific or germane to their areas of responsibility.

2. Bureaucracy: Decision making can become bogged down due to lack of immediate responses or a lack of understanding or comprehension of the problem or type of decision to be made. Too many reports are required by corporate from the field to the point where the field does nothing but complete reports.
3. Detailed decisions: Certain decisions are better off left up to local field personnel or delegated to them. Corporate staffs may tend to lose their original perspective.

Each of the five basic structures have their own advantages and disadvantages as organizational forms for the overall corporate structure. Again, it is important to note the structure a business selects can and will vary from one business to the next, even in similar industries.

International Division. This structure can provide an organizational umbrella for all the foreign activities of the business and a focal point for learning about the management of international operations. It is especially helpful for extending a company's activities internationally from a large domestic market like the United States that has dominated the company's attention. It permits centralized direction of a company's foreign operations, particularly during the development and expansion stages of the international program.[8]

The international division is usually headed by a vice president who reports directly to the president or chief executive of the company. Some companies form an international company headed by a president that plays essentially the same role as an international division. In most instances, the international division is responsible for policy and global strategic planning for international operations.[9] A representative organizational diagram for a company using an international division structure is shown in Figure 1–2. During its early stages, the corporate staff groups are likely to continue to be domestically oriented, except for certain finance and control functions (i.e., credit, accounting, and international finance). The international division will rely mainly on its own staff.

The international division usually has direct responsibility for all export and licensing activities of the parent company and is

FIGURE 1–2
International Division Structure

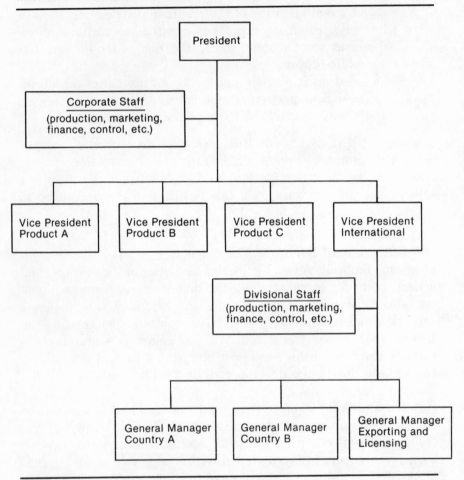

accountable, directly or indirectly, for the operations of overseas manufacturing and sales units. It has responsibility for improving total performance through the unification or synergy potentials of multinational operations.[10]

Where the products manufactured or sold abroad are the

products developed at home, as is normally the case, the international division is heavily dependent on the domestic product divisions. In this respect the international division has less autonomy than the product divisions and depends on their assistance more than they depend on each other, especially in regard to product allocation amounts and priority. As domestic product divisions become more familiar with international needs, the effectiveness of the communication and cooperation process improves. But, the inherent conflict between the goals of the domestic and international divisions is never completely eliminated.

The fact that the international division structure remains dominant in the majority of U.S. multinational companies, despite a strong move toward global structures and grid arrangements, suggests that many businesses have been able to work out informal arrangements or formal devices for resolving the problems inherent in dividing the international unit from the rest of the business.[11] One authority cites the example of a giant U.S. automobile manufacturer with plants in 20 countries, its own sales operations in 18 others, and more than 100,000 workers overseas. This manufacturer was able to continue to operate successfully with an international division structure by making adjustments within the structure for altering patterns of management decision making.[12] Another example is the International Business Machines Corporation (IBM), which continues to handle its extensive and rapidly growing international operations through its separate IBM World Trade Corporation while integrating basic research, product development, and manufacturing activities on a worldwide basis.

Advantages

1. Provides for centralized international responsibility.
2. Fosters development of an international executive cadre.
3. Establishes an organizational framework for a specific voice for international business at top management meetings.
4. Facilitates a companywide view of international opportunities.
5. Permits a sharper focus on international strategy.
6. Financial managers usually physically work side by side

which facilitates close communications across subfunctional lines and can foster a common approach to decision making, planning, and implementation. It helps coordinate an interchange of expertise regarding financial problems.
7. Financial managers can work in close physical proximity with nonfinancial managers to foster closer working relationships.
8. The cohesive and physically unified nature of an international division's finance department permits close working relationships with the corporate finance department.

Disadvantages

1. Can be a potential bottleneck. It cannot centralize many decisions because the competitive position of the subsidiary may be reduced by the time lag involved in securing decisions from the international division.
2. Exports may slow down because domestic producing divisions or units refuse to supply the international division for any number of reasons.
3. Transfer pricing problems can become a major headache between domestic and international.
4. Imbalances may arise between international and other divisions.
5. The division can foster a "we/they" syndrome between domestic and international management.
6. Weakens corporate finance from a global financial perspective.

As the international division structure increases in size relative to the total business, the same forces that led to its creation begin to work toward its dissolution. Senior management becomes aware that there are gains to be realized by coordinating production on a worldwide scale by taking advantage of economies of scale.

There are basically four global organizational structures that can eliminate or reduce the domestic-international dichotomy and pay no more attention to national boundaries than the realities of time and place require. A business may be structured along product, regional, or functional lines and even grid or matrix structures, which is discussed next.

Worldwide Product Division Structure. This product structure assigns worldwide product responsibility to product-group
executives. They are the primary line managers and coordinators
of activity for all products in a given geographic area and serve as
area specialists at the corporate staff level (see Figure 1–3).

This structure works best when a company's product line is
widely diversified, products go into a variety of end-use markets,
and when a relatively high technological capability is required. It is
also advantageous when high shipping costs, tariffs, country
import regulations, or other considerations dictate local manufacture of the goods.

Advantages

1. Emphasizes product know-how and technology, including
   the requirement to extend credit to make an export sale.
   Everyone understands the product or products. Information flows more easily from domestic parent product divi-

FIGURE 1–3
Product Structure

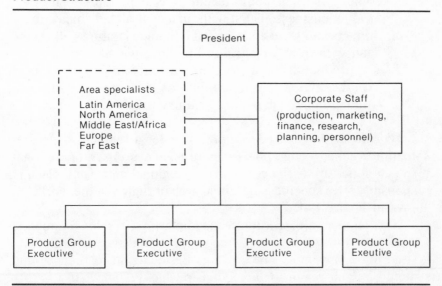

Source: Stefan H. Robock and Kenneth Simmonds, *International Business and Multinational Enterprises,* 4th ed. (Homewood Ill.: Richard D. Irwin, 1989), p. 265.

sions to overseas subsidiaries in the same product lines. Product planning is focused on a worldwide basis.

2. Domestic and international coordination in financial practices of the product division is much closer. It greatly reduces the we/they syndrome.
3. Alleviates profit center problems between domestic and international operations in the same product line business since both ultimately work for the same product division senior executive.
4. The division will have worldwide sales and profit responsibility for its own product line. Hopefully it will staff itself with financial people who have international expertise.

Disadvantages

1. Creates regional or environmental weaknesses. Managers can lack expertise in such areas as dealing with governments, public image, regulations, and credit problems.
2. In any given country, there may be several different product operations, each reporting back separately to its parent product division and each concerned with the local country risks of doing business as it pertains to its own product business. Thus, without a centralized finance function, certain local concerns of a financial nature will not be dealt with from a centralized perspective.
3. The product division structure does not pool together local expertise, regarding such things as local credit conditions, banking relationships, and country regulations.

Worldwide Regional Structure.   Under a regional structure, sometimes called geographic structures, the primary operational responsibilities are assigned to area or regional managers. Each is responsible for a specific geographic area or region of the world, as shown in Figure 1–4.

In this structure, corporate headquarters usually retains responsibility for worldwide strategic planning and control. The United States is simply one of a number of world markets in this structure. Each region or area division has responsibility for its own functions within the region or area for marketing, production, finance, and credit.

FIGURE 1–4
Regional or Area Geographic Structure

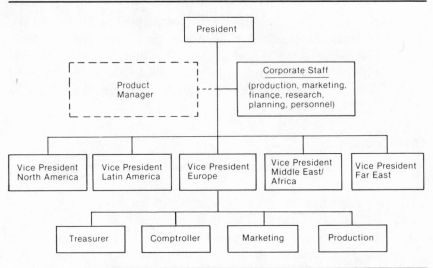

Source: Stefan H. Robock and Kenneth Simmonds, *International Business and Multinational Enterprises*, 4th ed. (Homewood, Ill.: Richard D. Irwin, 1989), p. 263.

Businesses that successfully use the regional or area structure have a narrow range of products whose end-use markets, local marketing requirements, technological base, and methods of manufacture tend to be similar, if not identical. The major oil companies generally use a variant of the geographic structure.

Advantages

1. All regions of the world, including the domestic market, are treated in principle equally as geographic units. This emphasizes regional decentralization in proximity to the marketplace.
2. Regional expertise is coordinated in a single management group for each region and coordinated across product and functional lines within each region. Managers focus on specific regions of the world rather than on the whole world.
3. Each country-level finance manager can be closely supported and monitored by regional financial executives.

4. Management can be physically located in the region and concentrate exclusively on it.
5. The close ties between finance managers and regional non-financial managers facilitates communications and the educational process to teaching local management latest techniques for improving their operations.
6. Facilitates the formulation and implementation of financial strategies that are sensitive to local needs, but also the region in scope.

Disadvantages

1. Can create relatively weak product emphasis and know-how.
2. Creates obstacles to the transfer of technology.
3. Sets up barriers between the regions.
4. Is a costly duplication of functional and product specialists.
5. Can create separate management structures for each region of the world which might lead to budget and capital expenditure problems when each region fights for its share of the overall pie.

Worldwide Functional Structure.   This has been the dominant organizational structure for international operations used by European companies. The division of responsibility at headquarters is organized by functions such as marketing, manufacturing, and finance; and the heads of these divisions have worldwide responsibilities as line executives (see Figure 1–5).

For example, the marketing/sales division has worldwide marketing responsibility, with direct control over all sales companies and distributors, wherever domiciled in the world.

Advantages

1. This structure is rarely used by businesses with more than one product line, but is well suited for single or narrow product line businesses.
2. The structure is well suited for the finance area because reporting lines are direct within the finance area. Financial managers are responsible to more senior financial managers

FIGURE 1–5
Functional Organization Structure

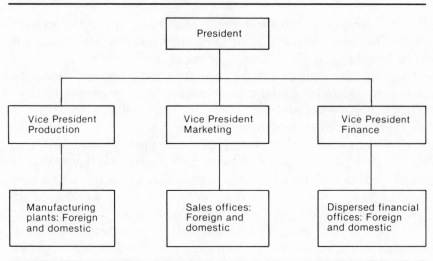

Source: Stefan H. Robock and Kenneth Simmonds, *International Business and Multinational Enterprises,* 4th ed. (Homewood, Ill.: Richard D. Irwin, 1989), p. 262.

rather than to regional or affiliate or other kinds of managers. It facilitates an economic and efficient management of the finance function on a worldwide basis. Their role is to support local management.

3. Tighter financial controls are emphasized under this structure.
4. Overall direction and leadership is done by senior financial executives at the corporate level on a worldwide integrated basis crossing all product lines and structures.

Disadvantages

1. Creates problems in effectively coordinating the various functions, no matter what the level (product, region, division).
2. Financial managers may become too narrow in their outlook or too financially oriented.
3. They are less forced organizationally to take part in team

management with other functional, product, or regional managers.

The Grid or Matrix Structure. Most recently businesses have moved to the matrix or grid form of organizational structure. It is an effort to gain the benefits of more than one of the global structures and requires a move away from the traditional hierarchy of power and unity of command management principles to more of a balance of power and the sharing of responsibility. Most multinational companies that have adopted this form of organization have developed a dual reporting structure along product and area lines. The grid structure, however, has still not been widely embraced. Forsaking traditional management principles for a new system, which does not yet have definite ways of working effectively, has been difficult for managers to accept.[13]

The General Electric Company (GE) provides an excellent example of the matrix form of organization. The company centered its foreign activities for many years in an international division that was organized as a separate company—International General Electric Company. Under pressure from changing internal and external forces, the company gradually moved to a structure that assigned worldwide responsibility to its domestic product groups. A reorganized International Group, however, continued to operate along with the product groups, as one company executive explained, "to provide a mechanism that would avoid the risk that 50 to 60 general managers might start at a furious pace reinventing the wheel, competing with each other in committing the same blunders instead of learning from each other's experience." The International Group had four overseas area managers who were responsible for governmental and business relations in their areas, and whose staff experts assisted operating departments on entry strategy and environmental assessment.

Through a form of grid arrangement, GE had assigned heavy international responsibility to units that contain product expertise while still trying to achieve coordination on a geographic area basis. The difficulties of finding a perfect organizational structure are demonstrated by the fact that a product organizational structure adopted by GE in 1964 was restructured within only five years by creating a strong International Group to review and coordinate all international operations of the company.

National Subsidiary Structure. The national subsidiary structure is an organizational structure whereby overseas affiliates report directly to parent headquarters and not through intermediate product-line or regional management structures. However, this type of structure is relatively rare.

The structure has long been used by European and Japanese companies, but now, even they are finding it inceasingly impractical and difficult to manage for reasons due to such things as size, the spread and number of overseas units, and the diversity of international operations. But, it has not entirely disappeared and is used by a few U.S. businesses as their primary form of international organization.

The national subsidiary structure generally entails a lean organization, but has an absence of intermediate layers of management. It puts great pressure on headquarters managers who must deal directly with overseas personnel. In addition, it requires a great deal of expertise on the part of headquarters personnel to keep up with worldwide events.

APPENDIX 1-A   DUTIES AND RESPONSIBILITIES OF AN INTERNATIONAL CREDIT DEPARTMENT

1. Continually keep abreast of country political, economic, and social changes, foreign exchange fluctuations and regulations, and country import regulations.
2. Develop a systematic collection follow-up sequence and technique for the collection of foreign accounts billed on: open account, documentary draft, notes, letters of credit, and other credit term arrangements.
3. Negotiate and maintain credit information agency contracts.
4. Prepare statistical and written reports for senior management on the condition of the accounts receivable investment and accounts.
5. Keep appropriate levels of senior management informed of the status of accounts receivable.
6. Contact banks and trade credit suppliers to exchange factual

credit information on mutual foreign customers, including information on country conditions.

7. Analyze domestic and foreign financial statements on customers.
8. Establish order limits, credit lines, or limits on individual customers for credit control purposes.
9. Develop an international commercial bank network to handle trade financing, documentary collections, letters of credit, and other services after evaluating the services of each bank.
10. Maintain liaison with government and private agencies, such as The Export-Import Bank (Eximbank), Overseas Private Investment Corporation (OPIC), American Insurance Group (AIG), and the U.S. Department of Commerce.
11. Identify and quantify areas to minimize bank float and improve cash flow, such as improving export documentation flow.
12. Review frequently, at least monthly, the status of current or past-due active foreign accounts.
13. Develop a statistical summary aging of accounts receivable reporting format to receive foreign subsidiary/affiliate trade accounts receivable information on a frequent basis (i.e., monthly, every other month, quarterly, etc.).
14. Perform overseas on-site credit reviews of foreign subsidiary/affiliate credit management of accounts receivable. Coordinate these visits with customer/country risk assessment visits.
15. Formulate and apply adequate controls where necessary to ensure the credit department operates efficiently and effectively.
16. Actively participate in industry trade credit groups and associations to exchange credit and collection experience on foreign account problems and country conditions.
17. Extend credit to foreign customers in accordance with established company policy and procedure.
18. Develop credit approval authority levels and procedures for the referral of accounts which exceed a credit person's authority level.
19. Develop and continually sponsor credit training programs, workshops, or seminars for worldwide credit and marketing/sales personnel, foreign customers, credit groups or associations, and outside companies or colleges/universities.
20. Attend in-house and outside training programs, seminars, and workshops to develop and improve credit skills and managerial techniques.
21. Order credit reports from credit reporting agencies when necessary.

22. Update and purge customer credit files on a regular basis.
23. Formulate a budget in accordance with company policy and procedure.
24. Manage the credit department within budget.
25. Develop sources of information to keep promptly informed of country conditions, such as, import regulations, foreign exchange regulations and political/economic conditions to assess country risk.
26. Establish, organize, and maintain country files.
27. Participate in credit and collection summary questionnaire surveys and/or obtain reports that provide information on worldwide collection experience and credit terms being offered by other exporters.
28. Participate in marketing/sales meetings when appropriate.
29. Meet with marketing/sales frequently to discuss risk accounts and country conditions.
30. Analyze unusual requests for extended credit terms beyond established credit terms.
31. Visit foreign customers whenever economically feasible to obtain additional credit and financial information, enhance relations, and counsel the customer to improve operations.
32. Prepare in advance of visiting foreign countries through letters of introduction, allocating sufficient time to accomplish objectives with well-thought-out agendas and plans.
33. Coordinate visits to foreign countries with visits to banks; other business firms; export development, Embassies, and Consulate offices of the U.S. Department of Commerce; credit reporting agencies, and export credit insurance agencies.
34. File incoming credit and financial information in appropriate customer credit files.
35. Properly organize and maintain customer credit files.
36. Automate the credit management function (if not in place and where necessary) or continually seek methods to improve existing systems to enhance productivity, information, and results by a cost/benefit justification.
37. Participate in the selection of a software system for the automation of credit and accounts receivable.
38. Continually seek methods to reduce paper flows, manual tasks, and clerical duties through automation by a cost/benefit justification.
39. Write job descriptions for each credit position.
40. Establish and monitor credit personnel performance.

41. Select individuals for credit positions based on the qualifications of each applicant.
42. Explain to customers the various types of trade finance arrangements offered by the company to enhance sales and customer goodwill.
43. Obtain security or collateral to minimize customer and/or country risks whenever feasible.
44. Respond to incoming inquiries, especially foreign customer inquiries, as expeditiously as possible.
45. Place accounts with collection agencies or attorneys after internal collection efforts are exhausted.
46. Formulate international credit policies and procedures.
47. Study and improve intra and interdepartmental relations, especially with marketing/sales and foreign customers.
48. Formulate international subsidiary/affiliate credit and collection policy guidelines.

APPENDIX 1–B EXPORT CREDIT AND COLLECTION GUIDELINE

Purpose
To establish a framework or guide for consistent credit decisions related in international credit directed toward attaining the strategies and goals established by the business, the objectives of sales and marketing, and the financial goals of treasury.

1. Objectives
Credit management is directed towards the following objectives:

1.1 Assist the sales and marketing functions to obtain credit sales while assuming reasonable credit risks.
1.2 Optimize cash receipts by collecting accounts at agreed on maturity dates.
1.3 Inform the sales and marketing functions regarding a customer's financial condition and payment history.
1.4 Maintain the accounts receivable investment at a level responsive to business and financial conditions.
1.5 Control bad-debt losses resulting from the extension of credit to customers within established objectives.
1.6 Utilize credit and accounts receivable systems for credit and

cash application control purposes to obtain optimum efficiency and effectiveness.

2. Credit Policy

2.1 *Payment terms.*

2.1.1 Standard export payment terms by product category or line will be the responsibility of sales and marketing management with the assistance and review of the credit manager.

2.1.2 In the case of export credit insurance, both credit and sales/marketing management are responsible for extending payment terms in accordance with the terms and conditions as stated in the policy by the insurer.

2.1.3 Credit, sales, and marketing should meet at least quarterly to determine the maximum export payment terms to extend per product category or line and per country, using a customer/country risk code classification or ranking (noncredit insured).

2.1.4 Terms and conditions offered by other competitive trade suppliers for comparable products sold in the same market must be taken seriously into consideration.

2.1.5 All deviations from standard payment terms should be closely monitored in view of any existing local country antitrust laws, regulations, or country risk conditions (now and in the future).

2.2 *Credit limits.*

2.2.1 Export credit management is responsible for establishing and monitoring credit limits (order and credit limits) granted to individual customers.

2.2.2 In the case of export credit insurance, both credit and sales/marketing management are responsible for extending credit limits in accordance with any of the terms and conditions as stated in the policy by the insurer.

2.2.3 Credit management and sales/marketing management will establish jointly country credit limits where and when necessary, unless established by an export credit insurer.

2.2.4 Credit management will authorize the release of customer orders, despite a high degree of risk or credit exposure to accomplish planned sales and marketing management objectives, if:

a. Cash or equivalent payment terms are unobtainable.

      b. Letter of credit, personal guaranties, debt subordination agreements, retention of title, or other forms of security are unavailable.

      c. If applicable, export credit insurance coverage cannot be obtained.

      d. Business considerations justify accepting the credit risk after reviewing the risks/rewards or costs/benefits by appropriate levels of management.

  2.3 *Coordination with other departments.*

    2.3.1 Credit management shall provide sales and marketing personnel with information concerning changes in the financial condition of customers which could potentially affect credit limits, sales, profit margins, and marketing plans. Similarly, sales and marketing personnel should provide credit management with customer and market information that may have an impact on the current and near-term business situation of customers and business plans.

    2.3.2 Credit management should participate in sales and marketing meetings, as appropriate, to promote and develop the interrelationships of these business functions.

    2.3.3 Credit management shall attend, whenever economically feasible, outside export trade credit organizational meetings for the exchange of credit information and credit training workshops or seminars (i.e., FCIB monthly or regional round table conferences, workshops, and seminars).

3. Procedures

  3.1 *Payment terms.*

    3.1.1 Sales and marketing personnel are encouraged to negotiate with customers for the shortest competitive export payment terms which deviate from standard export payment terms. Consideration should be given to the time value of money, existing market conditions, competitive situations, and profit margins.

    3.1.2 In cases regarding export credit insurance policies, sales and marketing personnel must take into consideration maximum permissible payment terms established by the insurer per customer or country.

3.1.3 Credit management is responsible for monitoring cash discount arrangements when offered to customers and for the collection of unearned (unauthorized) discounts taken by customers.

3.2 *Establishing customer credit.*

3.2.1 Sales personnel must initially obtain credit and financial information from prospective customers by using a customer profile form.

3.2.2 Credit management will extend credit to customers from credit and financial information obtained from the following sources: credit reports from no less than two credit reporting agencies, at least two bank references, customer financial statements, trade supplier references, and internally based on past payment experience and information obtained from sales personnel.

3.2.3 In the case of export credit insurance, prior approval must be obtained if the anticipated customer credit limit exceeds any discretionary credit limits established in the policy by its terms and conditions.

3.2.4 All customer credit and financial information will be maintained in a customer credit file. Such information will be updated at least annually or more frequently as the need arises.

3.3 *Credit controls.*

3.3.1 Order limits will be established on each customer based on historical ordering patterns or annual sales volume information obtained from sales personnel or direct from customers.

3.3.2 Credit limits will be assigned to each customer based on their financial credit worthiness as evidenced by an evaluation of the credit and financial information obtained from various reliable sources.

3.3.3 Credit authority limits will be assigned to credit department personnel as assigned by senior management.

3.4 *Collection activity.*

3.4.1 The collection of past due accounts shall be a joint effort of credit and sales personnel.

3.4.2 Collection of past due accounts will be performed in accordance with an established systematic collection follow-up sequence for customers billed on open account, drafts, or letters of credit.

3.4.3 In the case of export credit insurance, account past due balances must be followed up in accordance with the terms and conditions stated in the policy of the insurer.

3.4.4 In the case of documentary collections, international commercial banks will be used to control export title documents and assist in obtaining collection or acceptance of drafts in accordance with the stated export payment terms.

3.4.5 The credit manager will prepare written instructions for all concerned, especially freight forwarders, for the proper preparation of bank documentary collections and letters of credit.

3.4.6 Account balances deemed uncollectible, bankrupt, or unable to pay due to country conditions will be transferred to a suspense account ledger for further handling by a collection agency or attorney. In the case of country conditions, the prime example is an account unable to remit due to the unavailability of that currency in the country.

Therefore, the account is transferred to suspense until such point in time as the billing currency is made available or allocated to the customer to pay its debt obligation.

3.4.7 In the case of export credit insurance, claims will be filed against the insurer for commercial or political reasons in accordance with the terms and conditions of the policy.

3.5 *Accruals and write-offs to bad debts.*

3.5.1 The credit manager will work with accounting to determine the accrual provision to bad debts for doubtful accounts.

3.5.2 Bad debt reserves will be adjusted periodically throughout the year to provide an adequate reserve level in relation to the outstanding accounts receivable investment.

3.5.3 Customer balances over 180 days past due or transferred to suspense are to be reserved at 100 percent of the outstanding balance.

3.5.4 Bad debt reserve balances at year-end must meet the test of prudent accounting practices and tax regulations. In principle, this requires that the year-end reserve balance be either specified as to customer or identified by group of customers, whether recorded in trade or notes accounts receivable and/or suspense ledger.

APPENDIX 1–C   FOREIGN SUBSIDIARY CREDIT AND COLLECTION GUIDELINE

Purpose
To establish a framework or guide for establishing by each subsidiary credit function, local credit and collection policies and procedures.

1. Objectives
Local credit management at all foreign subsidiaries are directed towards the following objectives:

1.1 Assist the sales and marketing functions to obtain credit sales while assuming reasonable credit risks.

1.2 Optimize cash receipts by collecting accounts at agreed on maturity dates.

1.3 Inform the sales and marketing functions regarding a customer's financial condition and payment history.

1.4 Maintain the accounts receivable investment at a level responsive to business and financial conditions.

1.5 Control bad debt losses resulting from the extension of credit to customers within established objectives.

1.6 Develop credit and accounts receivable systems for credit and cash application control purposes to obtain optimum efficiency and effectiveness.

2. Responsibility and Organization

2.1 Local credit management is defined as any foreign subsidiary credit or accounting-related individual delegated the responsibility for credit approval and collection of accounts.

2.2 Local credit management is responsible for the day-to-day administration of receivables as well as establishing and maintaining effective credit and collection controls and procedures. Parent company credit manager(s) will review and make recommendations on all controls and procedures to be established by local credit management.

2.3 For foreign subsidiaries outside of Europe, local credit management will report functionally and organizationally to the local Controller (chief accountant) or General Manager, additionally to the parent company Credit Manager on a dotted-line basis.

2.4 In Europe, local credit management will report functionally and organizationally to the local Financial Director, Controller or General Manager, additionally to the parent company Credit Manager on a dotted-line basis.

2.5 The functional relationship between the parent company Credit Manager and local credit management at all foreign subsidiaries shall include direction, advice, guidance, training, and coordination on credit-related matters.

2.6 The parent company's Credit Manager will place special emphasis on multiple large exposure common customers who are sold by more than one foreign subsidiary. The purpose is to monitor these credit exposures to avoid unnecessary commercial or country risks.

3. Credit Policy

3.1 *Payment terms.*

3.1.1 Standard domestic payment terms by product category or line are established by local sales and marketing management with the assistance and review by local credit management.

3.1.2 In the case of export credit insurance, both credit and sales/marketing management are responsible for extending payment terms in accordance with the terms and conditions as stated in the policy by the insurer.

3.1.3 Local sales and marketing should meet at least quarterly with local credit management to determine the maximum export payment terms they are willing to extend per product category or line and per country. It is highly recommended they jointly assign export credit terms by using customer/country risk code classifications or rankings (noncredit insured).

3.1.4 Terms and conditions offered by other competitive trade suppliers for comparable products sold in the same market should be supplied by sales and marketing personnel.

3.1.5 All deviations from standard payment terms should be closely monitored in view of any existing local country antitrust laws, regulations, or country risk conditions.

3.2 *Credit limits.*

3.2.1 Local credit management is responsible for establishing and monitoring credit limits (order and credit limits) granted to individual customers.

3.2.2 In the case of export credit insurance, both credit and sales/marketing management are responsible for extending credit limits in accordance with the terms and conditions as stated in the policy by the insurer.

3.2.3 Local credit management and sales/marketing management will jointly establish country credit limits where and when necessary (within established country credit limits established by credit insurers).

3.2.4 Local credit management will authorize the release of customer orders, despite a high degree of risk or credit exposure to accomplish planned local management objectives, if:

a. Cash or equivalent payment terms are unobtainable.

b. Letters of credit, personal guaranties, debt subordination agreements, retention of title, or other forms of security are unavailable.

c. If applicable, credit insurance coverage cannot be obtained.

d. Business considerations justify accepting the credit risk after reviewing the risks/rewards or costs/benefits by appropriate levels of management.

3.3 *Coordination with other departments.*

3.3.1 Local credit management shall provide sales and marketing personnel with information concerning changes in the financial condition of customers which could potentially affect credit limits, sales, profit margins, and marketing plans. Similarly, sales and marketing personnel should provide local credit management with customer and market information that may have an impact on the current and near-term business situation of customers and business plans.

3.3.2 Local credit management should participate in sales and marketing meetings, as appropriate, to promote and develop the interrelationships of these business functions.

3.3.3 Local credit management shall attend (whenever economically feasible) outside trade credit organizational meetings for the exchange of credit information and credit training workshops or seminars (i.e., FCIB European conferences, workshops, and seminars).

4. Procedures

4.1 *Payment terms.*

4.1.1 Sales and marketing personnel are encouraged to negotiate with customers for the shortest competitive payment terms

which deviate from standard payment terms. Consideration should be given to the time value of money, existing
market conditions, competitive situations, and profit
margins.

4.1.2 In cases regarding export credit insurance policies, sales
and marketing personnel must take into consideration
maximum permissible payment terms established by the
insurer per customer or country.

4.1.3 When establishing export payment terms, all foreign subsidiary local credit management that is active in export
trade to nonrelated third party customers shall seriously
consider country credit risks (i.e., foreign exchange conditions and regulations, import regulations, political and
economic conditions). Local credit management and sales/
marketing personnel are encouraged to seek the advice and
guidance of the parent company's Credit Manager and
sales/marketing personnel.

4.1.4 All locations are encouraged to establish standard payment
terms by product categories or lines and by country, taking
into consideration industry standards, competitive practices, financial condition, and costs of capital.

4.1.5 Local credit management is responsible for monitoring
cash discount arrangements when offered to customers
and for the collection of unearned (unauthorized) discounts
taken by customers.

4.2 *Establishing customer credit.*

4.2.1 To obtain credit and financial information from customers,
local credit management is encouraged to implement a
Customer Profile Form (credit application) for use by sales
personnel to obtain such information.

4.2.2 Credit will be extended to domestic and foreign customers
from credit and financial information obtained from the
following sources: Credit reports from more than one
reliable credit reporting agency, banks, customer financial
statements, trade supplier references, and internally based
on past payment experience and information obtained from
sales personnel.

4.2.3 In the case of export credit insurance, prior approval must
be obtained if the anticipated customer credit limit exceeds
any discretionary credit limits established in the policy by
its terms and conditions.

4.2.4 Credit and financial information obtained on accounts shall be maintained in a customer credit file. The file should contain a copy of the Customer Profile Form. Such credit and financial information should be updated at least annually on an active purchasing customer or whenever applicable (i.e., to change a customer's credit limits, if the customer's financial condition has changed, or its purchasing requirements have increased).

4.3 *Credit controls.*

4.3.1 Order limits are to be assigned on each customer based on historical ordering patterns or annual sales volume information obtained from sales personnel or direct from customers.

4.3.2 Credit limits are to be assigned to each customer based on their financial creditworthiness as evidenced by an evaluation of the credit and financial information obtained from various reliable sources.

4.3.3 The local General Manager is responsible for establishing authority limits by subordinate credit personnel, Credit Manager, Chief Accountant, Financial Director, and General Manager.

4.4 *Collection activity.*

4.4.1 The collection of past due accounts shall be a joint effort of credit and sales personnel.

4.4.2 Local credit management will perform collection follow-up in line with approved payment terms by establishing a written systematic collection follow-up sequence.

4.4.3 In the case of export credit insurance, account past due balances must be followed up in accordance with the terms and conditions as stated in the policy by the insurer.

4.4.4 The use of formalized reminder letters adapted to the needs of individual locations and local country laws is encouraged, whether done manually or automatically by a credit-accounts receivable system.

4.4.5 Account balances deemed uncollectible are to be transferred to a suspense account ledger. An uncollectible account is defined as one in which the customer refuses to pay the outstanding debt obligation, a satisfactory payment arrangement cannot be agreed on, the account is transferred to a collection agency or attorney, or the account has filed for bankruptcy (country equivalent). This includes transferring accounts that are unable to pay due to the unavailability of the billing currency in its country or if allocation of the billing currency is not expected for some time.

4.4.6 In the case of export credit insurance, claims will be filed against the insurer for commercial or political reasons in accordance with the terms and conditions of the policy.

4.5 *Accruals and write-offs to bad debts.*

4.5.1 Local accounting management working in conjunction with local credit management and the General Manager shall determine the accrual provision to bad debts for doubtful accounts.

4.5.2 Bad debt reserves shall be adjusted periodically throughout the year to provide an adequate reserve level in relation to the outstanding accounts receivable investment, particularly to that portion aged 90 days and over or those accounts identified as large risks (a portion of the debt outstanding should be reserved).

4.5.3 Customer balances over 180 days past due or transferred to a suspense account (with collection agencies, domestic or export credit insurers, or solicitors, attorneys, lawyers) shall be reserved for 100 percent of the outstanding balance.

4.5.4 Bad debt reserve balances at year-end must meet the test of prudent local accounting practices and tax regulations. In principle, this requires that the year-end reserve balance be either specified as to customer or identified by group of customers, whether recorded in trade or notes accounts receivable and/or a suspense ledger.

5. Parent Company Credit Manager

5.1 *Multiple exposure accounts.*

5.1.1 The parent company Credit Manager will monitor and make recommendations to the local Credit Manager and General Manager regarding companywide multiple exposure accounts to minimize potential over-exposed situations or commercial and/or country risks.

5.1.2 From time to time, the parent company Credit Manager will request certain credit information concerning these accounts (i.e., account balances outstanding, condition of receivable balance outstanding, credit limits, latest credit and financial information).

5.2 *Management reports and systems.*

    5.2.1 Local credit management shall submit a monthly or quarterly (depends on the size of the A/R investment) accounts receivable aging statistics by local currency and U.S. dollars using the Accounts Receivable Management Report.

    5.2.2 The parent company Credit Manager will assist local credit management with the selection of automated credit and accounts receivable systems to obtain some uniformity and standardization worldwide with these systems.

5.3 *Local visits.*

    5.3.1 From time to time, the parent company Credit Manager will visit with local credit management and other personnel to perform an on-site review of the condition of receivable, credit controls, and adherence to this guideline.

    5.3.2 At the completion of each on-site review, local credit management and superiors, especially the General Manager, will be appraised of the review. Problem areas will be discussed to determine remedial action dates for completion. Follow-up visits will be made to ensure remedial action has been taken as agreed.

5.4 *Training.*

    5.4.1 The parent company Credit Manager will perform from time to time, especially when making on-site reviews, credit training programs for local company management (credit, accounting, sales/marketing, and senior managements) either at the local location or on a regional basis.

    5.4.2 At least once every two years, depending on budgetary constraints, local credit management will be invited to actively participate in a parent company Credit Managers' meeting for the sole purpose of jointly discussing an interchange of thoughts and ideas related to credit principles and practices and business practices.

REFERENCES

1. Clarence B. Nickerson, *Accounting Handbook for Non-Accountants,* 2nd ed. (Boston, Mass.: CBI Publishing Company, 1979), p. 151.
2. Ibid., p. 151.
3. George N. Christie and Albert E. Bracuti, *Credit Management,*

(Lake Success, N.Y.: The Credit Research Foundation, Inc., 1981), p. 27.

4. Ibid., p. 28.
5. Ibid., pp. 32–33.
6. George N. Christie, *Credit Department Operations: A Guide to Profits* (Lake Success, N.Y.: Credit Research Foundation, Inc., 1976), p. 2.
7. Stefan H. Robock and Kenneth Simmonds, *International Business and Multinational Enterprises,* 4th ed. (Homewood, Ill.: Richard D. Irwin, 1989), p. 270.
8. Ibid., p. 433.
9. Ibid., p. 433.
10. Ibid., p. 435.
11. Gilbert H. Clee and Wilbur M. Sachtjen, "Organizing a Worldwide Enterprise," *Harvard Business Review,* November–December 1964, pp. 57–59.
12. *Organizing the Worldwide Corporation,* New York: Business International, January 1970, pp. 12–13; and "Multinational Organizations," *Business Week,* March 24, 1975, p. 122.
13. W. D. Dance, "An Evolving Structure For Multinational Operations," *Columbia Journal of World Business,* November–December 1969, p. 29.

CHAPTER 2

IDENTIFYING THE RISKS

The exporter has two major concerns when selling goods and services internationally: What are the commercial or customer credit risks and what are the country or political risks?

Conducting business across national boundaries can involve unexpected payment delays or even foreign companies going bankrupt. The inability to assess the winds of change or understand a country's political or economic environment in some geographical parts of the world has resulted in nationalizations, expropriations, draconian foreign exchange controls, and other adverse problems that affect the performance of credit managers and the companies who employ them.

The challenges of the 1990s will place an increasing burden on exporters. Debt-servicing problems will undoubtedly be a dominant factor in years to come as debtor nations strive to curb imports while striving to improve their export performance.

Since World War II there has been a massive integrated increase in cross-border flows of goods, services, and investments. This has greatly assisted global economic growth, but it has also made companies highly vulnerable to fluctuations in foreign exchange risks.

This vulnerability has been especially painful to company credit managers, international finance managers, strategic financial planners, and marketing/sales management since the breakdown of the Bretton Woods Agreement in 1971, which caused foreign exchange markets to be plagued by a growing instability. Since then, large fluctuations in exchange rates, sometimes daily, have considerably complicated a company's short-term financial and long-term strategic decisions, imposing substantial resource costs on companies.

No credit person can really properly perform his or her duties and responsibilities without having a basic understanding of country risk conditions and foreign exchange in general. Many credit managers over the years have perfected the need for making sound credit decisions predicated on gathering, evaluating or analyzing factual information (i.e., historical payment experience or credit reports), received on a timely basis on foreign customers. In addition to the customer risk, the credit person must be concerned with country risk. It is a vital and integral part of the credit investigation process that many credit managers have not perfected. These risks are attributed to country political, economic, and foreign exchange risk conditions that prevail in many countries throughout the world. Many times, country conditions determine how and when an exporter will get paid. Indentifying the risks is one thing. Knowing what to do about them in the credit decision-making process is another.

In view of the world's current and future economic and political environment, it is important to stress the need on the part of credit managers to not only properly assess the creditworthiness of foreign customers, but to assess the country risk conditions as part of their credit decision-making process to assist their companies in promoting exports.

COMMERCIAL RISK

Determining commercial or customer risk employs an evaluation and analysis of information from a myriad of facts. It deals with obtaining answers to very important questions: Is the foreign customer creditworthy for the shipment? Will it be accepted? It is done to determine whether or not a foreign customer has the ability and willingness to pay maturing debt obligations as they come due. Is there a reasonable expectation for repayment made in accordance with terms and conditions mutually agreed on between the exporter and foreign customer? With the exception of unexpected country risk conditions, explained later, there is no substitute for making the right credit decision, on the right credit terms, and the establishment of proper and prudent credit controls.

Creditworthy or Financial Risk. This risk factor deals with the financial capability of the foreign customer to pay debt obligations as they come due for payment. Is the foreign customer suffering cash flow problems to the point where you will get paid slow or is it near insolvency or bankruptcy? The longer the length of the credit terms, the greater the degree of risk since it is difficult to determine if the foreign customer has the financial capacity to pay for the goods delivered three, six, or twelve months later— even longer in the case of capital goods exports.

Acceptance Risk. This risk factor deals with the foreign customer not accepting the goods after they are shipped. Nonacceptance may be justified by documents indicating the exporter did not comply with the sales contract due to price, quality, quantity, and description of the goods. Pricing problems sometimes occur in commodity shipments. The price may have declined since the sales contract was initially negotiated or prices might be gyrating almost daily, making it difficult to agree on price and when to ship.

Goods that are not accepted at the foreign port of destination might be left unclaimed at the foreign pier (which may accumulate large demurrage charges) or stored in a government warehouse (accruing large warehouse charges). The exporter may try to settle the dispute with the foreign customer either through direct negotiation or legal channels, ship the goods to its foreign office if one exists, find another buyer in the same country, reship the goods back to its country, or reship the goods to a foreign customer in another country. All of these alternatives are expensive and timely efforts due to the distances involved and the problems associated with legal systems in foreign countries, especially if the exporter elects to bring suit in the foreign country of the customer.

Domestic credit managers have a number of sources of credit and financial information to choose from, especially the ability to review and analyze customer financial statements. Credit managers who attempt to make credit decisions on foreign customers are hampered by limited and sometimes unreliable sources of credit and financial information received on a timely basis.

Despite the lack of sufficient and unreliable sources of information, making a credit decision about foreign customers employs a strong element of trust, logic, common sense, and good judgment. Although the element of trust exists in domestic credit, it may be all the credit manager has to go on in extending credit to foreign customers. Yet, the credit manager must be cognizant of the elements of country risk entering into the credit decision-making scenario. A foreign customer who is considered credit-worthy for open account terms, may not be extended these lenient payment terms if there is a high degree of country risk (i.e., lengthy foreign exchange delays due to shortages of the exporter's billing currency).

In effect, making a credit decision to foreign customers comprises an analysis of facts as shown in Table 2–1.

Admittedly, determining customer risk is difficult and time consuming—even costly. The propensity of each decision can vary from one extreme to the other. The credit manager is faced with extending credit limits of anywhere between cash to millions of dollars (or other currencies). The payment terms can range from open account, draft, or some sort of letter of credit payment terms, and the length of these terms can vary from discount to several years. They can be invoiced to many countries. This is one reason why companies should have written credit policies and procedures (guidelines). The intent is to encourage the development of consistent credit decision making.

Obviously, not all new or existing foreign customers will be approved or extended credit based on the same terms and conditions. This is especially true when country conditions enter into the credit decision. Not all foreign customers will pay on time and some will never pay, as evidenced by the interchange of information at credit group meetings (i.e., Finance, Credit, and International Business [FCIB] meetings, New York) and the reserve for doubtful accounts established on the balance sheets of companies

TABLE 2–1
Credit Decision Process

Internal/External Factors	Commercial Analysis	Country Analysis
Strategy	Antecedents	Political
Business plan	Payment record	Economic
Competition	Information sources	Social
	Nonfinancial/financial factors	F/X
		Regulations

throughout the world. While some companies will make credit sales and business decisions to sell goods and services to foreign customers and countries where elements of risk exist, others will not. Some will make credit sales only to the most financially strong and highly reputable companies in certain countries while others will sell to a combination of strong and weak businesses and countries throughout the world. It is important to note some countries are dependent on their industries to export goods and services (i.e., Japan and West Germany). This is done not only to generate export earnings, but because export business represents a high percentage of their country's gross domestic product (GDP).

Other approaches for identifying customer risk are to exchange payment experiences with other trade credit suppliers and to analyze customer financial statements by obtaining:

1. The names, addresses, and contact person of at least three or more local suppliers and three or more foreign suppliers; the names, addresses, and account officer of at least three bank references (account numbers are helpful); estimated yearly purchases and credit term requirements.
2. Consolidated year-end financial statements (balance sheet, income statement and notes) for the last three years for observing positive or negative trends as prepared by an outside CPA or reputable accounting firm, signed and dated by an officer, partner, or owner and/or the latest quarterly financial statement, prepared by an in-house accountant or outside CPA.

Although getting financial statements from foreign customers is difficult under many different types of circumstances, they are obtainable. Credit managers will be surprised at how many foreign customers will comply with a request for financial statements covering their last three years. When asked up front before business is transacted, it sets the trend and tone of how the exporter wishes to conduct its business from a credit and business perspective. Thereafter, asking for financial statements should be easier. Asking for financial statements after shipments have been made will be difficult. Asking for financial statements is one thing, especially for three years, getting it is another. Threats to put the foreign customer on letter of credit payment terms is not the answer—you will only lose the business to competition. A diplomatic and professional approach, explaining the reasons for the request, usually obtains positive results. The credit manager may have to extend credit in many instances without the benefit of financial statements and take a reasonable amount of risk. If the business relationship develops and prospers, and if the marketing/ sales department cooperates with the credit department in requesting financial statements from reluctant foreign customers, the chances of getting this valuable information are greatly enhanced.

Selling or entering into large sales contracts without knowing or having any idea about the financial strength or creditworthiness of the foreign customer doesn't make much sense. Marketing/sales should want to know whether or not a foreign customer is creditworthy for the transaction being considered or negotiated, especially long-term supply contracts or relationships. It is a waste of their time and effort to sell to someone that doesn't have the financial strength to increase purchases or pay its debt obligations timely. When sales volume increases and/or the credit terms lengthen, so will the risks and the possibility of a higher bad debt loss. Everyone in the exporter's operations needs reassurances the business relationship entered into will be a long and lasting one.

Getting credit and financial information in advance will help reduce the amount of time it takes for the credit department to approve a foreign customer. Getting this information on foreign customers can take several weeks. The sales department should inform the credit manager as early as possible of potential prospective customers, even if the sales department is only doing some preliminary investigating of potential foreign customers in certain countries. Why should the sales department get all excited about selling to certain customers if they aren't creditworthy or the country is considered a high risk from a credit point of view? The more lead time the credit manager has, the better it is for the sales department and customer in getting credit approval and goods shipped timely. The length of time it takes to gather sufficient amounts of credit and financial information on foreign customers to justify an extension of credit, especially if the sales orders are large and the payment terms long, is always an important consideration. Many times credit people are contacted at the last minute to make a credit decision on a new deal without having any prior knowledge of its details. This puts the credit manager in the position of making a hasty credit decision.

Analyzing foreign customer financial statements can best be accomplished by using some of the proven methods used on domestic financial statements. It can be done by using the same ratio tests to determine liquidity, activity, leverage, and profitability to assess the overall financial condition of foreign customers.

In summary, the entire international trading community is based on elements of trust, goodwill, and prudent judgment. Without these, international trade would deteriorate to the point of no return. It is important for credit managers to remember these elements because of the distances between buyers and sellers and the lack of sufficient amounts of credit and financial information on foreign customers. Credit inquiries should be conducted to determine if a foreign customer is acting in good faith and is not overestimating its future ability to pay. Again, the two questions uppermost in the mind of credit managers when considering commercial and country risks are (1) what is their ability to pay, and (2) are they willing to pay.

Identifying the risks has been made easier over the years by the development of some basic methods for evaluating the creditworthiness of foreign customers. Although some of these methods overlap, it is up to the credit manager to select a method which best suits the needs of his or her company and remains consistent.

The Eight Cs of Credit

In domestic credit, credit managers determine the ability and willingness of customers by carefully considering certain basic facts referred to as the Cs of credit:

- Character.
- Capacity or capability.
- Capital.
- Conditions.

In international trade, the credit manager should consider four additional Cs of credit:

- Country.
- Currency.
- Collateral.
- Computers.

By assessing and analyzing these eight Cs of credit, the credit manager can start to come up with some conclusions concerning the ability and willingness of foreign customers to repay maturing debt obligations timely.

Character. It consists of an account's reputation for honesty and dependability and the willingness of the foreign customer to pay promptly. It refers to past business experience and present standing, plus the salesperson's and credit manager's estimate of the account. When limited capital (net worth) is employed in a small- or medium-size business, credit is often granted on character alone. However, even with the largest foreign customer, character should be taken seriously and considered of prime importance, whether applied to individuals or the management of a company (corporation, joint venture partner, or limited partnership).

Capacity or Capability. This is the ability of the foreign customer, whether individual, partnership, or corporation, to conduct its business successfully. Training, experience, aggressiveness, and proven judgment are all important factors affecting capacity to operate. In addition, capability requires management ability and technical know-how for production, distribution, and the ability to manage. A lack of these qualities may result in a poor financial performance.

Capital. Important information on capital can be obtained directly from financial statements of the foreign customer or indirectly from other sources such as credit reporting agencies. Obtaining and understanding the capital account of foreign customers is difficult because capital account structures vary based on different industries, legal composition, accounting regulations, and countries. Many foreign customers in different countries have two or three different financial statements. Therefore, once you obtain a customer's financial statement, it is difficult to determine or believe the authenticity or accuracy of the numbers. (Which financial statement are you looking at: the one for the tax authorities, for creditors, or the real one!)

When substantial credit is involved, foreign customers should be encouraged to submit their financial statements at least quarterly (assuming they are obtainable).

Conditions.   External influences not traceable to any of the other credit factors which might aid or hinder the success of a foreign customer are referred to as *conditions.* Such influences may be good or bad, permanent or temporary. Aside from regular seasonal fluctuations, temporary situations that adversely affect a local country are drought, floods, tornadoes, fires, crop failures, and loss of industry. Individual accounts are sometimes affected by a poor location, competition, or periodic business fluctuations. A credit decision in such cases must take into consideration whether or not the venture may be expected to overcome the handicap.

Collateral.   To ensure payment, minimize a potential write-off, and to secure (security/collateral) the amount of credit extended, special written legal arrangements are made when a foreign customer appears weak and unacceptable after an evaluation of character, capacity, capital, and conditions. In export trade or cross-border transactions, this could consist of standby letters of credit, bank guarantees, retention of title (i.e., in European cross-border trade), or drafts accepted or paid in full in the billing currency before the original "to order" on-board ocean bill of lading is released to the obligor. Although collateral normally consists of a pledge of assets to secure the amount of credit extended by an exporter (such as, accounts receivable, inventory, or fixed assets), there is no uniform legal international means to register or differentiate which creditor has a first, second, or third lien on certain assets pledged to secure the debts of creditors. The Uniform Commercial Code (UCC) exists in the United States for this purpose. Even if an exporter obtains a pledge of certain assets from a foreign customer, the pledge may be meaningless if other creditors were given the same pledge of assets first.

Country. Those conditions within a country that could prevent or delay payment at maturity for goods and services delivered to a foreign customer are referred as *country*. It is the need to evaluate a foreign customer's risk within the context of the country's political, economic, social, and regulatory risks. The latter can directly influence the payment terms an exporter wishes to extend to foreign customers and the profitability of doing business with a country.

Currency. Discussed in detail later, currency concerns foreign exchange risk as it pertains to country risk conditions, including both a country's sovereign and transfer risks, in addition to exchange controls. It is the inability of a government to raise sufficient amounts of foreign exchange to service its debt obligations and the inability of local companies to raise foreign exchange. Currency can also pertain to an exporter's billing currency (i.e., billing in a currency other than its own for competitive or monetary reasons).

Computers. The automated systems used by a foreign customer are referred to as *computers*. They demonstrate a commitment to better record keeping or accounting of income statements, balance sheets, budgets, analysis of the business, controls, audit trails, and evaluation of performance. Depending on the size of the foreign customer, the systems could be mainframe or PC driven.

The Six Ps of Credit

Six factors that also influence credit decisions are:

- People
- Profit
- Payment
- Protection
- Politics
- Perspective

People. The reputation and character of the principals of the foreign customer, length of time in business, and the business background of the principals should be taken into consideration.

Who is running the business? Very often in international trade, the reputation of the foreign customer as a good or bad payer or creditworthy customer is the only factor or P to consider. Typically salespeople will stress the people factor more than anything else and forget to consider the creditworthiness of the foreign customer.

Profit.   What is the profit on the goods and services sold? In general, greater risks can be taken based on higher profits or higher gross margins. In this regard, consideration should be given to the objectives (short- and long-term) of marketing and the alternatives of supplying another foreign customer in the same market, if the first customer is considered a risk.

Payment.   This third P assesses your own payment experience and the payment experience of other suppliers. It also includes financial statement analysis, when available and reliable. It helps in determining what type of payment terms to extend and basically answers the question: Is there a reasonable expectation for repayment?

Protection.   After an assessment of the first three Ps, the credit manager might determine that some sort of collateral is needed in order to secure the credit sale. This could be a bank guarantee issued on its own letterhead, one that is issued in the form of a standby letter of credit, or the por aval (promise to pay) of a bank. Collateral can also take the form of a pledge or secured interest in certain assets of the foreign customer. (As previously stated, there is no international uniform financing statement or filing system similar to the U.S. Uniform Commercial Code. Assets used to secure a debtor might be previously pledged or secured to other creditors).

Politics.   This P takes into consideration country conditions as derived from political, economic, foreign exchange, social, and regulatory risks, any of which might inhibit a foreign customer's ability and willingness to pay maturing debt obligations. Country conditions can also affect the ability and willingness of a credit manager to extend certain credit terms as requested by a foreign customer or the credit manager's sales department. For example, the credit manager may deny credit if foreign exchange (F/X) delays are too long; the foreign customer's country has a history of political unrest due to war, riot, or revolution or if import regulations prohibit the exporter to sell on payment terms less than 90 days.

Perspective.   This is an assessment or appraisal of all the Ps mentioned above. Is the entire sale worthwhile in relation to market plans, objectives, and strategy? Do the rewards outweigh the risks in extending credit to the foreign customer? Will there be any rewards if the risks are high? What is the cost/benefit of the deal?

COUNTRY RISK

Perhaps one of the most important elements to consider in the credit approval process is country risk. Past, present, and future political and economic instabilities of countries throughout the world have affected the normal trade of goods and services between nations. Country risk creates slow accounts receivable turnover and foreign customer (commercial risk) problems to credit managers, as well as cash flow problems to cash managers and foreign exchange problems to international finance managers. It is a problem that cannot be ignored or taken mildly and must be given a much higher priority by credit people in the credit evaluation and approval process.

The risks, needs, and circumstances of country risk and its analysis vary from one person, group, or company to the next (i.e., international bankers, political risk consultants, and economists do a more indepth country risk analysis than would a credit manager). This means that companies are not entirely concerned about the same risks as banks. For example, a bank is more concerned about the repayment of a loan to a country over a long period of time. A company that sells goods to the same country is not as concerned because its payment terms are much shorter. Because a country is having repayment problems with bank loans does not necessarily mean the company who sold goods to a foreign customer in the same country will have payment problems. It could mean a change in foreign exchange policy that makes it difficult for the foreign customer to pay for goods on a timely basis. It does not necessarily mean the company should stop delivering goods to foreign companies in the same country. It could mean the potential tightening or withdrawal of export trade financing facilities and confirmation on export letters of credit by banks.

What is country risk analysis? In simplistic terms, it means accepting the risk of the customer's country when accepting or approving an export credit sale to a foreign customer. It means taking into consideration country conditions that could adversely affect the foreign customer's ability and willingness to pay maturing debt obligations timely. Will the customer accept your credit terms? Will the foreign customer be forced into bankruptcy or liquidation? To credit managers, the term *country risk analysis* means determining the "country creditworthiness" in terms of the ability and willingness of a foreign government to make available to local companies foreign exchange necessary to service their foreign currency denominated obligations or liabilities (debts) to foreign suppliers. In effect, it means the credit manager should consider the following broad interrelated country risk conditions as part of the credit approval process:

1. Political risks.
2. Economic risks.
3. Social risks.
4. Import/export regulations.
5. Foreign exchange risks.
6. Other internal/external conditions.

The importance of country risk analysis came to the forefront since the fall of the Shah of Iran and especially when the less developed countries (LDC) debt crisis, referred to as the "debt bomb" by economists, exploded on the world scene on August 20, 1982. At that time, the Mexican government announced it would be unable to pay its external debts of approximately $90 billion to creditors throughout the world. Since then, there has been a proliferation of information on country risks, including articles written at least weekly (if not daily), in newspapers, magazines, journals, and in speeches given by economists, consultants, politicians, business people, and bankers. It has been a prime topic, covered constantly at trade group organizations, and models have been developed to evaluate country risks.

In actuality, significant adverse country risk conditions date further back than the fall of the Shah of Iran or the LDC debt crisis. A few examples are:

• In 1970, Salvador Allende Gossens, a Marxist, became president of Chile with a third of the national vote. The Allende government furthered the nationalization of his predecessor. But, illegal and violent actions by extremist supporters of the government, the regime's failure to attain majority support, and poorly planned socialist economic programs led to political and financial chaos. A military junta seized power in September 11, 1973. Allende killed himself, succeeded by Augusto Pinochet Ugarte, a military leader still in power today.[1]

• The military overthrow (mainly by guerrilla fighting) of Fulgencio Batista in Cuba on January 1, 1959, resulted in a political vacuum in which Fidel Castro took power. The government, quickly dominated by extreme leftists, began a program of sweeping economic and social changes, without restoring promised liberties. Some 700,000 Cubans emigrated in the years after the Castro takeover, mostly to the United States. Cattle and tobacco lands were nationalized, while a system of cooperatives was instituted. By the end of 1960 all banks and industrial companies had been nationalized, mostly without compensation—including over $1 billion worth of U.S.-owned properties.[2]

• Argentina was one of the most prosperous, educated, and industrialized of the major Latin American nations, and one of the world's largest exporters, up until General Juan Peron was elected president in 1946. Although Peron and his wife Eva effected labor reforms, they ran the country into debt. A 1955 coup exiled Peron, who was followed by a series of military and civilian regimes. Peron returned in 1973, died 10 months later, and was replaced by his vice president elect wife, Isabel (Juan's second wife). A military junta ousted Mrs. Peron in 1976 amid charges of corruption. Under a continuing state of siege, the army battled guerrillas and leftists. Economic conditions worsened, which placed extreme pressure on the military government. It was not until the election of Raul Alfonsin in 1983 that democratic rule returned to Argentina.

Because of the aforementioned military regimes, the nation is plagued by severe financial problems and inflation soared to an annual rate of over 600 percent in 1985.[3]

Many other examples have taken place in other countries throughout the last three decades. The end results for companies and their credit managers are slow or partial payments (many times years after maturity date, without interest) from foreign companies, and perhaps no payments at all from those who have either gone bankrupt or liquidated themselves. In the worst examples, the countries nationalized certain industries, including foreign based companies, and the government refused to recognize their debts.

Although a foreign customer is creditworthy for whatever amount of credit to be extended and pays its debt obligations to banks and trade suppliers timely, payment may be delayed due to country conditions outside its control. This might be due to governmental foreign exchange regulations or restrictions, arbitrary changes in import/export regulations, or adverse political or economic conditions. For example, although an export sale might be invoiced to General Motors, IBM, BASF, or Mitsui, all considered excellent commercial credit risks, these companies might have foreign operations located in countries with adverse country risk conditions—Nigeria, the Philippines, Nicaragua, and COMECON countries (Eastern European nations), all of which historically had or currently have foreign exchange problems.

The process of country risk analysis requires the gathering, dissemination, and analysis of information pertaining to political, economic, social, and financial factors. This can best be accomplished by using basically three options: (1) gathering information in-house and analyzing it internally; (2) using the services of an outside consulting company for a fee; or (3) using a combination of the two methods.

There are several ideal analytical approaches toward evaluating the extent of each country's creditworthiness. One is to obtain statistical data. The second is to develop historical trends and growth patterns. The third is to list strengths and weaknesses. In this regard, there are a number of sources of information that can be useful to credit managers. Some of the typical sources used by experienced credit managers include information from governmental agencies, banks, the FCIB, economic and political reporting services, newspapers and magazines, and internal company reports. See Appendix 2-A for a partial listing of the sources of information offered by the aforementioned. Government agencies provide publications and news releases which contain information regarding a variety of statistics (i.e., balance of payments, import/export trade figures, current accounts), political, economic, social and trade data information.

Many banks are good sources of country-related information. These banks can be domestic or foreign based banks in an exporter's country. Their information can include statistics and background data on specific countries with key trends in any given country. Their information is usually available free or at a nominal cost. Credit managers are advised to consult their company's account officer first (if available) regarding the bank's services and information available. One excellent source of information is Global Business Communications, Inc., *The World Guide for Exporters* (formerly known as *The Chase World Guide for Exporters*). This guide includes such information on: import and foreign exchange regulations for more than 100 countries, updated with regular monthly bulletins; interest on credit terms granted for shipments abroad; bank charges in the United States and other countries for the handling of documentary collections and letters of credit; and, permissible credit terms.

The FCIB, a trade group organization is an excellent source of information. The Finance Credit and International Business (FCIB) organization is the international arm of the National Association of Credit Management (NACM) based in New York City. Its broadly based (multiple industry) membership constantly exchanges timely information relative to a given country's payment practices. The membership exchanges such information at monthly round table conferences as current country conditions which affects their companies ability to extend credit terms and collections at maturity dates. They discuss current import regulations (foreign exchange and credit terms). Representatives are usually present from FCIA (Foreign Credit Insurance Association) who explain the Export-Import Bank of the United States's (Eximbank) current position regarding certain countries, the availability of insurance coverage, and the terms and conditions of certain policies (in European round table conferences, representatives from European export credit insurers). The FCIB also offers to its members country credit reports (for a fee) and International Bulletins (part of the membership fee; issued bi-monthly), giving the membership a report of current events and changes affecting a credit manager's decision, collections and foreign exchange problems in countries. The bulletins also include topics on international trade financing techniques and international trade in general.

In addition, country risk consultants (i.e., S. J. Rundt's and Associates) also exchange information by giving advice and information regarding country conditions. The U.S. Department of Commerce also participates in this exchange of information and will explain or give country risk conditions from information obtained directly from a number of reliable sources, such as, U.S. and foreign embassies, their own foreign commercial service network, foreign banks, and trade missions.

Economic and political reporting services have large country information databanks and staffs of overseas analysts. They often furnish information needed to assess the extent of the risk of any one country. Their services are designed to assist decision making. Their reports concentrate more on comprehensive and analytical country studies of political, economic, and social factors at work in a country. Their services can either provide brief country risk information weekly based on current events in many countries and/or offer extensive country reports which are updated frequently. A large number of newspapers and magazines write on extensive topics which are germane to country risk assessment. These include not only American publications with sections devoted to international affairs, but international publications as well. Many of these are distributed worldwide.

A personal visit by the credit manager and marketing/sales personnel to countries can provide immeasurable insight and information into a country's conditions. Direct visits to the sources of information mentioned above (i.e., international commercial banks, domestic and foreign; embassies, commercial attaches, FCIB member companies) gives management a better base for economic analysis. It can also clarify the status of the country's condition to visit foreign customers and/or a parent company's own subsidiaries, branches or affiliate offices (another excellent source of country condition information). Large companies many times have economic and/or financial planning departments that perform a certain amount of country risk analysis, usually economic studies, on certain countries and subsequently issue certain types of reports.

The amount of information required to perform country risk analysis depends to a large extent on a number of factors. What is the total number of active foreign customers sold within one or two years? The total number of active foreign customers in each country? The total accounts receivable exposure per country outstanding at any one time? What is the total amount (currency exposures: credit sales might be in more than one currency) of credit sales per year per country? What are the credit terms and collection policy of your company? The credit terms extended to each foreign customer per country? The strategies of your company and the objectives of the marketing/sales department over the next three to five years? Where and why does your company want to export its goods and services? What is the experience of your company based on historical experience and that of other companies (i.e., collection problems were encountered in certain countries due to the lack of sufficient or poor sources of country risk information) with each country.

Generally, as the number of countries and customer base that are actively sold grows, the trade account and country receivable exposure will also grow, and the task of performing proper country risk assessments on a timely basis becomes more formidable. The credit manager should carefully weigh the costs/benefits and the risks/rewards of the three options mentioned above.

Specifying Country Risk Conditions

An assessment or evaluation of country risk conditions takes into consideration the probability of delayed payment or a credit loss (account write-off). This can result from any one or a combination of the four broad country risk conditions: (1) the resource base, (2) government policy, (3) external accounts, or (4) political risks.

A mistake made by many credit managers and companies is that they attempt to eliminate country risks rather than manage them. By eliminating the risk, they prefer to demand the most stringent credit terms available in international trade, that is, confirmed irrevocable sight letters of credit or simply the confirmation of a bank on L/Cs (asking for cash is usually out of the question due to competitive reasons and foreign exchange restrictions in certain countries). The aim of country risk analysis is to anticipate changes in country creditworthiness rather than merely react to them. Each company will have its own specific strategies, objectives, and motives for selling or not selling; extending credit or not extending credit to specific foreign customers and/or countries; to extend longer versus shorter payment terms or vice versa; and to increase or decrease collection techniques ("leading and lagging") when it concerns foreign exchange. It is difficult to obtain consistent and reliable country information on a timely basis. Many times, country conditions change radically (even irrationally) in short periods of time with very little prior notice. In addition, countries have been known to inflate their financial health to the international business community.

The following is an overview of the four conditions mentioned above. It is important to mention and remember that each one interrelates and overlaps with each other. Meaning, there is a cause and effect relationship of these country conditions.

In assessing the creditworthiness of a country, the analysis process should begin by looking at and understanding its resource base. The country's resource base is a good starting point to assess the appropriateness of a government's economic and financial policies. In addition, political trends or occurrences must be closely monitored and analyzed since it can have a major impact on the country's ability and willingness to repay its own foreign debt obligations and that of its companies who purchase goods from exporters.

The Resource Base.   The term *resource base* is loosely defined because of the lack of a better term. It comprises natural, human, and financial resources. The reason for the use of this term is that natural resources cannot per se make a positive contribution to a country's ability to earn or save foreign exchange with every country. The concept of resources must be taken into account in this regard—human and financial resources. A prime example of human and financial resource nations is Singapore, Taiwan, and

South Korea. They have consistently demonstrated the high quality use of human resources (skilled and cheap labor) and their ability to save enough to finance most of their own development needs.

While many countries have the ability to earn and save foreign exchange from their own natural resources, many other countries do not. This includes natural resources above or in the ground. A good example is the case of Zaire. This country has vast forest reserves, but in recent years Zaire has had limited success in utilizing this natural resource to earn enough foreign exchange to pay for its import bills. The problem lies in an inadequate transportation system that has been allowed to deteriorate so severely that timber can no longer be moved to appropriate trading centers. The point is that the adequacy of a country's natural resource base must be assessed in conjunction with the country's existing economic infrastructure.

Human resources refers to the extent to which a country's population can contribute to productive economic activity. This resource includes the health and literacy of the populace, a factor often inversely associated with the rate of population growth. Does the government have increasingly complex productivity development plans? What are the productivity plans of the public and private sectors? Does labor have the education and training to fit these plans? What about the availability of technical and managerial skills in all sectors? An entrepreneurial class is a key group that can provide the leading edge in technological advancements and development efforts. Does the country have an entrepreneurial class in all sectors?

The term *financial resources* deals with a country's ability to save—the ability to refrain from consuming all of its domestic production (a strong attribute and driving force behind Japan's rapid and strong growth to a world economic power). In simplistic terms, the more a country and its populace can save, the higher a proportion of a given investment level it can meet with its own resources. Thus, it needs to borrow less from abroad. When assessing country risk conditions, financial resources means analyzing the effectiveness of its financial institutions to perform their intermediary role between savers and investors.

A country's resource base as it relates to country risk analysis can only be viewed in light of the other country risk conditions. The utilization of a country's resource base must be looked at in terms of historical trends rather than simply present day circumstances. Its meaning depends on the quality and effectiveness of government, public, and private sectors over the medium and long run.

Government Policy.   Having assessed a country's resource base, the next step is to examine the present government's existing policies and its appropriate resource base. Government policies and attitudes can and do strongly influence the economic and business climate of any country. The political philosophy of any government affects not only economic policy, but the degree of regulation or assistance it exerts on internal commerce and external trade. It makes the difference between a dynamic business climate or economic stagnation. There are three basic aspects to consider:

1. The quality of the economic and financial management process.
2. Long-term development strategy.
3. Short-term policy measures.

The first aspect questions the competence of senior economic policy making officials. Given adequate and competent government leadership, do they have the ear of the political leadership? Or, does the political leadership have the political strength to implement decisions, particularly if they involve fiscal or monetary austerity measures once decisions are made, if ever? For example, if either or both the senior Central Bank and Ministry of Finance and Planning officials (typical titles in many countries, especially in Latin America) are incompetent, then a government policy is not likely to evolve into effective economic and/or financial policies. This problem is typical of many less developed countries. Another factor to consider is the line of communication between so-called technocrats and politicians. If these lines are poor, policies are either implemented slowly, partially, or not at all. The same thing can occur if a country's leadership feels unable to implement the recommendations of an economic policy team. No matter how good the advice of technocrats is, desirable policies may not be implemented or followed.

The second aspect questions the long-run development strategy of the country. How does this strategy relate to the country's human, natural, and financial resource base? A successful long-run development strategy results in reasonably rapid, balanced and sustainable economic growth with balance of payments (BOPs) and debt-servicing trends that are acceptable by the international financial community. For example, a country with a strong and large agricultural sector that employs a large labor force must give adequate attention to that sector for effective economic management. A dynamic agricultural sector typically provides the basis for well-balanced, sustained, rapid growth by:

1. Ensuring that the growing availability of agricultural and processed exports generates enough foreign exchange earnings to finance import needs—particularly capital goods.
2. Facilitating increased supplies of locally available inputs for the fledging industrial sector, so that economic growth does not imply an overly rapid rate of increase in imports.
3. Leading to rising incomes for rural people, typically the majority of the population, a trend which will have positive implications for social equity, and for the development of a broadly based domestic market for new industrial activity.

Industrial development should take place on the basis of efficiency, and not in support of prestige projects or of the economic interests of politically powerful groups. The appropriateness of a country's overall growth strategy is often reflected in its incremental capital-output ratio (ICOR), which is a measure of new output generated by new investment. In the better managed developing countries of East Asia, such as Thailand and South Korea, a unit of new investment seems to add around 0.4 units of new output per year, for an ICOR of 2.5. In a less well managed country, by contrast, particularly in those following a capital-intensive growth strategy, the ICOR might be as high as 6 or 7, which implies a relatively inefficient application of new investment.[4]

Third, there needs to be an assessment of how quickly and effectively a country's economic managers can respond to short-term policy measures to adverse cyclical developments, such as business cycles, crop failures, inflation, unemployment, higher oil prices, bad harvests, a recession in export markets, or a drop in export prices. In this regard, particular attention needs to be focused on fiscal, monetary, wage/price, and foreign exchange rate policies.

• *Fiscal policy* should be predicated on a rate of government expenditure increase that can be financed largely by a combination of domestic revenues and borrowing from sources other than monetary authorities (borrowing from the latter is potentially inflationary). In addition, fiscal policy should ensure that the public sector makes a reasonable contribution to national investment requirements; that is, government revenues should not be devoted entirely to payment for current consumption expenditures.

• *Monetary policy,* particularly in developing countries, tends to be dictated by a government's fiscal stance. But monetary policy should in effect, restrict money supply to a rate consistent with reasonable price stability, while assuring adequate credit availability to the key productive sectors.

• *Wage and price policies* should ensure that wage increases are kept roughly in line with productivity growth, with some allowance for levels of inflation already built into the economy. Of course, in cases in which past wage increases have been much greater than productivity growth, some downward adjustment in real wage levels may be necessary.

• Concerning *foreign exchange rate policies,* in many cases past trends in domestic prices relative to international prices may have led to a domestic price structure that is no longer competitive internationally. In such cases, a currency devaluation may be desirable in order to realign relative prices. Such devaluations should be followed by fiscal, monetary, and other measures aimed at improving future price competitiveness. This extremely important area of country risk, foreign exchange, is explained later.

Experience shows that some countries rich in resources, such as Argentina and Brazil, have suffered periods of prolonged slow growth and external payment imbalances. Others that are poor in resources, such as Singapore and Taiwan, have experienced very satisfactory growth and healthy external payment performances.

When the former situation occurs, it usually is the result of years of poor public policies; and vice versa. Analysis of the public economic and financial policy context almost always is the key element in country risk analysis.

Changes in government policies can occur as a result of regime change. A good example is the People's Republic of China (PRC), whose current leadership shifted government policy from heavy industry to light industry type investments. This was an attempt to develop an industrial base, by opening the economy toward foreign investment. In other countries, there are shifts from an agricultural to heavy or light industry or vice versa. These type of changes affect the kinds of exports companies are going to make.

In the case of underdeveloped countries, experienced credit managers are painfully aware of the dangers of rising nationalism and political unrest. Political uncertainties encompass the probability of war, riot, revolution, insurrection, confiscation, expropriation, civil commotions, inconvertibility of currencies, and restriction or cancellation of import licenses.

Hidden Trade Barriers.   Restrictive government policies are a more subtle form of risk and are less noticed because they are not newsworthy enough for mass media attention. For credit managers, government restrictions can pose more of a problem than either a change in regime or political turmoil.

In recent years, government restrictions have been imposed in many countries because of economic reasons. The usual reasons given include: to increase revenues, protect domestic businesses or jobs, maintain control over natural resources, or protect the value of the currency.

One particular restriction, a fixed exchange rate for the currency, creates a unique problem for credit managers. Fixed conversion rates are used to protect weak currencies from decline in a world market. Fixed exchange rates eventually lead to a massive devaluation and a weakened currency. The currency position may become so weak that the country cannot pay for its imports. If caught in this situation, the credit manager can encounter a delay in payment which lasts for years. (See Appendix 2–B and 2–C for some examples.)

External Accounts.   With the resource base and the policy context as defined here serving as background, and with a focus on international economic and financial developments, it then becomes possible to assess the outlook for a country's external financial situation. Therefore, there are several areas of a country's financial report card which should be monitored on an ongoing basis if the credit manager is to avoid finding its company's funds locked up by a country's financial problems. These are the external financial conditions of a country as related to (1) balance of payments, (2) external debt, (3) international reserves, and (4) potential access to external finance.

The *balance of payments* is a measurement of a country's financial condition which is important to credit managers. A negative balance of payments means that the value of imports exceeds the value of exports and must be financed either through foreign reserves or borrowings. A positive balance of payments means that the value of exports exceeds the value of imports, foreign reserves are created, and international debt may be repaid. For example:

- South Korea posted a trade surplus of $751 million for 1986's first eight months, in contrast to a year earlier deficit of about $1 billion, as reported by their Economic Planning Board.[5]
- Hong Kong's trade surplus widened in August 1986 to the equivalent of $247.4 million from $214 million a year earlier. Exports increased 22 percent to $3.26 billion, while imports 23 percent to $3.01 billion.[6]

In looking at the outlook for the balance of payments, it is important to look at the current account, the capital account and the debt service burden.

The current account measures the balance of a country's trade in goods and services, and as such, is a measure of the net change in its external indebtedness. What happens to the current account, of course, will depend on a number of factors, including the rate of growth of domestic demand in the country, the ability of a country to finance its own investment needs via domestic savings, the competitiveness of its exchange rate or rates, trends in world prices for its major export commodities, the degree of diversification and stability of its foreign exchange earnings.

Key aspects of the capital accounts of the balance of payments should also be assessed. Emphasis should be placed on the likely ease of finance to project current account deficits. For example, to the extent that such deficits are financed by official grants, say from OPEC countries, or by long-term, low interest rate loans from the World Bank or bilateral aid programs, then the repayment and debt service implications of such borrowings are lessened. Also of relevance is the question of whether international reserves must be drawn on in order to finance a projected current account deficit.

The *external debt* level of a country should be monitored due to the priority of debt repayments in the allocation of the availability of foreign currency. If a country's debt level becomes unmanageable, the exporter's risk of incurring blocked funds increases dramatically. Heavily indebted countries can become poor credit risks overnight if their balance-of-payment position suddenly becomes negative due to declining world prices of a major export. Recent declines in oil revenues have made poor credit risks of several heavily indebted countries that were considered good financial risks in the 1970s.

The debt service burden can be measured in a number of ways, but the most generally useful approach is to combine both projected repayment requirements on long-term debt and interest payments on total debt. That is then related to the total projected current account earnings. The anticipated debt service burden will be a function not only of the maturity structure and contractually-agreed interest rates or spreads on debt outstanding and projected new debt, but also the trends in money market rates in the case of LIBOR-based loans and the trends in a country's export outlook. Some attempt should be made to test the sensitivity of current account and debt burden projections to changes in key assumptions.

One also wants to keep an eye on trends in, and the adequacy of, a country's *international reserves*. A country generates foreign reserves from two sources: export earnings and foreign borrowing. If foreign reserves are declining, a problem may be approaching. Import coverage usually is evaluated on the number of months that normal imports are covered. Three or four months' coverage is usually considered adequate. Reserves, which may be defined to include external assets of the commercial banking system, should be sufficient to permit payment of normal trade-related liabilities without undue delay, and also to provide some cushion in the event of unanticipated adverse developments. In the short run, reserves can provide some cushion in the face of an unexpected shortfall in foreign exchange receipts or a sharp rise in import costs.

Also in this regard, it is important to assess a country's *potential access to external finance* in case of need. Here, one looks at country's drawing ability from the IMF, borrowing capacity from the World Bank, regional development banks, bilateral official sources, and international commercial banks. With respect to the latter, market perceptions of a country's credit-worthiness, and in particular, market confidence in its economic and financial management team are of paramount importance. Also important will be the availability of timely and comprehensive economic and financial statistics.

Financial information on countries is published by the International Monetary Fund (IMF) twice a year, and the data is available by subscription. Financial information on a country experiencing financial difficulty may be delayed suddenly or omitted completely. Therefore, an absence of information should be investigated when noted, since the country involved may be trying to keep bad news quiet. Table 2–2 contains some internal and external ratios for assessing internal and external accounts.

Political Risks.   Analysis of economic and financial matters, while essential in the assessment of country creditworthiness, cannot provide any final answers. The political outlook is equally if not more important.

In assessing domestic political risks, credit people should look for some reasonable assurance that political change, when it comes (and it always does, eventually) will be orderly, and that there will be reasonable continuity, if not an improvement, in fundamental economic and financial policies. Particular attention should be given to the possibility that political events could result in a moratorium on, or even a repudiation of, external debt—public and private.

TABLE 2–2
Economic Indicators

Internal

Gross Domestic Product (GDP)	Measure of the size of the economy
GDP composition	Indicator of the overall structure of the economy
Population	Measure of the potential size of the market
GDP/Population	Measure of the level of economic development
Savings/GDP	Indicator of growth prospects attributable to domestic savings
Investment/GDP	Indicator of current commitment to future economic growth and productivity
Government spending/GDP	Indicator of government involvement in the economy
External public debt/GDP	Indicator of overall exposure to the international economy and long-term debt burden
Money supply growth	Measure of economic activity and stability of the currency
Consumer Price Index and/or Wholesale Price Index	Measures of domestic inflation rate

External

Imports and/or exports/GDP	Measure of the openness of an economy
Exports/Imports	Called the coverage ratio; indicator of economy's rate of growth
Oil imports/main import	Rough measure of the terms of trade of an economy
Current account deficit/exports	Short-term measure of possible balance of payments difficulties
Total external debt/exports	Long-term indicator of country's liquidity
Interest payments/exports	Indicator of debt burden; reflects carrying costs of the external debt
International Reserves/Imports	Measure of short-term liquidity

Source: Edward G. Roberts, *Evaluating Country Risk,* Credit Research Foundation (Lake Success, N.Y.: April 1964), p. 5.

A change in regime can happen with the removal of a strong individual leader, or a change in political parties or political thought. The regime may change through orderly or disorderly elections, shifting coalitions, government reshuffling, assassination, coup d'etat, revolution, or the illness and death of a leader. The result is that monetary and fiscal policies are changed or affected. For example, when Turkey was run by the military, one cabinet minister, Ozal, followed austere policies which were needed to control the economy and the nation's fiscal affairs and Turkey had banker confidence worldwide. When Ozal left the government and was replaced by someone who reverted back to old Turkish policies (a lot of government spending, status policies), international creditors lost confidence.

Governments change when a coalition pulls out of a government, the government falls, and a new government is formed. Historically, Italy and Belgium (France in later years), typically undergo changes in government due to shifting coalitions. Each change brings about changes in foreign exchange (i.e., regulations and restrictions), and fiscal and monetary policies. Italy is a typical example of a nation that has nationalized many industries because the aforementioned has resulted in large continuous industry losses. Rather than see them fail, many of these industries that were vital to the economy as a whole were nationalized over the years. This created payment problems for credit people because like any other government, bureaucratic red tape (invoice/payment instrument processing time) typically creates payment slowness to foreign trade suppliers.

Credit people should also watch out for political risk regime changes such as coup d'etats. This type of change can occur radically and quickly. For example, Bolivia has undergone 299 coups in the last 150 years. Again, changes like this not only alter import regulations, but foreign exchange rates as well.

In addition, revolutions like those in Iran and Nicaragua can mean a complete change in the ruling elite. The regional political context should be such as not to endanger a country's economic or political viability. Thus an assessment is required of relations with neighboring countries, and in particular of the possibility of regional conflict, whether overt or covert.

If sudden or anticipated illnesses and deaths of government

leaders occurs, this can give rise to not only governments reshuffling themselves but, coup d'etats, revolutions, and even civil
strife. Even a rumored illness or potential death of a government
leader (i.e., Marcos, Khadafi, King Hussein, and even Khomeini)
can send the currency markets spinning and alter international
trade policies of nations and business firm exporters.

While the highly industrialized western nations have legal
methods of changing governments which provide for an orderly
transition, many lesser-developed nations accomplish a change in
governments only through extralegal methods. If the change in
government results in significant disruption of daily life or civil
war, necessary elements in the international trade process are
affected. The banks, custom houses, and the country's borders can
be closed or government officials may simply stop processing trade
documents. When this occurs, foreign trade suppliers are paid
slow.

A change in leadership can also change the way in which the
international investment community views the country's economic
future. The currency speculator's view of the country's economic
future under the new leadership may lead to wide fluctuations in
the currency markets. The result may be negative as when the
socialist, Francos Mitterand, won the French presidential election
in 1981, or the result may be positive as when the pro-business
politician, Edward Seaga replaced socialist Michael Manley in
Jamaica. Michael Manley was a left-winger and money spender,
but was disliked by business people because he created a lot of
instability. Edward Seaga on the other hand, established austere
policies which changed the business climate and won the confidence of business people.

When government policies threaten to destroy investments
and the property of commercial investors in a country, capital flight
is inevitable. The government usually retaliates by restricting
currency flow, and international trade is disrupted. In addition,
political turmoil should be considered in international trade more
than its immediate or direct effect. Prolonged political turmoil in a
country eventually begins to threaten the life and property of the
commercial lenders and investors, which results in the sustained
flight of capital. The flight of capital weakens the nation's currency
and leads to currency transfer restrictions, which in turn directly

affect the exporter's ability to receive timely payment for goods. If political turmoil is severe enough, it prevents the government from maintaining the routine procedures required for international trade and currency exchange.

Even more serious are the political and economic consequences which occur with the more violent changes in leadership. Political changes can be as extreme as the Iranian Revolution in 1979 which completely changed the rules of international trade in that country.

FOREIGN EXCHANGE RISK

A principle result of the various country risks previously mentioned are the effect these risks have on the ability and willingness of a foreign government to make enough foreign exchange available to its citizens, foreign residents, private and publicly owned companies (domestic and foreign owned) better known as the private sector, and government owned (partially or wholly) agencies to pay their foreign currency denominated liabilities or debts. This is defined as *foreign exchange risk*.

It is the probability that a country will fail to generate enough foreign exchange for all its country's debtors, public and private, to service maturing foreign debt obligations to creditors. Foreign exchange risk as it pertains to foreign equity investments, such as confiscation, nationalization, and restrictions on repatriation of earnings will not be discussed in this chapter because it typically is beyond the responsibility of credit people (usually a responsibility delegated to a company's international finance or foreign exchange manager). Also, the international monetary system, the foreign exchange market, forecasting foreign exchange rates, and measuring and managing foreign exchange exposure will not be discussed in this chapter or book. These are typically beyond the responsibilities of credit people and there is plenty of written material on these topics in the marketplace. For more information, a list of suggested readings is included at the end of this book.

When payment for the credit sale of goods and services is made across international boundaries, one currency must be exchanged for another. The need to exchange currencies would cause no problem if the currency of one country could always be bought and sold at a fixed and invariable price against the currency of all other countries. However, in the real world of today and in the foreseeable future, life in the world of foreign currency exchanges is more complicated than one can imagine. The price of one currency in terms of others usually undergoes continuous and sometimes drastic fluctuations simply because the currencies of the world, like any other commodity, follow laws of supply and demand which are subject to adverse political and economic conditions. On one day, there may be a strong demand for French francs, causing its price to rise against other currencies. This means that more dollars or other currencies may be required to buy a fixed quantity of francs. On another day, the demand for francs may be weak, causing its price in terms of dollars and other currencies to decline.

From a financial statement perspective, both the exporter and importer from the sale of goods and services, creates foreign exchange exposures when a mismatch of foreign currency assets and liabilities occurs. If an exporter sells goods in a foreign currency, it creates foreign currency receivables (the foreign customer or importer creates a foreign currency payable); if it is purchasing goods in a foreign currency, it creates a foreign currency payable (the exporter creates a foreign currency receivable). In either case, the foreign currency receivable or payable due is mismatched if it is not balanced by a corresponding foreign currency asset or liability. Foreign exchange exposure also results when a company borrows one currency and converts it to another, creating a liability (short- or long-term) and an asset in different currencies. In all cases, time intensifies the exposure.

The relationship that different currencies have to each other, i.e., the ratio or rate at which one currency can be sold for another, undergoes constant fluctuations. Rates may change many times in one day to reflect up-to-date supply and demand conditions of those who are in the market to buy or sell various currencies.

The term *foreign exchange risk* as it pertains to country risk conditions, includes both a country's sovereign and transfer risks, in addition to exchange controls. *Sovereign risk* refers solely to the inability of a government entity to raise sufficient amounts of foreign exchange to service its foreign currency debt obligations.

Transfer or convertibility risk pertains to the inability of companies in the private sector to raise foreign exchange, even though they are in good financial condition and operating profitably. *Exchange controls* refers to those countries that have resorted to some kind of exchange controls whose purposes vary from one country to the next and the major underlying reason is to stabilize their currencies by:

- Regulating the import and export of certain types of goods tied to specific exchange rates.
- Providing a means of allocating scarce foreign exchange resources.
- Preventing the flight of capital from a specific country or currency.
- Preventing an excessive inflow of foreign currencies.
- Preventing further drains of foreign exchange reserves.

Sovereign Risk

In international trade, a vast amount of business is conducted between trade credit suppliers and foreign governments through their various agencies, departments, ministries, trade companies, or offices. Business with foreign governments is usually conducted on a contract basis in which foreign suppliers submit bids (quotations based on price, terms of sale, credit terms, delivery time, quantities, quality) to foreign governments in order to get business.

In this regard, the credit person should not assume that the element of risk is diminished simply because the credit sale of goods and services is to a foreign government entity. When a given country is subject to adverse country risk conditions, the government entity is likely to be subject to many of the same adverse conditions as private sector companies. However, the fact that government entities are more likely to gain access to decreasing foreign exchange reserves varies from one government and country owned or operated industry to the next. For example, during the Mexican payment crisis in late 1982, the government-owned oil company, Petroleos Mexicanos (PEMEX), had a good payment record while payments from the private sector were slow. On the other hand, trade credit suppliers to government-owned companies in Venezuela waited nearly one and a half to two years (some are still waiting) to get paid on debts maturing prior to February 23, 1984 which were frozen by the government authorities.

Transfer or Convertibility Risk

A vast majority of international trade is carried on in U.S. dollars because many nations use the U.S. dollar as their base reserve currency. However, many business firms located in industrial countries throughout the world not only invoice their export credit sales in U.S. dollars, but other hard currencies (major trading currencies) as well and some soft currencies. For example, a Belgium company might bill its export of goods to Italy in Italian lira, U.S. dollars, and/or Belgium francs; A French company might invoice its exports to Belgium in not only French and Belgian francs, but German marks and U.S. dollars; a Japanese company might bill in U.S. dollars, Japanese yen, and German marks; a Brazilian company might bill its exports to Argentina, Chile, Uruguay, and Paraguay in not only cruzados, but U.S. dollars, australs, pesos, and guarani (all considered to be soft currencies except U.S. dollars).

Since the importing company must convert its local currency into U.S. dollars or another billing currency to pay for the imported goods, a transfer or convertibility risk is introduced into the export transaction. The transfer or convertibility risk is simply one where the invoiced currency may not be available when the importer seeks to settle the account or bill. This risk is particularly true with less developed countries (LDCs) and may be caused by a trade imbalance when imports greatly exceed exports. Lately, the dollar and multiple currency availability problem quite often results from high debt-repayment requirements of overextended countries.

The exporter can solve the problem of convertibility by arranging for the collection in advance or by transferring the risk to a third party. Collection in the desired currency can be arranged by requiring payment in advance before shipping the goods or by requiring an irrevocable letter of credit from the importer's bank. A letter of credit can then be confirmed by a bank in another country, preferably a bank in the exporter's country. However, this alternative may not be feasible if the exporter is facing a competitive price/credit terms situation whereby competition is offering better or more lenient prices and/or credit terms. Getting the L/C confirmed by a reputable bank might also pose a formidable task for the credit person because many bank credit lines are at their limits due to large country debts and banks want to limit their exposures.

Exchange Controls

Invoicing the sale of goods and services in foreign currencies must take into consideration country barriers or restrictions that may affect the ability and willingness of a foreign customer and exporter to engage in trade, to obtain or receive foreign exchange timely for payment or receipt of goods sold overseas, to obtain forward cover, or to borrrow or invest in foreign currencies.

These exchange controls are often imposed by a country's government authorities to:

- Minimize exchange rate fluctuations.
- Correct deficits in balance of payments current accounts.
- Control/support monetary and/or fiscal policies.
- Protect domestic industries.

Credit people must be cognizant of exchange controls that will affect their ability to extend credit, payment terms, and collections within normal credit policies. In effect, exchange controls in the form of import regulations and foreign exchange allocations can and will dictate how credit is extended, under what credit terms (type and length), and when payment is received—regulations that are beyond the control of credit people. These exchange controls also affect the willingness and ability of banks to structure and finance the sale of goods and services.

Internal economic conditions may cause a government to restrict its citizens from converting local currency into that of a foreign country's currency.

Exchange restrictions follow the same pattern in all countries when the countries restrict the free trade of their currency. A local government exchange authority, operating in conjunction with the country's central bank, becomes the only legal place for purchasing foreign currency. Similarly, all incoming foreign currency flows through the same exchange authority. When governments impose exchange restrictions, a black market inevitably develops.

The credit person should be as much concerned with exchange restrictions as with the credit risk of the customer. Exchange restrictions strongly influence the credit terms extended to foreign customers and may force an otherwise prime credit risk to accept restrictive credit terms. Credit terms will reflect the importer's ability to transfer local currency into U.S. dollars. The importer may be totally prevented by exchange controls from remitting dollars to the exporter.

Historically, most exchange controls have been imposed by countries with limited foreign exchange resources by regulating the outflow of exchange and those with poor track records of political and economic instability. Meanwhile, some industrially advanced countries have imposed some exchange restrictions to prevent the speculative inflow of foreign currencies.

One of the principle reasons why governments impose exchange controls is the unwillingness of the governments to allow market supply and demand force their free play in foreign exchange markets and trading. Without exchange controls, currencies would depreciate or appreciate against other currencies to their natural levels. Many times, the existence of exchange controls is justified in a number of circumstances.

The following will cite just a few of the types of exchange controls and examples of exchange controls imposed by some countries. It is nearly impossible to list all of the various types of exchange controls because foreign governments have been ingenious in thinking up new methods of preventing undesirable inflows and outflows of currencies. Exchange controls imposed by governments are further complicated when loopholes are found and the government imposes new restrictions to close the gaps.

It is important for the credit person to understand some of the basic types of controls imposed by foreign governments because they can have a substantial impact on the trading of goods and services, the credit terms extended, and collections. Many of these exchange control categories interrelate to each other.

Exchange Rate System and Foreign Exchange Markets. To discourage the importation of certain types of goods, some governments require that importers place a local currency cash deposit with a commercial or central bank for a fixed period of time before a valid import license is issued. This deposit is often non-interest bearing. These requirements vary from one country and industry to the next. Even the deposit percentages may vary from one type or class of goods to the next. The specific requirements can vary based on the country of origin of the goods to be imported (trade barriers). It is not uncommon for some governments to impose deposit requirements in excess of 100 percent of the value of the goods to be imported. These deposit requirements can either be used to pay for the imported goods at maturity or are refunded after maturity.

A number of countries over the years have resorted to a system of *multiple exchange rates* as a control mechanism. The system can be used to encourage or discourage imports and exports. In 1983, Belgium had a two-tier market for its franc as did South Africa for the rand and Argentina for the peso (now called the austral).

Current Example

In early December 1986, President Jaime Lusinchi announced a new differential exchange rate of Bs14.50:US$1 as part of a broad plan to:

- Curtail inflation.
- Halt reserve currency drains.
- Aid the government in financing 1987's budget.
- Stimulate domestic economic activity.
- Discourage excessive exports.

Included was the introduction of a three-tiered FX rate system:

1. A preferential rate or exchange of Bs7.50:US$1 for debt repayments and imports of essential imports including food, medicines, shoes, clothing, and raw materials for food and paper processing. A Bs7.50:US$1 rate for the sale to Banco Central of foreign currency income from exports of oil and iron, imports by these industries, and student expenses

abroad through December 1987. These rates are not changes from current policy.

2. A new rate of Bs14.50:US$1 for the bulk of imports and exports of goods and services that were transacted at the free rate, meaning that the bolivar for these purposes has been revalued by 72.4 percent or, conversely, the bolivar cost of purchasing dollars has been reduced by 42 percent from the roughly Bs25.00:US$1 at which the free rate had stood just before the announcement.

3. The free exchange rate is to be kept in existence, but will henceforth apply only to travel and to other nonessential transactions.

Source: *Rundt's Weekly Intelligence*, S. J. Rundt & Associates, Inc., No. 1,587 (New York: December 11, 1986), p. 17.

Countries imposing such a system to preserve and allocate scarce foreign exchange typically set a more favorable rate of exchange for more desirable imports such as essential food stuffs, commodities, and industrial equipment. In this regard, these imports are relatively cheap from a unit of currency point of view since less local currency is needed to pay for the imported goods. Conversely, undesirable goods are allocated a higher foreign exchange rate by the central bank.

Each government system of multiple exchange rates might include a government policy which only allows the rates of exchange to fluctuate within relatively narrow bands or margins (self-imposed or instituted by the IMF or financial institutions). If a rate threatens to move outside the band, the government intervenes on either the selling or buying side as necessary.

When a currency is relatively strong, local exporters may benefit from a dual rate structure since foreign importers can obtain the required currency at a supported price which may be lower than the freely floating rate. However, since rates established for trade transactions are allowed to fluctuate only within narrow limits, the chance of foreign exchange losses due to violent fluctuations is minimized.

Those countries with shortages of foreign exchange resources have resorted to the simple device of a *waiting list* to allocate the limited exchange available. Local importers wishing to pay for goods they purchased or plan to purchase from foreign suppliers have to apply at the local central bank or finance ministry for the necessary foreign exchange. They are then put on a waiting list. Once exchange becomes available, the necessary conversion may be made and the foreign exporter receives payment. Before that time, the payment in local currency remains in a blocked account in a local authorized bank, payable with or without interest. This waiting period could be weeks, months, or even years.

It is possible to regulate exchange rates by pegging the exchange rate of currency to that of another currency. This includes the setting of par values—central and official rates of exchange to another currency. Restrictions on the availability of forward contracts or limits on the time period are covered by forward contracts. This permits only authorized banks and non-bank institutions to deal in foreign exchange. In November 1986, Turkey implemented a change in its foreign exchange trading policy by permitting nonbank institutions to trade in foreign exchange. Under a ruling published in the Official Gazette, domestic companies with capital in excess of one billion liras or more, 50 percent paid-in, were allowed to set up exchange houses. Foreign firms are included in the new regulation, provided they bring in the equivalent of one billion lira or more.

Imports and Import Payments.   To prevent undesirable imports, especially luxuries or goods that would compete with infant, struggling, or mature local industries, some countries require importers to obtain a *government license or certificate* approving the specific import. Less desirable goods may be limited by quantity (quota) restrictions or excluded altogether.

To protect local industries from the importation of highly competitive goods, governments will impose high *tariffs* (a schedule of duties or taxes). In addition, the government might impose *quota* restrictions, tied to import licenses, which establishes the amount and/or quantity of goods an importer can bring into the country within a specified period of time (i.e., one calendar year). Again, tariff and quota restrictions may vary based on the country of origin of the goods. On the other hand, a low tariff and high quota may be charged on goods considered to be desirable imports that contribute to a country's economic development policies and do not compete with local industries. Certain country regulations specify the method of payment and length of time that may be used for imports (i.e., open account, letters of credit—confirmed or unconfirmed—payable at sight or 90 or 180 days, document against payment or acceptance—payable at 90 or 180 days). Regulations of this nature could include:

- Limits of extended payment terms and credit from foreign suppliers.
- Advance payment restrictions to foreign suppliers, such as, cash-in-advance or partial deposits cannot be made; payments can only be made within specified periods of time after shipment.
- Approval by exchange control authorities to the nature and length of credit by foreign suppliers; the billing currency; and the financing details.

In addition, imports and import payments could be restricted by:

- Foreign exchange allocated only to specific types of imports.
- The central foreign exchange authorities regulate and allocate official exchange reserves.
- Foreign exchange is allocated only against specific import licenses or certificates.
- Exchange is allocated in accordance with goods that are prioritized.

Forward exchange contracts are allocated for specific imports, certain currencies, and limited periods of time (i.e., three months). Procedures have been established that lead up to the allocation of foreign exchange for imports, such as, registering imports, filing documents with the exchange authorities, going only to authorized banks for the allocation of foreign exchange, and the filing of exchange control declaration forms.

Exports and Export Payments. Exports could be restricted by cost controls, export levies, excise taxes, quantitative controls, and global or single-country quotas. Conversely, export controls can be positive by promoting exports through subsidies, tax deferrals on exports, refunds of taxes or export levies. To restrict exported goods, only certain goods are permitted for export to certain countries at certain prices, credit terms, and types or forms of trade finance. Specifications are set on the maximum time in which export proceeds must be collected and repatriated back to the home country or country of origin of the goods.

Capital Inflows and Outflows. These measures affect the borrowing and lending of business firms and financial institutions, such as, restrictions on foreign borrowing to finance direct investments (locally or overseas), lending overseas subject to prior authorization by the exchange authorities, and the amount of interest charged on loans. They also set limitations on local banks' (domestic or foreign owned) access to foreign funds. Reserve requirements are set against a bank's external liabilities and banks are required to deposit or declare with the local exchange authorities and/or the central bank a specified percentage of their foreign exchange holdings or currency.

Nontrade-Related. These do not affect trade, but are restrictions on nonresident accounts, such as, authorized banks being the only banks permitted to open local currency accounts. Limitations are placed on the amount of remittances that can be remitted abroad. All amounts due from residents of other countries and all income earned in those countries from foreign assets are repatriated and surrendered within specified periods of time.

Examples of Country Exchange Controls

Argentina

In January 1984, the government issued a series of resolutions, implementing a new import control system which went into effect immediately.

IMPORTS: All imports into Argentina required an import certificate issued by the Secretariat of Commerce. When applying for a certificate, the importer must submit detailed information on the shipment, including a complete description of the product, price information, and other data (obtained from the foreign supplier).

Imports were classified into three lists:

1. List A covered prohibited items that may not be imported for a period of 180 days.
2. List B covered primarily capital goods, certain chemicals, plastics, and parts for goods on List A.
3. List C covered raw materials, inputs for the pharmaceutical industry and medical equipment. Imports of goods on Lists B and C require prior approval from appropriate government agencies. Once approval is granted, a certificate may be issued.

Items not on the above lists received the necessary certificates from the Secretariat of Commerce on an automatic basis.

Imports were subject to a local currency deposit approximately equivalent to the anticipated customs duties for the respective goods.

Exempt from the new import control system were:

1. Imports shipped under irrevocable letters of credit issued before December 29, 1983 and goods already in transit on that date.
2. Imports financed under agreements with international financial organizations signed prior to December 29, 1983.
3. Imports that do not require the transfer of foreign exchange.

IMPORT PAYMENTS: Imports required minimum credit terms of 180 days from the date of the bill of lading. Exempt from this requirement were imports of ALADI (Latin American Integration Association), negotiated items, and some other goods for which shorter terms were permissible. Extended credit terms were required for imports of capital goods exceeding U.S. $50,000, with the credit terms depending on the value of the shipment.

Source: *The Chase World Guide for Exporters*, copyright 1984, Chase Manhattan Bank, printed with permission of the publisher, Global Business Communications, Inc., P.O. Box 99, Gillette, N.J. 07933.

China (PRC—People's Republic of China)

Effective April 1, 1986, Mofert (the Ministry of Foreign Relations and Trade) issued new regulations for the four Special Economic Zones (SEZs) Shenzhen, Zhuhai, Shantou, and Xiamen. The regulations bar any goods imported into these territories from being resold anywhere else in China without explicit permission from the central government.

Shenzhen is being sealed off from the rest of the mainland, so that the Chinese will no longer be able to go into the zone to buy consumer items brought in from Hong Kong. Only imports necessary for production and consumption within the SEZs are now tax-free, while all other goods are subject to a 50 percent levy.

Items sold within China from the SEZs are subject to tax. Moreover, Mofert recently ordered specialized import/export firms in the PRC to accept only direct export orders from abroad, thereby closing an avenue through which some companies in Shenzhen (by buying from these firms for foreign exchange and using this leverage to force down prices) were able to fulfill their own centrally decreed export quotas without actually producing the needed volume.

While purchases abroad of capital goods and technology are to remain permissible as needed, the government will see to it that greater care is taken in avoiding duplication and low-quality items.

Generally, China is to take a less conventional approach to trade, promoting barter, entrepo, multilateral and "frontier" arrangements. Goods exchanges with Hong Kong and Macao, in particular, are to be more closely supervised. Price cutting by exporters is to be stopped. Even though local authorities have been promised more say in the use of foreign exchange, Peking's centralized control over foreign debt is to be toughened.

Source: *Rundt's Weekly Intelligence*, S. J. Rundt & Associates, Inc., No. 1,554 (New York: April 2, 1986), pp. 5–7.

Colombia

In March 1986, obligatory credit (payment) terms for imports, which used to range from 90 days (for some raw materials) up to three years (for certain capital goods) were abolished by the Junta Monetaria, so that Colombian buyers and their foreign suppliers could once again freely negotiate credit terms as they see fit.

It was also announced that exchange certificates, through which exchange surrender and outbound payments are generally effected, were cashable for hard currency prior to their maturity dates.

The 95 percent exchange license deposit for imports (consignacion), which must be lodged at the official certificate rate at least 20 calendar days prior to applying for an exchange license, remained in effect, but elimination of the requirement was said to be under consideration.

Source: *Rundt's Weekly Intelligence,* S. J. Rundt & Associates, Inc., No. 1,554 (New York: April 2, 1986), p. 7.

Nigeria

In October and November 1986, the import-duty rate structure was revised, thus reducing many tariffs appreciably, but the system of strict state control over incoming goods remained intact.

The government lowered customs rates on imports for consumption and manufacturing. Among other items, the tariff changes affected household appliances, foodstuffs, and automobiles:

- Televisions and radios were cut to 50 percent from 150 percent.
- Air-conditioning units were halved to 15 percent.
- Raw materials for soft-drink plants changed by one quarter to 30 percent.
- Automobile kits, destined for Nigeria's assembly plants, cut by one third to 20 percent.
- Cars assembled abroad, with engine capacities of 1,800.
- Cubic centimeters or more, down to 50 percent from 200 percent—250 percent.
- Finished trucks, four-wheel-drive vehicles, and tractors were halved to 30 percent.

Source: The Bank of Nigeria.

Implications for Credit People

What do the various sovereign, transfer or convertibility, and exchange control risks mean to credit people of exporting companies and their investments overseas? The following explains some of the basic implications.

Shortages of Foreign Exchange. Exporters who sell to countries with limited amounts of foreign exchange reserves or resources may find it difficult to collect receivables from foreign customers. Although local currency may be deposited with the appropriate government authorities, it may still have to wait for its billing currency to be allocated by the exchange control authorities. The waiting period for the local currency to be converted may be several weeks, months, or even years. An excellent source of information to warn credit people of potential foreign exchange delays is the information provided by the FCIB and exchanged by its members at frequently held round table conferences and those export credit group meetings held by affiliate offices of the NACM. Another good source is the country risk information provided by S. J. Rundt and Associates in *Rundt's Weekly Intelligence* and *The Financial Executive's Country Risk Alert* reports.

Continuing Uncertainty. Whatever new monetary system will evolve or be agreed on by nations, currency values (rates) will continue to fluctuate against each other to reflect supply and demand plus country conditions. It is inevitable that countries will continue to allow their currencies to float or be pegged to specific imports of goods for prolonged periods of time to help them overcome their fundamental debt obligations to external creditors. Credit people will, therefore, have to pay specific attention to a country's foreign exchange policies, risk propensity, and opportunities.

Price of Imports and Exports. Goods and services that are imported from countries whose currencies have been valued upward are likely to be more expensive. The reverse takes place when the exporter's foreign customer wants to export its goods to the country of the foreign supplier. In other words, it is cheaper for the export supplier to purchase goods from abroad if its currency strengthens vis-à-vis the currency of a foreign supplier. Conversely, goods exported to countries whose currencies have been valued downward are likely to be inexpensive to their foreign buyers. Therefore, the overall competitive position of exporters to world markets can change significantly based on the strength of its currency. A good example had been the U.S. dollar which strengthened some 40 percent to 60 percent between 1980 and 1985 against a basket of major trading currencies. This strengthening of the U.S. dollar versus other major trading currencies made companies who invoice their exports in U.S. dollars during this period uncompetitive in comparison to other nations who invoice in other major trading currencies that had weakened vis-à-vis the U.S. dollar.

Covering and Hedging.   Due to wider exchange rate fluctuations, greater uncertainties in the foreign exchange markets, the exchange controls imposed, and the exchange controls and regulations yet to be imposed, it may be more difficult for exporters and importers to cover or hedge certain currency risks. It may become more expensive to cover foreign exchange risks as banks and other financial institutions may require a wider profit margin to compensate for the additional foreign exchange risks. There is also the reality and probability that forward contracts for certain currencies and maturities may not be readily available. Exchange controls or restrictions in some countries may make it impossible or very expensive to cover or hedge by buying a foreign currency spot and depositing the proceeds at a local bank until needed.

For those foreign buyers who are subject to erratic and uncontrollable currency fluctuations without adequate protection or hedging techniques, the cost might mean bankruptcy, liquidation, severe liquidity/cash flow problems and delayed payments to trade credit suppliers.

The Market for Foreign Exchange

To understand the foreign exchange market, it is necessary to examine those factors that constitute the supply and demand for foreign exchange.

Supply.   The supply side begins with the export of goods and services to a foreign customer. The foreign customer must ultimately pay for the imported goods with its local currency. This means the foreign customer has to buy a currency for its own account, assuming the export is not invoiced in the foreign customer's local currency, or the trade credit supplier receives foreign currency as payment which it will sell against its own currency or another currency. In either case, the amount of foreign currencies offered in the market and exchanged between buyers and sellers increases.

The same effect results when foreigners purchase anything else from a country, such as real estate, stocks or bonds. Again, the billing currency must be bought (exchanged) for local currencies, thus putting more of these currencies on the market.

In addition, interest and dividends earned on capital lent or invested abroad will increase the supply of foreign exchange. The same is true for the repayment of currency loans made abroad and the repatriation of previously invested capital. In all cases, foreign currency has to be sold for another currency, if different, which augments the supply of foreign currencies in the foreign exchange markets.

Another source of supply is the exchange supplied by tourists which occurs when a tourist wishes to purchase something or repay something for which they need local currency. To do this, they exchange their currencies in the local marketplace thereby increasing the supply of foreign exchange. This is especially true and vital for such nations as Mexico, Italy, and Greece.

Demand.   The demand for foreign exchange is really the mirror image of supply. The demand side is created when there are imports of goods and services from abroad. Either the importer has to make payment in a foreign currency or the foreign exporter wishes to convert the billing currency it receives into its local currency. In either case there will be a market demand for foreign exchange.

A large source of demand for foreign exchange in the 1950s and 1960s has been U.S. investments abroad. The reverse is true today as foreign investment in the United States has increased substantially since 1980. This investment abroad means that foreign factories will be built with local labor and materials, thus using local currency. Consequently, the company investing overseas will wish to buy foreign exchange for their currency, thus generating demand.

Other factors causing increased demand include the spending of tourists abroad, interest and dividends on foreign capital invested in the country, and repayment of loans contracted in other currencies.

The Market Place.   A market place for foreign exchange is any place where foreign exchange is bought and sold in large amounts. The major markets today are in large cities—New York, London, Zurich, Singapore, Hong Kong, Amsterdam, and Tokyo. The exchange market consists of an enormous, highly sophisticated, and efficient global communications system in which most transactions are verbally arranged by two parties. The market places, as well as individual banks and dealers, are all linked by an integrated network of telecommunications which consists of telephones, telexes, cables, or SWIFT.*

The exchange market operates literally around the clock, 24 hours a day. After the European centers close, New York is still active for several hours. Via the trading rooms on the U.S. West Coast, the business then shifts to Far East centers like Tokyo, Hong Kong, and Singapore. From the Far East, activity moves on the Middle East—Bahrain—and from there back to Europe.[7]

An Example for the Export Trader

If a U.S. exporter sells goods and services abroad and receives payment in a foreign currency, whether in the form of a check, draft, or a cable transfer, it can arrange with the foreign exchange trader of its bank to sell its foreign exchange at the quoted market rate for the currency it holds. The seller of foreign exchange simply endorses the check or draft to the bank and receives a credit to its account for the equivalent U.S. dollar proceeds. If the U.S. exporter has received the foreign exchange in the form of a bank balance in a foreign country, it will have to arrange transfer of this balance to its bank. If it wishes to sell by cable, it will have to arrange the delivery of such balances by cable. The bank will then credit its account of the exporter's bank in U.S. dollars and receive the foreign currency balances in an account it maintains abroad.

It is also quite possible that the exporter does not yet possess this

---

* SWIFT—An acronym for Society for Worldwide Information and Funds Transfer. This international system and organization has been established to move funds and information among member banks.

foreign exchange, but knows that it is to receive certain amounts in the next few months. In this case it can contract to sell these amounts for future delivery (forward) to its bank at a specified rate. By doing so it assures itself of a fixed amount of dollars for the foreign currency it will receive. It may have fallen substantially in value by the maturity date of the contract, but the customer benefits from the rate previously established by means of its sale of exchange for future delivery.

An Example for the Foreign Customer

A German importer wants to buy goods from a U.S. supplier in U.S. dollars. It calls the foreign exchange trader of its bank to obtain the current market quotation and the U.S. dollar equivalent needed to make payments. If the amounts are small and time consideration is not important, payments can be arranged by bank drafts and/or mail-payment orders. The German importer will pay the German marks, for which the bank will issue a draft in U.S. dollars payable to the U.S. supplier to whom the importer owes the funds. This draft is then mailed by the German importer or its bank to the U.S. supplier as payment of the debt obligation. In the case of the mail-payment order, the German importer would pay the bank the equivalent dollars, and the bank would arrange to deliver the U.S. dollars due the beneficiary through a branch or a correspondent bank in the exporter's country. Necessary instructions would be provided by airmail.

If the amounts are sizable, and/or time consideration is important, the German bank can quote a rate, collect the marks from the importer, and make the payment abroad by cable or telex. In this case, the foreign beneficiary abroad normally will receive the funds on the next business day.

Paralleling what the exporter can do for his receivables, i.e., sell them in the forward market, the importer can buy for future delivery the amounts of foreign currency it may have to pay at some future date.

METHODS FOR IDENTIFYING COUNTRY RISKS

There are several proven methods for identifying the country conditions of any one given nation. The following is a synopsis of these methods.

The ASSERT Method

A method for determining whether or not to "go or no-go" with a credit decision, is for the credit manager to properly assess country risk conditions by the ASSERT method:

Analyze. Analysis starts with a good database to provide the credit manager with the most recent information on a country's condition. Data bases can be created internally or externally. Is the information from your database accurate? To create historical information on countries of interest to the company, credit managers should develop country files, similar to customer credit files, filed in alpha order by country or alpha order by country by region of the world (Europe, S.E. Asia, Latin America). The credit manager should classify all countries where an element of exposure exists according to a systematic risk classification, whether alphanumeric or descriptive (high risk; moderate risk). Country classifications can provide quantitative analyses of an exporter's receivable investment.

Strengthen. Database information, negative or positive, should be shared with other decision makers in the credit manager's company. This will serve the purpose of creating an early warning system or capability. In many companies, the decision to market goods in virgin countries or to increase market share in existing countries is usually determined well in advance of actual sales taking place, usually at planning meetings and/or senior management levels. Since country conditions are constantly in a state of flux or change, the credit manager and other line or staff personnel should consider regular quarterly or semiannual meetings to discuss key developments in certain countries of interest to the company.

Stress. The credit manager and company need to develop historical trends based on the company's past experience in dealing with certain countries. It means stressing the importance of getting back (selling again) into a country where the company and other company creditors had poor prior experience, especially if the country risk symptoms are similar. The experience of other companies in other industries, not just similar industries, should be examined. Many companies throughout the years of international trading and investing have been adversely affected by country conditions, such as, overseas properties (i.e., goods and/or plants) which were expropriated outright or been forced to sell at auctions or bargain prices for reasons related to government policies. Since historians always say that history repeats itself, companies or credit managers should not lead themselves into a false sense of security by believing that a country's external debt, which has been refinanced today, eradicates its sins of the past. Many country problems are deep rooted and simply will not disappear in relatively short periods of time. Some problems will take years. Textbooks and tenured international business people are full of cases and experiences of creditors who have been paid out with 15 or 20 year bonds that subsequently had to be sold at substantial discounts of face value or of debts that went into arbitration for years.

Expand. This means expanding or establishing a network of country information. It means being part of a community where information exists and is freely exchanged (i.e., the FCIB and APRA—the Association of Political Risk Analysis). Establishing contacts or business relationships with other credit managers in other companies is another good networking technique.

Resolve. Keep well informed of country developments. Apart from reading or relying on information or decisions from country risk consultants, the credit manager should continually keep abreast of country risk developments by subscribing to or reading material on countries or books on country risk assessment. It means reading such things as *The Wall Street Journal, New York Times, Financial Times of London, Euromoney, The Institutional Investor, Business Week,* and *Forbes,* and publications offered by many international banking institutions on economic developments in countries or the world economy in general. It means establishing a network of country and economic information from around the world.

Target. The bigger the company, the more complex the decision-making process becomes. By targeting, developing, and integrating oneself, the credit manager can share country risk assessment skills and network information with other appropriate individuals or groups within the company (i.e., senior executives, planning personnel, international finance managers). Even if the company decides to invest in a particular country by buying out an existing distributor or manufacturer or whatever, the importance of properly assessing country risk is certainly not diminished, but imperative. Here again, the information and expertise of the credit manager can be particularly beneficial, especially when consideration is given to the credit conditions and management of the overseas operations' own accounts receivable (direct credit sales domestically within the country or by exporting to other non-affiliated foreign customers in other countries).

The CAMEL Method[8]

In order to structure the variables that need to be collected, evaluated, forecasted, and compared for an effective assessment of country risk, credit people can use the CAMEL method.

Current Earnings This information encompasses past and present exports, imports and invisibles trade, and the current-account balance of payments of a country. It is easy to obtain from the country itself or from organizations like the International Monetary Fund (IMF).

Asset Quality. A country's natural, human, and general economic resources comprise their asset quality. Gross domestic product (GDP) figures reveal the size of an economy, and composition of GDP indicates its underlying structure. Natural resources can make an otherwise less-developed nation cash rich (i.e., countries in the Middle East as a result of petroleum prices). But, natural resources can have a negative effect on certain nations when their basic commodities for export earnings are affected by depressed commodity prices (i.e., Zambia, Zaire, and Bolivia from tin prices), while natural-resource-poor countries, such as Singapore, Taiwan, and South Korea, can thrive.

Management Quality. What is the ability of the government to manage its economy, or its attitude toward foreign investment and trade? If resources can make a nation, government policy can break it. How strong is its leadership? What about the level of social and political unrest, present and future?

Earnings Potential. The analyst should check the size of a country's domestic market (population, wealth distribution, protectionist tendencies, etc.). Can the government muster these resources to promote international business? Assess and project the probable/potential external-accounts prospects, factoring in such considerations as terms of trade, dependence of exports on uncontrollable influences (such as weather for cash crops or world market trends for commodities, both of which are major sources for export earnings and social stability).

Liquidity. Does the country have hard currency to which it can promptly service its external debt obligations? This is a crucial area for the analyst. It requires reliable up-to-date information which is often harder to come by than for any other part of the analysis. Yet, foreign exchange cash-flow prospects are frequently the most decisive indicators of sudden difficulties in international payments.

The IMPROVE Method[9]

Once an analysis is completed by the credit manager or analyst on a specific country or geographic area of the world, the analysis is of little value unless it is integrated into the strategies/goals of the company, the marketing/sales objectives, and the company's general exposure management. In this regard, a seven-point process can be used.

Identification. Discover and classify your exposures, whether they are transactions, currency translations, or general economic risks. The categories will overlap, but risks still need to be clearly defined and identified, especially as it concerns the objectives of the marketing/sales departments.

Measuring. Once identified, measure your exposures for determining the corporate resources needed to be assigned to meet the goals of the company and the objectives of marketing/sales.

Projected. Once measured, the exposures must be projected to guard against adverse country risk conditions as well as future opportunities if one takes advantage of them. Where is the marketing/sales department projecting to market its goods and services in the future? Have they even thought about it? If not, why not?

Risk Assessment. Only after such projections are made can the risk assessment be tailored to the situation in light of the differences between a mining enterprise in Zambia, a pharmaceutical manufacturer in Brazil, or a bank lending to the Philippines. To where and to whom does the marketing/sales department want to market its goods and services?

Options. Once risk is determined, managing it from a credit point of view means choosing among options ranging from cutting back or increasing export sales to certain countries targeted for growth, changing the payment terms (stricter or more lenient), establishing or increasing special reserves for doubtful accounts, or taking out export credit insurance coverage. The goals or objectives of treasury might conflict with those of marketing/sales. One wants to increase cash flow to reduce debt while the other wants to increase sales into new or old markets.

Valuation. The credit department and those of other departments (i.e., financial analysts, market analysts), should weigh each option through a cost/benefit and risk/reward analysis that is carefully prepared, comprehensive, and precise. Rather than focus on the short term, all concerned should carefully weigh the long term of the aforementioned.

Execution. Only after all of these steps have been taken can you proceed from analysis to execution and select and implement the best option.

CUSTOMER AND COUNTRY RISK
CODE CLASSIFICATIONS

The credit manager must incorporate a procedure for monitoring political risk into the export credit decision-making process. It may not be practical for him or her to establish their own research operation for this purpose. Many experienced credit managers evaluate country risk by classifying and assigning risk codes to countries. This minimizes a lot of guesswork and leaves little room for error on the part of department employees who have the authority to extend credit to foreign customers.

While systems for identifying risks vary from business to business, some of the elements involved are quite basic. First, it is well to classify accounts, since some are good, others are fair, and still others are marginal credit risks. In domestic credit, customers are usually ranked by numeric codes for consumer credit type customers and by alpha codes for business credit type customers. In international trade credit, foreign customers are assigned numeric or alpha codes which are primarily based on country risk determination variables and/or rankings. The codes (sometimes called classes) can range from A to E (A = excellent risk; E = high risk) or 1 to 5 (1 = excellent; 5 = high risk) or even higher depending on preference.

The goal is to select a set of variables which, when weighted, can provide an overall risk code or ranking for each country where an accounts receivable exposure exists. Unless you are totally dependent on an outside country consultant service which ranks countries, the credit manager, marketing/sales, and other appropriate decision makers must assess and evaluate country risk through their own sources of information. The assessment should include such quantitative factors as debt profile/servicing, international monetary reserve levels, fiscal and monetary indicators, and such ratios as debt-to-imports, debt-to-exports, and savings-to-investment. Qualitative factors such as political stability, economic conditions, and quality of life indicators (social risk conditions) should also be considered.

To assist in ranking countries and assigning country risk codes, there are basically three important and helpful sources of

TABLE 2–3
Institutional Investor's 1985 Country Credit Ratings

Rank Sept. 1985	Rank March 1985	Country	Institutional Investor Credit Rating	Six-Month Change	One-Year Change
1	1	United States	96.1	0.5	0.5
2	2	Japan	95.1	0.0	0.1
3	3	Switzerland	94.4	−0.3	−0.5
4	4	West Germany	93.2	0.1	0.1
5	5	United Kingdom	88.1	−0.7	−1.4
6	6	Canada	87.6	0.5	1.1
7	7	Netherlands	86.5	0.2	0.3
8	8	Norway	86.1	0.0	−0.7
9	10	Austria	82.4	−0.1	0.5
10	9	Australia	82.1	−1.8	−2.1
11	11	France	81.1	0.7	1.7
12	13	Sweden	78.4	−0.3	0.2
13	12	Singapore	78.1	−1.2	−1.5
14	14	Finland	77.3	0.1	1.6
15	15	Belgium	74.8	0.4	1.0
16	16	Italy	74.6	1.0	2.4
17	17	Denmark	72.1	−0.2	0.4
18	18	Taiwan	71.4	0.6	1.9
19	19	New Zealand	69.9	−0.8	−1.8
20	20	Saudi Arabia	69.8	0.2	−1.4
21	21	China	68.3	1.3	2.8
22	25	U.S.S.R.	67.4	2.8	3.4
23	24	Spain	67.0	2.0	2.8
24	22	Hongkong	66.9	0.7	2.6
25	23	Malaysia	64.5	−1.2	−2.8
26	26	Kuwait	64.2	0.3	0.5
27	27	Ireland	62.9	0.0	0.9
28	28	United Arab Emirates	60.4	−0.4	−0.6
29	29	South Korea	57.3	−0.6	0.4
30	30	Bahrain	57.0	0.6	1.4
31	32	Qatar	55.7	0.3	0.3
32	33	Algeria	54.1	0.9	0.6
33	31	South Africa	53.4	−2.2	−3.7
34	37	Oman	52.9	2.1	2.9
35	41	East Germany	52.8	5.2	8.1
36	35	Thailand	52.0	−0.1	−1.3
37	34	Iceland	51.5	−0.7	−0.6
38	36	Greece	51.2	−0.4	0.0

TABLE 2–3 (continued)

Rank			Institutional Investor Credit Rating	Six-Month Change	One-Year Change
Sept. 1985	March 1985	Country			
39	42	Hungary	50.6	3.3	5.0
40	43	Czechoslovakia	50.4	3.6	5.8
41	38	Portugal	49.7	0.2	0.9
42	39	Indonesia	49.6	0.3	−0.1
43	45	Bulgaria	48.5	3.3	5.3
44	44	India	46.3	0.4	−0.6
45	40	Trinidad and Tobago	45.2	−3.2	−4.3
46	46	Tunisia	41.8	−1.5	−3.0
47	48	Papua New Guinea	39.9	−0.9	−0.8
48	49	Mexico	39.2	0.1	1.1
49	50	Gabon	39.1	2.0	2.6
50	47	Colombia	38.6	−2.4	−6.3
51	52	Jordan	38.1	2.0	0.8
52	53	Cameroon	37.5	2.0	1.7
53	54	Cyprus	37.4	1.9	4.3
54	51	Venezuela	37.3	0.4	−0.1
55	55	Egypt	35.0	0.6	2.3
56	56	Turkey	34.8	0.5	4.2
57	59	Paraguay	32.7	0.1	−0.6
58	61	Libya	32.0	0.6	−0.2
59	58	Panama	31.1	−1.5	−2.0
60*	57	Barbados	30.9	−2.1	0.0
61*	60	Brazil	30.9	−0.7	1.2
62	62	Yugoslavia	29.9	−0.5	0.4
63	71	Rumania	28.4	3.5	7.4
64	63	Israel	28.3	−0.6	−1.7
	65	Kenya	28.3	0.8	1.6
66	68	Pakistan	27.7	1.5	3.9
67	64	Uruguay	27.5	−0.8	−1.3
68	67	Ivory Coast	26.0	−1.0	−3.3
69	66	Nigeria	25.4	−1.6	−4.4
70	72	Ecuador	25.0	0.9	0.8
71	69	Sri Lanka	23.9	−1.9	−2.4
72	70	Chile	23.3	−1.7	−3.1
73	73	Morocco	22.9	−0.4	−1.5
74	76	Mauritius	22.5	1.7	3.3
75	74	Argentina	21.0	−1.0	−2.3

TABLE 2–3 (concluded)

Rank			Institutional		
Sept. 1985	March 1985	Country	Investor Credit Rating	Six-Month Change	One-Year Change
76	80	Zimbabwe	19.7	1.1	0.6
77*	78	Iraq	18.8	−1.1	−0.6
78*	81	Syria	18.8	0.3	−1.3
79	82	Congo	18.7	0.5	1.6
80	79	Iran	18.4	−0.5	−0.3
	77	Philippines	18.4	−2.2	−3.8
82	75	Peru	18.2	−2.8	−5.1
83	83	Senegal	17.3	0.9	0.8
84	85	Malawi	16.6	1.2	1.0
85	87	Bangladesh	15.8	0.7	1.9
86	86	Costa Rica	14.2	−1.1	−0.4
87	91	Angola	13.9	0.7	0.5
	88	Poland	13.9	−0.3	2.8
89	84	Jamaica	13.8	−1.9	−0.6
90	90	Cuba	13.6	0.3	1.8
91	89	Dominican Republic	13.3	0.0	−0.2
92	92	Guatemala	12.4	−0.6	0.6
93	93	Lebanon	11.7	−0.7	−0.5
94	95	Seychelles	11.6	−0.1	0.3
95	94	Liberia	11.5	−0.4	0.5
96	96	Zambia	10.5	−0.2	0.8
97	98	Honduras	9.8	0.0	−0.2
98	100	Tanzania	9.7	0.8	1.5
99	97	Grenada	8.3	−1.6	0.1
100*	105	Zaire	8.0	−1.0	2.1
101*	102	Ethiopia	8.0	0.0	−0.5
102	99	Haiti	7.9	−1.6	−0.5
103	101	Bolivia	7.5	−0.8	−0.2
104	103	Sudan	7.4	−0.4	0.7
105	104	Sierra Leone	6.9	−0.2	−0.5
106	106	El Salvador	6.1	−0.6	−0.3
107	107	Uganda	5.9	0.6	1.6
108	109	North Korea	5.3	0.7	1.4
109	108	Nicaragua	4.4	−0.9	−0.3
Global average rating			40.3	0.1	0.4

* Order determined by the actual results before rounding.

Source: *Institutional Investor*, October 1985.

information which, when interrelated with each other, can prove extremely helpful in determining country risk codes:

1. Country credit ratings and rankings by international lenders from the magazine *Institutional Investor* (Table 2–3).
2. FCIB's *Credit and Collection Conditions in Export Markets* survey (Appendix 2–D).
3. Global Business Communications, Inc., *The World Guide for Exporters* (formerly known as *The Chase World Guide for Exporters*) and their quarterly statistical reports on credit terms and collection experience (Table 2–4).

This information, plus information from other sources, will assist in your efforts to establish risk codes by country. The next step is to analyze the total existing and anticipated (cash flow projections) accounts receivable investment by using the risk codes assigned to each country. It can be accomplished by using a Country-Risk Graph (Figure 2–1) which graphs where the bulk of an accounts receivable lies, and by using a County-Risk Matrix (Figure 2–2) which focuses on where a bulk of low-risk or high-risk accounts exists within quadrant rankings, can highlight potential write offs.

Risk Ranking.   The matrix in Figure 2–2 supplies the credit manager with an overall view of the company's accounts receivable country risk portfolio. The country of each foreign customer is plotted on the matrix (shown as Xs). Quadrant I contains high-dollar, low country risk accounts or the ideal accounts. Quadrant II contains high-dollar, high country risk account or the least desirable.

Country Credit Limit.   The next step is for the company to determine if it wants to limit its accounts receivable exposure per country based on an assessment of the data contained in the country risk matrix or graph. This can be further determined by assessing the risks/rewards of selling to countries where a high degree of accounts receivable exposure exists in addition to high delinquency rankings.

This assessment should include your company's direct investment in countries (means including the accounts receivable invest-

TABLE 2-4
Export Credit Reports

Crude Materials Including Mineral Fuels

Countries You Export to	Documentary Collections			Documentary Letters of Credit				Open Account	
	Sight Drafts—Documents against Payment	Time Drafts		Confirmed		Unconfirmed			
	Percent	Percent	Days	Percent	Days	Percent	Days	Percent	Days
Middle East									
Bahrain		100	(60–90)						
Egypt				100	(Sight–180)				
Iran				100	(180)				
Iraq				50	(30–90)				
Israel	28	18	(30–90)	45	(Sight–120)				
Jordan		50	(90)					50	(30)
Kuwait						100	(Sight)	9	(Sight–30)
Lebanon	50			50	(Sight)			50	(30)
Oman									
Qatar									
Saudi Arabia	34			33	(Sight)	33	(Sight)		
Syria	50			100	(Sight–90)				
United Arab Emirates						50	(Sight)		
Yemen Arab Republic									

Asia

Country				
Afghanistan	16			
Australia	17 (30–60)	17 (Sight)	8 (60)	42 (30–60)
China	43	40 (Sight)	40 (Sight)	20 (30–60)
Hong Kong	11	14 (Sight)	43 (Sight)	
India		78 (Sight–90)		11 (30)
Indonesia	27	67 (Sight)		33 (60)
Japan	9 (30)	41 (Sight–90)	9 (Sight)	14 (30–90)
Korea		60 (Sight–90)	40 (Sight–60)	
Malaysia	30		50 (Sight)	50 (60)
New Zealand	30 (30–90)			40 (30–90)
Pakistan		100 (Sight–90)		
Philippines	20 (60)	49 (Sight–90)	38 (Sight–60)	13 (60)
Singapore	20	20 (Sight)	20 (Sight)	20 (30)
Sri Lanka	16			
Taiwan	11 (30–90)	50 (Sight–90)	17 (Sight)	
Thailand	20 (90)	20 (30–90)	60 (Sight–60)	6 (30)

Africa

Country				
Algeria		100 (Sight)		
Angola				
Cameroon				
Ethiopia				
Gabon				
Ghana				
Ivory Coast				
Kenya		100 (30–90)		
Liberia				
Libya				
Malawi				

TABLE 2–4 (continued)

Crude Materials Including Mineral Fuels

Countries You Export to	Documentary Collections				Documentary Letters of Credit				Open Account	
	Sight Drafts—Documents against Payment		Time Drafts		Confirmed		Unconfirmed			
	Percent		Percent	Days	Percent	Days	Percent	Days	Percent	Days
Morocco										
Mozambique										
Nigeria										
Senegal										
Sierra Leone										
South Africa	34		33	(30–90)					33	(60–90)
Sudan										
Tanzania										
Togo										
Tunisia										
Uganda										
Zaire										
Zambia										

Chemicals and Fertilizers

Countries You Export to	Documentary Collections			Documentary Letters of Credit				Open Account	
	Sight Drafts—Documents against Payment Percent	Time Drafts		Confirmed		Unconfirmed			
		Percent	Days	Percent	Days	Percent	Days	Percent	Days
North America									
Bermuda	40							60	(30–60)
Canada								100	(30–90)
Europe									
Austria				22	(30–60)	11	(Sight)	67	(30–90)
Belgium				20	(Sight–30)			80	(30–90)
Bulgaria				100	(Sight–30)				
Cyprus		50	(120)	50	(30)				
Czechoslovakia				50	(Sight–30)	25	(90–120)	25	(180)
Denmark				50	(Sight–30)			50	(30–60)
Finland		17	(120)					83	(30–60)
France				17	(Sight)			83	(30–180)
Germany, D.R.								100	(60–90)
Germany, F.R.	37	9	(30)					91	(30–90)
Greece	25	25	(60–120)	13	(Sight)	25	(Sight)	25	(60–180)
Hungary	100			25	(Sight)			25	(30)
Iceland	20								
Ireland	9			20	(Sight)			60	(30–60)
Italy		9	(60)					82	(30–120)
Malta	100								
Netherlands								100	(30–90)
Norway	16					17	(Sight)	67	(30–90)

TABLE 2–4 (concluded)

Chemicals and Fertilizers

Countries You Export to	Documentary Collections			Documentary Letters of Credit				Open Account	
	Sight Drafts—Documents against Payment Percent	Time Drafts Percent	Days	Confirmed Percent	Days	Unconfirmed Percent	Days	Percent	Days
Poland								40	(60–90)
Portugal	40	20	(60)			100	(Sight)		
Romania				100	(Sight)				
Spain	12	13	(60)					75	(30–180)
Sweden	12							88	(30–60)
Switzerland								89	(30–60)
Turkey		14	(120)	43	(Sight–30)	11	(180)	14	(60)
USSR				75	(Sight–30)	29	(Sight–120)	25	(30)
United Kingdom				10	(30)			90	(30–90)
Yugoslavia				60	(Sight–60)	20	(90–120)	20	(60)
Latin America									
Argentina		35	(180)	60	(Sight–180)			5	(180)
Belize	20	60	(30–120)	20	(30)				
Bolivia				100	(Sight–30)				
Brazil	5	61	(30–180)	17	(Sight–180)	6	(90)	11	(30–90)
Chile		53	(120–180)	47	(Sight–120)				

Country									
Colombia	20	43	(30–180)	47	(Sight–180)	5	(120–180)	5	(30)
Costa Rica		40	(60–180)	33	(Sight–180)			7	(30)
Ecuador	10	18	(120)	45	(Sight–120)	9	(120)	18	(30–90)
El Salvador	9	9	(180)	73	(Sight–180)	9	(90)		
Guatemala	22	22	(30–60)	56	(Sight–90)				
Guyana	60	20	(30)	20	(30)				
Honduras		33	(120)	50	(Sight–30)			17	(Sight)
Mexico		5	(60)	28	(Sight–90)			67	(30–90)
Nicaragua				67	(Sight–30)			33	(30–90)
Panama	19	27	(30–120)	18	(Sight–60)	9	(60)	27	(30–120)
Paraguay				100	(Sight–30)				
Peru	7	36	(30–180)	50	(Sight–180)	7	(120)		
Suriname									
Uruguay		16	(120)	67	(Sight–180)			17	(30)
Venezuela		15	(120–180)	71	(Sight–180)			14	(60–90)
Caribbean									
Antigua	34	33	(60)	33	(30)			71	(30–60)
Bahamas	15			14	(30)			40	(30–90)
Barbados	20			20	(30)	20	(60)	15	(30–60)
Dominican Republic	16	15	(90–120)	46	(Sight–60)	8	(90)		
Haiti				80	(Sight–30)				
Jamaica	10	20	(90)	45	(Sight)	9	(Sight)	9	(30–60)
Martinique		27	(30–90)			100	(60)		
Netherlands Antilles	100								
Trinidad	25	25	(30)					50	(30–90)

Source: *The Chase World Guide for Exporters*, copyright 1987, Chase Manhattan Bank, printed with permission of the publisher, Global Business Communications, Inc., P.O. Box 99, Gillette, N.J. 07933, pp. 35–36.

FIGURE 2–1
Country Risk Graph

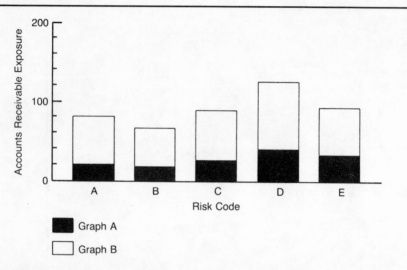

The graph is used to plot a company's overall accounts receivable country risk using risk rankings. The shaded areas represent accounts receivable in each rating group that are 60 days or more beyond maturity (30, 60, 90, 120 days can be used). The A rating is considered excellent; an E rating is poor.

ment of the local operation), exports from other company units, and whether or not the direct investment in a particular country is supplying materials to other company units.

Assignment of Credit Terms by Customer/Country Risk Codes

Before assigning credit terms by country, it is important to remember that different industries and, for that matter, even different product lines are subject to different country import and foreign exchange regulations. Depending on the level of experience, expertise and sophistication of the company and its credit manager, experiences will vary from one company and credit manager to the next as evidenced by the interchange of credit managers at credit group meetings.

FIGURE 2–2
Country Risk Matrix

Accounts Receivable Exposure		
I High		II Low
X X		X X
	X X	
X		
X		
Low IV	Moderate	High III

Example

Take two credit managers, both working for manufacturing type companies, who are exporting goods and services to the same country. The following is typical of what their experiences might be.

The first credit manager is reporting prompt payment experience from a number of countries while the second credit manager is reporting slow payment from the same countries. Their credit terms are even different.

1. The answer might lie in the first credit manager having a tighter collection policy than the second credit manager.
2. Their industries might be different and therefore both are subject to different foreign exchange and import regulations (F/X is allocated faster to the first credit manager's product lines because they are essential while the product lines of the second credit manager are not as essential).
3. The second company is willing to tolerate slow payments from its foreign customers to obtain market share.
4. The second credit manager sells to a financially weaker customer base than the first credit manager. This may be due

to its credit approval criteria or the industry itself, meaning, the second credit manager's industry is less prosperous than the first credit manager's.

It all means that just because one credit manager or company is operating in a certain industry with poor payment or business experience in one country, does not necessarily mean a similar or different company or credit manager will have exactly the same experiences. However, what is important are the trends each and every company and credit manager are experiencing in each country, especially Third World countries.

When establishing ratings, the first step is to establish a rating on each foreign customer based on commercial risk or the credit-worthiness of the account. If the foreign customer is financially weak for the amount of business (orders and sales volume) to be transacted with the account over a period of time, then perhaps restrictive credit terms of letter of credit might have to be assigned to the account. However, restrictive credit terms might be uncompetitive if competition is willing to extend less restrictive payment terms in which case the exporter needs to weigh the risk/rewards to extending less restrictive payment terms.

If less restrictive payment terms can be extended to a foreign customer, the next step is to evaluate country risk. This is based on pre-established country risk codes and an examination of country risk as it pertains to foreign exchange and import regulations to make sure these regulations have not changed since the country code was assigned. Experienced credit managers know that these regulations, especially in less developed or Third World countries, can change quite radically, quickly, and with little advance warning to external creditors. Figure 2–3 is an example of credit terms assigned to countries by risk code.

In summation, the credit manager and his or her staff must be alert to the danger signals in the pattern of economic policies of the countries of the world which create inflation. These policies are usually characterized by deficit spending and a pattern of heavy international borrowing. Although there may be many reasons for pursuing such policies, the most common is a desire to maintain political support. Governments tend to undertake heavy welfare payments and consumer subsidies as a means of achieving this purpose.

FIGURE 2–3
Credit Terms by Country Risk Code Classification

		Country Risk Code			
	A	B	C	D	E
C	O/A	O/A	SD/DAP	SD/DAP	CIA
R	C/D	CAD	TD/DA	CISBLLC	CWO
E	CAD	CAG	STD/DA	DEFPAY-LC	COD
D	CAG	DAP	ISLC	CISLC	CISLC
I	DAP	CONS	DEFPAY-LC	CITLC	CITLC
T	CONS	PROM.NOTE	CISLC		
	PROM.NOTE	SD/DAP	CITLC		
T		TD/DA	CISBLLC		
E		STD/DA			
R		ISLC			
M		ITLC			
S		ISBLLC			

Legend

Invoices, drafts, and time letters of credit can be payable within the standard length of times—30, 60, 90, 120, 150, 180 days and longer (longer for export sales of capital goods and commodities).

O/A—Open account payable against invoices with terms of discount, 30-to-180 days and over.

C/D—Clean draft.

CAD—Cash against documents.

CAG—Cash against goods.

DAP—Documents against payment.

CONS—Consignment.

PROM. NOTE—Promissory note.

SD/DAP—Sight draft, documents against payment.

TD/DA—Time draft, documents against acceptance.

STD/DA—Sight time draft, documents against acceptance.

ISLC—Irrevocable sight letter of credit.

ITLC—Irrevocable time letter of credit.

ISBLLC—Irrevocable stale bill of lading letter of credit.

DEFPAYLC—Deferred payment letter of credit.

CISLC—Confirmed irrevocable sight letter of credit.

CITLC—Confirmed irrevocable time letter of credit.

CISBLLC—Confirmed irrevocable stale bill of lading letter of credit.

CIA—Cash in advance.

CWO—Cash with order.

COD—Cash on delivery.

Example of Country Risk Code Classifications

A	B	C	D	E
Austria	Brazil	Argentina	Albania	Angola
Australia	Chile	India	Algeria	Bolivia
Bahamas	Cyprus	Indonesia	Bulgaria	Cuba
Belgium	Italy	Mexico	Cameroon	El Salvador
Finland	Spain	Paraguay	Costa Rica	Iran
France	South Korea	Saudi Arabia	Gabon	Iraq
Japan	Taiwan	Uruguay	Hungary	Lebanon
Luxembourg	Venezuela		Qatar	Liberia
New Zealand			Tunisia	Nicaragua
PRC			Turkey	Nigeria
Singapore			UAE	Peru
Switzerland				Philippines
USSR				Poland
				Romania
				Surinam
				Tanzania
				Uganda
				Zaire

Some governments suffer from poor economic management simply because of incompetence or because they pursue a political philosophy which is interwoven with faulty economic principles.

Finally, some underdeveloped countries lack an economic infrastructure of either natural resources or an industrial ability to generate exports sufficient to offset their basic imports. This guarantees an unfavorable balance of payments (BOP) position. The problem becomes more acute because these countries usually lack any significant dollar or gold reserves.

There is little doubt in the minds of many experienced credit managers that the task of customer and country risk analysis is difficult and complex and the risks can many times outweigh the rewards. They know that by checking and doublechecking many of the sources of information available to them, the rewards can far outweigh the risks. The idea is to manage the risks, not eliminate them. By managing risk, most foreign customer delinquency and country risk problems should be greatly reduced, thus resulting in an increase in cash flow, increased sales, and a reduction in bad debt losses.

APPENDIX 2–A SOURCES OF COUNTRY RISK INFORMATION

Governmental Agencies

U.S. Department of Commerce
Industry and Trade Administration
"Foreign Economic Trends and Their
  Implications for the United States"
Washington, D.C. 20402

U.S. Department of Commerce
International Trade Administration
"Business America"
Superintendent of Documents
U.S. Government Printing Office
Washington, D.C. 20402

U.S. Department of Commerce
International Trade Administration
"Country Market Sectorial Surveys"
Market Research Division,
  Room 1204
Washington, D.C. 20230

U.S. Department of Commerce
International Trade Administration
"Country Market Surveys"
Publications Sales Branch
  Room 1617
Washington, D.C. 20230

U.S. Department of Commerce
International Trade Administration
"International Economic Indicators
Superintendent of Documents
U.S. Government Printing Office
Washington, D.C. 20402

International Bank for Reconstruction
  and Development
(The World Bank)
"World Debt Tables"
External Public Debt of Developing
  Countries
1818 H Street N.W.
Washington, D.C. 20433

Bank for International Settlements
  (BIS)
"Maturity Distribution of
  International Bank Lending, and
  The External Position of Banks in
  Group of Ten Countries and
  Switzerland"
7 Central Gahnstrasse
Basle, Switzerland

Comptroller of the Currency
Federal Deposit Insurance
  Corporation
Federal Reserve Board
"Joint News Release, Country
  Exposure Lending Survey"
20th St. & Constitution Ave. N.W.
Washington, D.C. 20551

International Bank for Reconstruction
  and Development
(The World Bank)
"Borrowing in International Capital
  Markets and International Bond
  Issues, Publicized Eurocurrency
  Credits"
1818 H Street N.W.
Washington, D.C. 20433

International Monetary Fund (IMF)
"International Financial Statistics"
19th and H Streets N.W.
Washington, D.C. 20431

International Monetary Fund
"Balance of Payments Yearbook"
19th and H Streets N.W.
Washington, D.C. 20431

International Monetary Fund
"Direction of Trade Yearbook"
19th and H Streets N.W.
Washington, D.C. 20431

United Nations
"Monthly Bulletin of Statistics"
Between First Ave. & Roosevelt Dr.
    and E. 42nd St. & E. 48th St.
New York, N.Y. 10017

Economic and Political Reporting Services

S.J. Rundt & Associates Inc.
(World Risk Analysis Package)
130 East 63rd Street
New York, N.Y. 10021

Frost & Sullivan Inc.
(World Political Forecasts)
106 Fulton St.
New York, N.Y. 10038

Business International Corp.
(Country Assessment Service)
One Dag Hammarskjold Plaza
New York, N.Y. 10017

The Economist Intelligence Unit
(Quarterly Economic Reviews
    Service)
10 Rockefeller Plaza
New York, N.Y. 10020

International Reports Inc.
(International Country Risk Guide)
200 Park Avenue South
New York, N.Y. 10003

Magazines and Newspapers

The Economist (Weekly)
P.O. Box 2700
Woburn, MA 01888

Trade Finance (Monthly)
Euromoney
Subscription Dept.
Watling St.
Bletchley, Milton
Keynes MK2 2BW
United Kingdom

Institutional Investor (Monthly)
488 Madison Ave.
New York, N.Y. 10022

Far Eastern Economic Review
    (Weekly)
U.S. Mailing Agents
Data Movers Inc.
38 W. 36th Street
New York, N.Y. 10018

The Financial Times (Daily)
14 E. 60th Street
New York, N.Y. 10018

The Wall Street Journal (Daily)
Dow Jones & Company, Inc.
22 Courtlandt St.
New York, N.Y. 10007

The Asian Wall Street Journal
  (Weekly)
Dow Jones & Company, Inc.
22 Courtlandt St.
New York, N.Y. 10007

Banks

Morgan Guaranty Trust Company
  of N.Y.
"World Financial Markets"
International Economics Department
23 Wall Street
New York, N.Y. 10015

Security Pacific National Bank
"Economic Report"
International Edition
Economics Department, H8-13
P.O. Box 2097, Terminal Annex
Los Angeles, CA 90051

The Royal Bank of Canada
"Econoscope"
Economics Department
P.O. Box 6001
Montreal, Quebec
Canada H3C 3A9

The First National Bank of Boston
"UPDATE: Latin America"
P.O. Box 1784
Boston, MA 02105

APPENDIX 2–B IMPORT REGULATIONS—BRAZIL

Imports into Brazil are grouped into two major categories:

1. Imports that do not require an import permit titled *Guia de Importacao*. This group covers (*a*) shipments of samples without commercial value, and (*b*) shipments for the importer's own use of material for education or scientific purposes, including test animals, books, tapes, films, records and the like, some with limits as to value, others with no such limits.

2. Imports that require a *Guia de Importacao*. Guias are issued by the Foreign Trade Department (CACEX) of Banco do Brasil. To obtain a Guia, the importer must be registered at CACEX and furnish details on the foreign price of the merchandise and other information deemed necessary by CACEX. If the price declared by the importer is lower than the prevailing price for the respective goods in international markets, CACEX indicates on the Guia

the price to be used by the customs for the assessment of duties. There is a processing charge of up to 0.9 percent of the value of imports.

Guias may be issued in any convertible currency. Guias must be obtained prior to shipment for most imports. Exempt from this requirement is a list of some 80 essential items for which Guias may be obtained prior to customs clearance of the goods. This list covers animals for breeding, fruits and grains for seeding, minerals, vaccines and medicines, various educational material, and scientific apparatus for resale.

If an import is made under one of the following conditions, the Guia must be obtained prior to shipment whether or not the item concerned is included in the aforementioned list of 80 essentials:

1. Imports on credit terms exceeding 180 days.
2. Imports of merchandise verified as having no local equivalent and therefore benefiting from reduction or elimination of import duties.
3. Imports benefiting from duty concessions under special legislation.
4. Imports by governmental agencies.
5. Imports requiring prior permission from governmental agencies other than CACEX.
6. Imports for trade fairs and exhibits.
7. Imports of used machinery and equipment.

Validity periods of Guias are 60, 90, 180, or over 180 days, depending on the type of merchandise. Food, raw materials, and goods with customs duties over 55 percent are covered by 90-day Guias. Machinery and other capital goods are covered by 180-day Guias. Goods that are made to order are covered by over-180-day Guias.

Shipments must be made during validity periods of the Guia. Extension of validity periods may be required from CACEX prior to expiration dates. Application for extension must be accompanied by a letter from the supplier justifying the impossibility to ship the merchandise within the initially planned time period. A tolerance of 10 percent over the value and quantity stated on the Guia is permitted. Also, customs surcharges range from 0 percent to 300 percent of the FOB value of the goods. There are no stamp taxes on drafts or shipping documents.

Import Payments

Foreign exchange is obtained from any bank authorized to deal in foreign exchange by means of an exchange contract. Remittances abroad may be made only two business days prior to maturity of the obligation.

Imports under letters of credit require a deposit in Cruzados* equivalent to the FOB value of the letter of credit. CACEX may waive the deposit requirement for imports of certain agricultural products, such as fertilizer, insecticides, or seeds. Exempt from the deposit requirement are imports under drawback.

Payments prior to the shipment of the goods or before the arrival of the respective shipping documents require permission from the Foreign Exchange Department of Banco Central (the central bank).

The purchase of foreign exchange for remittances abroad in payment of goods and services is subject to a tax of 25 percent of the value of the exchange contracted. The tax is payable in Cruzados. It is only 20 percent for remittances covering imports of Latin American Integration Association (ALADI) that are negotiated items. Exempt from the remittance tax are payments for imports of petroleum, certain agricultural products (such as fertilizer, insecticides, seeds), some publications, and goods related to the Itaipu Dam.

Forward Foreign Exchange Contracts

For the purchase of foreign exchange, the importer must close an exchange contract, either spot or for future delivery.

For imports not subject to a Guia, foreign exchange may be closed only after customs clearance of the goods if the shipment is made under documentary drafts for collection. If such imports are made under letters of credit, foreign exchange must be closed prior to the opening of the L/C. Imports not requiring a Guia are allowed credit terms only up to 180 days from the date on the bill of lading. As a result, forward exchange contracts for the payment of such imports may not exceed 180 days.

For imports subject to a Guia made on a collection basis, foreign exchange may be closed only after the Guia has been obtained and shipping documents have been received by the collecting bank in Brazil. For imports made under L/Cs, foreign exchange must be closed at the time of opening of the L/C. Imports under letters of credit calling for credit terms exceeding 360 days are exempt from this requirement.

Foreign exchange contracts covering interest payments on suppliers credit may be closed spot only, and not earlier than two days preceding the maturity of the draft covering such payments.

---

* A new currency unit the *Cruzado* was introduced in Brazil, replacing the Cruzeiro at the rate of Cruzado 1 = Cruzeiros 1,000. The rate of exchange between the new unit and the U.S. dollar was US$1 = Cruzados 13.77 on March 4, 1986.

Credit Terms

Credit terms for imports not requiring a Guia are limited to 180 days maximum from the date on the bill of lading.

Some imports are subject to minimum credit terms regulated by Banco Central Resolution No. 638 of September 24, 1980 as amended by Banco Central Circular No. 674 of October 22, 1980. The Resolution covers imports made by individuals or enterprises for their own use or for resale and for which a Guia has been issued on or after September 24, 1980.

The minimum credit terms are listed below:

1. For imports of machinery, equipment, apparatus, instruments, vehicles, ships, boats and airplanes:

US$ FOB Value or Equivalent in Other Currencies	Minimum Credit Terms (Years)
Over 100,000 to 300,000	3
Over 300,000 to 1,000,000	5
Over 1,000,000	8

2. For parts, pieces, components and accessories for maintenance, assembly and repair:
   — Minimum term two years when the Guia has been issued up to December 31, 1980.
   — Minimum term one year when the Guia has been issued January 1, 1981 and thereafter.
3. For durable consumer products, raw materials and semi-finished products for the chemical and steel industries:
   — Minimum term 180 days when the ceiling to be imported in the year under consideration exceeds US $100,000 or the equivalent amount in another currency.
4. Exempt from the above minimum term requirements are imports:
   a. Under drawback.
   b. Of items for maintenance and repair by commercial aviation companies for their own use.
   c. By governmental agencies.
   d. By enterprises or organizations authorized by the National Council of Scientific and Technological Development.
   e. By enterprises that publish books, newspapers, and periodicals or items for own use.

Import Financing

No interest on suppliers' credit of up to 180 days may be remitted abroad, whether the import is invoiced in U.S. dollars or in other currencies.

Interest may be remitted abroad, irrespective of currency of invoice, at the rate of 0.625 percent per annum on credit terms exceeding 180 and up to 270 days, and at the rate of 0.875 percent per annum on terms exceeding 270 and up to 360 days. For terms exceeding 360 days the rate permissible to be remitted abroad is established on a case-by-case basis.

The interest need not be included on the commercial invoice, but may be shown in the form of a draft or other document. The rate of interest agreed on, however, must be included in the application for the Guia. CACEX will record this rate on the Guia. On the basis of this, a negotiable copy of the bill of lading, the commercial invoice and the draft, the importer may purchase the foreign exchange necessary for the interest payment.

Only interest payments recorded on the Guia may be remitted abroad. As a result, interest charged on past due payments cannot be remitted.

Foreign exchange contracts for interest payments may be closed spot only and not earlier than two days preceding the maturity of the draft covering the interest payment. Also, interest remittances are subject to a withholding tax of 25 percent. For interest payments on loans exceeding eight years, there is a rebate of 40 percent of the value of the withholding tax.

Local as well as foreign firms (subsidiaries, joint ventures, branches) may obtain loans from local banks in local and in foreign currency. Local as well as foreign firms may obtain loans from banks and suppliers abroad in foreign currency. However, the repayment of any type of loan in foreign currency is subject to exchange control regulations.

The avalizing of drafts covering import payments is not common practice at local banks.

Remarks

Marine insurance for shipments to Brazil must be placed with local insurance companies and may not be placed with companies abroad.

There are no restrictions on the choice of flagship vessels for shipments to Brazil.

Exporters must furnish the following shipping documents:

1. Full set of clean on-board bills of lading, marked "freight pre-paid" or "freight collect." All ocean or airway bills of lading must show the freight costs in figures and in words; the ocean B/L must show the number of the relative Guia and its expiration date. Where no Guia is required for any particular shipment, the B/L must be claused to that effect.
2. Signed commercial invoice, showing FOB value, freight and insurance separately, in six copies.
3. Marine insurance policy or certificate, valid up to 60 days after discharge of the goods at port of destination, covering all risks, including strike, riot, war, and with an extended transshipment clause in the case of a transshipment.
4. In case of L/C shipments, exporter's statement whether or not it will avail itself of the unused balance, if any, of the L/C. If the exporter will not avail itself of the balance, it must furnish its agreement to the cancellation of the balance of the L/C.
5. In the case of transshipment, both the certificate of origin issued in the producer's country and a B/L authenticated by the carrier certifying the transport of the merchandise from the country of origin to the country of transshipment to the country from whence shipment to Brazil is effected.

Shipments may be subject to quantity or quality inspection require-ments, depending on the type of goods. Bonded warehouse facilities are available in Brazil.

APPENDIX 2–C   IMPORT REGULATIONS—ECUADOR

In May 1986, the government authorities issued the following import regulations:

1. On application of an import license, importers must pay 80 percent of the customs duties for the anticipated import. The 80 percent is based on the FOB value of the goods as shown on the

Source: *The Chase World Guide for Exporters*, copyright 1986, Chase Manhattan Bank, printed with permission of the publisher, Global Business Communications, Inc., P.O. Box 99, Gillette, N.J. 07933.

respective import license. The remaining balance of 20 percent for duty is paid at customs clearance.

2. At the time of applying for foreign exchange, importers must make a Sucre deposit with Banco Central (the Ecuadorian Central Bank) equivalent to 100 percent of the FOB value of the goods, plus the freight charges. The deposit is non-interest bearing.

3. Imports are classified into "lists" according to essentials. The lists call for minimum credit terms and for payment of a foreign exchange commission as follows:

List	Minimum Credit Terms	Exchange Commission*
I (a)	120 days	25 percent
II		
I (b)	180 days	30 percent

* The percentage rate of the exchange commission is figured on the 100 percent Sucre deposit.
Lists I (a) and II cover essentials. List I (b) covers less essentials and goods competitive with locally produced items.

APPENDIX 2–D FCIB'S CREDIT AND COLLECTION CONDITIONS IN EXPORT MARKETS SURVEY

Source: Gerd-Peter E. Lota, *FCIB Survey of Credit and Collection Conditions in Export Markets*, FCIB-NACM Corporation, New York, August 31, 1988.

Credit Conditions during the First Half of 1988 (in percentage of replies)

Western Hemisphere	Good		Fair		Poor	
Argentina –	9.1%	(0–90+)	61.4%	(0–30)	29.5%	(0–90+)
Bahamas o	59.1	(0–10)	40.9	(0–35)	—	
Bolivia –	4.2	(0–90)	20.8	(0)	75.0	(0–90)
Brazil o	11.6	(0–90+)	58.1	(0–30)	30.3	(0–90+)
Canada +	95.6	(0–30)	4.4	(0)	—	
Chile o	27.3	(0–30)	56.8	(0–90+)	15.9	(0–90+)
Colombia –	15.9	(0–90)	56.8	(0–60)	27.3	(0–90)
Costa Rica +	11.1	(0–30)	52.8	(0–75)	36.1	(0–60)
Cuba +	—		12.5	(0–60)	87.5	(0–90+)
Dominican Republic +	16.7	(0–90+)	36.7	(0–50)	46.6	(0–90+)
Ecuador –	4.9	(0–10)	26.8	(0–90+)	68.3	(0–45)
El Salvador o	7.4	(0–10)	18.5	(0–60)	74.1	(0–90)
Guatemala o	11.1	(0–15)	37.0	(0–60)	51.9	(0–60)
Guyana o	10.0	(0–10)	20.0	(0–60)	70.0	(0–90+)
Haiti o	6.3	(0–10)	25.0	(0–90)	68.7	(0–60)
Honduras –	8.7	(0–10)	34.8	(0–90)	56.5	(0–90+)
Jamaica –	15.0	(0–60)	50.1	(0–90)	34.9	(0–60)
Mexico –	12.2	(0–10)	59.2	(0–60)	28.6	(0–90+)
Nicaragua –	—		12.5	(0–60)	87.5	(0–90+)
Panama –	6.1	(0–10)	18.2	(0–25)	75.7	(0–90+)
Paraguay –	7.1	(0–30)	35.7	(0–90)	57.2	(0–60)
Peru o	13.5	(0–90)	18.9	(0–90)	67.6	(0–90)
Surinam –	12.5	(0–10)	12.5	(0–30)	75.0	(0–90+)
N. Antilles +	47.1	(0–10)	47.0	(0–15)	5.9	(0–90)
Trinidad and Tobago o	21.7	(0)	52.2	(0–60)	26.1	(0–60)
United States of America +	94.6	(0–10)	5.4	(0–30)	—	
Uruguay o	18.2	(0–30)	54.5	(0–40)	27.3	(0–60)
Venezuela –	5.1	(0–30)	35.9	(0–90+)	59.0	(0–90+)

Europe

Country			
Albania +	90.0 —	48.1 (0–60)	51.9 (0–60)
Austria –	91.7 (0–45)	10.0 (0–60)	—
Belgium –	11.8 (0–15)	8.3 (0)	
Bulgaria o	55.6 (0)	76.4 (0–30)	11.8 (0–60)
Cyprus +	35.3 (0)	38.9 (0–10)	5.5 (0–60)
Czechoslovakia –	96.8 (0–10)	52.9 (0–20)	11.8 (0–60)
Denmark o	96.4 (0)	—	3.2 (0–90+)
Finland +	73.4 (0–45)	3.6 (0–10)	—
France –	65.0 (0–10)	24.4 (0–60)	2.2 (0–45)
Germany (East) –	99.8 (0–25)	25.1 (0–30)	9.9 (0–60)
Germany (West) +	23.1 (0–60)	0.2 (0)	—
Greece +	19.0 (0–10)	64.1 (0–45)	12.8 (0–60)
Hungary –	36.8 (0)	57.1 (0–30)	23.9 (0–90+)
Iceland –	54.2 (0–30)	42.1 (0–40)	21.1 (0–30)
Ireland –	44.7 (0–30)	41.7 (0–10)	4.1 (0–30)
Italy –	93.5 (0–30)	51.0 (0–30)	4.3 (0–90)
Luxembourg +	28.6 (0–10)	6.5 (0)	—
Malta +	92.1 (0)	42.9 (0–15)	28.5 (0–30)
Netherlands –	92.6 (0–10)	7.9 (0–60)	—
Norway –	4.7 (0)	7.4 (0–10)	47.7 (0–90+)
Poland –	31.2 (0–10)	47.6 (0–30)	9.4 (0)
Portugal +	—	59.4 (0–30)	72.7 (0–90+)
Romania –	57.8 (0–30)	27.3 (0–30)	8.9 (0–40)
Spain +	96.9 (0–15)	33.3 (0–30)	—
Sweden +	95.1 (0–15)	3.1 (0)	25.0 (0–90+)
Switzerland –	14.3 (0–30)	4.9 (0–10)	2.3 (0)
Turkey –	92.9 (0–30)	60.7 (0–60)	—
United Kingdom +	58.8 (0–60)	4.8 (0–10)	66.7 (0–90+)
U.S.S.R. –	14.3 (0–10)	41.2 (0–30)	
Yugoslavia +	14.3 (0–10)	19.0 (0–15)	

Credit Conditions during the First Half of 1988 (concluded)

Miscellaneous Markets	Good		Fair		Poor	
Afghanistan –	16.6%	(0–30)	—		83.4%	(0–90)
Algeria –	11.8	(0–30)	5.8%	(0–30)	82.4	(0–90+)
Angola +	—		16.6	(0–10)	83.4	(0–60)
Australia o	89.4	(0–10)	10.6	(0–30)	—	
Bahrain o	50.2	(0–10)	42.9	(0–60)	6.9	(0)
Bangladesh –	—		28.6	(0–10)	71.4	(0)
Cameroon +	—		16.6	(0–30)	83.4	(0–60)
Central African Republic o	—		—		100.0	(0–90+)
Egypt –	6.0	(0–90+)	32.3	(0–60)	61.7	(0–90)
Ethiopia –	—		20.0	(–10)	80.0	(0–90)
Gabon o	—		—		100.0	(0–90)
Ghana –	—		18.0	(0–10)	82.0	(0–90)
Guinea +	—		20.0	(0–10)	80.0	(0–75)
Hong Kong –	82.9	(0–20)	17.1	(0–30)	—	
India –	15.8	(0–10)	57.9	(0–90)	26.3	(0–90)
Indonesia –	14.7	(0)	64.7	(0–30)	20.6	(0)
Iran –	6.6	(0)	33.6	(0–10)	59.8	(0–90+)
Iraq +	—		10.0	(0)	90.0	(0–90+)
Israel o	41.3	(0–60)	56.5	(0–30)	2.2	(0–90)
Ivory Coast –	8.3	(0)	41.8	(0–30)	49.9	(0–60)
Japan +	99.7	(0–20)	0.3	(0)	—	
Jordan –	5.3	(0)	57.9	(0–30)	36.8	(0–60)
Kenya –	6.7	(0)	40.0	(0–45)	53.3	(0–30)
Kuwait –	32.1	(0–35)	53.6	(0–20)	14.3	(0–60)
Lebanon –	5.3	(0)	21.0	(0–10)	73.7	(0–60)
Liberia +	—		14.3	(0)	85.7	(0–90)
Libya –	—		17.1	(0–30)	82.9	(0–90)
Madagascar o	—		—		100.0	(0–90)
Malawi +	—		17.1	(0–10)	82.9	(0–90+)

Country	%	Cond.	%	Cond.	%	Cond.
Malaysia o	32.3	(0–10)	54.8	(0–60)	12.9	(0–60)
Morocco o	8.3	(0–75)	25.0	(0–35)	66.7	(0–90)
New Zealand –	87.9	(0–20)	9.0	(0)	3.1	(0)
Nigeria –			5.6	(0–10)	94.4	(0–90+)
Oman –	20.0	(0)	50.0	(0–90)	30.0	(0–60)
Pakistan –	9.4	(0)	50.4	(0–90)	40.2	(0–60)
Philippines –	9.8	(0–10)	24.4	(0–90)	65.8	(0–90)
Qatar –	22.2	(0)	33.4	(0–45)	44.4	(0–60)
People's Republic of China –	61.2	(0–90)	38.8	(0–30)		
Saudi Arabia –	38.4	(0–30)	56.4	(0–30)	5.2	(0–90)
Senegal –					100.0	(0–90+)
Sierra Leone +			20.0	(0–30)	80.0	(0–90)
Singapore –	62.1	(0–15)	37.9	(0–30)		
South Africa –	47.1	(0–30)	41.2	(0–10)	11.7	(0–30)
South Korea +	57.8	(0–30)	40.0	(0–30)	2.2	(0)
Sri Lanka –			33.6	(0)	66.4	(0–90)
Sudan +			29.5	(0–30)	70.5	(0–90+)
Syria –	10.0	(0)	10.0	(0–30)	80.0	(0–90+)
Taiwan –	60.4	(0–30)	39.6	(0–25)		
Tanzania –	8.3	(0)	25.0	(0–30)	66.7	(0–90)
Thailand –	20.0	(0–10)	70.5	(0–35)	9.5	(0–90)
Tunisia –	7.7	(0)	46.1	(0–30)	46.2	(0–30)
Uganda –			16.7	(0–30)	83.3	(0–90+)
United Arab Emirates –	33.3	(0–30)	57.1	(0–30)	9.6	(0–60)
Vietnam o					100.0	(0–90+)
Zaire o	11.1	(0–30)	11.1	(0–60)	77.8	(0–90)
Zambia +			25.4	(0–30)	74.6	(0–90)
Zimbabwe +			34.7	(0–10)	65.3	(0–90)
Yemen +			12.0	(0–30)	88.0	(0–90+)

Note: Conditions show percentage of credit rating plus number of days awaiting exchange.

Current Survey of Collections

Western Hemisphere	A	B	C	D	E
Argentina	56.4%	23.1%	7.6%	5.3%	7.6%
Bahamas	52.4	14.3	28.6	4.7	—
Bolivia	58.8	5.8	23.8	5.8	5.8
Brazil	44.7	36.8	8.1	5.2	5.2
Canada	59.6	29.8	8.5	—	2.1
Chile	47.4	36.8	13.2	7.1	2.6
Columbia	23.8	30.9	33.3	14.7	4.9
Costa Rica	20.6	35.3	26.5	24.5	2.9
Cuba	49.8	—	—	7.4	25.7
Dominican Republic	18.5	40.7	29.6	8.3	3.8
Ecuador	54.2	16.7	20.8	9.5	—
El Salvador	52.3	9.5	28.7	4.8	4.8
Guatemala	31.8	11.0	47.6	—	33.2
Guyana	16.6	—	50.2	7.9	—
Haiti	30.7	30.7	30.7	5.5	11.0
Honduras	44.4	5.5	33.6	10.6	5.3
Jamaica	21.3	26.4	36.4	8.9	6.7
Mexico	17.8	37.8	28.8	—	—
Nicaragua	55.9	—	44.1	12.9	29.0
Panama	25.8	6.5	25.8	—	—
Paraguay	58.3	8.3	33.4	—	—
Peru	36.1	38.9	25.0	—	20.5
Surinam	40.5	—	39.0	—	—
N. Antilles	43.7	25.0	25.0	—	6.3
Trinidad and Tobago	40.9	22.7	27.3	9.1	2.8
United States of America	48.6	45.9	—	2.7	—
Uruguay	62.6	17.6	19.8	—	9.7
Venezuela	41.9	22.6	16.1	9.7	9.7

Europe

Country	A	B	C	D	E
Albania	33.3	—	33.4	—	33.3
Austria	58.6	37.9	3.5	—	—
Belgium	44.4	50.1	5.5	—	—
Bulgaria	46.1	23.1	30.8	—	—
Cyprus	50.1	22.2	22.2	5.5	—
Czechoslovakia	62.4	29.0	—	8.6	—
Denmark	66.7	33.3	—	—	—
Finland	73.1	26.9	—	—	—
France	40.4	44.7	8.5	4.2	2.2
Germany (East)	63.3	30.4	6.3	—	—
Germany (West)	68.9	24.4	2.2	2.2	2.3
Greece	14.3	47.6	28.6	2.4	7.1
Hungary	35.3	41.1	11.7	—	11.9
Iceland	31.6	36.8	15.8	5.2	10.6
Ireland	30.4	52.2	8.6	8.8	—
Italy	28.0	42.0	24.0	6.0	—
Luxembourg	51.0	37.5	11.5	—	—
Malta	16.7	66.6	—	—	16.7
Netherlands	68.4	31.6	—	—	—
Norway	54.2	45.8	—	—	—
Poland	42.8	35.7	7.1	7.1	7.3
Portugal	25.8	45.2	19.4	3.2	6.4
Romania	—	50.4	49.6	—	—
Spain	28.3	56.5	13.0	—	2.2
Sweden	56.3	37.5	—	3.1	3.1
Switzerland	71.1	26.7	—	2.2	—
Turkey	26.9	23.1	34.6	3.8	11.6
United Kingdom	38.6	54.5	2.2	4.7	—
U.S.S.R.	33.3	27.8	33.3	—	5.6
Yugoslavia	23.5	29.4	29.4	5.9	11.8

Note: A = Prompt payment, B = 10–30 days slow, C = 31–60 days slow, D = 61–90 days slow, E = Over 90 days slow

Current Survey of Collections *(concluded)*

Miscellaneous Markets	A	B	C	D	E
Afghanistan	—	85.0%	12.6%	—	2.4%
Algeria	11.1%	22.2	—	11.1%	55.6
Angola	—	—	75.0	18.0	7.0
Australia	45.0	47.5	5.0	—	2.5
Bahrain	33.3	44.4	16.1	6.2	—
Bangladesh	33.3	50.2	16.5	—	—
Cameroon	—	50.6	45.4	—	4.0
Central African Republic	—	—	—	14.0	86.0
Egypt	47.8	30.4	13.0	4.3	4.5
Ethiopia	40.0	19.5	20.5	—	20.0
Gabon	—	24.0	—	10.5	65.5
Ghana	—	87.5	—	5.0	7.5
Guinea	27.4	33.0	—	—	39.6
Hong Kong	55.3	36.8	2.6	—	5.3
India	32.3	32.3	16.2	9.6	9.6
Indonesia	38.5	50.1	3.9	—	7.5
Iran	25.5	22.5	12.5	—	39.5
Iraq	40.0	19.5	20.5	—	20.0
Israel	32.6	41.3	10.9	10.9	4.3
Ivory Coast	37.5	50.0	12.5	—	—
Japan	77.1	22.9	—	—	—
Jordan	11.7	41.2	29.4	6.0	11.7
Kenya	27.3	9.1	36.3	—	27.3
Kuwait	23.5	52.9	17.6	6.0	—
Lebanon	41.7	16.7	—	24.9	16.7
Liberia	—	—	49.4	—	50.6
Libya	—	28.3	44.1	12.0	15.6
Madagascar	—	12.0	18.7	—	69.3

Malawi	—	42.0	14.0	—	44.0
Malaysia	48.1	25.9	14.8	7.4	3.8
Morocco	27.8	22.2	11.1	33.3	5.6
New Zealand	54.8	41.9	—	—	3.3
Nigeria	37.5	25.0	—	—	37.5
Oman	62.8	18.9	—	18.3	—
Pakistan	53.5	21.4	10.9	7.1	7.1
Philippines	55.5	20.3	13.7	3.4	7.1
Qatar	14.3	57.1	28.6	—	—
People's Republic of China	58.1	35.4	3.2	—	3.3
Saudi Arabia	22.8	48.6	25.7	2.9	—
Senegal	34.9	33.3	32.7	—	—
Sierra Leone	48.0	12.0	40.0	—	—
Singapore	48.3	41.3	6.8	—	3.6
South Africa	38.7	51.6	9.7	—	—
South Korea	62.2	24.3	10.8	—	2.7
Sri Lanka	42.8	28.6	14.3	—	14.3
Sudan	40.0	19.6	—	40.4	—
Syria	47.0	12.0	5.4	—	41.0
Taiwan	67.6	24.3	—	—	2.7
Tanzania	28.6	14.2	13.6	28.6	28.6
Thailand	45.4	27.3	18.2	4.3	9.3
Tunisia	18.2	45.4	44.5	—	18.1
Uganda	51.0	—	41.2	4.5	—
United Arab Emirates	23.5	29.4	8.4	5.9	25.6
Vietnam	54.0	12.0	—	—	16.3
Zaire	60.0	18.7	—	5.0	25.8
Zambia	48.7	24.9	—	0.6	25.8
Zimbabwe	52.7	24.1	—	—	23.2
Yemen	23.4	10.6	—	8.5	57.5

Survey of Terms Granted during the First Half of 1988 as Compared to the Second Half of 1987

Western Hemispere	No Change	More Liberal	Less Liberal
Argentina	92.5%	2.5%	5.0%
Bahamas	95.4	4.6	—
Bolivia	85.0	10.0	5.0
Brazil	87.1	5.1	7.8
Canada	97.6	—	2.4
Chile	87.2	12.8	—
Colombia	90.0	2.5	7.5
Costa Rica	84.8	—	15.2
Cuba	83.3	—	16.7
Dominican Republic	79.3	10.3	10.4
Ecuador	75.2	—	24.8
El Salvador	88.4	3.8	7.8
Guatemala	92.6	—	7.4
Guyana	88.9	—	11.1
Haiti	93.3	—	6.7
Honduras	81.8	—	18.2
Jamaica	90.0	5.0	5.0
Mexico	79.1	6.9	14.0
Nicaragua	85.7	—	14.3
Panama	53.3	—	46.7
Paraguay	100.0	—	—
Peru	70.3	2.7	27.0
Surinam	100.0	—	—
N. Antilles	100.0	—	—
Trinidad and Tobago	90.4	—	9.6
United States of America	93.9	3.0	3.1
Uruguay	95.2	4.8	—
Venezuela	88.8	2.8	8.4
Europe			
Albania	75.0	—	25.0
Austria	100.0	—	—
Belgium	94.3	2.5	3.2
Bulgaria	100.0	—	—
Cyprus	100.0	—	—
Czechoslovakia	94.1	5.9	—
Denmark	96.6	—	3.4
Finland	96.4	—	3.6
France	91.3	2.1	6.6
Germany (East)	100.0	—	—
Germany (West)	97.8	—	2.2
Greece	84.6	2.6	12.8
Hungary	61.9	9.5	28.6
Iceland	71.4	—	28.6
Ireland	95.2	—	4.8

Survey of Terms Granted during the First Half of 1988 as Compared to the Second Half of 1987 *(continued)*

Europe	No Change	More Liberal	Less Liberal
Italy	90.6%	2.3%	7.1%
Luxembourg	100.0	—	—
Malta	100.0	—	—
Netherlands	97.2	2.8	—
Norway	96.3	—	3.7
Poland	100.0	—	—
Portugal	100.0	—	—
Romania	66.7	—	33.3
Spain	92.8	—	7.2
Sweden	96.8	—	3.2
Switzerland	95.1	2.4	2.5
Turkey	65.4	19.2	15.4
United Kingdom	97.5	—	2.5
U.S.S.R.	87.5	—	12.5
Yugoslavia	52.6	—	47.4
Miscellaneous Markets			
Afghanistan	100.0	—	—
Algeria	70.6	—	29.4
Angola	100.0	—	—
Australia	97.6	2.4	—
Bahrain	100.0	—	—
Bangladesh	90.9	9.1	—
Cameroon	100.0	—	—
Central African Republic	100.0	—	—
Egypt	90.3	—	9.7
Ethiopia	100.0	—	—
Gabon	100.0	—	—
Ghana	83.3	16.7	—
Guinea	100.0	—	—
Hong Kong	94.7	2.8	2.5
India	86.1	5.6	8.3
Indonesia	93.5	3.2	3.3
Iran	83.3	—	16.7
Iraq	90.0	—	10.0
Israel	87.5	5.0	7.5
Ivory Coast	75.0	—	25.0
Japan	95.5	4.5	—
Jordan	73.7	5.3	21.0
Kenya	86.6	—	13.4
Kuwait	100.0	—	5.6
Lebanon	94.4	—	5.6
Liberia	83.3	—	16.7
Libya	100.0	—	—

Survey of Terms Granted during the First Half of 1988 as Compared to the Second Half of 1987 _(concluded)_

Miscellaneous Markets	No Change	More Liberal	Less Liberal
Madagascar	100.0%	—	—
Malawi	100.0	—	—
Malaysia	89.3	—	10.7%
Morocco	81.8	4.5%	13.7
New Zealand	96.6	—	3.4
Nigeria	85.7	—	14.3
Oman	100.0	—	—
Pakistan	94.1	2.9	3.0
Philippines	91.7	2.8	5.5
Qatar	100.0	—	—
People's Republic of China	100.0	—	—
Saudi Arabia	90.9	3.0	6.1
Senegal	83.3	—	16.7
Sierra Leone	100.0	—	—
Singapore	96.4	—	3.6
South Africa	93.3	—	6.7
South Korea	84.6	15.4	—
Sri Lanka	100.0	—	—
Sudan	100.0	—	—
Syria	100.0	—	—
Taiwan	91.7	5.5	2.8
Tanzania	100.0	—	—
Thailand	89.3	3.5	7.2
Tunisia	100.0	—	—
Uganda	100.0	—	—
United Arab Emirates	100.0	—	—
Vietnam	92.0	—	8.0
Yemen Rep.	100.0	—	—
Zaire	89.4	—	10.6
Zambia	74.9	—	25.1
Zimbabwe	94.5	—	5.5

Letter-of-Credit (L/C) Transactions Worldwide

The first percentage indicates the level of survey participants dealing on L/C in the country; the second percentage indicates the average volume of business done by these participating companies on L/C in each country.

Country	Company	Business	Country	Company	Business
Argentina	88.6%	68.5%	Afghanistan	89.8%	100.0%
Bahamas	18.2	52.5	Algeria	70.6	98.7
Bolivia	75.0	96.1	Angola	76.7	77.5
Brazil	51.2	52.2	Australia	25.5	23.3
Canada	4.2	3.5	Bahrain	42.9	79.2
Chile	72.7	56.3	Bangladesh	85.7	95.8
Columbia	64.6	71.4	Cameroon	64.8	100.0
Costa Rica	52.8	70.3	Central Af. Rep.	68.7	100.0
Cuba	87.5	100.0	Egypt	94.1	96.7
Dominican Republic	60.0	73.5	Ethiopia	70.4	88.6
Ecuador	63.4	76.3	Gabon	54.8	100.0
El Salvador	77.8	95.2	Ghana	76.7	98.8
Guatemala	66.7	78.6	Guinea	64.2	100.0
Guyana	70.0	100.0	Hong Kong	51.2	66.7
Haiti	58.7	100.0	India	89.5	82.8
Honduras	65.2	88.0	Indonesia	73.5	88.7
Jamaica	60.0	72.1	Iran	80.4	97.9
Mexico	48.0	53.3	Iraq	70.5	100.0
Nicaragua	72.5	100.0	Israel	41.3	53.1
Panama	39.4	96.5	Ivory Coast	58.3	84.3
Paraguay	71.4	89.6	Japan	30.6	32.7
Peru	89.2	79.3	Jordan	89.5	83.2
Surinam	76.5	100.0	Kenya	40.2	83.3
N. Antilles	23.5	65.0	Kuwait	50.2	62.9
Trinidad and Tobago	26.1	70.8	Lebanon	57.9	98.2
U.S.A.	27.0	10.0	Liberia	62.9	100.0
Uruguay	68.2	66.4	Libya	58.4	100.0
Venezuela	92.3	90.4	Madagascar	64.5	100.0

Letter-of-Credit (L/C) Transactions Worldwide (concluded)

Country	Company	Business	Country	Company	Business
Albania	54.4%	75.0%	Malawi	64.4%	83.3%
Austria	16.7	37.0	Malaysia	54.8	76.8
Belgium	8.3	23.3	Morocco	75.5	82.8
Bulgaria	82.4	86.0	New Zealand	33.3	44.3
Cyprus	22.2	81.3	Nigeria	78.8	98.9
Czechoslovakia	35.3	62.2	Oman	50.2	74.0
Denmark	3.2	20.0	Pakistan	91.9	97.1
Finland	10.7	24.0	Philippines	82.9	91.7
France	16.3	20.8	Qatar	44.4	75.0
Germany (East)	45.2	75.0	People's Republic of China	87.1	86.9
Germany (West)	14.6	26.4	Saudi Arabia	48.7	56.1
Greece	38.5	47.6	Senegal	66.8	90.0
Hungary	80.9	78.2	Sierra Leone	64.8	100.0
Iceland	21.1	62.8	Singapore	48.3	53.2
Ireland	12.5	51.7	South Africa	26.5	38.0
Italy	19.1	45.0	South Korea	84.4	92.3
Luxembourg	2.0	4.5	Sri Lanka	83.3	94.0
Malta	28.6	30.0	Sudan	80.8	100.0
Netherlands	5.3	32.5	Syria	84.4	100.0
Norway	7.4	75.0	Taiwan	87.5	76.5
Poland	85.7	90.4	Tanzania	66.8	100.0
Portugal	25.0	45.5	Thailand	83.3	85.4
Romania	81.8	98.9	Tunisia	76.9	78.1
Spain	22.2	37.2	Uganda	83.3	100.0
Sweden	3.1	40.0	United Arab Emirates	42.9	73.3
Switzerland	12.2	30.6	Vietnam	87.9	100.0
Turkey	60.7	64.8	Yemen Rep.	98.0	95.4
United Kingdom	11.9	42.0	Zaire	76.8	91.7
U.S.S.R.	11.8	87.5	Zambia	87.5	100.0
Yugoslavia	90.5	97.4	Zimbabwe	55.6	100.0

Participating Companies in This Survey and Their Percentage of Shipments to the Various Countries

Country	Present	Previous	Country	Present	Previous
Japan	62.9%	54.4%	Yugoslavia	26.9%	22.1%
France	62.8	57.4	Poland	26.9	19.1
Mexico	62.7	57.4	Jamaica	25.6	22.1
West Germany	61.5	54.4	N. Antilles	24.5	20.6
Australia	60.4	54.4	East Germany	24.5	16.2
Italy	60.3	48.5	Hungary	24.5	13.2
			Lebanon	24.4	9.8
Canada	57.6	66.2	Iceland	24.3	15.4
Israel	57.5	52.9	Jordan	24.3	14.7
Spain	57.5	51.5	Algeria	21.8	16.4
Argentina	56.4	48.5	Cyprus	21.8	16.2
Colombia	56.3	45.6	Czechoslovakia	21.8	15.3
South Korea	56.3	48.4	U.S.S.R.	21.7	15.0
Chile	56.2	47.1	Bulgaria	21.7	14.7
Brazil	55.1	58.8	Nigeria	21.6	12.0
United Kingdom	53.8	63.2	Haiti	20.5	16.1
Hong Kong	52.6	51.5			
Switzerland	52.6	45.5	Kenya	19.2	19.1
Philippines	52.6	35.3	Iran	19.2	16.2
Ecuador	52.5	33.8	Bahrain	17.9	16.4
Venezuela	51.2	45.5	Paraguay	17.9	11.8
Taiwan	51.1	42.6	Tunisia	16.7	17.5
Saudi Arabia	50.4	36.8	Bangladesh	16.5	7.4
Greece	50.0	30.8	Sri Lanka	15.8	16.2
			Ivory Coast	15.4	11.8
The Netherlands	48.9	42.6	Tanzania	15.4	11.6
India	48.7	48.4	Romania	14.1	14.7
U.S.A.	47.4	54.4	Iraq	12.8	11.8
Pakistan	47.4	25.0	Syria	12.8	11.8
Peru	47.3	35.3	Luxembourg	12.8	10.3
Belgium	46.8	38.2			

Participating Companies in This Survey and Their Percentage of Shipments to the Various Countries (concluded)

Country	Present	Previous	Country	Present	Previous
Costa Rica	46.2%	30.8%	Ethiopia	12.7%	9.8%
South Africa	43.6	41.2	Oman	12.7	9.5
Egypt	43.5	32.4	Zaire	11.5	7.4
Indonesia	43.5	30.8	Sudan	11.5	6.2
Panama	42.6	32.5	Guyana	11.5	5.8
New Zealand	42.3	33.8	Qatar	11.4	6.0
Sweden	41.8	33.8	Zambia	11.4	6.1
Portugal	41.0	36.8	Zimbabwe	11.2	8.4
Malaysia	39.7	18.2	Nicaragua	10.7	8.8
Denmark	39.7	35.3	Surinam	10.6	8.0
People's Republic of China	39.6	35.3	Cuba	10.4	7.3
Dominican Republic	38.5	32.4	Angola	9.4	4.9
Austria	38.5	24.6	Liberia	9.0	4.8
Thailand	38.4	23.6	Malta	8.9	6.9
Singapore	37.2	38.2	Yemen Rep.	8.2	7.4
Turkey	35.9	30.7	Ghana	7.9	8.8
Guatemala	35.8	30.7	Senegal	7.7	6.4
Norway	34.6	29.4	Libya	7.7	6.2
Kuwait	34.6	19.1	Cameroon	7.7	4.9
Finland	34.6	22.1	Uganda	7.6	5.2
El Salvador	34.6	19.3	Afghanistan	7.6	4.5
Ireland	30.7	26.5	Malawi	7.6	4.4
Bolivia	30.7	19.1	Central African Republic	7.3	5.8
Morocco	30.6	17.6	Sierra Leone	7.0	4.5
Trinidad and Tobago	29.5	22.2	Madagascar	6.9	4.4
Honduras	29.4	19.1	Vietnam	6.5	4.3
Bahamas	28.3	23.5	Guinea	6.4	4.3
Uruguay	28.2	19.1	Gabon	6.2	4.4
United Arab Emirates	26.9	23.5	Albania	5.1	4.9

Days Sales Outstanding (DSO) for International Transactions (Export Business)

Country	Present	Previous	Country	Present	Previous
Argentina	145 Days	(148)	Afghanistan	132 Days	(147)
Bahamas	61	(63)	Algeria	218	(258)
Bolivia	75	(77)	Angola	188	(185)
Brazil	128	(98)	Australia	98	(80)
Canada	47	(41)	Bahrain	90	(72)
Chile	92	(118)	Bangladesh	120	(133)
Colombia	118	(120)	Cameroon	89	(108)
Costa Rica	98	(110)	Central African Republic	120	(124)
Cuba	149	(161)	Egypt	89	(99)
Dominican Republic	91	(95)	Ethiopia	118	(115)
Ecuador	130	(135)	Gabon	124	(110)
El Salvador	86	(67)	Ghana	139	(140)
Guatemala	79	(54)	Guinea	140	(141)
Guyana	160	(93)	Hong Kong	68	(50)
Haiti	87	(98)	India	93	(95)
Honduras	84	(97)	Indonesia	59	(68)
Jamaica	59	(62)	Iran	184	(114)
Mexico	76	(66)	Iraq	240	(384)
Nicaragua	120	(75)	Israel	81	(82)
Panama	100	(100)	Ivory Coast	148	(88)
Paraguay	83	(85)	Japan	50	(57)
Peru	93	(81)	Jordan	100	(108)
Surinam	90	(84)	Kenya	94	(109)
N. Antilles	83	(72)	Kuwait	82	(76)
Trinidad and Tobago	72	(63)	Lebanon	114	(99)
United States of America	51	(56)	Liberia	161	(184)
Uruguay	112	(132)	Libya	184	(138)
Venezuela	135	(126)	Madagascar	156	(146)
			Malawi	181	(201)
Albania	146	(148)	Malaysia	74	(78)
Austria	42	(46)	Morocco	121	(134)

Days Sales Outstanding (DSO) for International Transactions (Export Business) (concluded)

Country	Present	Previous	Country	Present	Previous
Belgium	48	(49)	New Zealand	78	(81)
Bulgaria	66	(68)	Nigeria	144	(190)
Cyprus	81	(84)	Oman	90	(100)
Czechoslovakia	148	(179)	Pakistan	87	(114)
Denmark	55	(62)	Philippines	120	(93)
Finland	45	(48)	Qatar	56	(110)
France	72	(74)	People's Republic of China	82	(58)
Germany (East)	114	(122)	Saudi Arabia	121	(99)
Germany (West)	53	(40)	Senegal	175	(98)
Greece	91	(97)	Sierra Leone	65	(184)
Hungary	72	(78)	Singapore	62	(68)
Iceland	84	(99)	South Africa	52	(52)
Ireland	57	(52)	South Korea	113	(57)
Italy	89	(97)	Sri Lanka	190	(123)
Luxembourg	49	(40)	Sudan	89	(247)
Malta	103	(123)	Syria	91	(96)
Netherlands	46	(38)	Taiwan	124	(67)
Norway	47	(48)	Tanzania	71	(186)
Poland	102	(111)	Thailand	100	(78)
Portugal	88	(101)	Tunisia	148	(135)
Romania	121	(132)	Uganda	73	(144)
Spain	84	(91)	United Arab Emirates	210	(86)
Sweden	63	(49)	Vietnam	142	(212)
Switzerland	50	(40)	Yemen Rep.	120	(156)
Turkey	82	(97)	Zaire	187	(149)
United Kingdom	63	(59)	Zambia	120	(210)
U.S.S.R.	52	(59)	Zimbabwe		(128)
Yugoslavia	78	(85)			

Note: () indicate previous DSO.

REFERENCES

1. *The World Almanac and Book of Facts* (New York: Pharos Books, A Scripps Howard Company, 1987), p. 559.
2. Ibid., p. 562.
3. Ibid., p. 548.
4. Alexander J. Caldwell and Antonio J. Villamid, *Assessing Country Risk* (London, England: Euromoney Publications Ltd., 1981), p. 19.
5. "South Korea Posts Trade Surplus," *The Wall Street Journal,* September 15, 1986, p. 32.
6. "Hong Kong's Trade surplus Widens," *The Wall Street Journal,* September 26, 1986, p. 32.
7. Allen Sweeny and Robert Rachlin, *Handbook of International Financial Management* (New York: McGraw Hill, 1984), pp. 3–11.
8. Hans P. Belcsak, *A Treasurer's Guide to Country Risk, Cashflow* (Atlanta: Communication Channels, September 1987), pp. 43–44.
9. Ibid., p. 44.

CHAPTER 3

MECHANISMS OF
EXPORT TRADE

Exporting involves certain types of documentary procedures in order for a foreign customer to clear goods and take possession of them for customs officials, satisfy local financial obligations, and pay the export supplier. How these documents are prepared and sent to foreign customers very much determines and affects your relationship with them and payments at maturity.

Country documentary procedures have evolved over several centuries. These procedures are intended to clarify and specify the compliance or noncompliance with the sale of goods or services between exporters and importers in different countries. It directly relates to the sales contract. Importers and exporters need to understand the role of documents in international trade and their limitations.

In any export transaction there are basically four contracts:

1. The sales contract.
2. The contract of carriage.
3. The financial contract.
4. Cargo insurance contract.

The importance of preparing accurate documents sent on a timely basis cannot be over-emphasized. There is nothing more annoying to foreign customers than incurring inaccurate documents, missing documents, or late arrival of documents. I wonder how many export sales and foreign customers have been lost to competition (domestic and foreign) due to inefficient handling of export documentation.

This chapter will define and explain most of the important

documents used in international commercial trade. In this regard a company's personnel need to become familiar with the *Revised American Foreign Trade Definitions—1941,* adopted on July 30, 1941 by a Joint Committee representing the U.S. Chamber of Commerce, the National Council of American Importers, Inc., the National Foreign Trade Council, Inc., and especially the International Chamber of Commerce's (ICC) Publication Number 350, *Incoterms,* effective March 1980. These publications contain a complete listing of export trade term definitions used in international commerce (both are reprinted in Appendix 3–A and 3–B of this chapter). The trade terms defined in the American version constitute the customary basis in the United States for defining who is responsible for the goods during the transit period. The trade terms as defined by ICC Publication 350, is an attempt to standardize international trade practice and is now widely accepted outside the United States and by U.S. exporters. Although Incoterms are widely used internationally, and are gradually phasing out the *American Foreign Trade Definitions—1941 revision* because of U.S. exporter preference and its recognition worldwide, there are other standardized trade term rules and conditions in existence:

1. The Rules of Warsaw and Oxford were proposed by the International Law Association in 1932.
2. The General Conditions for Delivery of Merchandise— 1968, by the Council for Mutual Economic Assistance (COMCON) for the USSR and some Eastern European countries. These conditions were revised on January 1, 1976.
3. In 1969 the Combiterms were proposed to simplify costs and risks between exporters and foreign customers. They introduced code numbers for the unit costs contained in trade terms.

These rules and conditions are basically the same as those contained in *Incoterms.*

Incoterms can serve as a neutral ground when either party to the sales contract tries to impose its local laws and procedures on the other. Incoterms are based on the following principles[1]:

1. The terms are drawn from the most common practices of international trade so that they could be adopted by the greatest possible number of traders.
2. Where there were major differences in current practice, Incoterms would provide for the minimum liabilities on the part of the seller, leaving it to the parties to provide for greater liabilities in their contracts if they so desired.
3. References to the customs of a particular trade or port were kept to a minimum, although it was impossible to avoid them completely.

Incoterms were devised to concentrate on the most important trade terms used in international trade. It does not cover all of the trade terms used by exporters and importers.

To further assist all parties to export transactions, another helpful ICC publication is Number 354, *Guide to Incoterms*. This publication guide explains concretely, with the aid of diagrams and illustrations, the respective obligations of the foreign customer and exporter when they use one of the Incoterms in commercial sales contracts.

THE SALES CONTRACT

In most circumstances, the document which precedes a sales contract is the pro-forma invoice (explained later). It is a document which consists of an exporter's quoted price(s) for its goods based on CIF (cost, insurance, freight) or C&F (cost & freight) price from its port of departure. Sometimes FAS (free alongside ship) prices are quoted. Since the quotation in pro-forma invoice form sets forth the potential sale of goods by spelling out the basic essentials (cost of the goods, inland and ocean or air freight charges, insurance, etc.), the next step is to enter into a sales contract.

The sales contract is the legal document which details the terms and conditions mutually agreed on by an exporter and foreign customer. It can include other parties to the export transaction such as banks or credit insurers. Several different types of contracts can be used depending on the type of business of the foreign customer and the structure of the deal. Most companies have a set of standard contracts for distributors and commission sales agents, but large buy/sell deals require specialized complex contracts. Quite often, sales contracts need to be amended because of changing government import regulations that can affect such things as payment terms and the availability of foreign exchange.

There are basically two forms of contracts used by exporters. One is a "Standard" or "General Standard Terms and Conditions of Sale Contract," a preprinted contract which is stated on the reverse side of an exporter's purchase order form, commercial invoice, or issued as a separate document. This is usually a simplified contract that states basic terms, conditions, rights, and obligations of the parties to the sales contract. The second is a written form of contract that is prepared based on large buy/sell arrangements between two or more parties of the sale, based on specialized buy/sell deals, such as countertrade deals, products made to order, or complicated trade agreements or arrangements. The contract should state whose laws apply—the exporters or the importers. For example, goods sold from a U.S. Belgian subsidiary to a customer in Morocco are likely to be subject to the laws of Belgium and/or Morocco, not the United States. The U.S. Uniform Commercial Code (UCC) is not applicable to either Belgium or Morocco.

Unfortunately, many sales are consummated verbally either without a sales contract or before a foreign customer sees an exporter's sales contract. In this regard, the motivating factor between the two parties is to move goods. The buyer needs product and the seller has product to sell. It is assumed the sale is at competitive prices, the product meets market/customer specification, quality standards, and can be delivered within a specified period of time or deadline.

Although verbal agreements are legally binding, problems or misinterpretations can arise between both parties. To avoid or reduce misunderstandings, verbal agreements should be confirmed in writing. Even if a long-term business relationship exists between an exporter and foreign customer, no matter how large or small the deal, it is still advisable to obtain signed purchase orders from foreign customers that are acknowledged by the exporter. This can either be done in writing or by telexes or cables.

Many international sales are usually consummated through a series of letters, telexes, or cables. When an agreement is reached between both parties, the series of accumulated communication is considered a legally binding sales contract.

However, difficulties can and do arise between the two parties to the export transaction. Disagreements can arise when something goes wrong before the foreign customer uses the goods or until they are resold to the foreign customer's own customers, resulting in product disputes. It is only when a sales contract is negotiated to cover certain underlying assumptions and the sales department obtains input from its other internal departments (i.e., the credit department) that problems or disputes are reduced.

Elements of a Sales Contract

The major elements or provisions of a sales contract are:

Description of the goods.

Quantity.

Inspection and warranty.

Price.

Terms of sale.

Payment terms.

Financial responsibility.

Orders and delivery.

Force majeure.

Default.

Arbitration.

Law.

Description of the Goods.   The exporter and foreign customer need to agree to an exact description of the goods. This is because there are no precise common definitions for weights, measurements, and quality. This provision of the sales contract, in addition to a description of the goods, can include quantity (number, size, weight, and volume) and quality (grade, content, or any other features). However, some exporters make quantity and quality separate clauses.

Quantity. Specifies how much (the maximum amount) the foreign customer agrees to purchase from the exporter over specified periods of time during the life of the sales contract (i.e., 85,000 tons in year one, 145,000 tons in year two, and 195,000 tons in year three). This clause can also define certain weights (i.e., the term *ton* means a long ton of 2,240 pounds).

Inspection and Warranty. Discussed later, many countries are requiring independent inspection of goods to be imported into their countries based on quality, quantity, and price comparisons. This is usually done prior to shipment of the goods, either at a facility (warehouse or manufacturing plant) of the exporter or at the port of departure. In other instances, the inspection is done at the request of the foreign customer to ensure the goods are as specified in the sales contract. The exporter may also be required to provide the foreign customer with certain guarantees concerning the performance or quality of the goods to be imported. This is usually done in the form of a standby letter of credit (discussed in Chapter 4).

The sales contract may also include a clause that requests the exporter to issue a warranty or statement against product defects, merchantability, fitness, or any other warranty of any kind whatsoever. Usually the exporter specifies in the sales contract a period of time when the foreign customer can file claims for breach of warranty. In return, the sales contract specifies conditions for remedy of breach of warranty (i.e., if the goods are less than a certain quality, the exporter shall grant a pro rata reduction in the sales price of the goods).

Price. This is the price of the goods in terms of per unit, weight, or volume, expressed in an agreed on billing currency (i.e., German marks, French francs, Japanese yen). It is appropriate in this clause or in the "Payment Terms" clause of the sales contract to specify who will accept the foreign exchange risk. It is normal trade practice to quote a price and terms of sale (discussed below) together (i.e., FOB U.S. $50 per unit).

This clause of the sales contract might also include conditions for price changes or a price escalation or reduction clause within specificed periods of time during the life of the sales contract. In addition, this provision might include a clause for initial billings based on pro-forma invoices, followed by a final invoice price, based on a mathematical formula. This usually occurs in the commodity business.

Terms of Sale. This clause, terms of sale (also referred to as *shipping or selling terms,* but often confused with payment terms) of the sales contract defines the delivery term liability and responsibilities of the exporter and foreign customer. It establishes at specific points in time who is responsible for the goods, transportation costs, and insurance coverage during the transit period of the goods which switches from the exporter to the foreign customer at a specific period of time.

Trade terms are used in international trade to define these liabilities and responsibilities. It is important that the exporter specify in the sales contract which rules the trade terms or terms of sale are subject to (i.e., "Subject to the provisions of ICC Pub. 350, *Incoterm,* 1980 revision"). Some familiar trade terms are FOB, C&F, CIF, and FAS. It is important for exporters and foreign customers to become totally familiar with these terms of sale or trade terms. They are briefly explained at the end of this chapter. See Appendix 3–B, "Incoterms," for more information.

Negotiating trade terms depends on budgets (including, cash flows or financial strengths or weaknesses), competition, and industry practices.

Payment Terms. This provision of the sales contract specifies the payment terms agreed on between the exporter and foreign customer for payment of the goods. The payment terms selected depends principally on a number of factors.

One such factor is the *financial strength* of the foreign customer (commercial risk) and that of the exporter. If the foreign customer is determined to be in poor financial condition, the exporter's payment terms are likely to be short and more secured than unsecured (Chapter 4 covers payment terms). If the exporter is having financial difficulty, it may not be in a position to offer extended unsecured payment terms. On the other hand, if neither party is not in financial difficulty, extended unsecured payment terms might be permissible under certain circumstances (i.e., the exporter's cost of capital, profitability, or net present value on the sale). Both parties must abide by the foreign customer's import and foreign exchange regulations.

Competition is another factor. In order to compete overseas, there are many extended payment term situations (price discounts or exchange rate) offered not only to U.S. competitors, but foreign competitors as well. Although some extended payment term situations are due to industry practices, others are due to intense competition for companies attempting to hold or gain market share in certain countries or for strategic reasons.

Payment term arrangements may depend on *custom* practices in certain countries—such as, having to offer a cash discount for payment within a specified period of time. In a 1 percent 10 days, net 30 days arrangement, the foreign customer is entitled to a 1 percent cash discount if payment is made or received by the 10th day of the month. Otherwise, payment is due on the 30th of the month either from invoice or ship date. However, the custom might be to extend payment terms longer than 30 days or payment might be due at the end of the month which is typical in France domestically (i.e., 60 days EOM [end of month]). Many countries consider it customary to pay slow or late.

Political or country risks are another factor for determining payment terms. In certain situations, payment terms are dictated by country import regulations (i.e., certain imports into Brazil require extending 180 day payment terms to Brazilian importers or 120 to 180 days in the case of Ecuador). On the other hand, there may be shortages of your billing currency in the foreign customer's country (known as sovereign and transfer risks). Political or country risk takes into consideration the present or future possibility of war, riot, revolution, or insurrection and economic indications of a country's financial difficulties such as problems pertaining to balance of payments, unemployment, and high inflation. All of these conditions could affect your foreign customer's willingness and ability to remit payment on due date.

In addition, the sales contract should specify the exact payment terms by spelling out what the payment terms mean. For example, simply stating payment shall be net 30 days is insufficient. The payment terms should state that payment be made against presentation of commercial invoices representing the goods shipped 30 days from either the invoice date or ship date. Also, how will payment be remitted at maturity? Will it be by company check, bank draft, or telegraphic transfer? It should specify exactly where and how payment is to be remitted (i.e., the exporter's bank by specifying your bank account number and the telex or cable number of the bank). What if the exporter specifies letter of credit payment terms? Simply stating letter of credit is again insufficient. Do you want an irrevocable L/C? What about the confirmation of another bank? Is the L/C going to be payable at sight or in 30, 60, or 90 days (time L/C)? How will the drafts be drawn? What documents are to be presented and can the documentary requirements of the L/C be minimized? What about having the L/Cs advised and/or confirmed by certain designated banks? If payment is to be rendered against a draft (bill of exchange), the sales contract should specify either "documents against payment" or "documents against acceptance." It should also state that the exporter will retain title to the goods until the foreign customer either pays the draft or accepts it, whatever is the case. In this regard, the draft and title documents should be submitted to a bank or banks as documentary collections, in which case the bank or banks act as agent for the exporter in seeking payment and/or acceptance from the foreign customer. The role of banks in the collection process is discussed in Chapter 5. Letters of credit are discussed further in Chapter 4.

If the exporter charges interest for late payments, finance charges for export financing (i.e., discount charges) or any other fees or charges, these should be specified in the sales contract. In certain countries, the charging of interest is regulated by maximum permissible amounts and withholding taxes.

Financial Responsibility. This clause can either be included in the default clause or stated separately in the sales contract. The clause usually states that in the sole opinion of the exporter, if the foreign customer's financial responsibility or capability becomes impaired and/or unsatisfactory during the term of the contract, the exporter, may request the foreign customer to make cash payments before any further deliveries are made or the acceptance of alternative payment terms.

The clause should specify that "impaired" or "unsatisfactory" refers to either the financial deterioration of the foreign customer or is the result of adverse country risk conditions. An example of this would be the sovereign and transfer foreign exchange risks of the foreign customer's country or the implementation of minimum payment terms by the local country authorities which could extend the payment terms previously granted to the foreign customer.

This clause might further state that failure or refusal of the foreign customer to comply with the exporter's requirements will entitle the exporter, without liability to the foreign customer, to suspend deliveries during such failure or refusal or, as an alternative, to terminate the contract. The suspension of deliveries or termination of the contract under any of the said conditions shall not prejudice the exporter's claim against the foreign customer for damages.

Orders and Delivery. This clause specifies when purchase orders are to be submitted by the foreign customer and when the exporter shall deliver its goods against the purchase orders. This clause might refer to the quantities mentioned in the "Quantities" clause of the sales contract or it might specify the quantities under the "Order and Delivery Clause." There might also be a clause for shipping a certain percentage over/under the quantities specified in the purchase order.

Also specified are specific deadlines or delivery dates. Specific delivery dates usually refer to the on-board ocean bill of lading date. Meeting these delivery dates can be vitally important in instances where the goods to be shipped are seasonal, raw materials, or semi-processed goods required for further manufacturing. Missing these deadlines or delivery dates could prejudice a particular season, such as Christmas, the ability to keep a plant in operation, or delivery dates to the foreign customer's own customers. Included in this provision might be remedies for not meeting deadlines or delivery dates.

The foreign customer might want this clause to include certain shipping documents for the claiming and clearing of the goods through customs. The documents most frequently requested are the original on-board ocean bill of lading (properly consigned), the commercial invoice, consular invoice, and insurance policy or certificate. If the foreign customer's payment terms are draft-documents against payment or documents against acceptance, the documents are obtained once the foreign customer pays or accepts the draft from the designated local bank of the foreign customer. Therefore, the exporter may want to further specify the underlying conditions for the release of original documents to the foreign customer.

Force Majeure. This clause states that the exporter is not liable for any failure or delay in performance which may be due in whole or in part to things beyond its control. Force majeure clauses are fairly standard in most sales contracts. The clause might read as follows:

> The exporter is not liable for the exporter's failure or delay in obtaining normal production from its source due to fire, strike, or other labor difficulty, accident, breakdown of machinery or facilities including but not limited to, the transportation, handling and terminal facilities which may be used in making deliveries hereunder, transportation or handling difficulties, faults or errors in the management of the transportation, handling or terminal facilities including, but not limted to, any act or omission of terminal operators or carriers, act of God, or public enemy, restraint or hindrance by a governmental authority, war, insurrection, riot or any other causes of any nature reasonably beyond the control of the exporter, whether related or unrelated, similar or dissimilar to the foregoing. Likewise, the foreign customer shall not be liable for any failure or delay in performance (except with respect to payment for deliveries made and financial responsibility) due to similar causes reasonably beyond its control and affecting the receipt or transportation of the goods or its ability to use same. Any accepted order which, due to any such causes, shall not have been filled by the end of the primary term or any renewal term may be canceled by either party with respect to the goods not then delivered.

Default. The sales contract might also include, in addition to a clause for financial responsibility, a default clause. The clause might read as follows:

> In the event that the foreign customer becomes insolvent, commits any act of bankruptcy, takes advantage of any law for the benefit of debtors or the foreign customer's creditors, a receiver is appointed

for the foreign customer or for any of the foreign customer's property and, fails to comply with any of the terms or conditions of the contract, the exporter may then or thereafter, without legal process, and without further notice:

1. Refuse to make further deliveries.
2. Terminate the contract, but in such event the foreign customer shall remain liable for the payment of the goods delivered and for which payment has not been made.
3. Exercise such other and further rights and remedies as it may have pursuant to law.

Arbitration. There should be a clause providing for the settlement of any disputes which may arise between the parties to the international transaction. This clause should specify an arbitration tribunal for the referral of disputes such as, the International Chamber of Commerce, the American Arbitration Association, and the Inter American Commercial Arbitration Commission.

In addition, a place where the arbitration is to be held, how the costs for arbitration will be settled, and the scope of the arbitration should all be specified in the sales contract.

Law. The sales contract should contain a clause which provides for jurisdiction by the court of some other nation other than the United States, which many international sales contracts provide for. This is because U.S. laws only apply to sales contracts under which U.S. courts have jurisdiction.

EXPORT DOCUMENTS

Documents in international trade serve an important role in a number of functions. They serve such functions as obtaining payment, controlling and transferring title to the goods, clear goods through customs and indicate compliance with the terms and conditions of the sales contract.

Each document required in the export transaction should be spelled out in the sales contract. Generally, the burden falls on the exporter since documents are not only needed to export the goods out of the exporter's country, but they permit the foreign importer to import the goods into its country.

These documents can basically be divided into two broad categories: shipping documents and financial documents. Shipping documents can be subdivided into three different types: transport, commercial and official documents.

Shipping documents consist of:

- *Transport documents* are concerned with the movement of goods between the exporter and foreign customer.
- *Commercial documents* relate to the documents pertaining to the goods of the exporter.
- *Official documents* pertain to documents required by the exporter's and foreign importer's countries.

Financial documents relate directly to the exporter's demand for payment and financing transaction for the goods and services. There is very little room in international trade for inaccurate or incomplete documentation, especially as it pertains to the compliance or noncompliance with the terms and conditions of letters of credit (explained in Chapter 4).

Shipping Documents: Transport

The Dock Receipt.   A dock receipt is a document signed by the steamship company when goods are delivered to the pier for shipment by an exporter. It is prepared by the exporter on a blank form provided by steamship companies. It is also a shipping receipt used by suppliers selling goods to exporters on FAS (Free Alongside Ship) steamer terms. In such cases the dock receipt is the transfer of title document. It describes the goods, names the shipper, the ship's name, markings, number of packages, weights, and measurements.

Once the steamship company issues its permit to the exporter and a dock receipt has been prepared, the goods may be moved to the steamship pier. In actual practice, the dock receipt many times is in nonnegotiable form and cannot be used as a genuine transfer of title document. But, if necessary, it can be marked negotiable and used in that capacity. It is negotiable by inserting the notation on the dock receipt: "This is a negotiable dock receipt; bills of lading to be released only on surrender of same." It is replaced by the bill of lading once the goods are loaded on-board the ship.

Dock receipts can be issued as clean or unclean. Before the receiving clerk at the steamship's company pier signs the dock receipt, the clerk will make certain the exterior of the goods delivered is in good condition. If the goods appear in good order, the clerk signs the dock receipt without any notations, thus becoming a clean receipt. If the exterior of the goods is damaged, the clerk will note the facts on the receipt before signing it, thus making it an unclean receipt.

Mates Receipt. This is an old sailing term. It is a receipt issued by the master of the vessel. In many countries it is being replaced by the National Standard Shipping Note. It is still used in the Far East when shipping to an island not called on directly by the carrier. This document is issued in addition to the on-board bill of lading. It is a typewritten sheet of paper where the carrier confirms that the goods have been delivered to them. It is not a document of title. It also signifies that the owner of the vessel, usually an inter-island sailing vessel, has accepted the cargo in a given named port.

It is particularly used in grain and fertilizer trades where it is used for payment rather than a letter of credit. The document is then sometimes referred to as *cash against mate's receipt,* payment term. Once a mate's receipt has been issued by the owner of the vessel, indicating that the goods have been put on-board, the exporter can use it for collection purposes.

Air Waybill. The document used in air carriage or air shipments is the air waybill (AWB or air consignment note). It is issued only in nonnegotiable form. This document does not have the same characteristics as the ocean bill of lading. The air waybill merely evidences the air carrier's receipt of the goods and the terms of the contract of carriage. It does not represent the goods as does the bill of lading. At the destination, goods are delivered on arrival to the named consignee on presentation to the airline with a copy of the waybill and proper identification. Because air waybills are issued in nonnegotiable form, the exporter cannot retain title to the goods it ships by air. The air waybill is never an "order" lading. It is always in "straight," nonnegotiable form, mainly because air shipments only take a few hours or days and cannot reach the final destination before the goods arrive. Therefore, air waybills normally accompany air shipments.

An exporter's instructions to airlines or their agents must be clear and concise in order to obtain efficient service. This will depend on the accuracy and completeness of the air waybill. Many times, exporters use the "Shipper's Letter of Instruction," to facilitate the processing of air waybills. These forms may be obtained from any airline, forwarder, or approved IATA (International Air Transport Association) Cargo Agent.

The most important feature regarding the system of documentation for air cargo moving internationally is the standard International Air Transport Association (IATA) air waybill. This is the basic document evidencing the movement of goods by air. It was not until January 1, 1984 that a new Universal Air Waybill (UAWB) was introduced for mandatory use by airlines.

Exporters selling on a documentary draft collection basis (explained in Chapter 5) will not have the same protection and assurances of payment or acceptance of drafts as it does with properly consigned ocean bills of lading. In order for the exporter to protect itself, it can consign the goods to a well respected and trusted agent, customs house broker, branch office, subsidary/ affiliate or foreign customer in the country of destination, only if the exporter has excellent historical payment and trading experience with the aforementioned. It is not normally permissible to consign goods to a local commercial bank because most banks do not have warehouse facilities to store unclaimed goods. Exporters are advised to obtain the foreign bank's written permission before consigning the shipment to the foreign bank. Also, air carriers do not normally like to store goods at the airport of destination and they do not like to wait for an advice of acceptance or payment of drafts before releasing the goods. Therefore, when the exporter has made a contract with the air carrier, the foreign customer can protect itself against the exporter's rerouting of the goods by obtaining the shipper's copy of the air waybill (marked *for the shipper*). The air carrier may not accept instructions from any person other than the holder of such a copy of the air waybill, and, if this duty is not observed, the air carrier will be liable to pay compensation for the loss incurred.

All shipments forwarded by air can be insured. Most exporters cover air shipments through their regular marine insurance coverage. Airlines themselves offer insurance coverage for exporters under their open policies. The conditions of carriage are found on the reverse side of the air waybill and are subject to the Carriage by Air Act 1961 and supplementary provisions in the Carriage by Air Act 1962. Air carriers are not liable for damage caused by compliance with laws or government regulations or for any other cause beyond their control. The Warsaw Conventions of 1929 governs carriers' liability and provides for these limitations.[2] Air carriers are liable for loss, damage, or delay of goods, but only if the loss, damage, or delay can be proved by the exporter.

Exporters can use another alternative means for controlling the possession of goods shipped on air carriers. That is, they can use COD (cash on delivery) payment terms with air carriers. Under this payment term, the air carrier is supposed to collect the full value of the goods invoiced from the foreign customer before releasing the good. The air carrier then remits a net payment back to the exporter, after deducting a percentage commission. Exporters are advised to double check existing import and exchange control regulations before entering into this type of payment arrangement. It is also advisable for exporters to maintain a close collection follow-up sequence on air carrier COD shipments to ensure the air carrier remits the payment promptly to the exporter. Some air carriers have a tendency to delay payments.

Bill of Lading.   Of all the documents used in international trade, probably the most important is the bill of lading (B/L or "lading"), especially the "on-board" ocean bill of lading (see Figure 3-1). The B/L serves three main and separate functions:[3]

1. A receipt for goods delivered to a common carrier, signed by the person (or its agent) who contracts to carry the goods.
2. A contract for services rendered by a carrier which states the conditions in which the goods are to be delivered.
3. A document of title, acceptable for credit purposes, providing it is in a form which gives the holder of the lading title to the goods specified therein.

FIGURE 3-1
Ocean Bill of Lading

OCEAN BILL OF LADING

United States Lines, Inc.

SHIPPER/EXPORTER	DOCUMENT NO.	
GIBSON BROTHERS INTERNATIONAL, LTD P.O. BOX 152 PLYMOUTH, WISCONSIN 53202	712	3-20-81

	EXPORT REFERENCES	
FORWARDERS REF. NO.	A-630-10	
SHIPPERS REF. NO.	GBIL-780	

CONSIGNEE (IF "TO ORDER" SO INDICATE)	FORWARDING AGENT - FMC. NO.
A.B. TRYGG PRODUCTS TUNADALSGATAN 73101 KOPING, SWEDEN	RAY C. FISCHER CO., INC. FMC-4099 FMC222 312 E. WISCONSIN AVE. MILWAUKEE, WISCONSIN 53202
	POINT AND COUNTRY OF ORIGIN MILWAUKEE, WISCONSIN, US

NOTIFY PARTY	DOMESTIC ROUTING / EXPORT INSTRUCTIONS
SAME	HUB CITY - (MILWAUKEE/BALTIMORE)-VIA MILWAUKEE RAILROAD — CONRAIL PIER DELIVERY - ITO TRUCKING BOOKING #120-12688

PIER
DUNDALK MARINE TERMINAL

EXPORTING CARRIER (Vessel)	PORT OF LOADING	ONWARD INLAND ROUTING
AMERICAN ARCHER US	BALTIMORE	
PORT OF DISCHARGE HAMBURG	**FOR TRANSSHIPMENT TO** NORRKOPING	KOPING, SWEDEN

OUTWARD SHORT FORM BILL OF LADING - PARTICULARS FURNISHED BY SHIPPER - NOT NEGOTIABLE UNLESS CONSIGNED TO ORDER

MARKS AND NUMBERS	NO. OF PKGS.	DESCRIPTION OF PACKAGES AND GOODS	GROSS WEIGHT	MEASUREMENT
CONTAINER NO. USLU4965830 SEAL #00853 TRYGG PRODUKT KOPING VIA NORKOPING,SWEDEN P.O. #791 #1/93	1	HOUSE TO HOUSE CONTAINER SERVICE POINT TO POINT THROUGH BILL OF LADING ALL CHARGES ARE COLLECTED AT DESTINATION 40 FT. CONTAINER SAID TO CONTAIN 93 CARTONS OUTDOOR POWER EQUIP- MENT FOR LAWN AND GARDEN CARE CON- SISTING OF GARDEN TRACTORS, ROTARY TILLERS, SERVICE PARTS AND ADVERTI- SING MATTER THESE COMMODITIES LICENSED FOR DESTINATION SWEDEN DIVERSION CONTRARY TO US LAW PRO- HIBITED/SHIPPER'S LOAD AND COUNT	26,600 LBS	2062 CU FT.

(Clause 22 Of The United States Lines regular long form bill of lading effective July 1, 1974 will be subject to the York/Antwerp Rules 1974)

FREIGHT AND CHARGES PAYABLE AT KOPING, SWEDEN		ALL CHARGES EX TACKLE FOR ACCOUNT OF CARGO
26,600 LBS @	$	
$195.00 PER 2240	$ 2315.63	RECEIVED the goods or the containers, vans, trailers, palletized units or other packages said to contain goods herein mentioned, in apparent good order and condi- tion, except as otherwise indicated herein, to be transported to the port of discharge
	$	named (TERMS OF THIS BILL OF LADING CONTINUED ON REVERSE SIDE HERE- OF) IN WITNESS WHEREOF,
US INLAND FREIGHT	$ 644.00	THE MASTER OR AGENT OF SAID VESSEL HAS
	$	SIGNED 1 BILL(s) OF LADING, ALL OF THE SAME TENOR AND DATE, ONE OF WHICH BEING ACCOM- PLISHED, THE OTHERS TO STAND VOID.
	$	UNITED STATES LINES, INC.
	$	
TOTAL $ 2959.63		BY UNITED STATES LINES, INC.

	B/L No. 7402	FOR THE MASTER
703401 PLEASE REFER TO THIS INVOICE NUMBER WITH ALL REMITTANCES.		3 MO. 30 DAY 19 81 YEAR

Source: National Committee on International Trade Documentation.

There are basically two Acts which have played an integral part in the development of this important export document, the Bills of Lading Act 1855 and the Carriage of Goods by Sea Act 1924. The first Act established the following:[4]

1. It prevented the right of the original shipper to "stoppage in transit" (in transit). Moreover, not only did it give the right of conditional endorsement and of reserving the "jus disponendi" (law of disposal), but also the unpaid seller could resume possession of the goods by exercising the right of "stoppage in transitu."
2. It established the principle of transferability, permitting the transfer of a bill of lading from the holder to a person to whom the property in the goods passes, together with any rights and liabilities incorporated in the document.
3. It provided that once the bill of lading has been issued, it is prima facie evidence that the goods have been shipped.

Under the Carriage of Goods by Sea Act 1924, the carrier is under obligation to properly and carefully load, handle, stow, carry, keep, care for, and discharge the goods carried.[5]

Bills of lading are prepared, issued, and supplied by steamship companies and the form itself varies from one steamship company to the next. On the reverse side of each form are the conditions under which the carrier accepts the goods for transportation. The rules and agreements which the United States has accepted for the transportation of goods is the U.S. Carriage of Goods by Sea Act, 1936. However, many of the clauses contained in the act have been standardized by international agreements. Exporters should familiarize themselves with the provisions on the reverse side of B/Ls from time to time. Required on ladings are the following data:

Name of exporter (the shipper).

Vessel.

Type of goods (full description).

Weight or measurements.

Number of parcels and marks.

Port of shipment.

Destination (port of discharge).

Freight details.

Consignee or shipper's order.

Notify party on arrival of vessel.

Contract carriage terms.

Date goods received and/or loaded on the vessel.

Number of B/Ls.

Date and signature of the ship's master or his agent.

Bills of lading may be negotiable or nonnegotiable. The difference between the two is determined by the terminology in the clause dealing with the consignee. The B/Ls are either "Straight" or "To Order." If the words *To Order* are included, the B/L is negotiable. If the goods are consigned to a specific individual or company and the words *To Order* are omitted, the B/L is nonnegotiable.

Clean and Foul Bill of Lading. Bills of lading can be issued as either clean or foul. This depends on the condition of the goods when delivered to the steamship carrier by a transport company (i.e., railroad, motor truck, ocean vessel, or air carrier). Carriers are only responsible for delivering goods as received. The outward condition of the packaged goods is the determining factor of the condition of the goods. For example, if 50 cartons of goods are delivered to a carrier by a transport company and all 50 cartons are intact (no exterior damage), then the carrier will issue a clean bill of lading. If, on the other hand, the same 50 cartons are delivered to a carrier by a transport company, but only 40 are intact and 10 are damaged, the carrier will place a notation on the bill of lading that 10 cartons have been received as damaged and briefly describe the damage. In this case the B/L is unclean, foul, or claused.

The purpose of issuing clean or foul B/Ls is to protect the carrier from claims placed against them for exterior damages of goods delivered to them. Ascertaining the responsibility for exterior damage switches to the seller and transport company. Most shipments under letters of credit require clean ladings as banks favor this type of B/L for financial settlement purposes.

These terms, clean and foul, are applicable to any form of shipping receipt. It is important to emphasize that these terms are applicable only to the outward condition of packaged goods.

Straight Bill of Lading.   This type of bill of lading is nonnegotiable. When goods are shipped under a straight B/L, the goods are consigned to the foreign customer or its agent. The individual designated consignee on this form can take possession of the goods without presenting or surrendering the B/L to the carrier. This is because the carrier's agreement states merely that it is to transport the goods from the shipper (exporter) to the consignee (importer). On delivery of the goods to the consignee, the transport company legally fulfills its contractual obligation. A straight B/L does not protect the creditor against nonpayment or nonacceptance. In export trade, this type of B/L is principally used when accounts are extended open account payment terms. This means the customer can take possession of the goods without accepting or paying a draft or bill of exchange (B/E).

On a documentary draft collection basis the exporter can lose control over the goods when the carrier accepts the goods. If the exporter extended sight draft-documents against payment credit terms, the whole purpose of using this payment term would be self-defeating if a straight bill of lading is used because the foreign customer can take possession of the goods before paying the sight draft. When the exporter extends payment terms of time draft-documents against acceptance, the same situation exists and the exporter may not have an accepted draft prior to the consignee taking possession of the goods.

Through Bill of Lading.   This is a type of railroad bill of lading used only where the inland shipper is also the exporter. Although primarily a railroad B/L, it can be a combination railroad and ocean B/L. With this B/L, the inland shipper would route the goods from the inland railway terminal to a specified destination overseas. The through B/L is issued at the railway terminal and the charges for carrying the goods by rail from the terminal to seaport are added to the ocean freight charges from seaboard to the final destination.

To Order Bill of Lading.   The To Order B/L (see Figure 3–2) is a negotiable bill of lading. Only signed copies are negotiable and all signed copies are delivered to the exporter. The number of copies, signed by the steamship company originally, varies with the requirements of the exporter, the steamship company, and the

FIGURE 3–2
To Order Bill of Lading

SHIPPER (Principal or Seller licensee and full address)
XYZ Company

BOOKING NUMBER: 12345
B/L NUMBER: 12345

EXPORT REFERENCES
000000

CONSIGNEE (Name and Full Address/Non-negotiable Unless Consigned to Order)
(Unless provided otherwise, a consignment "To Order" means To Order of Shipper.)
TO THE ORDER OF
ZYX Company LTD
Seoul, Korea

FORWARDING AGENT (References, F.M.C. No.) FMC111111
AXX Company
, PA. US. 19106

POINT AND COUNTRY OF ORIGIN OF GOODS MLB
WEST CHESTER PA

NOTIFY PARTY/INTERMEDIATE CONSIGNEE (Name and Full Address)
SEO Company
Seoul, Korea

ALSO NOTIFY (Name and Full Address) /DOMESTIC ROUTING/ EXPORT INSTRUCTIONS/PIER — TERMINAL/ONWARD ROUTING FROM POINT OF DESTINATION
NO SED REQ/SECT.30.39 FTSR/S.A.S.

INITIAL CARRIAGE (MODE)*	PLACE OF RECEIPT*
EXECUTIVE HANDLG	8501 HAGERMAN
EXPORT CARRIER (Vessel, voyage, & flag)	PORT OF LOADING
PRES. GRANT V054 USA	PHILADELPHIA
PORT OF DISCHARGE	PLACE OF DELIVERY*
BUSAN	

PARTICULARS FURNISHED BY SHIPPER

MKS.& NOS./CONTAINER NOS.	NO. OF PKGS.	H M	DESCRIPTION OF PACKAGES AND GOODS	GROSS WEIGHT	MEASUREMENT
Container No. SEO Company Emblem EX Busan, Korea #1/UP	44		1 20' CONTAINER SAID TO CONTAIN DRMS A)LF39-0340 SLAC CY/CY SYNTHETIC RESIN, NES L L/C COVERING:TRIMETHYLOLPROPANE TRIMETHACRYLATE (SR-350) 21120 LBS AT USD1 USA ORIGIN C AND F BUSAN L/C NO.:M1906507ES02243/514079 CLEAN ON BOARD "FREIGHT PREPAID" SHIPPER'S LOAD.COUNT & STOWAGE EX- PORT LIC. G-DEST ON BOARD HOUSE/HOUSE CONTAINERIZATION	10313KG 22743LB	33.930M 1200.000CF
CTR NBR* APLS275164	****SEAL NBR**** T/S MODE QUANT/TYPE 2691		D20 CY/CY 44 DRMS		

THESE COMMODITIES LICENSED BY U.S. FOR ULTIMATE DESTINATION KOREA. DIVERSION CONTRARY TO U.S. LAW PROHIBITED. ** ORIGINAL BL **

B/L TO BE RELEASED AT: PHILADELPHIA
OCEAN FREIGHT PAYABLE AT

FREIGHT RATES CHARGES, WEIGHTS AND/OR MEASUREMENTS (SUBJECT TO CORRECTION)	PREPAID U.S. $	COLLECT U.S. $	Local Currency

SHIPPED ON BOARD
DATE 8-1-85
BY

The undersigned Carrier hereby acknowledges recei[pt of] the sealed container or packages or other shipping u[nits] said to contain the Goods described above in appar[ent] external good order and condition unless other[wise] stated. The Shipper agrees, and the Consignee and ev[ery] person purchasing this instrument for value, if neg[oti]able, or otherwise having an interest in the Good[s is] advised that the receipt, custody, carriage and deli[very] of the Goods are subject to all the terms and condi[tions] set forth and incorporated by reference on this side [and] the reverse hereof, whether written, stamped or prin[ted].

A set of 3 originals of this bill of lading is he[reby] issued by the Carrier. Upon surrender to the Ca[rrier] of any one negotiable bill of lading, properly endo[rsed] all others shall stand void.

By:
Authorized Rep/of Carrier or Ma[ster]
Date and AUG. 1 1
Place Issued: PHILADELPHIA

75	054	72	TOTAL PREPAID
Vessel	Voyage	Office	TOTAL COLLECT

FCC	FORWARDER	SHIPPER	CONSIGNEE	LD. PORT	DIS. PORT	DEST.	NOTIFY	CSC	B/L NUMBER
									12345

*APPLICABLE ONLY WHEN USED AS MULTI MODAL BILL OF LADING

D-15 B/L 5/84 Reorder Stock No. 20-1[...]

Source: The Philadelphia National Bank.

consular authorities. All original signed copies of the ladings are known as *a full set* to the party to whom title to the goods are transferred. Most bills of lading are issued in sets of at least three signed negotiables, but more can be made up. This is because the set is broken up and each one is mailed separately in the event the first one is lost in the mail, but usually one is kept by the exporter. Banks in letter of credit financing request at least two original bills of lading (it appears on the L/C as 2/3 bills of lading). It only takes one properly endorsed original B/L to obtain the goods from the carrier at the foreign port of destination. The original shipper can have the goods shipped to order of a second party or the shipper itself. It means the goods are controlled and remain the property of the exporter until the consignee endorses and delivers an original negotiable "To Order of . . . (name of exporter)" or "To Order of Shipper" B/L to the carrier. It is advisable to add to the To Order Bill of Lading, "Notify . . ." by inserting the name of the foreign customer, the exporter's agent (in the country of destination), the customs house broker or its own subsidiary, whichever is the case. Any "to order" bill of lading which is made out this way is called a *to order, notify* bill of lading. This type of B/L instructs the steamship company to notify a specific named party of the arrival of the goods at the foreign port of destination which helps reduce warehouse charges (demurrage), pilferage, or theft.

It is important to note Venezuela, Colombia, and the Dominican Republic have import regulations that do not permit To Order Bills of Lading. Straight B/Ls are used in these markets which creates problems for credit managers and marketing/sales personnel. While the credit manager may not feel comfortable with either the financial capability of the foreign customer or the country itself, his or her marketing/sales department may want to sell on open account or draft credit terms to be competitive, while taking into consideration market share considerations. Because of the risks, the credit manager might prefer letter of credit type payment terms. However, in the event of discrepant documents under an L/C in these countries, the exporter does not have the protection of an L/C because the B/L must be straight ladings, and is in effect now dealing with the foreign customer on open account because the foreign customer can take possession of the goods before the exporter as beneficiary to the L/C is paid.

If the exporter consigns the goods to itself, the inland shipper endorses the bill of lading with its signature, just as a check might be endorsed. This is known as endorsing in blank. Anyone holding an endorsed in blank B/L holds title to the goods. The order B/L, endorsed in blank, is often used as a means of transferring title.

When an inland shipper ships goods on an order B/L, consigned to the order of the exporter, the exporter holds title to the goods until it places its endorsement on the B/L. When the latter procedure is followed, the actual original B/L must be in the possession of the consignee when the goods arrive at the foreign port of destination in order to take possession of the goods.

The order B/L is mostly used when the exporter draws a draft on foreign customers. When the exporter extends sight draft-documents against payment credit terms, the only way for the consignee to obtain possession of the goods (obtain the original B/L) is to pay the amount stated on the sight draft (documents against payment). If the payment terms are time draft-documents against acceptance, the consignee must accept the draft in order to obtain the original B/L and take possession of the goods. The subject of drafts payable "at sight" or "against acceptance" is further explained in Chapters 4 and 5.

Carriers will not release goods covered by a To Order B/L until an original negotiable endorsed B/L is delivered to the carrier. This is important because it protects not only the shipper, but all intermediary parties to the transaction. To Order B/Ls are required for the discounting of drafts by banks since the order B/L represents the collateral (title) supporting the draft. The order B/L is also a requirement for L/C financing.

When bills of lading arrive after the arrival of goods at the foreign port of importation, customs officials in some countries may release the goods to the foreign customer against a bond or bank guaranty which often costs the importer twice the amount of the invoice value. Bonds and bank guarantees are explained in Chapters 4 and 8.

Exporters should always instruct the inland shipper to mark on the face of the B/L the phrase *For Export*. This is necessary so that federal transportation taxes which are sometimes levied only on domestic movements are waived, and also so that the benefits of free lighterage can be enjoyed if a lighterage problem is present.[6]

On-Board Ocean Bill of Lading.   Many times, bills of lading are signed by the steamship company before the goods are loaded on-board the steamship carrier (see Figure 3–3). It is conceivable for a vessel named in the lading to be withdrawn or substituted for one reason or another. Because of this reason, many shippers of record (exporters) require a second signature of the master of the steamship company or its agent on the lading which evidences that the goods are actually on-board the vessel (also known as a received-for-shipment bills of lading). A rubber stamp statement is used in this instance on the bill of lading that the cargo is on-board the vessel. The statement must be signed and dated by the master or other authorized agent of the steamship company. Under this type of B/L the steamship company agrees to move the goods of the exporter on a named steamship to a designated foreign port. Many international commercial banks request the presentation of on-board ocean bills of lading as a condition of letters of credit. Experienced exporters prefer on-board ocean bills of lading to determine precise due dates in conjunction with documentary cash mobilization techniques (discussed in Chapter 5).

Each ocean bill of lading also contains a section for a statement of freight charges. They will be stamped *freight prepaid* or *freight payable at destination* as appropriate. Steamship companies prefer the freight charges be prepaid because of collection problems at the port of discharge (destination) from importers and/or because of their foreign exchange problems. While in some cases exporters prefer these charges to appear only on the nonnegotiable copies of a bill of lading (except when required under letters of credit), sometimes these charges are also on the negotiable ladings, particularly when freight charges are collected as a separate expense from a foreign buyer.[7]

Transshipment Bill of Lading.   This is another type of B/L used by shipping companies when there is no direct service between two ports, but the steamship company is prepared to transship the goods (cargo) at an intermediate port at its expense.

With the development of combined transport operations there is an increasing volume of both linear cargo trade and bulk cargo shipment of goods which involves the bill of lading being issued in association with a selected Charter Party (i.e., the Combined Transport Bill of Lading 1971 or "Combinconbill").

FIGURE 3–3
On-Board Ocean Bill of Lading

BILL OF LADING

SHIPPER/EXPORTER		DOCUMENT NO. XE 2345
Fabritech, Inc. 900 Avenue of the Americas New York, NY		EXPORT REFERENCES
CONSIGNEE		FORWARDING AGENT · REFERENCES Brown, Jenkinson & Company
To Order of Shipper		POINT AND COUNTRY OF ORIGIN U.S.A.
NOTIFY PARTY		DOMESTIC ROUTING/EXPORT INSTRUCTIONS
Jose D'Amato S.A.R.L. Av. Fernando de Sousa Lisbon		N/A
PIER OR AIRPORT #39 New York		
EXPORTING CARRIER (Vessel/Airline) SS "Hope"	PORT OF LOADING New York	ONWARD INLAND ROUTING
AIR/SEA PORT OF DISCHARGE Lisbon	FOR TRANSSHIPMENT TO N/A	N/A

PARTICULARS FURNISHED BY SHIPPER

MARKS AND NUMBERS	NO. OF PKGS.	DESCRIPTION OF PACKAGES AND GOODS	GROSS WEIGHT	MEASUREMENT
Made in U.S.A.	16	Steel Wardrobes containing garments		14' X 18'
		Original ON BOARD 3/15/8X		

FREIGHT CHARGES PAYABLE AT **Lisbon**   BY **Jose D'Amato, Lisbon**

Land Origin Charges	PREPAID	COLLECT
Port Charges		
SUB TOTAL		
Ocean Freight		
SUB TOTAL		
Port Charges		
Land Destination Charge		
SUB TOTAL		
GRAND TOTAL		

SHORT FORM BILL OF LADING

Received the goods or packages said to contain goods herein mentioned, in apparent good order and condition unless otherwise indicated, to be transported and delivered, or trans-shipped as herein provided

This carriage is subject to the provisions of the U.S. Carriage of Goods by Sea Act of 1936. This Short Form Bill of Lading is issued pursuant to 46 U.S.C. 844, as amended. All the terms and conditions of the Carrier's regular form Bill of Lading, as filed with the Federal Maritime Commission and posted on board the vessel and available to any shipper or consignee upon request, are incorporated with like force and effect as if they were written at length herein, and all such terms and conditions so incorporated by reference are agreed by Shipper to be binding and to govern the relations whatever they may be between those included in the words 'Shipper' and 'Carrier' as defined in Carrier's regular form Bill of Lading.

IN WITNESS WHEREOF, the Carrier Master or Agent of said vessel has signed and the Shipper has received this one original bill of lading

Dated At _____ New York _____ NAME OF CARRIER

March 15, 19XX ____ By _____
MO   DAY   YEAR

B/L No. _____

Source: *Dynamics of Trade Finance*, copyright 1984, The Chase Manhattan Bank, printed with permission of the publisher, Global Business Communications, Inc., P.O. Box 99, Gillette, N.J. 07933, p. 30.

Short Form Bill of Lading.   On a short form bill of lading the carrier's normally detailed conditions shown on the reverse side of the long form B/L are written into a brief incorporated clause on the front of the form. This short form is recognized by the International Chamber of Shipping (ICS) and its use is supported by the United Nations. The short form B/L saves indirect costs by improving efficiency. It is acceptable for documentary credits under article 26 b.ii., of the Uniform Customs and Practice of Documentary Credits (UCP), Publication No. 400 (unless otherwise specified in the letter of credit). The UCP is discussed in Chapter 5.

Sea Waybill.   This is a nonnegotiable alternative to the bill of lading. It provides for delivery to a named consignee without presentation of the documents at destination. It helps to solve some of the problems caused by late arrival of documents after arrival of the goods. It is particularly useful when selling goods on open account or between long-established trading partners or foreign customers where trust has been established. It can be used with documentary credits, if the L/C specifically authorizes its acceptance.

SPECIAL NOTE

Presenting the right type of B/L is vitally important to the export creditor. Presenting a straight B/L defeats one of the significant purposes for extending credit to foreign customers on documents against payment or documents against acceptance draft payment terms. The intent of using these payment terms is to either receive payment at sight or obtain an acceptance on drafts prior to the release of goods to the foreign customer.

It is important to mention at this point that the right type of B/L be spelled out in the sales contract to coincide with the payment terms. To do otherwise may create problems. Written procedures and/or automated internal controls are very important. Experienced exporters know that irrespective of what is agreed on in the sales contract regarding terms of sale and payment terms, foreign customers many times submit purchase orders that specify that at least one original negotiable To Order B/L be sent direct to them. Foreign customers do this because they are fearful of late arrival of original title documents. It is especially true when they have had poor prior experience with exporters. Many countries abroad have strict pilferage regulations (i.e., Colombia), steep demurrage charges and regulations stating that goods must be cleared through customs within limited periods of time.

Many times a foreign customer may encounter any one of the above mentioned problems. This might be due to an exporter's inefficiency in expediting original documents, or to sales departments who are fearful of losing the foreign customer to competition. The sales department may cater to the wishes of their foreign customers by accepting purchase orders or direct requests to submit at least one original negotiable B/L to them. The sales department may be justified—why lose a foreign customer to competition due to their company's inefficiency to expedite original title documents? But then again, why take on a collection problem or possible bad debt?

Shipping Documents: Commercial

Commercial/Proforma Invoice.   This document illustrated in Figure 3–4, is a bill addressed to the foreign customer which clearly describes the goods and indicates:

1. The total cost of the goods sold.
2. A description of the goods.
3. The price per unit of the goods.
4. The terms of sale: FOB, FAS, or CIF.
5. Payment terms specifically spelled out (i.e., 90 days draft from the on-board ocean B/L date, not 90 days draft).
6. Bear the marks and number of packages as they appear in the bill of lading and consular invoice, when required, and on the insurance certificate.
7. Show any charges and fees connected with the shipment.
8. Show any other requirements on the commercial invoice such as, signed, marked paid, notarized, or consularized or any combination thereof as stipulated in the terms and conditions of the sale contract, and country import regulations.

FIGURE 3–4
Commercial Invoice

COMMERCIAL INVOICE

COMMERCIAL INVOICE
(1)

SHIPPER/EXPORTER/MANUFACTURER/SELLER (2)	DOCUMENT NO. (5)	INVOICE NO. AND DATE
ABC INDUSTRIES 349 FRALEY STREET KANE, PA 21760	2415	INT 306 9/1/ 81
	OTHER REFERENCES (6) CUST. ORDER • 5078	

CONSIGNED TO ORDER OF SHIPPER/PORT AGENT/BANK (3A)	BUYER (7)
ORDER OF SHIPPER BILBRO VENSKT 609 40 BAGERSTEN STOCKHOLM, SWEDEN	BILBRO VENSKT 609 40 BAGERSTEN STOCKHOLM SWEDEN
	COUNTRY OF ORIGIN OF GOODS (8) U.S.A.

NOTIFY PARTY/INTERMEDIATE CONSIGNEE (4)	TERMS (9) (15)
OLSON FORWARDING CO. 1000 ULMERSTRAZ STOCKHOLM, SWEDEN	CIF STOCKHOLM SIGHT DRAFT, 30 DAYS NO DISCOUNT
PIER OR AIRPORT (10) PACKER AVE.	ABC INDUSTRIES 349 FRALEY ST. KANE, PA 21760
EXPORTING CARRIER (VESSEL /AIRLINE) (11) / PORT OF LOADING (12) STAGHOUND / PHILADELPHIA	U.S. CURRENCY
AIR/SEA PORT OF DISCHARGE (13) / FOR TRANSSHIPMENT TO (14) STOCKHOLM	

PARTICULARS FURNISHED BY SHIPPER

MARKS AND NUMBERS (16)	NO. OF PKGS. (17)	DESCRIPTION OF PACKAGES AND GOODS (18)	GROSS WEIGHT (19)	MEASUREMENT (20) (CUBE)
ABC STKHLM 1–150 CONT. No. 6785 1–40 FT. CONT.	150	WOODEN DISHES	38,550	1800 CFT.

John L. Jones CERTIFIED CORRECT AND JUST PER
_____, CHIEF CLERK.
THESE COMMODITIES LICENSED BY U.S. FOR
ULTIMATE DESTINATION SWEDEN. DIVERSION
CONTRARY TO U.S. LAW PROHIBITED.

COMMODITY DESCRIPTION COUNTRY OF ORIGIN OF GOODS (NOT SHOWN ABOVE) (PRODUCT CODES, CATALOG & SERIAL NOS., MEASUREMENT, ETC., AS APPLICABLE)	ITEM. NO.	NET WT.	NO. PIECES	NO. UNITS	UNIT PRICE	GROSS PRICE
WOODEN DISHES – 6" DIAM.	1	18,000	15,000		1.25	$18,750.00
WOODEN DISHES – 8" DIAM.	2	20,000	18,000		2.10	37,800.00
OPTIONAL AREA (21)						

PACKING	DOM. FREIGHT	INT'L. FREIGHT	OTHER CHARGES (SPECIFY)	INSURANCE	TOTAL EXTRA CHARGES (B)
		$3,813.75	FORWARDER $40.00	450.00	$4,303.75

TOTAL GROSS PRICE	DISCOUNT	TOTAL NET PRICE (A)	INVOICE TOTAL (A) + (B)
$56,550.00	NONE	$56,550.00	$60,853.75

Source: Philadelphia National Bank.

9. Specifically spell out where payment is to be remitted. This pertains more to foreign customers billed on open account.
10. It should be dated, and show the names and addresses of the exporter and foreign customer, the "ship to" location, port of shipment, vessel, and as a matter of courtesy to the foreign customer (unless specifically spelled out in a letter of credit, import regulation, or customer purchase order), signed by the exporter.

It is not a title document in contrast to the bill of lading and is nonnegotiable. This document must describe the goods exactly as it appears in letter of credit terms and conditions. Inaccurate commercial invoices are the cause of many difficulties when banks are negotiating letters of credit.

The commercial invoice is basically a document concerning the foreign customer and exporter. But, there are instances where a third party has a legitimate interest in the commercial invoice. These could be customs officials in the country of destination, banks (especially with letter of credit financing, or buyer financing), insurance companies, and third-party financiers.

Also, as mentioned above, country regulations may specify the commercial invoice show weights and measurements in metric and/or linear units, in the language of their nation, or certain statements.

Great care must be exercised by those people responsible for completing commercial invoices. They must comply specifically to the terms and conditions of the letter of credit, the UCP, country import regulations, and customer purchase orders. If you comply with these regulations you will avoid delays, inconveniences, and unnecessary costs to the foreign customer when clearing goods through customs or applying for foreign exchange for the respective import.

In some circumstances an exporter may be required to submit a pro-forma invoice before shipping the goods to a foreign customer. This is actually a form of quotation by an exporter to foreign customers which gives details of the shipment. Pro-forma invoices are more likely to be a country import regulation in advance of shipments to:

1. Assess custom duties.
2. To obtain an import license.
3. Obtain pre-allocation of foreign exchange.

This invoice must meet all of the regulations of the importing country and especially the terms and conditions of a letter of credit.

Acceptance on the part of the foreign customer to the pro-forma invoice can become the basis for a contract as to price and terms. Both the commercial and pro-forma invoices must agree identically with each other. When a pro-forma invoice is submitted to a foreign customer, later followed by shipment of the goods and a commercial invoice, the commercial invoice must agree with the previously submitted pro-forma invoice. It is also conceivable the exporter may be required to certify on the commercial invoice that the "goods are in accordance with the pro-forma invoice."

Certificate of Inspection.   This is a pre-inspection of the goods by independent surveillance companies which more and more countries are requiring as part of their import regulation scheme. These independent companies or firms carry out preshipment inspections based on quality, quantity, and perform price comparisons.

The purpose is to ensure that the goods comply with the importer's contractual requirements and/or conform to accepted trade standards and norms.

The Societe Generale du Surveillance S.A. (SGS) and its affiliates have been the principle appointed inspection company by many countries. Other companies have recently been used by countries, namely: Intertek, Swede Control, Bureau Veritas, Thionville, Cotecna, Griffiths, and Omic. Figure 3–5 contains a history of preshipment inspection programs.

On completing the inspection, a Report of Findings is completed which expresses an opinion by the inspecting company to their principals. A Clean Report of Findings (CRF) is issued only after the inspecting company is satisfied with the quantity, quality, and price of the goods to be shipped. The Clean Report of Findings, together with other commercial documents, is required by the foreign customer in order to obtain payment from commer-

FIGURE 3–5 History of Preshipment Inspection Programs

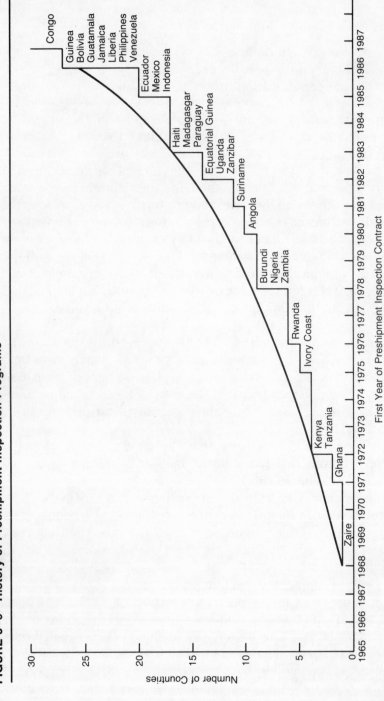

Source: Gerd P. Lota, "Special Bulletin on Preshipment Inspection—Part 2," FCIB International Bulletin, no. 6614–15 (September 10, 1987). p. 3. Copyright 1987 by the FCIB-NACM Corporation. All rights reserved.

cial banks and/or to clear goods through customs. If a Nonnegotiable Report of Findings (NNRF) is issued by the inspecting company, the exporter should discuss the matter with the foreign customer who will probably have to discuss the NNRF with their foreign exchange and customs officials.

Over the years, many countries have required pre-inspection in accordance with their summary authority which vary by the importing country without notice (exporters are advised to check with your international commercial bankers and/or a country import regulation publication). Appendix 3–C lists those countries that require pre-inspection as of December 31, 1987.

Combined Transport Documents. These are rapidly growing types of bills of lading (or what are called intermodal B/Ls) involving container shipments, through road haulage services (trucking companies), and through rail services (railroad companies). Combined Transport B/Ls means the goods will be moved by more than one means of transportation, such as by truck to a railroad to a port, then by a steamship carrier. They can emanate from the following:

1. Combiconbill or combined transport bills of lading which is the carriage of goods by at least two modes of transportation.
2. CMR (Convention relative au contrat de transport internationale des Marchandies par vois de Route) consignment note which involves the movement of goods through international road transport services (mostly used in Europe).
3. CIM (Convention International concernant is transport de Marchandise par chemin de fer) consignment note which involves the movement of goods on a through international rail service (mostly used in Europe).
4. FIATA combined transport bill of lading, a transport document used by FIATA members which provides for a combined transport by at least two different modes of transport.

These documents do not evidence shipment of the goods on board a carrier destined for an overseas location, unlike the ocean bill of lading. They simply evidence the carrier's receipt for the goods and obligation (liability) to ship the goods to a place of delivery.

These documents are acceptable for presentation under Article 25 of the UCP 400 of the International Chamber of Commerce.

Certificate of Origin.   A certificate of origin specifies quality/quantity since it is interrelated to price of the goods for ensuring that the goods comply with an importer's contractual requirements and/or conform to accepted trade standards and norms. A few countries require a separate document (certificate) even though the commercial invoice contains a statement of origin of the goods. The purpose of this document is to verify the origin of the goods and enable the importing country officials to levy the proper import tariff rate, if required, perhaps under a "most-favored-nation" arrangement. Sometimes this document requires the countersignature of a chamber of commerce or a visa from the country's resident consul located at or near the port of export. Some governments have a special form for this purpose or sometimes accept a statement certifying the origin of the goods on the exporter's own stationery or on the commercial invoice will suffice.

Packing List.   This document lists the contents of packages/consignments. It will include the number and type of packages, their contents, the net and gross weights in kilograms and/or linear measurements, dimensions of the packages such as height/width/length, and markings. It is sometimes referred to as a packing note. It can be a duplicate of the commercial invoice, only without prices.

Health and Purity Certificates.   Most foreign countries require that shipments of plants and unmanufactured plant products be accompanied by Phytosanitary Certificates of Inspection which certify conformity with their plant quarantine import regulations. These types of certificates are not a requirement of the United States, but is provided as a service at the request of a shipper. After inspection, the certificates certify that the commodity to be exported to a particular country is substantially free from pests and plant diseases considered harmful by the importing country.

Exports of certain types of food and agricultural products may require certificates by the importing country. For example, the U.S. Grain Standards Act and the Agricultural Marketing Act require USDA inspection of grain exports.

Insurance Policy and Certificate.   Because of the risk against loss or damage during the transit period of goods from plant or warehouse to the foreign port of discharge, having sufficient insurance coverage is very important. Appropriate insurance coverage is an integral part of the export trade process regardless of whether the goods are transported by land, sea, or air. It is important to note that steamship carriers are not insurers of goods and are exempted by law from certain types of losses. These are contained in the Carriage of Goods by Sea Act of 1936. The Act limits ocean carrier's liability to $500 per package for certain types of losses.

It is vitally important for exporters and foreign customers to specifically spell out in the export sales contract, who is responsible for insurance coverage from the time the goods leave the exporter's point of origin until the foreign customer takes possession of the goods.

The goods are usually insured against loss or damage in transit by ocean cargo insurance. Unlike domestic cargo insurance, this type of coverage is much broader and applies to shipments by rail, air, and steamship carriers. There are two basic types of coverage offered by insurers:

1. One-time cargo insurance which covers specific shipments. This type of policy is expensive because the insurer cannot spread its risks over a number of different shipments to different countries. Sometimes infrequent exporters insure their overseas shipments under a freight forwarder's policy for a fee.
2. An open (blanket) cargo insurance policy which grants continuous coverage on all shipments made by an exporter. This type of policy is more commonly used by exporters who ship frequently. It is also less expensive than having to take out cargo insurance to cover each export shipment and less time consuming when it comes to export documentation preparation.

Under open policies, the exporter can use certain methods to report export shipments to the insurer. These are the short form declaration, a special marine policy, and the monthly report of shipments on a bordereau (a special form used to detail and summarize export shipments).

The short form of declaration is used infrequently by exporter's but, when a claim needs to be filed by a foreign customer, the short form must be returned to the exporter for processing.

Because exporters must provide evidence of insurance coverage for the goods exported to foreign customers, banks (especially when CIF terms of sale are quoted), and other third parties (lease arrangements, credit insurers), special marine insurance policies are used for this purpose. This is used in addition to the information on the short form of declaration. This policy lists the following:

1. The name of the party to whom loss or losses are payable to (these are usually made out in "to order" forms which are then negotiable and can be endorsed over).
2. The numbers and marks of the shipment.
3. All applicable policy provisions.

There are usually four copies to the special marine insurance policy, two negotiables and two nonnegotiable copies. The negotiable copies are sent with the shipping documents and the others are for the beneficiary and the insurer (underwriter). It is important the insurer (underwriter) countersign it by an authorized representative.

The special marine insurance policy is now used in place of an insurance certificate under most letters of credit or, it is rapidly replacing it. This is because of objections with certificates not constituting an insurance policy.

Although most policies will cover goods from the point of origin of the exporter until the goods arrive at the warehouse of the foreign customer (usually 15 days from the time goods are off-loaded from the steamship carrier at the port of destination), most experienced exporters will take out "all risk" policies which are more comprehensive in coverage.

However, because of the potential unforeseen risks of transporting goods to foreign customers, sometimes in identifiable or unidentifiable risk markets, such as war, riot, revolution, insurrection, strikes, theft, or pilferage problems, experienced exporters will take out separate policies or include additional clauses in their policies to cover some of these potential risks. These clauses are explained below.* In addition, exporters should investigate the possibility of taking out export credit insurance, explained and examined in Chapter 6.

It is also important to note that some countries mandate through local law that foreign customers take out cargo insurance in its country. Under FOB (Free on Board) or C&F (Cost and Freight) terms, the foreign customer is responsible for arranging insurance for at least a portion of the transit period of the goods. There are situations when the foreign customer is responsible for insuring the goods, but the exporter actually makes all the insurance arrangements. Under this method, the exporter will charge the cost of the insurance to the foreign customer as a separate item on the commercial invoice. When foreign customers are responsible for insuring the goods, experienced exporters do not always assume adequate insurance is in place, especially with new foreign customers not commonly known in its trade. These situations can result either from neglect on the part of the foreign customer to obtain full coverage or inadequate coverage which can perhaps be due to high premium costs or limitations on coverage. Also, having one insurer eliminates the risk of disputes between two insurers. Overlooking this potential risk could result in major financial losses to exporters. Because of this potential and recurring problem, experienced exporters take out Contingency Insurance to safeguard against these risks. This permits the exporter to file a claim on goods if the importer has failed to insure them. The cost for this coverage is usually one third the cost of a normal policy.

The standard method used by insurers and exporters for computing the cost of coverage needed is to take the total of the cost of the goods, freight, the cost of the insurance itself, plus 10

---

*These are some special clauses exporters can include in their policies to cover special risks:

F.C. & S. clause (free of capture and seizure) is war risk insurance not covered by the insurance company unless definitely agreed on in each instance. The shipper must weight the current risk of war.[8]

The S.R. & C.C. clause refers to strikes, riots, and civil commotions. It is not covered unless the company makes a current agreement on existing conditions.[9]

The Warehouse to Warehouse clause covers the movement of the cargo from the warehouse of the exporter to the carrying vessel, and at the destination port to the inland warehouse of the importer.[10]

percent of the total. This will cover incidentals and unexpected costs.

Once the foreign customer pays for the goods or accepts a draft, the title document and insurance policy or certificate are turned over to the foreign customer. This provides the foreign customer with a clean, insurable interest in the goods. If the goods are still intransit, but damaged, the exporter is still assumed to have adequate coverage and can file a claim with the insurer.

In addition, exporters should consider taking out fire insurance in the event goods must be stored in a warehouse at the foreign port of destination or the goods are held in consignment (bonded warehouse). Insurance coverage in the event of fire is obtained in various countries only against policies issued in local currency. If the goods are held in storage or bond for their benefit, then normally they are charged for the insurance coverage, otherwise it is charged to the foreign customer(s).

Warehouse Receipt. This is a document of title issued by a warehouseman which covers goods stored in a terminal or warehouse. Warehouse receipts are either issued in negotiable or nonnegotiable form.

A warehouse receipt becomes negotiable when it is made out "to order" of a named person or "to bearer." It is considered negotiable commodity paper that can be used as collateral and for trade financing.

A warehouse receipt becomes nonnegotiable when it is made out to a specific party. Only that party may authorize release of the goods from the warehouse. But, it can be transferred or assigned to another party. A nonnegotiable warehouse receipt is not a title document and cannot be used as collateral.

Shipping Documents: Official

Consular Invoice. This document is provided by most countries who have their own special blank forms at their consular offices. The principle function of a consular invoice is to enable the authorities of the country of destination to keep accurate records of the type, quantity, and value of the goods to be imported into their country. It is also a vital document for customs clearance of the goods.

There are generally two principle purposes of the consular invoice. The first is to assess import duties and the second is for general statistical purposes (i.e., to categorize or classify goods and determine their balance of trade and payment situation).

Different countries have different rules for the preparation of consular invoices. It is extremely important that the details of the document be accurate and, for this reason, heavy fines are levied against those who allow or make errors and omissions.

A consular invoice can list the value of the goods (cost, insurance, and freight), and the country of origin. Most governments that require preparation of this document charge a fee for their form. Once the document is presented to the local consulate office in your area for verification, another fee is assessed. These fees are usually negotiated with the foreign customer.

Certified Invoice.   Importers on occasion will require exporters to supply a certified invoice. It is usually a normal commercial invoice signed by the exporter certifying, for example, that its goods are in accordance with the terms and conditions of a letter of credit, or that its terms of sale agree with the sales contract, that the goods originated in a certain country (country of the exporter), or other statements which the importer requires.

Export License: Validated and General.   The United States controls the flow of goods and services overseas from its country by the implementation of export license restrictions and requirements and foreign country governments, by consular regulations and requirements.

With the exception of U.S. territories and possessions and, in most cases, Canada, all items for export require an export license. There are two basic licenses: Validated and General Licenses.[11]

The United States controls the export of certain commodities, technical data, and high-technology for reasons of national security, short supply, or foreign policy. The Validated Export License can be obtained from the Commerce Department's Office of Export Administration (OEA) for each order of these items for export. This requirement can apply to shipments of certain commodities to all countries.

It is important to pay particular attention to the preparation of applications for Validated Licenses when required. Under the jurisdiction of OEA, exporters of commodities are guided by the Export Administration Regulations which sets forth all licensing requirements including a complete list (the Commodity Control List) of commodities. The regulations identify the countries for which export license documents are required for each listed commodity. Copies of the Export Administration Regulations and the supplementary Export Administration Bulletins are available by subscription. Subscription forms can be obtained from your nearest Commerce District Office or from the Commerce's Office of Export Administration, Washington, D.C. Violations of Export Administration Regulations are subject to fines and/or imprisonment, as well as the revocation of export privileges.

According to the U.S. Department of Commerce *A Basic Guide to Exporting,* items requiring a Validated License include, but are not limited to, certain chemicals, special types of plastics, sophisticated electronic and communications equipment, scarce materials, and related technical data. Articles of war (i.e., arms, ammunition, implements of war) fall under the licensing jurisdiction of the U.S. State Department. (A few commodities specifically listed in the regulations, such as narcotics, dangerous drugs, and endangered fish and wildlife, are under the jurisdiction of other agencies.) By reviewing the Commodity Control List of the Export Administration Regulations, you can determine whether a Validated Export License is needed to export a particular commodity to a particular country.[12]

There are five special licensing procedures that may be used, when appropriate, in lieu of the individual license. Four of these may sometimes be used to reduce the number of individual licenses required for multiple exports; one reduces documentation requirements for certain types of activities. These procedures are described in the Export Administration Regulations. Re-exports of U.S.-origin commodities from one foreign country to another are controlled by requiring a re-export authorization, either specifically issued by OEA or as permitted by the regulations.

The following basically outlines some of the procedures for obtaining a Validated Export License:

1. Before an order is quoted, it is advisable to check with a U.S. Department of Commerce District Office to determine

the type of export license required for the country of destination.

2. If a Validated License is needed and the value of the shipment exceeds a certain amount or more (generally $5,000), there are special forms that must generally be supplied by the purchaser or obtained by the purchaser from the government of that country to support the request for an export license.
3. Requesting forms in advance will help reduce delays.
4. Before applying for an export license, it is generally necessary to have actually received an order.
5. After the required forms are received, an Application for Export License (Form ITA-622P) must be prepared and submitted to the Office of Export Administration with the forms obtained from the purchaser.
6. If everything is in order, a Validated Export License will generally be issued.

There are several types of *General Licenses*. These are published authorizations that cover the export of commodities not subject to Validated License requirements. Most items shipped overseas fall into one of these general classifications. It is not necessary to submit a formal application or receive written authorization to ship these products; they can be shipped by merely inserting the correct General License symbol on the export control document known as the Shipper's Export Declaration (discussed later).

If an export item does not require a validated export license, no formal application is necessary. Your Commerce District Office can advise as to the correct General License to use. You can also refer to the Export Administration Regulations described previously for a complete description of the purposes of each type of General License, restrictions on its use, and the special requirements for each. In general, however, it is a good idea to check with your District Office for assistance on export regulation problems.

In addition to the licensing requirements, it is necessary to show on ocean and air waybills of lading and commercial invoices, a destination control statement or antidiversion clause. This statement permits distribution and resale of the exported commodities or technical data to all destinations in the world other than those specifically exempted. There are different statements that must be used depending on the country of destination and the type of commodity or technical data to be exported.

Shipper's Export Declaration. This document has two purposes. It is a declaration (Commerce Form 7525-V*) by the exporter that the shipment is in accordance with U.S. export control regulations and that the commodity described is authorized for export under the validated or general license identified in the declaration by meeting all of the conditions of the license and the regulations. It also is a source of statistical information that appears in "FT 410," the Bureau of the Census' monthly foreign trade report ("U.S. Exports: Commodity by Country").[12]

The form contains information about the shipment, such as, the port of export, and the names of the exporter, importer (consignee), carrier, and describes the goods. Most ocean carriers now include the export declaration on their bills of lading, so this requirement can be completed when the ocean bill of lading is completed.

Import License. Like the export license regulations and requirements of the United States, many nations abroad impose import license regulations and requirements on their importers when importing goods and services from foreign suppliers (the same holds true for U.S. importers of goods and services from foreign suppliers). These regulations vary from country to country and change quite frequently. Import license (also used are import certificates which serve the same purpose as import licenses) regulations and requirements serve many of the same purposes: To control the flow of imports into their countries, to assess custom duties, limit certain types of imports, and the control and allocation of foreign exchange. The following are some examples of current import license regulations in some countries.

---

* These forms are available from the Government Printing Office, the District Office of the U.S. Department of Commerce International Trade Administration, or an office of the Collector of Customs.

South Korea

All imports require licenses and are obtainable only by registered traders. Their imports are classified into items: (1) "automatic approval" items, and (2) restricted "negative list" items. Licenses for goods under the automatic approval category (which covers a vast majority of goods) are issued by authorized banks. Imports classified as restricted items require the recommendation of the trade association plus the approval of the Ministry of Commerce and Industry (MCI) before an authorized bank can grant its approval.

The application for a license must be accompanied by a firm offer or a contract from the foreign supplier and legalized by the exporters local Consul of Korea or a local Chamber of Commerce. The validity of licenses is normally six months, but can be longer depending on the credit terms granted by the foreign supplier or on the manufacturing period required for the goods to be imported. All goods must be cleared through customs before the expiration date of the license.

In the case of letter of credit payment terms, licenses must be obtained prior to the opening of the letter of credit covering the shipment, regardless of the shipping date. Licenses may be extended for three months, sometimes for six months in certain circumstances. A tolerance on the licenses is allowed after dispatch of the goods for adjustment of the final quantity and value of the goods. The licenses may not be transferred from one importer to another.

Each importer must obtain approval from an authorized bank or import authorization from MCI for the respective import of goods at the time an import license is obtained. The maximum permissible credit terms for most imports is 120 days.

Foreign exchange for remittances abroad are bought from authorized banks on the strength of the import license against payment in Won or against payment in U.S. dollars obtained from an authorized foreign exchange business. Advance payment for imports require a license from an authorized bank and a guarantee from the government or a banking institution in the exporter's country for the refund of the advance.

Argentina

The following depicts some the import license regulations imposed on local Argentine importers over a period of time.

During the first quarter of 1984, the local government issued a series of resolutions for implementing a new import control system: Effective in January 1984, all imports into the country required an import certificate issued by the Secretariat of Commerce. Prior to applying for the certificate, the local importers were required to obtain from the foreign supplier: details of the shipment, a complete description of the goods, price information, and other information.

Imports were classified into three lists:

1. List I covered prohibited goods that could not be imported for a period of 180 days.
2. List II covered primarily capital goods, certain chemicals, plastics, and parts on List I.
3. List III covered raw materials and imports for the pharmaceutical industry plus medical equipment.

Imports covered by Lists I and II require prior approval from appropriate government agencies. Certificates were issued after approval was granted.

Any goods not on the above lists received certificates from the Secretariat of Commerce on an automatic basis.

FINANCIAL DOCUMENTS

The Promissory Note

A promissory note is an unconditional promise in writing, signed by the maker agreeing to pay on demand or in a definite time a sum certain in money to order or to bearer.[14] Generally, notes are used by U.S. exporters to cover shipments of goods with maturities of one year and longer (usually capital equipment or project financing type deals). They can also be used for refinancing past due receivables of foreign customers, unless a country does it for you by a renegotiation of its private debts (a result of shortages of hard currency).

In Europe, notes are preferable to bills of exchange or drafts. Many of the national laws governing promissory notes and bills of exchange are based on the Geneva Conventions of 1930 (Uniform Law Governing Bills of Exchange and Promissory Notes) which is discussed later in the chapter. It is preferable because a draft cannot be legally waived. Stamp taxes (i.e., Italy) imposed on drafts in certain countries is another factor that favors the use of promissory notes.

The instrument must be legally negotiable to give the purchaser the benefits of holder-in-due-course stature.[15] If the bill (note or draft) is denominated in a currency other than that of the currency of the exporter's country, the word *effective* should be written before the numeric and written amounts in letters on the note or bill of exchange. If not, the payment of claims (default of an obligation) in the currency of the foreign customer's country, converted at the relative rate of exchange, cannot in terms of the uniform law be refused by the creditor. The purpose of the word *effective* is to reduce the currency risk, but it offers no protection to the creditor in the United States. It is more commercially acceptable to specify that "payment is to made in U.S. dollars or other billing currency."

The Draft

The draft or sole/bill of exchange, commonly referred to as a bill of exchange (B/E) or simply a bill in Europe, is the instrument most widely used in international commercial trade to effect payment from foreign customers (see Figure 3–6). The international practice of using drafts differs from the domestic practice of selling merchandise on open account payment terms, in which payment is effected by a commercial invoice. A draft is an unconditional

FIGURE 3–6
An Example of a Draft

	NO._____
EXCHANGE FOR_____	DATE_____
_____ DAYS AFTER _____ PAY THIS **SOLE OF EXCHANGE**	
TO THE ORDER OF	
VALUE RECEIVED AND CHARGE SAME TO ACCOUNT OF	
TO	

order, in writing, signed by a person (seller), and addressed to a foreign customer (importer) or its agent to pay a specified amount of money on presentation (sight) of the instrument or at some specified future date (time). Drafts can be drawn in any currency. The normal practice for U.S. exporters is to draw drafts in U.S. dollars for the sale of goods and services.

The draft indicates to whom such payment is to be made, which is usually "to the order of . . . (seller's name)" or "to the order of . . . (name of the U.S. bank handling the collection of the draft on the seller's behalf)." The words *to the order of* are required along with other factors to make the instrument negotiable. An instrument so drawn can be transferred from one person to another simply by endorsement on the reverse side of the draft.

The party (seller or exporter) and the person who signs the draft is the *drawer*. The party or person to whom payment is to be made is the *payee*. Drawer and payee are usually the same person. The party to whom the draft is addressed is the *drawee*.

Drafts may be drawn at sight or time. Sight drafts are payable on presentation to the foreign customer. Time drafts are payable on a certain date after presentation (sight), after the date of the draft by using a document date (i.e., if the bill of lading date were August 21, 1988 and the payment terms were 90 days from B/L date, the due date would be November 21, 1988), or a fixed maturity date which specifies on the draft the date payment is due. The time period permitted in time drafts is often referred to as the *usance* time period of the draft. The due date or date payment is due, is often called the *maturity date* or *maturity* of the time draft. The drawee becomes the acceptor on time drafts as soon as the drawee has signed his name across the bill, along with writing the word *accepted* and date the draft was accepted, thereby signifying a *willingness* to pay the draft at maturity. When this occurs on time drafts, an *acceptance* is created. It is important for the exporter or supplier to note that the creation of an acceptance on a time draft is not a guarantee of payment from either the foreign customer, the foreign bank, or the U.S. collecting bank handling the draft for collection. Drafts may be drawn for any period of time. The most usual are 30, 60, 90, 120, 150, or 180 days after sight, or after date, including a fixed maturity date of the time draft. Other usances of 45 or 75 days or whatever after sight or after date are also used.

If an accepted draft is properly drawn, title to it (including right to payment) can be transferred from one party to the next. The seller who holds accepted drafts can obtain financing by selling them to a third party (usually commercial banks). This assumes the third party who purchases the drafts, expects payment from the drawee at maturity.

Drafts that are payable to bearer may be transferred by delivery of the draft to another party. A draft which is payable to order of a named party may be transferred by endorsement of the payee (often the same party as the drawee) and delivery of the instrument. Thus, the process of transfer from one party to another until the final holder is entitled to payment of the face amount at maturity.

Any one party that endorses the draft to another party is liable for the face amount of the draft. Under this type of circumstance, if the drawee of the draft does not accept it or pay it, the present holder of the draft would seek payment from the last endorser, who in turn seeks payment from the prior endorser, and on down the line to the drawer of the draft.

An endorsement consists of a signature and any related comments by or on behalf of the owner of a negotiable instrument. Therefore, the following warranties are implied:

- The instrument is genuine in all respects in what it purports to be, to the owner's knowledge.
- There is complete title to the holder of the instrument.
- That all prior parties to the instrument had the capacity to contract.
- The negotiable draft, at the time of endorsement, is a valid enforceable obligation.
- If the instrument is dishonored, and if all necessary procedures are taken, the endorser is obliged to pay the holder the face amount of the draft, except to the extent the endorser may have limited its liability (discussed below).

There are basically four types of endorsements. The effect of liability on the endorser or the further negotiability of the draft depends on the type of endorsement.

Blank Endorsement.   This is the most common type of endorsement. It consists only of the endorser's signature and specifies no endorsee. Therefore, it becomes payable to bearer and any further negotiation can be effected by mere delivery. The endorser in blank becomes liable to all subsequent holders should the drawee dishonor the instrument at maturity (due date). An endorser of a draft before acceptance warrants that it will be accepted and paid at maturity.[16]

Special Endorsement.   This type of endorsement specifies the name to whom or to whose order (done by writing *pay to the order of* [name of party] before the signature) the instrument is being transferred to and paid at maturity. The holder to whom the instrument is endorsed must endorse it before it can become further negotiable. This means that the holder of a blank endorsed instrument can make it payable to a specific person by filling in above the signature of the endorser *pay to the order of* followed by the name of the endorsee. This changes a blank to a special endorsement.[17]

Restrictive or Conditional Endorsement.   The holder of an instrument can make it restrictive or conditional by including a special phrase before the signature. For example, the phrase may read *pay to Mr. Z only,* or *for deposit to account number only.* It is also conceivable for the endorsee to be appointed the agent of the endorser with the restriction on the instrument *for collection,* or *as agent.* Transfer of the instrument can also be made based on some stated condition.

Qualified Endorsement.   An endorser can limit its liability by including a phrase before its signature such as *without recourse.* The endorser only is then eliminated from any secondary liability should the drawee dishonor the instrument. This means the holder of the instrument will look to all prior endorsers for payment should the ultimate obligor refuse to pay and/or accept the instrument.

Chapter 5 will explain the rights of a qualified holder in due course in instances when the foreign customer (drawee) refuses to pay a draft drawn by an exporter (drawer) on the drawee.

International Law for Drafts/Bills of Exchange

Internationally there is no unified law that defines the draft or bill of exchange. To a large extent most country laws covering negotiable instruments either base their definitions on the U.K. Bills of Exchange Act of 1882 or on the European system which is the Uniform Law on Bills of Exchange and Promissory Notes, drafted by the Geneva Conventions on Bills of Exchange of 1932.

The U.K. Bills of Exchange Act of 1882 defines a bill of exchange as:[18]

> An unconditional order in writing addressed by one person to another, signed by the person giving it, requiring the person to whom it is addressed to pay on demand or at a fixed or determinable future time a certain sum in money to or to the order of a specified person or to bearer.

The Uniform Law on Bills of Exchange and Promissory Notes as drafted by the Geneva Conventions on Bills of Exchange of 1932 stipulates that:[19]

A bill of exchange contains:

1. The term *bill of exchange* inserted in the body of the instrument and expressed in the language employed in drawing up the instrument.
2. An unconditional order to pay a determinant sum of money.
3. The name of the person who is to say (*drawee*).
4. A statement of the time of payment.
5. A statement of the place where payment is to be made.
6. The name of the person to whom or to whose order payment is to be made.
7. A statement of the date and of the place where the bill is issued.
8. The signature of the person who issues the bill (*drawer*).

Countries that are members of the Geneva Convention are:

Belgium	France	Italy	Norway
Brazil	Greece	Japan	Austria
Denmark	Poland	Luxembourg	Switzerland
Germany	Portugal	Monaco	U.S.S.R.
Finland	Sweden	Netherlands	Hungary

Other countries have signed the Geneva Convention with certain reservations, and others have included similar wordings in their laws.

The Draft Uniform Law on International Bills of Exchange and International Promissory Notes as drawn up by the United Nations Commission on International Trade in 1973 stipulated that:

An international bill of exchange is a written instrument which:[20]

1. Contains, in the text thereof, the words *Pay against this International Bill of Exchange, drawn subject to the Convention of* . . . (or words of similar import).
2. Contains an unconditional order whereby one person (the drawer) directs another person (the drawee) to pay a definite sum of money to a specified person (the payee) or to his order.
3. It is payable on demand or at a definite time.
4. It is signed by the drawer.
5. It shows that it is drawn in a country other than the country of the drawee or of the payee or of the place where payment is to be made.

The principal difference between the U.K. Act and the Geneva Law is that the Geneva Law requires the words *Bill of Exchange* to be included in the text and a statement of the date and of the place where the bill is issued. The Draft Law of the United Nations Commission is aimed at providing rules for a special negotiable instrument for optional use in international transactions.

For the interest of the reader, article 3 of the U.S. Uniform Commercial Code (UCC) is the statutory law in the United States governing commercial paper (checks, promissory notes, bills of exchange, trade acceptances, and similar instruments). It covers the various elements and requirements of a negotiable instrument in all states, except Louisiana, which is governed by Code Napoleon (French Code), its legal effect, the rights of the parties thereof, and other related legal matters.

Under the Commercial Paper Article of the Code a writing to be a negotiable instrument must:[21]

A. Be signed by the maker or the drawer—("signed" includes any symbol executed by a party with intention to authenticate a writing).

B. Contain an unconditional promise or order to pay a sum certain in money and no other promise, order, obligation or power given by the maker or drawer except as authorized by the Code. A sum certain in money includes foreign money. A promise or order otherwise unconditional is not made conditional by the facts, among others, that the instrument:

1. is limited to payment out of a particular fund or the proceeds of a particular source, of the instrument issued by a government or governmental agency or unit.

2. is limited to payment out of the entire assets of a partnership, unincorporated association, trust or estate by or on behalf of which the instrument is issued.

C. Be payable on demand or at definite time.

1. Instruments payable on demand include those at sight or on presentation and those in which no time for payment is stated.

2. Instruments payable at a definite time include those which by their terms are payable on or before a stated date or at a fixed period after a stated date or at a fixed period after sight or at a definite time subject to any acceleration.

3. Instruments which by their terms are payable only upon an act or event uncertain as to time of occurrence are not payable at a definite time even though the act or event has occurred.

D. Be payable to order or to bearer.

A writing which conforms to the above provisions is defined in the Commercial Paper Article as:[22]

1. A *draft* ("bill of exchange") if it is an order.
2. A *check* if it is a draft drawn on a bank and payable on demand.
3. A *certificate of deposit* if it is an acknowledgement by a bank of receipt of money with an engagement to repay it.
4. A *note* if it is a promise other than a certificate of deposit.

Some examples of drafts that would not meet the UCC requirements would be: A draft whose maturity date on the face of it reads, *payable 60 days after clearance of goods through customs.* Another is a draft that contains a clause which makes payment contingent, *the goods must meet acceptable performance standards.*

APPENDIX 3–A: AMERICAN FOREIGN TRADE DEFINITIONS

Adopted July 30, 1941, by a joint committee representing the Chamber of Commerce of the United States of America, the National Council of American Importers, Inc., and the National Foreign Trade Council, Inc.

FOREWORD

Since the issuance of American Foreign Trade Definitions in 1919, many changes in practice have occurred. The 1919 Definitions did much to clarify and simplify foreign trade practice, and received wide recognition and use by buyers and sellers throughout the world. At the 27th National Foreign Trade Convention, 1940, further revision and clarification of these Definitions was urged as necessary to assist the foreign trader in the handling of his transactions.

The following Revised American Foreign Trade Definitions–1941 are recommended for general use by both exporters and importers. These revised definitions have no status at law unless there is specific legislation providing for them, or unless they are confirmed by court decisions. Hence, it is suggested that sellers and buyers agree to their acceptance as part of the contract of sale. These revised definitions will then become legally binding upon all parties.

In view of changes in practice and procedure since 1919, certain new responsibilities for sellers and buyers are included in these revised definitions. Also, in many instances, the old responsibilities are more clearly defined than in the 1919 Definitions, and the changes should be beneficial both to sellers and buyers. Widespread acceptance will lead to a greater standardization of foreign trade procedure, and to the avoidance of much misunderstanding.

Adoption by exporters and importers of these revised terms will impress on all parties concerned their respective responsibilities and rights.

GENERAL NOTES OF CAUTION

1. As foreign trade definitions have been issued by organizations in various parts of the world, and as the courts of countries have interpreted these definitions in different ways, it is important that sellers and buyers agree that their contracts are subject to the Revised American Foreign Trade Definitions–1941 and that the various points listed are accepted by both parties.

2. In addition to the foreign trade terms listed herein, there are terms that are at times used, such as Free Harbor, CIF & C (Cost, Insurance, Freight, and Commission), CIFC & I (Cost, Insurance Freight, Commissions, and Interest), CIF Landed (Cost, Insurance, Freight, Landed), and others. None of these should be used unless there has first been a definite understanding as to the exact meaning thereof. It is unwise to attempt to interpret other terms in the light of the terms given herein. Hence, whenever possible, one of the terms defined herein should be used.

3. It is unwise to use abbreviations in quotations or in contracts which might be subject to misunderstanding.

4. When making quotations, the familiar terms *hundredweight* or *ton* should be avoided. A hundredweight can be 100 pounds of the short ton, or 112 pounds of the long ton. A ton can be a short ton of 2,000 pounds, or a metric ton of 2,204.6 pounds, or a long ton of 2,240 pounds. Hence, the type of hundredweight or ton should be clearly stated in quotations and in sales confirmations. Also, all terms referring to quantity, weight, volume, length, or surface should be clearly defined and agreed upon.

5. If inspection, or certificate of inspection, is required, it should be agreed, in advance, whether the cost thereof is for account of seller or buyer.

6. Unless otherwise agreed upon, all expenses are for the account of seller up to the point at which the buyer must handle the subsequent movement of goods.

7. There are a number of elements in a contract that do not fall within the scope of these foreign trade definitions. Hence, no mention of these is made herein. Seller and buyer should agree to these separately when negotiating contracts. This particularly applies to so-called "customary" practices.

DEFINITIONS OF QUOTATIONS

(I) Ex (Point of Origin)
"Ex Factory", "Ex Mill", "Ex Mine", "Ex Plantation", "Ex Warehouse", (named point of origin)

Under this term, the price quoted applies only at the point of origin, and the seller agrees to place the goods at the disposal of the buyer at the agreed place on the date or within the period fixed.

Under this quotation:

Seller must

1. Bear all costs and risk of the goods until such time as the buyer is obliged to take delivery thereof.
2. Render the buyer, at the buyer's request and expense, assistance in obtaining the documents issued in the country of origin, or of shipment, or of both, which the buyer may require either for purposes of exportation, or of importation at destination.

Buyer must

1. Take delivery of the goods as soon as they have been placed at his disposal at the agreed place on the date or within the period fixed.
2. Pay export taxes, or other fees or charges, if any, levied because of exportation.
3. Bear all costs and risks of the goods from the time when he is obligated to take delivery thereof.
4. Pay all costs and charges incurred in obtaining the documents issued in the country of origin, or of shipment, or both, which may be required either for purposes of exportation, or of importation at destination.

(II) F.O.B. (Free on Board) *

(II-A) "FOB (named inland carrier at named inland point of departure)". Under this term, the price quoted applies only at inland shipping point, and the seller arranges for loading of the goods on, or in, railway cars, trucks, lighters, barges, aircraft, or other conveyance furnished for transportation.

Under this quotation:

---

* See Comments on all F.O.B. Terms on page 227.

Seller must

1. Place goods on, or in, conveyance, or deliver to inland carrier for loading.
2. Provide clean bill of lading or other transportation receipt, freight collect.
3. Be responsible for any loss or damage, or both, until goods have been placed in, or on, conveyance at loading point, and clean bill of lading or other transportation receipt has been furnished by the carrier.
4. Render the buyer, at the buyer's request and expense, assistance in obtaining the documents issued in the country of origin, or of shipment, or of both, which the buyer may require either for purposes of exportation, or of importation at destination.

Buyer must

1. Be responsible for all movement of the goods from inland point of loading, and pay all transportation costs.
2. Pay export taxes, or other fees or charges, if any, levied because of exportation.
3. Be responsible for any loss or damage, or both, incurred after loading at named inland point of departure.
4. Pay all costs and charges incurred in obtaining the documents issued in the country of origin, or of shipment, or of both, which may be required either for purposes of exportation, or of importation at destination.

(II-B) "FOB (named inland carrier at named inland point of departure) Freight Prepare To (named point of exportation)"*. Under this term, the seller quotes a price including transportation charges to the named point of exportation and prepays freight to named point of exportation, without assuming responsibility for the goods after obtaining a clean bill of lading or other transportation receipt at named inland point of departure.

Under this quotation:

Seller must

1. Assume the seller's obligations as under II-A, except that under (2) he must provide clean bill of lading or other transportation receipt, freight prepaid to named point of exportation.

Buyer must

1. Assume the same buyer's obligations as under II-A, except that he

does not pay freight from loading point to named point of exportation.

(II-C) "FOB (named inland carrier at named inland point of depature) Freight Allowed To (named point)"*.   Under this term, the seller quotes a price including the transportation charges to the named point, shipping freight collect and deducting the cost of transportation, without assuming responsibility for the goods after obtaining a clean bill of lading or other transportation receipt at named inland point of departure.

Under this quotation:

Seller must

1. Assume the same seller's obligations as under II-A, but deducts from his invoice the transportation cost to named point.

Buyer must

1. Assume the same buyer's obligations as under II-A, including payment of freight from inland loading point to named point, for which seller has made deduction.

(II-D) "FOB (named inland carrier at named point of exportation)"*.   Under this term, the seller quotes a price including the costs of transportation of the goods to named point of exportation, bearing any loss or damage, or both incurred up to that point.

Under this quotation:

Seller must

1. Place goods on, or in, conveyance, or deliver to inland carrier for loading.
2. Provide clean bill of lading or other transportation receipt, paying all transportation costs from loading point to named point of exportation.
3. Be responsible for any loss or damage, or both, until goods have arrived in, or on, inland conveyance at the named point of exportation.
4. Render the buyer, at the buyer's request and expense, assistance in obtaining the documents issued in the country of origin, or of shipment, or of both, which the buyer may require either for purposes of exportation, or of importation at destination.

Buyer must

1. Be responsible for all movements of the goods from inland conveyance at named point of exportation.

2. Pay export taxes, or other fees or charges, if any, levied because of exportation.
3. Be responsible for any loss or damage, or both, incurred after goods have arrived in, or on, inland conveyance at the named point of exportation.
4. Pay all costs and charges incurred in obtaining the documents issued in the country of origin, or of shipment, or both, which may be required either for purposes of exportation, or of importation at destination.

(II-E) "FOB Vessel (names port of shipment)"*.   Under this term, the seller quotes a price covering all expenses up to, and including, delivery of the goods upon the overseas vessel provided by, or for, the buyer at the named port of shipment.

Under this quotation:

Seller must

1. Pay all charges incurred in placing goods actually on board the vessel designated and provided by, or for, the buyer on the date or within the period fixed.
2. Provide clean ship's receipt or on-board bill of lading.
3. Be responsible for any loss or damage, or both until goods have been placed on board the vessel on the date or within the period fixed.
4. Render the buyer, at the buyer's request and expense, assistance in obtaining the documents issued in the country of origin, or of shipment, or of both, which the buyer may require either for purposes of exportation, or of importation at destination.

Buyer must

1. Give seller adequate notice of name, sailing date, loading berth of, and delivery time to, the vessel.
2. Bear the additional costs incurred and all risks of the goods from the time when the seller has placed them at his disposal if the vessel named by him fails to arrive, or to load, within the designated time.
3. Handle all subsequent movement of the goods to destination:
   a. provide and pay for insurance.
   b. provide and pay for ocean and other transportation.
4. Pay export taxes, or other fees or charges, if any, levied because of exportation.
5. Be responsible for any loss or damage, or both, after goods have been loaded on board the vessel.
6. Pay all costs and charges incurred in obtaining the documents, other than clean ship's receipt or bill of lading, issued in the country of origin, or of shipment, or of both, which may be required either for purposes of exportation, or of importation at destination.

(II-F) "FOB (named inland point in country of transportation)"*.   Under this term the seller quotes a price including cost of the merchandise and all costs of transportation to the named inland point in the country of importation.

Under this quotation:

Seller must

1. Provide and pay for all transportation to the named inland point in the country of importation.
2. Pay export taxes, or other fees or charges, if any, levied because of exportation.
3. Provide and pay for marine insurance.
4. Provide and pay for war risk insurance, unless otherwise agreed upon between the seller and buyer.
5. Be responsible for any loss or damage, or both, until arrival of goods on conveyance at the named inland point in the country of importation.
6. Pay the costs of certificates of origin, consular invoices, or any other documents issued in the country of origin, or of shipment, or of both, which the buyer may require for the importation of goods into the country of destination and, where necessary, for their passage in transit through another country.
7. Pay all costs of landing, including wharfage, landing charges, and taxes, if any.
8. Pay all costs of customs entry in the country of importation.
9. Pay customs duties and all taxes applicable to imports, if any, in the country of importation.

Note: *The seller under this quotation must realize that he is accepting important responsibilities, costs, and risks, and should therefore be certain to obtain adequate insurance. On the other hand, the importer or buyer may desire such quotations to relieve him of the risks of the voyage and to assure him of his landed costs at inland point in country of importation. When competition is keen, or the buyer is accustomed to such quotations from other sellers, seller may quote such terms, being careful to protect himself in an appropriate manner.*

Buyer must

1. Take prompt delivery of goods from conveyance upon arrival at destination.
2. Bear any costs and be responsible for all loss or damage, or both, after arrival at destination.

---

* See Note and Comments on all F.O.B. Terms on page 226–27.

COMMENTS ON ALL F.O.B. TERMS

In connection with F.O.B. terms, the following points of caution are recommended:

1. The method of inland transportation, such as trucks, railroad cars, lighters, barges, or aircraft, should be specified.
2. If any switching charges are involved during the inland transportation, it should be agreed, in advance, whether these charges are for account of the seller or the buyer.
3. The term *FOB (named port),* without designating the exact point at which the liability of the seller terminates and the liability of the buyer begins, should be avoided. The use of this term gives rise to disputes as to the liability of the seller or the buyer in the event of loss or damage arising while the goods are in port, and before delivery to or on board the ocean carrier. Misunderstandings may be avoided by naming the specific point of delivery.
4. If lighterage or trucking is required in the transfer of goods from the inland conveyance to ship's side, and there is a cost thereof, it should be understood, in advance, whether this cost is for account of the seller or the buyer.
5. The seller should be certain to notify the buyer of the minimum quantity required to obtain a carload, a truckload, or a barge load freight rate.
6. Under FOB terms, excepting "FOB (named inland point in country of importation)", the obligation to obtain ocean freight space, and marine and war risk insurance, rests with the buyer. Despite this obligation on the part of the buyer, in many trades the seller obtains the ocean freight space, and marine and war risk insurance, and provides for shipment on behalf of the buyer. Hence, seller and buyer must have an understanding as to whether the buyer will obtain the ocean freight space and marine and war risk insurance, as is his obligation, or whether the seller agrees to do this for the buyer.
7. For the seller's protection, he should provide in his contract of sale that marine insurance obtained by the buyer include standard warehouse to warehouse coverage.

(III) FAS (Free Along Side)

Note: *Seller and buyer should consider not only the definitions but also the "Comments" given at the end of this section in order to understand fully their respective responsibilities and rights under "FAS" terms.*

"FAS Vessel (named port of shipment)". Under this term, the seller quotes a price including delivery of the goods along side overseas vessel and within reach of its loading tackle.

Under this quotation:

Seller must

1. Place goods along side vessel or on dock designated and provided by, or for, buyer on the date or within the period fixed; pay any heavy lift charges, where necessary, up to this point.
2. Provide clean dock or ship receipt.
3. Be responsible for any loss of damage, or both, until goods have been delivered along side the vessel or on the dock.
4. Render the buyer, at the buyer's request and expense, assistance in obtaining the documents issued in the country of origin, or of shipment, or of both, which the buyer may require either for purposes of exportation, or of importation at destination.

Buyer must

1. Give seller adequate notice of name, sailing date, loading berth of, and delivery time to, the vessel.
2. Handle all subsequent movement of the goods from along side the vessel.
   a. Arrange and pay for demurrage or storage charges, or both, in warehouse or on wharf, where necessary.
   b. Provide and pay for insurance.
   c. Provide and pay for ocean and other transportation.
3. Pay export taxes, or other fees or charges, if any, levied because of exportation.
4. Be responsible for any loss or damage, or both, while the goods are on a lighter or other conveyance along side vessel within reach of its loading tackle, or on the dock awaiting loading, or until actually loaded on board the vessel, and subsequent thereto.
5. Pay all costs and charges incurred in obtaining the documents, other than clean dock or ship receipt, issued in the country of origin, or of shipment, or of both, which may be required either for purposes of exportation, or of importation at destination.

FAS COMMENTS

1. Under FAS terms, the obligation to obtain ocean freight space, and marine and war risk insurance, rests with the buyer. Despite this obligation on the part of the buyer, in many trades the seller obtains ocean freight space, and marine and war risk insurance, and provides for

shipment on behalf of the buyer. In others, the buyer notifies the seller to make delivery along side a vessel designated by the buyer and the buyer provides his own marine and war risk insurance. Hence, seller and buyer must have an understanding as to whether the buyer will obtain the ocean freight space and marine and war risk insurance, as is his obligation, or whether the seller agrees to do this for the buyer.

2. For the seller's protection, he should provide in his contract of sale that marine insurance obtained by the buyer include standard warehouse to warehouse coverage.

(IV) C&F (Cost and Freight)

Note: *Seller and buyer should consider not only the definitions but also the "C&F Comments" and the "C&F and CIF Comments" (pages 230–33), in order to understand fully their respective responsibilities and rights under "C&F" terms.*

"C&F (named point of destination)".   Under this term, the seller quotes a price including the cost of transportation to the named point of destination.

Under this quotation:

Seller must

1. Provide and pay for transportation to named point of destination.
2. Pay export taxes, or other fees or charges, if any, levied because of exportation.
3. Obtain and dispatch promptly to buyer, or his agent, clean bill of lading to named point of destination.
4. Where received-for-shipment ocean bill of lading may be tendered, be responsible for any loss or damage, or both, until the goods have been delivered into the custody of the ocean carrier.
5. Where on-board ocean bill of lading is required, be responsible for any loss or damage, or both, until the goods have been delivered on board the vessel.
6. Provide, at the buyer's request and expense, certificates of origin, consular invoices, or any other documents issued in the country or origin, or of shipment, or of both, which the buyer may require for importation or goods into country of destination and, where necessary, for their passage in transit through another country.

Buyer must

1. Accept the document when presented.
2. Receive goods upon arrival, handle and pay for all subsequent movement of the goods, including taking delivery from vessel in

accordance with bill of lading clauses and terms; pay all costs of landing, including any duties, taxes, and other expenses at named point of destination.

3. Provide and pay for insurance.
4. Be responsible for loss of or damage to goods, or both, from time and place at which seller's obligations under (4) or (5) above have ceased.
5. Pay the costs of certificates of origin, consular invoices, or any other documents issued in the country of origin, or of shipment, or of both, which may be required for the importation of goods into the country of destination and, where necessary, for their passage in transit through another country.

C&F COMMENTS

1. For the seller's protection, he should provide in his contract of sale that marine insurance obtained by the buyer include standard warehouse to warehouse coverage.

2. The comments listed under the following CIF terms in many cases apply to C&F terms as well, and should be read and understood by the C&F seller and buyer.

(V) CIF (Cost, Insurance, Freight)

Note: *Seller and buyer should consider not only the definitions but also the "Comments", at the end of this section, in order to understand fully their respective responsibilities and rights under "CIF" terms.*

"CIF (named point of destination)".   Under this term, the seller quotes a price including the cost of the goods, the marine insurance, and all transportation charges to the named point of destination.

Under this quotation:

Seller must

1. Provide and pay for transportation to named point of destination.
2. Pay export taxes, or other fees or charges, if any, levied because of exportation.
3. Provide and pay for marine insurance.
4. Provide war risk insurance as obtainable in seller's market at time of shipment at buyer's expense, unless seller has agreed that buyer provide for war risk coverage (See Comment 10 (c), page 233).
5. Obtain and dispatch promptly to buyer, or his agent, clean bill of lading to named point of destination, and also insurance policy or negotiable insurance certificate.

6. Where received-for-shipment ocean bill of lading may be tendered, be responsible for any loss or damage, or both, until the goods have been delivered into the custody of the ocean carrier.
7. Where on-board ocean bill of lading is required, be responsible for any loss or damage, or both, until the goods have been delivered on board the vessel.
8. Provide, at the buyer's request and expense, certificates of origin, consular invoices, or any other documents issued in the country of origin, or of shipment, or both, which the buyer may require for importation of goods into country of destination and, where necessary, for their passage in transit through another country.

Buyer must

1. Accept the documents when presented.
2. Receive the goods upon arrival, handle and pay for all subsequent movement of the goods, including taking delivery from vessel in accordance with bill of lading clauses and terms; pay all costs of landing, including any duties, taxes, and other expenses at named point of destination.
3. Pay for war risk insurance provided by seller.
4. Be responsible for loss of or damage to goods, or both, from time and place at which seller's obligations under (6) or (7) above have ceased.
5. Pay the cost of certificates of origin, consular invoices, or any other documents issued in the country or origin, or of shipment, or both, which may be required for importation of the goods into the country of destination and, where necessary, for their passage in transit through another country.

C&F AND CIF COMMENTS

Under C&F and CIF contracts there are the following points on which the seller and the buyer should be in complete agreement at the time that the contract is concluded:

1. It should be agreed upon, in advance, who is to pay for miscellaneous expenses, such as weighing or inspection charges.
2. The quantity to be shipped on any one vessel should be agreed upon, in advance, with a view to the buyer's capacity to take delivery upon arrival and discharge of the vessel within the free time allowed at the port of importation.
3. Although the terms C&F and CIF are generally interpreted to provide that charges for consular invoices and certificates of origin are for the account of the buyer, and are charged sepa-

rately, in many trades these charges are included by the seller in his price. Hence, seller and buyer should agree, in advance, whether these charges are part of the selling price, or will be invoiced separately.

4. The point of final destination should be definitely known in the event the vessel discharges at a port other than the actual destination of the goods.

5. When ocean freight space is difficult to obtain, or forward freight contracts cannot be made at firm rates, it is advisable that sales contracts, as an exception to regular C&F or CIF terms, should provide that shipment within the contract period be subject to ocean freight space being available to the seller, and should also provide that changes in the cost of ocean transportation between the time of sale and the time of shipment be for account of the buyer.

6. Normally, the seller is obligated to prepay the ocean freight. In some instances, shipments are made freight collect and the amount of the freight is deducted from the invoice rendered by the seller. It is necessary to be in agreement on this, in advance, to avoid misunderstanding which arises from foreign exchange fluctuations which might affect the actual cost of transportation, and from interest charges which might accrue under letter of credit financing. Hence, the seller should always prepay the ocean freight unless he has a specific agreement with the buyer, in advance, that goods can be shipped freight collect.

7. The buyer should recognize that he does not have the right to insist on inspection of goods prior to accepting the documents. The buyer should not refuse to take delivery of goods on account of delay in the receipt of documents, provided the seller has used due diligence in their dispatch through the regular channels.

8. Sellers and buyers are advised against including in a CIF contract any indefinite clause at variance with the obligations of a CIF contract as specified in these Definitions. There have been numerous court decisions in the United States and other countries invalidating CIF contracts because of the inclusion of indefinite clauses.

9. Interest charges should be included in cost computations and should not be charged as a separate item in CIF contracts, unless otherwise agreed upon, in advance, between the seller and buyer; in which case, however, the term CIF and I (Cost, Insurance, Freight and Interest) should be used.

10. In connection with insurance under CIF sales, it is necessary that seller and buyer be definitely in accord upon the following points:

a. The character of the marine insurance should be agreed upon in so far as being WA (With Average) or FPA (Free of Particular Average), as well as any other special risks that are covered in specific trades, or against which the buyer may wish individual protection. Among the special risks that should be considered and agreed upon between seller and buyer are theft, pilferage, leakage, breakage, sweat, contact with other cargoes, and others peculiar to any particular trade. It is important that contingent or collect freight and customs duty should be insured to cover Particular Average losses, as well as total loss after arrival and entry but before delivery.

b. The seller is obligated to exercise ordinary care and diligence in selecting an underwriter that is in good financial standing. However, the risk of obtaining settlement of insurance claims rests with the buyer.

c. War risk insurance under this term is to be obtained by the seller at the expense and risk of the buyer. It is important that the seller be in definite accord with the buyer on this point, particularly as to the cost. It is desirable that the goods be insured against both marine and war risk with the same underwriter, so that there can be no difficulty arising from the determination of the cause of the loss.

d. Seller should make certain that in his marine or war risk insurance, there be included the standard protection against strikes, riots and civil commotions.

e. Seller and buyer should be in accord as to the insured valuation, bearing in mind that merchandise contributes in General Average on certain bases of valuation which differ in various trades. It is desirable that a competent insurance broker be consulted, in order that full value be covered and troubled avoided.

(VI) "Ex Dock (named port of importation)"

Note: *Seller and buyer should consider not only the definitions but also the "Ex Dock Comments" at the end of this section, in order to understand fully their respective responsibilities and rights under "Ex Dock" terms.*

Under this term seller quotes a price including the cost of the goods and all additional costs necessary to place the goods on the dock at the named port of importation, duty paid, if any.

Under this quotation:

Seller must

1. Provide and pay for transportation to named port of importation.
2. Pay export taxes, or other fees or charges, if any, levied because of exportation.
3. Provide and pay for marine insurance.
4. Provide and pay for war risk insurance, unless otherwise agreed upon between the buyer and seller.
5. Be responsible for any loss or damage, or both, until the expiration of the free time allowed on the dock at the named port of importation.
6. Pay the costs of certificates of origin, consular invoices, legalization of bill of lading, or any other documents issued in the country or origin, or of shipment, or of both, which the buyer may require for the importation of goods into the country of destination and, where necessary, for their passage in transit through another country.
7. Pay all costs of landing, including wharfage, landing charges, and taxes, if any.
8. Pay all costs of customs entry in the country of importation.
9. Pay customs duties and all taxes applicable to imports, if any, in the county of importation, unless otherwise agreed upon.

Buyer must

1. Take delivery of the goods on the dock at the named port of importation within the free time allowed.
2. Bear the cost and risk of the goods if delivery is not taken within the free time allowed.

Ex Dock Comments

This term is used principally in United States import trade. It has various modifications, such as "Ex Quay", and "Ex Pier" but it is seldom, if ever, used in American export practice. Its use in quotations for export is not recommended.

APPENDIX 3–B: INCOTERMS

Purpose of Incoterms

1. The purpose of "Incoterms" is to provide a set of international rules for the interpretation of the chief terms used in foreign trade contracts, for the optional use of businessmen who prefer the certainty of uniform international rules to the uncertainties of the varied interpretations of the same terms in different countries.

2. Frequently parties to a contract are unaware of the differences of trading practice in their respective countries. The existing diversity of interpretation is a constant source of friction in international trade, leading to misunderstandings, disputes and references to the courts with all the waste of time and money that these entail. It was with the object of making available to traders a means of overcoming the worst causes of this friction that the International Chamber of Commerce first published in 1936 a set of international rules for the interpretation of trade terms. These rules were known as "Incoterms 1936." Amendments and additions were later made in 1953, 1967, 1976 and 1980 in order to provide an up-to-date set of rules broadly in line with the current practice of a majority of the businessmen engaged in international trade.

3. The chief difficulties met with by importers and exporters are of three kinds. First, uncertainty as to the law of what country will be applicable to their contracts, second, difficulties arising from inadequate information, and, third, difficulties arising from diversity in interpretation. These handicaps to trade can be much reduced by the use of "Incoterms."

Provision for the Custom of the Particular Trade or Port

4. On some points, it has been found impossible to give an absolutely definite ruling. In that case, the rules have left the matter to be decided by the custom of the particular trade or port. Every endeavor has been made to limit such references to custom to the absolute minimum, but it has been impossible to avoid them altogether.

In order to avoid misunderstandings and disputes, the seller and the buyer would be well advised to keep such general and particular customs in mind when negotiating their contract.

Special Provisions in Individual Contracts

5. Special provisions in the individual contract between the parties will override anything provided in the rules.

6. Parties may adopt "Incoterms" as the general basis of their contract, but may also specify particular variations of them or additions to them, such as may be suited to the particular trade or the circumstances of the time or their individual convenience. For instance, some merchants require a CIF supplier to provide war risk insurance as well as marine insurance. In that case, the purchaser may specify "Incoterms CIF plus war risk insurance". The seller will then quote his price on that basis.

Some abbreviations in common use in domestic trade may not be readily understood in international trade. It is recommended that for the sake of clarity the use of such domestic abbreviations should be avoided.

Variations of C&F and CIF Contracts
7. Merchants should be extremely cautious in using, in their contracts of sale, variations of the terms C&F and CIF such as C&F and CIF Cleared and Customs Duty Paid or similar expressions. The addition of a word or even a letter to C&F and CIF may sometimes have an entirely unforeseen result, and the character of the contract may be changed. Merchants may find that a court will refuse to recognize certain variations as being C&F or CIF contracts at all. It is always safer in such cases explicitly to state in the contracts what obligations and charges each party is meant to assume.

"Incoterms" and the Contract of Carriage
8. Merchants adopting these rules in their contracts should keep clearly in mind the fact that they refer solely to the relationship between seller and buyer, and that none of the provisions affect, either directly or indirectly, the relations of either party with the carrier as defined in the contract of carriage.

However, the law of carriage of goods will determine how the seller should fulfill his obligation to deliver the goods "to the carrier". The terms FOB, C&F and CIF, which have been retained unchanged in the present version of "Incoterms", all conform with the practice of delivering the goods on board the vessel. Nowadays goods are usually delivered by the seller to a carrier before shipment on board takes place. In such cases merchants should use the new and amended terms: Free-carrier (named point), Freight/Carriage paid to, or Freight/Carriage and Insurance paid to. A definition of "carrier" has been inserted in a note to the term Free carrier (named point).

"Delivered . . ." Terms
9. Unless there is a clear agreement to the contrary expressed in the contract of sale, it is no part of the duties of the seller to procure a policy of insurance available for the benefit of the buyer.

However, in certain circumstances, such as those contemplated in article A.5 of the rules relating to the sale of goods on "Delivered at Frontier" terms, the parties might be well advised jointly to consider what duties, if any, the seller or the buyer should assume in matters pertaining to the insurance of the goods from the point of departure in the country of dispatch to the point of final destination chosen by the buyer.

Unless there is a clear agreement to the contrary expressed in the contract of sale, any document of transport placed by the seller at the disposal of the buyer must be clean[1].

Unless the context otherwise requires, the following expressions have the meanings hereby assigned to them, that is to say:

"Country of dispatch" means the country from which the seller has to dispatch the goods to the named placed of delivery at the frontier, or in the country of importation, as the case may be, whether by public carrier or by his own means of transport.

"Expenses" means any cost, charges and expenses of or incidental to the performance by the parties of their respective duties and which shall be incurred, borne and paid by parties in accordance with the rules applicable.

Definition of Bill of Lading

10. As used in these rules the term "bill of lading" is a shipped bill of lading, issued by or on behalf of the carrier, and is evidence of a contract of carriage as well as proof of delivery of the goods on board the vessel.
11. A bill of lading may be either freight prepaid or freight payable at destination. In the former case the document is usually not obtainable until freight has been paid.

Simplified Documentary Practices

12. In liner trade, bills of lading are frequently replaced by nonnegotiable documents ("sea waybills", "liner waybills", "freight receipts", "combined or multimodal transport documents") and the feasibility of transmitting the relevant information by automatic data processing is presently being investigated. When bills of lading are not used in the relevant trade, the parties should either use the Free carrier (named point) or Freight/ Carriage paid to terms or alternatively, stipulate in the FOB, C&F and CIF terms that the seller should provide the buyer with the usual document or other evidence of the delivery of the goods to the carrier. Merchants wishing to see these rules should specify that their contracts will be governed by the provisions of "Incoterms". If they wish to refer to a term in a previous version they should specifically so state.

---

[1] For the definition of the term "clean shipping document" in banking practice, references should be made to Article 18 of "Uniform Customs and Practice for Documentary Credits" (ICC Publication 290). For the possibility of agreement between the parties to the contract of sale as to what clauses about condition, quality or quantity superimposed by the carrier on the document of transport would be acceptable to the seller and the buyer, attention is invited to Publication 283 "The Problem of Clean Bills of Lading."

Ex Works*

Ex Factory, Ex Mill, Ex Plantation, Ex Warehouse

"Ex Works" means that the seller's only responsibility is to make the goods available at his premises (i.e., works or factory). In particular he is not responsible for loading the goods on the vehicle provided by the buyer, unless otherwise agreed. The buyer bears the full cost and risk involved in bringing the goods from there to the desired destination. This term thus represents the minimum obligation for the seller.

A. *The seller must:*

1. Supply the goods in conformity with the contract of sale, together with such evidence of conformity as may be required by the contract.
2. Place the goods at the disposal of the buyer at the time as provided in the contract, at the point of delivery named or which is usual for the delivery of such goods and for their loading on the conveyance to be provided by the buyer.
3. Provide at his own expense the packing, if any, that is necessary to enable the buyer to take delivery of the goods.
4. Give the buyer reasonable notice as to when the goods will be at his disposal.
5. Bear the cost of checking operations (such as checking quality, measuring, weighing, counting) which are necessary for the purpose of placing the goods at the disposal of the buyer.
6. Bear all risks and expense of the goods until they have been placed at the disposal of the buyer at the time as provided in the contract, provided that the goods have been duly appropriated to the contract, that is to say, clearly set aside or otherwise identified as the contract goods.
7. Render the buyer, at the latter's request, risk and expense, every assistance in obtaining any documents which are issued in the country of delivery and/or of origin and which the buyer may require for the purposes of exportation and/or importation (and, where necessary, for their passage in transit through another country).

B. *The buyer must:*

1. Take delivery of the goods as soon as they are placed at his disposal at the place and at the time, as provided in the contract, and pay the price as provided in the contract.

---

* This term came into force 1953.

2. Bear all charges and risks of the goods from the time when they have been so placed at his disposal, provided that the goods have been duly appropriated to the contract, that is to say, clearly set aside or otherwise identified as the contract goods.
3. Bear any customs duties and taxes that may be levied by reason of exportation.
4. Where he shall have reserved to himself a period within which to take delivery of the goods and/or the right to choose the place of delivery, and should he fail to give instructions in time, bear the additional costs thereby incurred and all risks of the goods from the date of the expiration of the period fixed, provided that the goods shall have been duly appropriated to the contract, that is to say, clearly set aside or otherwise identified as the contract goods.
5. Pay all costs and charges incurred in obtaining the documents mentioned in Article A.7, including the cost of certificates of origin, export license and consular fees.

For/Fot*

Free on Rail/Free on Truck (Named Departure Point)
FOR and FOT mean "Free on Rail" and "Free on Truck". These terms are synonymous, since the word "Truck" relates to the railway wagons. They should only be used when the goods are to be carried by rail.

A. *The seller must:*

1. Supply the goods in conformity with the contract of sale, together with such evidence of conformity as may be required by the contract.
2. In the case of goods constituting either a wagonload (carload, truckload) lot or a sufficient weight to obtain quantity rates for wagon loading, order in due time a wagon (car, truck) of suitable type and dimensions, equipped, where necessary, with tarpaulins, and load it at his own expense at the date or within the period fixed, the ordering of the wagon (car, truck) and the loading being carried out in accordance with the regulations of the dispatching station.
3. In the case of a load less than either a wagonload (carload, truckload) or a sufficient weight to obtain quantity rates for wagon loading, deliver the goods into the custody of the railway either at the dispatching station or, where such facilities are included in the rate of freight, into a vehicle provided by the railway, at the date or within the period fixed, unless the regulations of the dispatching

---

* This term came into force 1953.

station shall require the seller to load the goods on the wagon (car, truck).

Nevertheless, it shall be understood that if there are several stations at the point of departure, the seller may select the station which best suits his purpose, provided it customarily accepts goods for the destination nominated by the buyer, unless the buyer shall have reserved to himself the right to choose the dispatching station.

4. Subject to the provisions of article B.5 below, bear all costs and risks of the goods until such time as the wagon (car, truck) on which they are loaded shall have been delivered into the custody of the railway or, in the case provided for in article A.3, until such time as the goods shall have been delivered into the custody of the railway.

5. Provide at his own expense the customary packing of the goods, unless it is the custom of the trade to dispatch the goods unpacked.

6. Pay the costs of any checking operations (such as the checking quality, measuring, weighing, counting) which shall be necessary for the purpose of loading the goods or of delivering them into the custody of the railway.

7. Give notice, without delay, to the buyer that the goods have been loaded or delivered into the custody of the railway.

8. At his own expense, provide the buyer, if customary, with the usual transport document.

9. Provide the buyer, at the latter's request and expense (see B.6), with the certificate of origin.

10. Render the buyer, at the latter's request, risk and expense, every assistance in obtaining the documents issued in the country of dispatch and/or of origin which the buyer may require for purposes of exportation and/or importation (and, where necessary, for their passage in transit through another country).

B. *The buyer must:*

1. Give the seller in time the necessary instructions for dispatch.

2. Take delivery of the goods from the time when they have been delivered into the custody of the railway and pay the price as provided in the contract.

3. Bear all costs and risks of the goods (including the cost, if any, of hiring tarpaulins) from the time when the wagon (car, truck) on which the goods are loaded shall have been delivered into the custody of the railway or, in the case provided for in article A.3, from the time when the goods shall have been delivered into the custody of the railway.

4. Bear any customs duties and taxes that may be levied by reason of exportation.

5. Where he shall have reserved to himself a period within which to give the seller instructions for dispatch and/or the right to choose

the place of loading, and should he fail to give instructions in time, bear the additional costs thereby incurred and all risks of the goods from the time of expiration of the period fixed, provided, however, that the goods shall have been duly appropriated to the contract, that is to say, cleary set aside or otherwise identified as the contract goods.

6. Pay all costs and charges incurred in obtaining the documents mentioned in articles A.9 & 10 above, including the cost of certificates or origin and consular fees.

FAS*

Free Alongside Ship (named Port of Shipment)

FAS means "Free Alongside Ship". Under this term the seller's obligations are fulfilled when the goods have been placed alongside the ship on the quay or in lighters. This means that the buyer has to bear all costs and risks of loss of or damage to the goods from that moment. It should be noted that, unlike FOB, the present term requires the buyer to clear the goods for export.

A. *The seller must:*

1. Supply the goods in conformity with the contract of sale, together with such evidence of conformity as may be required by the contract.
2. Deliver the goods alongside the vessel at the loading berth named by the buyer, at the named port of shipment, in the manner customary at the port, at the date or within the period stipulated, and notify the buyer, without delay, that the goods have been delivered alongside the vessel.
3. Render the buyer at the latter's request, risk and expense, every assistance in obtaining any export license or other governmental authorization necessary for the export of the goods.
4. Subject to the provisions of articles B.3 and B.4 below, bear all costs and risks of the goods until such time as they shall have been effectively delivered alongside the vessel at the named port of shipment, including the costs of any formalities which he shall have to fulfill in order to deliver the goods alongside the vessel.
5. Provide at his own expense the customary packing of the goods, unless it is the custom of the trade to ship the goods unpacked.
6. Pay the costs of any checking operations (such as checking quality, measuring, weighing, counting) which shall be necessary for the purpose of delivering the goods alongside the vessel.

---

* This term came into force 1953.

7. Provide at his own expense the customary clean document in proof of delivery of the goods alongside the named vessel.
8. Provide the buyer, at the latter's request and expense (see B.5), with the certificate of origin.
9. Render the buyer, at the latter's request, risk and expense, every assistance in obtaining any documents other than that mentioned in article A.8, issued in the country of shipment and/or of origin (excluding a bill of lading and/or consular documents) and which the buyer may require for the importation of the goods into the country of destination (and, where necessary, for their passage in transit through another country).

B. *The buyer must:*

1. Give the seller due notice of the name, loading berth of and delivery dates to the vessel.
2. Bear all the charges and risks of the goods from the time when they shall have been effectively delivered alongside the vessel at the named port of shipment, at the date or within the period stipulated, and pay the price as provided in the contract.
3. Bear any additional costs incurred because the vessel named by him shall have failed to arrive on time, or shall be unable to take the goods, or shall close for cargo earlier than the stipulated date, and all the risks of the goods from the time when the seller shall place them at the buyer's disposal provided, however, that the goods shall have been duly appropriated to the contract, that is to say, clearly set aside or otherwise identified as the contract goods.
4. Should he fail to name the vessel in time or, if he shall have reserved to himself a period within which to take delivery of the goods and/or the right to choose the port of shipment, should he fail to give detailed instructions in time, bear any additional costs incurred because of such failure and all the risks of the goods from the date of expiration of the period stipulated for delivery, provided, however, that the goods shall have been duly appropriated to the contract, that is to say, clearly set aside or otherwise identified as the contract goods.
5. Pay all costs and charges incurred in obtaining the documents mentioned in articles A.3, A.8 and A.9 above.

FOB*

Free on Board (named port of shipment)
FOB means "Free on Board". The goods are placed on board a ship by the seller at a port of shipment named in the sales contract. The risk of

---

* This term came into force 1953.

loss of or damage to the goods is transferred from the seller to the buyer when the goods pass the ship's rail.

A. *The seller must:*

1. Supply the goods in conformity with the contract of sale, together with such evidence of conformity as may be required by the contract.
2. Deliver the goods on board the vessel named by the buyer, at the named port of shipment, in the manner customary at the port, at the date or within the period stipulated, and notify the buyer, without delay, that the goods have been delivered on board.
3. At his own risk and expense obtain any export license or other governmental authorization necessary for the export of the goods.
4. Subject to the provisions of articles B.3 and B.4 below, bear all costs and risks of the goods until such time as they shall have effectively passed the ship's rail at the named port of shipment, including any taxes, fees or charges levied because of exportation, as well as the costs of any formalities which he shall have to fulfull in order to load the goods on board.
5. Provide at his own expense the customary packing of the goods, unless it is the custom of the trade to ship the goods unpacked.
6. Pay the costs of any checking operations (such as checking quality, measuring, weighing, counting) which shall be necessary for the purpose of delivering the goods.
7. Provide at his own expense the customary clean document in proof of delivery of the goods on board the named vessel.
8. Provide the buyer, at the latter's request and expense (see B.6), with the certificate of origin.
9. Render the buyer, at the latter's request, risk and expense, every assistance in obtaining a bill of lading and any documents, other than that mentioned in the previous article, issued in the country of shipment and/or origin and which the buyer may require for the importation of the goods into the country of destination (and, where necessary, for their passage in transit through another country).

B. *The buyer must:*

1. At his own expense, charter a vessel or reserve the necessary space on board a vessel and give the seller due notice of the name, loading berth of and delivery dates to the vessel.
2. Bear all costs and risks of the goods from the time when they shall have effectively passed the ship's rail at the named port of shipment, and pay the price as provided in the contract.
3. Bear any additional costs incurred because the vessel named by him shall have failed to arrive on the stipulated date or by the end of the period specified, or shall be unable to take the goods or shall close

for cargo earlier than the stipulated date or the end of the period specified and all the risks of the goods from the date of expiration of the period stipulated, provided, however, that the goods shall have been duly appropriated to the contract, that is to say, clearly set aside or otherwise identified as the contract goods.

4. Should he fail to name the vessel in time or, if he shall have reserved to himself a period within which to take delivery of the goods and/or the right to choose the port of shipment, should he fail to give detailed instructions in time, bear any additional costs incurred because of such failure, and all the risks of the goods from the date of expiration of the period stipulated for delivery, provided, however, that the goods shall have been duly appropriated to the contract, that is to say, clearly set aside or otherwise identified as the contract goods.

5. Pay any costs and charges for obtaining a bill of lading if incurred under article A.9 above.

6. Pay all costs and charges incurred in obtaining the documents mentioned in articles A.8 and A.9 above, including the costs of certificates of origin and consular documents.

C&F*

Cost and Freight (named port of destination)

C&F means "Cost and Freight". The seller must pay the costs and freight necessary to bring the goods to the named destination but the risk of loss of or damage to the goods, as well as of any cost increases, is transferred from the seller to the buyer when the goods pass the ship's rail in the port of shipment.

A. *The seller must:*

1. Supply the goods in conformity with the contract of sale, together with such evidence of conformity as may be required by the contract.

2. Contract on usual terms at his own expense for the carriage of the goods to the agreed port of destination by the usual route, in a seagoing vessel (not being a sailing vessel) of the type normally used for transport of goods of the contract description, and pay freight charges and any charges for unloading at the port of discharge which may be levied by the regular shipping lines at the time and port of shipment.

3. At his own risk and expense obtain any export license or other governmental authorization necessary for the export of the goods.

---

* This term came into force 1953.

4. Load the goods at his own expense on board the vessel at the port of shipment and at the date or within the period fixed or, if neither date nor time has been stipulated, within a reasonable time, and notify the buyer, without delay, that the goods have been loaded on board the vessel.

5. Subject to the provisions of article B.4 below, bear all risks of the goods until such time as they shall have effectively passed the ship's rail at the port of shipment.

6. At his own expense furnish to the buyer without delay a clean negotiable bill of lading for the agreed port of destination, as well as the invoice of the goods shipped. The bill of lading must cover the contract goods, be dated within the period agreed for shipment, and provide by endorsement or otherwise for delivery to the order of the buyer or buyer's agreed representative. Such bill of lading must be a full set of "on board" or "shipped" bills of lading, or a "received for shipment" bill of lading duly endorsed by the shipping company to the effect that the goods are on board, such endorsement to be dated within the period agreed for shipment. If the bill of lading contains a reference to the charter-party, the seller must also provide a copy of this latter document.

   Note: A clean bill of lading is one which bears no superimposed clauses expressly declaring a defective condition of the goods or packaging.

The following clauses do not convert a clean into an unclean bill of lading:

   a. Clauses which do not expressly state that the goods or packaging are unsatisfactory, e.g., "second-hand cases", "used drum".

   b. Clauses which emphasize carrier's nonliability for risks arising through the nature of the goods or the packaging.

   c. Clauses which disclaim on the part of the carrier knowledge of contents, weight, measured, quality, or technical specification of the goods.

7. Provide at his own expense the customary packaging of the goods, unless it is the custom of the trade to ship the goods unpacked.

8. Pay the costs of any checking operations (such as checking quality, measuring, weighing, counting) which shall be necessary for the purpose of loading the goods.

9. Pay any dues and taxes incurred in respect of the goods, up to the time of their loading, including any taxes, fees or charges levied because of exportation, as well as the costs of any formalities which he shall have to fulfill in order to load the goods on board.

10. Provide the buyer, at the latter's request and expense (see B.5), with the certificate of origin and the consular invoice.

11. Render the buyer, at the latter's request, risk and expense, every assistance in obtaining any documents, other than those mentioned

in the previous article, issued in the country of shipment and/or of origin and which the buyer may require for the importation of the goods into the country of destination (and, where necessary, for their passage in transit through another country).

B. The buyer must:

1. Accept the documents when tendered by the seller, if they are in conformity with the contract of sale, and pay the price as provided in the contract.
2. Receive the goods at the agreed port of destination and bear, with the exception of the freight, all costs and charges incurred in respect of the goods in the course of their transit by sea until their arrival at the port of destination, as well as unloading costs, including lighterage and wharfage charges, unless such costs and charges shall have been included in the freight or collected by the steamship company at the time freight was paid.
   Note: If the goods are sold "C&F landed", unloading costs, including lighterage and wharfage charges, are borne by the seller.
3. Bear all risks of the goods from the time when they shall have effectively passed the ship's rail at the port of shipment.
4. In case he may have reserved to himself a period within which to have the goods shipped and/or the right to choose the port of destination, and he fails to give instructions in time, bear the additional costs thereby incurred and all risks of the goods from the date of the expiration of the period fixed for shipment, provided always that the goods shall have been fully appropriated to the contract, that is to say, clearly set aside or otherwise identified as the contract goods.
5. Pay the costs and charges incurred in obtaining the certificate of origin and consular documents.
6. Pay all costs and charges incurred in obtaining the documents mentioned in article A.11 above.
7. Pay all customs duties as well as any other duties and taxes payable at the time of or by reason of the importation.
8. Procure and provide at his own risk and expense any import license or permit or the like which he may require for the importation of the goods at destination.

CIF*

Cost, Insurance, and Freight (named port of destination)
CIF means "Cost, Insurance and Freight". This term is the same as C&F but with the addition that the seller has to procure marine insurance

---

* This term came into force 1953.

against the risk of loss of or damage to the goods during the carriage. The seller contracts with the insurer and pays the insurance premium. The buyer should note that under the present term, unlike the term "Freight/ Carriage and Insurance paid to", the seller is only required to cover insurance on minimum conditions (so-called FPA conditions).

A. The seller must:

1. Supply the goods in conformity with the contract of sale, together with such evidence of conformity as may be required by the contract.
2. Contract on usual terms at his own expense for the carriage of the goods to the agreed port of destination by the usual route, in a seagoing vessel (not being a sailing vessel) of the type normally used for the transport of goods of the contract description, and pay freight charges and any charges for unloading at the port of discharge which may be levied by regular shipping lines at the time and port of shipment.
3. At his own risk and expense obtain any export license or other governmental authorization necessary for the export of the goods.
4. Load the goods at his own expense on board the vessel at the port of shipment and at the date or within the period fixed or, if neither date nor time has been stipulated, within a reasonable time, and notify the buyer, without delay, that the goods have been loaded on board the vessel.
5. Procure, at his own cost and in a transferable form, a policy of marine insurance against the risks of carriage involved in the contract. The insurance shall be contracted with underwriters or insurance companies of good repute on FPA terms, and shall cover the CIF price plus ten per cent. The insurance shall be provided in the currency of the contract, if procurable[1].

   Unless otherwise agreed, the risks of carriage shall not include special risks that are covered in specific trades or against which the buyer may wish individual protection. Among the special risks that should be considered and agreed upon between seller and buyer are theft, pilferage, leakage, breakage, chipping, sweat, contact with other cargoes and others peculiar to any particular trade.

   When required by the buyer, the seller shall provide, at the buyer's expense, war risk insurance in the currency of the contract, if procurable.
6. Subject to the provisions of article B.4 below, bear all risks of the

---

[1] CIF A.5 provides for the minimum terms (FPA) and period of insurance (warehouse to warehouse). Whenever the buyer wishes more than the minimum liability to be included in the contract, then he should take care to specify that the basis of the contract is to be "Incoterms" with whatever addition he requires.

goods until such time as they shall have effectively passed the ship's rail at the port of shipment.

7. At his own expense furnish to the buyer without delay a clean negotiable bill of lading for the agreed port of destination, as well as the invoice of the goods shipped and the insurance policy or, should the insurance policy not be available at the time the documents are tendered, a certificate of insurance issued under the authority of the underwriters and conveying to the bearer the same rights as if he were in possession of the policy and reproducing the essential provisions thereof. The bill of lading must cover the contract goods, be dated within the period agreed for shipment, and provide by endorsement or otherwise for delivery to the order of the buyer or buyer's agreed representative. Such bill of lading must be a full set of "on board" or "shipped" bills of lading, or a "received for shipment" bill of lading duly endorsed by the shipping company to the effect that the goods are on board, such endorsement to be dated within the period agreed for shipment. If the bill of lading contains a reference to the charter-party the seller must also provide a copy of this latter document.

Note: A clean bill of lading is one which bears no superimposed clauses expressly declaring a defective condition of the goods or packaging.

The following clauses do not convert a clean into an unclean bill of lading:

a. Clauses which do not expressly state that the goods or packaging are unsatisfactory (e.g., "second-hand cases," "used drums").

b. Clauses which emphasize the carrier's nonliability for risks arising through the nature of the goods or the packaging.

c. Clauses which disclaim on the part of the carrier knowledge of contents, weight, measurement, quality, or technical specification of the goods.

8. Provide at his own expense the customary packing of the goods, unless it is the custom of the trade to ship the goods unpacked.

9. Pay the costs of any checking operations (such as checking quality, measuring, weighing, counting) which shall be necessary for the purpose of loading the goods.

10. Pay any dues and taxes incurred in respect of the goods up to the time of their loading, including any taxes, fees or charges levied because of exportation, as well as the costs of any formalities which he shall have to fulfill in order to load the goods on board.

11. Provide the buyer, at the latter's request and expense (see B.5), with the certificate of origin and the consular invoice.

12. Render the buyer, at the latter's request, risk and expense, every assistance in obtaining any documents, other than those mentioned in the previous article, issued in the country of shipment and/or of origin and which the buyer may require for the importation of the

goods into the country of destination (and, where necessary, for their passage in transit through another country).

B. *The buyer must:*

1. Accept the documents when tendered by the seller, if they are in conformity with the contract of sale, and pay the price as provided in the contract.
2. Receive the goods at the agreed port of destination and bear, with the exception of the freight and marine insurance, all costs and charges incurred in respect of the goods in the course of their transit by sea until their arrival at the port of destination, as well as unloading costs, including lighterage and wharfage charges, unless such costs and charges shall have been included in the freight or collected by the steamship company at the time freight was paid.

   If war insurance is provided, it shall be at the expense of the buyer (see A.5).

   Note: If the goods are sold "CIF landed", unloading costs, including lighterage and wharfage charges, are borne by the seller.
3. Bear all risks of the goods from the time when they shall have effectively passed the ship's rail at the port of shipment.
4. In case he may have reserved to himself a period within which to have the goods shipped and/or the right to choose the port of destination, and he fails to give instructions in time, bear the additional costs thereby incurred and all risks of the goods from the date of the expiration of the period fixed for shipment, provided always that the goods shall have been duly appropriated to the contract, that is to say, clearly set aside or otherwise identified as the contract goods.
5. Pay the costs and charges incurred in obtaining the certificate of origin and consular documents.
6. Pay all costs and charges incurred in obtaining the documents mentioned in article A.12 above.
7. Pay all customs duties as well as any other duties and taxes payable at the time of or by reasons of the importation.
8. Procure and provide at his own risk and expense any import license or permit or the like which he may require for the importation of the goods at destination.

Ex Ship*

Named Port of Destination

"Ex Ship" means that the seller shall make the goods available to the buyer on board the ship at the destination named in the sales contract.

---

* This term came into force 1953.

The seller has to bear the full cost and risk involved in bringing the goods there.

A. *The seller must:*

1. Supply the goods in conformity with the contract of sale, together with such evidence of conformity as may be required by the contract.
2. Place the goods effectively at the disposal of the buyer, at the time as provided in the contract, on board the vessel at the usual unloading point in the named port, in such a way as to enable them to be removed from the vessel by unloading equipment appropriate to the nature of the goods.
3. Bear all risks and expense of the goods until such time as they shall have been effectively placed at the disposal of the buyer in accordance with article A.2, provided, however, that they have been duly appropriated to the contract, that is to say, clearly set aside or otherwise identified as the contract goods.
4. Provide at his own expense the customary packing of the goods, unless it is the custom of the trade to ship the goods unpacked.
5. Pay the costs of any checking operations (such as checking quality, measuring, weighing, counting) which shall be necessary for the purpose of placing the goods at the disposal of the buyer in accordance with article A.2.
6. At his own expense, notify the buyer, without delay, of the expected date of arrival of the named vessel, and provide him in due time with the bill of lading or delivery order and/or any other documents which may be necessary to enable the buyer to take delivery of the goods.
7. Provide the buyer, at the latter's request and expense (see B.3), with the certificate of origin and the consular invoice.
8. Render the buyer, at the latter's request, risk and expense, every assistance in obtaining any documents, other than those mentioned in the previous articles, issued in the country of shipment and/or of origin and which the buyer may require for the importation of the goods into the country of destination (and where necessary, for their passage in transit through another country).

B. *The buyer must:*

1. Take delivery of the goods as soon as they have been placed at his disposal in accordance with the provisions of article A.2, and pay the price as provided in the contract.
2. Bear all risks and expense of the goods from the time when they shall have been effectively placed at his disposal in accordance with article A.2, provided always that they have been duly appropriated to the contract, that is to say, clearly set aside or otherwise identified as the contract goods.

3. Bear all expenses and charges incurred by the seller in obtaining any of the documents referred to in articles A.7 and 8.
4. At his own risk and expense, procure all licenses or similar documents which may be required for the purpose of unloading and/or importing the goods.
5. Bear all expenses and charges of customs duties and clearance, and all other duties and taxes payable at the time or by reason of the unloading and/or importing of the goods.

Ex Quay

Duty Paid . . . Named Port[1]

"Ex Quay" means that the seller makes the goods available to the buyer on the quay (wharf) at the destination named in the sales contract. The seller has to bear the full cost and risk involved in bringing the goods there.

There are two "Ex Quay" contracts in use, namely Ex Quay "duty paid" and Ex Quay "duties on buyer's account" in which the liability to clear the goods for import is to be met by the buyer instead of by the seller.

Parties are recommended always to use the full descriptions of these terms, namely Ex Quay "duty paid" or Ex Quay "duties on buyer's account", or else there may be uncertainty as to who is to be responsible for the liability to clear the goods for import.

If the parties wish that the seller should clear the goods for import but that some of the costs payable upon the import of the goods should be excluded—such as value added tax (VAT) and/or other similar taxes—this should be made clear by adding words to this effect (e.g., "exclusive of VAT and/or taxes").

A. The seller must:

1. Supply the goods in conformity with the contract of sale, together with such evidence of conformity as may be required by the contract.
2. Place the goods at the disposal of the buyer on the wharf or quay at the agreed port and at the time, as provided in the contract.

---

[1] **Ex Quay (duties on buyer's account).**

There are two "Ex Quay" contracts in use, namely Ex Quay (duty paid) which has been defined above and Ex Quay (duties on buyer's account) in which the liabilities specified in A.3 are to be met by the buyer instead of by the seller.

Parties are recommended always to use the full descriptions of these terms, namely Ex Quay (duty paid) or Ex Quay (duties on buyer's account), or else there may be uncertainty as to who is to be responsible for the liabilities in A.3.

3. At his own risk and expense, provide the import license and bear the cost of any import duties or taxes, including the costs of customs clearance, as well as any other taxes, fees or charges payable at the time or by reason of importation of the goods and their delivery to the buyer.
4. At his own expense, provide for customary conditioning and packing of the goods, regard being had to their nature and to their delivery from the quay.
5. Pay the costs of any checking operations (such as checking quality, measuring, weighing, counting) which shall be necessary for the purpose of placing the goods at the disposal of the buyer in accordance with article A.2.
6. Bear all risks and expense of the goods until such time as they shall have been effectively placed at the disposal of the buyer in accordance with article A.2, provided, however, that they have been duly appropriated to the contract, that is to say, clearly set aside or otherwise identified as the contract goods.
7. At his own expense, provide the delivery order and/or any other documents which the buyer may require in order to take delivery of the goods and to remove them from the quay.

B. The buyer must:

1. Take delivery of the goods as soon as they have been placed at his disposal in accordance with article A.2, and pay the price as provided in the contract.
2. Bear all expense and risks of the goods from the time when they have been effectively placed at his disposal in accordance with article A.2, provided always that they have been duly appropriated to the contract, that is to say, clearly set aside or otherwise identified as the contract goods.

Delivered at Frontier*

Named Place of Delivery at Frontier[1]

"Delivered at Frontier" means that the seller's obligations are fulfilled when the goods have arrived at the frontier—but before "the customs border" of the country named in the sales contract.

---

* This term came into force 1967.

[1] To avoid misunderstandings, it is recommended that parties contracting according to this trade term should qualify the word *frontier* by indicating the two countries separated by that frontier, and also the named place of delivery. For example: "Delivered at Franco-Italian frontier (Modane)".

The term is primarily intended to be used when goods are to be carried by rail or road but it may be used irrespective of the mode of transport.

A. The seller must:

1. Supply the goods in conformity with the contract of sale, together with such evidence of conformity as may be stipulated in the contract of sale.
2. At his own risk and expense:
   a. Put the contract goods at the disposal of the buyer at the named place of delivery at the frontier on the date or within the period stipulated in the contract of sale, and at the same time supply the buyer with a customary document of transport, warehouse warrant, dock warrant, delivery order, or the like, as the case may be, providing by endorsement or otherwise for the delivery of the goods to the buyer or to his order at the frontier, and also with an export license and such other documents, if any, as may be strictly required at that time and place for the purpose of enabling the buyer to take delivery of the goods for their subsequent movement, as provided in articles B.2 and 2.

      The goods so put at that disposal of the buyer must be clearly set aside or otherwise identified as the contract goods.
   b. Comply with all formalities he may have to fulfull for these purposes, and pay any Customs fees and charges, internal taxes, excise duties, statistical taxes, and so on, levied in the country of dispatch or elsewhere, which he may have to incur in discharge of his duties up to the time when he puts the goods at the disposal of the buyer in accordance with article A.2*a.*
3. Bear all the risks of the goods up to the time when he has fulfilled his obligations under article A.2*a.*
4. Procure, at his own risk and expense, in addition to the documents contemplated in article A.2*a*, any exchange control authorization or other similar administrative document required for the purpose of clearing the goods for exportation at the named place of delivery at the frontier and any other documents he may require for the purpose of dispatching the goods to that place, passing them in transit through one or more third countries (if need be), and putting them at the disposal of the buyer in accordance with these Rules.
5. Contract on usual terms, at his own risk and expense, for the transport of the goods (including their passage in transit through one or more third countries, if necessary) to the named place of delivery at the frontier, bear and pay the freight or other costs of transport to that place and also, subject to the provisions of articles A.6 and 7, any other expenses of or incidental to any movement

whatsoever of the goods up to the time when they are duly put at the disposal of the buyer at that place.

Nevertheless, the seller shall, subject to the provisions of articles A.6 and 7 at his own risk and expense, be at liberty to use his own means of transport, provided that in the exercise of such liberty he shall perform all his other duties under these Rules.

If no particular point (station, pier, quay, wharf, warehouse, or as the case may be) at the named place of delivery at the frontier is stipulated in the contract of sale or prescribed by the regulations of the Customs or other competent authority concerned, or by the regulations of the public carrier, the seller may, if there are several points to choose from, select the point which suits him best, provided it offers such Customs and other proper facilities as may be necessary to enable the parties to perform their respective duties under these Rules.[2] The point so chosen by the seller must be notified to the buyer[3], and thereupon that point shall be deemed for the purposes of these Rules to be the point at the named place of delivery at which the goods shall be put at the disposal of the buyer and the risk of the goods shall pass.

6. Provide the buyer, at the buyer's request and risk, with a through document of transport normally procurable in the country of dispatch covering on usual terms the transport of the goods from the point of depature in that country to the point of final destination in the country of importation named by the buyer, provided that in so doing the seller shall not be deemed to assume any duty or to incur any risks or expenses other than those he would normally be called upon to incur, perform, bear and pay under these Rules.

7. If it is necessary or customary for the goods to be unloaded, discharged or landed on their arrival at the named place of delivery at the frontier, bear and pay the expenses of such operation (including lightering and handling charges).

If the seller elects to use his own means of transport for sending the goods to the named place of delivery then, in such case, he shall bear and pay all the expenses of or incidental to the necessary or customary operations contemplated in the last preceding paragraph.

8. Notify the buyer at seller's expense that the goods have been dispatched to the named place of delivery at the frontier. Such notice must be given in sufficient time to allow the buyer to take

---

[2] If at the named place of delivery at the frontier there are two customs-posts of different nationalities, it is recommended that the parties should either stipulate which one has been agreed upon, or leave the choice to the seller.

[3] See article A.8 footnote.

such measures as are normally necessary to enable him to take delivery of the goods.[4]

9. Provide, at his own expense, packaging customary for the transport of goods of the contract description to the named place of delivery, unless it is the usage of the particular trade to dispatch goods of the contract description unpacked.

10. Bear and pay the expenses of or incidental to any checking operations, such as measuring, weighing, counting or analyzing of quality, which may be necessary to enable him to transport the goods to the named place of delivery at the frontier and to put them at the disposal of the buyer at that place.

11. Bear and pay in addition to any expenses to be borne and paid by the seller in accordance with the preceding articles, any other expenses of or incidental to the performance of the seller's duty to put the goods at the disposal of the buyer at the named place of delivery at the frontier.

12. Render to the buyer, at buyer's request, risk and expense, a reasonable amount of assistance in obtaining any documents other than those already mentioned, which may be obtainable in the country of dispatch or of origin, or in both countries and which the buyer may require for the purposes contemplated in articles B.2 and 6.

B. *The buyer must:*

1. Take delivery of the goods as soon as the seller has duly put them at his disposal at the named place of delivery at the frontier, and be responsible for handling all subsequent movements of the goods.

2. Comply at his own expense with any Customs and other formalities that may have to be fulfilled at the named place of delivery at the frontier, or elsewhere, and pay any duties that may be payable at the time or by reason of the entry of the goods into the adjoining country or of any other movement of the goods subsequent to the time when they have been duly put at his disposal.

3. Bear and pay the expenses of or incidental to unloading, discharging or landing the goods on their arrival at the named place of

---

[4] Such notice may be served by the seller upon the buyer by sending it through the post by air mail and address to the buyer at his place of business given in the contract of sale. But if the goods have been dispatched by air, or if the distance between the point of departure of the country of dispatch and the named place of delivery at the frontier is short, or if the business addresses of the seller and the buyer are so far apart as to be likely to cause undue delay in the delivery of notice sent through the post then, in any such case, the seller shall be bound to give such notice to the buyer by sending the same by cable, telegram or telex.

delivery at the frontier, in so far as such expenses are not payable by the seller in accordance with the provisions of article A.7.

4. Bear all risks of the goods and pay any expenses whatsoever incurred in respect thereof including Customs duties, fees and charges from the time when they have been duly put at his disposal at the named place of delivery at the frontier.

5. If he fails to take delivery of the goods as soon as they have been duly put at his disposal, bear all the risks of the goods and pay any additional expenses incurred, whether by the seller or by the buyer, because of such failure, provided that the goods shall have been clearly set aside or otherwise identified as the contract goods.

6. Procure, at his own risk and expense, any import license, exchange control authorization, permits or other documents issued in the country of importation, or elsewhere, that he may require in connection with any movement of the goods subsequent to the time when they have been duly put at his disposal at the named place of delivery at the frontier.

7. Bear and pay any additional expenses which the seller may have to incur for the purpose of obtaining a through document of transport in accordance with article A.6.

8. At seller's request and at buyer's expense, place such import license, exchange control authorization, permits and other documents, or certified copies thereof, at the disposal of the seller for the limited purpose of obtaining the through document of transport contemplated in article A.6.

9. Supply the seller, at his request, with the address of the final destination of the goods in the country of importation, if the seller requires such information for the purpose of applying for such licenses and other documents as are contemplated in articles A.4 and A.6.

10. Bear and pay the expenses incurred by the seller in providing the buyer with any expert third-party certificate of conformity of the goods stipulated in the contract of sale.

11. Bear and pay any expenses the seller may incur in or about his endeavors to assist the buyer in obtaining any of the documents contemplated in article A.12.

Delivery Duty Paid*

Named Place of Destination in the Country of Importation

While the term *Ex Works* signifies the seller's minimum oligation, the term *Delivered Duty Paid,* when followed by words naming the buyer's

---

* This term came into force 1967.

premises, denotes the other extreme—the seller's maximum obligation. The term *Delivered Duty Paid* may be used irrespective of the mode of transport.

If the parties wish that the seller should clear the goods for import but that some of the costs payable upon the import of the goods should be excluded—such as value added tax (VAT) and/or other similar taxes— this should be made clear by adding words to this effect (e.g., "exclusive of VAT and/or taxes").

A. *The seller must:*

1. Supply the goods in conformity with the contract of sale, together with such evidence of conformity as may be stipulated in the contract of sale.
2. At his own risk and expense:
   a. Put the contract goods at the disposal of the buyer, duty paid, at the named place of destination in the country of importation on the date or within the period stipulated in the contract of sale, and at the same time supply the buyer with a customary document of transport, warehouse warrant, dock warrant, delivery order, or the like, as the case may be, providing by endorsement of otherwise for the delivery of the goods to the buyer or to his order at the named place of destination in the country of importation and also with such other documents, if any, as may be strictly required at that time and place for the purpose of enabling the buyer to take delivery of the goods, as provided in article B.1.

   The goods so put at the disposal of the buyer must be clearly set aside or otherwise identified as the contract goods.

   b. Provide the import license or permit and bear the cost of any import duties or taxes, including the cost of Customs clearance, as well as any other taxes, fees or charges payable at the named place of destination at the time of the importation of the goods, so far as such payments are necessary for the purpose of enabling the seller to put the goods duty paid at the disposal of the buyer at that place.

   c. Comply with all formalities he may have to fulfill for these purposes.
3. Bear all the risks of the goods up to the time when he has fulfilled his obligations under article A.2 a).
4. Procure at his own risk and expense, in addition to the documents contemplated in article A.2 a), any export license or permit, exchange control authorization, certificates, consular invoice and other documents issued by the public authorities concerned, which he may require for the purposes of dispatching the goods, exporting them from the country of dispatch, passing them in transit through

one or more third countries (if necessary), importing them into the country of the named place of destination, and putting them at the disposal of the buyer at the place.

5. Contract on usual terms, at his own risk and expense, for the transport of the goods from the point of departure in the country of dispatch to the named place of destination, bear and pay the freight or other costs of transport to that place, and also, subject to the provisions of article A.6, any other expenses of or incidental to any movement whatsoever of the goods up to the time when they are duly put at the disposal of the buyer at the named place of destination.

Nevertheless, the seller shall, at his own risk and expense, be at liberty to use his own means of transport provided that in the exercise of such liberty he shall perform all his other duties under these Rules.

If no particular point (station, pier, quay, wharf, warehouse, or as the case may be) at the named place of destination in the country of importation is stipulated in the contract of sale or prescribed by the regulations of the Customs or other competent authority concerned, or by the regulations of the public carrier, the seller may, if there are several points to choose from, select the point which suits him best, provided it offers such Customs and other proper facilities as may be necessary to enable the parties to perform their respective duties under these Rules. The point so chosen by the seller must be notified to the buyer,[5] and thereupon that point shall be deemed for the purposes of these Rules to be the point at the named place of destination at which the goods shall be put at the disposal of the buyer and the risks of the goods shall pass.

6. If it is necessary or customary for the goods to be unloaded, discharged or landed on their arrival at the named place of destination for the purpose of putting them duty paid at the disposal of the buyer at that place, bear and pay the expenses of such operations, including any lightering, wharfing, warehousing and handling charges.

7. Notify the buyer, at seller's expense, that the goods have been placed in the custody of the first carrier to dispatch to the named place of destination, or that they have been dispatched to that destination by the seller's own means of transport, as the case may be. Any such notice must be given in sufficient time to allow the buyer to take such measures as are normally necessary for the purpose of enabling him to take delivery of the goods.[6]

---

[5] See article A.7, footnote.

[6] Such notice may be served by the seller upon the buyer by sending it through the post by air mail, and addressed to the buyer at his place of business given in the contract of sale. But if the goods have been dispatched by air, or if the business addresses of the seller and the

8. Provide, at his own expense, packaging customary for transport of goods of the contract description to the named place of destination, unless it is the usage of the particular trade to dispatch goods of the contract description unpacked.

9. Bear and pay the expenses of or incidental to any checking operations, such as measuring, weighing, counting or analyzing of quality, which may be necessary to enable him to transport the goods to the named place of destination and to put them at the disposal of the buyer at that place.

10. Bear and pay, in addition to any expenses to be borne and paid by the seller in accordance with articles A.1 to 9 inclusive, any other expenses of or incidental to the performance of the seller's duty to put the goods at the disposal of the buyer at the named place of destination in accordance with these Rules.

B. The buyer must:

1. Take delivery of the goods as soon as the seller has duly put them at his disposal at the named place of destination, and be responsible for handling all subsequent movement of the goods.

2. Bear and pay the expenses of or incidental to unloading, discharging or landing the goods on their arrival at the named place of destination, in so far as such expenses are not payable by the seller in accordance with the provisions of article A.6.

3. Bear all the risks of the goods and pay any expenses whatsoever incurred in respect thereof from the time when they have been put at his disposal at the named place of destination in accordance with article A.2 a.

4. If he fails to take delivery of the goods as soon as they have been duly put at his disposal, bear all the risks of the goods and pay any additional expenses incurred, whether by the seller or by the buyer, because of such failure, provided that the goods shall have been clearly set aside or otherwise identified as the contract goods.

5. Supply the seller, at his request, with the address of the final destination of the goods in the country of importation, if the seller requires such information for the purpose of applying for such documents as are contemplated in article A.2 b.

6. Bear and pay the expenses incurred by the seller in providing the buyer with any expert third-party certificate of conformity of the goods stipulated in the contract of sale.

7. Render to the seller, at seller's request, risk and expense, a reasonable amount of assistance in obtaining any documents which

---

buyer are so far apart as to be likely to cause undue delay in the delivery of notice sent through the post then, in any such case, the seller shall be bound to give such notice to the buyer by sending the same by cable, telegram or telex.

may be issued in the country of importation and which the seller may require for the purpose of putting the goods at the disposal of the buyer in accordance with these Rules.

FOB Airport*

Named Airport of Departure

The rules set forth hereunder for delivery on FOB terms for carriage of the goods by air have been carefully drafted to reflect the usages usually observed in trade. It will be noted that the expresson "FOB"—properly meaning "free on board"—is not, in relation to air transportation, to be taken literally but rather as announcing that the next word constitutes the point where the seller's responsibility is to terminate.

A. The seller must:

1. Supply the goods in conformity with the contract of sale, together with such evidence of conformity as may be required by the contract.
2. Deliver the goods into the charge of the air carrier or his agent or any other person named by the buyer, or, if not air carrier, agent or other person has been so named, of an air carrier or his agent chosen by the seller. Delivery shall be made on the date or within the period agreed for delivery and at the named airport of departure in the manner customary at the airport or at such other place as may be designated by the buyer in the contract.
3. Contract at the buyer's expense for the carriage of the goods, unless the buyer or the seller gives prompt notice to the contrary to the other party. When contracting for the carriage as aforesaid, the seller shall do so, subject to the buyer's instructions as provided for under article B.1, on usual terms to the airport of destination named, to the nearest airport available for such carriage to the buyer's place of business, by a usual route in an aircraft of a type normally used for the transport of goods of the contract description.
4. At his own risk and expense obtain any export license or other official authorization necessary for the export of the goods.
5. Subject to the provisions of articles B.6 and B.7 below, pay any taxes, fees and charges levied in respect to the goods because of exportation.
6. Subject to the provisions of articles B.6 and B.7 below, bear any further costs payable in respect of the goods until such time as they will have been delivered, in accordance with the provisions of article A.2 above.

---

* This term came into force 1976.

7. Subject to the provisions of articles B.6 and B.7 below, bear all risks of the goods until such time as they will have been delivered, in accordance with the provisions of article A.2 above.
8. Provide at his own expense adequate protective packing suitable to dispatch of the goods by air unless it is the custom of the trade to dispatch the goods unpacked.
9. Pay the costs of any checking operations (such as checking quality, measuring, weighing, counting) which shall be necessary for the purpose of delivering the goods.
10. Give the buyer notice of the delivery of the goods without delay by telecommunication channels at his own expense.
11. In the circumstances referred to in articles B.6 and B.7 below, give the buyer prompt notice by telecommunication channels of the occurrence of said circumstances.
12. Provide the buyer with the commercial invoice in proper form so as to facilitate compliance with applicable regulations and, at the buyer's request and expense, with the certificate of origin.
13. Render the buyer, at his request, risk and expense, every assistance in obtaining any document other than those mentioned in article A.12 above issued in the country of departure and/or of origin and which the buyer may require for the importation of the goods into the country of destination (and, where necessary, for their passage in transit through another country).
14. Render the buyer, at his request, risk and expense and subject to the provisions of article B.9 below, every assistance in bringing any claim against the air carrier or his agent in respect of the carriage of the goods.

B. The buyer must

1. Give the seller due notice of the airport of destination and give him proper instructions (where required) for the carriage of the goods by air from the named airport of departure.
2. If the seller will not contract for the carriage of the goods, arrange at his own expense for said carriage from the named airport of departure and give the seller due notice of said arrangements, stating the name of the air carrier or his agent or of any other person into whose charge delivery is to be made.
3. Bear all costs payable in respect of the goods from the time when they have been delivered in accordance with the provisions of article A.2 above, except as provided in article A.5 above.
4. Pay the price invoiced as provided in the contract as well as the cost of air freight if paid by or on behalf of the seller.
5. Bear all risks of the goods from the time when they have been delivered, in accordance with the provisions of article A.2 above.
6. Bear any additional costs incurred because the air carrier, his agent

or any other person named by the buyer fails to take the goods into his charge when tendered by the seller, and bear all risk of the goods from the time of such tender, provided, however, that the goods will have been duly appropriated to the contract, that is to say, clearly set aside or otherwise identified as the contract goods.

7. Should he fail to provide proper instructions (where required) to the seller for the carriage of the goods, bear any additional costs incurred because of said failure and all risks of the goods from the date agreed for delivery or from the end of the period agreed for delivery, provided, however, that the goods will have been duly appropriated to the contract, that is to say, clearly set aside or otherwise identified as the contract goods.

8. Bear all costs, fees, and charges incurred in obtaining the documents mentioned in article A.13 above, including the costs of consular documents, as well as the costs of certificates of origin.

9. Bear all costs, fees and charges incurred by the seller in bringing and pursuing any claim against the air carrier or his agent in respect of the carriage of the goods.

Free Carrier*

Named Point

This term has been designed to meet the requirements of modern transport, particularly such "multimodal" transport as container or "roll on-roll off" traffic by trailers and ferries.

It is based on the same main principle as FOB except that the seller fulfills his obligations when he delivers the goods into the custody of the carrier at the named point. If no precise point can be mentioned at the time of the contract of sale, the parties should refer to the place or range where the carrier should take the goods into his charge. The risk of loss of or damage to the goods is transferred from seller to buyer at that time and not at the ship's rail.

"Carrier" means any person by whom or in whose name a contract by road, rail, air, sea or a combination of modes has been made. When the seller has to furnish a bill of lading, waybill or carrier's receipt, he duly fulfills this obligation by presenting such a document issued by a person so defined.

A. *The seller must:*

1. Supply the goods in conformity with the contract of sale, together with such evidence of conformity as may be required by the contract.

2. Deliver the goods into the charge of the carrier named by the buyer

---

* This term came into force 1980.

on the date or within the period agreed for delivery at the named point in the manner expressly agreed or customary at such point. If no specific point has been named, and if there are several points available, the seller may select the point at the place of delivery which best suits his purposes.

3. At his own risk and expense obtain any export license or other official authorization necessary for the export of the goods.
4. Subject to the provisions of article B.5 below, pay any taxes, fees and charges levied in respect of the goods because of exportation.
5. Subject to the provisions of article B.5 below, bear all costs payable in respect to the goods until such time as they will have been delivered in accordance with the provisions of article A.2 above.
6. Subject to the provisions of article B.5 below, bear all risks of the goods until such time as they have been delivered in accordance with the provisions of article A.2 above.
7. Provide at his own expense the customary packing of the goods, unless it is the custom of the trade to dispatch the goods unpacked.
8. Pay the cost of any checking operations (such as checking quality, measuring, weighing, counting) which shall be necessary for the purpose of delivering the goods.
9. Give the buyer without delay notice by telecommunication channels of the delivery of the goods.
10. In the circumstances referred to in article B.5 below, give the buyer prompt notice by telecommunication channels of the occurrence of said circumstances.
11. At his own expense, provide the buyer, if customary, with the usual document or other evidence of the delivery of the goods in accordance with the provisions of article A.2 above.
12. Provide the buyer with the commercial invoice in proper form so as to facilitate compliance with applicable regulations and, at the buyer's request and expense, with the certificate of origin.
13. Render the buyer, at his request, risk and expense, every assistance in obtaining any document other than those mentioned in article A.12 above issued in the country of departure and/or of origin and which the buyer may require for the importation of the goods into the country of destination (and, where necessary, for their passage in transit through another country).

B. *The buyer must:*

1. At his own expense, contract for the carriage of the goods from the named point and give the seller due notice of the name of the carrier and of the time for delivering the goods to him.
2. Bear all costs payable in respect of the goods from the time when they have been delivered in accordance with the provisions of article A.2 above, except as provided in article A.4 above.

3. Pay the price as provided in the contract.
4. Bear all risks of the goods from the time when they have been delivered in accordance with the provisions of Article A.2 above.
5. Bear any additional costs incurred because the buyer fails to name the carrier, or the carrier named by him fails to take the goods into his charge, at the time agreed, and bear all risks of the goods from the date of expiry of the period stipulated for delivery, provided, however, that the goods will have been duly appropriated to the contract, that is to say, clearly set aside or otherwise identified as the contract goods.
6. Bear all costs, fees and charges incurred in obtaining the documents mentioned in article A.13 above, including the cost of consular documents, as well as the costs of certificates of origin.

Freight Carriage—Paid To*

Named Point of Destination
Like C&F, "Freight/Carriage paid to . . ." means that the seller pays the freight for the carriage of the goods to the named destination. However, the risk of loss or damage to the goods, as well as of any cost increases, is transferred from the seller to the buyer when the goods have been delivered into the custody of the first carrier and not at the ship's rail. It can be used for all modes of transport including multimodal operations and container or "roll on-roll off" traffic by trailers and ferries. When the seller has to furnish a bill of lading, waybill or carrier's receipt, he duly fulfills this obligation by presenting such a document issued by the person with whom he has contracted for carriage to the named destination.

A. *The seller must:*

1. Supply the goods in conformity with the contract of sale, together with such evidence of conformity as may be required by the contract.
2. Contract at his own expense for the carriage of the goods by a usual route and in a customary manner to the agreed point at the place of destination. If the point is not agreed or is not determined by custom, the seller may select the point at the place of destination which best suits his purpose.
3. Subject to the provisions of article B.3 below, bear all risks of the goods until they shall have been delivered into the custody of the first carrier, at the time as provided in the contract.
4. Give the buyer without delay notice by telecommunication chan-

---

* This term came into force 1980.

nels that the goods have been delivered into the custody of the first carrier.

5. Provide at his own expense the customary packing of the goods, unless it is the custom of the trade to dispatch the goods unpacked.

6. Pay the costs of any checking operations (such as checking quality, measuring, weighing, counting) which shall be necessary for the purposes of loading the goods or of delivering them into the custody of the first carrier.

7. At his own expense, provide the buyer, if customary, with the usual transport document.

8. At his own risk and expense obtain any export license or other governmental authorization necessary for the export of the goods, and pay any dues and taxes incurred in respect of the goods in the country of dispatch, including any export duties, as well as the costs of any formalities he shall have to fulfill in order to load the goods.

9. Provide the buyer with the commercial invoice in proper form so as to facilitate compliance with applicable regulations and, at the buyer's request and expense, with the certificate of origin.

10. Render the buyer, at the latter's request, risk and expense, every assistance in obtaining any documents, other than those mentioned in the previous article, issued in the country of loading and/or of origin and which the buyer may require for the importation of the goods into the country of destination (and, where necessary, for their passage in transit through another country).

B. *The buyer must:*

1. Receive the goods at the agreed point at the place of destination and pay the price as provided in the contract, and bear, with the exception of the freight, all costs and charges incurred in respect of the goods in the course of their transit until their arrival at the point of destination, as well as unloading costs unless such costs and charges shall have been included in the freight or collected by the carrier at the time freight was paid.

2. Bear all risks of the goods from the time when they shall have been delivered into the custody of the first carrier in accordance with article A.3.

3. Where he shall have reserved to himself a period within which to have the goods forwarded to him and/or the right to choose the point of destination, and should he fail to give instructions in time, bear the additional costs thereby incurred and all risks of the goods from the date of expiry of the period fixed, provided always that the goods shall have been duly appropriated to the contract, that is to say, clearly set aside or otherwise identified as the contract goods.

4. Bear all costs and charges incurred in obtaining the documents mentioned in article A.10 above, including the cost of consular documents, as well as the costs of certificates of origin.

5. Pay all customs duties as well as any other duties and taxes payable at the time of or by reasons of the importation.

Freight Carriage and Insurance*

Paid To (named point of destination)
This term is the same as "Freight/Carriage paid to . . ." but with the addition that the seller has to procure transport insurance against the risk of loss or of damage to the goods during the carriage. The seller contracts with the insurer and pays the insurance premium.

A. *The seller must:*

1. Supply the goods in conformity with the contract of sale, together with such evidence of conformity as may be required by the contract.
2. Contract at his own expense for the carriage of the goods by a usual route and in a customary manner to the agreed point at the place of destination. If the point is not agreed or is not determined by custom, the seller may select the point at the place of destination which best suits his purpose.
3. Subject to the provisions of article B.3 below, bear all risks of the goods until they shall have been delivered into the custody of the first carrier, at the time as provided in the contract.
4. Give the buyer without delay notice by telecommunication channels that the goods have been delivered into the custody of the first carrier.
5. Provide at his own expense the customary packing of the goods, unless it is the custom of the trade to dispatch the goods unpacked.
6. Pay the costs of any checking operations (such as checking quality, measuring, weighing, counting) which shall be necessary for the purpose of loading the goods or of delivering them into the custody of the first carrier.
7. At his own expense, provide the buyer, if customary, with the usual transport document.
8. At his own risk and expense obtain any export license or other governmental authorization necessary for the export of the goods, and pay any dues and taxes incurred in respect of the goods in the country of dispatch, including any export duties, as well as the costs of any formalities he shall have to fulfill in order to load the goods.
9. Provide the buyer with the commercial invoice in proper form so as

---

* This term came into force 1980.

to facilitate compliance with applicable regulations and, at the buyer's request and expense, with the certificate of origin.

10. Render the buyer, at the latter's request, risk and expense, every assistance in obtaining any documents, other than those mentioned in the previous article, issued in the country of loading and/or of origin and which the buyer may require for the importation of the goods into the country of destination (and, where necessary, for their passages in transit through another country).

11. Procure, at his own cost, transport insurance as agreed in the contract and upon such terms that the buyer, or any other person having an insurable interest in the goods, shall be entitled to claim directly from the insurer, and provide the buyer with the insurance policy or other evidence of insurance cover. The insurance shall be contracted with parties of good repute and, failing express agreement, on such terms as are in the seller's view appropriate having regard to the custom of the trade, the nature of the goods and other circumstances affecting the risk. In this latter case, the seller shall inform the buyer of the extent of the insurance cover so as to enable him to take out any additional insurance that he may consider necessary before the risks of the goods are borne by him in accordance with article B.2.

The insurance shall cover the price provided in the contract plus ten per cent and shall be provided in the currency of the contract, if procurable. When required by the buyer, the seller shall provide, at the buyer's expense, war risk insurance in the currency of the contract, if procurable.[7]

B. The buyer must:

1. Receive the goods at the agreed point at the place of destination and pay the price as provided in the contract, and bear, with the exception of the freight and the cost of transport insurance, all costs and charges incurred in respect of the goods in the course of their transit until their arrival at the point of destination, as well as unloading costs, unless such costs and charges shall have been included in the freight or collected by the carrier at the time freight was paid.

2. Bear all risks of the goods from the time when they shall have been delivered into the custody of the first carrier in accordance with article A.3.

3. Where he shall have reserved to himself a period within which to have the goods forwarded to him and/or the right to choose the point

---

[7] It should be observed that the insurance provision under A.11 of the present term differs from that under A.5 of the CIF term.

of destination, and should he fail to give instructions in time, bear the additional costs thereby incurred and all risks of the goods from the date of expiry of the period fixed, provided always that the goods shall have been duly appropriated to the contract, that is to say, clearly set aside or otherwise identified as the contract goods.

4. Bear all costs, fees and charges incurred in obtaining the documents mentioned in article A.10 above, including the cost of consular documents, as well as the costs of certificates of origin.

5. Pay all customs duties as well as any other duties and taxes payable at the time of or by reason of the importation.

APPENDIX 3–C: COUNTRIES REQUIRING PRE-INSPECTION

COUNTRY	REGULATION/DECREE
ANGOLA, Bance Nacional de	Decree No. 18/80 of February 15, 1980.
BOLIVIA	Decrete Supremo No. 21170 dated January 10, 1986.
BURUNDI, Banque de la Republique du	Bank Regulations C—Imports—Second Chapter—Section II and Third Chapter, June 5, 1978.
ECUADOR, Central Bank of	Junta Monetaria Regulation No. 230/85 of February 28, 1985.
EQUATORIAL GUINEA, Bank of	Decree No. 81/1982 of December 1, 1982.
GHANA, Bank of	Bank Notice published in the Ghana Commercial and Industrial Bulletin June 1, 1971 (No. 38) and May 12, 1972 (No. 44).
GUATEMALA	Government Agreement 254/86 of June 18, 1986, published in Official Papers June 23, 1986.

HAITI, Central Bank of	Presidential Decree of October 31, 1983 and Interministerial Communique of November 3, 1983.
INDONESIA, Government of	Joint Decree of the Ministers of Trade, Finance and the Governor of Bank Indonesia Nos. 656/Kpb/85, 329/KMK.05/1985 and 18/2/KEP/GBI of April 11, 1985.
IVORY COAST, Government of	Presidential Decree 75-422 of June 12, 1975, revised by Decree No. 76-281 of April 20, 1976. The Ministry of Commerce Ordinance 0137/MC, June 26, 1975.
JAMAICA	Notice to Importers and Commercial Banks, January 1986.
KENYA, Central Bank of	Exchange Control Notice No. 10 (revised November 81) and subsequent notices.
LIBERIA	Notice to Importers and Commercial Banks, July 4, 1986.
MADAGASCAR, Democratic Republic of Ministere de L'Industrie et du Commerce	Official regulations effective July 1, 1983.
MEXICO, Direccion General de Norms Sobre Adquisiciones y Almacenes	Diario Official May 2, 1985.
PARAGUAY, Central Bank of	D.C. Circular No. 52/83 of August 30, 1983.
RWANDA, Banque National du	Regulation III/No. 19 of April 29, 1977.
SURINAM, Ministry of Transport, Trade and Industry	Decree 30 of December 3, 1981. Notice to Importers of December 11, 1981.
TANZANIA, Bank of	Exchange Control Circulars 109, 202, 203 and subsequent notices.

UGANDA, Bank of	Statutory Instruments 1982 No. 90 of May 19, 1982 and Notice to Importers of June 16, 1982.
VENEZUELA	Government Decree 1072 of April 17, 1986, and 1109 of May 21, 1986.
ZAIRE, Banque du	Circular 120 of October 3, 1968. Circular 124 of June 6, 1969 and subsequent notices.
ZAMBIA, Bank of	Notice to Importers of January 18, 1978 and circular A.D. No. 13/78 to all authorized dealers in foreign exchange.
ZANZIBAR, People's Bank of	Circular No. PBZ/102/49 of August 26, 1982.

REFERENCES

1. *Guide to Incoterms,* 2nd ed. (Paris, France: International Chamber of Commerce Services S.A.R.L., 1980), p. 8.
2. Peg Wieland, *Chase World Guide for Exporters: Methods of Export Financing,* 3rd ed. (New York: Chase World Information Corporation 1979), p. 69.
3. *International Trade Procedures: An Introduction to Doing Business Abroad,* 7th ed. (Philadelphia: Philadelphia National Bank, 1985), p. 18.
4. Alan E. Branch, *Elements of Export Practice* (New York: Chapman & Hill, 1985), p. 254.
5. Ibid., p. 254.
6. Philip MacDonald, *Practical Exporting and Importing,* 2nd ed. (New York: The Ronald Press Company, 1959), p. 232.
7. Ibid., p. 240.
8. A.B. Manring, *Exporting From The U.S.A.: How to Develop Export Markets and Cope with Foreign Customs* (North Vancouver, Canada: Self-Counsel Press Inc., 1981), p. 83.
9. Ibid., p. 83.
10. Ibid., p. 83.
11. *A Basic Guide to Exporting,* (Washington, D.C.: U.S. Department of Commerce, International Trade Administration, 1981), p. 43.
12. Ibid., p. 43.

13. Ibid., p. 45.
14. *Negotiable Instruments, Endorsements and Documents of Title: Basic Introductory Outline* (New York: The Chase Manhattan Bank, N.A.), p. 6.
15. Louis J. Celi and I. James Czechowicz, *Export Financing: A Handbook of Sources and Techniques* (Morristown, N.J.: Financial Executives Research: Business International Corporation, 1985), p. 203.
16. Gerhard W. Schneider, *Export-Import Financing: A Practical Guide* (New York: The Ronald Press Company, 1974), p. 202.
17. Ibid., p. 202.
18. Charles J. Gmur, *Trade Financing* (London: Euromoney Publications Ltd., 1981), p. 29.
19. Ibid., p. 30.
20. Ibid., p. 30.
21. *Negotiable Instruments, Indorsements and Documents of Title, Basic Introductory Outline* (New York: The Chase Manhattan Bank, N.A.), pp. 1–2.
22. Ibid., p. 2.

CHAPTER 4

EXPORT PAYMENT TERMS

PART A
NONLETTER OF CREDIT PAYMENT TERMS

International trade always involves an element of risk between an exporter and foreign customer over the trading of goods and services. The exporter wants payment for its goods promptly and extends the shortest payment terms possible. On the other hand, the foreign customer wants goods and documents received in good condition on a timely basis, many times on the longest payment terms possible. Foreign customers, like any other domestic customer, are usually reluctant to pay for goods before they have a chance to inspect them. They will request some type of extended payment term from exporters. It is probably one of the most important elements of international trade because most foreign customers either customarily obtain extended payment terms from their foreign suppliers and/or their country's import or foreign exchange regulations require or obligate them to obtain extended payment terms from their suppliers. Besides, most foreign customers are reluctant to finance the transit time of goods.

Payment terms, also referred to as credit terms or terms of payment, specify the conditions for payment of the goods and services between an exporter and foreign customer. That is, the length of time for which credit is to be extended by the exporter before payment is due by the foreign customer. Terms of sale on the other hand, discussed in Chapter 3, deals with the delivery terms liabilities and responsibilities between both parties (exporter and importer). How the salesperson quotes a customer (i.e., FOB, C&F, or CIF to a named port or point) determines when title transfer takes place. It will also determine who is responsible for the goods and pays for the transportation expenses. This important fact has a direct correlation and effect on credit terms, collections, and the management of accounts receivables.

Payment terms and terms of sale should be described in some detail as an integral part of the sales contract. In addition, they should be stated on such important documents as price lists, purchase orders and commercial invoices.

The practice for settling payment between exporters and importers differs from domestic practice. Export transactions are usually settled with drafts or bills of exchange together with supporting shipping documents. Domestically, payment is settled by presentation of a commercial invoice, bill of lading (proof of delivery) on open account or a promissory note for equipment or capital goods.

In domestic trade, the buyer normally obtains possession of the goods without signing a formal document which directly indicates an obligation to pay. Exceptions are the sale of equipment or project type financing, financed by the use of promissory notes and marketable securities and/or debt financing, repayable up to five years and longer. However, promissory notes, marketable securities, and/or debt financing techniques are usually backed by security and/or collateral plus the financial capability of the debtor to service the debt. Export payment terms on the other hand, can require a "formal promise to pay," known as Documents against Acceptance of a draft or bill of exchange (D/A financing) or against payment in full, known as Documents against Payment of a draft or bill of exchange (D/P financing) before the foreign customer obtains possession of the goods. A draft or bill of exchange can be accepted or paid prior to release of the goods when the original on-board ocean bill of lading along with other shipping documents are retained by the exporter who uses the intermediary of a commercial banks' overseas correspondents or subsidiary banks (explained in Chapter 5).

In international trade there are many different types of payment terms an exporter can negotiate with foreign customers. Some are less restrictive than others. In this chapter, I will take you from the less restrictive to the most restrictive or secured types of payment terms—mainly letters of credit. This is discussed in Part B and its other uses are discussed in Part C of this chapter.

Consignment

This type of payment terms is a method for selling goods overseas whereby title to the goods is retained by the exporter until the goods are actually sold. In most cases, the goods are stored in a free port or bonded warehouse (private or government controlled) in the foreign customer's (consignee's) country. This way, the goods do not actually enter into the country for duty purposes. The purpose of consignment payment terms is to place an inventory of goods at the immediate disposal of the consignee for sale to third parties or the consignee itself. Under most consignment arrangements, the goods are usually consigned to the exporter (consignor) as "in custody of" an overseas private or government bonded warehouse company or overseas commercial bank who is experienced in handling consignment arrangements. The consignment arrangement is usually entered into with anyone of the following consignees: An exporter's subsidiary, affiliate, branch, joint venture or related office overseas; a foreign sales commission agent; or overseas distributor.

There are many risks and administrative details to consignment arrangements:

1. Detailed terms and conditions between all parties to the consignment arrangement must be spelled out in a consignment contract. It is customary for exporters to seek the services of retained counsel in the country of the foreign customer for the proper drawing of a legally binding consignment contract (as with other sales contracts). This is done because of the different commercial laws and practices between countries concerning such things as property rights, tax liabilities, duty, and the wording and transfer of the all important negotiable bills of lading. The drawing of the contract should be a coordinated effort between the exporter's legal, credit, and sales departments, the foreign customer, retained counsel in the market of the consignee, and other interested parties to the consignment arrangement.

2. The goods stored in a warehouse for consignment must be stored separately from all other goods not part of the consignment stock, but imported by the foreign customer.

3. The goods should be insured by either the foreign customer or the exporter, but preferably the foreign customer. In either case, your risk management department should assess and/or obtain adequate insurance protection to protect itself.

4. Most importantly, the integrity and financial capability of the importer must be unquestioned, especially if a distributor or foreign commissioned sales agent is the consignee.

5. Proper accounting methods and procedures must be established. Because title remains the property of the exporter until the goods are actually sold, each sale made by the exporter, whether they are goods in transit or goods stored in a bonded warehouse, must be accounted for as inventory of the exporter. Once all or part of the goods held in consignment for the consignee are sold, an accounts receivable is created on the books of the exporter. If the goods are taken into the consignee's own inventory from the consignment stock or sold direct to a third party, then an inventory or an accounts payable is created on the books of the consignee.

6. Accounting records of the parties to the consignment arrangement must be compared and reconciled. On site reviews and constant monitoring are a must on the part of the exporter. At least twice per year the sales, credit, and accounting departments should perform on-site audits. Frequency depends on the size of the stock. All departments, especially the sales and credit departments, must be assured the goods held in consignment stock are moving (being sold) to third parties of the consignee and not simply moved into its own warehouse as unsold inventory. Goods sold direct to third parties by the consignee should evidence changes on the financial statement of the consignee. Goods moved out of the consignment stock direct to third parties on a timely basis also means that inventory losses from the consignment stock are minimized (assuming all of the goods in the stock are being moved). Because consignees have a tendency to sell new consignments rather than older goods, inventory problems will be created.

7. The exporter should verify that unsold goods can be readily returned to the country of origin, if necessary, or resold some place else. Local tax laws and custom regulations must be investigated.

8. Consignment arrangements should be limited to countries that do not have burdensome foreign exchange restrictions. There should be no question of foreign exchange availability.

In conclusion, this type of payment arrangement is very risky and difficult to administrate from the point of view of many experienced credit managers throughout the world.

Open Account

This payment term is the same as domestic open account payment terms. Open account payment terms are highly desirable from the foreign customer's standpoint because the foreign customer can obtain title documents (especially the original bill of lading) direct from the exporter without the intermediary of banks or other third parties. Exporters use open account payment terms in order to gain market share, meet competitive situations, or to minimize documentation flows and expenses encountered when selling under documentary collections or letters of credit through banks. It is possible to sell under these payment terms only when the exporter has the utmost confidence in the foreign customer's ability and willingness to pay and in the customer's country. The problem of selling on open account terms is the lack of a tangible obligation (i.e., draft), that removes the principal basis for positive action against the foreign customer in the event of default.

Despite the credit manager feeling comfortable with the risk of a foreign customer, it is extremely important for the exporter to carefully weigh all of the political and economic risks of the importer's country. This means including an analysis of both the availability of the billing currency and the foreign exchange regulations of the importer's country before granting open account payment terms to the foreign customer. Assessing country risk is discussed in Chapter 2.

Some exporters credit insure their exports in order to minimize their risks when selling on open account or other payment terms. If insured, the insurer may place a credit limit on the foreign customer and/or the country with maximum permissible payment terms (discussed in Chapter 6).

While an exporter must exercise prudent judgment through a careful analysis of commercial and country risks inherent by selling on open account to nonrelated companies overseas, traditionally, open account has normally been extended to foreign branches, subsidiaries, or related companies of the exporter. However, many parent companies with related companies overseas are reevaluating their open account payment terms (intercompany receivables) because of the unavailability of their billing currency. This is due in part to some of the severe country risk situations existing in many countries throughout the world.

Cash against Documents, Cash against Goods, and Documents against Payment

Cash against Documents (CAD), Cash against Goods (CAG) and Documents against Payment (DAP) are payment terms used by exporters (especially the use of CAD by Europeans), that have basically the same meaning. These payment terms do not require the drawing of a draft for collection. Exporters use these methods of payment for competitive reasons and to avoid stamp taxes on sight or time drafts which are applicable in some foreign countries (i.e., Italy). Normally, it is the foreign customer that complains about the use of drafts in cases where the exporter refuses to pay the stamp taxes.

In the case of CAG payment terms, experienced exporters will recall these payment terms were requested by Turkish importers during the country's severe banking and liquidity crisis in the mid 1970s. Under this type of payment term, the goods are shipped and, on arrival at the foreign port of destination in Turkey, the goods are stored in a bonded warehouse until the foreign customer withdraws the goods from the warehouse, approximately 70 days from withdrawal, at which time the foreign customer pays for the goods.

Control of the documents under these payment terms is normally done through the intermediary of banks by submitting the documents with a letter of instruction or letter of transmittal (see Chapter 5 for more information on these letters). In other instances, the documents can be sent to a confirming house, the exporter's agent or the foreign customer's agent in the exporter's country. CAD payment terms with a foreign customer's agent is normally done because of foreign exchange shortages in the foreign customer's country or with government agencies. In some instances the foreign customer designates a related or affiliated company in the country of the exporter or another country to coordinate purchases of the project related business.

Release of the documents to the foreign customer takes place on payment of the exporter's billing currency as stated on its commercial invoice. This usually occurs almost concurrently with the arrival of the goods at the foreign port of destination. This assumes the negotiable bills of lading are not consigned direct to the foreign customer. Payment for the goods is remitted to the exporter the same as open account or documentary drafts for collection.

The problem for the exporter selling under any of these types of payment terms is the same as selling under open account. This problem is the lack of a tangible obligation, as mentioned under open account payment terms, that removes the principal basis for positive action against the purchaser in the event of default. The commercial or foreign customer risk, and the risk of the importer's country (country risk) need to be investigated and thoroughly analyzed or reviewed before the goods are shipped.

Clean Collection

Under a clean draft, the exporter sends the shipping documents directly to the foreign customer and submits only an invoice(s) and draft drawn on the foreign customer to its bank for collection. This type of payment term, like open account or cash against documents, should only be used when the exporter has complete confidence in the foreign customer and its country after both have been carefully investigated and analyzed.

Clean drafts are more commonly used between subsidiaries, affiliates, or related offices of the exporter, generally with long-standing relationships. One advantage for the use of the clean draft is to expedite the flow of documents to the foreign customer, especially when the transportation time between the two parties is short.

Time Draft–Documents against Acceptance

A Time Draft–Documents against Acceptance (D/A) payment term is more restrictive than consignment, open account or CAD, CAG, DAP, but is less restrictive than documents against payment or letter of credit. Under this payment term, a draft together with original shipping documents, are presented through commercial banking channels in most cases. The role of commercial banks pertaining to drafts for collection is discussed in Chapter 7. (See Figure 4–1 for an example.) Provided the draft is drawn on the

FIGURE 4–1
Time Draft

```
FORM 01-2127

                                              NO.    BG 009126

EXCHANGE FOR   U.S. $75,000.00               DATE      October 28, 1987

XXXXXNINETYXXXXXXXX DAYS AFTER    B/L DATE          PAY THIS  SOLE OF EXCHANGE

TO THE ORDER OF   THE PHILADELPHIA NATIONAL BANK
XXXXXXXXXXXXXXX SEVENTY-FIVE THOUSAND U.S. DOLLARS XXXXXXXXXXXXXXXXXXXXXXXX
VALUE RECEIVED AND CHARGE SAME TO ACCOUNT OF

                                         EWP International Corporation
          XYZ International Company       Houston, Texas
   TO     16 Street
          Brussels, Belgium                 Eugene W Perry
                                         Eugene W. Perry
```

---

foreign customer, it requires the foreign customer to accept the draft, usually on arrival of the goods at the port of destination, thus creating a Trade Acceptance (T/A). By accepting the draft, the foreign customer promises to pay the time draft at its maturity. For example, if the time draft is payable 90 days from the date of the draft, then the foreign customer by accepting the time draft, promises to pay it 90 days from the date of the time draft. It is not a guarantee of payment at the maturity date. Payment is predicated on the credit and financial capability and willingness of the foreign customer to pay the drafted obligation at maturity.

On acceptance of the draft by the foreign customer, the intermediary party (i.e., bank) will release the original shipping documents to the foreign customer. The exporter can give instructions to the intermediary party to accept a provisional payment in local currency on the condition that shortages of the billing currency are the sole responsibility of the importer.

NOTE: Overseas collecting banks abroad will not automatically deliver title documents to a foreign customer against payment in local currency unless instructed by the exporter. Exporters should carefully evaluate or consider whether or not to authorize the release of title documents against payment in local currency. Exporters who instruct overseas collecting banks to deliver title documents against payment in local currency should do so with a written commitment from the foreign customer to assume all exchange risks. Most bank forms contain wording similar to the following:

> A provisional deposit in local currency may be accepted with drawee's written understanding to assume full responsibility for all exchange risks and to take such steps with your exchange control authorities as may be necessary to bring about final settlement in the currency in which the draft is drawn at the earliest possible date, in the event such exchange is not immediately obtainable.

Since August 1971, the dollar no longer could be used as the basis for the gold exchange standard, meaning the exchange rates of most of the leading trading countries were allowed to float in relation to the dollar and thus indirectly in relation to gold. This was a break from the so-called gold exchange standard under the Bretton Woods Agreement established in 1944, which lasted until 1971. Because of the aforementioned, exporters who authorize the release of title documents against payment in local currency from a foreign customer run an "exchange risk" because of the possibility that the rate of exchange of the local currency might depreciate before the billing currency is allocated to pay the draft. Also, the foreign customer's country may not be able to allocate the appropriate foreign exchange (billing currency) due to a shortage of that billing currency, thus creating a "transfer risk."

Sight Time Draft–Documents against Acceptance

A Sight Time Draft–Documents against Acceptance is a draft drawn on the foreign customer. (See Figure 4–2 for an example.) It is created almost exactly the same way as a time draft–documents against acceptance with one major exception regarding how and when the maturity date is determined. The maturity date of a sight time draft is determined by the overseas collecting bank when the foreign customer actually "sights" the draft and accepts it, creating a trade acceptance (TA). Most foreign customers will normally wait for the arrival of the steamship carrier at the port of destination before accepting the draft. For example, if the ocean voyage time to South Africa, Argentina, or Australia is approximately 30 days and the payment terms as stated on the draft are 90 days sight, then the maturity date would be 120 days if the foreign customer waits for the arrival of the steamship carrier at the port of

FIGURE 4–2
Sight Time Draft

FORM 01 2127		
	NO.	TW 0011292
EXCHANGE FOR U.S. $25,000.00	DATE	October 28, 1987

XXXXXXXXXXXXXXX120 **DAYS AFTER** _____SIGHT_____ **PAY THIS SOLE OF EXCHANGE**

TO THE ORDER OF THE PHILADELPHIA NATIONAL BANK

XXXXXXXXXXXXXXXXXX TWENTY-FIVE THOUSAND U.S. DOLLARS XXXXXXXXXXXXXXXXXXX

VALUE RECEIVED AND CHARGE SAME TO ACCOUNT OF

TO
123 Importer Ltd.
3rd & 20th Avenue
Taipei, Taiwan

EWP International Corporation
Houston, Texas
Eugene W. Perry
Eugene W. Perry

destination. In many circumstances, these payment terms are used in order to gain a competitive advantage. However, the payment terms create some difficulty for exporters because the maturity date is not fixed like in dated documents–documents against acceptance payment (DA) terms. The exporter has to estimate the maturity date. The same risks and conditions exist to the exporter when accepting payment in local currency (see above Note).

On acceptance of the draft by the foreign customer, the overseas collecting bank will release the title documents to the foreign customer and notify whoever sent the documents and draft that the draft was accepted to mature on "X" date.

Sight Draft–Documents against Payment

A Sight Draft–Documents against Payment (D/P) is a more restrictive payment term than consignment, open account, or documents against acceptance type payment terms. (See Figure 4–3 for an example.) It is restrictive because the foreign customer must pay the face amount of the draft before it can obtain the original shipping documents to clear the goods pertaining to the shipping documents through customs. For this payment term to work effectively, the exporter must retain and hold title to the goods in its name.

Under this payment term the exporter draws a draft on the

FIGURE 4–3
Sight Draft

FORM 01-2127

NO. ___AR 001296___

EXCHANGE FOR ___U.S. $50,000.00___

DATE ___October 28, 1987___

XXXXXXXXXXXXXXXXXXX DAYS AFTER ___SIGHT___ PAY THIS **SOLE OF EXCHANGE**

TO THE ORDER OF ___THE PHILADELPHIA NATIONAL BANK___

XXXXXXX FIFTY THOUSAND U.S. DOLLARS XXXXXXXXXXXXXXXXXXXXXXXXXXXXXXXXXXXXXXXX

VALUE RECEIVED AND CHARGE SAME TO ACCOUNT OF

TO ABC Company, Ltd.
123 Street
Hamburg, W. Germany

EWP International Corporation
Houston, Texas

Eugene W. Perry
Eugene W. Perry

---

foreign customer and presents it, together with the original shipping documents, through commercial banking channels in most
cases. When using banks, it is important to obtain the name and
address of the foreign customer's bank.

The foreign customer must pay the full amount of the billing
currency or the foreign customer will not receive the original
shipping documents or the cargo pertaining thereto. If the documents are lost or delayed in the mail, the foreign customer may
obtain the cargo with a bond from a bank, and issue it to either the
customs authorities or the steamship company who delivered the
goods, with or without the consent of the exporter.

When an intermediary party, such as a bank, is used, the
exporter may give instructions to the intermediary party to deliver
the original shipping documents to the foreign customer against
provisional payment in local currency although the draft calls for
payment in another currency (see preceding Note). Exporters use
this type of instruction to countries where their billing currency is
scarce (shortages of foreign exchange) and import payments must
wait for an allocation of the billing currency or foreign exchange
from the local exchange control authorities. This provision makes
it the foreign customer's responsibility to pay the billing currency
in full despite shortages of local currency.

Note: When the foreign customer presents the title documents to the customs officials, it can proceed with the withdrawal of its goods through customs, deliver the goods direct to a customer, inventory the goods, or immediately use the goods in its manufacturing process.

Drafts for collection accompanied by shipping and other documents, commonly called *documentary collections,* are usually guided by certain rules governing how banks should process them. These rules have been established by the International Chamber of Commerce (ICC), in their publication No. 322, effective January 1, 1979. The rules are to assist and set forth basic responsibilities between companies and banks as parties in the collection process. This publication does not have the force of law. However, most major trading countries do adhere to the ICC publication. There are two fundamental rules described in the publication:

1. Banks are not responsible for the validity of the documents presented.
2. Banks must follow the exporter's instructions.

It is important that exporters be familiar with the provisions of this publication which is reprinted in Chapter 5.

Cash in Advance

A payment term whereby the buyer abroad makes a purchase of merchandise against a cash deposit or cash in advance (pre-payment) sent to the exporter in advance of an entire shipment or part of a shipment. The volume of international commerce conducted under this type of payment arrangement is infrequent and insignificant. This type of payment term is advantageous for the exporter since it eliminates both the commercial and country risks. However, in a buyer's market where competition among worldwide exporters is competitive, exporters ask for cash in advance arrangements only if the risk of nonpayment is high due to severe country or customer risks. Prepayment is sometimes used when merchandise is made to a buyer's specifications and the manufacturer has to lay out a large amount of money for the production of the respective merchandise. Asking for prepayment is not always the logical answer to eliminate or reduce risks. In many countries the local exchange authorities implement regulations that would prohibit importers or buyers to make purchases under this payment term.

If an exporter is credit insured, the credit insurance agency might remove the country from its list of eligible export countries because of country or buyer risks. In this case, the agency might insist on cash in advance.

Foreign customers are sometimes reluctant to purchase merchandise from an exporter under cash in advance because of some of the following reasons

1. Merchandise may not be shipped or not shipped timely. A problem for importers under strict or rigid import regulations (i.e., import permits with short expiration dates).
2. Merchandise shipped by the supplier was not in accordance with the customer's order.
3. All of the correct documents were not forwarded.
4. Shipment of the merchandise is delayed.

PART B
DOCUMENTARY LETTERS OF CREDIT

In Part A to this chapter, I mentioned international trade involves an element of risk. The two most prominent risks are the risks of delayed or nonpayment arising from the poor financial condition of foreign customers and the risks associated with the foreign customer's country, known as country risk.

There is a possible solution for minimizing these problems, perhaps not always on a mutually satisfactory basis to the parties involved in the export transaction. It is the use of a documentary letter of credit. It is called *documentary* because of the use of export documents in the sale of goods.

Based on my years of experience, it is by all means an integral and vital tool for minimizing the risks associated with international trade. It is also one of the least understood and most abused forms for obtaining payment in international trade. For one thing, it is not a guarantee of payment from banks. Also, it is not a substitute for good credit judgment on the part of credit managers and supporting staff. It is not the "answer" for salespeople who think their credit department or even senior management will dictate or want a letter of credit to cover the sale of goods or services. Even if the situation warrants a letter of credit, it must be the right type of letter of credit and it must be in conformity with the sales contract. As many experienced credit managers will attest, Murphy's Law certainly applies when it comes to getting paid under a letter of credit.

When letter of credit payment terms are warranted, it is vitally important for both the marketing/sales and credit departments to understand what type of letter of credit is necessary to cover the sale of goods and services to a foreign customer and the country involved.

Most letters of credit are documentary. This means that payment will be made against the beneficiary's draft and any documents (commercial invoices, packing lists, and bills of lading) called for in the credit. The payment terms under a letter of credit are either sight or time (usance) drafts or other demands for payment (no draft). Sight drafts are payable on presentation of the credit instrument to the paying bank. Time or usance drafts from sight or date under the credit are payable at some future date.

This part of the chapter will explain the different types of documentary letter of credit instruments that can be used to finance international trade. For more information about getting paid from banks under a letter of credit transaction, refer to Chapter 5.

LETTERS OF CREDIT

A letter of credit (L/C) is a written undertaking by a bank (the issuing bank), made in accordance with instructions from the foreign customer (the applicant), issued to the exporter (the beneficiary) to honor drafts or effect payment in accordance with the payment terms of the credit to the exporter or beneficiary who is to comply with the terms and conditions of the credit. The International Chamber of Commerce defines letters of credit as:[1]

> In simple terms, a documentary credit is a conditional bank undertaking of payment.
>
> Expressed more fully, it is a written undertaking by a bank (issuing bank) given to the exporter (beneficiary) at the request, and

on the instructions, of the buyer (applicant) to pay at sight or at a determinable future date up to a stated sum of money, within a prescribed time limit and against stipulated documents.

Letters of credit for international trade are often referred to as L/C, LOC for letter of credit, commercial letters of credit, commercial credit, documentary letters of credit, documentary credit, or just simply a credit.

There are principally three to four major parties to a letter of credit with different names to describe their different roles to the letter of credit transaction:

Buyer	Seller	Buyer's Bank	Seller's Bank
Applicant	Beneficiary	Issuing	Advising
Importer	Exporter	Negotiating	Confirming
Account party	Shipper	Paying	Negotiating
Consignee	Consignor		Paying

A letter of credit has many purposes in international trade. The primary purpose is to finance a commercial transaction between an exporter and a foreign customer that provide a bank's assurance for money to be paid to an exporter or beneficiary of a credit when goods are shipped. This is predicated on the beneficiary of the credit complying with the terms and conditions of the credit. But, there are certain things which a letter of credit is not intended to accomplish.

Contrary to what most people believe about letters of credit, they are not "money in the bank" or "guarantees" of payment, as many experienced exporters have learned. In many instances, credits contain stipulations or conditions that are difficult or nearly impossible to comply with. Some of these will be discussed in this chapter. Most others are discussed in Chapter 5.

A letter of credit does not ensure that the goods shipped to the foreign customer will be those evidenced in a commercial invoice and bill of lading. Banks only deal in documents and not in goods when dealing with commercial letters of credit. That is, the bank is obligated to pay the beneficiary of the credit against drafts drawn against the credit, provided the documents and draft comply with the terms and conditions of the credit. The bank assumes no liability or responsibility for the exact and correct quality, quantity, description, condition, value, or existence of the goods as stated in the accompanying documents to the letter of credit. It is not the bank's responsibility to ensure that the goods shipped are as described in the documents. For example, if the letter of credit calls for documents (commercial invoice, bill of lading, packing list) covering a shipment of minerals and books, the bank will pay the beneficiary (exporter) provided it has complied with the terms and conditions of the credit. A letter of credit is no substitute for confidence and integrity between the exporter and foreign customer. There is very little substitute for quality goods, price, extended credit terms, financing, and efficient and effective operations of an exporter now and in the future due to the worldwide competitive marketplace. Because of the problem of quality, quantity, and price, many nations and/or foreign customers are requiring that the goods and documents be inspected by independent agencies prior to shipment as a condition in letters of credit (includes other payment term transactions), an aspect discussed in Chapter 3.

The letter of credit is a separate contractual agreement between the bank which opens the credit and the applicant (foreign customer). It is a separate contract from the sales contract between the exporter and foreign customer.

It is vitally important to note that all parties to the letter of credit instrument (exporter [beneficiary], foreign customer [applicant], applicant's bank [opening bank], and the beneficiaries bank [advising/negotiating/paying/confirming bank]) are all subject to the Uniform Customs and Practice for Documentary Credits, known in trade circles as "UCP" (1983 revision), publication number 400 of the International Chamber of Commerce (ICC) (see Chapter 5, for a reprint), except to the extent to which the parties may expressly otherwise agree. The 1983 revision of the UCP supersedes UCP publication No. 290. These governing general principles, definitions, and provisions were developed over a period of time as a result of customary banking practice and changes in international trade.

Most letters of credit issued by banks in countries throughout the world subscribe to the UCP. Since some nations do not subscribe to the UCP (such as the People's Republic of China), it is advisable to check with the ICC, commercial banks, or the U.S. Department of Commerce. Exporters and foreign customers should be totally familiar with its provisions.

TERMS AND CONDITIONS OF SALES CONTRACT

In order to avoid and minimize misunderstandings between the exporter (beneficiary) and foreign customer (applicant), sales of goods and services should be evidenced by a terms and conditions of sales contract or simply sales contract. The agreement should specifically spell out what is agreed on between the foreign customer and the exporter. Among other terms and conditions of sale applicable to the trading of goods or services in the sales contract (i.e., prices, quantities) are the terms and conditions listed below which serve to minimize discrepancies (discussed in chapter 5) and bad relationships between the parties to the export transaction and the letter of credit:

- Payment terms.
- Terms of sale.
- Expiration date.
- Shipment date.
- Late presentation of documents date, if any.
- The opening bank.
- Advising/confirming bank preference.
- Minimum title documentary requirements.
- Amount of the credit.
- Date to open the L/C.
- Partial shipments, yes or no.
- How the L/C will be transmitted to the beneficiary.

The exporter should negotiate with the foreign customer for the least amount of terms, conditions, and documents to be required in the letter of credit. This will assist the exporter (beneficiary) in expediting the processing, banking, and payment of the letter of credit and minimize discrepancies. To the foreign customer it means receiving documents in good order, without delays in the shipment of the goods, and clearance through customs. However, it is important to note that irrespective of the terms and conditions mutually agreed on in a sales contract, there can still be discrepancies or problems with complying to certain terms and conditions in the letter of credit. The two answers to minimizing problems with letter of credit transactions is to minimize the presenting of discrepant documents and the relationship between the parties to the letter of credit transaction. This means not just having a good working relationship between the exporter and the foreign customer, they must have a good relationship with the banks. The better the relationship, the better are the chances of getting paid.

On complete negotiation of a sales contract, the foreign customer applies to its bank for the issuance of a commercial letter of credit in favor of the exporter (beneficiary). The application (Figure 4–4) for the letter of credit outlines specific information to be included in the letter of credit itself. It should at least be synonymous to the information contained in the sales contract. By signing the application form, the applicant could also sign a security agreement (depending on the creditworthiness of the applicant), which is normally contained on the reverse side of the application. The application is in itself a separate contractual agreement between the bank which opens the credit and the applicant (foreign customer), separate from the sales contract between the exporter and foreign customer. The application will be used for issuances of the letter of credit by the applicant's bank who will enter into yet another contract by issuing the letter of credit itself. In effect, the applicant's bank, by issuing the letter of credit has substituted its own credit standing for that of the applicant (foreign customer) who it has credit assessed. Therefore, it would be appropriate for the beneficiary of the letter of credit to ensure itself that the opening bank who irrevocably commits itself to pay against a letter of credit is creditworthy. This can be done by asking a bank in the country of the exporter to add its "confirmation" to that of the opening bank if the exporter is unsure of the creditworthiness of the opening bank or its country. Also, large international commercial banks are more than willing to give advice on opening banks if you are unfamiliar with the bank.

FIGURE 4–4
Application for Letter of Credit

**Philadelphia
National Bank**

A CoreStates Bank

International Operations
PO Box 13866
Philadelphia PA 19101

**APPLICATION AND AGREEMENT
COMMERCIAL LETTER OF CREDIT**

DATE

Gentlemen:

The undersigned hereby requests you (as its agent) to open your irrevocable Letter of Credit via:

☐ Air Mail   ☐ Short Teletransmission   ☐ Full Teletransmission
                                  (Details by Air Mail)   (Operative Transmission)

through your correspondent or ....

In Favor of (Beneficiary)   For Account of (Applicant)

up to an aggregate amount of ....
available by drafts at .... for: ☐ 100%   ☐ _____ % of the
invoice value, drawn at your option, on you or your correspondent, and presented not later than _____
                                                                                                                      (credit expiration date)

DOCUMENTS REQUIRED AS INDICATED BY "X"

☐ Commercial Invoice ....

☐ U.S. Special Customs Form #5515 ....

☐ Insurance Policy/Certificate ....

☐ Other Documents ....

☐ Air Way Bill consigned to ....

☐ Full set clean on board ocean Bills of Lading issued or endorsed to the order of The Philadelphia National Bank,

marked "Freight   ☐ Collect   ☐ Prepaid"   Latest Shipping Date ....

Notify...

Evidencing shipment of ....
                                          (PLEASE MENTION COMMODITY ONLY, OMITTING DETAILS ON PRICE, GRADE, QUALITY, ETC.)

From ....   To ....

Partial shipments   ☐ are   ☐ are not permitted.   Transhipments   ☐ are   ☐ are not permitted.

Indicate shipping terms: (FOB, C&F, CIF) ....   Container shipments   ☐ are   ☐ are not permitted.

Insurance to be effected by ourselves, if Insurance Policy/Certificate is not checked above.
The negotiating Bank is to be authorized to forward all documents in one registered airmail.
Documents must be presented for payment, acceptance or negotiation within .... days after the date of issuance of the Bill
of Lading or other shipping documents.

All banking charges outside USA are for account of   ☐ Beneficiary   ☐ Account Party

Customer/Bank Telephone number ....   Charge PNB Account No. ....

SPECIAL INSTRUCTIONS:

THIS APPLICATION MUST BE SIGNED ON REVERSE SIDE

Source: Philadelphia National Bank.

The bank opening the credit will undertake to pay the beneficiary of the letter of credit by its irrevocable commitment as stated on the actual credit and therefore, the exporter will look to that bank for payment or acceptance. It assumes the beneficiary has complied with the terms and conditions of the letter of credit. The exporter will not look to the foreign customer for payment or acceptance unless the exporter encounters discrepancies that it cannot correct. In this case, the obligations of the issuing and/or confirming banks under the letter of credit cease to exist. The exporter is now dealing with the foreign customer on open account terms—hopefully the foreign customer is a good credit risk, and the country risk is small.

TYPES OF LETTERS OF CREDIT

There are many different types and versions of letters of credit that can be used in international trade. It is important, not only for credit people, but for all parties to an export sales transaction to thoroughly understand the limitations and purposes of each.

Revocable Letter of Credit

A revocable letter of credit is an L/C issued by the foreign customer's bank and advised by a U.S. or foreign bank (see Figure 4–5). The issuing bank may amend or cancel the credit at any time, without the approval of the beneficiary. If a credit is revocable and designates a bank other than the opening bank as the paying bank, the paying bank can revoke its agreement to pay under the credit on receipt of a notice of revocation from the opening bank provided payment has not been made. Therefore, the revocable credit gives the exporter no protection prior to negotiation of the credit. This type of credit is only a means of arranging payment between the foreign customer and exporter. The revocable credit is less frequently used than the confirmed or unconfirmed irrevocable credits. It is sometimes used for trade between parents and subsidiaries or as a mechanism to ensure currency allocation under foreign exchange regulations.

FIGURE 4–5
An Example of a Revocable Letter of Credit

TEXAS COMMERCE BANK
NATIONAL ASSOCIATION
International Banking Division
P. O. BOX 2558
HOUSTON, TEXAS 77001

CABLE: TEXCOMBANK

TELEX: 775418

REVOCABLE CREDIT NO. EC-00091-E

May   , 19—

ABC
717 Travis
Houston, Texas 77001   REVOCABLE SPECIMEN

Gentlemen:

We are instructed by The Cho-Heung Bank, Ltd., Seoul, Korea to advise you that
they have issued their Revocable Letter of Credit No. 900000 in your favor for
account of Korean Importers, Seoul, Korea and operative on November , 19—,
for a sum not exceeding in all Four Hundred Seventy Five Thousand Dollars United
States currency ($475,000.00USC), available by your draft(s) on us at sight,
accompanied by your officially signed receipt in duplicate, marked" "Received
under The Cho-Heung Bank, Ltd. Revocable Credit 900000 of Advice No. EC-00091-E".

✱ This advice is subject to revocation or modification, with or without a notice
to you, at any time before or after presentation to us of the drafts and documents.

Draft(s) so drawn with documents as specified must be present at this office
not later than January , 19—.

✱ This is solely an advice of a Revocable Credit opened by the above mentioned
correspondent and conveys no engagement by us.

This credit is subject to the "Uniform Customs and Practice for Documentary
Credit (1974 Revision), International Chamber of Commerce, Publication No. 290".

VERY TRULY YOURS,

TEXAS COMMERCE BANK NATIONAL ASSOCIATION

_____
Authorized Signature

REVOCABLE SPECIMEN

Source: Texas Commerce Bank National Association.

Advice of Authority to Pay is a revocable credit as indicated by the terms in the credit. A bank advises the beneficiary and does not engage or commit itself to pay under the credit. The beneficiary by presenting the required draft and documents is entitled to payment only if the credit has not been previously revoked.

Authority to Purchase is another revocable type credit, which is frequently issued and almost exclusively used by Far Eastern banks. Its purpose is to finance imports from the United States and other countries by providing a place (advising bank) where an exporter may present a draft on the foreign customer and obtain payment. Unless otherwise specified in the Authority, the exporter's draft will be negotiated by the advising bank with recourse (advance funds) to the exporter until the issuing bank is fully paid by the foreign customer. It is important to note that under an Authority, drafts are actually drawn by the beneficiary on the foreign customer. Most Far Eastern banks, however, are willing to offer to negotiate the drafts without recourse. If the Authority to Purchase is irrevocable and drafts may be drawn without recourse, the instrument becomes, in effect, a letter of credit in that it offers the exporter both security and a credit facility. The logical rejoinder is: "If everything is equal, why not cover the sale with a regular commercial credit?" The answer is simply that most Far Eastern foreign customers are more familiar with the Authority to Purchase and as a result prefer to utilize it to finance their purchases. If an exporter or beneficiary of an irrevocable Authority to Purchase entertains a doubt as to the standing of the issuing bank, the exporter may obtain the confirmation of a bank in the exporter's country (assuming a bank will grant confirmation). The Authority than becomes identical to a confirmed irrevocable letter of credit.

Irrevocable Letter of Credit

An irrevocable letter of credit is an L/C issued by the foreign customer's bank abroad or a bank outside its country. This is usually a bank in the exporter's country and is advised by a U.S. or foreign bank, without the confirmation of the notifying or "advising" bank (see Figure 4–6). The advising bank is one which simply notifies a beneficiary (exporter) of the opening of an L/C in its favor without any undertaking or obligation on its part, except that the bank must use reasonable care to check the authenticity of the credit which it advises (Article 8 of UCP 400), usually on its

FIGURE 4–6

An Example of an Irrevocable Letter of Credit

TEXAS COMMERCE BANK
NATIONAL ASSOCIATION
International Banking Division
P. O. BOX 2558
HOUSTON, TEXAS 77001

CABLE: TEXCOMBANK

TELEX: 775418

IRREVOCABLE CREDIT NO. EC-00092-E

May , 19--

ABC
717 Travis
Houston, Texas 77001

IRREVOCABLE UNCONFIRMED SPECIMEN

Gentlemen:

We are instructed by Banco Nacional de Comercio Exterior, S.A., Mexico D.F., Mexico to advise you that they have issued their Irrevocable Letter of Credit No. 9876 in your favor for account of ZYX Importers, Mexico D.F., Mexico for a sum or sums not exceeding in all USDlrs. Five Hundred Twenty Nine Thousand and no/100 (US$529,000.00) available by your drafts on us at sight for full invoice value of merchandise to be accompanied by:

- Commercial Invoice in original and three copies issued in name of Zyx Importers Mexico D.F., Mexico, relative to shipment of the merchandise for final destination in mexico delivered FOB tank cars at Laredo, Texas.

COVERING: "3 Carros Tanques conteniendo 20,000 galones 140,000 libras approximadamente de Oxido de Etileno, cada uno. F.O.B. Laredo, Texas".

Partial shipments of not less than 20,000 galons each, are permitted.

We are advised that insurance will be covered by buyers.
Invoices dated prior to July , 19--, are acceptable.

The above mentioned correspondent engages with you that all drafts drawn under and in conformity with the terms of this advice will be duly honored. Upon delivery of documents as specified if presented at this office (Commercial Letter of Credit Department, International Banking Division, P.O. Box No. 2558, Houston, Texas 77001, on or before August , 19--.

★ This is solely an advice of an Irrevocable Credit opened by the above mentioned correspondent and conveys no engagement by us.

This credit is subject to the Uniform Customs and Practice for Documentary Credits (1974 Revision) International Chamber of Commerce Publication No. 290.

Very truly yours,

TEXAS COMMERCE BANK NATIONAL ASSOCIATION

_____
Authorized Signature

Source: Texas Commerce Bank National Association.

own stationery. The terms and conditions of the credit cannot be changed without the consent of the opening bank. The opening bank will ask a bank, usually in the exporter's country, to notify the exporter that an L/C has been issued in favor of the exporter. This bank is called the advising bank. The advising bank will notify the beneficiary in writing with a notation that it makes "no engagement" (or words to that effect), making the credit unconfirmed. The advising bank may volunteer to negotiate the exporter's draft drawn against the credit. This means the advising bank acts as a paying agent for the opening bank (maybe with recourse to the beneficiary). This type of credit may be designated as a Correspondent (unconfirmed) Irrevocable Letter of Credit. The advising bank is under no obligation to honor drafts against the credit. The foreign customer's bank is irrevocably committed to pay the exporter on any drafts drawn against the credit, provided the exporter complies with all of the terms and conditions of the credit. An unconfirmed irrevocable credit cannot be changed without the agreement of all parties to the credit. Beneficiaries to these type credits are entirely dependent on the creditworthiness of the opening bank because of their irrevocable obligation under the credit. The beneficiary must still be concerned about the creditworthiness of the opening bank and the political risks of the opening bank's country, especially its foreign exchange availability. This type of irrevocable commitment on the part of the opening bank relieves the exporter of the commercial risk of the foreign customer, again, provided it complies with the terms and conditions of the credit. If it does not, the exporter will, in effect, be dealing on open account payment terms with the foreign customer.

Confirmed Letter of Credit

This is an L/C issued by the foreign customer's bank abroad but confirmed by a bank in the United States or in another country (see Figure 4–7). This means that a bank other than the opening bank of the credit irrevocably commits itself to honor drafts drawn against the credit, assuming the exporter or beneficiary complies with the terms and conditions of the credit. However, simply because another bank adds its irrevocable commitment to a credit does not

FIGURE 4–7

An Example of a Confirmed Letter of Credit

TEXAS COMMERCE BANK
NATIONAL ASSOCIATION
International Banking Division
P. O. BOX 2558
HOUSTON, TEXAS 77001

CABLE: TEXCOMBANK

TELEX: 775418

Irrevocable Confirmed Credit No. EC-00093-C   May , 19--

ABC
717 Travis
Houston, Texas 77001   IRREVOCABLE CONFIRMED SPECIMEN

Gentlemen:

We are instructed by Banco de Santa Cruz de la Sierra, Santa Cruz, Bolivia to advise
you that they have issued their Irrevocable Confirmed Credit No. 4567 in your favor
for account of Paz y Gomez, Santa Cruz, Bolivia for a sum or sums not exceeding in
all USDlrs. Twenty Five Thousand and no/100 (US$25,000.00) available by your draft(s)
at sight on us for full invoice value of goods to be described in invoice as:

       Steel Structure. F.O.B. Houston.

Your draft(s) must be accompanied by:

1. Commercial Invoice in original and 4 copies.
2. Full set on clean on board ocean bills of lading issued to order of shipper, blank
   endorsed, dated latest August , 19--.

Evidencing shipment of the merchandise from Houston to Santa Cruz, Bolivia.
Partial shipments not permitted.
Insurance covered by buyers in Bolivia.

The above mentioned correspondent engages with you that all drafts drawn under and
in conformity with the terms of this advice will be duly honored upon delivery of
documents as specified if presented at this office (Commercial Letter of Credit,
International Banking Division, P.O. Box No. 2558, Houston, Texas 77001, on or
before August , 19--.

We confirm the credit and hereby undertake that all drafts drawn and presented as
above specified will be duly honored.

This credit is subject to the Uniform Customs and Practice for Documentary Credits
(1974 Revision) International Chamber of Commerce Publication No. 290.

                Very truly yours,

                TEXAS COMMERCE BANK NATIONAL ASSOCIATION

                Authorized Signature

Source: Texas Commerce Bank National Association.

guarantee payment and it would be a misconception on the part of beneficiaries to think it does. Some of the reasons why an exporter might want a foreign bank's credit confirmed by another bank are:

1. Exporters are not totally familiar with the credit standing of opening banks.
2. The opening bank is in a country which is considered a country risk (i.e., the country is having economic difficulties).
3. The foreign customer is considered to be a commercial or customer risk.
4. There is a shortage of the exporter's billing currency in the country of the opening bank. This is considered part of country risk, but needs to be mentioned separately because of the misconception of exporters who assume irrevocable obligations on the part of opening banks do not include foreign exchange shortages. However, experienced exporters and commercial banks know that international trades financed by letters of credit do receive foreign exchange priority from government authorities. In most instances this is true because the goods being financed by L/Cs are categorized as priority or essential imports.

When another bank adds its confirmation, the beneficiary does not have to be concerned about the ability or willingness of the overseas bank to fulfill its irrevocable obligation under the credit. However, before another bank adds its confirmation, the confirming bank will satisfy itself that the opening bank has the financial capability to fulfill its irrevocable obligation and will carefully evaluate the opening bank financially and its country through a country risk analysis. Banks who are asked to add their confirmation to credits will evaluate their lines of credit with opening banks and their country credit limits. These lines and/or limits are established by country desk officers and/or committees. Normally the establishment of these lines of credit leads to relationships with overseas banks known as "correspondent" bank relationships (discussed in Chapter 7).

In most cases banks will attach a cover letter to the opening bank's credit, stating whether it is acting in merely an advisory capacity or is adding its confirmation to the credit.

Simply stated, if you are not sure whether a bank has added its confirmation or not, look for the word *confirm*. If you do not see it on the letterhead of the bank who received the credit from an overseas bank, chances are the letter of credit is **not** confirmed. A typical confirmation clause might be: "We confirm this credit and thereby undertake that all drafts drawn and presented as specified above will be duly honored."

The problem is that many exporters or beneficiaries of credits might assume that the following clauses are the advising bank's confirmation to the credit:

> We hereby agree with bona fide holders that all drafts drawn under and in compliance with the terms of this credit shall meet with due honor upon presentation and delivery of documents as specified to the drawee if drawn and presented for negotiation on or before expiration date of this credit,[2] or;
>
> We hereby engage with drawers and/or bona fide holders that drafts drawn, negotiated and presented in conformity with the terms of this credit will be duly honored on presentation, and that drafts accepted within the terms of this credit will be duly honored at maturity.[3]

The two above mentioned clauses are the engagement clauses of the issuing bank. Specifically, the opening bank agrees to honor drafts in favor of drawers, endorsers, and bona fide holders.

However, beneficiaries of credits should exercise caution against accepting the following wording as confirmation of an advising bank:

> We confirm the credit and hereby undertake that all drafts drawn and presented as above will be duly honored by us. The opening bank states, Payment shall be effected two working days after (negotiating bank's) telex to opening bank stating that all documents conform to the terms of the credit. Payment will be effected to you upon receipt of funds from (a N.Y. reimbursing bank, third bank, not the negotiating bank).

Exporters should **not** consider this to be a confirmed letter of credit. How the negotiating bank is going to get reimbursed is of no concern to the exporter. Either the credit is confirmed or it is not confirmed. The reimbursing instructions are of interest only to banks. If these instructions were in the cover letter to the opening bank's credit, they would clearly be procedural. However, in the context of the body of the credit, these are reversing instructions—reversing the confirmation and making it contingent to reimbursement from the reimbursing bank over which the exporter and the negotiating bank have no control.

The above-mentioned credit might be considered as acceptable to the beneficiary. This is because the country of issuance from a country like Argentina might be acceptable. In countries where there is a priority schedule for the release of foreign exchange, the above-mentioned claused letter of credit moves toward the top of the priority scale for release of foreign exchange. This is typical of most Latin American countries, underdeveloped countries, or Third World countries that are short of foreign exchange for the importation of essential goods. Therefore, accepting a claused letter of credit might be better than not having a letter of credit or not making a sale to a country at all. This may require a business decision (meaning a mutually agreed on decision between the department heads of marketing/sales, credit/finance and perhaps the controller's area) to determine if the rewards outweigh the risks.

The following explains most of the various types of irrevocable letters of credit instruments in use by international commercial banks. Basically, there are two types, straight credits and negotiation credits.

Straight Credits. This type of credit can be used by exporters in cases where the beneficiary negotiates drafts drawn against the credit with the opening bank or confirming bank. Advising banks may negotiate drafts drawn against credits of the beneficiary, but act solely as the agent of the beneficiary. The letter of credit conveys no legal undertaking to protect such parties.

Negotiation Credits. This type of credit enables the beneficiary to either specifically nominate a bank (or any bank, if the credit reads *freely negotiable by any bank* or words to that effect) to check the documents against the credit. If the beneficiary has complied with the terms and conditions of the credit, the bank will pay the beneficiary the amount of the drawing against the credit less interest for the time it takes to obtain reimbursement from the issuing bank, unless the credit specifically states that negotiation charges are for the foreign customer's account. Beneficiaries should require negotiation credits where the currency of the credit is not their own currency or where the beneficiary can obtain preferential rates or service from another bank.

In other words, the negotiating bank now becomes a legally recognized party to the credit. Negotiating banks will pay the beneficiary of the credit on a recourse basis in the event anything goes wrong. Under any other type of credit there is no recourse to the beneficiary.

Beneficiaries of credits payable in a freely convertible currency, are payable at banks in the billing currency, can obtain funds prior to the actual payment by the opening bank. This will occur when drafts are negotiated under the credit of the overseas bank in which the overseas bank advances funds to the beneficiary and forwards the draft and documents to the opening bank for payment.

Banks can negotiate a beneficiary's draft under unconfirmed straight or negotiation credits "with recourse" to the beneficiary. Some credits may provide for the beneficiary to draw drafts "without recourse." When drawings are made against credits with recourse, the beneficiary receives funds in advance from the negotiating bank or paying bank. The advance is repaid when the negotiating bank receives reimbursement from the paying bank. Until the negotiating bank is reimbursed, the beneficiary may remain indebted to the negotiating or paying bank for the advance. The negotiating bank will look to the beneficiary for repayment of the advance in the event reimbursement is not made by the paying bank.

Paying banks will effect payment to the beneficiary under confirmed, unconfirmed, revocable, or irrevocable letters of credit. Banks negotiating drafts for beneficiaries under letters of credit do so under the laws existing within the country by advancing funds to the beneficiary with recourse. Negotiating banks have no recourse to the beneficiary after it has honored the beneficiary's draft. The negotiating bank looks to the designated paying bank for reimbursement. The bank designated in the credit as the paying bank will reimburse the negotiating bank for its "without recourse" negotiation after satisfying itself that the drafts and documents comply with the terms and conditions of the credit.

It is important that the beneficiary of credits know the purpose and intent of the credit instrument. The entire credit should be read and clearly understood. Make sure as beneficiary you know what the bank's obligations are under each credit. If you have any doubts, call an appropriate person at the advising, paying, or confirming bank's letter of credit department (such as the letter of credit supervisor or manager) to obtain a clear interpretation.

There are other types of credit instruments issued by banks to describe the needs and requirements of all parties concerned:

- Correspondent's Irrevocable Credit.
- Confirmed Irrevocable Straight Credit.
- Confirmed Irrevocable Negotiation Credit.
- Correspondent's Irrevocable Straight Credit.
- Correspondent's Irrevocable Negotiation Credit.

(A correspondent bank is a commercial bank in one city or country which agrees to handle certain transactions for a bank in another city or country, discussed in Chapter 7.)

The various types of credit instruments mentioned above may gradually disappear in favor of the standardized credit instrument format recommended by the International Chamber of Commerce. These standard credit formats will be designated on its face as irrevocable and usually will be advised to the beneficiary on the stationery of the issuing bank and not retyped on the form of the bank who is advising the credit. Banks issuing credit instruments in this format will include legal language which allows for the *negotiation* of drafts under the credit. Most forms adapted to the standard format will include a provision for a bank in the beneficiary's country to indicate on the form whether that bank is merely advising the terms to the beneficiary *without recourse* or whether it has *confirmed* the credit on behalf of the issuing bank.

SPECIAL TYPES OF LETTERS OF CREDIT

Most documentary letters of credit are issued to meet the traditional documentary requirements of a shipment. Some commercial type letters of credit, however, may be classified as special types because they vary somewhat from the usual type of transactions and can perform special functions. Under this subheading, we will discuss the principle types of credits classified as special which are not uncommon in international trade finance.

Transferable

A transferable letter of credit, issued in transferable form (the credit must state it is transferable), enables the original beneficiary to request the paying bank of the credit to transfer the credit by issuing one or more credits in favor of other beneficiaries up to the total value of the original credit (see Figure 4–8). The transfer must be made by means of an advice given by a named bank, effecting the transfer to the second beneficiary (could be more than one) in exactly the same wording as the original credit, with only three possible changes:

1. The transferee's name and address is substituted for the beneficiary's.
2. The unit price and amount of the credit may be reduced to allow for the first beneficiary's profit.
3. The expiry date may be brought forward to allow for movement of documents from the bank effecting the transfer to the issuing bank.

In effect, the original beneficiary (exporter) is the middleman in a transferable credit, and usually has the credit transferred to one or more of its own suppliers. When the credit is transferred, the exporter is actually using the creditworthiness of the opening bank, thus avoiding having to borrow or use its own funds to buy the goods from its own suppliers.

A transferable credit may be transferred only once. Transferable credits are generally used by middle men (agents or distributors) desiring to keep their identity secret from the exporter so as to protect their trade connections from becoming known. Normally, transferable credits work well and are not as complicated as they might seem at first sight, particularly if partial transfers are permissible. However, to ensure the first beneficiary's profit under a partial transfer, the first beneficiary must make certain that it presents on time its invoice for the full amount of the original credit to the bank effecting the transfer. If it fails to do so, the bank will

FIGURE 4-8

An Example of a Transferable Letter of Credit

TEXAS COMMERCE BANK
NATIONAL ASSOCIATION
International Banking Division
P. O. BOX 2558
HOUSTON, TEXAS 77001

CABLE: TEXCOMBANK

TELEX: 775418

IRREVOCABLE CREDIT NO.
Irrevocable Transferable Credit No. EC-00097-E   May , 19⁜

ABC Corporation
717 Travis
Houston, Texas 77001   TRANSFERABLE SPECIMEN

Gentlemen:

We are instructed by Albank Alsaudi Alhollandi, Dammam, Saudi Arabia to inform you that they have issued their irrevocable letter of credit No. D-6111X in your favor for account of Messrs. Commercial Enterprises ,Dammam, Saudi Arabia for a sum or sums not exceeding a total of USDlrs. Two Hundred Seventy Thousand and no/100 (US$270,000.00) available by your drafts in duplicate on us at sight drawn for 100% of the C&F invoice value showing No. and date of credit to be accompanied by:

-Full set of CLEAN ON BOARD OCEAN BILLS OF LADING to order, endorsed in blank, dated not later than June 30, 1980, marked "Freight Prepaid", indicating rates and amounts of ocean freight surcharges paid.

-Invoice in six fold in English, duly signed by beneficiaries, of which two copies are to be certified by Chamber of Commerce.

-Packing list in quadruplicate.

Covering: 250,000 lbs of American Rice

From Houston to Dammam, Saudi Arabia.
Part shipments are allowd. Transhipment not allowed.

We are advised that insurance will be covered by buyers.

Invoices dated prior to June , 19⁜ are acceptable.

✱ This letter of credit is transferable however, no transfer shall be effective unless in the form as per specimen attached and notice of transfer endorsed hereon by us and our customary charges therefore paid. The correctness of the signature and title of the persons signing instructions must be verified by your bank.

The above mentioned correspondent engages with you that all drafts drawn under and in compliance with the terms of this advice will be duly honored upon delivery of documents as specified if presented at this office (Commercial Letter of Credit Department, International Banking Division, P.O. Box No. 2558, Houston, Texas 77001, on or before July , 19⁜.

This letter is solely an advice of of an Irrevocable credit opened by the above mentioned correspondent and conveys no engagement by us.
This credit is subject to the "Uniform Customs and Practice for Documentary Credit (1974 Revision) International Chamber of Commerce Publication No. 290".

TEXAS COMMERCE BANK NATIONAL ASSOCIATION

Authorized Signature

Source: Texas Commerce Bank National Association.

present the second beneficiary's invoice direct to the issuing bank, and obviously this invoice will not include the first beneficiary's profit.

Example

A credit which is transferable, valued at $100,000 is transferred by the original beneficiary to two other beneficiaries for $45,000 each. The paying bank in this case would issue two separate credits for $45,000 each in favor of the beneficiary designated by the transferor (original beneficiary). Each credit would have the same documentary requirements as the original credit except for the expiration dates of the two credits. The expiry dates of the two credits would in most cases be dates prior to the expiration dates of the original credit. Assuming the two beneficiaries present drafts each for $45,000 and comply with the terms and conditions of the credit, the paying bank will pay each $45,000 or a total of $90,000. This invoice submitted with other documentary requirements by the two beneficiaries would be turned over by the paying bank to the original beneficiary, who would then submit an invoice and draft for a total of $100,000. The paying bank would pay the original beneficiary $10,000 representing its profit. Figure 4–9 illustrates the path of a typical transferable L/C.

Back-to-Back

The principle of a back-to-back credit is that the exporter, as beneficiary of the first credit, offers its credit as security in order to

FIGURE 4–9
Transferable Letter of Credit Routing

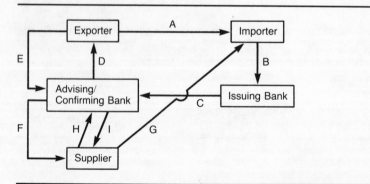

finance the opening of a second credit in favor of the exporter's own supplier or manufacturer of the goods needed for shipment under the first or original credit from the advising bank. Figure 4–10 illustrates the route of a typical back-to-back L/C.

This type of financing arrangement sounds simple, but in reality it is difficult to structure and justify from the point of view of banks. The difficulty banks have with this arrangement is that performance under the original credit is subject to the second credit being banked on a timely basis and in accordance with terms and conditions of the second credit. Some other reasons for a banker's reluctance to enter into this type of arrangement are:

1. The bank issuing the second credit is not familiar with the original beneficiary's manufacturer or supplier.
2. The second credit usually has conditions which are similar to the first credit which may be difficult for the manufacturer or supplier to comply with.
3. The applicant of the second credit must agree with amendments to the first credit which may become difficult to comply with from the point of view of the manufacturer or supplier of the second credit. This is especially true if the

FIGURE 4–10
Back-to-Back Letter of Credit Routing

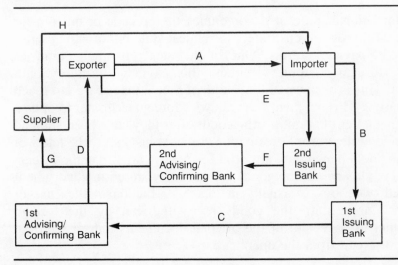

original beneficiary does not inform the second beneficiary of amendments.

Banks usually confine back-to-back credits to situations where they know the beneficiary of the second credit and are comfortable with its financial resources (ability to pay). Beneficiaries who prefer this type of financing are recommended to explore its availability with the bank or banks. Alternatives to this type of arrangement would be a transferable credit or an assignment of proceeds under a letter of credit, both of which are explained in this chapter.

The bank which issues a back-to-back credit is actually not only assuming the risk of the exporter, but also the risk of the bank issuing the primary credit. If the exporter is unable to produce documents or the documents contain discrepancies, the bank issuing the back-to-back credit may not be able to obtain payment under the credit since the foreign customer is not obligated to accept discrepant documents of the ultimate supplier under the back-to-back credit. The bank is still obligated to fulfill its commitment under the back-to-back credit. It is because of these reasons that many banks are reluctant to issue back-to-back credits.

Stale Bill of Lading

In international trade, it is sometimes the practice or custom for Far Eastern foreign customers to request stale bill of lading letter of credit payment terms. One of the most prevalent countries where foreign customers request this payment term is South Korea. This is because of the length of time it takes cargo to reach this nation. This payment term allows a foreign customer to open a covering letter of credit for the goods after they have been shipped or arrive at the port of destination. In most instances, the letter of credit is not opened until after the goods have arrived in the foreign country. On arrival, the goods are normally stored in government bonded warehouses, usually in Pusan or Inchon in the case of South Korea, until the goods are withdrawn by the foreign customer after receipt of the original documents lodged with the letter of credit from the opening bank.

Selling under this payment term has its risks and rewards, but experienced exporters know that the risks far outweigh the rewards. The principle major risks are:

1. The foreign customer may not open a letter of credit to cover the goods shipped.
2. The timeliness of opening the covering letter of credit may be delayed after the goods arrive in a country.
3. The credit may not provide for the acceptance of stale bills of lading.
4. The original negotiable bill of lading must be held by the banks until the letter of credit is presented to the negotiating and/or paying bank.
5. The foreign customer or its country has not been properly investigated by marketing/sales or credit departments.

In order to minimize the above mentioned risks and tighten controls, the following should be included in the terms and conditions of sale contract for this type of payment term:

1. Most exporters specify a specific number of days from the bill of lading date for the letter of credit to be opened (i.e., 60 days from B/L date).
2. The payment terms should be specific (i.e., 60 days stale B/L, unconfirmed L/C). Requesting confirmation on the L/C is at the discretion of the exporter, depending on the risks.
3. The L/Cs should be opened for 100 percent of full invoice value for each shipment, unless it is feasible for either or both parties to deal with one L/C covering several recent export shipments. Opening credits for 100 percent of full invoice value will prevent the foreign customer from turning the bonded warehouse into a consignment arrangement (i.e., the foreign customer may not want to withdraw 100 percent of the goods of one shipment from the bonded warehouse, but instead may make partial withdrawals of the goods stored in the bonded warehouse. Therefore, several intermittent credits may be opened against one shipment).
4. The letter of credit should provide for:

      a. Acceptance of stale bills of lading.*

      b. Sufficient time to present documents under the credit.

      c. Allow for a sufficient expiration date.

      e. Provide for original negotiable on-board ocean bills of lading.

      f. Payment terms of sight draft; or time draft from after sight or after date if necessary to meet import regulations or competition.

      g. Presentation of commercial invoices.

      h. Partial shipments/payments.

5. It is essential that the exporter use its own freight forwarder and not a forwarder preferred or designated by the foreign customer. This will eliminate any confusion as to who the shipper of record is on the original negotiable bill of lading. It will also help reduce the possibility of collusion between the foreign customer and its forwarder.

6. A designated party should be responsible for holding the original negotiable on-board ocean bill of lading. This can be either the exporter or the exporter's freight forwarder. There is a tendency for distribution/traffic departments and freight forwarders to close their files after receipt of freight bills. In this case the files must remain active until the L/Cs arrive to cover the shipments.

7. The exporter should designate someone to follow-up to ensure that letters of credit are opened timely or in accordance with the terms and conditions mutually agreed on.

8. The foreign customer should pay the costs associated with storing the goods in the bonded warehouse (i.e., warehousing fees, insurance).

9. These payment terms tend to create problems with the aging of accounts receivable, especially with automated systems. The original negotiable on-board bill of lading

---

* Article 24, UCP 400, allows banks to accept documents with a date of issuance prior to the date of the L/C. Article 47 of UCP 400 says that in the absence of specific instructions on how long after the issuance of transport documents they must be accepted, banks will refuse documents presented to them later than 21 days after the issuance of the transport document(s), and, of course, prior to the expiry date of the credit. This is true unless the credit specially allows for the acceptance of stale documents.

does not transfer to the foreign customer until payment is executed by the paying bank under the letter of credit. Therefore, receivables tend to age prematurely unless a provision is made within the system to compensate for the ocean voyage time and title transfer. Another technicality is that since the exporter holds title to the goods until the bill of lading is presented under the letter of credit to the negotiating or paying bank, the goods actually represent goods or inventory "in-transit," and not an accounts receivable.

The difference between accepting or not accepting to sell under these payment terms could be the gain or loss of a sale to competition, a lost customer(s), a lost market, reduced market share, and loss of profit.

Deferred Payment

Under this type of letter of credit, payment is delayed to the beneficiary until after the stipulated number of days quoted in the credit has elapsed (i.e., after 180-days). More simply, it permits payment terms in excess of those payment terms normally associated with commercial trade type letters of credit. When the number of days has elapsed, the beneficiary presents a sight draft on the paying bank (issuing, advising, or confirming bank). The credit will require the beneficiary to present shipping documents promptly after shipment. Figure 4–11 is an example of an irrevocable deferred payment credit.

This type of credit instrument is specifically designed to extend the payment terms beyond 180-day time or usance credits that create bankers' acceptances. Under Federal Reserve regulations, payment terms beyond 180 days are ineligible for discount with a Federal Reserve bank (bankers' acceptances and the regulations pertaining thereto are covered in Chapter 8). The regulations do not prohibit the creation of ineligible bankers' acceptances due to payment terms extended beyond 180 days. Acceptances of this type are simply not eligible for rediscounting at the discount window of a Federal Reserve bank. Therefore, the beneficiary undertakes to finance the shipment on behalf of the

FIGURE 4–11
An Example of an Irrevocable Deferred Payment Credit

TEXAS COMMERCE BANK
NATIONAL ASSOCIATION
International Banking Division
P. O. BOX 2558
HOUSTON, TEXAS 77001

CABLE: TEXCOMBANK

TELEX: 775418

Irrevocable Deffered Credit No. EC–0095–D   May , 19--

Tools International
717 Travis
Houston, Texas 77001   DEFFERED SPECIMEN

Dear Sirs:

   We are instructed to advise you of the establishment by Bank of Madrid, Madrid, Spain, of their Irrevocable Credit No. 9876, in your favor, for account of Lamar & Co., Madrid, Spain

for MAXIMUM U.S.$6,000.00 (SIX THOUSAND U.S. DOLLARS)

available as follows and after presentation to us not later than August   , 19* of the following documents:

Signed commercial invoice in seven copies, quoting Spanish License No. 12345, and describing the merchandise as indicated below

Certificate of U.S.A. origin, visaed by the Spanish Chamber of Commerce

Full set of on board ocean steamer bills of lading to order of shipper, blank endorsed and marked "Notify: Lamar & Co., Madrid, Spain" and "Freight Collect"

evidencing shipment of Tools, F.O.B. Vessel Houston, form Houston to Bilbao, not later than June , 19*.

 Payment to be effected to you 90 days after the date of the relative bills of lading, at which time you must present your clean drafts at sight on us. Therefore, when presenting documents hereunder please include your letter authorizing us to forward documents to our principals prior to payment.

   The above bank engages with you that all drafts drawn under and in compliance with the terms of this advice will be duly honored if presented to our Commercial Letter of Credit Department, International Banking Division, P.O. Box 2558, Houston, Texas 77001, on or before August , 19* on which date this credit expirees, however the documents must be presented not later than July , 19*

   Fxcept as otherwise expressly stated herein, this credit is subject to the "Uniform Custoı ı and Practice for Documentary Credits (1974 Revĩsion) International Chamber of Commeı ıe, Publication No. 290".

                              Very truly yours,

                              TEXAS COMMERCE BANK NATIONAL ASSOCIATION

_____
Authorized Signature

foreign customer until the sight draft is honored by the paying bank.

It is important to note that shipping documents are released to the foreign customer (opener of the credit instrument) before the beneficiary is paid.

If the beneficiary (exporter) needs cash flow, despite the terms and conditions of a deferred payment credit, it can ask the bank to finance the credit. In this case the bank grants a loan to the beneficiary by using the deferred payment credit as collateral.

Like any other credit instrument, unless the credit instrument is confirmed, the exporter only has the irrevocable obligation of the foreign (opening) bank which is subject to country risk.

Under a time payment credit, the documents and draft are presented to the paying/negotiating bank immediately after shipment. Under a deferred payment credit the exporter (beneficiary) does not present its draft until after the stipulated number of days elapses in the payment terms. For example, if the payment terms are 210 days from B/L date in a deferred payment credit, the exporter (beneficiary) cannot present its draft until the 210 days has elapsed from the B/L date. The exporter is out of funds (cash flow) until it presents its draft and gets paid from the paying bank.

Red Clause

In its original concept, this type of letter of credit contained a clause written in red ink either across the face of the credit or as a separate paragraph in the credit. It came into being during the early days of international trade when a foreign customer (applicant) did not want its capital or cash tied up before the actual purchase and shipment of the goods it purchased. In order to accomplish this, a credit was opened in favor of the foreign customer's (applicant) own representative traveling abroad or its buying agent, and this credit could contain the so-called *Red Clause*. (See Figure 4–12 for an example of the Red Clause.)

The purpose of the Red Clause is to allow the beneficiary of the credit to obtain advance funds or a loan from a negotiating bank in the country where the beneficiary is traveling or located. The advanced funds are to be used for the purpose of purchasing goods to be shipped to the foreign customer (applicant). In this regard,

FIGURE 4–12
Example of Letter of Credit Containing a Red Clause

FIGURE 4–12 *(concluded)*

TEXAS COMMERCE BANK
NATIONAL ASSOCIATION
International Banking Division
P. O. BOX 2558
HOUSTON, TEXAS 77001

CABLE: TEXCOMBANK   TELEX: 775418

IRREVOCABLE CREDIT NO. EC-00099-E   May   , 19*

Page Two

Page two of two pages forming an integral part of this credit.

Drafts accompanied by documents in conformity with the terms and conditions of this credit will be honored either upon receipt of notification to us by our principals that the goods have passed inspection by U.S. Department of Health, Education, and Welfare and Food and Drug Administration or at the latest 45 days after bill of lading on board date unless Texas Commerce Bank N.A. is notified in writing by the accountee that the goods have not passed on first inspection by the U.S. Department of Health, Education and Welfare and Food and Drug Administration, such notification must be accompanied by a certificate or statement issued by New-FDA indicating rejection.

Drafts and documents must be accompanied by a letter of a negotiating or collecting bank:

(1) Authorizing Texas Commerce Bank N.A. to release the documents before honoring the draft to: ABC Import Company, 7676 Travis, Houston, Texas, free of payment, for the purpose of efecting customs entry and obtaining inspection by the U.S. Department of Health, Education and Welfare, Food and Drug Administration;

(2) Giving instructions for the disposal of the remaining documents and/or of the goods in the event that the goods do not pass on first inspection.

★Banks or Bankers to whom this credit must be presented are hereby authorized to advance to the beneficiary, such sum or sums as he may require to the extent of US$150,000.00, to pay for merchandise, upon the execution of a Guaranty by the beneficiary stating that the advances are to pay for merchandise to be shipped in accordance with the terms of the letter of credit, and that the relative documents are to be handed to the bank or bankers making such advances when completed at which time the advances with interest are to be deducted from the proceeds of drafts drawn under such letter of credit. We hereby guarantee the reimbursement of advances so made, up to the amount stated above and in the currency of this credit, and undertake and agree that in the event that such advances with interest shall not be repaid to the bank or banker by the beneficiary of such credit during the currency thereof, we will repay them with interest to the date of such payment.

Very truly yours,

TEXAS COMMERCE BANK NATIONAL ASSOCIATION

_____
Authorized Signature

Source: Texas Commerce Bank National Association.

Red Clause credits are sometimes referred to as *packing credits*—they allow for the purchase and packing of goods for shipment.

Red Clause credits are restricted for negotiation to one bank or its branches to prevent the beneficiary from taking down an advance at one bank, negotiating the required shipping documents at a second bank, and obtaining payment a second time for the same goods. This is one of the reasons why some authorized banks who can make Red Clause advances, if they so elect, require the beneficiary to lodge the original credit instrument with them when the advance is made and endorsed on the reverse side of the credit. The usual wording of a Red Clause is:

> In the event the beneficiary informs you (the negotiating bank) that they require temporary advances up to ____ percent not exceeding $ ____ to enable them to pay for the goods for the purchase and shipment for which this letter of credit is opened, you are hereby authorized to make such advances which are to be repaid with interest from the payment to be made under this credit. We undertake that should they not be repaid to you by the beneficiary in terms of and during the currency of this credit, we will repay them with interest accrued to date. Please, advise us by airmail of each advance made by you.

Banks who choose to issue a credit with a Red Clause provision usually protect themselves by having the applicant present an addendum to or incorporate in its credit application an agreement with the following clauses:

Gentlemen:

Re: ____ percent Red Clause Letter of Credit

> You are hereby authorized to instruct your correspondent, in the event the beneficiary informs your correspondent that they require temporary advances to enable it to make purchases and shipments of the goods for which this credit is opened prior to the time it may draw under the credit, to make such advances which are to be repaid with interest from the draft(s) to be drawn by the beneficiary under the credit. We hereby agree to make to you as you may direct, upon demand, prompt payment, with accrued interest to date of such payment, of such advances if not repaid to your correspondent by the beneficiary before the expiration of this credit.

Some banks (the restricted negotiating banks) may not fully understand the purpose of the Red Clause and treat such advances as actual negotiations under the credit. They might call on the issuing bank to reimburse them immediately. In any event, the negotiating bank should be instructed on the use of the Red Clause and advised that such advances are to be carried by them as a loan on their books until the beneficiary ships and presents its draft and required documents. At this point, the negotiating bank then deducts from the payment to the beneficiary the amount of previous advances plus accrued interest currently being charged by the negotiating bank. At best, the Red Clause must be considered by the foreign customer (applicant) and opening bank as a "blank check" arrangement. It should be given serious consideration before incorporating this clause in the credit, especially if the amount is sizable or in favor of anyone who does not enjoy the complete confidence of the foreign customer (applicant).

The negotiating bank which makes the advance in accordance with the Red Clause terms is under no responsibility nor do they obligate themselves in any way to seek out the beneficiary to have their advance repaid. The responsibility to pay the advance rests strictly with the beneficiary. The bank's customer carries the risk until the advance is liquidated, with interest being paid to the bank that made the advance. The name *Red Clause* today connotes a definite meaning to those in the everyday work of letter of credit operations. The clause may not be written in red ink or red type, but it carries the same responsibilities even if written in black ink.

Green Ink Clause

The Green Ink Clause credit is somewhat similar to the Red Clause credit in that it provides for advances to the beneficiary prior to shipment. However, they differ in one very important aspect. The Green Ink Clause requires the beneficiary to lodge warehouse receipts covering the required goods with the restricted negotiating bank until the beneficiary is ready to ship. Furthermore, the local bank making the advance is authorized to release the warehouse receipts back to the beneficiary against the beneficiary's written undertaking that they will deliver to the bank within the life of the credit the required shipping documents in good order. The Green Ink Clause is worded as follows:

As the beneficiary(ies) may have to pay for and incur expenses in connection with goods before shipments, and therefore before it/they can lodge bills of lading for such goods with you, I/we authorize your aforementioned office(s) to grant advances by way of overdraft or otherwise to the beneficiary(ies) to the extent of $ _____ , such advances to be treated as being part of the sum first aforementioned as being repayable by the proceeds of such draft(s) when negotiated. It is distinctly understood that you are not to be responsible for the application of the moneys so advanced, and in the event and in consideration of your aforementioned office(s) making such advances, I/we hereby undertake to repay you on demand and sum or sums owing to you by the said beneficiary(ies) in respect of such advances and interest thereon at the bank's current rate and for this purpose the statement of account of your aforementioned office(s) shall be regarded as conclusive proof of my/our indebtedness. Should your aforementioned office(s) be requested by the beneficiary(ies) to allow the goods to be stored in _____ or _____ as the case may be before shipment, the bank is hereby authorized to agree to the goods being so stored during the pleasure of the bank, provided that warehouse receipts in the bank's name covering the goods are being held by the bank. The bank is also authorized at the request of the beneficiary(ies) to deliver up from time to time to the beneficiary(ies) the said warehouse receipts or such of them as may be required provided that the beneficiary(ies) furnishes a written undertaking to deliver to the bank in due course shipping documents covering the goods or such part of the goods as are represented by the warehouse receipts so delivered up. The bank is not responsible in the event of any error or irregularity in the warehouse receipts or documents or any wrong description of the goods or any mistake or misrepresentation as to the quality, quantity, size, or value thereof. We undertake to keep the goods so stored fully covered by insurance in the following manner until payment for same has been made to you:

The insurance thereon with _____ percent added is to be effected.

1. Beneficiary(ies) to your satisfaction, policy/policies to be handed to your aforementioned office(s), or by
2. You on my/our account, the cost of which I/we hereby engage to pay, or
3. We/us to your satisfaction, policy/policies to be handed to you, and I/we assign you the full benefit of such insurance and the monies payable thereunder.

It is advisable for customers and/or opening banks to investigate the warehouse they allow the beneficiary to use. They should instruct the restricted negotiating bank to accept warehouse receipts only from responsible, licensed, bonded or government bonded warehouses. It would be a risk to neglect this precaution and allow the beneficiary to obtain advances against warehouse receipts issued by a warehouse for which the beneficiary has access to or holds the keys to the warehouse.

Again, the international customer and the opening bank are urged to use caution in establishing a credit with either a stipulated Green Ink Clause or a Red Clause incorporated therein.

Evergreen Clause

The Evergreen Clause is a letter of credit that represents an automatic extension of the credit itself. For example, if a credit expires on July 31, it may have a clause saying, "This credit will automatically be extended for one (1) year (or whatever time period), unless we notify you otherwise three (3) months (or whatever period) in advance." The Evergreen Clause stipulates that if the opening bank does not notify the beneficiary that the credit has expired, and this is a clause right in the wording of the credit, then it is automatically extended for a certain period of time as mentioned previously. It's like a deferred payment credit, but it stipulates a time frame. There is an option given to the beneficiary to draw under the credit if the credit is not extended or renewed for an additional period of time. This form of credit is often used where a company is bidding and it requires a surety bond. The surety company would issue a bond without an expiration date, backed up by the letter of credit from a bank.

Legislative changes in both the states of California and New York have resulted in a lot of letters of credit in favor of insurance companies now requiring that they have an Evergreen Clause put into them.

Foreign Currency

Although letters of credit can be opened in a foreign currency, traditionally U.S. exporters denominate their commercial invoices and letters of credit in U.S. dollars. Because of this practice, I have purposely classified foreign currency letters of credit as special, since it deviates from normal practice. However, foreign currency L/Cs can assist in promoting export sales as a means of trade finance since many foreign customers prefer to be billed/invoiced in their currency or that of another hard currency. In this regard, the exporter (beneficiary) must seriously consider the risks/rewards of billing in another currency because of fluctuating exchange rates between its currency and that of another country.

The exporter (beneficiary) can make any one of the following requests with the negotiating/paying bank, assuming it complies with the terms and conditions of the credit:

1. Request the paying bank to issue you a draft in the currency of the credit, to be used for the beneficiaries own foreign exchange accounts.
2. Request the paying bank to convert the currency of the credit at the current rate of exchange (spot contract) to U.S. dollars.
3. Enter into a forward exchange contract with the bank if the beneficiary makes the determination that it is better to hedge its position.

Revolving

Exporters can minimize time-consuming operations, confusion, and inefficiency in dealing with repetitive shipments over extended periods of time to the same foreign customer if their payment terms are *revolving* letter of credit.

This type of letter of credit specifies that either the tenor (maturity) or amount of the credit is automatically renewed pursuant to its terms and conditions. A letter of credit with a revolving maturity may be either cumulative or noncumulative. When cumulative, any amount not utilized during a given period may be applied or added to the subsequent period. If a credit is noncumulative, any unused amount is simply no longer available. Figure 4–13 is an example of a revolving letter of credit.

A credit is revolving when the amount is automatically rein-

FIGURE 4–13
Example of Revolving Letter of Credit

TEXAS COMMERCE BANK NATIONAL ASSOCIATION

Telex: 77-5418   International Banking Division
Cable Address: TEXCOMBANK   P. O. Box 2558
Telephone: (713) 236-4220   Houston, Texas 77001   DATE OF ISSUE: May , 19*

☐ This credit confirms the cabled advice to the advising bank which advice must be attached hereto.

☐ THIS CREDIT IS FORWARDED TO THE ADVISING BANK BY AIRMAIL.

REVOLVING SPECIMEN

IRREVOCABLE DOCUMENTARY CREDIT

— CREDIT NUMBER —
OF ISSUING BANK | OF ADVISING BANK
EC-00098

— ADVISING BANK —

— APPLICANT —

Banco de Chile
Santiago, Chile

ABC Import Company
1234 Main Street
Houston, Texas 77001

— BENEFICIARY —

— AMOUNT —

Chilean Export Company
877 Avenida
Santiago, Chile

Two Hundred Twenty Thousand Five Hundred
and no/100 USDlrs. (US$220,500.00)

DATE September , 19*
— EXPIRY —
AT THE COUNTERS OF: ourselves

Dear Sirs,

    We hereby inform you we have opened our irrevocable credit in your favour available for payment/acceptance of your draft(s) at 120 days———————sight drawn on ourselves for the sum as shown above.

accompanied by the following documents:
    Commercial Invoice(s) in original and 3 copies.
    Customs Invoice(s) in duplicate.
    On board Original Ocean bills of lading (if more than one original has been issued all are required)
        made out to our order and notify applicant.
    Packing List.
    Weight Note.
    Signed statement tht insurance covering all risks has been provided under your open
policy.
For invoice value of merchandise to be described in invoice as:
P.V.D. BRISTLE AS PER SPECIFICATIONS ON PURCHASE ORDER No. 89674 DATED APRIL 30, 19*
C AND F HOUSTON, TEXAS.

Bills of lading must be dated not later than August , 19*
Drafts must be presented to the drawee bank within 21 days after the on board date of bills of lading, but not later than
Each draft accompanying documents must indicate the credit number and name of issuing bank

SHIPMENT FROM Chile
To Houston, Texas

PARTIAL SHIPMENTS	TRANSHIPMENTS
permitted	permitted

SPECIAL CONDITIONS This letter of credit is Revolving to the extent that the amount drawn by you not exceeding US$220,500.00 may become available to you again but only upon receipt by you of our formal advice of reinstatement. Total drawings under this credit are not to exceed US$661,500.00.

We hereby engage with drawers and/or bona fide holders that drafts drawn and negotiated in conformity with the terms of this credit will be duly honoured on presentation and that drafts accepted within the terms of this credit will be duly honoured at maturity.
The amount of each draft must be endorsed on the reverse of this credit by the negotiating bank. IF THE DRAFT IS NOT NEGOTIATED THIS CREDIT AND ALL REQUIRED DOCUMENTS MUST ACCOMPANY THE DRAFT.
The advising bank is requested to notify the beneficiary with/without adding their confirmation.
    Yours faithfully,

ADVISING BANK'S NOTIFICATION

AUTHORIZED SIGNATURE

PLACE, DATE, NAME AND SIGNATURE OF ADVISING BANK

Source: Texas Commerce Bank National Association.

stated on presentation of drafts and documents throughout the life of the credit and assuming the beneficiary complies with the terms and conditions of the credit. A maximum limit on the amount is usually agreed on by the exporter (beneficiary), the foreign customer (applicant), and the issuing bank because of its potential for the amount to be continuously increased and the bank's credit position concerning the applicant.

In most cases, there are three different clauses for exporters to consider which make the credit revolving:

1. This credit is "revolving," to the extent of $ _____ per month (cumulative)/(noncumulative). However, maximum drawings under this credit may not exceed $ _____ .
2. This credit is "revolving" in that all drafts paid automatically become available to you with the provision that the total drawings hereunder may not exceed $ _____ .
3. This credit is "revolving," in that all drafts paid are again available to you on receipt by us of instructions to that effect from our customer and provided we have notified you to this effect by an amendment to this credit.

Assignable

A normal credit which an exporter originally receives that contains the added clause in the wording of the credit, "This credit is assignable," is an Assignable Letter of Credit. It means the credit is assignable in whole or in part to one or more additional beneficiaries, in the full amount or in divided amounts of the proceeds of the credit to another party, depending on whether the credit allows for partial shipments. It differs from a transferable credit because unlike the transferable credit (in which the beneficiary has the right to instruct the paying or opening bank to make the credit available to one or more secondary beneficiaries), the assignable credit only assigns the proceeds of the original letter of credit.

Like the Transferable Letter of Credit, it is used when an exporter (beneficiary) primarily acts as the middleman. The assignee (other beneficiaries), therefore, have no control over whether or not proper documentation as required by the credit will be submitted correctly in whole or in part by the primary (original) beneficiary. Therefore, an assignment is not as safe for the assignee as a transfer. The beneficiary of an assignment usually has to turn control of the goods and shipping documents over to the original beneficiary. Payment under the credit is only received after the original beneficiary complies with all of the conditions in the credit. If the documents do not comply with the credit, no payments are made. It is always conceivable that the original beneficiary may choose not to ship the goods under the original credit, but instead sell the goods to a third party. The assignee who is a seller of goods to the original beneficiary should have complete confidence in the latter's honesty before making shipment.

An assignment of proceeds may be requested by the original beneficiary when a credit is not transferable but some confidence of payment must still be given to the assignee. Normally, the assignee should not put too much faith in such an assignment. The important thing to note is that the original beneficiary is responsible for performance under the letter of credit. This could be a responsibility that it is not capable of handling or may not wish to exercise. Moreover, the assignee has no assurances that no previous assignments of the credit have been entered into that conflict with its own rights. In reality, assignments of this nature are not any safer then selling an open account payment terms. Therefore, this vehicle is not used very frequently. Banks even prefer not to get involved in assignments because of the possible risks and conflicts.

Assignment of Proceeds

The beneficiary of a credit instrument may wish to instruct the paying bank to assign and pay the proceeds in whole or in part to a third party. This is not to be construed as a transfer of the credit instrument or a transferable credit. The assignment of proceeds has no monetary value to third parties until the beneficiary of the credit complies with the terms and conditions of the credit.

To effect an assignment, the beneficiary can either include an assignment of proceeds in the actual credit instrument by requesting the opener to include it in the credit or submit a written notice of the assignment to the negotiating or paying bank, with the original credit. An example of such a written notice is shown in Figure 4–14.

FIGURE 4–14
Example of Written Notice of Assignment of Proceeds (Letter of Credit)

ASSIGNMENT OF PROCEEDS
(LETTER OF CREDIT)

**TEXAS COMMERCE BANK
NATIONAL ASSOCIATION**
International Banking Division
P.O. BOX 2558
HOUSTON, TEXAS 77001

Date _____

Re: Letter of Credit _____ issued by

_____

Advice No. _____

Gentlemen:

We hereby authorize and direct you to pay the proceeds of each draft drawn by us, payable to your order, under and in compliance with the above described Letter of Credit (herein called the "Credit"), if and when such draft is honored by you, as follows: —

(1) _____ %; not exceeding $ _____ or

(2) at the rate of $ _____ per _____ ; not exceeding $ _____ or

(3) $ _____ to:

_____ whose address is

_____ (herein called

the "Designated Payee"), and to pay the balance, if any, of such proceeds to us.

This instrument, and your acceptance thereof, is not an assignment of the Credit, does not give to the Designated Payee any interest therein and does not affect our or your right to agree to amendments thereto, the cancellation thereof, or any substitution therefor.

We warrant to you that we have not, and will not, by negotiation of drafts or otherwise, assign the right to receive the whole or any part of such proceeds or give any other authorization or direction to make any payment thereof to any third party.

Please advise the Designated Payee of your acceptance of this instrument and, in consideration thereof, we agree that this instrument is irrevocable.

We transmit to you herewith the Credit (including all amendments, if any) and request you to note thereon the foregoing authorization and directions, and also enclose our check for $ _____ to cover your charges.

Very truly yours,

_____
(Name of Beneficiary)

By: _____
(Authorized Signature and Title)

We accept the foregoing instrument

**TEXAS COMMERCE BANK
NATIONAL ASSOCIATION**

The above signature with title as stated conforms with that on file with us and is authorized for the execution of such instruments.

_____
(Name of Bank)

By: _____
(Authorized Signature and Title)

By: _____
(Authorized Signature and Title)

F-220-00064 (10/78)

Source: Texas Commerce Bank National Association.

PART C
NONDOCUMENTARY LETTERS OF CREDIT, BONDS, AND GUARANTEES

Exporters of certain types of goods and services (depending on the industry) are many times requested to guarantee their performance or delivery under supply or construction contracts. The beneficiary (foreign customer in this case) wants the added assurance that the commercial contract entered into will yield expected results and wishes to minimize nonperformance, default, or dishonesty. The practice of guaranteeing is normally done through commercial banks, insurance companies, and other financial institutions. Over the last several years, the various forms of guarantees are becoming more and more standardized with the issuance of international commercial bank standby letters of credit (now covered by the UCP 400 as issued by the ICC). This practice of guaranteeing performance or delivery exists and is growing in importance and use because:

- Country risks have increased in importance and severity since the quadrupling of OPEC oil prices in 1973/74 and again in 1978/79 (which triggered a severe liquidity crises with many nations around the world), plus many other factors associated with political and economic risks.
- Supply and construction contracts have been increasing over the past decade and will probably continue to increase in the Far East (i.e., China), Latin America, and Africa as their liquidity crisis weakens and political risks are minimized.

It is not the intent of this chapter to deal will all of the various types of supply and construction contracts, and the guarantees and bonds that pertain to them. It is nearly impossible to cover all of these aspects because of varying country laws, negotiations between exporters and foreign customers, and product lines or services. This chapter is intended to give the reader a general idea and awareness of the subject.

CLEAN CREDITS

Letters of credit without the requirement for presentation of documents (i.e., negotiable bills of lading, consular commercial invoices) are called *clean letters of credit* and can be made payable on simple demand by the beneficiary. These credits are very flexible and can be used in a variety of situations (i.e., construction bonding). Clean credits can be used for Bid and Performance Bonds, Overseas Bank Guarantees, Escrow Arrangements, Security Purchases, Steamship Conference Credits, Surety Credits, and Carnets.

There are basically two types of clean credits: the guaranty type and the payment type. One type of clean credit is one that is issued in lieu of a guarantee to protect the exporter/beneficiary financially from default by the bank's customer. Documents normally called for are evidence of the underlying transaction (such as nonnegotiable copies of bills of lading), and the beneficiary's certificate of nonpayment by the applicant. An example of where such credits are useful is in the purchase of crude oil, where it is particularly difficult to present negotiable documents speedily.

An example of a payment type clean credit would be one that requires the exporter/beneficiary to draw a draft on the bank in accordance with the terms and conditions of the clean credit.

STANDBY CREDITS

Standby letters of credit are extremely versatile instruments and can be used for the following:

- Payments for merchandise shipped on open account.
- Bid and performance bonds.
- Advance payment guarantees.
- Other financial obligations.

A standby letter of credit is issued in the same manner as a commercial letter of credit. (See Figure 4–15 for an example of the standby L/C.) At this point it is important to mention that standby credits are now under the auspices of the UCP 400 issued by the ICC. They previously were not under the auspices of any previously existing UCPs issued by the ICC.

U.S. banks are generally precluded under the law from issuing guarantees, but can issue guarantees if they have a substantial interest in the performance of the transaction involved or a

FIGURE 4–15

Example of Standby Letter of Credit for Non-Payment of Invoices

```
OUR CREDIT NO   CR NO ADVISING BK      DATE        EXPIRY DATE    LETTER OF CREDIT AMOUNT
599999                                 XX/XX/XX     XX/XX/XX       USDXXXXXXXXXXXXXXXXX
RF:Lmw
ADVISED VIA:    U.S. MAIL    FULL TELEX


     BENEFICIARY                           APPLICANT

     XYZ COMPANY                           ZYX INCORPORATED


                      NON-PAYMENT OF INVOICES
                      EXAMPLE 5 - NON-NEGOTIATBLE


Gentlemen:

We hereby issue this Irrevocable Standby Letter of Credit which is available by your drafts
drawn on us at SIGHT bearing the clause: "Drawn under Standby Letter of Credit No.:599999 of
the Philadelphia National Bank", accompanied by:

1) A STATEMENT ON THE LETTERHEAD OF AND PURPORTEDLY SIGNED BY AN AUTHORIZED OFFICER OF XYZ
COMPANY STATING THAT, "ZYX INCORPORATED HAS FAILED TO PAY INVOICE(S) WHEN DUE RELATING TO THE
SUPPLY OF _____ PURSUANT TO PURCHASE ORDER _____ AND/OR CONTRACT
NO. _____ DATED _____ AND THAT _____ DAYS HAVE PASSED SINCE THE
INVOICE(S) DATE.

2) COPY(S) OF RELEVANT UNPAID INVOICE(S).

3) COPY(S) OF COMMON CARRIER BILL OF LADING SHOWING MERCHANDISE CONSIGNED TO ZYX INCORPORATED.

THIS LETTER OF CREDIT SETS FORTH IN FULL THE TERMS OF OUR UNDERTAKING, AND SUCH UNDERTAKING
SHALL NOT IN ANY WAY BE MODIFIED, AMENDED OR AMPLIFIED BY REFERENCE TO ANY DOCUMENT OR
INSTRUMENT REFERRED TO HEREIN OR IN WHICH THIS LETTER OF CREDIT IS REFERRED TO OR TO WHICH
THIS LETTER OF CREDIT RELATES AND ANY SUCH REFERENCE SHALL NOT BE DEEMED TO INCORPORATE
HEREIN BY REFERENCE ANY DOCUMENT OR INSTRUMENT.

IT IS REQUIRED THAT THIS ORIGINAL LETTER OF CREDIT AND ALL AMENDMENTS, IF ANY, BE PRESENTED
AT THE TIME OF ANY DRAWINGS FOR OUR ENDORSEMENT.

WE ENGAGE WITH YOU THAT ALL DOCUMENTS PRESENTED IN COMPLIANCE WITH THE TERMS OF
THIS LETTER OF CREDIT WILL BE DULY HONORED BY US IF DELIVERED TO OUR LETTER OF CREDIT
DEPARTMENT LOCATED AT ONE NORTH FIFTH STREET, TENTH FLOOR PHILADELPHIA, PA 19106 PRIOR TO
3 P.M. ON OR BEFORE THE EXPIRATION DATE.

EXCEPT SO FAR AS OTHERWISE EXPRESSLY STATED, THIS DOCUMENTARY CREDIT IS SUBJECT TO THE
"UNIFORM CUSTOMS AND PRACTICE FOR DOCUMENTARY CREDITS:  (1983 REVISION), INTERNATIONAL
CHAMBER OF COMMERCE, PUBLICATION NO. 400.

THIS LETTER OF CREDIT IS AVAILABLE BY SIGHT PAYMENT AT THE COUNTERS OF THE PHILADELPHIA
NATIONAL BANK, PHILADELPHIA.



     AUTHORIZED SIGNATURE
```

Source: Philadelphia National Bank.

segregated deposit sufficient in amount to cover the bank's potential liability. As an alternative, U.S. banks can issue standby and
performance letters of credit. Their overseas branches are permitted to issue guarantees, where permitted by local law, but are

subject to the limitations in Regulation K of the Board of Governors of the Federal Reserve System.*

The U.S. Comptroller of the Currency has defined standby credits, L/Cs or any other similar arrangements, however named or designated, which represents an obligation to the beneficiary on the part of the insurer as:[4]

1. To repay money borrowed by or advanced to or for the account of the account party.
2. To make payment on account of any indebtedness undertaken by the account party.
3. To make payment on account of any default by the account party in the performance of any obligation.

In both instances, both types of clean credits are similar in that they should be issued as irrevocable obligations on the part of the issuing bank. Clean credits are primarily issued to protect and assure the exporter/beneficiary that someone will fulfill its contractual obligation. In many instances, the clean credit is issued as and is called a *standby* letter of credit, issued to satisfy performance and protect beneficiaries against default under a contractual arrangement.

Sometimes the standby credit is coupled with a credit in favor of the applicant, used in lieu of negotiable documents as security for the issuing bank, which represents a particularly tricky instance of the back-to-back credit. The issuing bank will probably have to rely more on its knowledge of the parties and the transaction than on the goods in such transactions.

Standby credits can be issued to indemnify steamship companies for missing documents, so that they will release merchandise to the applicant/importer. This is a document of long standing in itself. Increasingly shipping companies are requesting such indem-

---

* Regulation K (amended August 1983), in defining International Operations of U.S. Banking Organizations (Subject A Section 211.3) reads in part ". . . a foreign branch of a member bank may . . . guarantee customer's debts or otherwise agree for their benefit to make payments on the occurrence of readily ascertainable events if the guarantee or agreement specified a maximum monetary liability . . ."

nities to have long expiry periods or no expiry date, and to be for a considerable multiple of the CIF value of the cargo, if at any time in the future the real owner of the cargo should appear.

Clearly, banks must know their applicants well before issuing such indemnities. Such large contingent risks, unlimited in time, are undesirable from both the banks' and the applicant's point of view, and it may be that the ease with which such indemnities have been issued will diminish. Standby credits create an obligation of the issuing bank that involves a credit risk and could result, if the credit is drawn against by the beneficiary, in an outflow of funds from the bank at a later date. It is a contingent liability of the issuing bank and thus represents an extension of credit to their customers. Federal Reserve Bank Regulation "H" requires that these credits be given the same credit considerations as loans to a customer.[5]

It is important to recognize the difference between a commercial documentary letter of credit and a standby letter of credit. The commercial credit finances the movement or storage of goods and is normally payable against the presentation of shipping documents conveying or securing title to the goods (such as bills of lading). In theory the commercial credit is secured by the goods being shipped.[6] The standby credit is in effect an unsecured credit instrument which, in many instances, is payable against a simple statement of default or for nonperformance. This form of letter of credit lacks the stability provided by the tangible goods underlying the commercial letter of credit transaction.[7]

It is a fundamental law that in commercial letter of credit transactions, banks deal in documents and not in goods. When a standby credit calls for some written representation to accompany the demand for payment, as is normally the case, the bank's duty to examine those representations should be equated with its duty to examine documents under a conventional commercial letter of credit.

Both the documentary and standby credits are, of course, to be regarded as entirely separate and distinct from the underlying contracts because with neither instrument does the bank have any involvement whatsoever in disputes arising between its customer and the beneficiary of the credit.[8]

TYPES OF BONDS AND GUARANTEES

Bid Bonds

It is quite common in international trade, as in domestic trade, for companies to bid on such things as construction projects, or the supplying of medium or heavy capital equipment. The purpose of the bid bond is to ensure that the contractor or supplier who was awarded a contract will accept the award to contract, supply, and service its obligation under the terms and conditions of the awarded contract. Normally, each bid is accompanied with some form of collateral or a commitment from the bidder to cover a percentage of the bid price, traditionally 10 percent (could be 1 to 15 percent). The percentage is a down payment and represents an honest commitment on the part of the bidder to supply its goods or services. In this regard the percentage is covered by a bid bond issued in the form of a clean standby credit or bank guaranty. (Examples of bid bonds are included in Figures 4–16 and 4–17.) This is done instead of using cash or other forms of payment, thus utilizing credit instead of short-term funds. There is a fixed expiry date associated with the bid bond which corresponds to the expected contract award date. Normally in the Middle East, the government exercises its discretion for extension and the amount for public tendering. The bid bond is usually returned when the contract is signed and when the performance bond is issued. The bid bond can be called by the beneficiary (buyer/importer) when the contractor or supplier fails to accept the contract.

Performance Bonds

On awarding the bid, it is normally required that the supplier/exporter of goods or services guarantee the performance of its goods or services until the contract is completed. The supplier/exporter will issue a performance bond which can be issued by surety/bonding companies. However, it is becoming normal business practice throughout the world to issue the performance bond in the form of a standby letter of credit from a reputable bank (see Figure 4–18). Most beneficiaries prefer standby credits because the

FIGURE 4–16

Example of Standby Letter of Credit for Bid Bonds

OUR CREDIT NO	CR NO ADVISING BK	DATE	EXPIRY DATE	LETTER OF CREDIT AMOUNT
599999		XX/XX/XX	XX/XX/XX	USDXXXXXXXXXXXXXXXX
RF:Lmw				

ADVISED VIA: U.S. MAIL   FULL TELEX

BENEFICIARY

XYZ COMPANY

APPLICANT

ZYX INCORPORATED

BID BOND
EXAMPLE 1 - NON-NEGOTIABLE

Gentlemen:

We hereby issue this Irrevocable Standby Letter of Credit which is available by your drafts drawn on us at SIGHT bearing the clause: "Drawn under Standby Letter of Credit No.:599999 of the Philadelphia National Bank", accompanied by:

1) A STATEMENT ON THE LETTERHEAD OF AND PURPORTEDLY SIGNED BY AN AUTHORIZED OFFICER OF XYZ COMPANY STATING THAT, "ZYX INCORPORATED WITHDREW BID SUBMITTED BY THEM RELATIVE TO THE SUPPLY OF _____ UNDER TENDER OFFER NO. _____.

OR

THAT ZYX WITHDREW SAID BID AFTER IT HAD BEEN ACCEPTED BY THEM.

OR

THAT ZYX FAILED TO ESTABLISH THE RELATIVE PERFORMANCE BOND IN THE REQUIRED PERCENTAGE OF THE OFFERED PRICE WITHIN THE PERIOD DESIGNATED AFTER THEY WERE AWARDED THE CONTRACT

AND/OR IN LIEU OF ABOVE:
A STATEMENT ON THE LETTERHEAD OF AND PURPORTEDLY SIGNED BY AN AUTHORIZED OFFICER OF XYZ COMPANY STATING THAT, "ZYX INCORPORATED DID NOT ABIDE WITH THE TERMS AND CONDITIONS OF TENDER NO. _____ FOR THE SUPPLY OF _____."

NOTE: THIS LETTER OF CREDIT IS ISSUED TO SATISFY THE REQUIREMENT OF A _____ % BID BOND UNDER RELATIVE TENDER OFFER NO. _____."

THIS LETTER OF CREDIT SETS FORTH IN FULL THE TERMS OF OUR UNDERTAKING, AND SUCH UNDERTAKING SHALL NOT IN ANY WAY BE MODIFIED, AMENDED OR AMPLIFIED BY REFERENCE TO ANY DOCUMENT OR INSTRUMENT REFERRED TO HEREIN OR IN WHICH THIS LETTER OF CREDIT IS REFERRED TO OR TO WHICH THIS LETTER OF CREDIT RELATES AND ANY SUCH REFERENCE SHALL NOT BE DEEMED TO INCORPORATE HEREIN BY REFERENCE ANY DOCUMENT OR INSTRUMENT.

IT IS REQUIRED THAT THIS ORIGINAL LETTER OF CREDIT AND ALL AMENDMENTS, IF ANY, BE PRESENTED AT THE TIME OF ANY DRAWINGS FOR OUR ENDORSEMENT.

WE ENGAGE WITH YOU THAT ALL DOCUMENTS PRESENTED IN COMPLIANCE WITH THE TERMS OF THIS LETTER OF CREDIT WILL BE DULY HONORED BY US IF DELIVERED TO OUR LETTER OF CREDIT DEPARTMENT LOCATED AT ONE NORTH FIFTH STREET, TENTH FLOOR PHILADELPHIA, PA 19106 PRIOR TO 3 P.M. ON OR BEFORE THE EXPIRATION DATE.

EXCEPT SO FAR AS OTHERWISE EXPRESSLY STATED, THIS DOCUMENTARY CREDIT IS SUBJECT TO THE "UNIFORM CUSTOMS AND PRACTICE FOR DOCUMENTARY CREDITS: (1983 REVISION), INTERNATIONAL CHAMBER OF COMMERCE, PUBLICATION NO. 400.

THIS LETTER OF CREDIT IS AVAILABLE BY SIGHT PAYMENT AT THE COUNTERS OF THE PHILADELPHIA NATIONAL BANK, PHILADELPHIA.

AUTHORIZED SIGNATURE

Source: Philadelphia National Bank.

FIGURE 4–17
Example of Standby Letter of Credit for Bid Bonds

OUR CREDIT NO	CR NO ADVISING BK	DATE	EXPIRY DATE	LETTER OF CREDIT AMOUNT
599999		XX/XX/XX	XX/XX/XX	USDXXXXXXXXXXXXXXXX

RF:Lmw
ADVISED VIA: U.S. MAIL   FULL TELEX

BENEFICIARY

LOST AND FOUND BANK
EGYPT

APPLICANT

ZYX INCORPORATED
USA

BID BOND
EXAMPLE 1A
NON-NEGOTIABLE

Gentlemen:

We hereby issue this Irrevocable Standby Letter of Credit which is available by your drafts drawn on us at SIGHT bearing the clause: "Drawn under Standby Letter of Credit No.:599999 of the Philadelphia National Bank", accompanied by:

1) A STATEMENT ON THE LETTERHEAD OF AND PURPORTEDLY SIGNED BY AN AUTHORIZED OFFICER OF YOUR BANK STATING THAT YOU HAVE BEEN CALLED UPON TO EFFECT PAYMENT UNDER YOUR GUARANTEE ISSUED IN FAVOR OF XYZ COMPANY, CAIRO, EGYPT FOR THE ACCOUNT OF ZYX INCORPORATED, USA TOGETHER WITH A CERTIFICATE SIGNED BY AN AUTHORIZED OFFICER OF XYZ COMPANY STATING THAT XYZ COMPANY WITHDREW BID SUBMITTED BY THEM RELATIVE TO THE SUPPLY OF _____ UNDER THEIR OFFER NO. _____ BEFORE THE EXPIRATION OF THE LETTER."

OR

THAT ZYX WITHDREW SAID BID AFTER IT HAD BEEN ACCEPTED BY THEM.

OR

THAT ZYX FAILED TO ESTABLISH THE RELATIVE PERFORMANCE BOND IN THE REQUIRED PERCENTAGE OF THE OFFERED PRICE WITHIN THE PERIOD DESIGNATED AFTER THEY WERE AWARDED THE CONTRACT.

AND/OR IN LIEU OF ABOVE:

A STATEMENT ON THE LETTERHEAD OF AND PURPORTEDLY SIGNED BY AN AUTHORIZED OFFICER OF XYZ COMPANY STATING THAT, "ZYX INCORPORATED DID NOT ABIDE WITH THE TERMS AND CONDITIONS OF TENDER NO. _____ FOR THE SUPPLY OF _____ ."

NOTE: THIS LETTER OF CREDIT IS ISSUED TO SATISFY THE REQUIREMENT OF A _____ % BID BOND UNDER RELATIVE TENDER OFFER NO. _____ ."

SPECIAL INSTRUCTIONS:

A) PLEASE ISSUE YOUR GUARANTEE TO EXPIRE _____ .

THIS LETTER OF CREDIT SETS FORTH IN FULL THE TERMS OF OUR UNDERTAKING, AND SUCH UNDERTAKING SHALL NOT IN ANY WAY BE MODIFIED, AMENDED OR AMPLIFIED BY REFERENCE TO ANY DOCUMENT OR INSTRUMENT REFERRED TO HEREIN OR IN WHICH THIS LETTER OF CREDIT IS REFERRED TO OR TO WHICH THIS LETTER OF CREDIT RELATES AND ANY SUCH REFERENCE SHALL NOT BE DEEMED TO INCORPORATE HEREIN BY REFERENCE ANY DOCUMENT OR INSTRUMENT.

IT IS REQUIRED THAT THIS ORIGINAL LETTER OF CREDIT AND ALL AMENDMENTS, IF ANY, BE PRESENTED AT THE TIME OF ANY DRAWINGS FOR OUR ENDORSEMENT.

SEE CONTINUATION

FIGURE 4–17 *(concluded)*

ATTACHED TO AND FORMING PART OF DOCUMENTARY CREDIT NO. 599999   DATE: XX/XX/XX
PAGE· TWO

WE ENGAGE WITH YOU THAT ALL DOCUMENTS PRESENTED IN COMPLIANCE WITH THE TERMS OF
THIS LETTER OF CREDIT WILL BE DULY HONORED BY US IF DELIVERED TO OUR LETTER OF CREDIT
DEPARTMENT LOCATED AT ONE NORTH FIFTH STREET, TENTH FLOOR PHILADELPHIA, PA 19106 PRIOR TO
3 P.M. ON OR BEFORE THE EXPIRATION DATE.

EXCEPT SO FAR AS OTHERWISE EXPRESSLY STATED, THIS DOCUMENTARY CREDIT IS SUBJECT TO THE
"UNIFORM CUSTOMS AND PRACTICE FOR DOCUMENTARY CREDITS: (1983 REVISION), INTERNATIONAL
CHAMBER OF COMMERCE, PUBLICATION NO. 400.

THIS LETTER OF CREDIT IS AVAILABLE BY SIGHT PAYMENT AT THE COUNTERS OF THE PHILADELPHIA
NATIONAL BANK, PHILADELPHIA.

AUTHORIZED SIGNATURE

Source: Philadelphia National Bank.

backing of a bank is preferred over the creditworthiness of a surety/bonding company which is more difficult to assess.

In the Middle East, Asia, and most Latin American countries, the standby credit is not readily acceptable to back up a bid or performance bond. Regulations in these areas require that a guarantee must be issued by a local bank in favor of a buyer of a service or goods. In this case most commercial banks would issue a standby credit in favor of a local bank requesting them to issue a guarantee in favor of a buyer. These regulations apply for both bid and performance bonds.

There are two ways that bonds are established. Either the exporter's bank issues the standby credit directly to the beneficiary's bank overseas or the exporter's bank standby credit can be used as an inducement for the local overseas bank to issue its own local bank guarantee. The difference is that the banking charges are minimal when the exporter's bank issues the credit.

FIGURE 4–18
Example of Standby Letter of Credit for Performance Bond

OUR CREDIT NO	CR NO ADVISING BK	DATE	EXPIRY DATE	LETTER OF CREDIT AMOUNT
599999		XX/XX/XX	XX/XX/XX	USDXXXXXXXXXXXXXXXX

RF:Lmw

ADVISED VIA: U.S. MAIL   FULL TELEX

BENEFICIARY	APPLICANT
XYZ COMPANY	ZYX INCORPORATED

PERFORMANCE BOND
EXAMPLE 2 - NON-NEGOTIABLE

Gentlemen:

We hereby issue this Irrevocable Standby Letter of Credit which is available by your drafts drawn on us at SIGHT bearing the clause: "Drawn under Standby Letter of Credit No.:599999 of the Philadelphia National Bank", accompanied by:

1) A STATEMENT ON THE LETTERHEAD OF AND PURPORTEDLY SIGNED BY AN AUTHORIZED OFFICER OF XYZ COMPANY STATING THAT, "ZYX INCORPORATED HAS FAILED OR REFUSED TO PERFORM IN ACCORDANCE WITH THE TERMS AND CONDITIONS OF CONTRACT NO. _____ DATED _____ BETWEEN XYZ COMPANY AND ZYX INCORPORATED FOR THE SUPPLY OF _____.

NOTE: THIS LETTER OF CREDIT IS ISSUED TO SATISFY THE REQUIREMENT OF A _____ % PERFORMANCE BOND UNDER RELATIVE CONTRACT NO. _____ DATED _____.

PLEASE NOTE:

IF A PERFORMANCE BOND IS BEING ISSUED TO SATISFY THE REQUIREMENT AS PER SAMPLE 1A, USE THE SAME FORMAT.

THIS LETTER OF CREDIT SETS FORTH IN FULL THE TERMS OF OUR UNDERTAKING, AND SUCH UNDERTAKING SHALL NOT IN ANY WAY BE MODIFIED, AMENDED OR AMPLIFIED BY REFERENCE TO ANY DOCUMENT OR INSTRUMENT REFERRED TO HEREIN OR IN WHICH THIS LETTER OF CREDIT IS REFERRED TO OR TO WHICH THIS LETTER OF CREDIT RELATES AND ANY SUCH REFERENCE SHALL NOT BE DEEMED TO INCORPORATE HEREIN BY REFERENCE ANY DOCUMENT OR INSTRUMENT.

IT IS REQUIRED THAT THIS ORIGINAL LETTER OF CREDIT AND ALL AMENDMENTS, IF ANY, BE PRESENTED AT THE TIME OF ANY DRAWINGS FOR OUR ENDORSEMENT.

WE ENGAGE WITH YOU THAT ALL DOCUMENTS PRESENTED IN COMPLIANCE WITH THE TERMS OF THIS LETTER OF CREDIT WILL BE DULY HONORED BY US IF DELIVERED TO OUR LETTER OF CREDIT DEPARTMENT LOCATED AT ONE NORTH FIFTH STREET, TENTH FLOOR PHILADELPHIA, PA 19106 PRIOR TO 3 P.M. ON OR BEFORE THE EXPIRATION DATE.

EXCEPT SO FAR AS OTHERWISE EXPRESSLY STATED, THIS DOCUMENTARY CREDIT IS SUBJECT TO THE "UNIFORM CUSTOMS AND PRACTICE FOR DOCUMENTARY CREDITS: (1983 REVISION), INTERNATIONAL CHAMBER OF COMMERCE, PUBLICATION NO. 400.

THIS LETTER OF CREDIT IS AVAILABLE BY SIGHT PAYMENT AT THE COUNTERS OF THE PHILADELPHIA NATIONAL BANK, PHILADELPHIA.

AUTHORIZED SIGNATURE

Source: Philadelphia National Bank.

A performance bond has two principle purposes:

1. It assures the importer/buyer (employer) that the supplier/ exporter of goods and services is creditworthy.

2. It gives access to additional resources in the event the

supplier of goods and services fails to perform or encounters difficulties in the fulfillment of its contractual obligations. In this regard there is a difference between surety company performance bonds and guarantees or performance bonds issued by banks or other financial institutions. A surety company will commit itself to the performance of its customer and guarantees completion. Banks or financial institutions commit themselves only to the payment of an amount on written demand based on a simple notice of nonperformance or noncompletion.

Performance bonds issued for major construction or turn-key contracts are usually replaced with a maintenance bond when the work is accepted by the client or on its expiry. However, beneficiaries in the Middle East do request expiry date extensions. The issuing bank cannot refuse the re-issuance or extension because refusal is usually sanctioned with a call of the bond involved.

Advanced Payment Guarantee

It is not uncommon for the importer/buyer (employer) to make funds available to the exporter/seller (employee). The purpose of advancing funds is to permit the employee to cover certain costs of the employee, such as:

- Hiring and housing of labor.
- Initial transportation costs.
- Purchase of equipment.
- Organizational costs.

This type of guarantee is usually issued by banks in the form of a standby letter of credit (see Figure 4–19). The advance payment guarantee (APG) must be properly used. On breach of contract, nonperformance, or improper use of the guarantee, the amount outstanding in the APG will be called. How long the APG remains outstanding depends on the contractor's/supplier's performance under the contract. It is common practice to consider a fraction of the progress certificate as representing works or expenses, possibly for cash outlays or noncash items such as depreciation relative to equipment acquired with the advance payment, previously covered by the APG.[9] This will evidence the proper use of the APG

FIGURE 4–19
Example of Standby Letter of Credit for Advance Payment

OUR CREDIT NO	CR NO ADVISING BK	DATE	EXPIRY DATE	LETTER OF CREDIT AMOUNT
599999		XX/XX/XX	XX/XX/XX	USDXXXXXXXXXXXXXXXX

RF:Lunw
ADVISED VIA: U.S. MAIL   FULL TELEX

BENEFICIARY

XYZ COMPANY

APPLICANT

ZYX INCORPORATED

ADVANCE PAYMENT
EXAMPLE 3 - NON-NEGOTIABLE

Gentlemen:

We hereby issue this Irrevocable Standby Letter of Credit which is available by your drafts drawn on us at SIGHT bearing the clause: "Drawn under Standby Letter of Credit No.:599999 of the Philadelphia National Bank", accompanied by:

1) A STATEMENT ON THE LETTERHEAD OF AND PURPORTEDLY SIGNED BY AN AUTHORIZED OFFICER OF XYZ COMPANY STATING THAT, "THIS DRAWINGS REPRESENTS THE AMOUNT OF AN ADVANCE PAYMENT MADE BY US AND DUE US BECAUSE OF ZYX INCORPORATED'S FAILURE TO COMPLY WITH THE TERMS AND CONDITIONS OF CONTRACT NO. _____ DATED _____ BETWEEN XYZ COMPANY INCORPORATED FOR THE SUPPLY OF _____."

2) A COPY OF A REGISTERED LETTER SENT BY AIRMAIL TO ZYX INCORPORATED, SIGNED BY AN AUTHORIZED OFFICER OF XYZ COMPANY TOGETHER WITH A COPY OF THE REGISTERED MAIL RECEIPT ISSUED BY THE _____ POSTAL AUTHORITIES, EVIDENCING MAILING AT LEAST THIRTY (30) DAYS PRIOR TO ANY DRAFT(S) DATE, NOTIFYING ZYX INCORPORATED AT _____ ATTENTION: _____ OF YOUR INTENTIONS TO DRAW UNDER THIS LETTER OF CREDIT AND OUTLINING THE REASONS FOR THE DRAWING.

NOTE: THIS LETTER OF CREDIT REPRESENTS _____ % OF TOTAL CONTRACT VALUE.

SPECIAL INSTRUCTIONS:

A) THIS LETTER OF CREDIT IS CURRENTLY INOPERATIVE. IT WILL BECOME OPERATIVE BY SPECIFIC AMENDMENT UPON THE PHILADELPHIA NATIONAL BANK RECEIPT OF A LETTER SIGNED BY AN AUTHORIZED OFFICER OF ZYX INCORPORATED STATING THAT THEY ARE IN RECEIPT OF USD. _____ FROM XYZ COMPANY PURSUANT TO CONTRACT NO. _____ DATED _____ AND AUTHORIZING THE PHILADELPHIA NATIONAL BANK TO AMEND THE LETTER OF CREDIT TO MAKE OPERATIVE.

THIS LETTER OF CREDIT SETS FORTH IN FULL THE TERMS OF OUR UNDERTAKING, AND SUCH UNDERTAKING SHALL NOT IN ANY WAY BE MODIFIED, AMENDED OR AMPLIFIED BY REFERENCE TO ANY DOCUMENT OR INSTRUMENT REFERRED TO HEREIN OR IN WHICH THIS LETTER OF CREDIT IS REFERRED TO OR TO WHICH THIS LETTER OF CREDIT RELATES AND ANY SUCH REFERENCE SHALL NOT BE DEEMED TO INCORPORATE HEREIN BY REFERENCE ANY DOCUMENT OR INSTRUMENT.

IT IS REQUIRED THAT THIS ORIGINAL LETTER OF CREDIT AND ALL AMENDMENTS, IF ANY, BE PRESENTED AT THE TIME OF ANY DRAWINGS FOR OUR ENDORSEMENT.

WE ENGAGE WITH YOU THAT ALL DOCUMENTS PRESENTED IN COMPLIANCE WITH THE TERMS OF THIS LETTER OF CREDIT WILL BE DULY HONORED BY US IF DELIVERED TO OUR LETTER OF CREDIT DEPARTMENT LOCATED AT ONE NORTH FIFTH STREET, TENTH FLOOR PHILADELPHIA, PA 19106 PRIOR TO 3 P.M. ON OR BEFORE THE EXPIRATION DATE.

EXCEPT SO FAR AS OTHERWISE EXPRESSLY STATED, THIS DOCUMENTARY CREDIT IS SUBJECT TO THE "UNIFORM CUSTOMS AND PRACTICE FOR DOCUMENTARY CREDITS: (1983 REVISION), INTERNATIONAL CHAMBER OF COMMERCE, PUBLICATION NO. 400.

THIS LETTER OF CREDIT IS AVAILABLE BY SIGHT PAYMENT AT THE COUNTERS OF THE PHILADELPHIA NATIONAL BANK, PHILADELPHIA.

AUTHORIZED SIGNATURE

Source: Philadelphia National Bank.

because of the number of progress certificates produced. As the APG is drawn down, it is sometimes the issuing bank (or insurance company if issued by them) that will handle the administration of confirming reductions of the APG to the applicant. Therefore, the APG is reduced as the contract proceeds. Advance payments can either be made in a lump sum payment or for fixed percentages of the contract.

There are several important factors that must be mentioned regarding bonds, guarantees, and standby letters of credit. One such factor is the sales contract—the basis for the performance bond. Whatever is stated in the standby credit must agree with what is stated in the sales contract.

Also a definite settlement date must be set in the contract which should be stated in the standby credit (i.e., the bond is active on opening, and settlement is calculated six months from the bill of lading date. Material must be examined within 45 days from date of title transfer).

The legal/contractual rights and liabilities vary between suppliers of goods and services and importers/buyer or employers from one country to the next. Get your banker's input when putting together the sales contract, the bonds, other bonds, or guarantees. They can be extremely helpful and so can the people in your credit department. It is important the credit department be involved in the negotiation of these contracts and bonds because of their experiences from traveling abroad or participating in credit group meeting such as the FCIB. Seek legal advice both at home and abroad.

It is a good idea to include in your sales contract and in the performance bond, an arbitration clause as recommended by the International Chamber of Commerce ([ICC] refer to their publication Nos. 291, 382, 414, 412, and 419). The American Arbitration Association and the International Chamber of Commerce Arbitration are arbitration organizations that are recognized by most countries around the world, especially those countries that subscribe to the U.N. Convention on the Recognition & Enforcement of Foreign Arbitral Awards (ratified in January 1980 by some 58 countries). In this regard, you should delegate a certain authority in a certain country to actually review what has gone on at the project site or whatever circumstances may be regarding performance of your goods or services. Have the authority submit a statement as part of the documentation required under the performance bond. The authority statement should state whether or not the work has or has not been completed or that the goods perform or do not perform by verifying performance within the specific agreed on date. Depending on local law, this may not be permissible. Therefore, the consultation of retained local counsel in the country of the beneficiary is recommended.

It is important to note that the issuance of performance bonds in the form of standby credits ties up the issuing bank's credit lines with the country of the beneficiary and/or its correspondent bank. One of the problems that standby credits create for themselves is that many credits issued in this form have an "open-endedness" to them. Meaning, beneficiaries continually have the credits extended because either the project is not completed or the beneficiary is not satisfied with the performance of the goods or services. This is particularly true with projects involving the Middle East (i.e., Pakistan law gives the importer 60 years to determine performance. Other examples of long expiry dates on standby credits are Iran and Iraq).

Bank charges, especially those of foreign banks who advise standby credits to beneficiaries can be high. Exporters recommend a clause in the sales contract and likewise in the performance bond that states all bank charges outside the issuing bank are for the beneficiary's account. Eastern Europe and Middle East countries have historically had high charges. If the charges cannot be worked into the sales contract, have the issuing bank determine the charges (before the credit is issued) by cabling the advising bank of the beneficiary and ask them the charge for issuing a bank guarantee on behalf of the supplier. This way, you will have an idea of the charges. Rates depend on the overseas bank, the country risk, tenor of the standby credit, and how long it will be outstanding. It is advisable for the exporter to shop around for the lowest rates in the banking community. Prices or rates vary from day to day. Rates also depend on the goods involved, the buyer (*especially* the buyer), and the experience of the exporter in the market.

Sometimes performance bonds have to be opened in the currency of the buyer's country (check with local counsel).

Because of the "open-endedness" of standby credits, some

exporters take out insurance against unlawful calling of the credits. The Overseas Private Insurance Corporation (OPIC), discussed in Chapter 6, is one insurer that provides coverage for the issuance of performance bonds. Amendments to a standby credit should be accepted by the customer in writing or by telex.

Comments

It is becoming increasingly common for potential customers (particularly in the Middle East) to stipulate, as part of the contract or tender terms, that suppliers must take out Performance Bonds whereby a bank guarantees to a bank nominated by the customer a percentage of the contract value (from 2.5 up to 10 percent) as security to the customer against failure by the seller to meet the supply terms of the contract. (As previously mentioned, the normal business practice today is for the exporter/supplier to open a standby credit with its bank in lieu of a performance bond opened by other means.) The seller would give the bank a counter-guarantee to protect the bank in the event the performance bond is called up. The wording of such performance bonds is usually laid down as part of the contract term, often with very one-sided wording, such as, "X bank guarantees to pay on first demand without proof of conditions."

The courts have held that, as in international banking practice one bank must honor their bond to another, a guaranteeing bank must pay up on demand (if that is the wording of the bank or guarantee) regardless of any dispute that there may be between seller and buyer. Neither proof of default by the buyer or seller nor genuine claim would need to be produced if the guarantee had a "without proof or conditions" clause. Even in force majeure circumstances, or if the buyer were in default (e.g., through the buyer failing to provide seller with an acceptable letter of credit), this would not be of concern to the bank. It would be the concern of the seller whose recourse would be legal action under the applicable law pertaining to the contract (which might be very difficult in certain countries).

Against this background, it is important that companies that might be subject to such a possibility of one-sided performance bonds take appropriate precautions.

1. Avoid the need for such bonds wherever possible.
2. If performance bonds are insisted on by the customer:
    a. Try to arrange a modified form of wording that requires the customer to produce evidence of the seller's default in meeting the contract terms.
    b. Minimize the level of the bond relative to proceeds (e.g., to 2.5 percent of the contract value).
    c. Limit/minimize the period during which such bonds remain in force.
    d. Take the greatest care to ensure the seller can indeed fulfill the contract terms (e.g., inspection, supply dates) and that its exposure will be minimized by obtaining confirmed irrevocable letters of credit (standby).

One way of attempting to prevent a beneficiary from drawing against a standby credit after the completion of a contract is to get a court injunction to prevent payment. A court injunction is simple—it takes too long. Another way is to negotiate a settlement directly with the buyer.

In addition to the above mentioned factors to assist exporters or bidders of goods and services in dealing with performance bonds, it is recommended exporters/bidders become familiar with the ICC's Uniform Rules for Contract Guarantees (Publication Number 325). The Rules are designed to regulate contract guarantees, and include an introduction explaining their use. The Rules invest these guarantees with a moral content and strive to achieve a fair balance between the legitimate interests of the parties involved.

Repayment of a Loan/Line of Credit

This type of letter of credit is issued in favor of the bank or lending institution and is usually issued in the local currency of the lender. The customer of the issuing bank must accept the exchange risk should there be a drawing unless otherwise negotiated beforehand between the lending institution and applicant.

This credit is issued to guarantee the lending institution repayment of loan(s) granted to a subsidiary of the applicant. If money loaned is not paid with interest as agreed between the parties involved, the lending institution will draw against the credit for principal plus interest owed by the borrower.[10]

Nonpayment of Invoices

This type of standby credit is used to guarantee payment to the seller of goods. Its main purpose is to provide a second source of payment for the seller in case the buyer does not pay for the invoiced goods. The seller ships the goods to a buyer on a collection basis (open account) requesting it to pay invoices within X days for either the invoice due date or B/L date. If the buyer fails to pay on the agreed on due date, the seller would draw against the standby credit.

Insurance Premium Default

From time to time insurance companies require standby credits to guarantee payment(s) of insurance premiums by the insured party. In this case the insurance company is trying to make sure that cash flows are not interrupted by failure of the insured to pay or the inability of the insured to pay. Therefore, they request that a standby credit be issued in their favor to assure that payments under the policies (workman compensation policy, product liability policy, and a host of others) will be paid on a timely basis. If the insured party (applicant) does not make the payments, then the insurance company can draw against the standby credit.[11]

Surety Bonds

Contract guarantees are issued by surety companies on rare occasions for international contracts. The purpose of the surety company when issuing a bond in favor of an overseas beneficiary is to indemnify the beneficiary only when the contractor or applicant of the bond fails to perform. Before the bond is called by the beneficiary, usually the contractor or supplier has a grace period to remedy the situation. The surety company will want written proof of default which may be difficult to obtain. If the contractor or supplier is unable to remedy the situation, the surety company will call on the services of other resources. These surety bonds are generally worded as commitments to pay. This means that the surety company by issuing its bond, commits itself to pay on demand a sum of money to the beneficiary. Generally, the bond is a fraction of the total contract value because of the demand feature.

This fraction is a deposit or promise to deposit liquid funds with the surety company.

Bank Guarantees

A guarantee is defined as a commitment to pay a sum of money in consideration of the nonfulfillment or breach of contractual terms by the account party.[12] Foreign firms or government agencies are not very familiar with surety companies. They are more familiar with the international banking system. Because beneficiaries of goods or services prefer unconditional commitments to pay over conditional commitments, as with surety companies, the bank guarantee (payable on demand) is preferred.

There are certain laws or regulations prevailing in some countries which make a guarantee or undertaking issued in favor of a national (overseas company or government agency) permissible only if a local institution issues the guarantee such as a local bank. This means that if a U.S. company were required to guarantee its contractual performance to a company or government agency domiciled in another country having such requirements, it would not be possible for the U.S. company to arrange a clean credit (unconditional) directly in favor of the overseas national with a U.S. bank. Under these circumstances, a U.S. company can request a U.S. bank to issue a clean credit (either in U.S. dollars or in local currency) in favor of its correspondent bank or branch in the overseas country of the importer/buyer. The terms of this type of clean credit will request the overseas correspondent or branch to issue its own local guarantee/undertaking to the local importer or buyer. Therefore, local laws will be observed since the guarantee/undertaking is issued locally. The issuing overseas bank or branch who issued its guarantee will be protected by the clean credit of the U.S. bank. In the United States, nationally (federal) chartered banks may not issue guarantees on the letterhead of their head office.[13] This is a regulation of the U.S. Treasury Department. This is the reason why these types of banks have to substitute the word guarantee with a standby letter of credit. Only state chartered banks may issue guarantees. U.S. Edge Act banks can issue guarantees, but this varies from state to state according to local state banking regulations.

It is important to exercise care in the wording of clean credits because local laws in some overseas countries provide that a guarantee or undertaking covering a contract cannot terminate prior to the termination of the contract itself, or prior to formal acceptance by the beneficiary of the product or project to which the contract relates. A clean credit issued to protect a local bank for issuing its guarantee or undertaking should not be permitted to expire on its stated expiration date. Instead, the clean credit in favor of the local bank will need to be extended (assuming the local indemnity has not been released). Otherwise, payment under the clean credit may be claimed by the local bank to obtain funds needed to cover its guarantee or undertaking. Clean credits in certain countries must have expiration dates not earlier than the expected period of the underlying contract. Many international commercial banks are unwilling to issue clean credits on a long-term basis covering long-term contracts.

COMPARISON: SURETY BONDS—BANK GUARANTEES (Simplified Case)

	Surety Bond	Bank Guarantee
Type of obligation	Obligation to perform	Obligation to pay
Usual form	Guarantee	Letter of credit
Strength of commitment	Conditional	Unconditional legal
Legal nature	Surety	Indemnity
Call is triggered by	Existence of default	Statement
Type of contract	Ancillary relative	Independent absolute

Source: Trade Finance, Euromoney.

REFERENCES

1. ICC Pub. No. 415, *Guide To Documentary Credit Operations* (Paris, France: ICC Publishing S.A., 1985), p. 6.
2. Bank of America International Services (San Francisco: Bank of America, NT&SA, 1981), p. 26.
3. A. Leonard Back, *Introduction to Commercial Letters of Credit* (New York: CitiBank, N.A., 1980), p. 7.
4. Antimo Cancelliere, *Stand-By Letters of Credit* (Philadelphia: The Philadelphia National Bank, 1985), p. 2.

5. Ibid., p. 3
6. Ibid., p. 3
7. Ibid., p. 3
8. Ibid., p. 3
9. Charles J. Gmur, *Trade Financing* (London: Euromoney Publications Ltd., 1981), p. 158.
10. Antimo Cancelliere, *Stand-By Letters of Credit,* p. 6
11. Ibid., p. 7.
12. H. Harfield, *Bank Credits and Acceptances,* 5th ed. (New York: The Ronald Press Company, 1974), p. 149.
13. Ibid., pp. 154–67.

CHAPTER 5

COLLECTION TECHNIQUES

In international trade, as in domestic trade, it is a fact of life that not all foreign customers pay their debt obligations timely. This is even true with the most highly regarded and financially sound companies from around the world, especially when foreign governments tie up payments in bureaucracy. This may sound hard to believe, but it is true. Many companies, big or small, make occasional attempts (some more frequent than others), to gain additional cash flow advantages by holding their money as long as possible.

Collecting past due debts from foreign customers can be a formidable and complex task, warranting the best collection skills and techniques a credit manager can muster. Unlike domestic credit, there are language barriers, long distances, procedures, foreign laws (i.e., foreign exchange regulations), and customs to wade through. All of this is particularly true when dealing with foreign customers in Third World countries where the timely collection of debts is constantly hampered by shortages of hard currency in the importer's market. Debtors can do little about this.

Delinquent foreign receivables has been and will continue to be a formidable task for export creditors. It is not only attributed to and perpetuated by unsettling political and economic conditions in many parts of the world but, from mismanaged, under-capitalized, highly leveraged, and loss-ridden companies. Due to the nature of international business, export shipments are generally made for higher amounts of goods than in domestic trade. Without easy access to supplies, orders must be placed for larger quantities and freight costs are higher. These factors necessitate greater amounts of credit to approve. There is also a tendency for foreign customers and export shippers to consolidate shipments based on agreed-on terms and conditions. The object is to minimize costs, create efficiency, and minimize confusion over what is shipped versus not shipped against purchase orders. If extended credit terms are offered, as is the norm in international trade, receivable balances outstanding or owing at any one time get large per foreign customer. Past-due balances complicate things by making the total balance outstanding abnormally higher. It means a lot more working capital is tied up for longer periods of time—which increases the risks when a high level of country risk exists.

The collection procedures and techniques used in international trade depend largely on the payment terms and method of distribution and the selling technique for the underlying export credit sale. In general, selling goods and services by indirect methods that assume payment obligations (i.e., export management companies [EMCs], export trading companies [ETCs], export merchants, or export-import houses, who collect their own foreign receivables) usually requires shorter payment terms, such as net 30 days from invoice date. In this case, collection techniques are similar to domestic. On the other hand, the use of direct methods (i.e., selling direct to foreign customers or agents) for selling goods and services usually involve extended payment terms to foreign customers who are billed at a location in their country of domicile.

FORMS OF PAYMENT

Various types of payment or credit terms used in international trade were previously discussed. Of equal importance is the means by which payment is remitted from foreign customers or their banks.

Credit personnel will come across different types of payment instruments and methods from foreign customers. It is important to recognize them to minimize confusion in differentiating whether or not you have a valid form of payment. The following describes most common forms or types you are likely to come across, especially when selling on an open account basis.

Company Check. In reality, this is a special type of draft. In its most common form, it is a sight draft. In this case, the drawee is the person signing the check, on its bank (drawee) account, directing it to pay a specific sum of money (currency) on demand to the order of the payee who is the beneficiary (i.e., the exporter as payment for goods purchased). The check is often used to pay for goods purchased on such payment terms as open account, cash-in-advance (CIA), cash with order (CWO), or goods delivered on cash on delivery (COD).

Bank Draft. This is a different type of draft than the company check. It is an order from one bank (the drawer), in this case the importer's bank, to another bank (the drawee), a U.S. bank in the case of a U.S. exporter, with whom it normally maintains a correspondent relationship, to pay to a named person (the payee) a specified sum of money (currency) on demand.[1] This type of draft is sometimes used to pay for goods imported on draft payment terms used in documentary collections or letters of credit.

Bank Money Order. A bank money order is almost like a banker's draft in which a bank orders money (currency) to be paid to a named person or to bearer. There is no separate drawee and the order is drawn on the issuing bank itself.

Airmail Payment Order. This is an instruction mailed from a foreign bank to a U.S. bank authorizing the U.S. bank to debit its account and pay the exporter.

Telex/SWIFT. Almost all banks have telex, and many are getting SWIFT (Society for Worldwide Information and Funds Transfer) capabilities. SWIFT is an automated telex system that imposes certain standards for procedures and message formats. It has the ability to transmit and receive messages in computer form, eliminating many opportunities for clerical error.

TYPES OF COLLECTIONS

In international trade there are basically three types of collections which correlate to the following export payment terms.

1. Open account.
2. Drafts: documentary collections.
3. Letters of credit.

Each requires its own systematic collection follow-up sequence, a process complicated by the term or number of days associated with each. For example, an exporter could be extending payment terms of 30, 60, 90, or 180 days to any given number of foreign customers at any one given period of time on open account, documentary, or nondocumentary collections and letters of credit in more than one country. Depending on the volume of sales and amount of receivables, an exporter could have a data base of anywhere between 30 to 60 or more different types of payment terms. In other words, an exporter's receivable portfolio in any given month could contain a myriad of different types of payment terms. It differs greatly from domestic trade credit whereby payment terms are usually net 30 days; 1 percent 10th, net 30 days; or 1 percent 15th, EOM (end of month), or anything similar thereto. Problems occur when an exporter lacks a sophisticated automated receivable system and related accounting procedures to handle invoicing, inventory, and the booking of credit sales to receivables. Although the problem exists to a certain extent in domestic, it is more complex in international trade. A typical predicament facing credit managers and their companies is explained in the example below.

Example

Assume the following:
Payment terms: 90 days date draft from B/L date
Terms of sale: FAS, Houston, Texas
Sourced from: El Paso, Texas
Date: February 1
Amount of sale: U.S. $50,000
Transport times: 5 days from El Paso to Houston
30 days from Houston to Valparaiso, Chile
On-board B/L date: February 10
ETA: March 10

In this case:

1. The sales department wants credit for the sale as soon as it departs the sourcing location—El Paso, Texas. An invoice must be generated to account for the sale.
2. The accounting department credits inventory, debits accounts receivable, and accounts for the sale once the goods depart Texas. Problems exist for companies with distinct and separate international groups or departments who source from similar locations. Who gets priority? International sales usually represent a small percentage of the capacity of domestically located plants. In this case, allocation of goods to the international group (sales, distribution and accounting) will want their orders prioritized and invoiced as soon as possible, before the sale is lost to another sales group (domestic or international).
3. The foreign customer's payment terms for this sale are calculated from bill of lading date (note the payment terms do not state or begin from invoice date). Why not calculate the due date from invoice date? The problem lies over the delivery of goods to a port of departure in sufficient time to meet a scheduled steamship departure date. Sometimes their scheduled dates are delayed because other suppliers are late in delivering their goods to the pier, the steamship may run into mechanical problems, weather may be bad in the area or, there may be a port strike, among other reasons. These are some prime reasons why the bill of lading date is preferred in international trade versus an invoice date.

The problem:

1. If the sale is booked to receivables using the invoice date with a domestically oriented automated receivable system, the system will automatically calculate the due date from invoice date. But what if the payment terms do not begin until the on-board ocean bill of lading date? Suppose the foreign customer does not want to assume liability for the goods until they pass over the rail of the steamship (the terms of sale are FAS Houston)?

    Under the aforementioned, the real due date is: May 10 (90 days from the B/L date of February 10) and not May 1 (90 days from the invoice date of February 1).

2. Accounting and especially sales will not want to wait for the on-board ocean bill of lading to be issued and received by their company. To book the shipment as a sale could add another week if the B/Ls are received by the company's freight forwarder untimely or if its freight forwarder sends the B/Ls untimely to them. What about mail time?

3. Unless your credit department takes the aforementioned problems into consideration for calculating the actual due date, a collection letter (called *dunning* letter in the credit profession) or a telex/cable could be sent prematurely to foreign customers for collection of debts not even due for payment. It upsets foreign customers and could lose customers to competition or disrupt sales volume. A foreign customer might lower its purchase order requirements of the exporter's products. Many foreign customers are sensitive to over-zealous collectors.

4. Weekly or monthly cash flow projections are complicated by this problem. The accounts receivable aging management reports can mislead credit managers into believing that a certain amount of invoices are due in a specific week or month.

5. The summary aging of accounts receivable is distorted because invoices can age prematurely.

6. The credit manager is subject to negative reports issued by auditors resulting from opinions that accounts are followed up untimely for collection and/or the condition of accounts receivable needs improving based on a review of a portfolio of receivables over a period of time.

Solutions:

1. Do a cost/benefit analysis (cash flow analysis and cost of capital) of direct computer link-ups with freight forwarders with your accounts receivable system and order processing system.

2. Consider electronic data interchanges (EDI) of bills of lading, including other export documents, between your freight forwarders, freight forwarders with ocean carriers, shippers, and port authorities. Most major ocean carriers, shippers, forwarders, and port authorities are currently working on projects that will allow them to exchange information with each other via direct computer to computer link-ups. If the B/L is received electronically by the exporter

from the forwarder, the amount of time it takes to receive the B/L via mail can be cut at least in half. Once received electronically, your distribution and accounting departments can enter the actual on-board ocean bill of lading date into the accounts receivable system.

3. On receipt of the actual on-board ocean bill of lading date by your accounting and distribution departments, the B/L date can be entered into a separate file on the accounts receivable system and once or twice per month (more frequently if necessary) to correct the due dates generated from invoices.

Although there are other possible solutions for this problem, it is important to remember not to collect amounts owing from foreign customers prematurely. Once the problem of due dates is solved, the credit manager is in a position to improve cash flow by accurately following up on delinquent foreign customers.

Open Account

Like domestic trade, the exporter ships the goods and sends the bill of lading (made out or consigned direct to the foreign customer) and invoice directly to the foreign customer. The buyer takes possession of the goods on arrival and customs clearance of the goods in its country, and settles the payment obligation as agreed. Payment usually is made via mail, but preferably by telex or cable if large enough or over a specified amount, to a designated bank lock box of the exporter.

Perhaps one of the most persuasive factors is the lack of a tangible obligation, made mostly by banks, which removes the principal basis for positive action against the foreign purchaser in the event of default. In the event of nonpayment at maturity (due date), collection may be difficult. Experienced exporters know that legal procedures abroad to enforce payment under open account payment terms are more complicated and difficult than enforcing payment under a draft for nonpayment, especially if an accepted time draft is protested. Past experience of bankers and export creditors has shown that imports covered by documentary drafts for collection do receive priority over open account payment terms in countries where the local government authorities allocate foreign exchange for the respective import on a priority basis. This is especially true under tight foreign exchange allocations. Letters of credit for payment are usually given highest priority when a country prioritizes the allocation of foreign exchange.

When this method of payment is used, merchandise is shipped by the exporter to the foreign customer and a bill is rendered in the form of an invoice which is paid at some future date. Some open account arrangements provide for settlement at monthly intervals (progress payments), but other arrangements require payment at less frequent periods. Sometimes, discounts for early payment are offered depending on the product, competition, and profitability of the exporter. The due date (maturity date) is preferably calculated from the ship date rather than the invoice date. Payment by the foreign customer may come in the form of foreign draft, remittance order, or the customer's own check.

Documentary Collections

Frequently exporters want to control their goods until the foreign customer has paid for or formally promised to pay for the goods. In this case, the original bill of lading must be consigned to "order of shipper" and controlled until payment in full is received by the exporter or a promise of payment is made. In international trade, the Documentary Collection is used as a banking service to achieve this goal.

Outward Foreign Collections. One of the most typical and practical means for controlling the flow of title documents, obtaining payment or acceptance on drafts, and transfer of funds between an exporter and foreign customer is using the services of commercial banks. This is done by using a bank documentary collection form. You can use one or a combination of two methods: Regular Collection or Direct Collection. Most banks have their own collection forms for use by exporters.

Under **regular collections,** the exporter sends a draft and documents to its remitting bank (usually a bank in its country). It also sends an instruction letter explaining exactly how the draft is to be collected. The collecting bank in turn, enters certain data from the collection of the exporter into its computer (if automated) and forwards the Export Collection together with the draft, documents, and instructions to the overseas collecting bank.

When the exporter's shipment is being made by air, or there are other time constraints like a short shipping voyage time (i.e., shipments on the East Coast of the United States to ports in the Caribbean, Central America, and Northern South America), the exporter may mail the draft, documents, and instructions directly to the overseas collecting bank. The collection in this case is called a **direct collection** or what most banks have, a Direct Collection Letter (DCL), used for this specific purpose. The Philadelphia National Bank/Philadelphia International Bank Universal Collection Form example (Figure 5–1) may be used for both the regular and direct collection methods. It is a method used by many exporters to improve cash flow and assure that the documents required for customs clearance of the goods arrive at the port of entry prior to the goods. Although the original documents and draft are sent direct to the overseas collecting bank, a copy of the DCL is usually sent to the remitting bank of the exporter for collection follow up with, and receipt of funds from, the overseas collecting bank.

It is a method of settlement for collecting and controlling payments and documents of an exporter in one country for the sale of goods and services to a foreign customer in another country by utilizing bank networks. In this regard, banks act as an exporter's agent to obtain acceptance and/or payment/collection of drafts from foreign customers located in other countries. A collection for payment at maturity (due date) is many times referred to as *documentary* when title (shipping and/or financial) documents used in international trade are delivered to the drawee (foreign customer) for payment or acceptance of a draft. Sometimes drafts are not presented for payment under a Documentary Collection. This is called a *Clean Collection*. The documents typically sent to a foreign customer are shipping and financial documents since most overseas shipments are transported via steamship or air cargo carriers.

More specifically, a documentary collection is the process whereby shipping and financial documents, and in most cases, a draft are drawn on a foreign customer and ultimately sent to a foreign bank for acceptance and/or payment. There are basically three methods for transmitting documents to an overseas collecting bank. In the first method, an exporter sends its draft and documents to a designated bank in its country, called the remitting

FIGURE 5–1
Example of Direct Collection Letter

Philadelphia International Bank

$_____   _____ 19____ **NO. DCX** 12577

(TENOR)_____PAY TO THE ORDER

OF_____

                                                                                            DOLLARS

Value received and charge the same to account of
            (Drawee)   (Drawer)
To

                                                        _____
                                                        AUTHORIZED SIGNATURE

X-6272 9/84

Philadelphia International Bank
A CoreStates Bank
World Trade Center
Suite 1332
Baltimore Md 21202

ORIGINAL (Attach To Original Shipping Documents)

EXPORT COLLECTION

TO (Send to Bank or Buyer) | FROM (Drawer)

ACCOUNT NUMBER | SUB CODE

ADVISE BY PIB REF. NO. **DCX** 12577 | SUPPLIER'S INVOICE/REF NO | DATE | AMOUNT $

TYPE OF COLLECTION

☐ **OPEN ACCOUNT**
The enclosed invoice(s) have been sent to you directly by the supplier. Please remit payment to The Philadelphia International Bank, Baltimore, quoting PIB's Reference No. above.

☐ **DIRECT COLLECTION**
The enclosed draft and documents have been sent to you for collection directly from the drawer, or drawer's agent for account of The Philadelphia International Bank, Baltimore, quoting PIB's Reference No. and are to be handled in accordance with the instructions specified below.

☐ **REGULAR COLLECTION**
we enclose for collection

Please follow the instructions indicated (x) below

☒ Send all PAYMENTS and Correspondence directly to:

Philadelphia International Bank
World Trade Center, Suite 1332
Baltimore, MD. 21202

TELEX 4422022
SWIFT PNBPUS3B

	DOCUMENTS ENCLOSED	BILL OF LADING	COMM INV	INS POLICY	WGT	CON INV	CERTIF OF ORIGIN	OTHER
ORIGINALS								
DUPLICATES								

IN CASE OF NEED REFER TO

508 ☐ Deliver documents against payment.
509 ☐ Deliver documents against acceptance.
511 ☐ All charges for account of drawee including stamps, exchange, taxes and our charge of $_____
512 ☐ Waive charges if refused.
563 ☐ All charges must be paid prior to release of documents and may not be waived.
510 ☐ All charges for account of drawer.
500 ☐ Protest for non payment.
501 ☐ Protest for non acceptance.

502 ☐ Do not protest
505 ☐ Cable advice of non payment
506 ☐ Cable advice of non acceptance.
504 ☐ Advise acceptance and due date by airmail.
535 ☐ Advise acceptance and due date by telex or SWIFT.
516 ☐ Remit payments by airmail.
534 ☐ Remit payment by tested telex or SWIFT.
521 ☐ Hold for arrival of merchandise.
520 ☐ A provisional deposit in local currency may be accepted under drawee's written obligation to assume all exchange risks

Who is authorized
530 ☐ To obtain honoring of the draft as drawn
565 ☐ To give instructions unconditionally
OTHER INSTRUCTIONS

                                                        _____
                                                        AUTHORIZED SIGNATURE

"Subject to Uniform Rules for Collections (1978 Revision), International Chamber of Commerce, Publication No. 322".

Source: Philadelphia National Bank.

bank. They, in turn, send the draft and documents to a foreign bank, called the collecting or presenting bank. Preferably, the collecting or presenting bank is designated by the foreign customer. Unless the foreign customer designates its own bank in its country, exporters run the risk that their remitting bank may designate a foreign bank in the city of the foreign customer that is not in close proximity to the foreign customer, or a foreign bank that the foreign customer has no relationship with. Imagine having to travel to the other side of New York City or Houston to accept or pay a draft, obtain title documents, and travel to the port to claim the goods. If you have ever traveled across Mexico City or Sao Paulo, you can well imagine what an inconvenience you've created for your foreign customer. Consider the repercussions if the foreign customer is a new customer—one that was obtained from competition and that you have been nurturing for several years. The solution is to obtain the name and address of your customer's designated bank on receipt of its purchase order. The salesperson and/or the distribution/order processing department should immediately contact the foreign customer for the full name and address of the bank if it is missing.

The collecting or presenting bank will contact the obligor (importer) to inform them the draft and title documents have arrived at their bank.

The second method is where the exporter sends the documents and draft indirectly by using a bank's Direct Collection Letter (DCL), previously discussed.

As the third method, the exporter sends the documents and draft directly to the customer's overseas bank, completely by-passing a bank in the country of the exporter.

Title documents and drafts should be accompanied by a collection letter or letter of instruction to the bank or banks. It is another integral part of the collection process. Most banks have their own blank printed letter of instruction forms and/or Direct Collection Letters (DCL). The exporter can make use of these forms by simply and carefully completing the instructions it wants that pertain to the export collection transaction, explained later.

The letter of instructions will detail the requirements of the exporter (drawee) pertaining to such information as the paying or handling of bank collection charges, the title documents, and the remittance instructions. In addition, other important instructions could pertain to procedures to be followed by the bank or banks, especially the overseas collecting bank, in the event difficulties arise with respect to nonacceptance or nonpayment of the draft. The banks should know the appropriate person to contact if there are problems.

The foreign bank (collecting bank), following the exporter's instructions, releases the title documents to the foreign customer on payment of a sight draft–documents against payment (D/P) or the acceptance of a time draft, better known as documents against acceptance (D/A). In the event a draft is not accepted or paid, the foreign bank should follow the exporter's instructions as to whom to notify for further instructions.

A sight draft–documents against payment (D/P) type collection should be paid once presented to or "sighted" by the foreign customer before the collecting bank in the country of import. The word *sighted* for sight draft–documents against payment (D/P) payment terms means the customer physically sights the draft and title documents at the counters of the overseas collecting bank. Under this payment term, the exporter, by controlling the original document, retains control of the goods until the foreign customer pays the sight draft. Thus, the exporter controls the title documents (retains title), provided the on-board ocean bill of lading is properly consigned and endorsed.

Under certain circumstances, a foreign customer can obtain possession of the documents before acceptance or payment of a draft drawn against it. This can occur when a foreign customer needs to meet certain legal requirements of its country or when it needs to obtain a government permit for foreign exchange. The foreign customer can also post a bond or bank guarantee with the collecting bank.

Exporters should become familiar with these country practices in order not to operate under a false sense of security. Also, D/P or D/A payment terms are not practical with air freight shipments since air waybills are nonnegotiable and can only be consigned direct to the consignee (foreign customer). Therefore, foreign customers can take possession of the goods before sighting or accepting a draft. It is possible to consign air waybills to overseas banks, but the bank must give written permission prior to shipment of the goods. Banks are not equipped to store goods in warehouses.

The foreign customer, when sighting the draft and documents, pays the face amount of the draft. The collecting bank then transmits the funds to the remitting bank for payment to the exporter. Once the full amount of the draft is paid, the overseas collecting bank will release the title documents to the foreign customer. However, experienced exporters know most foreign customers will not sight the draft until the goods arrive at the customer's designated port of importation, irrespective of the documents arriving before the arrival of the steamship carrier, unless the goods are shipped via air cargo. This is a technique used by foreign customers to improve cash flow, obtain favorable exchange rates when necessary, ensure that the goods arrive without disruption, and for other reasons. It is important this payment term is specifically spelled out in the sales contract. When the draft and documents arrive before the steamship carrier, the overseas collecting bank will inform the foreign customer of the arrival of the draft and documents at its bank and immediately start to request the foreign customer to sight the draft and documents. If it does not sight the draft and documents promptly, waiting for the vessel to arrive, the bank may consider the drafted obligation in default. The solution to this potential problem is for the exporter and foreign customer to agree in the sales contract to wait for the arrival of the goods at the port of importation before sighting the draft. The letter of instructions to the bank or banks should state that the draft and documents are to be presented on arrival of the steamship carrier by stating an ETA date. The aforementioned may not be feasible, depending on the financial strengths of both parties. The exporter may want its payment on presentation of the draft and documents and not want to wait until the vessel arrives at the port of destination. This may be true under situations where the ocean voyage time is long (i.e., goods shipped via New York and destined to Japan, Australia, or South Africa). If at that time, the foreign customer does not pay the sight draft for whatever reasons, the overseas collecting bank will consider the drafted obligation as unpaid and in default.

Under the payment term, time draft–documents against acceptance (D/A), the foreign collecting bank will release title documents to the foreign customer on "acceptance" of the draft. This is done by writing *accepted* across the face of the draft, dating and signing it. Once accepted, the draft becomes a trade acceptance (T/A) and the title documents are released to the foreign customer. Note, the title documents can only be released when the draft is accepted. By accepting the draft the foreign customer recognizes and acknowledges its legal obligation to pay the face amount at maturity (due date). A draft, once accepted by the obligor, is only a promise to pay. It does not mean an automatic payment at maturity of the draft. The foreign customer as obligor is still responsible for making sure the draft is paid at maturity. Once accepted, the draft or trade acceptance (T/A) is a legally binding obligation of the foreign customer to pay at maturity.

The above mentioned procedure is complicated by a credit person who does not understand the role and significance of shipping and financial documents, the payment terms and draft pertaining thereto, and its instructions to the banks. In summation, the procedure of documentary collection works when the exporter submits to its designated bank, the following after shipping the goods:

- Shipping documents, including the important original bill of lading that conveys title to the goods, in addition to other important title documents to the shipment.
- A draft (a demand for payment, not a promise of payment), demanding acceptance or payment from the foreign customer. Depending on the agreed on payment terms, the draft might be payable on "sight" (demanding payment on presentation) or a time draft (demanding payment at some stipulated time in the future after presentation—sight—or after the bill of lading date).
- Instructions to the banks on how to handle the transaction. Proper and accurate instructions are extremely important. They may be any one of a combination of the following:

  1. Release of documents to a foreign customer under cash against documents (CAD), cash against goods (CAG), or documents against payment (DP or DAP) payment terms, without a sight draft, against receipt of payment.
  2. Release documents to the foreign customer on payment of the sight draft (known as a documents against payment, or D/P collection).

3. Release documents to the buyer on acceptance of the time draft (a documents against acceptance, or D/A collection).

Inward Foreign Collections. The converse of outward foreign collections is commonly called an *inward collection*. In the reverse manner from that outlined above, foreign collecting banks receive from remitting banks, documentary collection items payable to the originator. The inverse of this in the United States would be a U.S. bank receiving from a foreign bank, a documentary collection item payable to the originator in a foreign country. Documents are delivered to the foreign customer in accordance with the instructions given by the remitting bank. Normally, those accompanied by a sight draft are delivered against payment, while those accompanied by a time or "usance" draft are delivered against acceptance. If it is necessary for the buyer to obtain clearance of goods before paying or accepting a draft (usually due to local regulations), the remitting bank will instruct the collecting bank to release the goods against a trust receipt. The trust receipt provides for the bank to retain title to the goods. The foreign customer receives the goods as trustee for the bank and agrees to hold them, or the proceeds if they are sold, at the disposal of the bank. The foreign customer generally is required to pay the amount of the draft to the bank not later than the business day before the maturity date of the draft, or sooner if it sells the goods.

If the merchandise arrives before the documents, the foreign customer may, on the strength of a guarantee given by its bank, obtain a carrier's certificate from the transportation company on which the goods were shipped. The certificate is used to make customs entry and to take delivery of the goods without the permission of a bill of lading.[2]

Advantages and Disadvantages of Documentary Collections: Exporter and Foreign Customer. *Advantages:* The primary advantage of using drafts with documentary collections is that under D/P payment terms, the exporter can use overseas collecting banks to enforce payment from its foreign customer, provided the on-board ocean bill of lading is properly consigned and controlled by the exporter. For a documentary draft collection to work properly, an original bill of lading should not be sent direct to the foreign customer by someone in the sales or distribution department, or even the freight forwarder. It also provides a means when time drafts are used, to obtain an acceptance on the draft which creates an enforceable debt instrument in the form of a trade acceptance. The exporter's rights to payment are protected under the negotiable instruments law of the foreign customer's country. In the event the foreign customer defaults or delays payment at maturity, the possession of a trade acceptance may put the exporter in a stronger position before the foreign court if the exporter had sold under open account payment terms. The only evidence of indebtedness under open account is the unpaid commercial invoice. Also, if the exporter sends the draft and documents to an overseas collecting bank designated by the foreign customer, the chances of acceptance or payment default should be diminished because the foreign customer would not want to put itself in an embarrassing position with its own banker.

The exporter can use trade acceptances (T/As), which are negotiable instruments, to obtain financing from a number of sources. Trade acceptances can be discounted with or without recourse. They are a good tool to use for exporters needing cash flow.

An overseas collecting bank presenting a collection on behalf of an exporter may obtain payment quicker from a foreign customer who might otherwise be inclined to delay payment if the exporter were invoicing under open account payment terms. This is especially true when an exporter uses a bank designated by the foreign customer.

Disadvantages: There are certain disadvantages to the use of documentary collections to a foreign customer. The customer must rely on the exporter's reputation, honesty, and ability to deliver the draft and documents (especially the original bill of lading) timely before the goods arrive at its country. The foreign customer must rely on the exporter shipping products of good quality and quantity as ordered. The foreign customer cannot inspect the goods before paying the sight draft or accepting the time draft. However, it can examine the documents at the collecting bank before it releases them.

Documentary collections may be more cost competitive than

letter of credit payment terms because they are less costly and do not require the foreign customer to tie up its local bank credit lines. On the other hand, documentary collections are more expensive than open account payment terms not only for the exporter, but for the foreign customer as well. Banks do not perform their services and responsibilities free of charge—there are remitting and collecting bank collection charges. Normally, remitting collection bank charges are usually for the account of the exporter. Collecting bank charges are usually for the account of the foreign customer. Problems can arise when a decision is made to change a foreign customer's payment terms from open account to draft type payment terms. The foreign customer may be reluctant to pay bank collection charges in its country. In many countries, these charges can be quite expensive. Bank collection charges are discussed later.

The foreign customer and/or the exporter's sales department may be reluctant to accept documentary type payment terms if competition is offering open account payment terms or the foreign customer has had poor prior experience with local banks handling an exporter's draft and documents from other suppliers. This could include a persistent and aggravating problem to exporters of collecting banks not remitting payments timely (done frequently to gain the use of funds and float).

The documentary collection process is not a guarantee of payment of acceptance of drafts. Banks do not guarantee payment or acceptances of drafts. They only attempt to obtain acceptances and payment in either D/A or D/P payment terms in accordance with the instructions of exporters.

Like any other sale of goods, there is always the risk that the foreign customer, on inspection of the documents, might reject the documents presented by the collecting bank and refuse to pay or accept the draft. Rejection of the shipment may be justified by the foreign customer based on such documentary discrepancies as an increase in the price of the goods, incorrect packaging and markings, incorrect quantities, and the wrong goods. In other instances, the documents may arrive late because the exporter is inefficient and the foreign customer's import license expired before the goods were shipped and the customer cannot obtain foreign exchange to pay for the goods even if it still wanted them.

Despite the stated reasons for nonacceptance of the goods and whether or not it is justified, the exporter is in an exposed position. If it sold goods to a country or foreign customer with a high degree of risk with export credit insurance protection, it may not receive protection or payment of its claim by the insurer, depending on the type of coverage. If it is unable to work out the problem, it can warehouse the goods in the country of the original foreign customer or elsewhere until another buyer is located, or absorb the expense of shipping the goods back, or ship the goods to another country where another buyer has been found and absorb the shipping expenses (probably at a discount from the original price).

The exporter must rely on the integrity of the foreign customer's ability and willingness to complete the export transaction and make acceptances and payments as agreed. Likewise, exporters should comply with the terms and conditions of the sales contract. Deviations or changes should be mutually agreed on before the goods are shipped. This potential problem can be minimized by the credit person properly and thoroughly assessing the creditworthiness of foreign customers. Checking the experiences of other trade suppliers might reveal acceptance or payment problems or credit information reporting agencies might report or reveal a record of dishonored protested drafts.

In the case of air shipments, the foreign customer, as direct cosignee, can claim the goods on their arrival. Possession or surrender of the nonnegotiable air waybill is not required. Although control over the goods can be effected by consigning the air waybill to the exporter's agent, branch, or subsidiary, it can be consigned to the overseas collecting bank. This is not usually a recommended or an acceptable practice because most banks are not equipped to take possession of incoming air shipments and are reluctant to do it. Their written permission is highly recommended. If the foreign customer does not accept or pay the draft timely, the exporter runs the risk that the bank may authorize appropriate government officials to impound the goods or sell them at auction.

In extending credit terms under documents against acceptance or documents against payment credit terms to a foreign customer using a documentary collection, the exporter must make sure the foreign customer has the ability and willingness to pay maturing debt obligations as they come due. Possession of a trade acceptance (T/A), as an enforceable debt instrument may strengthen the exporter's legal position, but it does not guarantee payment. If the exporter discounted the T/A on a recourse basis, it may wind up with the debt obligation back on its books which could mean an additional receivable on top of any other shipments or debts outstanding representing drafts yet to be accepted or unaccepted by the same foreign customer.

Even if the foreign customer is creditworthy for the amount of business to be transacted between the sales department and foreign customer over a specified period of time, the transfer of funds from the buyer's country may be blocked by the government authorities of the country for economic or political reasons or as a consequence of war or civil disturbances. Payment may be delayed due to unavailability of foreign exchange in the buyer's country. When an exporter's draft is denominated in a currency other than that of the foreign customers' country, the foreign customer must exchange its local currency for the required foreign currency to pay the collection. There is the risk that the required foreign currency may not be immediately available in its country and the buyer must wait for an allocation of this currency. Depending on the buyer's country conditions, the waiting period could be several weeks, months, and even years before the proper amount of foreign exchange is allocated. Also, there is always the risk of exchange rate fluctuations. If a country devalues its currency against the currency of the exporter and the foreign customer is not properly protected, the foreign customer could wind up having to put up more of its currency than it originally anticipated to pay the exporter's draft. These are some of the reasons why exporters seek to obtain export credit insurance or the alternative of shipping under a letter of credit, with or without the confirmation of another bank. Also, exporters should never place themselves in the position of accepting a deposit in local currency as payment in full. It is simply a local currency deposit, not payment of an exporters billing currency.

Completing the Documentary Collection Form. Once the exporter has completed its documents in accordance with the foreign customer's purchase order, these documents should be assembled and submitted to either the remitting or collecting bank (in the case of direct collections) together with a completed draft drawn on the foreign customer (drawee) if called for, along with instructions on how the documentary collection is to be handled and what procedures to follow in the event difficulties arise. As previously mentioned, many banks provide preprinted collection forms, some with drafts attached for the exporter's use in submitting collections. If using a preprinted bank collection form, which is usually the norm for most experienced exporters, it should be noted that the larger section of these forms is called the *transmittal* section of the collection. The remaining section is usually the draft. Most bank documentary collection forms are multi-part forms, consisting of the original front part of the form, to be sent to the remitting bank for Regular Collections or direct to the collecting bank under Direct Collections. The second copy is sent to the drawer's remitting bank for Direct Collections. It enables the drawer's bank to follow up with the collecting bank. The third and fourth copies are sent to the drawer (exporter) for collection follow-up purposes with the drawee (foreign customer) and the banks. Most exporters retain one copy for their traffic department files pertaining to the respective shipment. The other copy is obviously sent to the credit department. The fifth copy is retained by the freight forwarder handling the respective shipment. Discussed later is the role freight forwarders play in the documentary collection and letter of credit process.

It is imperative the exporter's instructions be as precise and accurate as possible. The following is an explanation of the various entries that are seen on most bank collection forms (refer to Figure 5–2).

Draft

1. The U.S. Dollar or the foreign currency denominated amount covered by the draft. This amount should agree with the invoice amount or be the foreign currency equivalent.
2. The date of the draft should agree with the payment terms. If the payment terms are D/P or D/A, the preferable method is to date the draft the same day as the on-board ocean bill of lading date (the payment terms should reflect when the terms begin as agreed on with the foreign customer to avoid disputes or misunderstandings).

FIGURE 5–2

Draft and Transmittal Sections of Bank Collection Form

DOCUMENTARY COLLECTION

1. List the U.S. $ or the foreign currency amount covered by this draft. This amount should match the invoice amount or be the foreign currency equivalent.

2. Use the date the draft is prepared.

3. Reference number used for tracing and all correspondence regarding this collection.

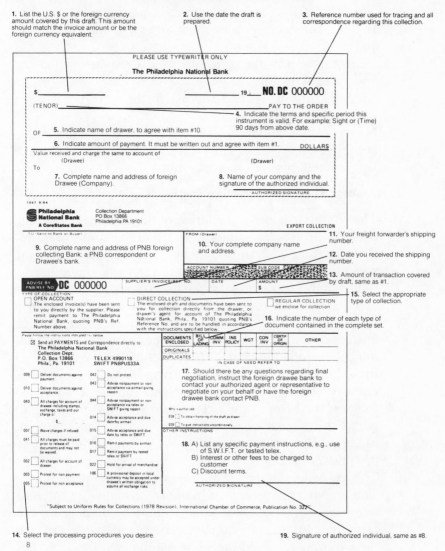

11. Your freight forwarder's shipping number.

12. Date you received the shipping number.

13. Amount of transaction covered by draft, same as #1.

15. Select the appropriate type of collection.

16. Indicate the number of each type of document contained in the complete set.

17. Should there be any questions regarding final negotiation, instruct the foreign drawee bank to contact your authorized agent or representative to negotiate on your behalf or have the foreign drawee bank contact PNB.

18. A) List any specific payment instructions, e.g., use of S.W.I.F.T. or tested telex.
B) Interest or other fees to be charged to customer
C) Discount terms.

14. Select the processing procedures you desire.

19. Signature of authorized individual, same as #8.

Source: Philadelphia National Bank.

3. The remitting bank's reference number used for tracing and all correspondence regarding the collection.

4. The payment terms and specific period the draft is valid. For example, Sight or (Time) 90 days from date thereof (the date of the draft) or from B/L date.

5. Indicate the name of drawer (exporter), to agree with Item 10.

6. Indicate the amount of payment. It must be spelled out and agree with Item 1.

7. Complete the name and address of the foreign customer (drawee).

8. Name of your company (exporter) and the signature of the authorized individual. The draft should be endorsed on the reverse side by the same individual.

Transmittal Section: Collection Instructions

9. The complete name and address of the overseas collecting bank of the drawee. Under Article 3 of the Uniform Rules, the exporter can designate an overseas bank to handle the collection. However, this is often the bank suggested by the foreign customer as stipulated on its purchase order whether telexed or mailed. Exporters should provide a space on their purchase order forms for the foreign customer's collecting bank. If the exporter does not indicate a collecting bank, the remitting bank will forward the collection to its branch or correspondent in the buyer's country. This could create problems for the foreign customer if the bank is not located near it. Imagine having to go to the opposite side of town in Sao Paulo, Tokyo, Mexico City, or Calcutta. It's just like going from one end of New York City to the other—but worse!

10. The exporter's complete business name and address.

11. The exporter's reference number (usually an invoice number) or a freight forwarder's shipping number.

12. Date the documentary collection was prepared or the date the exporter received the shipping number.

13. Amount of the transaction covered by the draft (same as # 1).

14. Select the processing procedures desired by the exporter:

a. Check *Deliver documents against payment,* (D/P) if the payment terms are sight draft, cash against documents, cash against goods, or a simple documents against payment (clean collection).

b. Check *Deliver documents against acceptance,* (D/A) if the payment terms are time draft or sight time draft (i.e., 90 days draft from B/L date or 120 days sight draft from B/L date).

c. Check *All charges for account of drawee including stamps, exchange (foreign exchange commissions), taxes and our charges of:* _____ , if you want the foreign customer to be responsible for these charges. Usually in international trade, the foreign customer is responsible for its own bank collection charges or any charges assessed to it within their country.

d. Check *Waive charges if refused,* if you want to absorb the charges in the above mentioned point. The exporter will have to make a business decision if the foreign customer refuses to pay any or part of the overseas bank collection charges. In this regard, it makes much more common sense for the exporter to absorb the foreign bank's collection charges if refused by the foreign customer, than to hold up prompt receipt of funds. The cash flow can be put to use by the exporter. Also, unless you are billing in the buyer's currency, it is best to get the foreign customer to deposit funds with the collecting bank in the event there are foreign exchange delays. Disputing or negotiating who pays foreign bank collection charges is something that should have been negotiated up-front when the sales contract was negotiated. In general, it is more advantageous for exporters to absorb disputed charges than run the risk of delayed cash flow or never getting paid at all.

e. Check *All charges must be paid prior to release of documents and may not be waived,* only if the foreign customer agreed in writing to absorb these charges before the goods are shipped.

f. Check *All charges for account of drawer,* if the

exporter agreed prior to shipment of the goods to absorb these charges.

g. Check *Protest for nonpayment,* only if agreed to by the foreign customer before the goods are shipped, or if you had poor prior payment experience or, if there is undoubted commercial creditworthiness risk with the foreign customer. Protesting is a serious action for exporters to take, discussed later.

h. Check *Protest for nonacceptance,* the same as above.

i. Check *Do not protest,* if the exporter feels comfortable with the commercial risk or has had good prior payment experience with a foreign customer.

j. Check *Advise nonpayment or nonacceptance via airmail giving reasons,* as a good and prudent measure to always want reported. However, the credit department will have to determine if it wants to receive these notices via mail. It could take one or more weeks.

k. Check *Advise nonpayment or nonacceptance via telex or SWIFT giving reasons,* is usually the preferable method since it eliminates mail time and promptly informs the credit department of any potential problems with the collection so it can take prompt and prudent measures to correct the problem.

l. Check *Advise acceptance and due date by airmail,* is the same problem as that mentioned above.

m. Check *Advise acceptance and due date by telex or SWIFT,* the preferable method, promptly informs the credit department.

n. Check *Remit payment by airmail,* if the amounts are small.

o. Check *Remit payment by tested telex or SWIFT,* the preferable method because it speeds up cash flow. Most credit managers usually have a cut-off dollar or currency figure amount to determine when funds should be wire transferred based on a cost/benefit analysis.

p. Check *Hold for arrival of merchandise,* is usually a good measure to take, since most foreign customers in reality will not accept or sight the documents held by overseas collecting banks until the goods arrive in their country anyway.

q. *A provisional deposit in local currency may be accepted under drawee's written obligation to assume all exchange risks,* should always be checked as a matter of credit department and company policy if the exporter is billing the foreign customer in a currency other than its own. The exporter should never put itself in the position of having to pay for losses in foreign exchange. This prudent measure is always taken when the credit person knows the country is experiencing foreign exchange problems or is simply a country risk.

15. Select the appropriate type of collection.

16. Indicate the number of each type of documents contained in the complete set. This is the number of documents the exporter has submitted to the banks with the documentary collection.

17. *In case of need refer to,* should be completed if there are any questions regarding final negotiation or collection assistance. Usually exporters designate the credit department or a foreign agent or representative when applicable.

18. *Other instructions,* could include a list of any specific payment instructions, e.g., use of SWIFT or tested telex; interest or other fees to be charged to the foreign customer; discount terms.

Defaults and Protests.   In the event the foreign customer refuses to pay or accept a draft, the collecting bank should notify the exporter, through the remitting bank if used, of the dishonor or default and the stated reasons. If the exporter has elected not to protest nonacceptance or nonpayment, the exporter should immediately determine the reasons for nonacceptance or nonpayment with assistance from: (1) the foreign customer and/or foreign sales agents; (2) distributors (if the export sale is an indent type sale, sometimes called a *drop* shipment or direct sale to a customer of a distributor); or (3) its own local branch or subsidiary.

If the exporter elects to instruct the overseas collecting bank to protest and pursue nonacceptance or nonpayment in the buyer's country, the exporter should be absolutely sure it thoroughly understands the protesting procedures in the buyer's country.

Protesting is a legal procedure of officially registering the fact that a draft was presented for acceptance or payment and was dishonored by the drawee. The initial protest is usually followed by further legal actions taken against the defaulting drawee. A certificate is prepared by a local lawyer or notary public and they present the draft a second time to the defaulting drawee with a certificate of protest (the dishonored draft is attached), giving the date and place of presentation of the draft to the drawee. This certificate states that the drawee refused to accept or pay the draft on presentation. Copies of the certificate of protest are filed with the appropriate officials.

In most countries protesting is a serious offense and credit managers who elect to instruct their banks to protest for nonacceptance or nonpayment should be absolutely sure they know what they are doing. Notices of protest are published in official gazettes or trade journals in some countries. Such public notices can significantly damage the defaulting drawee's credit reputation because in effect they are "blacklisted" and local creditors will be cautious about dealing any further with the defaulting drawee. Also, if the exporter's credit department has a habit of protesting in a specific marketplace or area of the world, other foreign customers will be cautious about dealing with you as an overseas supplier. You will develop a bad reputation as an exporter to the local market area.

It is important to note that protesting procedures vary from country to country and most have time limitations that are relatively short, sometimes only a few days, in which the exporter can file a protest for nonacceptance or nonpayment.

Once a draft is protested, all parties to the export transaction (including subsequent endorsers) will be notified. This notification serves to establish the holder's right of recourse against the drawer and subsequent endorsers (in case someone has financed the export sale by purchasing a trade acceptance from the exporter as original drawer).

After a second attempt is made to honor a defaulted draft for nonacceptance or nonpayment, the exporter as drawer or subsequent holder of such dishonored draft must decide if it wants to pursue further legal action against the drawee to obtain payment or to write-off the amount of the transaction as a bad debt. Or, if the holder of the defaulted draft is credit insured, it can file a claim with the insurer (assuming it has commercial risk coverage). Legal action in most, if not all cases, must be litigated in a court of law under the legal jurisdiction of the drawee's country. Experience has taught foreign creditors that for a judgment to be made in favor of the creditor (holder or drawer), there must be a valid and enforceable claim against the defaulting party (drawee). Unpaid sight drafts or unaccepted time drafts that were protested have little or no value because the drawee has not acknowledged the debt obligation, it is one-name paper and unenforceable on its face. Foreign courts will make reference to the underlying sales contract between both parties to the export transaction in deciding on the drawee's obligation. In the case of trade acceptances, the T/A in itself represents the drawee's acknowledgement of the debt obligation by accepting it, thus creating the T/A (an accepted time draft), a legally enforceable debt instrument.

In certain countries there are some legal benefits that can be obtained from protesting. For example:

- In Brazil, the holder of a protested draft can institute bankruptcy proceedings against the drawee.
- In Scotland, the holder can take "summary diligence," which is a quick and inexpensive method of enforcing payment.
- In Algeria, the holder of the protested draft can attach the personal property of the drawee (if there is any value).

Exporters and credit managers must realize that legal fees can be quite costly and protesting small amounts is often cost prohibitive. Discounters or financers of T/As will not finance these export transactions if the exporter instructed the banks to protest for nonpayment.

Bank Responsibilities: Uniform Rules For Collection.   What obligates banks used by exporters around the world to comply with the instructions of exporters and between themselves? The answer lies with those nations who abide by the Uniform Rules for Collection (Appendix 5–A), issued by the International Chamber of Commerce's Publication Number 322 of January 1, 1979. The Uniform Rules comprise an accepted body of practice, define the terms used in collections, set out the procedures to be followed by all parties, and establish liabilities and responsibilities. Exporters who ship goods under documentary collections should become as familiar as possible with the provisions of these rules. Since not all countries and/or banks comply with these rules, exporters are encouraged to check with their bankers and the International Chamber of Commerce.

It is important to note these rules replace the "Uniform Rules for the Collection of Commercial Paper" (ICC Publication Number 354) which were widely used since their introduction in 1967.

In addition to ICC's Uniform rules, each country has its own legal code or body of court decisions governing bank collections. These laws, while generally not in conflict with the ICC's Uniform Rules, do take precedence when conflicts arise.

The importance and thrust of the Uniform Rules and the laws governing collections (import and export) is that a bank which undertakes a role in a documentary collection is acting as an agent of the exporter and is subject to its general control and instructions. Because banks act only on the instructions of the exporter (discussed later), it is important that these instructions be as complete and precise as possible, leaving little room for error or interpretation.

The Uniform Rules basically state that the remitting bank (if used) is responsible for verifying that the documents submitted appear on their face to be those listed in the collection and that no documents are missing. The overseas collecting bank that receives the collection from the remitting bank or direct from the exporter is responsible for presenting the draft and documents to the foreign customer for acceptance or payment, whatever is the case, and remitting payment. Should the foreign customer refuse to accept or pay the draft, the collecting bank will notify the remitting bank and/or exporter and follow any further instructions to protect the goods or to protest the dishonored draft.

Bank Fees for Documentary Collections. Below are some typical fees charged by banks for the handling of drafts for collection (documentary collections) covering export shipments from the United States.

Amount	Rate	Minimum/Maximum
Any amount	1/10%*	Minimum U.S. $75
Any amount	Flat†	U.S. $65

* The above rates apply to items when an exporter uses a bank's collection form to accompany the documents, or when the exporter uses its own form.
† The above rate applies to items when a bank's Direct Collection Letter (DCL) is used.

Letters of Credit

One of the most frequently used payment terms in international trade is the letter of credit (L/C). Yet in reality, it is one of the most least understood. Many letter of credit instruments are difficult to comply with. All too often, many exporting companies think it is a guarantee of payment, which, in fact, it is not.

Complying with its terms and conditions can prove to be a formidable task for the beneficiary (exporter) of the letter of credit. It requires meticulous handling on the part of all those involved with it. Particularly, an exporter's credit department needs a strict collection follow-up sequence to ensure compliance to and payment of the L/C.

Payment under letters of credit is conditional on the exporter's (beneficiary) compliance with the terms and conditions as specified in the body of the letter of credit from the issuing bank. These terms and conditions require the exporter as beneficiary to present certain stipulated documents and drafts, which are usually those associated with the export transaction for transport, commercial, and official purposes (i.e., commercial invoices, bills of lading, certificates of origin, and insurance certificates).

If the exporter as beneficiary has complied with the terms and conditions or documentary and financial requirements of the letter of credit, it at least has some assurances of payment. But, assurance of payment depends on the creditworthiness of the issuing bank and/or its country. In the event the exporter does not feel comfortable with either, it can ask for another bank to confirm the issuing bank's letter of credit. Asking for this confirmation is one thing—getting it is another. This is because of country risk conditions with certain nations, especially Third World nations who cannot pay their debt obligations to foreign creditors (especially banks). Because of this, many banks around the world have reached their debt capacity and cannot extend any further credit to these nations or banks.

Presentation of Documents for Payment.   Once the exporter has been advised that a letter of credit has been issued in its favor, many exporters make the mistake of starting to prepare or fulfill the requirements of the foreign customer's purchase order before actually receiving the actual letter of credit from the opening or issuing bank. Unless the exporter has had good or excellent prior experience with the foreign customer and its issuing bank, the exporter runs the risk of having the goods ready for shipment from the sourcing location or worse yet, at the pier ready to board a steamship, without receiving the original letter of credit. The exporter runs a risk because it may or may not be able to comply with certain terms and conditions contained in the actual original letter of credit. It is always conceivable new conditions might be added to the credit instrument. Or, the goods might be shipped and arrive at the overseas port of destination without any original documents because the original L/C arrived late. Thus, the foreign customer will be unable to clear goods through customs, and the goods will be stored in a customs warehouse to accrue expensive demurrage charges.

The answer to the above mentioned problem which affects collections and cash flow projections for credit managers, is to have the opening bank issue the letter of credit via tested telex or SWIFT to the advising or negotiating bank as the "original operative instrument" which can be presented for payment by the beneficiary. The exporter must make sure the negotiating or confirming bank, usually the advising bank, is willing to accept the aforementioned as the original operative instrument. Sometimes advising, negotiating, and even confirming banks who pay on behalf of issuing banks, still want to wait for the original written letter of credit to be received by them via mail. This might indicate a financial problem with the opening bank or some sort of technical problem between the banks which the exporter should investigate immediately. The solution helps reduce or eliminate any delays in processing the foreign customer's orders and banking the letter of credit timely for payment after shipment of the goods. Remember, in many cases banks want the original on-board ocean bill of lading presented to them with the original L/C.

On receipt of the original or copy of the letter of credit, the exporter should always carefully review it to ensure that the terms and conditions of the credit instrument are in agreement with the original terms and conditions of the sales contract with the foreign customer (applicant), and that the exporter can comply with all of the terms and conditions of the credit. If not, the credit needs to be amended before shipment takes place. In this regard, it is a good idea for the credit, sales, and traffic/distribution departments to each receive a copy of the letter of credit to ensure compliance.

Once the goods are shipped and the exporter assembles the required documents as stipulated in the letter of credit, it is then in a position to draw the required draft, and present it and the documents to the respective bank for payment. It is important to remember the obligations of the local bank in your market area that advised the opening bank's letter of credit. Depending on the language contained in the advising bank's covering letter to the opening bank's letter of credit, it may not be under any obligation to review the documents or pay the draft presented under the letter of credit. Its obligation might simply be to check the authenticity of the original letter of credit to determine if it is a bona fide letter of credit. Or, the advising bank might assume the obligation of negotiating the opening bank's letter of credit on its behalf and not pay it without authorization from the opening bank. Or, the advising bank might assume the obligation of negotiating and paying the beneficiary's draft and documents, assuming the exporter as beneficiary complied with the terms and conditions of the opening bank's letter of credit. In this regard, it will get reimbursed from the opening bank based on the payment term in the letter of credit. However, if another bank confirms the opening bank's letter of credit, then it is obligated to pay the beneficiary if the beneficiary (exporter) has complied with the terms and conditions of the letter of credit.

When exporters as beneficiaries to letters of credit get paid depends entirely on the payment terms contained in the letter of credit. Banks who pay under letters of credit get reimbursed from the opening bank on the same payment terms.

If it is a D/P (i.e., sight draft) letter of credit, the negotiating or confirming bank negotiates and pays it, providing immediate payment to the exporter as beneficiary. The paying bank gets reimbursed from the opening bank after it examines the documents. Exporters must be careful not to construe language written in the body of original letters of credit regarding reimbursement clauses, as previously mentioned. These clauses are written simply for banks. If the exporter is not sure, it should contact the advising bank for an interpretation. Again, if discrepancies are encountered by the paying or checking bank, you won't get paid until the discrepancies are corrected.

If it is a D/A (i.e., time draft—90 days draft from B/L date), the bank holds it to maturity (draft drawn on the foreign customer) and then pays it. Or, the bank may accept it (draft drawn on the negotiating or confirming bank) by discounting the draft which provides immediate payment to the beneficiary or, the beneficiary can elect to have the bank hold it until maturity or, it can elect to have the accepted draft returned to it for discounting at another financial institution. The accepted time draft by a bank is called *a bankers' acceptance* (BA). It represents the obligation of the bank to pay the face amount at maturity, less an acceptance commission and discount charges. Bankers' acceptances (an export trade financing instrument) is discussed in Chapter 8. The paying bank is reimbursed at the maturity of the bankers' acceptance. Again, if discrepancies are encountered by the paying or checking bank, an acceptance will not be created until the discrepancies are corrected.

Once the bank, other than the opening bank, has fulfilled its obligation, it then forwards the documents to the issuing bank. Exporters as beneficiaries should always request the bank to forward the documents via the quickest means possible. Many exporters believe that they have fulfilled their obligation simply because they have been paid under a letter of credit. This is not true because in documentary collections and even in open accounts, it is still imperative that the foreign customer be in a position to claim and withdraw its goods through customs. Therefore, it is still important for the original documents negotiated under letter of credit to be expedited as quickly as possible. Once the issuing bank examines or verifies the documents to ensure compliance, the issuing bank turns over the documents to the foreign customer (applicant) on presentation of the amount due, or on terms agreed to between the buyer and the issuing bank. These payment terms could differ from the payment terms stipulated in the actual letter of credit. The foreign customer then presents the shipping documents to the carrier and takes possession of the goods on customs clearance.

Common Letter of Credit Discrepancies. Banks have found there are a number of common discrepancies, a term used in banking to describe a beneficiary's noncompliance with certain terms and conditions of the letter of credit on examination of the beneficiary's draft and documents drawn against the credit. All parties to the letter of credit instrument are subject to the Uniform Customs and Practice for Documentary Credits (UCP) of the International Chamber of Commerce (ICC), issued under their Publication Number 400 (1983 revision). Refer to Appendix 5–B for a reprint of these rules and regulations. It is important for credit personnel to become totally familiar with the UCP 400 when a bank or banks claim discrepancies on presentation of your documents for acceptance and/or payment under a letter of credit instrument. Discrepancies, on the initial submission of documents under a letter of credit affect the beneficiary three ways:

1. *Cost:* Cable charges for messages sent between the applicant/beneficiary; the opening bank to the advising bank and/or paying bank to amend the credit.
2. *Loss of Cash Flow:* A sight L/C would effectively mean no prompt payment shortly after the documents and draft are presented to the paying or negotiating bank; payment made on due date under a time draft L/C if the discrepant documents are not corrected and/or the applicant will not authorize payment; or the availability to discount a bankers' acceptance when created; and, not to mention the interest expense associated with the loss of funds until the discrepant documents are corrected or payment is authorized by the applicant, issuing bank, or confirming bank in the case of a confirmed L/C.
3. *Unresolved Discrepancies:* Unless the applicant is willing to authorize discrepant documents, the beneficiary is in effect dealing on open account payment terms with the applicant and its country who were initially considered either a commercial (customer) and/or country risk.

The most frequently found discrepancies between letters of credit and the drafts and documents presented under letters of credit are mentioned below.

Drafts and documents are presented after the expiration date of the credit (UCP 400, Article 46a & b) is a common discrepancy. This usually occurs when the exporter (beneficiary) cannot get a properly prepared document in time, especially if certain documents require consularization (legalization). Sometimes local consulate offices are backlogged or have stringent legalization procedures. In other instances, the exporter has done a poor job in coordinating and consolidating all of the documentary requirements under a credit. The situation requires authorization from the foreign customer (applicant) to extend the credit.

Sometimes a partial shipment is made when the credit requires one shipment (UCP 400, Article 44). This usually happens when the foreign customer (applicant) increases the order without amending the credit or when the exporter overships or underships without amending the credit.

Documents may be presented late (UCP 400, Article 47a). Drafts and documents must be presented within 21 business days after the shipment of the goods to the paying or negotiating bank. This is known as *stale documents*. The credit should call for the acceptance of stale documents or the acceptance of documents and drafts after 21 business days.

Another common discrepancy is when the goods stated on the invoice are described differently then the B/L and/or versus the credit (UCP 400, Article 41c). Or, the invoice value and/or the quantity of merchandise might exceed the amount and/or quantity available under the credit (UCP 400, Article 15).

If goods are shipped after the credit expires and/or the latest shipping date expires (UCP 400, Article 45b), it can cause a discrepancy. The exporter should have gotten the L/C amended to extend it. Perhaps the carrier was not readily available within the stipulated expiry dates and that another carrier was not available. But, if a carrier was available after the expiry dates, but the date or dates in the L/C were not extended, a business decision to ship or not to ship should be made. Is it better to lose the sale, foreign customer, and/or market share? What happens if the applicant (account) refuses to authorize payment because of discrepancies?

In the event the applicant does not authorize payment, then it is conceivable they do not need your goods or perhaps have found another supplier. What is stated in the sales contract? Is the foreign customer acting in good faith and is it an account you are dependent on for a long-term relationship and market share?

Sometimes the exporter overships, which happens when the importer increases the original order or the exporter confuses similar orders placed by the same foreign customer. This inadvertent shipment will involve more goods than required under the credit without amending the credit to increase its value and quantity under the credit.

Missing documents is another problem (UCP 400, Article 2). The incorrect amount of documents are presented—one or more documents is missing. The exporter can still have a late submission of documents until the one or more missing documents are submitted even though a bulk of the documents are submitted under the credit. This assumes the documents are presented within the expiry dates.

Another discrepancy is when the bill of lading has numerous problems or errors, such as not marked *on board* (Article 26a, UCP 400) or *freight prepaid* when the credit covers C & F or CIF shipments (Article 31, UCP 400). Sometimes changes on the B/L are not signed by the steamship company or its agent or are not initialed by the party who signed the B/L. The B/L does not show the consignment (goods shipped) exactly as required in the credit. The B/L is not clean or claused, when the credit requires clean B/Ls (Article 34, UCP 400). The B/L is marked *on deck,* but not authorized in the credit (Article 28, UCP 400). The on-board endorsement on the B/L is not signed or initialed and/or is not dated by the steamship carrier or its agent (Article 27(b), UCP 400). Information is missing on the B/L as specified in the credit. The shipment is incorrectly consigned.

The stated price on the credit may differ from the stated price on the commercial invoice and/or on the B/L. This sometimes occurs with exporters selling commodities or other products when prices are determined by a formula method based on averages or commodity prices for a period. This can be difficult to determine and a final price of the goods is not ready at the time of shipment. In this case, the credit should allow a price based on presenting a pro-forma invoice. The final price on a final commercial invoice versus the pro-forma price can be settled outside the credit between the exporter and foreign customer.

A discrepancy can occur with insurance documents, if the insurance certificate or policy does not cover the risks specified in the credit (Article 37(a), UCP 400). Another type of insurance is used other than that required in the credit. The currency stated on the insurance documents may differ from that stated in the credit (Article 37(a), UCP 400). The insurance document may not show the consignment exactly as required in the credit, or the endorsement may not be correct and/or issued by insurance companies or their agents or by underwriters (Article 35, UCP 400). The value on the insurance documents is less than the CIF value of the goods or, if such value cannot be determined, the amount of drawing on the commercial invoice whichever is greater (Article 37(b), UCP 400). The coverage might only be effective after the bill of lading or other shipping document dates (Article 35, UCP 400).

All documents must conform and relate to each other and to the letter of credit. The documents must have all the "I"'s dotted and the "T"'s crossed. If the terms and conditions of the credit differ from the purchase order or sales contract, the paying or negotiating bank is certainly not aware of these differences and cannot recognize such differences when examining documents presented under a letter of credit.

It should be noted that corrections made to discrepancies must be done prior to the time (expiry dates) permitted in the letter of credit for presentation of documents. If no specific time for presentation of documents is mentioned in the credit, then the beneficiary automatically must correct the discrepancies within 21 days from the shipping date.

It is important to remember that banks deal in documents and not in goods. Product descriptions on commercial invoices, bills of lading, and other documents versus the letter of credit is one source of discrepancies which creates controversy between the beneficiary and the bank examiner. The way in which products are described on documents very much determines the amount of duty assessed as listed under tariffs. The problem is further complicated by automated systems which use product codes to describe products geared towards the domestic market rather than the export marketplace. This is especially true for companies who source their products from domestic plant locations that are automated for domestic business purposes and cannot change product codes easily without affecting its domestic business. It is a problem for shipments destined for Europe and Japan where most duty rates are based on CIF or C&F prices, which if improperly described can affect freight bills.

There are several alternative approaches the exporter (beneficiary) can use to get paid when discrepancies are encountered.

1. The beneficiary, after examining the draft and documents versus the credit, but before they are presented to the paying or negotiating bank, notices some differences between the documents and the credit. In this case, the beneficiary can either cable the applicant/buyer to amend the credit so the beneficiary can comply with the credit. If the applicant agrees, the beneficiary can try to correct the discrepant documents before the credit or latest shipment date expires or without creating stale documents.

2. The beneficiary can submit the draft and documents to the paying, negotiating, or advising bank with a request that the draft and documents be sent to the opening bank on an "approval" or "approval to pay" basis, despite the discrepant documents. The paying or negotiating bank will examine the documents before forwarding them on an approval basis as requested by the beneficiary. The paying bank will pay the beneficiary once it receives approval from the opening bank, which will come only after the opening bank has received the draft and documents and the applicant has approved the draft and documents containing discrepancies. The beneficiary should request the approval be made by cable reply.

3. If the bank examiner at the paying or negotiating bank advises the beneficiary of discrepancies which were overlooked by the beneficiary, the beneficiary, unable to correct the discrepancies, may instruct the paying or negotiating bank to cable the opening bank for "payment authorization" or "cable authority to pay" all discrepancies. In this case, the paying or negotiating bank will list the

discrepancies in its cable to the opening bank. The opening bank will request the applicant to approve the discrepancies, and assuming it does, approves the discrepancies. The opening bank will cable the paying bank to pay the beneficiary.

4. If the beneficiary cannot correct the discrepancies found by the bank examiner, the beneficiary may request that the paying or negotiating bank pay its draft against its guarantee. This means that the beneficiary, by offering its guarantee, agrees to indemnify the paying or negotiating bank against any loss or damage it may sustain by reason of such payment. The beneficiary further agrees to repay the bank on demand in the event such payment is not approved by the issuing bank. Banks will normally accept guarantees from beneficiaries only for their own customers in satisfactory financial condition. What this all means in effect is that the beneficiary by issuing its guarantee to obtain payment of its draft, is substituting its credit standing for that of the applicant. Therefore, it is important for the beneficiary of the credit to have previously performed a credit-financial analysis on the applicant/buyer and that of its country by a country risk analysis whenever economically feasible and practical. When the beneficiary receives immediate payment for issuing its guarantee, such payment is subject to the approval by the issuing bank which may or may not reimburse the paying bank for paying under the guarantee.

Most commercial banks can be helpful in resolving documentary problems, especially if a relationship exists between the beneficiary and the bank. Sometimes account officers at a bank can be quite helpful when letter of credit checkers or examiners are being unreasonable with respect to minor disputed discrepancies.

Choosing the appropriate instructions to the paying or negotiating bank to either "send documents on approval to pay" or "cable authority to pay" basis is extremely important. A good exporter will use the instructions "send documents on approval to pay" basis only when the steamship carrier is arriving shortly at the overseas port of destination of the foreign customer. Otherwise, the instruction "cable authority to pay" is to be used.

Remember the importer/buyer needs the original documents to clear goods through customs and to arrange or settle payment with its local exchange authorities. It has to either fulfill its own customer purchase orders or needs the goods for its own manufacturing process.

It is conceivable that the opening or confirming banks may find discrepancies after payment is made to the exporter/beneficiary. Although the banks have no recourse to the exporter/beneficiary, more than likely there may be discrepant or missing documents. Therefore, it may be in the best interest for the exporter to resolve the problems in keeping with the best interests of the foreign customer involved in the transaction. A disgruntled foreign customer will be a customer lost to competition or may result in a reduction in the foreign customer's purchase order requirements, a subsequent loss in market share, loss of profit, or even detrimental effects on production/capacity at plants of the exporter.

Letter of Credit Check List

Although banks have their own application forms and procedures in connection with the issuance of credits, there is no substitute for the detailed work that must be performed by the exporter (beneficiary) in order to comply with the terms and conditions of the credit instrument. Therefore, it is important for the credit department to check the credit and documents with the sales contract to ensure all specific terms and conditions agreed on between the commercial parties do not disagree.

Major commercial banks throughout the world have staffs of trained letter of credit specialists. These bank people are not only there to handle bank operations pertaining to letters of credit, but can assist exporters in resolving problems or questions with their credits. In order to minimize problems, increase efficiency and increase cash flow by getting paid promptly on first presentation, the following check list may be beneficial to exporters to minimize letter of credit discrepancies.

Credit Instrument

1. Is the credit irrevocable?
2. What bank has committed itself to pay? As the beneficiary

are you satisfied that this bank can pay (what about country risk)? If not, can the credit be confirmed by a prime bank?

3. If the credit is confirmed, what type of bank confirmed the credit? Are you satisfied with its financial standing? If the bank is foreign owned, are you satisfied with its financial standing and its country risk in the event of discrepancies?

4. Is your name and address as well as that of your foreign customer complete and spelled correctly?

5. Is the amount of the credit sufficient to cover the shipment? Exporters should take into consideration factors that depend on the terms of sale, such as FOB or CIF; the cost of goods plus profit; inland transportation to the steamer (including wharfage and handling charges at port of loading); ocean freight charges; forwarding fees; consular, insurance, inspection, and/or miscellaneous charges.

6. Is the credit transferable if required?

7. Does the credit contain any negative clauses or statements related to boycotts? Refer to Appendix 5–C for an explanation and additional information concerning this very important issue to U.S. exporters and their overseas operations.

Invoices

1. Is the merchandise, price(s), and terms of payment described exactly in the credit as specified in the sales contract?

2. Is there sufficient tolerance allowed on the quantity to be shipped? If not, have the quantity preceded by the word *about* or *approximate,* which is customarily understood to mean that the credit is available for the quantity indicated plus or minus 5 percent.

3. Are the invoices issued in the name of the account party for whose account the credit was opened?

4. Does the total amount of the invoices exceed the amount of the credit or remaining balance in the credit, unless the credit allows a tolerance? The amount must be preceded by the word *about* or *approximately,* which means the credit amount indicated is available plus or minus 10 percent. If yes, the credit needs to be increased by an amendment to the credit.

5. Are the marks and number of packages on the invoice identical to those on other documents?
6. Are partial shipments permitted, if required?

Drafts

1. Is the draft drawn by the beneficiary on parties as specified in the credit?
2. Does the draft exceed the credit amount or remaining balance of the credit and agree with stated amounts on other documents?
3. Is the draft worded to conform with what is stated in the credit?
4. If appropriate, is the draft drawn payable to parties other than the beneficiary, except in those cases where payment is to be made to banks acting on behalf of the beneficiary?
5. Is the draft properly endorsed on the reverse side?

Bills of Lading

1. Are they prepared in full sets as specified in the credit?
2. Is the lading marked "on board" with notation dated and signed by the steamship company or its agents?
3. Is the B/L endorsed when issued to the shippers order?
4. Is it stamped "freight prepaid" when required or when C&F and CIF terms of sale are specified or where freight is being invoiced?
5. Is the B/L dated later than the latest ship date as specified in the credit? If yes, the credit should be amended to extend the ship date. If no ship date is specified, the B/L must be dated and presented within the validity of the credit.
6. Is the lading clean? Documents should not bear a notation qualifying the receipt of the goods in apparent good order and condition.
7. Is shipment permitted from the place you intend to ship from?
8. Does the port of destination quoted by the exporter agree with the credit?
9. Is transshipment permitted, if required?

10. If the exporter is chartering a vessel, does the credit allow charter party bills of lading?
11. Does the credit stipulate shipment to be effected on a named vessel or vessel of a named steamship company or flag vessel and can the exporter comply with this requirement?

Insurance (if required).

1. Does the insurance cover the risks specified in the credit and at least the value of the shipment?
2. Is the insurance issued in negotiable form, countersigned, and endorsed?
3. Is it in complete form (the original and duplicate)?
4. Does the insurance show that the date appearing on the insurance document is not later than the date appearing on the B/Ls?
5. If the exporter is shipping "on deck," does the insurance policy or certificate, under CIF terms, cover on-deck shipment? Also, does the credit allow for on-deck shipment?

Other Documents

1. Are all other documents in compliance with the requirements of the credit? Are these documents issued and presented in accordance with the terms and conditions of the credit?
2. Does the exporter require an export or exchange license?
3. Can the exporter obtain properly executed shipping, consular, and other documents to comply with the terms and conditions of the credit and before the above mentioned expiry dates? The documentation requirements of the credit may include:
    a. Consular invoice and certificate of origin. (Is an import license required to secure consular papers?)
    b. An inspection certificate or analysis. (Is a specified agency required to issue the certificate, i.e., SGS— Societe Generale de Surveillance?)
    c. Properly consigned or to order "on board" bills of lading, air waybill, parcel post receipt.
    d. A mill certificate.

e. Weights and assays report of findings.

f. A commercial invoice and packing list (Are these properly signed and executed, indicating proper goods description, marks, numbers, or other identifying information?)

Expiry Dates, also referred to as latest presentation date, date for presenting documents are from the ship date and latest shipping date.

1. Are all of the drafts and documents to be presented under the credit dated within the expiration dates and are the drafts and documents being presented within the expiry dates? Such documents must be presented within the number of days specified or within 21 days if the dates are unspecified.

If you are not sure what the credit instrument is telling you, call the advising bank and get an interpretation! Read and reread the terms and conditions of the credit. Make sure the terms and conditions of the credit agree with the purchase order and the terms and conditions of the sales contract. If there are differences between the credit, purchase order, and sales contract, cable the buyer immediately for an amendment to the credit.

Before presenting documents for negotiation, have them checked by a second experienced person and make sure that the documents not only comply with the credit instrument, but also include the required number of copies.

The Payment.   Beneficiaries should note Article 16 (c) of the UCP 400 which states that banks have a reasonable time in which to examine the documents banked under a letter of credit. Assuming there are no discrepancies in the documents of a confirmed letter of credit or a credit negotiated by an advising bank "without recourse," beneficiaries can usually expect the bank to pay the credit instrument within three working bank business days from the date of presentation of the documents under the credit instrument.

The Uniform Commercial Code (UCC) of the State of New York indicates that banks must decide whether to pay or not to pay within 72 hours. Exporters are advised to doublecheck the UCC laws of other states to be used for a majority of their letter of credit business from time to time. Ask your lawyers or banks to confirm what a reasonable time is under state law.

Banking Fees for Letters of Credit. All letter of credit transactions are subject to a number of fees and charges which vary from bank to bank and country to country. When the sales department negotiates letter of credit payment terms, it is important for them to clearly spell out in the sales contract who is responsible for what charges. The easiest method is simply to state the foreign customer is responsible for all bank letter of credit charges in its country and the exporter (beneficiary) for charges in *its* country.

However, on the surface and in reality, it is not always possible to negotiate a letter of credit transaction based on the aforementioned because:

1. The opening of a letter of credit meets with resistance or reluctance on the part of the foreign customer because it feels it is financially creditworthy for the purchase. The exporter's credit department has determined the element of country risk is too high.
2. Letter of credit opening fees and depository requirements are high and restrictive.
3. The depository requirements of the importer's country and/or that of its bank tie up the working capital of the foreign customer.
4. In the case of usance (time) letter of credit transactions, the foreign customer is unwilling or reluctant to absorb the costs for creation of a bankers' acceptance (BA). The exporter may want to discount the BA for cash flow reasons. In addition, exporters won't feel obligated to pay all of the costs associated with the creation of the BA in cases where the import regulations of the foreign customer's country require the exporter to extend long payment terms (i.e., 90 or 180 days).

The following is an example of costs and fees associated with an export letter of credit transaction. For precise cost information, the exporter is advised to check with its banker before the sale of goods is consummated. Chase Manhattan's *World Guide for Exporters* is an excellent source containing country bank charges for the handling of letters of credit.

Procedure	Fee
Confirmation commission	1/20 percent, minimum $50 for each three months or fraction thereof
Advising commission	$30
Amendment commission	$30 per amendment
Negotiation commission	1/10 percent, minimum $50 or if reimbursed on a third bank 1/8 percent, minimum $50
Discrepancy charge	$30 per presentation of discrepant documents
Acceptance or deferred payment commission	1.5 percent per annum, minimum $50
Reimbursement commission	$30
Cancellation of unused letters of credit	$30
Postage and/or cable charges	If applicable

COLLECTION PROCEDURES

A complete business transaction involves five major steps. Someone has to:

1. Make a product or create a service.
2. Sell the product or service.
3. Deliver the product to a customer.
4. Pay for the product or service.
5. Collect for it if unpaid from a customer, according to the payment terms.

In international trade, there is no doubt that 8 out of 10 export sale transactions will be affected by Murphy's Law. Because of all the documentary requirements, laws, regulations, distances, and the number of parties to the export transaction, foreign customers somehow always seem to find a problem or excuse for not paying timely. Some of these are:

- Incorrect or missing documents.
- Pricing errors or problems.
- Description of the goods is incorrect.
- The quantity delivered is incomplete versus the purchase order (shortages).
- The goods are damaged.
- The purchase order number is incorrect or missing on some or all of the documents.
- The draft is incorrect or not endorsed.
- The foreign customer claims its computer is down and they are unable to remit payment until this is corrected or backup.
- The foreign customer claims to have lost the documents.
- Terms of sale disputes (i.e., shipping costs, insurance, and freight charges).
- Foreign customer claims to have returned part or all of the goods.
- The goods cannot be cleared through customs timely.

One of the best methods of ensuring timely payments and minimizing delinquencies is to pay prompt and close attention to all of the five steps mentioned above. Credit people must constantly act as policemen, troubleshooters, and problem solvers. They must and should constantly insist on accurate and precise export documents to ensure efficiency and consistency to increase cash flow by minimizing float.

It is extremely important that credit managers develop, in writing, a Systematic Collection Follow-up Sequence Procedure for all types of export payment term transactions. It ensures prompt collection follow-up on invoices, drafts, and letters of credit as they come due for acceptances or payment. Just as important, it serves as a means for ensuring there aren't any problems with the export documents, the shipment, or cash flow problems with the foreign customer. In order to obtain acceptances and payments as they come due timely, the credit department must receive a copy of the documentary collection and letter of credit collection sent to the banks.

The effort to collect past due obligations should be a coordinated team effort with many of the parties to the export transaction, especially the marketing and sales department. For example, an overseas distributor who submits an order for billing to a foreign customer in its market area, earning a commission, should be responsible for assisting in obtaining an acceptance on a draft for payment. The commission should not be paid until payment is collected from the foreign customer and applied to the customer's account. The same applies to foreign agents. They should not be paid their commission until the actual payment from the customer is applied to the customer's account. Your distribution and freight forwarders should assist in correcting or attempting to solve export documentation problems with foreign customers as expeditiously as possible. Remitting and collecting banks should coordinate their collection follow-up sequences with that of the exporter and follow the exporter's instructions explicitly. And, marketing/sales people should insist on prompt acceptances and payments timely from their foreign customers. Product or pricing disputes should be corrected or settled as quickly as possible. To assist in obtaining acceptances or payment from customers, overseas branches or subsidiaries of the exporter should participate in the collection process.

Some of the typical collection tools used by experienced credit managers to assist their respective department personnel with collections are copies of the letter of instructions for letters of credit and documentary collections submitted to banks by their traffic/distribution department (most are the same) or freight forwarders (explained later). Some credit departments are responsible for preparing and banking the aforementioned themselves. Also the credit department's mailing of monthly statements—which are only sent to foreign customers on open account payment terms—can assist the collection process. Statements mailed to customers on draft or letter of credit payment terms are meaningless because a draft or L/C could represent several invoices. However, they may be requested for audit purposes. The respective salesperson, overseas distributor, or foreign agent, should be kept promptly informed of the status of non-acceptances or past-due foreign customers. They should be sent copies of all correspondence. The telephone is a most useful collection tool, especially with remitting banks. The telephone is also an effective

collection tool with foreign customers, particularly if the credit
person is fluent in the foreign customer's language. Many foreign
customers speak English—some well, others not so well. A
telephone conversation is expensive and can be difficult because of
bad connections or language problems. This is one of the reasons
why it is important to use distributors, foreign agents, branches, or
subsidiaries if applicable. They are experts in their respective
countries. Form collection letters are fine for routine collection
follow-up purposes, but not effective because of the distances
involved, the language barriers, and inefficient mail service in
many countries. Collection letters can serve to document the
collection follow-up efforts of the credit person. Telexes and
cablegrams are probably the credit person's most effective and
efficient collection tools. They do involve an expense, but the
benefits far outweigh the costs.

Whatever the collection technique, it is important to remember the customs and practices of many countries regarding the
collection of past due debt obligations of debtors. Many countries
do not have actual credit people per se. The effort to collect past
due debts in many countries is done by part- or full-time accountants who do not have the experience or time to perform
efficient and effective collections. Many times the principals of the
business perform collection activity when they have time. Principals of foreign businesses are less likely to use firmness on their
past due accounts for fear of losing the account to competition.
Remember that aggressive and increasingly tough collection techniques used in the United States do not always apply to customers
located overseas. They will easily become insulted, won't understand, and will complain to your marketing/sales department.
Worse, the foreign customer may either threaten to or actually go
to competition with its business. Good tact and diplomacy is
always advisable.

Role of the Freight Forwarder

Formerly called a shipping or forwarding agent (sometimes mistak-
enly called foreign freight forwarders), the freight forwarder is
another integral part of the export process. Freight forwarders,
concerned with the transport of goods between international

boundaries, are not foreign companies, but U.S. companies licensed by the U.S. Federal Maritime Commission. They perform a number of services for exporters as the exporter's agent, including:

1. Arranging for the shipment of goods to foreign customers.
2. Booking shipments on appropriate carriers.
3. Preparing shipping documentation (i.e., bills of lading, obtain consularization of documents).
4. Advising and/or training exporters on export documentation preparation and procedures.
5. Arranging for marine insurance on the goods.
6. Coordinating, preparing and banking (forward to banks) export collection documents (letters of credit and documentary collections) in accordance with an exporter's instructions.
7. Arranging for warehousing goods at the port of departure.
8. Providing information on ocean freight rates determining cost and freight (C&F) charges for CIF costs.
9. Advising on the routing of goods, including inland route and carriage to the port of departure and ocean routing to the port of destination.

Freight forwarders earn their income from fees charged to exporters for their services, as those mentioned above, including freight brokerage received from shipping lines for booking cargo. In addition, freight forwarders can act as custom house brokers for importers (not to be confused with foreign customers) by clearing incoming goods through customs and/or other governmental agencies.

As part of the collection process, someone must be responsible for preparing and consolidating all of the documents pertaining to each and every export shipment and banking the draft and documents for documentary collections and letters of credit. Although this decision is normally the responsibility of the exporter's traffic and distribution manager, the credit manager's input is extremely important to not only the collection process, but your company's cash mobilization (cash flow) as well. Once a decision is made to utilize the services of one or more freight forwarders, it is important to prepare a written set of explicit and concise procedures for the forwarder which explains in detail exactly how bank documentary collections and letters of credit are to be prepared and to whom they will be sent (i.e., which banks).

Once freight forwarders are selected, the credit manager should personally visit each forwarder to develop a good rapport and ensure the procedures are thoroughly understood.

EXPORT CASH MOBILIZATION

Export cash mobilization refers to how money moves from the payer (foreign customer) to the payee (exporter) in the least amount of time possible. Cash mobilization starts with a company's domestic and international cash management functions. At small- to medium-size companies, the functions are typically delegated to a finance manager or controller. The larger the company, the more the two functions of domestic and international cash management are separated between managers of domestic and international finance. Domestically, the cash manager's responsibilities include, but are not limited to, the functions of short-term investments, cash receipts, disbursements, banking relationships, and bank reconcilement. The function includes the appointment and maintenance of bank lock boxes. The international finance manager is usually concerned with such international cash management and finance functions as the cross-border cash movements of foreign exchange, dividends, royalties, and disbursements; foreign exchange management; intra-country corporate funds flow; banking relationships, investments; and cash receipts and disbursements.

Typically, domestic and international cash managers at most companies do not have the time, understanding, education, or desire to handle the cash mobilization problems of a credit manager's export related collection activities with foreign customers (third-party sales). When the question is asked, "Who is in control of your export third-party receipts?" the answer is, "Our export receipts from third-party sales are too small to be that concerned about." (That is, as a percent of total sales, it is too small.)

For 40 years, domestic cash and credit managers have reached a point in time when the inherent efficiency of today's system (i.e., increasing funds availability with well-placed lockboxes, accounts receivable systems, prompt and correct invoicing) lends itself to only marginal improvements. On the export side, the opportunity for substantial increases in funds flow is greater because the system is flawed with inefficiencies. Even though larger exporters are increasingly using or changing foreign customer habits from check mail remittances to telegraphic transfers, a great number of checks still arrive in U.S. lockboxes from abroad that are drawn on foreign banks. These checks make a return trip before the funds become available to the exporter.

The roles of both the credit and cash managers must be re-examined to ensure they are working toward mutual goals or objectives with complementing measures of performance. Too often company lines of responsibility between credit and cash management conflict. Each pursue different diverse objectives which can hamper cash mobilization. One good example of their counterproductive activities is the bank selection process. Often, credit managers exercise control over which banks will handle their documentary export collections. Their overriding reasons for selecting one bank over another are better service, low collection fees, overseas correspondent networks, and automated systems. These reasons are not only persuasive, but valid as far as the credit manager is concerned. But, they lack the sensitive issue of the value of cash receipts on hand for immediate access by cash management. It assumes the credit manager hasn't taken care of the issue. By combining forces, the credit and cash managers can jointly select banks to meet the objectives of each.

Yet, experienced credit managers know they must assume the responsibility to maintain effective and efficient control of their export receivable portfolios. Unless the credit manager steps in and assumes responsibility by implementing effective procedures and controls, the problems will become insurmountable. Let's reexamine some of the problems that can occur when not enough attention or the proper procedures are not implemented regarding the management of third-party export receipts. Properly completed export documents done on a timely basis is important. A missing or inaccurate customer purchase order number on a commercial invoice can cause payment delays. Many customers, especially government entities, will not pay unless the PO (purchase order) number is correctly stated on invoices (including other documents used in export trade). This especially holds true for export sales made on open account. Where and how payment is to be remitted must be clearly stated on all appropriate documents, including commercial invoices, letters of instructions to banks on documentary collections and letters of credit, and promissory notes. Improper "remit to" instructions will result in an increase in bank float (i.e., a foreign customer will mail a large check instead of making a wire transfer); lost receipts (without proper instruction on where foreign customers send their payments, cash receipts will be sent almost anywhere; i.e., the exporter's foreign subsidiary, to a salesperson, or a manufacturing plant). A lack of remittance information on what the foreign customer is paying can be a problem. That is, what invoices and drafts, or deductions, if any, has the customer taken for such things as incorrect prices, damaged goods, or incomplete orders. Without invoice numbers and amounts pertaining to the remittance, it will be difficult for your accounts receivable department to apply the remittance and for the credit department to know what is paid. Delinquencies can increase when proper procedures are not followed due to the increase in bank float and the problem of lost receipts. Cash application to customer accounts will be done untimely, and accounts receivable performance measurements will be adversely affected (i.e., days sales outstanding and collection efficiency will decrease). Customer receivable balances outstanding will increase, affecting order and credit limits. New customer orders might be held until the cash receipts paying current or past due invoices and/or drafts is applied to the customer's account.

Yet, because it is so intimately connected with cash management, credit managers should always strive to coordinate the two functions. The reasoning behind the coordination is simple: in domestic sales, payment instructions are straightforward and the float time can be minimized with a standard cash management practice, such as use of a lockbox. But for foreign sales, the credit manager will have much less control unless proper instructions and controls are implemented and adhered to. Many times, the credit manager must act as policeman to make sure instructions are being followed.

A creative credit manager working with a cooperative cash

manager can find solutions to collection receipt delays that affect export cash mobilization. The following are some of techniques and ideas that have helped many experienced credit managers speed up export receipt collections for open account, documentary collection, and letters of credit, thus improving export receivable turnover performance:

1. Use your domestically located bank accounts as a confirming bank for letters of credit. If the confirming bank is also the bank you have an account with, it can credit your account directly and minimize the float.
2. Make sure your order processing department(s) maintain adequate backup documentation. Foreign customers often withhold payment due to discrepant or missing documents. These delays can be minimized by maintaining good files on the export transaction (i.e., copies of commercial invoices, bills of lading, and other documents). Of course, completing accurate documents in the first place is the answer to payment delays.
3. Communicate payment instructions clearly and concisely. To ensure that foreign customers pay via the most cost-effective mechanism, exporters should print conspicuous "remit to" payment instructions, preferably in the importer's language, on the commercial invoice and where appropriate on letters of instruction to banks for documentary collections and letters of credit. If the foreign customer mails you a check drawn on its bank overseas, a delay of four to six weeks will occur before you get good funds. Upon receipt of the check, your bank will mail the check to the overseas bank for collection. You are better off instructing your customer to send you a bank draft drawn on a U.S. bank. Better yet is to have your customer wire the payment by telex or SWIFT.
4. Cultivate good relations in the importer's country. Spend time nurturing relations with local embassies, consulates, central banks, commerce ministries, and trade associations to cut red tape and to ease government approvals for trade transactions and foreign exchange.
5. Use discounts and penalty fees where possible. While the

practice of offering discounts for early payment is common, some exporters have also successfully charged interest on overdue accounts without losing sales.

6. Implement and consistently review a systematic collection follow-up sequence procedure. Institute standard procedures to handle overdue accounts pertaining to open account, documentary collection, and letters of credit. The sequence should consist of a series of phone calls, telexes, letters, and even, when necessary, personal visits. Always include and inform all appropriate salespeople in the sequence. They can prove to be extremely effective collectors—sometimes the best collectors.

7. Use direct collection letters. This will accelerate the flow of documentation which increases funds flow, especially as it pertains to goods shipped on a sight draft basis.

8. Take advantage of courier services offered by banks and independent companies. Have the original documents airmailed or courier documents to the overseas bank designated by the foreign customer on documentary collections. The overall benefits will far outweigh the costs.

9. Make sure your export payment terms are clearly spelled out on commercial invoices, contracts, communications with customers, and letters of instruction to banks. Unless when the payment terms begin is specified, disputes will arise with the foreign customer on the due date of a related export transaction. Banks will also have a problem knowing who is right or wrong, the exporter or foreign customer, when it pertains to documentary collections. Clearly spell out if the payment terms begin from invoice date, on-board ocean bill of lading date, or from receipt of goods. Most exporters use the ocean bill of lading date whenever possible for documentary collections and letter of credit payment term type transactions. Many times invoices are completed too early, sometimes one or two weeks in advance of the actual steamship departure date.

10. Use the following U.S. bank instructions for the collecting and remitting banks:
    a. Cable advise nonpayment and/or non-acceptance.
    b. Cable advise payment or acceptance.

    c. Do not protest (unless absolutely necessary).

    d. All foreign bank charges are for the account of the drawee.

    e. Waive foreign bank charges if refused.

    f. Special instructions:

        (1) Funds over a specified amount should be remitted via SWIFT or wire to your designated U.S. collecting bank. They in turn should be instructed to remit funds via CHIPS or wire to your bank depository account unless they are a depository account.

        (2) When using bank Direct Collection Letters (DCLs), be sure your "remit to" instructions to the U.S. collecting bank are NOT typed on the original (first copy) of the DCL form. This first original is supposed to be sent directly to the foreign collecting bank. In this case, funds will bypass the U.S. collecting bank and it will continue to pursue collection until otherwise notified.

11. Investigate the use of freight forwarders to prepare and present documents with documentary collections and letters of credit for presentation to banks. Experienced and efficient freight forwarders can prove to be extremely valuable.

12. Set up lockboxes/intercept points to reduce mail delays. The importer can mail its check to a post office box operated by the exporter's bank. For example, a pharmaceutical exporter established a lockbox in Hong Kong to cut down on the float generated by having Asian customers mail checks directly to New York.

13. Establish foreign currency accounts to accumulate export proceeds. Many exporters use hold accounts to reduce foreign exchange costs and exposure, and to shorten float time in countries with stable currencies.

14. Take a close look at netting, reinvoicing, and other cross-border cash management vehicles to control intra-company trade. Netting, or the offsetting of creditor and debtor positions within a firm, accelerates export sales by eliminating bank float. Reinvoicing centers, which buy

products from manufacturing subsidiaries and resell them to sale subsidiaries, can be used to centralize intracompany export management as well as managing receivable exposures and liquidity.

15. Consider using a trading company. It can help you to concentrate trade activities and expertise, to carry out consistent pricing and marketing plans, and to improve cash and exposure management. Trading companies are widely used in Asia, especially in Hong Kong, Japan, Singapore, Korea, and Taiwan.

Many experienced credit managers over the years have gone through a myriad of banks to handle their export collections, switching their collections from one bank to the next from time to time, trying to find a bank with the best services to meet their needs. One bank that has introduced excellent and innovative services and systems is The Philadelphia National Bank, Philadelphia, Pennsylvania. The following describes some of its innovative products, namely, their Reimbursement Collection Service (RCS), Collection Concentration System, and International Receivables Reporting. These programs and systems were introduced by the bank to assist exporters with their export collections while increasing the mobilization of their funds. Other U.S banks such as Chase Manhattan, Security Pacific, and Northern Trust have similar products and services, just to mention a few.

The Philadelphia National Bank

Reimbursement Collection Service: Letter of Credit Presentation/Collection and Concentration Systems. The following is an outline of the features and benefits of the Philadelphia National Bank's (PNB) Reimbursement Collection Service (RCS) for the collection of proceeds under letters of credit which are advised and payable at U.S. banks other than PNB. The name *PNB* refers to the operational capabilities of both PNB (Philadelphia) and its New York Edge Act affiliate, the Philadelphia International Bank (PIB).

The concentration of export letters of credit to a particular U.S. bank has always been difficult. Although an exporter may request that a certain bank be designated for negotiation, the routing is ultimately controlled by the issuing bank in the foreign country of the exporter's foreign customer. Because of PNB's extensive correspondent bank network, a company would be successful in having many of its letters of credit directed to PNB, that is, PNB could be designated the negotiating and/or confirming bank because the foreign bank maintains a U.S. dollar deposit account with them. The benefits of directing letters of credit in this fashion will be reviewed later.

When the opening bank does not direct letters of credit through PNB, they offer exporters the use of a Reimbursement Collection Service, which facilitates the monitoring and collection of proceeds under these letters of credit. The service of that bank has been designed to:

- Enhance the cash flow of exporters.
- Provide a means for monitoring outstanding receivable obligations.
- Improve the concentration of funds.

The service is especially beneficial in cases where the letter of credit is presentable and drawn on large money center banks as many of these banks are prone to negotiation and payment delays. However, substantial benefits may also be realized for letters of credit drawn on any U.S. bank.

The operating procedures for utilizing this service are as follows:

1. On shipment, all documents required in the credit are sent to the U.S. bank where the accompanying drafts are to be presented. The freight forwarder (or your traffic/ distribution department) remits a copy of PNB's specially designed four-part form (their pink copy) with the documents which designates that the funds be wired to PNB for a company's account. Alternatively, if the negotiating bank is in New York City, all documents may be sent (or delivered) directly to PNB (or PIB), from which they will be presented to the appropriate bank.

2. A second copy of the form is sent to PNB where all the appropriate information is entered into their automated

processing system, CompuDraft, thereby creating an "expected receive" file in which all information germane to the individual collection item is maintained (including your item reference number[s]).

3. Two days after the documents are presented to the negotiating bank, PNB will commence tracing (collection follow-up by mail, telex, or cable) for payment and/or status by telephone. After the initial call, they will follow up daily.

4. If there are discrepancies in the documents, PNB will notify whoever is designated on the collection by telephone to provide them with the name and telephone number of the appropriate contact person at the reimbursing bank. It will be the exporter's responsibility to resolve the problem (discrepancy) directly with them.

5. On payment, PNB will credit your account and notification will be sent via a printed paper advice. Payment amounts and other transaction details (such as your reference/invoice number and name of customer) can also be transmitted electronically via PNB's CompuLink System.

PNB also has a standard "outstanding and paid" report package available for this service to exporters. It includes a periodic summary listing of all of an exporter's outstanding and paid items over a given period (from the date of the previous report) in whatever format required. PNB charges no additional fee for these reports.

The Benefits. The benefits of this service are summarized below:

• Problems of follow-up are reduced because PNB has accepted that role and assumed that responsibility. Thus, the credit department can spend more time doing a better job of approving credit or handling other types of collection.

• Improves an exporter's cash flow because PNB is generally able to extract the payment from the negotiating bank more quickly, especially when the credit is payable at many of the money center banks.

• Improves cash flow because mailed checks will be eliminated in favor of direct wire transfers to an exporter's account at PNB.

• Improves information and concentration benefits as described earlier.

Experienced credit managers report that the PNB service has saved them between two and eight days cash flow—sometimes more depending on the exporter's leverage with advising banks and the company's existing monitoring procedures. Additionally, the savings make no allowance for the reduction/elimination of the problems exporters face in having to deal with the operating departments of many banks.

PNB does charge a modest fee for RCS. Most experienced credit managers report that the cost savings and increased cash flow more than offset the fee. However, since the fee may be paid for on an analysis basis, typically PNB's larger corporate customers incur no direct charge to utilize the service. The fee is structured in this fashion since typically payment under letters of credit are received from the negotiating bank late in the day after notification and investment deadlines have passed.

Collection Concentration System. It is important that any exporter receive rapid cash availability and accurate information to post and monitor its receivables position. Recognizing these requirements for speed and accuracy, PNB has designed a concentration system under which payment for all of an exporter's international payment transactions—open account, documentary collections, export letters of credit—would flow through one account covering both U.S. dollar and foreign currency remittances. Availability under foreign currency denominated receipts, of course, would depend on completion of a spot trade. U.S. dollar checks drawn on foreign banks would have to be entered for collection.

PNB's system would utilize the bank's automated collection service, information reporting function, and tracing capabilities. The following basically outlines their system.

1. *Export Letters of Credit.* Previously mentioned, PNB has an extensive foreign correspondent bank network which makes it possible for an exporter to direct L/Cs via PNB as the negotiating and/or confirming bank. A good target percentage for directing credit is 50 percent according to PNB. For letters of credit negotiable at PNB, documents are required to be negotiated within

three days by law (in New York banks have a reasonable amount of time). For large dollar negotiations over $100,000, PNB will negotiate in 24 hours, if advance notification of presentment is given. A specific individual in the bank's Letter of Credit Department will be assigned as the exporter's primary contact to handle questions and problems.

Where the opening bank does not direct the letter of credit through PNB, the bank can offer exporters the use of their Reimbursement Collection Service (RCS), which is designed to facilitate the presentation and collection of proceeds under other bank's Export Letters of Credit negotiated at other U.S. banks. The service is designed to improve the control of funds flows and also monitor outstanding receivable obligations.

There are two methods by which this service can be utilized:

Regular RCS

1. On shipment, all documents called for in the letter of credit are sent to PNB's Collection Department along with a completed instruction form (letter of transmittal). PNB will provide your freight forwarders or your traffic/distribution departments with a collection form.
2. PNB enters all appropriate information into the automated processing system which produces an instruction letter requesting payment to PNB via CHIPS/wire from the New York City negotiating bank.
3. The instruction letter, along with the letter of credit documents, is then presented to the New York paying bank by courier.

Direct RSC

1. On shipment, all documents required by the letter of credit are sent to the U.S. bank where the accompanying drafts are to be presented. The freight forwarder remits with the documents the copy of PNB's specially designed three-part form. This form also contains instructions requesting payment to PNB via CHIPS/wire.
2. A second copy of the form is sent to PNB where all appropriate information is entered into the automated processing system.

Once entered into the system (under either of the two methods discussed above), the follow up would be the same. The mechanics of this follow-up service are as follows:

1. Two days after presenting documents, their Collection Department begins tracing by telephone to obtain payment and/or status. After the initial call, they telephone at least once every day.
2. If there are discrepancies in the documents, the exporter will be notified by telephone. You will also be given the name and telephone number of the contact person at the New York paying bank. It will then be the exporter's responsibility to resolve the problem directly.
3. Their standard outstanding and paid report package is available for this service. This includes a summary listing of all your outstanding and paid items over a given period (from the date of the previous report) in whatever format you require. There is no additional charge for these reports.
4. On payment, your account is credited and notification of the payment is mailed and/or delivered via a balance reporting system

Benefits of this service are the same as those previously mentioned under PNB's Reimbursement Collection Service.

Experience has shown that in most cases PNB is able to save between two and eight days cash flow for exporters. This savings makes no allowance for the reduction/elimination of the problems exporters face in having to deal with the operating departments of the large money center banks.

   2. *Documentary Collections.* Documentary processing is available on either a direct or regular collection basis, at the exporter's option. On receipt of the collection item, PNB would create an "expected file" which would be confirmed back to an exporter's credit department via a hard copy acknowledgment similar to that shown in Figure 5–3. This data file would include amount, customer name, and various reference numbers of the exporter (i.e., invoice or customer receivable numbers) for each collection. Their operating system can accommodate two separate alphanumeric data fields for an exporter's information; one field contains 22 digits and the other 19 digits.

FIGURE 5-3
Example of Acknowledgment

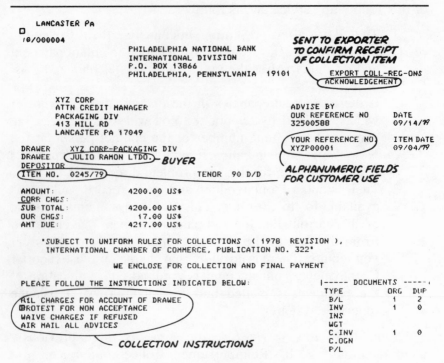

Source: Philadelphia National Bank.

Information regarding individual collections is accumulated and a periodic outstanding item report would be created in a format selected by an exporter (i.e., by customer name, your reference number, or country). A sample of this report is shown in Figure

5–4. A summary paid item report covering specific intervals may also be generated at an exporter's request. Figure 5–5 is an example of this report.

PNB makes available an automated tracing capability for acceptance and payments as part of the service package. To use this feature, credit personnel would specify a tracer interval (i.e., 10 to 15 days) for each collection item. Also, their standard air mail tracer may be overridden with a cable tracer by an exporter's credit personnel. Should an exporter choose not to control the tracing process, PNB's system will automatically trace late non-acceptances or late payment drafts every 21 days by air mail. Recently, PNB introduced a new enhancement whereby the item may be traced by telephone locally from their representative office. This feature is available on a country-specific basis, primarily in countries where the banking system is especially prone to processing delays. PNB has found this tracing method often results in substantial cash flow improvements. As PNB's collection department receives information germane to specific outstanding collections, the information is immediately passed on to each appropriate exporter's collection item in the form of a "status" report (Figure 5–6).

As noted earlier, cash availability and payment information are vital system considerations for an exporter's treasury and credit personnel. In the PNB system, all payments received by 4:00 P.M. EST are electronically posted with transaction details available the same day via their balance reporting system, which can be accessed by an exporter's operating area either by data terminal or telex. Any payments received after 4:00 P.M. EST are credited the same day, although transaction details are not available until the following morning.

3. *Open Account.*   Similar to the documentary (draft) and letter of credit (Corporate RCS) collection services currently made available to exporters under PNB's automated collection system, this product not only provides a means to route foreign open account remittances to one U.S. collecting bank, but it also enables an exporter to receive "full-detail" credit information via electronic transmission.

The procedures for handling individual transactions are similar to those followed for documentary collection items. Once shipment and invoicing are completed by an exporter, a copy of PNB's

FIGURE 5-4 Outstanding Item Report

```
11/10/88                    I N T E R N A T I O N A L   C O L L E C T I O N   S Y S T E M                    PAGE   1

                                          O U T S T A N D I N G   R E P O R T

XYZ CORPORATION                              PHILADELPHIA NATIONAL BANK
ATTN: CREDIT MANAGER
CONSTRUCTION DIV                             REPORTS SELECTED: ALL PRODUCTS        REPORT SEQUENCE: COUNTRY
1013 SUMMERVILLE RD.                                                                               REFERENCE NUMBER
TRENTON, NJ 08034

YOUR REFERENCE       |- - - - - - - - - - - YOUR  INFORMATION - - - - - - - - - |  | - - - - - -  | |- OUR INFORMATION -|

804267               ITEM NO:        804267                          COLLECT: USD        15,387.42    OUR REF:    DC053372
                     ITEM DATE:      06/01/88                            NET: USD        15,387.42    ENTERED:    06/03/88
                     TENOR:          D030ST                                                           LOCATION:   PNB
                     MATURITY DATE:  07/10/88                                                         TRACED:     08/01/88
                     DRAWER/MAKER    ▓▓▓▓▓▓▓▓▓▓▓▓▓▓▓  XYZ CORPORATION                                              08/22/88
                     DRAWEE          STERKO BV                                                                    09/12/88
                     DEPOSITOR                                                                                    10/03/88
                     COUNTRY:        NETHERLANDS                                                                  10/24/88
                     BANK NAME       RABOBANK NETHERLANDS
                     STATUS:         06/15/88 THIS ITEM HAS BEEN ACCEPTED TO MATURE ON 07/10/88.

806122 & 806123      ITEM NO:        806122 & 806123                 COLLECT: USD        28,575.17    OUR REF:    DC053385
                     ITEM DATE:      06/27/88                            NET: USD        28,575.17    ENTERED:    06/30/88
                     TENOR:          D030ST                                                           LOCATION:   PNB
                     MATURITY DATE:                                                                   TRACED:     08/03/88
                     DRAWER/MAKER    ▓▓▓▓▓▓▓▓▓▓▓▓▓▓▓  XYZ CORPORATION                                              08/24/88
                     DRAWEE          STERKO BV                                                                    09/14/88
                     DEPOSITOR                                                                                    10/05/88
                     COUNTRY:        NETHERLANDS                                                                  10/26/88
                     BANK NAME       RABOBANK NETHERLANDS

809010               ITEM NO:        809010                          COLLECT: USD        21,572.84    OUR REF:    DC034305
                     ITEM DATE:      09/16/88                            NET: USD        21,572.84    ENTERED:    09/21/88
                     TENOR:          D060ST                                                           LOCATION:   PNB
                     MATURITY DATE:  11/21/88                                                         TRACED:
                     DRAWER/MAKER    ▓▓▓▓▓▓▓▓▓▓▓▓▓▓▓  XYZ CORPORATION
                     DRAWEE          STERKO BV
                     DEPOSITOR
                     COUNTRY:        NETHERLANDS
                     BANK NAME       RABOBANK NETHERLANDS
                     STATUS:         09/23/88 THIS ITEM HAS BEEN ACCEPTED TO MATURE ON 11/21/88.

809011               ITEM NO:        809011                          COLLECT: USD        24,429.30    OUR REF:    DC034306
                     ITEM DATE:      10/05/88                            NET: USD        24,429.30    ENTERED:    10/14/88
                     TENOR:          D060ST                                                           LOCATION:   PNB
                     MATURITY DATE:  12/09/88                                                         TRACED:
                     DRAWER/MAKER    ▓▓▓▓▓▓▓▓▓▓▓▓▓▓▓  XYZ CORPORATION
                     DRAWEE          STERKO BV
                     DEPOSITOR
                     COUNTRY:        NETHERLANDS
                     BANK NAME       RABOBANK NETHERLANDS
                     STATUS:         10/17/88 THIS ITEM HAS BEEN ACCEPTED TO MATURE ON 12/09/88.
```

I N T E R N A T I O N A L   C O L L E C T I O N   S Y S T E M

O U T S T A N D I N G   R E P O R T

PHILADELPHIA NATIONAL BANK

XYZ CORPORATION
ATTN: CREDIT MANAGER
CONSTRUCTION DIV.
1013 SUMMERVILLE RD.
TRENTON, NJ 08034

REPORTS SELECTED: ALL PRODUCTS

REPORT SEQUENCE: COUNTRY
REFERENCE NUMBER

YOUR REFERENCE | - - - - - - - - - YOUR INFORMATION - - - - - - - | |- OUR INFORMATION -|

810103
ITEM NO: 810103
ITEM DATE: 10/24/88
TENOR: D000ST
MATURITY DATE:
DRAWER/MAKER   BOSO B.V.   XYZ CORPORATION
DRAWEE
DEPOSITOR
COUNTRY: NETHERLANDS
BANK NAME   AMSTERDAM ROTTERDAM BANK N.A.

COLLECT: USD   17,216.90
NET: USD   17,216.90

OUR REF: DC034307
ENTERED: 11/07/88
LOCATION: PNB
TRACED:

810241
ITEM NO: 810241
ITEM DATE: 11/01/88
TENOR: D000ST
MATURITY DATE:
DRAWER/MAKER   BOSO B.V.   XYZ CORPORATION
DRAWEE
DEPOSITOR
COUNTRY: NETHERLANDS
BANK NAME   AMSTERDAM-ROTTERDAM BANK N.A.

COLLECT: USD   18,632.50
NET: USD   18,632.50

OUR REF: DC034309
ENTERED: 11/09/88
LOCATION: PNB
TRACED:

FIGURE 5-4 (concluded)

INTERNATIONAL COLLECTION SYSTEM

OUTSTANDING REPORT

PHILADELPHIA NATIONAL BANK

REPORTS SELECTED: ALL PRODUCTS

REPORT SEQUENCE: COUNTRY
REFERENCE NUMBER

XYZ CORPORATION
ATTN: CREDIT MANAGER
CONSTRUCTION DIV.
1013 SUMMERVILLE RD.
TRENTON, NJ 08034

YOUR REFERENCE |- - - - - - - - - - - - YOUR INFORMATION   - - - - - - - - - - - | |- - - - - - - - - - - - - | |- OUR INFORMATION -|
|- - - TOTAL OUTSTANDING COLLECTIONS - - - | |- - - - NON TIME ITEMS - - - - -| |- - - - - AGING OF TIME ITEMS - - - - - -|

TOTAL NUMBER: 6   OUTSTANDING: $ 64,424.57   OUTSTANDING: $ 61,389.56

TOTAL NET OUTSTANDING: $ 125,814.13   OVER 30 DAYS: $ 65,535.43   1 - 30 DAYS PAST DUE: $ .00

                                                                          31 - 90 DAYS PAST DUE: $ .00

                                                                          OVER 90 DAYS PAST DUE: $ 15,387.42

DOLLAR TOTALS ARE U.S. DOLLARS ONLY

Source: Philadelphia National Bank.

FIGURE 5–5
Summary Paid Item Report

```
                                        PHILADELPHIA NATIONAL BANK
                                             P A I D   R E P O R T

XYZ CORPORATION
ATTN: CREDIT MANAGER
CONSTRUCTION DIV.                REPORTS SELECTED: ALL PRODUCTS          REPORT SEQUENCE: REFERENCE NUMBER
1013 SUMMERVILLE RD.                                                                     ITEM NUMBER
TRENTON, NJ  08034                                                                       COUNTRY
                                                                                         DRAWEE
                                                                                         DRAWER/MAKER
                                                                                         MATURITY DATE

YOUR REFERENCE   |- - - - - - - - - - -  YOUR  INFORMATION  - - - - - - - |   |-OUR INFORMATION-|

3758             ITEM NO:        000913            EX. CONV:                    OUR REF:  67577786
                 ITEM DATE:      09/29/88          AMT OUTS:       USD  400.00  ENTERED:  10/26/88
                 TENOR:                            CORR CHGS:      USD    9.85  LOCATION: PNB
                 MATURITY DATE:                    OTHER CHGS:            .00
                 DRAWER/MAKER    XYZ CORPORATION   AMT REC'D:      USD  390.15
                 DRAWEE          CHASE BANK AG, GERMANY  OUR CHGS:        30.00      ** PAID **
                 DEPOSITOR       1LT STEPHANIE EBNER     NET PROCEEDS:USD 360.15
                 COUNTRY:        GERMANY
                 CREDIT DATE:    11/10/88
                 ACCOUNT:        09010707
```

FIGURE 5–5 (concluded)

```
11/10/88         INTERNATIONAL COLLECTION SYSTEM                    PAGE   2
                          PAID REPORT
                    PHILADELPHIA NATIONAL BANK
                    REPORTS SELECTED: ALL PRODUCTS      REPORT SEQUENCE: REFERENCE NUMBER
                                                                         ITEM NUMBER
XYZ CORPORATION                                                          COUNTRY
ATTN: CREDIT MANAGER                                                     DRAWEE
CONSTRUCTION DIV.                                                        DRAWER/MAKER
1013 SUMMERVILLE RD.                                                     MATURITY DATE
TRENTON, NJ  08034

YOUR REFERENCE      |- - - - - - - - YOUR INFORMATION - - - - - - - - - |  |-OUR INFORMATION-|

  # OF PAYMENTS:     1                 TOTAL CORR CHGS:        $        9.85

  # CLOSED:          0                 TOTAL OTHER DEDUCTIONS: $         .00

                                       TOTAL AMT RECEIVED:     $      390.15

                                       TOTAL OUR CHGS:         $       30.00

                                       TOTAL NET PROCEEDS:     $      360.15


              DOLLAR   TOTALS   ARE   U. S.   DOLLARS   ONLY
```

Source: Philadelphia National Bank.

410

FIGURE 5–6
Status Report

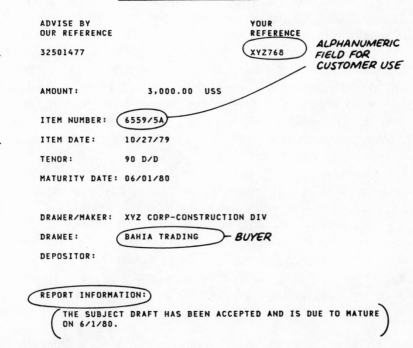

```
                    PHILADELPHIA NATIONAL BANK
                    INTERNATIONAL DIVISION
                    P.O. BOX 13866
                    PHILADELPHIA, PENNSYLVANIA  19101


XYZ CORP
ATTN CREDIT MANAGER                             DATE
CONSTRUCTION DIV
1013 SUMMERVILLE RD                             03/14/80
TRENTON NJ 08034



                    S T A T U S   R E P O R T


      ADVISE BY                        YOUR
      OUR REFERENCE                    REFERENCE

─     32501477                         XYZ768      ALPHANUMERIC
                                                   FIELD FOR
                                                   CUSTOMER USE

      AMOUNT:          3,000.00  US$

      ITEM NUMBER:   6559/5A

─     ITEM DATE:      10/27/79

      TENOR:          90 D/D

      MATURITY DATE: 06/01/80



      DRAWER/MAKER:  XYZ CORP-CONSTRUCTION DIV

      DRAWEE:        BAHIA TRADING      — BUYER

      DEPOSITOR:


  REPORT INFORMATION:

      THE SUBJECT DRAFT HAS BEEN ACCEPTED AND IS DUE TO MATURE
      ON 6/1/80.
```

Source: Philadelphia National Bank.

collection form (accommodates open account items) is sent to
PNB. The original of the form, invoice(s), and other documentation required by the foreign customer are sent directly to the
foreign customer as is currently done by an exporter for open
account transactions. Once PNB receives its copy, its collection

staff will input the appropriate information of the exporter's open account collection into its collection system thereby creating an electronic "expected receive" file.

The due date applied will be taken from the form. Tracers, similar to those utilized to follow up past due documentary collection items, will not be generated as that responsibility rests with the exporter. PNB's experience has shown that most exporters, by the very nature of their export sales methods of open account, prefer not to have the bank involved in dunning for past due payments. However, if an item becomes past due, PNB can, if desired, automatically advise an exporter that the payment due has not yet been received. Their standard past due notification is on a 21-day cycle, although when PNB's copy of the collection letter is originally submitted for computer entry, an exporter can designate a notification cycle of its preference (i.e., 5, 10, 15 days). The primary benefit of this feature is that using this status information, an exporter can take appropriate action to initiate collection follow-up action. A secondary benefit may be realized in that this information would enable exporters to track individual customer payment histories over time to determine who regularly pays in accordance with payment terms.

On payment, PNB posts the credit to the exporter's account and the details (i.e., reference numbers, customer names) are available to exporters the same day if received prior to 4:00 P.M. EST via PNB's electronic information reporting system, Compu-Link. A summary full detail electronic report is available the next day. Also a paper payment advice is mailed. Information would appear on a CompuLink report, which may, if required, be accessed from multiple locations.

SUMMARY

The PNB systems described above offers the following benefits to exporters:

- Convenience of using one bank to collect all international remittances.
- Consolidated payment and receivables information delivered

electronically to exporter location(s) in many cases on a same day basis.

- Improved cash flow as a result of prompt crediting of all payments received.
- Improved customer service by virtue of the fact that specific personnel would be assigned to handle an exporter's account.
- Prompt application of remittances to an exporter's receivables thus reducing foreign receivables outstanding with its foreign customers, placing the exporter's credit department in a better position to release pending customer orders.

International Receivables Reporting: Data Transmission for Open Account, Documentary Collection, and Letter of Credit Receivables. Rapid collection of an exporter's receivables is a major need that must be supplemented by timely delivery of detailed information. The faster an exporter receives complete data on its individual transactions, the more accurately it can reflect its actual Days Sales Outstanding, by applying the funds on the same day the bank gives it credit. The fastest way to receive the detail is via computer-to-computer or tape-to-tape transmission from your bank to your corporate receiving site. Data transmission saves time and money as it speeds the update to your accounts receivable system, reduces errors, and improves an exporter's credit controls. Many exporters use PNB's Data Transmission Service for reporting domestic receivables (i.e., Lockbox, DTC). Now, using PNB's Data Transmission Service, an exporter can receive information from PNB on international receivables. Figure 5–7 illustrates how this transmission of data is accomplished.

International receivables are not routinely reported via data transmission. Payments for international receivables come from many sources (SWIFT, CHIPS, Fedwire, Telex). The information is not usually in a standardized format and must be reformatted for entry into an exporter's accounts receivable system, creating opportunities for errors and delaying accurate posting of receivable information to foreign customer accounts. PNB has an answer to this problem.

PNB has automated the delivery of an exporter's international receivables information in conjunction with their international

FIGURE 5–7 International Receivables Reporting Flow Chart: Data Transmission for Open Account, Documentary Collection and Letter of Credit Receivables

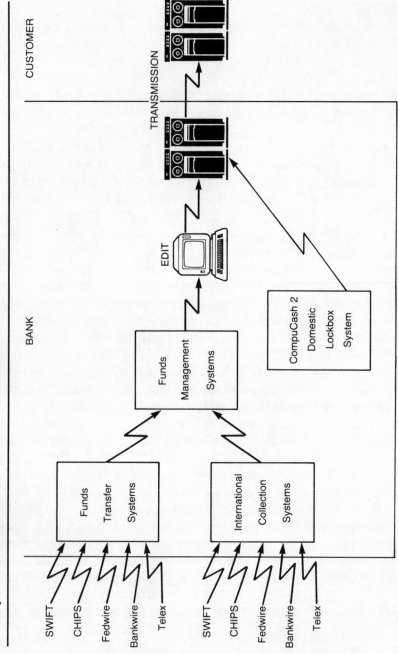

Source: Neil Leary, PNB International Collection Concentration System, (Philadelphia, Pa.: The Philadelphia National Bank, 1987).

collections and funds transfer systems. Some of the advantages of this system include:

- Eliminates the need for manual entry of international data by their customers.
- Consolidates international receipts with an exporter's other receivables (i.e., Lockbox).
- Standardizes international receivable information to conform with an exporter's individual automated system's requirements.
- Speeds the receipt of information for accounting, credit, and cash management purposes.
- Give the credit manager information on the same day as the treasurer.
- Maximizes an exporter's investment in its automated accounts receivable system.

HOW THE SYSTEM WORKS AT PNB

1. An exporter's foreign customer sends a payment to its account at PNB using any payment vehicle (i.e., SWIFT, CHIPS, Fedwire, Telex) under open account, documentary collection, or letter of credit.
2. PNB electronically passes the credit transactions which have entered an exporter's account from its funds management and automated collection systems into a communications editing and formatting process.
3. The transactions are put into a standard format you have specified, and are then sent electronically to their communications scheduler to be forwarded daily at the agreed on transmission time.
4. This service can operate on a stand-alone basis or in conjunction with their normal data transmission for their lockbox customers.

BAD DEBT WRITE-OFFS

The Reserve for Doubtful Accounts

From an accounting point of view, when a foreign account receivable balance outstanding is considered doubtful for collection, usually after all collection techniques are exhausted, the amount in question is written off against a monetary reserve account. This reserve is usually debited against the income of the respective product line or sales department responsible for the product or products sold to the foreign customer and credited to accounts receivable. When gross receivables are net of reserve for doubtful accounts this is called *net accounts receivable*.

There are several acceptable methods used singularly or in combination for determining an adequate reserve for doubtful accounts, including:

1. Historical experience regarding the reserve provision and actual write-offs.
2. A fixed amount with added provision to cover estimated write-offs.
3. Amounts allowed under local tax regulations (i.e., a foreign subsidiary's experience may indicate an adequate reserve provision of 1 percent of receivables, while parent company fiscal and tax regulations may permit a reserve up to 5 percent).

When it has been decided at planning time what the total pending year's accrual will be, the credit department will determine the most advantageous method whereby the expense is to be debited and the reserve account credited:

1. Calendarized on the basis of 1/12 per month.
2. Accrual on the basis of sales patterns, i.e., if 30 percent of sales volume is in the first half of the year and 70 percent on the second half, the accrual may be booked on the same 30 percent–70 percent basis.

Doubtful Account Determination

When an account is deemed uncollectable by the credit manager, the account and receivable balance outstanding might be accounted for in a receivable aging category or "bucket" called suspense or suspense account. The suspense account contains those accounts and balances that are placed with collection agencies, attorneys, bankrupt, or collection is delayed beyond one year from due date awaiting allocation of foreign exchange (the exporter's billing currency). The aforementioned assumes the foreign customer paid the maturing debt obligation in local currency.

After all possible efforts have been taken to collect an outstanding account and it is deemed uncollectible, the account is then considered a bad debt and is written off on securing the proper approvals (internal).

Accounts should be written off promptly following determination as uncollectible when:

1. The foreign customer becomes bankrupt.
2. The foreign customer is referred to an outside party for collection (i.e., collection agency, solicitor, or attorney, etc.).
3. The account has not been collected within a reasonable period of time and future collection is doubtful. The time element may vary, depending on the business area involved. But, as a general rule, accounts 6 to 12 months overdue for payment should be thoroughly reviewed for possible write-off. In the event of funds tied up due to country risk conditions (i.e., shortages of your billing currency in the importer's country), a business decision might be necessary, depending on the amount, to determine if the account balance needs to be written off. In the case of certain debts owing from Iran, Venezuela, and Nigeria, exporters having been waiting several years for these countries to allocate foreign exchange to pay their debt obligations with importers in these countries.

   In some countries, local regulations prohibit bad debt write-offs and consequent tax deductions until the account has been adjudicated bankrupt or where a specific opinion of counsel has been issued. In those cases, management should review the matter to determine whether or not write-off is still appropriate with a deferred tax benefit, reclassify the receivable, or carry the amount in accounts receivable while retaining the offsetting reserve credit in the reserve for bad debts (discussed later).
4. Small deductions, disputes, and shortages. These items do not usually qualify as being considered bad debt amounts.

Therefore, any subsequent write-off should not be made against the bad debt reserve. It is up to the appropriate sales department to make the necessary adjustments to the foreign customer's account.

All items approved for write-off will be debited to the reserve for doubtful accounts and credited to the individual foreign customer's trade or note receivable.

Costs, fees, and other expenses related to bad debt write-offs are to be charged to the reserve account. For example, an attorney handling an account for collection requests payment of $50 for court costs and an advance of $250 against his or her fee. The amount of $300 will be debited to the reserve account (assuming it has been determined that significant recovery is possible and that the expenses should be incurred).

Recoveries of bad debts written off will be credited back to the reserve account. The amount credited should be the amount of the gross write-off less any nonrecoverable costs, fees, or other collection expenses.

Most credit managers or companies require write-offs over specified amounts to be fully documented and approved for write-off by senior management (i.e., the senior credit manager, sales manager, treasury executive, operations vice-president). The documented write-off explains the circumstances leading up to the request to write-off the amount and foreign account in question. It is important for senior management to approve the write-off of certain amounts (i.e., amounts exceeding $10,000, $20,000 or $25,000) to determine any weaknesses within the organization or problem market countries or areas.

Each exporter should make adjustments at year-end to the reserve for doubtful accounts, as required. It is conceivable the reserve might be too excessive in relation to its potential write-offs. If a reduction is made to the reserve for doubtful accounts, the credit department could be making a profit contribution to the operating areas of its company.

Over the past 10 or 15 years, there have been a vast number of bankruptcies or near bankruptcies around the globe to warrant senior management's attention to the importance of maintaining or securing the best professional people possible to manage its investment in accounts receivable. Many of these and others might have overseas operations you could have sold to. The following are just a few examples:

AM International, U.S.	McLouth Steel, U.S.
Grupo Alfa, Mexico	Wickes Companies, U.S.
GHK, U.S.	AEG-Telefunken, W. Germany
Johns Manville, U.S.	Rumasa, Spain
Penn Square Bank, U.S.	Continental Airlines, U.S.
Drysdale, U.S.	Dome Petroleum, Canada
Banco Ambrosiano, Italy	Massey Ferguson, Canada
Freddie Laker, U.K.	Sanko Steamship, Japan
Braniff Airlines, U.S.	Explosives Rio Tinto, Spain

Despite these bankruptcies or near bankruptcies and many, many others, the aforementioned does not take into consideration the many foreign exchange or "hidden trade barrier" situations an exporter's credit department encounters. Even the most professional credit managers cannot predict or control these situations. The end result is a frustrating effort to collect maturing debt obligations that become nothing but a delinquency problem for credit managers.

APPENDIX 5-A   UNIFORM RULES FOR COLLECTIONS

FOREWORD

These new ICC "Uniform Rules for Collections" enter into force as from 1st January 1979.

This development will interest bankers throughout the world since the new Rules replace the existing "Uniform Rules for the collection of Commercial Paper " (Publication No. 254), which have been widely used since their introduction in 1967.

The new title was chosen since, in practice, documents collected are as likely to have as much a financial as a commercial character.

In making this revision, the ICC's Banking Commission has taken into account both the evolution in practice since 1967 and specific problems that have arisen that could not be solved by the existing rules. An example is the course of action presenting banks should follow when the collection order requires the payment of interest that the drawee refuses to pay. The revised Rules give a clear ruling on this problem.

This revision reflects the policy of the ICC to stay abreast of changes in international commerce.

Carl-Henrick Winqwist
Secretary General of the ICC

GENERAL PROVISIONS AND DEFINITIONS

A. These provisions and definitions and the following articles apply to all collections as defined in (**B**) below and are binding upon all parties thereto unless otherwise expressly agreed or unless contrary to the provisions of a national, state or local law and/or regulation which cannot be departed from.

B. For the purpose of such provisions, definitions and articles:
   1. i "Collection" means the handling by banks, on instructions received, of documents as defined in **ii** below, in order to
      a) Obtain acceptance and/or, as the case may be, payment, or
      b) Deliver commercial documents against acceptance and/or, as the case may be, against payment, or
      c) Deliver documents on other terms and conditions.
      ii "Documents" means financial documents and/or commercial documents:
      a) "Financial documents" means bills of exchange, promissory notes, cheques, payment receipts, or other similar instruments used for obtaining the payment of money;
      b) "Commercial documents" means invoices, shipping documents, documents to title, or other similar documents, or any other documents whatsoever, not being financial documents.
      iii "Clean collection" means collection of financial documents not accompanied by commercial documents.
      iv "Documentary collection" means collection of
      a) Financial documents accompanied by commercial documents;

b) Commercial documents not accompanied by financial documents.

2. The "parties thereto" are:
   i The "principal" who is the customer entrusting the operation of collection to his bank;
   ii The "remitting bank" which is the bank to which the principal has entrusted the operation of collection;
   iii The "collecting bank" which is any bank, other than the remitting bank, involved in processing the collection order;
   iv The "presenting bank" which is the collecting bank making presentation to the drawee.
3. The "drawee" is the one to whom presentation is to be made according to the collection order.

C. All documents sent for collection must be accompanied by a collection order giving complete and precise instructions. Banks are only permitted to act upon the instructions given in such collection order, and in accordance with these Rules.

If any bank cannot, for any reason, comply with the instructions given in the collection order received by it, it must immediately advise the party from whom it received the collection order.

LIABILITIES AND RESPONSIBILITIES

Article 1—Banks will act in good faith and exercise reasonable care.

Article 2—Banks must verify that the documents received appear to be as listed in the collection order and must immediately advise the party from whom the collection order was received of any documents missing.

Banks have no further obligation to examine the documents.

Article 3—For the purpose of giving effect to the instructions of the principal, the remitting bank will utilize as the collecting bank:
   i The collecting bank nominated by the principal, or, in the absence of such nomination,
   ii Any bank, of its own or another bank's choice, in the country of payment or acceptance, as the case may be.

The documents and the collection order may be sent to the collecting bank directly or through another bank as intermediary.

Banks utilizing the services of other banks for the purpose of giving effect to the instructions of the principal do so for the account of and at the risk of the latter.

The principal shall be bound by and liable to indemnify the banks against all obligations and responsibilities imposed by foreign laws or usages.

Article 4—Banks concerned with a collection assume no liability or responsibility for the consequences arising out of delay and/or loss in transit of any messages, letters or documents, or for delay, mutilation or other errors arising in the transmission of cables, telegrams, telex, or communication by electronic systems, or for errors in translation or interpretation of technical terms.

Article 5—Banks concerned with a collection assume no liability or responsibility for consequences arising out of the interruption of their business by Acts of God, riots, civil commotions, insurrections, wars, or any other causes beyond their control or by strikes or lockouts.

Article 6—Goods should not be dispatched direct to the address of a bank or consigned to a bank without prior agreement on the part of that bank.

In the event of goods being dispatched direct to the address of a bank or consigned to a bank for delivery to a drawee against payment or acceptance or upon other terms without prior agreement on the part of that bank, the bank has no obligation to take delivery of the goods, which remain at the risk and responsibility of the party dispatching the goods.

PRESENTATION

Article 7—Documents are to be presented to the drawee in the form in which they are received, except that remitting and collecting banks are authorized to affix any necessary stamps, at the expense of the principal unless otherwise instructed, and to make any necessary endorsements or place any rubber stamps or other identifying marks or symbols customary to or required for the collection operation.

Article 8—Collection orders should bear the complete address of the drawee or of the domicile at which presentation is to be made. If the address is incomplete or incorrect, the collecting bank may, without obligation and responsibility on its part, endeavour to ascertain the proper address.

Article 9—In the case of documents payable at sight the presenting bank must make presentation for payment without delay.

In the case of documents payable at a tenor other than sight the presenting bank must, where acceptance is called for, make presentation for acceptance without delay, and where payment is called for, make presentation for payment not later than the appropriate maturity date.

Article 10—In respect of a documentary collection including a bill of exchange payable at a future date, the collection order should state whether the commercial documents are to be released to the drawee against acceptance (D/A) or against payment (D/P).

In the absence of such statement, the commercial documents will be released only against payment.

PAYMENT

Article 11—In the case of documents payable in the currency of the country of payment (local currency), the presenting bank must, unless otherwise instructed in the collection order, only release the documents to the drawee against payment in currency which is immediately available for disposal in the manner specified in the collection order.

Article 12—In the case of documents payable in a currency other than that of the country of payment (foreign currency), the presenting bank must, unless otherwise instructed in the collection order, only release the documents to the drawee against payment in the relative foreign currency which can immediately be remitted in accordance with the instructions given in the collection order.

Article 13—In respect of clean collections partial payments may be accepted if and to the extent to which and on the conditions on which partial payments are authorized by the law in force in the place of payment. The documents will only be released to the drawee when full payment thereof has been received.

In respect of documentary collections partial payments will only be accepted if specifically authorized in the collection order. However, unless otherwise instructed, the presenting bank will only release the documents to the drawee after full payment has been received.

In all cases partial payments only will be accepted subject to compliance with the provisions of either Article 11 or Article 12 as appropriate.

Partial payment, if accepted, will be dealt with in accordance with the provisions of Article 14.

Article 14—Amounts collected (less charges and/or disbursements and/or expenses where applicable) must be made available without delay to the bank from which the collection order was received in accordance with the instructions contained in the collection order.

ACCEPTANCE

Article 15—The presenting bank is responsible for seeing that the form of the acceptance of a bill of exchange appears to be complete and correct, but is not responsible for the genuineness of any signature or for the authority of any signatory to sign the acceptance.

PROMISSORY NOTES, RECEIPTS, AND OTHER SIMILAR INSTRUMENTS

Article 16—The presenting bank is not responsible for the genuineness of any signature or for the authority of any signatory to sign a promissory note, receipt, or other similar instrument.

PROTEST

Article 17—The collection order should give specific instructions regarding protest (or other legal process in lieu thereof), in the event of non-acceptance or non-payment.

In the absence of such specific instructions the banks concerned with the collection have no obligation to have the documents protested (or subjected to other legal process in lieu thereof) for non-payment or non-acceptance.

Any charges and/or expenses incurred by banks in connection with such protest or other legal process will be for the account of the principal.

CASE-OF-NEED (PRINCIPAL'S REPRESENTATIVE) AND PROTECTION OF GOODS

Article 18—If the principal nominates a representative to act as case-of-need in the event of non-acceptance and/or non-payment the collection order should clearly and fully indicate the powers of such case-of-need.

In the absence of such indication banks will not accept any instructions from the case-of-need.

Article 19—Banks have no obligation to take any action in respect of the goods to which a documentary collection relates.

Nevertheless in the case that banks take action for the protection of the goods, whether instructed or not, they assume no liability or responsibility with regard to the fate and/or condition of the goods and/or for any acts and/or omissions on the part of any third parties entrusted with the custody and/or protection of the goods. However, the collecting bank must immediately advise the bank from which the collection order was received of any such action taken.

Any charges and/or expenses incurred by banks in connection with any action for the protection of the goods will be for the account of the principal.

ADVICE OF FATE, ETC.

Article 20—Collecting banks are to advise fate in accordance with the following rules.

   i *Form of advice.* All advices or information from the collecting bank to the bank from which the collection order was received, must bear appropriate detail including, in all cases, the latter bank's reference number of the collection order.

   ii *Method of advice.* In the absence of specific instructions, the collecting bank must send all advices to the bank from which the collection order was received by quickest mail but, if the collecting bank considers the matter to be urgent, quicker methods such as cable, telegram, telex, or communication by electronic systems, etc. may be used at the expense of the principal.

   iii *a) Advice of payment.* The collecting bank must send without delay advice of payment to the bank from which the collection order was received, detailing the amount or amounts collected, charges and/or disbursements and/or expenses deducted, where appropriate, and method of disposal of the funds.

   b) Advice of acceptance. The collecting bank must send without delay advice of acceptance to the bank from which the collection order was received.

   c) Advice of non-payment or non-acceptance. The collecting bank must send without delay advice of non-payment or advice of non-acceptance to the bank from which the collection order was received.

The presenting bank should endeavour to ascertain the reasons for such non-payment or non-acceptance and advise accordingly the bank from which the collection order was received.

On receipt of such advice the remitting bank must, within a reasonable time, give appropriate instructions as to the further handling of the documents. If such instructions are not received by the presenting bank within 90 days from its advice of non-payment or non-acceptance, the documents may be returned to the bank from which the collection order was received.

INTEREST, CHARGES, AND EXPENSES

Article 21—If the collection order includes an instruction to collect interest which is not embodied in the accompanying financial document(s), if any, and the drawee refuses to pay such interest, the presenting bank may deliver the document(s) against payment or acceptance as the case may be without collecting such interest, unless the collection order expressly states that such interest may not be waived. Where such interest is to be collected the collection order must bear an indication of the rate of interest and the period covered. When payment of interest has been refused the presenting bank must inform the bank from which the collection was received accordingly.

If the documents include a financial document containing an unconditional and definitive interest clause the interest amount is deemed to form part of the amount of the documents to be collected. Accordingly, the interest amount is payable in addition to the principal amount shown in the financial document and may not be waived unless the collection order so authorizes.

Article 22—If the collection order includes an instruction that collection charges and/or expenses are to be for the account of the drawee and the drawee refuses to pay them, the presenting bank may deliver the document(s) against payment or acceptance as the case may be without collecting charges and/or expenses unless the collection order expressly states that such charges and/or expenses may not be waived. When payment of collection charges and/or expenses has been refused the presenting bank must inform the bank from which the collection order was received accordingly. Whenever collection charges and/or expenses are so waived they will be for the account of the principal, and may be deducted from the proceeds.

Should a collection order specifically prohibit the waiving of collection charges and/or expenses then neither the remitting nor collecting nor presenting bank shall be responsible for any costs or delays resulting from this prohibition.

Article 23—In all cases where in the express terms of a collection order, or under these Rules, disbursements and/or expenses and/or collection charges are to be borne by the principal, the collecting bank(s) shall be entitled promptly to recover outlays in respect of disbursements and expenses and charges from the bank from which the collection order was received and the remitting bank shall have the right promptly to recover from the principal any amount so paid out by it, together with its own disbursements, expenses and charges, regardless of the fate of the collection.

APPENDIX 5–B: UNIFORM CUSTOMS AND PRACTICE FOR DOCUMENTARY CREDITS (1983) REVISION

FOREWORD TO THE 1983 REVISION

This foreword is written exactly 50 years since the ICC adopted the first edition of the Uniform Customs and Practice for Documentary Credits (UCP) at its 7th Congress in Vienna in 1933.

Innumerable aspects of international trading operations have changed radically over the intervening years. Yet the UCP remain a vital element in world trade. An ever increasing number of banking and other executives still need to know their provisions thoroughly and use them every day.

How can the UCP have become and remained so indispensable over such a long period—a period which moreover seems certain to extend well into the 21st century?

I see two reasons. First, the realities of international trade continue to require documentary credits and therefore an internationally accepted set of standards governing their use.

Just as 50 years ago, sellers still hesitate to release their goods before receiving payment, while buyers prefer to have control over the goods before parting with their money. But matching payment with physical delivery is rarely possible, so a compromise is normally agreed—payment against "constructive delivery", the handing over of documents transferring title to, or control over, the goods.

Creditworthiness then becomes important, and bankers are required to intervene, giving their conditional undertaking to the seller to pay against presentation of documents and compliance with conditions stipulated by the buyer. Hence the continuing need for documentary credits.

Secondly, the UCP are fortunately a living text which has been regularly updated by the ICC Banking Commission since its initial introduction.

Prior to 1962 the UCP were primarily designed to safeguard the banker when the buyer gave incomplete or imprecise instructions. In the 1962 revision—the first to achieve global acceptance—stress was laid on the buyer's duty to specify what he wanted, setting out "international banking customs and other rules that facilitate banking functions".

The 1974 revision gave effect to changes in documentation and procedures caused by the progress of trade facilitation and the revolution in maritime transport—containerization and the resultant development of combined transport. The forward looking approach we adopted reflected banking practices, but also dictated "the most prudent course of behaviour irrespective at times of existing usage, course of dealing or custom".

For the 1983 revision we have again had "to look to the future—because that is where we shall have to live". So, while the interests and problems of the buyer and the seller remain paramount, notes has also been taken of:

- The continuing revolution in **transport technology,** and the geographical extension of containerization and combined transport;
- The increasing influence of **trade facilitation** activities on development of new documents and new methods of producing documents;
- The **communications revolution,** replacing paper as a means of transmitting information (data) relating to a trading transaction by methods of automated or electronic data processing (ADP/EDP);
- Development of new types of documentary credits, such as the **deferred payment credit** and the **stand-by credit.**

In addition, for the UCP to give the maximum possible guidance and assistance to all parties, three basic principles have been born in mind:

- That the buyer is responsible for stipulating, clearly and precisely, the documents required and the conditions to be complied with;
- The increasing interest and influence in international trade of nations which are less developed and, therefore, less experienced in this area;
- Misunderstandings and interpretive problems caused by the 1974 text, necessitating amplification or simplification in the 1983 version.

Finally, thought has been given to the current major problem of fraud, while recognizing that fraud originates when a commercial party first contracts with a rogue, and that the documentary credit merely pays for the commercial transaction and cannot "police" it.

The revision has been carried out by a Working Party—with representatives of commerce and industry, insurers, forwarders and carriers as well as bankers—reporting to the Banking Commission.

ICC National Committees, countries without National Committees reached primarily through the United Nations Commission on International Trade Law (whose support and participation have been of extreme importance and value), other UN bodies concerned with the facilitation of international trade procedures, and banking circles in countries represented in ICC's East/West Committee, have all played an active role in the work, both through the Working Party and the Commission and in over four thousand individual items of written comment.

Sincere thanks are given to them all; but their real reward will be the knowledge of their major contribution to the facilitation of international trade through this 1983 revision of the UCP.

Bernard S. Wheble
Chairman,
ICC Commission on Banking Technique and Practice
June 1983

A. GENERAL PROVISIONS AND DEFINITIONS

Article 1—These articles apply to all documentary credits, including, to the extent to which they may be applicable, standby letters of credit, and are binding on all parties thereto unless otherwise expressly agreed. They shall be incorporated into each documentary credit by wording in the credit indicating that such credit is issued subject to Uniform Customs and Practice for Documentary Credits, 1983 revision, ICC Publication No. 400.

Article 2—For the purposes of these articles, the expressions "documentary credit(s)" and "standby letter(s) of credit" used herein (hereinafter referred to as "credit(s)"), mean any arrangement, however named or described, whereby a bank (the issuing bank), acting at the request and on the instructions of a customer (the applicant for the credit),

i Is to make a payment to or to the order of a third party (the beneficiary), or is to pay or accept bills of exchange (drafts) drawn by the beneficiary,
or
ii Authorizes another bank to effect such payment, or to pay, accept or negotiate such bills of exchange (drafts), against stipulated documents, provided that the terms and conditions of the credit are complied with.

Article 3—Credits, by their nature, are separate transactions from the sales or other contract(s) on which they may be based and banks are in no way concerned with or bound by such contract(s), even if any reference whatsoever to such contract(s) is included in the credit.

Article 4—In credit operations all parties concerned deal in documents, and not in goods, services and/or other performances to which the documents may relate.

Article 5—Instructions for the issuance of credits, the credits themselves, instructions for any amendments thereto and the amendments themselves must be complete and precise.

In order to guard against confusion and misunderstanding, banks should discourage any attempt to include excessive detail in the credit or in any amendment thereto.

Article 6—A beneficiary can in no case avail himself of the contractual relationships existing between the banks or between the applicant for the credit and the issuing bank.

B. FORM AND NOTIFICATION OF CREDITS

Article 7—

a. Credits may be either
   i Revocable, or
   ii Irrevocable.
b. All credits, therefore, should clearly indicate whether they are revocable or irrevocable
c. In the absence of such indication the credit shall be deemed to be revocable.

Article 8—A credit may be advised to a beneficiary through another bank (the advising bank) without engagement on the part of the advising bank, but that bank shall take reasonable care to check the apparent authenticity of the credit which it advises.

Article 9—

a. A revocable credit may be amended or cancelled by the issuing bank at any moment and without prior notice to the beneficiary.
b. However, the issuing bank is bound to:
 i Reimburse a branch or bank with which a revocable credit has been made available for sight payment, acceptance or negotiation, for any payment, acceptance or negotiation made by such branch or bank prior to receipt by it of notice of amendment or cancellation, against documents which appear on their face to be in accordance with the terms and conditions of the credit.
 ii Reimburse a branch or bank with which a revocable credit has been made available for deferred payment, if such branch or bank has, prior to receipt by it of notice of amendment or cancellation, taken up documents which appear on their face to be in accordance with the terms and conditions of the credit.

Article 10—

a. An irrevocable credit constitutes a definite undertaking of the issuing bank, provided that the stipulated documents are presented and that the terms and conditions of the credit are complied with:
 i If the credit provides for sight payment—to pay, or that payment will be made;
 ii If the credit provides for deferred payment—to pay, or that payment will be made, on the date(s) determinable in accordance with the stipulations of the credit;
 iii If the credit provides for acceptance—to accept drafts drawn by the beneficiary if the credit stipulates that they are to be drawn on the issuing bank, or to be responsible for their acceptance and payment at maturity if the credit stipulates that they are to be drawn on the applicant for the credit or any other drawee stipulated in the credit;
 iv If the credit provides for negotiation—to pay without recourse to drawers and/or bona fide holders, draft(s) drawn by the beneficiary, at sight or at a tenor, on the applicant for the credit or on any other drawee stipulated in the credit other than the issuing bank itself, or to provide for negotiation by another bank and to pay, as above, if such negotiation is not effected.
b. When an issuing bank authorizes or requests another bank to confirm its irrevocable credit and the latter has added its confirmation, such confirmation constitutes a definite undertaking of such bank (the confirming bank), in addition to that of the issuing bank, provided that

the stipulated documents are presented and that the terms and conditions of the credit are complied with:

i If the credit provides for sight payment—to pay, or that payment will be made;

ii If the credit provides for deferred payment—to pay, or that payment will be made, on the date(s) determinable in accordance with the stipulations of the credit;

iii If the credit provides for acceptance—to accept drafts drawn by the beneficiary if the credit stipulates that they are to be drawn on the confirming bank, or to be responsible for their acceptance and payment at maturity if the credit stipulates that they are to be drawn on the applicant for the credit or any other drawee stipulated in the credit;

iv If the credit provides for negotiation—to negotiate without recourse to drawers and/or bona fide holders, draft(s) drawn by the beneficiary, at sight or at a tenor, on the issuing bank or on the applicant for the credit or on any other drawee stipulated in the credit other than the confirming bank itself.

c. If a bank is authorized or requested by the issuing bank to add its confirmation to a credit but is not prepared to do so, it must so inform the issuing bank without delay. Unless the issuing bank specifies otherwise in its confirmation, authorization or request, the advising bank will advise the credit to the beneficiary without adding its confirmation.

d. Such undertakings can neither be amended nor cancelled without the agreement of the issuing bank, the confirming bank (if any), and the beneficiary. Partial acceptance of amendments contained in one and the same advice of amendment is not effective without the agreement of all the above named parties.

Article 11—

a. All credits must clearly indicate whether they are available by sight payment, by deferred payment, by acceptance or by negotiation.

b. All credits must nominate the bank (nominated bank) which is authorized to pay (paying bank), or to accept drafts (accepting bank), or to negotiate (negotiating bank), unless the credit allows negotiation by any bank (negotiating bank).

c. Unless the nominated bank is the issuing bank or the confirming bank, its nomination by the issuing bank does not constitute any undertaking by the nominated bank to pay, to accept, or to negotiate.

d. By nominating a bank other than itself, or by allowing for negotiation by any bank, or by authorizing or requesting a bank to add its

confirmation, the issuing bank authorizes such bank to pay, accept or negotiate, as the case may be, against documents which appear on their face to be in accordance with the terms and conditions of the credit, and undertakes to reimburse such bank in accordance with the provisions of these articles.

Article 12—

a. When an issuing bank instructs a bank (advising bank) by any teletransmission to advise a credit or an amendment to a credit, and intends the mail confirmation to be the operative credit instrument, or the operative amendment, the teletransmission must state "full details to follow" (or words of similar effect), or that the mail confirmation will be the operative credit instrument or the operative amendment. The issuing bank must forward the operative credit instrument or the operative amendment to such advising bank without delay.

b. The teletransmission will be deemed to be the operative credit instrument or the operative amendment, and no mail confirmation should be sent, unless the teletransmission states "full details to follow" (or words of similar effect), or states that the mail confirmation is to be the operative credit instrument or the operative amendment.

c. A teletransmission intended by the issuing bank to be the operative credit instrument should clearly indicate that the credit is issued subject to Uniform Customs and Practice for Documentary Credits, 1983 revision, ICC Publication No. 400.

d. If a bank uses the services of another bank or banks (the advising bank) to have the credit advised to the beneficiary, it must also use the services of the same bank(s) for advising any amendments.

e. Banks shall be responsible for any consequences arising from their failure to follow the procedures set out in the preceding paragraphs.

Article 13—When a bank is instructed to issue, confirm, or advise a credit similar in terms to one previously issued, confirmed or advised (similar credit) and the previous credit has been the subject of amendment(s), it shall be understood that the similar credit will not include any such amendment(s) unless the instructions specify clearly the amendment(s) which is/are to apply to the similar credit. Banks should discourage instructions to issue, confirm, or advise a credit in this manner.

Article 14—If incomplete or unclear instructions are received to issue, confirm, advise, or amend a credit, the bank requested to act on such instructions may give preliminary notification to the beneficiary for information only and without responsibility. The credit will be issued, confirmed, advised or amended only when the necessary information has been received and if the bank is then prepared to act on the instructions. Banks should provide the necessary information without delay.

C. LIABILITIES AND RESPONSIBILITIES

Article 15—Banks must examine all documents with reasonable care to ascertain that they appear on their face to be in accordance with the terms and conditions of the credit. Documents which appear on their face to be inconsistent with one another will be considered as not appearing on their face to be in accordance with the terms and conditions of the credit.

Article 16—

a. If a bank so authorized effects payment, or incurs a deferred payment undertaking, or accepts, or negotiates against documents which appear on their face to be in accordance with the terms and conditions of a credit, the party giving such authority shall be bound to reimburse the bank which has effected payment, or incurred a deferred payment undertaking, or has accepted, or negotiated, and to take up the documents.

b. If, upon receipt of the documents, the issuing bank considers that they appear on their face not to be in accordance with the terms and conditions of the credit, it must determine, on the basis of the documents alone, whether to take up such documents, or to refuse them and claim that they appear on their face not to be in accordance with the terms and conditions of the credit.

c. The issuing bank shall have a reasonable time in which to examine the documents and to determine as above whether to take up or to refuse the documents.

d. If the issuing bank decides to refuse the documents, it must give notice to that effect, without delay by telecommunication or, if that is not possible, by other expeditious means, to the bank from which it received the documents (the remitting bank), or to the beneficiary, if it received the documents directly from him. Such notice must state the discrepancies in respect of which the issuing bank refuses the documents and must also state whether it is holding the documents at the disposal of, or is returning them to, the presentor (remitting bank or the beneficiary, as the case may be). The issuing bank shall then be entitled to claim from the remitting bank refund of any reimbursement which may have been made to that bank.

e. If the issuing bank fails to act in accordance with the provisions of paragraphs (c) and (d) of this article and/or fails to hold the documents at the disposal of, or to return them to, the presentor, the issuing bank shall be precluded from claiming that the documents are not in accordance with the terms and conditions of the credit.

f. If the remitting bank draws the attention of the issuing bank to any discrepancies in the documents or advises the issuing bank that it has paid, incurred a deferred payment undertaking, accepted or negotiated under reserve or against an indemnity in respect to such discrepancies, the issuing bank shall not be thereby relieved from any of its obligations under any provision of this article. Such reserve or indemnity concerns only the relations between the remitting bank and the party towards whom the reserve was made, or from whom, or on whose behalf, the indemnity was obtained.

Article 17—Banks assume no liability or responsibility for the form, sufficiency, accuracy, genuineness, falsification or legal effect of any documents, or for the general and/or particular conditions stipulated in the documents or superimposed thereon; nor do they assume any liability or responsibility for the description, quantity, weight, quality, condition, packing, delivery, value or existence of the goods represented by any documents, or for the good faith or acts and/or omissions, solvency, performance or standing of the cosignor, the carriers, or the insurers of the goods, or any other person whomsoever.

Article 18—Banks assume no liability or responsibility for the consequences arising out of delay and/or loss in transit of any messages, letters or documents, or for delay, mutilation or other errors arising in the transmission of any telecommunication. Banks assume no liability or responsibility for errors in translation or interpretation of technical terms, and reserve the right to transmit credit terms without translating them.

Article 19—Banks assume no liability or responsibility for consequences arising out of the interruption of their business by Acts of God, riots, civil commotions, insurrections, wars or any other causes beyond their control, or by any strikes or lockouts. Unless specifically authorized, banks will not, upon resumption of their business, incur a deferred payment undertaking, or effect payment, acceptance or negotiation under credits which expired during such interruption of their business.

Article 20—

a. Banks utilizing the services of another bank or other banks for the purpose of giving effect to the instructions of the applicant for the credit do so for the account and at the risk of such applicant.

b. Banks assume no liability or responsibility should the instructions they transmit not be carried out, even if they have themselves taken the initiative in the choice of such other bank(s).
c. The applicant for the credit shall be bound by and liable to indemnify the banks against all obligations and responsibilities imposed by foreign laws and usages.

Article 21—

a. If an issuing bank intends that the reimbursement to which a paying, accepting or negotiating bank is entitled shall be obtained by such bank claiming on another branch or office of the issuing bank or on a third bank (all hereinafter referred to as the reimbursing bank) it shall provide such reimbursing bank in good time with the proper instructions or authorization to honour such reimbursement claims and without making it a condition that the bank entitled to claim reimbursement must certify compliance with the terms and conditions of the credit to the reimbursing bank.
b. An issuing bank will not be relieved from any of its obligations to provide reimbursement itself if and when reimbursement is not effected by the reimbursing bank.
c. The issuing bank will be responsible to the paying, accepting or negotiating bank for any loss of interest if reimbursement is not provided on first demand made to the reimbursing bank, or as otherwise specified in the credit, or mutually agreed, as the case may be.

D. DOCUMENTS

Article 22—

a. All instructions for the issuance of credits and the credits themselves and, where applicable, all instructions for amendments thereto and the amendments themselves, must state precisely the document(s) against which payment, acceptance or negotiation is to be made.
b. Terms such as "first class", "well known", "qualified", "independent", "official", and the like shall not be used to describe the issuers of any documents to be presented under a credit. If such terms are incorporated in the credit terms, banks will accept the relative documents as presented, provided that they appear on their face to be in accordance with the other terms and conditions of the credit.
c. Unless otherwise stipulated in the credit, banks will accept as originals documents produced or appearing to have been produced:

  i By reprographic systems;

  ii By, or as the result of, automated or computerized systems;

  iii As carbon copies, if marked as originals, always provided that, where necessary, such documents appear to have been authenticated.

Article 23—When documents other than transport documents, insurance documents and commercial invoices are called for, the credit should stipulate by whom such documents are to be issued and their wording or data content. If the credit does not so stipulate, banks will accept such documents as presented, provided that their data content makes it possible to relate the goods and/or services referred to therein to those referred to in the commercial invoice(s) presented, or to those referred to in the credit if the credit does not stipulate presentation of a commercial invoice.

Article 24—Unless otherwise stipulated in the credit, banks will accept a document bearing a date of issuance prior to that of the credit, subject to such document being presented within the time limits set out in the credit and these articles.

D.1—Transport Documents (Documents Indicating Loading on Board or Dispatch or Taking in Charge)

Article 25—Unless a credit calling for a transport document stipulates as such document a marine bill of lading (ocean bill of lading or a bill of lading covering carriage by sea), or a post receipt or certificate of posting:

a. Banks will, unless otherwise stipulated in the credit, accept a transport document which:

  i Appears on its face to have been issued by a named carrier, or his agent, and

  ii Indicates dispatch or taking in charge of the goods, or loading on board, as the case may be, and

  iii Consists of the full set of originals issued to the consignor if issued in more than one original, and

  iv Meets all other stipulations of the credit.

b. Subject to the above, and unless otherwise stipulated in the credit, banks will not reject a transport document which:

  i Bears a title such as "Combined transport bill of lading", "Combined transport document", "Combined transport bill of lading or port-to-port bill of lading", or a title or a combination of titles of similar intent and effect, and/or ii Indicates some or all of the conditions of carriage by reference to a source or document other than the transport document itself (short form/blank back transport document), and/or

iii Indicates a place of taking in charge different from the port of loading and/or a place of final destination different from the port of discharge, and/or

iv Relates to cargoes such as those in containers or on pallets, and the like, and/or

v Contains the indication "intended", or similar qualification, in relation to the vessel or other means of transport, and/or the port of loading and/or the port of discharge.

c. Unless otherwise stipulated in the credit in the case of carriage by sea or by more than one mode of transport but including carriage by sea, banks will reject a transport document which:

   i Indicates that it is subject to a charter party, and/or

   ii Indicates that the carrying vessel is propelled by sail only.

d. Unless otherwise stipulated in the credit, banks will reject a transport document issued by a freight forwarder unless it is the FIATA Combined Transport Bill of Lading approved by the International Chamber of Commerce or otherwise indicates that it is issued by a freight forwarder acting as a carrier or agent of a named carrier.

Article 26—If a credit calling for a transport document stipulates as such document a marine bill of lading:

a. Banks will, unless otherwise stipulated in the credit, accept a document which:

   i Appears on its face to have been issued by a named carrier, or his agent, and

   ii Indicates that the goods have been loaded on board or shipped on a named vessel, and

   iii Consists of the full set of originals issued to the consignor if issued in more than one original, and

   iv Meets all other stipulations of the credit.

b. Subject to the above, and unless otherwise stipulated in the credit, banks will not reject a document which:

   i Bears a title such as "Combined transport bill of lading", "Combined transport document", "Combined transport bill of lading or port-to-port bill of lading", or a title or a combination of titles of similar intent and effect, and/or

   ii Indicates some or all of the conditions of carriage by reference to a source or document other than the transport document itself (short form/blank back transport document), and/or

   iii Indicates a place of taking in charge different from the port of loading and/or a place of final destination different from the port of discharge, and/or

iv Relates to cargoes such as those in containers or on pallets, and the like.

c. Unless otherwise stipulated in the credit, banks will reject a document which:

i Indicates that it is subject to a charter party, and/or

ii Indicates that the carrying vessel is propelled by sail only, and/or

iii Contains the indication "intended", or similar qualification in relation to

- The vessel and/or the port of loading—unless such document bears an on board notation in accordance with Article 27(b) and also indicates the actual port of loading, and/or
- The port of discharge—unless the place of final destination indicated on the document is other than the port of discharge, and/or

iv Is issued by a freight forwarder, unless it indicates that it is issued by such freight forwarder acting as a carrier, or as the agent of a named carrier.

Article 27—

a. Unless a credit specifically calls for an on board transport document, or unless inconsistent with other stipulation(s) in the credit, or with Article 26, banks will accept a transport document which indicates that the goods have been taken in charge or received for shipment.

b. Loading on board or shipment on a vessel may be evidenced either by a transport document bearing wording indicating loading on board a named vessel or shipment on a named vessel, or, in the case of a transport document stating "received for shipment", by means of a notation of loading on board on the transport document signed or initialed and dated by the carrier or his agent, and the date of this notation shall be regarded as the date of loading on board the named vessel or shipment on the named vessel.

Article 28—

a. In the case of carriage by sea or by more than one mode of transport but including carriage by sea, banks will refuse a transport document stating that the goods are or will be loaded on deck, unless specifically authorized in the credit.

b. Banks will not refuse a transport document which contains a provision that the goods may be carried on deck, provided it does not specifically state that they are or will be loaded on deck.

Article 29—

a. For the purpose of this article transhipment means a transfer and reloading during the course of carriage from the port of loading or place of dispatch or taking in charge to the port of discharge or place of destination either from one conveyance or vessel to another conveyance or vessel within the same mode of transport or from one mode of transport to another mode of transport.

b. Unless transhipment is prohibited by the terms of the credit, banks will accept transport documents which indicate that the goods will be transhipped, provided the entire carriage is covered by one and the same transport document.

c. Even if transhipment is prohibited by the terms of the credit, banks will accept transport documents which:

 i Incorporate printed clauses stating that the carrier has the right to tranship, or

 ii State or indicate that transhipment will or may take place, when the credit stipulates a combined transport document, or indicates carriage from a place of taking in charge to a place of final destination by different modes of transport including a carriage by sea, provided that the entire carriage is covered by one and the same transport document, or

 iii State or indicate that the goods are in a container(s), trailer(s), "LASH" barge(s), and the like and will be carried from the place of taking in charge to the place of final destination in the same container(s), trailer(s), "LASH" barge(s), and the like under one and the same transport document.

 iv State or indicate the place of receipt and/or final destination as "CFS." (container freight station) or "CY" (container yard) at, or associated with, the port of loading and/or the port of destination.

Article 30—If the credit stipulates dispatch of goods by post and calls for a post receipt or certificate of posting, banks will accept such post receipt or certificate of posting if it appears to have been stamped or otherwise authenticated and dated in the place from which the credit stipulates the goods are to be dispatched.

Article 31—

a. Unless otherwise stipulated in the credit, or inconsistent with any of the documents presented under the credit, banks will accept transport documents stating that freight or transportation charges (hereinafter referred to as "freight") have still to be paid.

b. If a credit stipulates that the transport document has to indicate that freight has been paid or prepaid, banks will accept a transport document on which words clearly indicating payment or prepayment of freight appear by stamp or otherwise, or on which payment of freight is indicated by other means.

c. The words "freight prepayable" or "freight to be prepaid" or words of similar effect, if appearing on transport documents, will not be accepted as constituting evidence of the payment of freight.

d. Banks will accept transport documents bearing reference by stamp or otherwise to costs additional to the freight charges, such as costs of, or disbursements incurred in connection with, loading, unloading or similar operations, unless the conditions of the credit specifically prohibit such reference.

Article 32—Unless otherwise stipulated in the credit, banks will accept transport documents which bear a clause on the face thereof such as "shipper's load and count" or "said by shipper to contain" or words of similar effect.

Article 33—Unless otherwise stipulated in the credit, banks will accept transport documents indicating as the consignor of the goods a party other than the beneficiary of the credit.

Article 34—

a. A clean transport document is one which bears no superimposed clause or notation which expressly declares a defective condition of the goods and/or the packaging.

b. Banks will refuse transport documents bearing such clauses or notations unless the credit expressly stipulates the clauses or notations which may be accepted.

c. Banks will regard a requirement in a credit for a transport document to bear the clause "clean on board" as complied with if such transport document meets the requirements of this article and of article 27(b).

d. Shipments made by modes of transport other than those referred to in paragraphs (b) and (c) of this article will not be regarded as partial shipments, provided the transport documents are issued by one and the same carrier or his agent and indicate the same date of issuance, the same place of dispatch or taking in charge of the goods, and the same destination.

D.2—Insurance Documents

Article 35—

a. Insurance documents must be as stipulated in the credit, and must be issued and/or signed by insurance companies or underwriters, or their agents.

b. Cover notes issued by brokers will not be accepted, unless specifically authorised by the credit.

Article 36—Unless otherwise stipulated in the credit, or unless it appears from the insurance document(s) that the cover is effective at the latest from the date of loading on board or dispatch or taking in charge of the goods, banks will refuse insurance documents presented which bear a date later than the date of loading on board or dispatch or taking in charge of the goods, indicated by the transport document(s).

Article 37—

a. Unless otherwise stipulated in the credit, the insurance document must be expressed in the same currency as the credit.
b. Unless otherwise stipulated in the credit, the minimum amount for which the insurance document must indicate the insurance cover to have been effected is the CIF (cost, insurance and freight . . . "named port of destination") or CIP (freight/carriage and insurance paid to "named point of destination") value of the goods, as the case may be, plus 10 percent. However, if banks cannot determine the CIF or CIP value, as the case may be, from the documents on their face, they will accept as such minimum amount the amount for which payment, acceptance or negotiation is required under the credit, or the amount of the commercial invoice, whichever is the greater.

Article 38—

a. Credits should stipulate the type of insurance required and, if any, the additional risks which are to be covered. Inprecise terms such as "usual risks" or "customary risks" should not be used; if they are used, banks will accept insurance documents as presented, without responsibility for any risks not being covered.
b. Failing specific stipulations in the credit, banks will accept insurance documents as presented, without responsibility for any risks not being covered.

Article 39—Where a credit stipulates "insurance against all risks", banks will accept an insurance document which contains any "all risks" notation or clause, whether or not bearing the heading "all risks", even if indicating that certain risks are excluded, without responsibility for any risk(s) not being covered.

Article 40—Banks will accept an insurance document which indicates that the cover is subject to a franchise or an excess (deductible), unless it is specifically stipulated in the credit that the insurance must be issued irrespective of percentage:

D.3—Commercial Invoice

Article 41—

a. Unless otherwise stipulated in the credit, commercial invoices must be made out in the name of the applicant for the credit.
b. Unless otherwise stipulated in the credit, banks may refuse commercial invoices issued for amounts in excess of the amount permitted by the credit. Nevertheless, if a bank authorized to pay, incur a deferred payment undertaking, accept, or negotiate under a credit accepts such invoices, its decision will be binding upon all parties, provided such bank has not paid, incurred a deferred payment undertaking, accepted or effected negotiation for an amount in excess of that permitted by the credit.
c. The description of the goods in the commercial invoice must correspond with the description in the credit. In all other documents, the goods may be described in general terms not inconsistent with the description of the goods in the credit.

D.4—Other Documents

Article 42—If a credit calls for an attestation or certification of weight in the case of transport other than by sea, banks will accept a weight stamp or declaration of weight which appears to have been superimposed on the transport document by the carrier or his agent unless the credit specifically stipulates that the attestation or certification of weight must be by means of a separate document.

E. MISCELLANEOUS PROVISIONS

Quantity and Amount
Article 43—

a. The words "about", "circa" or similar expressions used in connection with the amount of the credit or the quantity or the unit price stated in the credit are to be construed as allowing a difference not to exceed 10 percent more or 10 percent less than the amount or the quantity or the unit price to which they refer.
b. Unless a credit stipulates that the quantity of goods specified must not be exceeded or reduced, a tolerance of 5 percent more or 5 percent less will be permissible, even if partial shipments are not permitted, always provided that the amount of the drawings does not exceed the amount

of the credit. This tolerance does not apply when the credit stipulates the quantity in terms of a stated number of packing units or individual items.

Partial Drawings and/or Shipments
Article 44—

a. Partial drawing and/or shipments are allowed, unless the credit stipulates otherwise.
b. Shipments by sea, or by more than one mode of transport but including carriage by sea, made on the same vessel and for the same voyage, will not be regarded as partial shipments, even if the transport documents indicating loading on board bear different dates of issuance and/or indicate different ports of loading on board.
c. Shipments made by post will not be regarded as partial shipments if the post receipts or certificates of posting appear to have been stamped or otherwise authenticated in the place from which the credit stipulates the goods are to be dispatched, and on the same date.

Drawings and/or Shipments by Instalments

Article 45—If drawings and/or shipments by instalments within given periods are stipulated in the credit and any instalment is not drawn and/or shipped within the period allowed for that instalment, the credit ceases to be available for that and any subsequent instalments, unless otherwise stipulated in the credit.

Expiry Date Presentation
Article 46—

a. All credits must stipulate an expiry date for presentation of documents for payment, acceptance or negotiation.
b. Except as provided in Article 48 (a), documents must be presented on or before such expiry date.
c. If an issuing bank states that the credit is to be available "for one month", "for six months" or the like, but does not specify the date from which the time is to run, the date of issuance of the credit by the issuing bank will be deemed to be the first day from which such time is to run. Banks should discourage indication of the expiry date of the credit in this manner.

Article 47—

a. In addition to stipulating an expiry date for presentation of documents, every credit which calls for a transport document(s) should also stipulate a specified period of time after the date of issuance of the transport document(s) during which presentation of documents for payment, acceptance or negotiation must be made. If no such period of time is stipulated, banks will refuse documents presented to them later than 21 days after the date of issuance of the transport document(s). In every case, however, documents must be presented not later than the expiry date of the credit.

b. For the purpose of these articles, the date of issuance of a transport document(s) will be deemed to be:

i In the case of a transport document evidencing dispatch, or taking in charge, or receipt of goods for shipment by a mode of transport other than by air—the date of issuance indicated on the transport document or the date of the reception stamp thereon whichever is the later.

ii In the case of a transport document evidencing carriage by air—the date of issuance indicated on the transport document or, if the credit stipulates that the transport document shall indicate an actual flight date, the actual flight date as indicated on the transport document.

iii In the case of a transport document evidencing loading on board a named vessel—the date of issuance of the transport document or, in the case of an on board notation in accordance with article 27(b), the date of such notation.

iv In cases to which Article 44(b) applies, the date determined as above of the latest transport document issued.

Article 48—

a. If the expiry date of the credit and/or the last day of the period of time after the date of issuance of the transport document(s) for presentation of documents stipulated by the credit or applicable by virtue of Article 47 falls on a day on which the bank to which presentation has to be made is closed for reasons other than those referred to in Article 19, the stipulated expiry date and/or the last day of the period of time after the date of issuance of the transport document(s) for presentation of documents, as the case may be, shall be extended to the first following business day on which such bank is open.

b. The latest date for loading on board, or dispatch, or taking in charge shall not be extended by reason of the extension of the expiry date and/or the period of time after the date of issuance of the transport document(s) for presentation of document(s) in accordance with this article. If no such latest date for shipment is stipulated in the credit or amendments thereto, banks will reject transport documents indicating a date of issuance later than the expiry date stipulated in the credit or amendments thereto.

c. The bank to which presentation is made of such first following business day must add to the documents its certificate that the documents were presented within the time limits extended in accordance with Article 48(a) of the Uniform Customs and Practice for Documentary Credits, 1983 revision, ICC Publication No. 400.

Article 49—Banks are under no obligation to accept presentation of documents outside their banking hours.

Loading on Board, Dispatch, and Taking in Charge (Shipment)
Article 50—

a.—Unless otherwise stipulated in the credit, the expression "shipment" used in stipulating an earliest and/or a latest shipment date will be understood to include the expressions "loading on board", "dispatch" and "taking in charge".

b. The date of issuance of the transport document determined in accordance with Article 47(b) will be taken to be the date of shipment.

c. Expressions such as "prompt", "immediately", "as soon as possible", and the like should not be used. If they are used, banks will interpret them as a stipulation that shipment is to be made within 30 days from the date of issuance of the credit by the issuing bank.

d. If the expression "on or about" and similar expressions are used, banks will interpret them as a stipulation that shipment is to be made during the period from five days before to five days after the specified date, both end days included.

Date Terms
Article 51—The words "to", "until", "till", "from", and words of similar import applying to any date term in the credit will be understood to include the date mentioned. The word "after" will be understood to exclude the date mentioned.

Article 52—The terms "first half", "second half", or a month shall be construed respectively as from the 1st to the 15th, and the 16th to the last day of each month, inclusive.

Article 53—The terms "beginning", "middle", or "end" of a month shall be construed respectively as from the 1st to the 10th, the 11th to the 20th, and the 21st to the last day of each month, inclusive.

F. TRANSFER

Article 54—

a. A transferable credit is a credit under which the beneficiary has the right to request the bank called upon to effect payment or acceptance or any bank entitled to effect negotiation to make the credit available in whole or in part to one or more other parties (second beneficiaries).

b. A credit can be transferred only if it is expressly designated as "transferable" by the issuing bank. Terms such as "divisible", "fractionnable", "assignable", and "transmissible" add nothing to the meaning of the term "transferable" and shall not be used.

c. The bank requested to effect the transfer (transferring bank), whether it has confirmed the credit or not, shall be under no obligation to effect such transfer except to the extent and in the manner expressly consented to by such bank.

d. Bank charges in respect of transfers are payable by the first beneficiary unless otherwise specified. The transferring bank shall be under no obligation to effect the transfer until such charges are paid.

e. A transferable credit can be transferred once only. Fractions of a transferable credit (not exceeding in the aggregate the amount of the credit) can be transferred separately, provided partial shipments are not prohibited, and the aggregate of such transfers will be considered as constituting only one transfer of the credit. The credit can be transferred only on the terms and conditions specified in the original credit, with the exception of the amount of the credit, of any unit prices stated therein, of the period of validity, of the last date for presentation of documents in accordance with Article 47 and the period for shipment, any or all of which may be reduced or curtailed, or the percentage for which insurance cover must be effected, which may be increased in such a way as to provide the amount of cover stipulated in the original credit, or these articles. Additionally the name of the first beneficiary can be substituted for that of the applicant for the credit, but if the name of the applicant for the credit is specifically required by the original credit to appear in any document other than the invoice, such requirement must be fulfilled.

f. The first beneficiary has the right to substitute his own invoices (and drafts if the credit stipulates that drafts are to be drawn on the applicant for the credit) in exchange for those of the second beneficiary, for amounts not in excess of the original amount stipulated in the credit and for the original unit prices if stipulated in the credit, and upon such substitution of invoices (and drafts) the first beneficiary can draw under the credit for the difference, if any, between his invoices and the second beneficiary's invoices. When a credit has been transferred and the first beneficiary is to supply his own invoices (and drafts) in exchange for the second beneficiary's invoices (and drafts) but fails to do so on first demand, the paying, accepting or negotiating bank has the right to deliver to the issuing bank the documents received under the credit, including the second beneficiary's invoices (and drafts) without further responsibility to the first beneficiary.

g. Unless otherwise stipulated in the credit, the first beneficiary of a transferable credit may request that the credit be transferred to a second beneficiary in the same country, or in another country. Further, unless otherwise stipulated in the credit, the first beneficiary shall have the right to request that payment or negotiation be effected to the second beneficiary at the place to which the credit has been transferred, up to and including the expiry date of the original credit, and without prejudice to the first beneficiary's right subsequently to substitute his own invoices and drafts (if any) for those of the second beneficiary and to claim any difference due to him.

Assignment of Proceeds

Article 55—The fact that a credit is not stated to be transferable shall not affect the beneficiary's right to assign any proceeds to which he may be, or may become, entitled under such credit, in accordance with the provisions of the applicable law.

The Uniform Customs and Practice for Documentary Credits were prepared by the ICC Commission on Banking Technique and Practice.

This Commission brings together bankers from throughout the world with the object of:

- Defining, simplifying and harmonizing the practices and terminology used in international banking.
- Expressing the views of bankers before relevant international organizations, in particular the United Nations Commission on International Trade Law (UNCITRAL).
- Serving as a forum for bankers to discuss common problems.

Each ICC National Committee may appoint members of the Banking Commission, and of the twenty other ICC Commissions covering most subject areas of interest to international business.

Seminars and conferences on practical aspects of the application of the UCP are also held every year in numerous countries: details on application from National Committees.

APPENDIX 5-C: BOYCOTTS

The following is an interpretation of only certain boycotts, the primary one concerning U.S. exporters being the Arab boycott of Israel, and U.S. laws and regulations concerning the aforementioned. For exact interpretations and guidance, U.S. exporters are encouraged to seek legal advice and to contact the offices of commerce and treasury mentioned below.

U.S. companies have to contend with two basic elements if they are going to do business in the Middle East.

1. The first is the boycott of Arab countries against Israel, whereby the Arab countries refuse to deal directly with Israel or to accept Israeli goods from any source. This is enforced by Arab countries through the use of the certificate of origin, which can be used in either negative or positive forms. The negative form shows that the goods or merchandise is not of Israeli origin, the positive states where the goods came from and the origin of all components.
2. The second element, the so-called secondary boycott, deals with 13 Arab countries who refuse to do business with third-country firms that have business relationships with Israel that contribute to Israel's economic or military capability (i.e., investments, licensing agreements, technical assistance, etc.).

Although the Arab boycott of Israel is the most significant one U.S. companies will encounter, many other countries have from time to time employed some kind of primary boycott against some other country. It is a very common international practice. There have been conditions in documents from India, Pakistan, and Bangladesh that have prohibited imports of goods from Israel, South Africa, and Rhodesia.

However, the secondary boycott concerns the United States because it attempts to influence the way U.S. companies make decisions about who they can do business with (i.e., Israel) or not to do business with (i.e., black-listed companies boycotted by the Arabs, such as freight forwarders, steamship companies, or manufacturers who have done business with Israel despite the Arab boycott of Israel). This secondary boycott created an intrusion into U.S. sovereignty and raised concern leading to the enactment of U.S. law.

Two sets of anti-boycott compliance rules and regulations were enacted for U.S. domestically based operations and their overseas operations. The first are the anti-boycott provisions of the Export Administration Act. These were enacted in 1977 as an amendment to the act. They are administered by the U.S. Department of Commerce, which has issued a rather comprehensive set of regulations to implement the law

(Part 369 of the Export Administration Regulations). These prescribe the types of conduct that are prohibited or permitted by U.S. companies in complying with the requirements of the boycott. The second anti-boycott provisions are those inserted in the tax code by the so-called Ribicoff amendment to the Tax Reform Act of 1976 (sect. 999 of the Internal Revenue Code). They are administered by the U.S. Treasury Department and the IRS. The Treasury Department has issued a rather comprehensive set of guidelines to implement these provisions.

In general, U.S. exporters seem to encounter Arab boycott clauses mostly when they request letters of credit from Middle Eastern foreign companies (private, public, or government owned/operated). The documentary requirements in these letters of credit usually contain boycott language that must be used in certain documents. However, U.S. exporters can encounter boycott language when dealing with Arab countries not involving letter of credit payment terms.

Because the laws and regulations implemented by the U.S. Commerce and Treasury departments are complex and difficult to interpret, many U.S. exporters have established internal procedures whereby a person or persons in their in-house legal departments or outside counsel are responsible for interpreting and coordinating Arab boycott clauses. The procedures require the credit and traffic/distribution managers to report any and all Arab boycott clauses to this person or persons. In this regard, both the U.S. Departments of Commerce and Treasury have established offices to answer questions, seek advice, and give direction concerning questionable clauses:

Treasury Department

Office of the General Counsel
Room 2004
Department of the Treasury
Washington, D.C. 20220

(202) 566-8401

Commerce Department

Director, Compliance Policy Division
Office of Antiboycott Compliance
Department of Commerce
Washington, D.C.

(202) 377-4559

Exporters to the Middle East are encouraged to become familiar with rules and regulations established by the U.S. Commerce and Treasury Departments.

REFERENCES

1. Gerhard W. Schneider, *Export-Import Financing: A Practical Guide* (New York: The Ronald Press Company, 1974), p. 202

2. *International Trade Procedures: An Introduction To Doing Business Abroad* (Philadelphia, PA.: The Philadelphia International Bank, 1985), p. 14.

CHAPTER 6

U.S. PROGRAMS

PART A

FCIA/EXIMBANK

If there is any one area where the credit manager can excel, it is the ability to come up with the best and cheapest export trade finance package available to help make the export sale. Maneuvering through the maze to find the right program, qualify for assistance, and hope the foreign customer accepts the financing can be a nightmare for the inexperienced and unsophisticated credit manager.

The U.S. government offers a variety of export credit insurance and guarantee programs. Part A gives the reader a better understanding of what is available in the marketplace from our own government—specifically those programs and guarantees offered by FCIA and Eximbank—and explains how to use them. Part B covers those programs and guarantees offered by the private sector.

In effect, these government and private programs can greatly assist U.S. exporters in promoting international trade in market areas of the world considered large risks without some sort of credit or guarantee protection. The descriptions of each program are designed for clear understanding and easy reference.

Since there are many alternative sources, the prudent credit manager needs to know which program offers the right protection without being cost prohibitive. Unless the credit manager has a thorough understanding of just what is available and how these programs can assist his or her company, many export sales will be lost to competition, or a more expensive alternative will be used when a cheaper one would suffice.

EXPORT-IMPORT BANK OF THE UNITED STATES (EXIMBANK)

The Export-Import Bank of the United States (Eximbank), was created February 2, 1934, to finance trade with the Soviet Union. A second bank was created on March 9, 1934, to assist trade with all other countries. Because agreement was not reached on Soviet repayment of old debts owed to the United States, the first bank did not extend any loans. The second bank lent $4 million for the Cuban purchase of silver bullion and its minting in Philadelphia into 10 million Cuban silver pesos. The two banks were merged May 7, 1936. Created by a Presidential Executive Order, the bank was established on a statutory basis in 1945 with the passage of the Export Import Bank Act.

The Bank helped to prime the pump with exports during the Depression. It later financed strategic projects, such as construction of the Burma Road. It helped U.S. companies to participate in the post-war reconstruction of Europe and Asia before the Marshall Plan was in place. It also helped U.S. contractors to build the Inter-American Highway linking us with our continental neighbors.

Eximbank's services are generally broken down into two financing areas. The first is the buyer credit or project financing area, which provides direct loans at fixed rates and extended terms of repayment, as well as financial guarantees of private source loans for heavy equipment and capital-intensive projects. The second is the supplier credit area, which offers assistance through the Cooperative Financing Facility (an established network of foreign banks that work with Eximbank), discount loans, medium-term commercial bank guarantees, and numerous other programs.

The Eximbank charter lays down the following basic operating principles:

- The bank should supplement and encourage, not compete with, private capital.

- The bank loans should generally be for specific purposes and offer reasonable assurance of repayment.
- The Bank is a self-supporting organization; therefore, fees and premiums charged should be commensurate with the risks undertaken.

Meeting foreign competition is also an important statutory requirement for the Bank. The Bank has been authorized to offer financing at rates and terms which are competitive with official foreign export credit agencies. Recent legislation has stressed this policy.

Before digresssing further on the various types of coverage and policies offered by the Foreign Credit Insurance Association and Eximbank (FCIA is discussed later), it is important to understand that Eximbank operates under certain political and economic constraints which are interrelated to the policies of the administration in office in Washington, D.C. Eximbank is not an international commercial bank; it operates under political considerations from the U.S. Congress on up to the executive level of the U.S. government. Thus, it has less flexibility than commercial bank and most foreign official credit agencies. Eximbank's ability to provide loans, guarantees, or insurance can be separated into three basic categories:[1]

1. *Mandated Economic Criteria.* Eximbank's credit assistance programs are limited to U.S. firms and foreign exporters doing business in the United States. Eximbank will finance exports to foreign subsidiaries of U.S.-based companies when the United States goods and services are provided by other U.S. suppliers, but it will not normally finance deals made directly between related firms. However, such deals are usually eligible only for political risk coverage under the medium-term guarantee program and under the policies of FCIA. Eximbank will not offer direct loan assistance when private institutions can provide comparable financing on "reasonable terms."[2]
2. *Political and Military Constraints.* As defined in the 1974 Trade Act, Eximbank may not provide export assistance to Communist countries, except those that have bilateral trade agreements with the United States (effectively, those

with "most favored nation" [MFN] status) and those that allow their citizens to emigrate freely. Eximbank also faces restrictions imposed by Congress on doing business in South Africa (including transactions that help the South African government maintain or enforce apartheid).

As a matter of policy (though not law), Eximbank does not support sales of military equipment or services to industrial countries. It is specifically prohibited by law from supporting sales of such equipment to Third World countries, unless the U.S. president declares such sales to be in the national interest.

The Export Administration Act also prevents Eximbank from operating in countries designated as "supporters of international terrorism."[3]

3. *Restrictions on Products.* Partially for foreign policy reasons and partially for domestic economic and political reasons, Eximbank treats equipment exports for nuclear energy, telecommunications, and media differently than exports of products.

The bulk of Eximbank's resources in dollar terms are devoted to long-term financing of five years and longer (direct loans and financial guarantees), mainly to support the sales of exporters of power plants, commercial jet aircraft, and locomotives, as well as other heavy capital goods and major projects. In terms of number of programs however, there are many programs which provide medium-term financing—181 days to five years. Exporters benefiting most from these other programs are mining and refining equipment, construction equipment, agricultural equipment, and general aviation aircraft. In addition, there is also short-term coverage and financing —up to 180 days—for exporters of consumer goods, small manufactured products, replacement parts, and natural resources. The following exhibits will give you an idea of where the Bank's resource dollars went in fiscal year 1985 in terms of loans, guarantees, and Export Credit Insurance (Figure 6–1). These loans are further broken down by Authorizations by Market (Figure 6–2), Authorizations by Area (Figure 6–3), and major Direct Credits and Financial Guarantees (Figure 6–4) funded by the bank in fiscal 1985.

FIGURE 6–1 Authorization Summary, Export-Import Bank of the United States ($ millions)

	FY 1985			FY 1984		
	Number of Authorizations	Amount Authorized	Export Value	Number of Authorizations	Amount Authorized	Export Value
Loans						
Direct credits	13	$ 320.2	$ 460.4	29	$1,122.1	$ 1,880.7
Medium-term credits*	175	315.8	114.6	186	302.3	170.0
Small business credits*	64	23.4	19.2	77	40.6	22.1
Total loans	252	659.4	594.2	292	1,465.0	2,072.8
Guarantees						
Financial†						
Related to direct credits	4	52.8	—	16	226.3	—
Unrelated to loans	18	719.7	986.8	13	672.9	1,023.2
Local cost	2	6.8	—	—	—	—
Bank	140	514.1	605.8	195	415.6	489.5
Working capital	32	26.7	50.4	10	18.4	19.5
Total guarantees	196	1,320.1	1,643.0	234	1,333.2	1,532.2
Export Credit Insurance						
Short-term	896	5,840.4	5,840.4	997	4,710.0	4,710.0
Medium-term	58	126.9	149.2	84	302.4	347.6
Combined short- and medium-term	16	79.0	79.0	1	2.0	2.0
Master policies	23	483.2	992.5	28	803.2	1,765.6
Total insurance	993	6,529.5	7,061.1	1,110	5,817.6	6,825.2
Grand total	**1,441**	**$8,509.0**	**$9,298.3**	**1,636**	**$8,615.8**	**$10,430.2**

* Export value for loans which are guaranteed or insured are included in the guarantee and insurance details.
† Export value for Financial Guarantees related to specific loans are included with the appropriate loan details.

FIGURE 6–2 Authorizations by Market (Export-Import Bank of the United States)

			October 1, 1984 through September 30, 1985		
	Loans	Guarantees	Medium-Term Insurance	Total	Exposure 9/30/85
Algeria		$ 16,874,000		$ 16,874,000	$ 686,227,503
Angola		2,640,000		2,640,000	214,061,650
Antigua					828.733
Argentina					733,483,665
Australia		17,619		17,619	355,639,710
Austria					65,232,355
Bahamas		492,915		492,915	7,063,256
Bahrain					684,809
Barbados					9,005,155
Belgium					65,295,364
Belize					188,120
Bermuda					1,283,948
Bolivia					29,977,360
Brazil	$ 37,400,000	270,125,100	$ 35,964,857	343,489,957	2,028,255,991
Brunei					592,025
Burkina Faso			2,975,000	2,975,000	3,082,860
Burma, Union of					2,550,000
Burundi					53,577
Cameroon					60,522,617
Canada		41,093	657,313	698,406	848,244,913
Canary Islands					56,064
Cayman Islands					7,394,111
Central African Republic					3,422,142
Chile	1,275,000	23,318,480	7,859,375	32,452,855	131,884,451

FIGURE 6–2 (continued)

	October 1, 1984 through September 30, 1985				Exposure 9/30/85
	Loans	Guarantees	Medium-Term Insurance	Total	
China					$ 26,386,019
Mainland					51,001,184
Taiwan					1,427,747,760
Colombia	$130,000,000	$237,585,117	$3,453,210	$371,038,327	1,171,444,752
Congo	12,075,000	4,621,959		16,696,959	65,097,380
Costa Rica					26,711,322
Cuba					36,266,581
Cyprus					3,835,684
Denmark					37,913,267
Djibouti					131,630
Dominica					81,150
Dominican Republic			145,047	145,047	132,473,880
Ecuador		5,625,000		5,625,000	75,446,794
Egypt		44,985,937	3,428,020	48,413,957	332,980,735
El Salvador		5,682,727		5,682,727	20,096,532
Ethiopia					77,720,893
Fiji Islands					3,331,552
Finland					73,590,704
France					201,399,472
Gabon	435,000	2,093,280		2,528,280	27,893,344
Germany, Federal Republic of					29,897,201
Ghana					4,027,632
Greece					68,940,684

Country					
Greenland					23,768
Grenada					74,500
Guatemala		3,877,454	11,422,414	15,299,868	25,947,305
Guiana-French					213,658
Guinea					8,724,531
Guyana					4,507,250
Haiti					11,722,179
Honduras					15,885,137
Hong Kong					62,723,920
Hungary	17,000,000		53,040	17,053,040	23,183,722
Iceland	74,100			74,100	8,208,237
India					158,710,149
Indonesia	23,562,500			32,382,500	786,388,903
Iraq					5,411,588
Ireland					91,433,240
Israel	21,280,291	127,500	9,941,818	31,222,109	1,016,046,681
Italy	127,500		127,500	127,500	355,794,181
Ivory Coast					97,660,431
Jamaica			998,263	998,263	85,569,012
Japan	12,595,307	134,000,000		146,595,307	665,839,377
Jordan			220,938	220,938	258,844,092
Kenya					6,333,882
Kiribati					7,781
Korea, Republic of	35,750,000	5,100,000	3,862,822	40,850,000	2,979,055,519
Kuwait				3,862,822	16,578,606
Lebanon					207,736
Lesotho					1,700,000
Liberia					8,207,812
Liechtenstein					2,221,592
Luxembourg					337,812

FIGURE 6–2 (continued)

			October 1, 1984 through September 30, 1985		
	Loans	Guarantees	Medium-Term Insurance	Total	Exposure 9/30/85
Macao					$ 391,804
Madagascar					30,594,413
Malawi			$ 87,468	$ 87,468	2,000,049
Malaysia, Federation of					69,313,145
Mali					30,242
Malta					689,702
Mauritania					4,741,686
Mexico	$ 10,140,500	$ 112,779,675	82,998,790	205,918,964	2,476,945,889
Monaco					4,543
Montserrat					15,871
Morocco		2,707,500	264,593	2,972,093	131,652,719
Mozambique					19,094,678
Nepal					3,000
Netherlands					25,140,511
Netherlands Antilles		6,899,721		6,899,721	38,267,921
New Caledonia					8,549
New Zealand		1,152,537		1,152,537	38,420,180
Nicaragua					18,284,204
Niger					5,317,941
Nigeria		137,700,000		137,700,000	625,732,173
Norway					125,676,344
Oman					964,045
Pakistan					112,147,907
Panama		382,500	395,005	777,505	24,892,105
Papua New Guinea					5,103

Paraguay	6,200,723	4,015,740	2,550,000	1,465,740	
Peru	179,560,817	30,000,000	30,000,000	30,000,000	
Philippines	1,358,109,215				
Poland	241,809,418				
Portugal	176,541,311				
Qatar	10,450,251				
Reunion Island	6,646				
Romania	121,782,502				
Saudi Arabia	86,730,454	11,681,085	11,681,085		
Senegal	5,248,663	1,127,913		1,127,913	
Sierra Leone	23,286,604				
Singapore	214,714,705	15,817,970			15,817,970
South Africa	18,051,510				
Spain	1,065,426,507				
Sri Lanka	48,177,801	997,050		997,050	
St. Christopher (Kitts)-Nevis	893,850	1,700,000		1,700,000	
St. Lucia	195,168				
St. Vincent	206,959				
Sudan	28,246,331				
Suriname	8,893,910	8,500,000	8,500,000		
Sweden	49,603,510				
Switzerland	9,097,646				
Syria	27,453				
Tahiti	467,972				
Tanzania	13,723,639				
Thailand	111,508,570	294,746	294,746		
Togo	2,401,751				
Tr. Terr. Pac. Is. (U.S.)	72,039				
Trinidad and Tobago	277,144,857	16,544,691	294,691		16,250,000

FIGURE 6–2 (concluded)

	October 1, 1984 through September 30, 1985				Exposure 9/30/85
	Loans	Guarantees	Medium-Term Insurance	Total	
Tunisia	$ 7,860,270	$ 18,877,636		$ 26,737,906	$ 102,002,312
Turkey		98,138,635	$ 5,257,675	103,396,310	754,933,282
Uganda					1,428,657
Union of Soviet Socialist Rep.					302,712,284
United Arab Emirates					7,488,753
United Kingdom		135,801	206,909	342,709	580,723,999
Uruguay		637,500		637,500	19,512,840
Vanuatu					1,422
Venezuela			271,541	271,541	227,253,215
Virgin Islands-British					249,501
West Indies-British					1,314,317
West Indies-French					337,006
Western Samoa					47,509
Yemen Arab Republic			1,105,000	1,105,000	1,105,000
Yugoslavia		91,315,558	11,099,300	102,414,858	954,949,936
Zaire					694,895,957
Zambia					77,848,004
Zimbabwe					35,254,394
L.A. Multinational Financial Inst.					13,259,035
Private Export Funding Corp.					85,387,948
Working capital guarantees		26,730,835		26,730,835	40,229,180
Total all markets	**$320,235,647**	**$1,320,057,070**	**$205,988,920**	**$1,846,281,637**	**$27,556,859,242**

FIGURE 6–3
Authorizations By Area (Export-Import Bank of the United States)

	October 1, 1984 through September 30, 1985				Exposure 9/30/85
	Loans	Guarantees	Medium-Term Insurance	Total	
Africa/Middle East	$ 20,370,270	$ 351,047,150	$ 38,824,420	$ 410,241,839	$ 5,691,083,708
Asia	87,799,877	180,790,156	294,746	268,884,780	8,361,214,912
Europe/Canada	17,000,000	92,617,001	12,016,562	121,633,563	5,529,710,407
Latin America	195,065,500	668,871,928	154,853,192	1,018,790,620	7,849,233,087
Miscellaneous		26,730,835		26,730,835	5,617,128
Total all areas	320,235,647	1,320,057,070	205,988,920	1,846,281,637	27,556,859,242
Medium-term credits	315,766,033			315,766,033	463,857,192
Small business credits	23,415,089			23,415,089	43,557,297
Discount loans					164,058,287
Multibuyer insurance					
Authorized				6,323,560,000	6,424,393,026
Unshipped					344,205,606
All other					
Total authorizations	**$659,416,769**	**$1,320,057,070**	**$205,988,920**	**$8,509,022,759**	**$35,001,930,650**

FIGURE 6–4

FY 1985 Direct Credits and Financial Guarantees. (Export-Import Bank of the United States)

Obligor (Guarantor) Supplier	Purpose	Eximbank's Interest Rate (in percent)	Direct Credit	Financial Guarantee
Brazil				
Government of the State of São Paulo (Federative Republic of Brazil) Various suppliers	Medical, dental and optical equipment	11.200% 4.460	$ 27,412,000 9,988,000	$ 6,600,000
Furnas Centrais Eletricas, S.A. (Federative Republic of Brazil) Westinghouse Electric, Bechtel Corp., and various other suppliers	Nuclear power engineering services and equipment			59,330,000
Itaipu Binacional (ITAIPU) (Federative Republic of Brazil) International Engineering Company	Hydroelectric engineering services			8,500,000
Rede Ferroviaria Federal, S.A. (Federative Republic of Brazil) General Motors Corporation and General Electric Company	New locomotive component sets and rehabilitation of existing equipment			53,635,000
Empresa Brasileira de Telecomunicacoes (Federative Republic of Brazil) U.S. Aircraft Insurance Group and International Technology Underwriters	Communications satellite launch insurance			7,194,825
Total for Brazil			37,400,000	135,259,825

Chile				
Cia. Chilena de Generacion Electrica, S.A. (Government of Chile) PRC Engineering	Engineering services and studies	10.700	1,275,000	225,000
Corporacion Nacional del Cobre de Chile Dresser/WABCO	Trucks for Chuquicamata copper mine			14,763,480
Total for Chile			**1,275,000**	**14,988,480**
Colombia				
Carbones de Colombia S.A. (Republic of Colombia) Various suppliers	Coal mine project	11.200	130,000,000	40,000,000
Republic of Columbia General Electric Co.	Radio communications system			13,364,384
Republic of Colombia Motorola, Inc. Calmaquip Engineering Corp. and various other suppliers	Radio communications system			4,367,657
Empresa Colombiana de Petroleos Overseas Bechtel, Willbros. Int'l. and various other suppliers	Oil pipeline construction project and marine terminal			115,005,000
Total for Colombia			**130,000,000**	**182,360,084**

FIGURE 6–4 (continued)

Obligor (Guarantor) Supplier	Purpose	Eximbank's Interest Rate (in percent)	Direct Credit	Financial Guarantee
Congo				
People's Republic of the Congo	Agricultural services	9.500%	$ 12,075,000	$ 1,610,000
CRS Sirrine, Inc.				
Total for Congo			**12,075,000**	**1,610,000**
Gabon				
Republic of Gabon	Amendment of a direct	10.700	435,000	
Various suppliers	credit previously			
	authorized for			
	locomotives (6)			
	component parts			
Total for Gabon			**435,000**	
Hungary				
National Bank of Hungary	Line of credit	11.550	17,000,000	
(Ministry of Finance)				
Various suppliers				
Total for Hungary			**17,000,000**	
India				
Cement Corporation of India Ltd.	Amendment of a direct	10.000	74,100	
(Government of India)	credit previously			
Fuller International, Inc.	authorized for			
	expansion of cement plant			
Total for India			**74,100**	

	Description	Rate	Amount	Amount
Indonesia				
Government of Indonesia / Various suppliers	Various equipment for nuclear research and training	9.500	5,200,000	
Government of Indonesia / Bell Helicopter Textron, Inc.	Components for the manufacture of helicopters	9.850	18,362,500	
Total for Indonesia			**23,562,500**	
Israel				
Bank Leumi Le-Israel B.M. / Various suppliers	Manufacturing equipment			19,653,896
Total for Israel				**19,653,896**
Japan				
All Nippon Airways Co. Ltd / General Electric Company	Aircraft engines, commercial jet	12.000	12,595,307	
All Nippon Airways Co. Ltd (Various) / Boeing Company	Aircraft, commercial jet (8)767-200			134,000,000
Total for Japan			**12,595,307**	**134,000,000**
Korea, Republic of				
Kukdong Oil Company, Ltd. (Korea Development Bank) / The Badger Company, Inc, and Various other suppliers	Petroleum refining and processing plant	10.700	35,750,000	
Total for Korea, Republic of			**35,750,000**	

FIGURE 6–4 (continued)

Obligor (Guarantor) Supplier	Purpose	Eximbank's Interest Rate (in percent)	Direct Credit	Financial Guarantee
Mexico				
Nacional Financiera, S.A. General Electric Co.	Locomotive kits	11.200%	$ 10,140,500	$ 10,140,500
Banco Nacional de Mexico Gulfstream Aerospace Corp.	Aircraft, small jet (1) Gulfstream III			10,625,000
Aeronaves de Mexico, S.A. (Nacional Financiera, S.A.) McDonnell Douglas	Aircraft, commercial jet (3)DC-9-80			63,930,933
Nacional Financiera, S.A. Various suppliers	Amendment of a financial guarantee previously authorized for communications satellite project			4,335,000
Total for Mexico			**10,140,500**	**89,031,433**
Nigeria				
Federal Republic of Nigeria General Electric Company	Generators and turbines			93,500,000
Total for Nigeria				**93,500,000**
Singapore				
Cubic Corporation (Various) Cubic Western Data	Automatic fare card system	10.350	15,817,970	
Total for Singapore			**15,817,970**	

Trinidad and Tobago				
Trinidad and Tobago Telephone Co. (Government of Trinidad and Tobago)	Telephone and telegraph installations	11.200	16,250,000	
Various suppliers				
Total for Trinidad and Tobago			**16,250,000**	
Tunisia				
Regie des Sondages Hydrauliques (Republic of Tunisia)	Water well drilling rigs (8)	10.350	7,860,270	1,048,036
AMCA International & Various Other Suppliers				
Total for Tunisia			**7,860,270**	**1,048,036**
Turkey				
Dogus Construction Group (Ziraat Bank)	Construction equipment			11,602,500
Caterpillar Overseas, S.A.				
Undersecretariat for the Treasury and Foreign Trade	Engineering services and studies			25,500,000
Foster Wheeler Energy Corp.				
Total for Turkey				**37,102,500**

FIGURE 6-4 (concluded)

Obligor (Guarantor) Supplier	Purpose	Eximbank's Interest Rate (in percent)	Direct Credit	Financial Guarantee
Yugoslavia				
Jugoslovenski Aerotransport (Udruzena Beogradska Banka) Boeing Company	Aircraft, commercial jet (2)737-300			$ 51,680,000
Inex Adria Aviopromet (Ljubljanska Banka) McDonnell Douglas Corp.	Aircraft, commercial jet (1)DC-9			19,052,750
Total for Yugoslavia				70,732,750
Total			$320,235,647	$779,287,004

Note: In FY 1985, Eximbank authorized no loans for the purchase of goods from a U.S. entity by a foreign subsidiary of that entity.

In mid-1986, Eximbank announced a new organizational structure which is of primary importance to users of its services. In the past, its structure retarded communication and services, an important element to contacting the right person for precise, accurate, and timely information regarding programs and current events. In Figure 6–5 the most recent organizational chart of the Export-Import Bank of the United States is illustrated.

The following changes were made at the bank:

1. The reorganization places all international lending and guarantee responsibilities under a new International Lending Division. By putting all the international lending programs under one roof, and moving contract administration into this division, the bank will be able to handle any request for loans or guarantees from start to finish.

2. The new Insurance and Banking Division includes a new U.S. division which will be responsible for loans and guarantees to U.S. borrowers (includes Section 1912 to counter foreign subsidized credit imports). Other sections of this division (insurance, claims and recoveries, and marketing and program development) will continue to work with state export promotion agencies, trade associations, and other entities and will concentrate on new programs to be developed.

3. A new Country Risk Analysis Division staffed by the Bank's economists is being established to enable Eximbank to understand better the markets in which they take risk, and manage the risk more effectively. The Bank has accepted the fact that they must not be afraid to take risks, but must develop an even sharper capacity to understand and appreciate the risks that they take.

4. A new Policy and Planning Division is responsible for industry analysis, adverse impact studies, advisory committee issues, and forward planning.

5. A new Information Management Division will be responsible for the Bank's computer operations and systems development.

In addition, the Bank has established two on-line services called Eximbank Bulletin Board. One is a listing that offers

FIGURE 6–5
Export-Import Bank of the United States: Organizational Chart

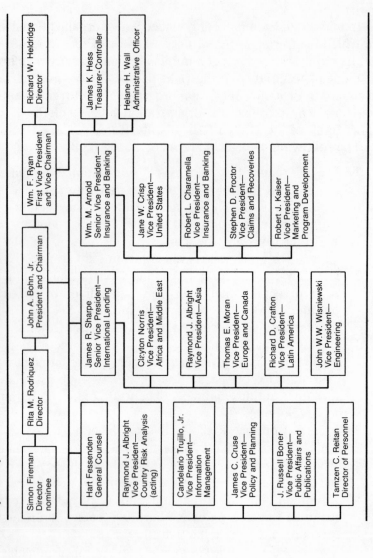

Source: The Export-Import Bank of the United States.

472

Eximbank programs, and the other is the country limitation schedule. To log on to the Bank's bulletin board for banks interested in handling the Bank's export trade finance or for banks and exporters to review the current country limitation schedule, call via computer with modem (202-566-4602). For help in walking through the logging-on procedure call (202-566-4690).

THE FOREIGN CREDIT INSURANCE ASSOCIATION (FCIA)

The Foreign Credit Insurance Association was created in 1961 to give U.S. exporters the means to become internationally competitive. It is an association of leading insurance companies, operating in cooperation with and as agents of the Export-Import Bank of the United States (Eximbank). It offers policies insuring U.S. exports against commercial (foreign customer) and political risks. Such coverage helps the exporter to offer credit terms and to obtain financing of foreign receivables.

The advantages of FCIA insurance to the exporter are quite clear. The fundamental reason for export credit insurance is the protection it gives a company on the riskiest part of its portfolio: foreign receivables. Such insurance, of course, is not a substitute for an exporter's good in-house credit management. However, overseas political and commercial developments can unfold, despite the exercise of sound credit judgment, and can generate losses for otherwise prudent manufacturers or financial institutions. In these instances, export credit insurance serves a vital function. It protects the U.S. exporter against overseas events that are beyond its control.

Once the exporter has protected his foreign receivables, it is free to conduct its export activity with greater flexibility. With this insurance, for example, the exporter can compete vigorously for overseas markets, entering even those it might otherwise consider too risky. It can match foreign-supported selling terms. In a world of high costs and fierce competition for export markets, the ability to offer attractive credit terms to a foreign customer increasingly spells the difference between winning or losing a sale.

The exporter can undertake such new business with existing

capital because risk is minimized. This leveraging of a firm's productive facilities translates into enhanced profitability and additional job opportunities.

At the same time, an exporter's bank will normally extend more liberal export trade financing when the receivables being offered as collateral are insured. Discounting of receivables to obtain financing is one of the widely used benefits of export credit insurance for FCIA customers. The proceeds of FCIA policies may be assigned to a commercial bank or other financial institution as security against discounted receivables.

The benefits of FCIA coverage can be summed up this way:

- It protects the exporter against the failure of the foreign customer to pay his dollar obligation (or other currency, if so requested and approved) for commercial or political reasons.
- It encourages the exporter to offer competitive terms of payment to the foreign customer.
- It supports the exporter's prudent penetration of higher risk foreign markets.
- It gives the exporter greater financial liquidity and flexibility in administering its foreign receivable portfolio.

What Basic Losses Are Covered?

Commercial defaults may result from nonpayment by a foreign customer, bankruptcy or economic deterioration in the foreign customer's market area, fluctuations in demand, unanticipated competition, shifts in tariffs, and technological changes. One of the principals or key management members of the foreign customer may die or become inactive, causing the company to close. A foreign customer's own government or one of its major customers may alter purchasing patterns. The foreign customer may be subject to an unexpectedly sharp increase in operating expenses. Natural disasters, such as floods and earthquakes, can also affect the ability of a foreign customer to operate in a market.

Superimposed on an exporter's commercial risks are risks of a political or noncommercial nature. Political risks are beyond the control of either buyer or seller. War, revolution, riot, and insurrection are all legitimate fears of exporters. In the aftermath of political upheavals, the assets of an importer may be confiscated, a shipment may be detained or diverted, or licenses may be revoked.

Overall, the risks of extending credit to customers in other countries are typically much greater than the risks of granting credit to domestic customers. The U.S. exporter needs to be insured against these risks, and FCIA helps.

FCIA'S POLICIES, PROGRAMS, AND GUARANTEES

What are the different types of coverage and policies offered by FCIA and Eximbank? The following policies, programs, and guarantees offered by Eximbank and FCIA are intended as a descriptive summary only. The complete terms and conditions of coverage are set forth in the policy declarations and endorsements of FCIA and the terms and conditions of Eximbank offered by the bank in its programs and guarantees. Figure 6–6 is a Program Selection Chart which briefly outlines each program in summary form. It can be used as a quick and immediate reference tool.

Master Deductible Policy

The Master Policy enables U.S. exporters to expand international sales in a substantial manner through the use of competitive credit terms. This policy also helps insureds attract and retain good customers in higher risk markets. It gives exporters the flexibility to finance insured receivables with financial institutions. In short, the Master Policy allows the exporter to compete in markets around the world.

The policy is written for shipments during a one-year period and insures all, or a reasonable spread, of an exporter's eligible sales. Both short-term sales, with repayment terms generally up to 180 days, and medium-term sales, with repayment stretching out to five years (and longer under certain circumstances), can be insured under the Master Policy.

The policy is subject to limits. The aggregate limit represents the insurers' maximum liability under the policy. The exporter makes credit decisions for shipments up to the amount of a discretionary credit limit (DCL) applicable to the policy after

FIGURE 6–6 Program Selection Chart

Program	Eligible Nonmilitary U.S. Products and Services	Description	Eligible Applicants
1. Eximbank Working Capital Guarantee Program	All products and services.	Loan guarantee program designed to provide eligible exporters with access to working capital loans from commercial lenders.	Commercial lenders extending export-related working capital loans principally for creditworthy small- to medium-sized businesses.
2. FCIA New-To-Export Insurance Policy	Consumables, raw materials, spare parts, agricultural commodities, capital goods, consumer durables, and services.	One-year blanket policy insuring all eligible short-term export credit sales.	Companies which are just be-ginning to export or have an average annual export credit sales volume of less than $750,000 for past two years. Exporters must not have used FCIA in the past two years.
3. FCIA Umbrella Insurance Policy	Consumables, raw materials, spare parts, agricultural commodities, capital goods, consumer durables, and services.	One-year blanket policy insur-ing all eligible short-term ex-port credit sales of exporters with average annual export credit sales of less than $2,000,000 for the past two years and who have not used FCIA in the past two years.	Any entity capable of administering a policy on behalf of multiple exporters.
4. Bank Letter of Credit Policy	Consumables, raw materials, spare parts, agricultural commodities, capital goods, consumer durables, and services.	One-year blanket policy insur-ing all eligible commercial banks against loss on irrevocable letters of credit issued by foreign banks in favor of U.S. exporters.	Approved commercial banking institutions in the United States.

5. FCIA Multi-Buyer Policy	All products and services eligible for short-term or medium-term insurance.	One-year blanket policy insuring all eligible short- and medium-term export credit sales.	Exporters of U.S. goods and services who conduct a sizeable export business.
6. FCIA Medium-Term Insurance Policy	Capital equipment and services including automobiles/trucks, general aviation aircraft, mining, construction and agricultural equipment, processing and communications equipment, and planning/feasibility studies.	Single-buyer policy insuring individual medium-term export credit sales.	Exporters of U.S. goods and services of financial institutions in the United States.
7. FCIA Combined Short-Term/Medium-Term Insurance Policy	Capital equipment including automobiles/trucks, construction, mining and agricultural equipment, and general aviation aircraft.	Single-buyer policy for repetitive export sales to a dealer or distributor. Policy provides insurance for short-term inventory financing followed by medium-term coverage for receivables financing.	Exporters of U.S. goods or financial institutions in the United States.
8. Eximbank Medium-Term Bank Guarantee Program	Capital equipment and services including automobiles/trucks, general aviation aircraft, mining, construction and agricultural equipment, processing and communications equipment, and planning/feasibility studies.	Guarantee by Eximbank to commercial bank covering export financing extended to individual foreign buyers. Covers either single or repetitive sales to single buyer.	Approved commercial banking institutions in the United States.

FIGURE 6–6 (continued)

Program	Eligible Nonmilitary U.S. Products and Services	Description	Eligible Applicants
9. Eximbank Small Business Credit Program	Capital equipment and services produced by eligible small businesses.	Eximbank funding commitment to enable U.S. banks to offer medium-term fixed rate export loans at the lowest rates permitted under the internationally agreed export credit guidelines.	Approved commercial banking institutions in the U.S. financing exports produced by small businesses (as defined by the Small Business Administration).
10. Eximbank Medium-Term Credit Program	Capital goods and services including automobiles/ trucks, general aviation aircraft, mining, construction, agricultural processing and communications equipment, and planning/feasibility studies.	Same as Small Business Credit Program except (a) the exporter need not be a small business, (b) the exporter must face officially supported subsidized foreign competition.	Approved commercial banking institutions in the United States.
11. Eximbank Preliminary Commitment	Major procurement including power generation/ transmission projects, mining and industrial projects, project-related services, commercial jet aircraft, and locomotives.	Offer from Eximbank detailing, in advance of a particular transaction, the terms and conditions for direct loan/financial guarantee support.	Exporters, financial institutions or foreign buyers.

Program		
12. Engineering Multiplier Program	Project-related feasibility studies and preconstruction design and engineering services.	Medium-term, fixed interest rate direct loans to support up to $10 million of services for projects with potential for procurement of U.S. equipment and services worth $10 million or twice the amount of the original contract, whichever is greater.	Foreign buyers (exporters or financial institutions may also apply for Preliminary Commitment).
13. Eximbank Direct Loan	Major procurement including power generation/transmission projects, mining and industrial projects, project-related services, commercial jet aircraft, and locomotives.	Long-term, fixed interest rate loans to finance export sales usually worth at least $10 million and facing officially supported foreign competition.	Same as Engineering Multiplier Program.
14. Eximbank Financial Guarantee	Major procurement including power generation/transmission projects, mining and industrial projects, project-related services, commercial jet aircraft, and locomotives.	Guarantee by Eximbank of export financing extended to foreign buyers.	Same as Engineering Multiplier Program.
15. Private Export Funding Corporation (PEFCO)	Major procurement including power generation/transmission projects, mining and industrial projects, project-related services, commercial jet aircraft, and locomotives.	Medium- and long-term fixed interest rate loans of at least $1 million guaranteed by Eximbank.	Same as Engineering Multiplier Program.

FIGURE 6–6 (continued)

Program	Maximum Coverage	Maximum Repayment Period	Fees and Premiums	Minimum Buyer Cash Payment
1. Eximbank Working Capital Guarantee Program	Guarantee applies up to 90% of the principal amount of the loan and interest up to the U.S. Treasury rate plus 1%.	Generally up to 12 months.	One percent of the loan amount for loans of 180 days or less; 0.5% for each additional 6 months or portion thereof.	Not applicable.
2. FCIA New-To-Export Insurance Policy	• 100% political risk protection. • 95% commercial risk protection (98% for bulk agricultural sales). • Interest up to prime rate minus 0.5%.	180 days (360 days for bulk agricultural commodities and consumer durables).	• Varies with each sale but is usually priced 0.25% to 1.00% of sales value. • Minimum annual premium of $500.	None.
3. FCIA Umbrella Insurance Policy	• 100% political risk protection. • 90% commercial risk protection (98% for bulk agricultural sales). • Interest up to prime rate minus 0.5%.	180 days (360 days for bulk agricultural commodities and consumer durables).	• Same fee rates as FCIA New-to-Export Policy. • $500 minimum annual premium is paid by the Umbrella Policyholder/ Administrator in advance.	None.

480

	Coverage	Terms	Premium	Deductible
4. Bank Letter of Credit Policy	• 95% political risk protection. • 95% commercial risk protection (98% for bulk agricultural sales). • Interest up to prime rate minus 0.5%.	180 days (360 days for bulk agricultural commodities and consumer durables).	Minimum annual premium of $2,000.	None.
5. FCIA Multi-Buyer Policy	• Three options for short-term coverage: (1) 100% political/90% commercial risk protection after first-loss deductible; (2) 95% combined political/commercial risk protection after all-risk deductible; (3) 80% combined political/commercial risk protection (95% on letter of credit sales) with no deductible. • Bulk agriculture sales 98% commercial risk protection for all options. • Medium-term	• Same as FCIA Short-Term Policy for short-term sales. • Same as FCIA Medium-Term Policy for medium-term sales.	• Premium rate is determined by factors such as insured's sales profile, history of export credit losses, average term of repayment and size of first-loss commercial deductible. • Minimum annual premium of $500.	• None for short-term sales. • 15% for medium-term sales.

FIGURE 6–6 (continued)

Program	Maximum Coverage	Maximum Repayment Period	Fees and Premiums	Minimum Buyer Cash Payment
	commercial/political risk options are: 90/100%; 90/90%; 80/80%. • Interest up to prime rate minus 0.5% for short-term: Treasury rate plus 1% for medium-term sales.			15% at shipment.
6. FCIA Medium-Term Insurance Policy	• 100% political risk protection. • 90% commercial risk protection. • Interest up to U.S. Treasury rate plus 1%.	Contract Value — Maximum Term Up to $50,000 — 2 years $50,000 to $100,000 — 3 $100,000 to $200,000 — 4 Over $200,000 — 5 (Exceptionally up to 7 years).	Varies from 1% to 6.5% of export receivable depending on term and nature of buyer.	
7. FCIA Combined Short-Term/Medium-Term Insurance Policy	• 100% political risk protection. • 90% commercial risk protection. • Interest up to prime rate minus 0.5% for short-term, U.S. Treasury rate plus 1% for medium-term sales.	Up to 270 days for inventory phase followed by up to three years for receivables financing (exceptionally five years).	Varies from 1.25% to 6.5% of export receivable depending on term and nature of buyer.	• None for short-term financing. • 15% when rolled over to medium-term.

Program	Coverage		Fees	Cash Payment
8. Eximbank Medium-Term Bank Guarantee Program	• 100% political risk protection. • For commercial risk, after the exporter retains a 10% participation, the financing bank assumes 5% or 15% participation and Eximbank covers the balance. • Interest up to U.S. Treasury rate plus 1%.	Same as FCIA Medium-Term Policy.	Same as FCIA Medium-Term Policy.	15% at shipment.
9. Eximbank Small Business Credit Program	The outstanding balance of the export loan.	Same as FCIA Medium-Term Policy.	Eximbank charges financial institution a one-time commitment fee at beginning of transaction of 0.15% to 0.75%, depending on term of loan.	15% at shipment.
10. Eximbank Medium-Term Credit Program	The outstanding balance of the export loan.	Same as FCIA Medium-Term Policy.	Same as Small Business Credit Program.	15% at shipment.
11. Eximbank Preliminary Commitment	Not applicable.	Not applicable.	None.	Not applicable.
12. Engineering Multiplier Program	• Loan for 85% of U.S. costs. • Financial guarantee for local costs up to 15% of the eligible U.S. costs.	Same as FCIA Medium-Term Policy.	Same as Eximbank Direct Loan and Financial Guarantee (see below).	15% prior to concurrently with disbursement of Eximbank loan.

FIGURE 6–6 (continued)

Program	Maximum Coverage	Maximum Repayment Period	Fees and Premiums	Minimum Buyer Cash Payment
13. Eximbank Direct Loan	Loan for up to 85% of U.S. costs.	Generally five to ten years beginning at delivery or start up.	Eximbank charges borrower a one-time fee of 2% of loan value and a 0.5% per annum commitment fee on the undisbursed balance.	15% prior to concurrently with disbursement of Eximbank loan.
14. Eximbank Financial Guarantee	• Guarantee for up to 85% of U.S. costs. • 100% political and commercial risk protection. • Interest up to the U.S. Treasury rate plus 1%.	Same as Eximbank Direct Loan.	Eximbank charges the lender a financial guarantee fee of 0.5% per annum on the outstanding balance and a commitment fee of 0.125% per annum on the undisbursed balance.	15% prior to or concurrently with disbursement of guaranteed loan.
15. Private Export Funding Corporation (PEFCO)	Loan for up to 85% of U.S. costs.	Usually five to ten years.	Eximbank charges PEFCO the fees indicated for a Financial Guarantee. PEFCO charges borrower a commitment fee of 0.5% per annum on the undisbursed balance.	15% prior to or concurrently with disbursement of PEFCO loan.

Program	Financing Characteristics	Special Features
1. Eximbank Working Capital Guarantee Program	• Guarantee is made with recourse to exporter. • The exporter must provide the lender with sufficient collateral so that the loan balance does not exceed 90% of the collateral value. • The guarantee can be either for a single export-related loan or for a revolving line of credit.	• May be combined with the Small Business Administration's Export Revolving Line of Credit (ERLC) Program. • Approved banks can commit Eximbank's guarantee on a discretionary basis by assuming a 15% risk participation.
2. FCIA New-To-Export Insurance Policy	• Policy proceeds are assignable for financing purposes. • Under special assignment, financial institutions are assured of repayment up to policy limits in event of default.	• Political risk only coverage also available. • Initially no annual commercial risk deductible required. • Maximum eligibility five years, with commercial risk protection dropping to 90% after two years.
3. FCIA Umbrella Insurance Policy	Same as FCIA New-to-Export Policy.	• Policy Administrator relieves exporter of administrative responsibilities by providing for all required reporting to/from FCIA, including premium payment. • No exporter commercial risk deductible or minimum annual premium required of exporters.

FIGURE 6–6 (continued)

Program	Financing Characteristics	Special Features
4. Bank Letter of Credit Policy	Policy applies only to irrevocable letters of credit issued by a foreign bank which has an approved issuing bank credit limit (IBCL).	• No annual commercial risk deductible. • Coverage available for refinancing of payments by insured bank under a sight irrevocable letter of credit. • Pre-presentation coverage available. • Coverage available for fixed and floating interest rates.
5. FCIA Multi-Buyer Policy	• Policy proceeds are assignable for financing purposes.	• Political risk only coverage is also available. • Reduced premium rate due to blanket policy and risk deductible requirements. • Exporter can insure most sales without clearing buyers through FCIA. • Short-term only and medium-term only coverages are available. • Deductible may be fixed for the policy year or vary with volume of sales.
6. FCIA Medium-Term Insurance Policy	• Policy proceeds are assignable for financing purposes. • Medium-term obligations are in the form of notes which usually carry a floating market rate of interest, paid at least semi-annually.	• Political risk only coverage also available. • No annual commercial risk deductible required. • Covers either single or repetitive sales to a single buyer. • 95% commercial risk protection for small businesses. • Special coverages are available for export finance leases and export operating leases of new or used equipment.

7. FCIA Combined Short-Term/Medium-Term Insurance Policy

- Dealers can purchase inventory for resale without making a cash payment for up to 270 days (360 days if no rollover to medium-term).
- Policy proceeds are assignable for financing purposes.
- Usually issued to cover a one-year revolving sales plan.
- No annual commercial risk deductible required.

8. Eximbank Medium-Term Bank Guarantee Program

- Except for specified exporter's commercial risk participation, the financing must be provided without recourse to the exporter.
- Medium-term obligations are in the form of notes which usually carry a floating market rate of interest, paid at least semi-annually.
- Political risk only coverage also available.
- Qualified banks can commit Eximbank's guarantee on a discretionary basis by assuming a 15% commercial risk participation.
- Small businesses retain only 5% commercial risk participation.
- Available for loans in selected foreign currencies.

9. Eximbank Small Business Credit Program

- The interest rate may be as mutually agreed but must not yield less than the following consensus rates: 10.95% for rich countries, 9.65% for intermediate countries, and 8.8% for poor countries (as of 1/15/86). Eximbank will lend or purchase the export loan with recourse to the commercial bank at 1% below the rate charged.
- The repayment risk on the foreign obligation is borne by the financial institution unless that obligation is also insured or guaranteed by Eximbank/FCIA.
- Maximum contract value is $2.5 million per transaction.
- Aggregate commitment cannot exceed $10 million per buyer, per year.

10. Eximbank Medium-Term Credit Program

- Same as Small Business Credit Program.
- The repayment risk on the foreign obligation is borne by the financial institution unless that obligation is also guaranteed or insured by Eximbank/FCIA.
- Maximum contract value is $10 million per transaction.

FIGURE 6–6 *(concluded)*

Program	Financing Characteristics	Special Features
11. Eximbank Preliminary Commitment	Enables borrower, exporter, and financial institution to establish terms of financing for more effective planning or marketing.	Generally valid for 180 days but may be renewed at discretion of Eximbank. Buyer must apply to Eximbank to convert a Preliminary Commitment to a loan or a Financial Guarantee.
12. Engineering Multiplier Program	• Eximbank's interest rates (as of 1/15/86) for two- to five-year loans are: 10.95% for rich countries, 9.65% for intermediate countries and 8.8% for poor countries. • If Eximbank finances final project, loan can be rolled over into long-term financial package.	• Contract amounts over $10 million eligible for Eximbank's Direct Loan and Financial Guarantee. • Available for negotiated contracts if foreign competition would be encountered if given the opportunity to bid.
13. Eximbank Direct Loan	Eximbank's interest rates for over five-year loans (as of 1/15/86) are as follows: 11.20% for rich countries, 10.15% for intermediate countries and 8.80% for poor countries. Special rates apply to commercial jet aircraft and nuclear power projects.	• If Eximbank loan is blended with commercial bank or PEFCO loan, Eximbank portion generally will apply to the later maturities.
14. Eximbank Financial Guarantee	Eximbank can blend its direct loan with its Financial Guarantee to provide a complete financing package. Guarantee may extend up to 85%, depending on the amount of Eximbank's loan, if any.	• Financial Guarantee also available for loans in selected foreign currencies. • Special coverages are available for export finance leases and export operating leases of new or used equipment.

488

15. Private Export Funding Corporation (PEFCO)

- PEFCO is often co-lender with commercial banks lending the earlier maturities, PEFCO the middle maturities and Eximbank financing the later maturities.
- Interest rate to borrower usually averages 1% to 2% over comparable U.S. Treasury rate.

Several different options are available to the applicant for determining when PEFCO's interest rate is set.

Source: Export-Import Bank of the United States.

489

confirming the creditworthiness of the buyer. A special buyer credit limit (SBCL) is available for larger amounts on application to FCIA.

Normally, FCIA covers 90 percent of a commercial loss and 100 percent of a political loss. For short-term transactions, this coverage applies to the gross invoice value. Medium-term sales require a minimum 15 percent cash payment by the buyer on or before delivery, so the coverage applies to the balance, or financed portion, of the transaction. The buyer's interest obligation is covered at a specified rate up to a limited time after the due date.

The Master Policy also has a deductible feature similar to that of major medical or other forms of insurance. This deductible applies only to commercial coverage on an annual cumulative basis. The deductible does not generally apply to political coverage since political risks are often unforeseen, and losses in this area should not penalize the exporter's full scope of coverage.

Certain agricultural commodities may be insured under this policy with terms extended to one year (if needed), with commercial coverage increased to 98 percent.

The Master Policy offers lower premiums, quicker credit decisions on the part of the exporter, faster service to foreign customers, and reduced paperwork.

Medium-Term Policy

The medium-term policy covers capital and quasi-capital goods primarily of U.S. manufacture sold in international trade on terms for six months to five years, and occasionally longer. The policy is written on a case-by-case basis. There is no requirement that the exporter insure all his medium-term transactions. The exporter may insure either a single or repetitive sale to a foreign customer.

What Is Covered?   FCIA medium-term policies cover credit sales in which the terms of repayment range between 181 days and five years after arrival of the goods at the port of importation. Policies can be tailored to accommodate three types of transactions:

1. Single sales—one-time transactions.
2. Repetitive sales—ongoing relationships, generally with a dealer or distributor.

3. Combination short-term/medium-term sales of capital equipment and related spare parts to dealers and distributors.

Under the terms of the policy, the foreign customer must make a 15 percent cash payment on or before delivery. The remaining financed portion is to be covered by a promissory note requiring payment in approximately equal installments on a monthly, quarterly, or semiannual basis.

What Types of Losses Are Covered?   The policies cover two types of loss: commercial and political. Commercial losses are those which can affect businesses anywhere, such as a buyer's insolvency or failure to pay an obligation within six months after the due date. Political losses can be caused by war, revolution, cancellation of import or export licenses, and currency inconvertibility. Normally, the policy covers 90 percent of commercial credit risk and 100 percent of political risks. Also covered are interest charges, as described earlier.

Combined Short-Term/Medium-Term Policy
A combination of short- and medium-term insurance is available, mainly to protect U.S. exporters in transactions with foreign dealers and distributors. The combination policy affords commercial and political risk protection in three areas:

1. Parts and accessories on terms up to 180 days.
2. Inventory financing, where the exporter may ship goods under a "floor plan" arrangement. Initial coverage is for up to 270 days with no down payment.
3. Receivables financing, with terms typically up to three years following the minimum cash payment on resale by the dealer or at the end of the inventory period.

In sum, commercial credit risks are covered to 90 percent and political risks to 100 percent under both the short- and medium-term portions of dealer sales. However, before policy conversion to medium term is effective, the normal 15 percent cash payment must be received, with FCIA coverage available for the financed portion, including interest as described earlier.

The Single Sale Policy

Exporters can insure single sales with a foreign customer by submitting an application, complete with appropriate information on the buyer to support the request. In general, requests for coverage on amounts below $100,000 require two current favorable credit reports from such sources as Dun & Bradstreet International, World Traders Data Reports (WTDRs) from the U.S. Department of Commerce, reports from a domestic or foreign bank, or other domestic or foreign credit agency reports. On requests above $100,000, financial statements on the foreign customer will also be required—in some cases for the past two or three years.

FCIA issues a commitment notice on the transaction stating the parameters of coverage, including their limit of liability for the transaction, the amount and schedule of repayment terms, the premium rate, the policy period, and any special conditions required.

Although the single sale policy covers only one specific transaction with a particular buyer, more than one shipment can be made in order to complete the transaction. Promissory notes for the financed portion must be executed with repayment of principal and interest made in equal monthly, quarterly, or semiannual installments.

Repetitive Sales Policy

An exporter can submit an application for coverage of a transaction with a particular buyer containing the same information as detailed above. However, in place of a commitment notice, FCIA issues a policy with a transaction endorsement stating the parameters of coverage.

The same cash down payment and promissory note requirements apply. However, this policy carries a final shipment date, usually one year from the effective date of the policy. Following shipment, the exporter submits a monthly shipment report form, accompanied by the appropriate premium check, stating the shipments made during the prior month.

Although both the medium-term and combination policies are offered by FCIA on a single buyer basis, exporters should consider the advantages of insuring all shipments of capital goods under a single Master Policy. This approach will lower the average premium rate and curtail much of the paperwork by providing a discretionary credit limit under the policy for most medium-term transactions.

Coverage for the Services Industry

FCIA offers export credit insurance to cover sales of services (U.S. expertise and technology) to foreign customers. FCIA developed this program to encourage U.S. companies to expand their foreign business during a period when there is a very strong overseas demand for goods and services.

Industries benefiting from this coverage include management consultants, engineering service firms, transportation companies, and other firms offering the services of U.S. based personnel to foreign customers with repayment being made in U.S. dollars in the United States.

Up to now, service exports have generally been done on a restrictive credit basis. FCIA offers coverage to companies willing to extend prudent terms to gain a greater share of the services market. It protects a company performing a contracted service against failure of its customers to make agreed on payments because of unforseen commercial or political reasons.

Services Covered. It covers services performed by U.S.-based personnel or U.S. personnel temporarily assigned in a host country, and paid for in U.S. dollars. It can be tailored to the needs of any U.S. company performing services and receiving progress payments at regular intervals ranging from payment on receipt of invoice to payment at 180 days after the invoice date.

Coverage. FCIA indemnifies a company for 90 percent of an insured obligation in the event of a commercial loss, and for 100 percent coverage on political loss. In addition to the 10 percent retention on commercial losses, service policies also contain a first loss deductible for commercial losses. The deductible is applied to the cumulative amount of commercial losses which relate to transactions attributable to a given policy year.

It determines its premium charges for the Services Industry Program primarily from the terms of repayment being offered by the company, although the total volume to be insured and the

service exporter's past experience are also considered. The longer
the terms of repayment, the higher the premium rate will be.
Premium generally involves a composite rate for all projects to be
insured during a policy year. At the beginning of each policy year,
an advance minimum premium of $2,000 is required.

Expanded Programs for Banks

To keep pace with the ever-increasing role financial institutions
play in expanding U.S. exports, FCIA offers several programs to
suit the particular needs of U.S. commercial banks. Edge Act
corporations, U.S. subsidiaries, and agencies of foreign banks can
also become insureds under FCIA policies. FCIA bank programs
offer insurance protection against potential default by foreign
customers, banks, and sovereignties for either commercial or
political reasons, giving the bank needed risk coverage in expanding export related business. Banks can profit from this increased
marketing and leveraging flexibility by:

- Participating in irrevocable letter of credit sales.
- Extending credit lines directly to foreign companies to
  finance purchases of U.S. goods.
- Providing financing or guarantees to a U.S. exporter on the
  firm's overseas receivables portfolio.

Under a short-term policy, a bank may receive discretionary
authority up to $500,000 depending on experience and need.
Coverage may vary from 70 to 90 percent commercial and 100
percent political, with a deductible feature based on FCIA's
experience with the bank. A specified retention may be shared with
the exporter.

In mid-1985 Eximbank issued a new bank credit insurance
program for banks which allows for coverage of transactions under
letters of credit. Banks that have run up against country limitations
can use the policy to insure their exposure, and therefore increase
their capacity in a given market. Eximbank or FCIA must give
prior approval to each transaction, but coverage is 95 percent for
most transactions, 98 percent for agricultural commodities, and 100
percent for soveriegn obligations. The following outlines some of
the terms and conditions of cover:

Sovereign

100 percent cover
Interest cover: P − 1/2 percent
Default—60 day waiting period before claim filing
Cover commences at commitment
No DCL

Bank-to-Bank*

Old Policy	New Policy
90/100 percent cover 98/100 percent Bulk AG	95 percent cover/98 percent Bulk AG
Interest cover: T +1 percent	Interest cover: P −½ percent
Passback—1/2 of retention	Passback—all of retention
Commercial default—180 days waiting period before claim filing	Commercial default—60 day waiting period before claim filing
DCL (maximum $500,000)	No deductible
Cover commences at shipment	No DCL
	Up to 360 days

* Covers all types of transactions, including open account/drafts—old policy; covering just L/Cs and sovereign L/Cs, straight coverage—new policy.

Financial Institution Buyer Credit Policy. Financial institutions can reduce their risks on a direct buyer credit loan or a reimbursement loan made to a foreign customer for the financing of U.S. exports through this policy, otherwise called the Buyer Credit Policy.

A direct buyer credit loan is a loan extended to a foreign entity by a financial institution for the importation of U.S. manufactured or produced goods. A reimbursement loan is the financial institution's reimbursement of a buyer's payments to the U.S. supplier. In both cases, repayment of the loan is based on a buyer's obligation to the financial institution. This policy affords coverage against commercial defaults and political events which result in nonpayment under a buyer obligation.

What Percentages of Cover Is Offered under This Policy? This policy provides coverage against specified political risks such as war, revolution, expropriation or confiscation by a government authority, cancellation of import or export licenses and foreign exchange inconvertibility, and commercial losses due to protracted default, insolvency of the buyer, or failure to reimburse for other reasons. Coverage is underwritten for three classes of buyers:

Class I Sovereign obligors or guarantors; political-only transactions, as determined by FCIA.

Class II Nonsovereign public sector obligors or guarantors, as determined by FCIA.

Class III Private sector obligors or guarantors.

The policy is issued in one or two formats depending on the class of obligor and type of coverage: a documentary policy for comprehensive coverage (Class I and II) and all political-only transactions, and a nondocumentary policy for comprehensive coverage (Class III). The documentary format requires the financial institution to obtain specific documents such as a signed buyer obligation, transport document, invoice, and an exporter certificate (certifying, among other things, that a buyer obligation has been established, and that the goods are manufactured or produced in and shipped from the United States). If the beneficiary of the funding is foreign, additional certificates may be required. Having obtained documents which on their face satisfy the policy requirements, the insured financial institution can be assured that defects in the underlying commercial transaction will not cause claim denial.

Under the documentary format, the principal risk assumed is the uninsured retention (if any). Under the nondocumentary format, the financial institution remains at risk for not only the uninsured retention, but also certain events, such as fraud in the transaction, nonshipment of products, dispute in the transaction or the discovery of non-U.S. goods.

Both policy formats offer equalized coverage for commercial and political risks (comprehensive cover). Political-only coverage is available under the documentary format. Maximum percentages of cover are indicated below:

	Documentary Format*	Nondocumentary Format†
Sovereign obligors or guarantors	100%	n.a.
Nonsovereign obligors or guarantors	90	90%
Approved agricultural commodities	98	98
Letter of credit transactions	Excluded	Excluded

n.a. = Not applicable.
* Class I, II, and all political-only transactions.
† Class III comprehensive.

What is covered under the policy? Coverage applies to credit terms extended, under a direct loan or reimbursement agreement, to a foreign customer named in the policy declarations for any goods produced and shipped for the United States during the policy period. The maximum period between the date of shipment and the date of the buyer obligation will generally be 45 days. Cover is typically provided for credit terms up to 180 days for consumer items, parts, and raw materials. On a case-by-case basis, agricultural commodities, capital equipment, and quasi-capital equipment may be insured on terms up to 360 days. Products which are less than 50 percent U.S. content and certain defense products are not eligible for cover. Principal amounts are covered up to the maximum insured percentages stated above or specified in the policy declarations.

Documented interest is covered at the applicable rate for the approved currency specified in the policy up to a maximum of 180 days after the due date.

Is there a risk retention factor to the insured? The insured may pass back the uninsured portion to a third party only under the documentary format. The insured must stay at risk for the uninsured percentage under the nondocumentary format. There is no first loss deductible provision in either format of the policy.

Are there any other obligations of the insured? The insured agrees with the insurer to:

• Pay the minimum premium in full before the policy is issued.

- Report and pay premium on insured funding on or before the last business day of the month in which the funding occurred.
- Not enter into any transaction with a buyer who is insolvent or has any debts payable to the insured which are 90 days or more past due.
- Report to FCIA, in writing, if the buyer has not paid any amount for 90 days after it was due.
- Do everything reasonable to collect from the buyer any amounts owing on the due date.
- Obtain FCIA's prior written approval for rescheduling any insured transaction.
- Cooperate with the insurers to effect recoveries.

What are the premiums and how are they determined? A risk-based pricing system is utilized. A disciplined formula provides a premium rate that reflects the major elements of each transaction. The pricing system does not provide for published rates; financial institutions or insurance brokers may obtain a nonbinding rate indication by contacting FCIA's Buyer Underwriting Department with the specifics of the contemplated transaction. Changing conditions may result in a different rate being finally offered than is initially indicated.

Premium is paid on the total principal volume amount to be insured. The premium rate is paid per $100 of invoice value. The following minimum premium rates apply:

Class I and political-only transactions	$ 2,500
Class II	$ 5,000
Class III	$10,000

Umbrella Policy. Eximbank's Umbrella Policy, offered through its agent, FCIA, enables state and local government agencies, banks, export trading companies, freight forwarders, and other financial and professional organizations to become administrators of short-term credit risk insurance covering the export sales of numerous exporters. These administrators assume responsibility for collecting premiums, reporting shipments, filling out forms and processing claims on behalf of the exporters insured under their Umbrella Policy.

The Umbrella Policy gives new exporters greater access to foreign credit risk protection and lessens their paperwork burdens. It also helps exporters get financing because the policy proceeds are assignable to any financial institution as collateral on a hold harmless basis.

Administrators of Umbrella Policies benefit as well. The policy enables them to offer an important service to their small- and medium-size business customers.

Here are answers to questions most frequently asked about the Umbrella Policy:

What coverage does an Umbrella Policy provide? The policy covers the exporter against a foreign customer's failure to pay for goods or services for political or commercial reasons. If the buyer does not pay because of war, revolution, expropriation of business, cancellation of import licenses or currency inconvertibility, the loss is considered political and 100 percent of it is covered. If the buyer does not pay for commercial reasons such as insolvency, the policy provides coverage for 90 percent of the loss and the exporter retains 10 percent of the risk. No deductible is required. (Certain agricultural exports qualify for 98 percent commercial risk coverage and 100 percent political risk coverage.)

What are the premiums for an Umbrella Policy? Premiums are calculated from the FCIA "new-to-export" rate table and paid by the administrator to FCIA. The administrator may recoup these premiums, including the minimum annual payment of $500, from fees agreed to by the administrator and covered exporters. The fees need not be the same as the FCIA premiums.

Credit limits must be approved by FCIA on each export credit transaction, and there is no maximum transaction size. Neither the administrator nor the covered exporter may commit FCIA to insuring any export transaction without prior FCIA approval.

Maximum credit extension term. The policy covers shipments up to 180 days from arrival at port of importation. Certain products qualify for 360 day terms (certain bulk agricultural products).

All shipments. An exporter must cover all its export shipments unless ineligible under the policy or sold for cash or on confirmed irrevocable letter of credit terms.

Policy Period is 12 months.

What exporters are eligible for coverage under the policy?

Any manufacturing, service, or trading firm is eligible that has had annual export sales averaging $2.0 million or less in the preceding two years (not including goods sold on a cash basis or with a confirmed irrevocable letter of credit) and has not been insured by FCIA during that time.

What are the responsibilities of the administrator of the policy? The administrator of the policy agrees to submit to FCIA:

- Applications for approval of exporters and foreign customers.
- Monthly reports of exporter shipments, overdue payments, and buyers in financial difficulty.
- Premium payments.
- Claim forms in the event that a buyer does not pay.

The administrator does not have responsibility for the underlying export transactions or for determining the creditworthiness of exporters or buyers. FCIA reviews each exporter and buyer for approval.

What organizations are eligible to become policy administrators? Eligible organizations include:

- Financial institutions, such as commercial and savings banks, commercial finance companies, small business investment companies.
- Export companies, such as export trading companies, export management companies, export financing cooperatives.
- Service firms, such as insurance brokers, accounting firms.
- Trade organizations, such as chambers of commerce, industry trade organizations, other business or professional groups with a staff capable of administering a policy.
- Government entitites, such as state export finance or development agencies.

Can administrators hold FCIA policies of their own? Yes, administrators may hold other FCIA policies for their own account in addition to the Umbrella Policy for other exporters.

What is the cost of being an Umbrella Policy administrator? Administrators make an annual premium payment of $500 which is applied to the actual premium costs of insuring exporter shipments.

What fees can the policy administrators charge for the duties they perform? Eximbank does not limit the fees, if any, administrators charge their insured exporter customers.

What are the other important policy terms? The usual term for covered shipments will be up to 180 days from arrival of the goods at the port of importation. Certain goods qualify for 360 day terms. Any exporter insured under an Umbrella Policy must cover all eligible shipments under that policy unless they are sold for cash or confirmed irrevocable letter of credit.

Short Term/Case-by-Case Program

In the latter part of October 1986, FCIA announced a new insurance program called the Short Term/Case-by-Case Program. The new program is aimed at offering insurance on short-term transactions on a case-by-case or "one-off" basis (**Note:** FCIA up to this point in time was only willing to insure short-term transactions on a whole turnover basis, i.e., all eligible export credit sales to foreign customers, irrespective of the size of the transaction). The new program is a new source of insurance for short-term transactions which provides much needed insuring capacity for many foreign countries who have otherwise been difficult to insure with private-sector insurers.

What this new program means is that your company can now obtain from FCIA/Eximbank a policy of insurance to cover selected short-term transactions provided such transactions meet FCIA's basic eligibility guidelines i.e., insured products must be made in and shipped from the United States, your foreign customer(s) must be deemed creditworthy for the amount and terms, the insured products can contain foreign content, but not in excess of 50 percent exclusive of price mark-up and, lastly, credit terms generally can be up to, but not in excess of, 180 days from date of arrival at port of importation, except for agricultural commodities and quasi-capital equipment which can be up to 360 days.

FCIA will have no standard rate schedule for such transactions. Rather, FCIA is prepared to quote a premium rate solely on the basis of their analysis and perception of the risk, i.e., the country in which the buyer is domiciled, the creditworthiness of the buyer and/or the buyer's country and the proposed credit terms.

Although premium rates will be quoted on a case-by-case basis, there will be a minimum premium requirement as follows:

- $2,500 minimum premium for sovereign buyers (class I).
- $5,000 minimum premium for class II (nonsovereign public buyers, and private buyers able to provide a suitable bank guarantee).
- $10,000 minimum premium for private buyers.

FCIA will provide a verbal nonbinding indication of a premium rate on prospective transactions; however, as precondition to issuing a written commitment, they will require the submission of a formal application. These applications can be supplied by FCIA or credit insurance brokers on request, including specimen policies.

Multibuyer Insurance Policy
This policy is one of the most advanced policies FCIA is offering. It permits the insured to select a percentage of cover from two options, increasing or decreasing coverages to suit its particular circumstances and needs.

What options are offered for percentages of cover? All options afford coverage against different categories of risk, but the degree of coverage and amount of deductibles vary. The categories of risk include losses caused by events such as war, revolution, seizure of goods, revocation of licenses, foreign exchange inconvertibility, insolvency, and protracted default.

Option A: Split coverage, with deductible. Provides 100 percent coverage against loss due to specified political events and 90 percent coverage against loss due to most commercial events, with a deductible amount applying only to commercial risk losses.

Option B: Equalized coverage, with deductible. Insures against 95 percent of loss due to any insured event, either political or commercial, and a deductible applies to any loss. Receivables from sovereign obligors are 100 percent insured without application of a deductible.

Insured Percentage of Coverage Options

	Option A Split Coverage (deductible applies to commercial risks only)		Option B Equalized Coverage (deductible)
	Risk 1, 2, 3, 5 Political	Risk 4 Commercial	All Risks 1 through 5
Sovereign obligors	100%	100%	100%
Bulk agricultural transactions	100	98	98
Letters of credit	100	90	95
Medium term	100	90	90
All other	100	90	95

For an additional premium, the insured may elect Preshipment Coverage, which is valuable in cases where goods are special ordered, or there is a long manufacturing run prior to shipment.

What is covered? Coverage applies to credit sales for any goods produced and shipped from the United States during the policy period. Receivables for products which are less than 50 percent U.S. content and certain defense products are not eligible for cover. Services can also be included. A valid written obligation (such as a written purchase order) from the foreign customer is required.

Principal amounts are covered up to the percentages shown in the options chart—those percentages depending on the options selected by the exporter.

Documented interest is also covered up to rates specified in the interest coverage endorsement of the policy. It is fully covered up to 180 days after the due date (or fewer days when the claim is settled earlier).

Coverage of documented post-maturity interest is limited to the lesser of:

• The rate specified in the obligation.
• The rate legally valid in the buyer's country.

- The rate below applicable to the approved currency designated in the sales contract:

U.S. dollars; *The Wall Street Journal,* New York, published prime rate minus 0.5 percent.

Swiss francs, French franc, West German deutsche marks, U.K. pounds sterling, Canadian dollars and Japanese yen; the six month Euro offered rate plus 0.5 percent.

What credit terms are covered to foreign debtors? The terms that may be extended are up to: 180 days for consumer items, parts, and raw materials; 360 days for agricultural commodities and industrial and commercial products; for insureds with medium-term coverage, the terms that may be extended are up to five years (sometimes longer) for certain capital equipment.

What is the deductible amount? A deductible applies per policy year and is negotiated separately with each insured.

Are there any credit limit limitations? There are two types of credit limits: the first is the discretionary credit limit. It permits the insured to extend insured credit without the prior approval of FCIA subject to several conditions contained in the terms and conditions of the policy. The second type of limit is the Special Buyer Credit Limit (SBCL). Insured must apply for these limits to FCIA, typically when the discretionary credit limit is too low or constrained by the country limitation schedule.

What is the premium rate for this policy? Premium rates are based on many factors including length of terms offered, debtor type, spread of country risk, transaction type, and previous export collection experience. A minimum annual premium of $500 is paid for each policy period. An advance premium equal to one month's estimated premium is collected on issuing the policy.

Comprehensive Insurance Policy for Financing or Operation Leases

Companies engaged in leasing products of U.S. origin outside the United States can reduce their risks by insuring both their stream of lease payments and the fair market value of the leased product themselves through lease policies underwritten by FCIA. The policy covers the insured against both commercial and political risks. Coverage is available for a cross-border lease (a lease in which the lessor and lessee are in two different countries) or an international lease (a lease in which both the lessor and lessee are in the same country, other than the United States). For additional information concerning leasing, refer to Chapter 8.

FCIA offers two credit insurance policies for the leasing industry: an Operating Lease Policy and a Financing Lease Policy. Each one provides a unique system of coverage which is described below. It is important to note that the terms *operating lease* and *financing lease* are used by FCIA as descriptive titles for the purposes of the policies only. Definitions of an operating lease, true lease, financing or full payout lease vary depending on whether one is speaking in the context of accounting, taxes, commercial law, or international trade. These definitions do not determine one's choice between the two FCIA policies. The choice of the Operating Lease or Financing Lease policies is solely the lessor's and is based on its evaluation of which coverage structure best fits the specific transaction.

How does FCIA define an eligible lessor? An eligible lessor is defined as any leasing company, manufacturer, bank, trust, partnership or other entity, foreign or domestic, that leases or participates in the financing of leases of U.S. manufactured equipment and related services outside the United States.

What transactions are eligible for coverage? Lease coverage can apply to new or used equipment and related services. Generally, no more than 10 percent of the value of the leased products, exclusive of price mark-up, may consist of labor, raw materials, component parts or any combination thereof originating or manufactured outside the United States. The transaction must be subject to a lease agreement between the lessee and lessor, which is valid and enforceable in the lessee's country at the time it is executed by both parties. Additionally, the lease agreement must contain certain specific obligations of the lessee which are set forth in the policies themselves.

Operating Lease Policy. Coverage for operating leases was designed around the general concept of a lease transaction in which:

- Payments total less than full value of the leased product.
- There is residual value of the leased product.
- There is usually an intention of the lessor to repossess that residual and release, sell, or otherwise dispose of it.
- The lessor keeps the risk that the residual will decline in market value at a greater rate than expected.

The Operating Lease Policy divides coverage into two distinct parts which may be purchased together, or separately:

1. Coverage for Stream of Payments (Policy Risks 1, 2, 3, and 4): The policy provides coverage for the stream of payments which fall due during a repossession efforts period after default of the lessee. This part of the overall coverage is intended to maintain the insured's stream of payments while action is taken to repossess the leased products. Although the length of the repossession efforts period is underwritten on a case-by-case basis, it will generally extend to cover both periodic and nonperiodic payments which fall due during a maximum period of five months after the default.
   Coverage for the stream of payments is usually provided at 100 percent for sovereign lessees and 90 percent for all others.
2. Coverage against Government Prevention of Repossession (Policy Risk 5): As a second part of coverage, FCIA will insure the political risk of prevention of repossession of the leased product due to specific government actions including, but not limited to, expropriation, confiscation, and cancellation of export licenses. This coverage comes into effect only after the end of the repossession efforts period. It is limited to the fair market value of the leased product at the time of claim.

Premium for the two parts of the coverage are paid separately, thus allowing the insured to request the amounts of coverage deemed appropriate.

Finance Lease Policy. This policy was designed around the concept of a lease where there is generally little residual value remaining in the leased product, the ownership of which is transferred to the lessee at the end of the lease. Accordingly, FCIA views the structure as similar to a medium-term sale transaction and requires a 15 percent advance payment from the lessee to the lessor on or before delivery of the leased products. Although the advance payment may be financed, it may not be financed by the insured or by a financial institution which requires any share of the leased products as security against the loan. FCIA will only insure the remaining 85 percent of the lease transaction.

Should the lessee default, coverage is provided for the insured percentage of each lease payment as it falls due until the end of the lease term. Coverage is usually provided at 100 percent for all others. Defaults are covered not only for commercial risks, but also political risks including expropriation. At the time of claim payment, the insured is obligated to transfer to FCIA all remaining obligations of the lease as well as title to the leased products. Although the policy requires that the policyholder make an effort to repossess the leased products, the coverage of lease payments as they become due remains effective regardless of FCIA's own subsequent repossession of a leased product which has lost its market value.

There is no first loss deductible provision in the policy; however, the policyholder must stay at risk for the amount exceeding the insured percentage of coverage specified in the policy declarations.

The premium rate is determined by the length of the lease and the type of lessee (sovereign, nonsovereign public sector or private-sector) and is payable per $100 of the credit limit. Due to the different structures of the policies and the application of the limits concepts to the operating coverage, premium for a single transaction could greatly vary depending on the policy chosen. One should therefore carefully study the premium schedules when considering the policy most suited to the transaction.

FCIA's Small- and Medium-Size Business Programs

For small- and medium-sized businesses, successful exporting often depends on finding financing for themselves and their foreign customers. These companies face several challenges in financing their exports. First, they need working capital to market and produce goods and services for export. Second, they need to convince commercial lenders to extend the credit their foreign customers need to buy their goods. Many potential buyers cannot buy without a deferred (extended credit terms) payment plan.

Eximbank offers four programs that are especially helpful to small- and medium-sized businesses and to those who are new to exporting. A brief description of these programs follows.

Working Capital Guarantee Program. Eximbank designed the Working Capital Guarantee Program to help exporters get financing for their own pre-export activities. It is intended to help creditworthy exporters when they cannot secure working capital any other way.

How it works: The program works by guaranteeing a private lender that, if the exporter defaults, Eximbank will repay 90 percent of the outstanding loan. By reducing the lender's risks, Eximbank provides incentives for the lender to finance these essential working capital activities.

Eligible transactions: The Working Capital Guarantee may be used to support production for a specific transaction or as a revolving line of credit to support marketing, inventory, and production activities for potential export sales.

Requirements and fees: The loan term will generally range from one month to one year, but can be longer. Eximbank requires that the loan not exceed 90 percent of the collateral required to secure the loan.

Eximbank's guarantee will cover 90 percent of the principal amount of the loan and will cover interest up to the lesser of the stated rate of the loan or 1 percent above the U.S. Treasury borrowing rate for comparable maturities up to the date of claim payment. The lender will be at risk for 10 percent of the principal amount of the loan, interest in excess of the guarantied rate, and later interest, if any.

Eximbank charges a one-time, up-front guarantee fee calculated against the term of the loan. For loans with a maturity of up to 180 days, the fee is 1 percent. For loans with longer maturities, 0.5 percent is added for each additional six-month period or portion thereof.

Coordination with SBA loans: If an exporter qualifies as a small business, his bank may request a guarantee for loans up to

$1.0 million under the Small Business Administration's Export Revolving Line of Credit (ERCL) Program. Eximbank participates in the ERCL program by guarantying half of such loans in excess of $200,000. The ERLC Program has a different fee and interest rate structure from Eximbank's Working Capital Guarantee Program.

Answers to some questions concerning this program:

1. What businesses are eligible for the Working Capital Guarantee Program?

The program was specifically developed to promote exports by small, medium-size, minority, and agricultural concerns. It may, however, be used to cover working capital loans made to any U.S. business as long as the lender certifies that the guaranty is essential for the loan to go forward and Eximbank determines that the exporter is creditworthy.

2. Which lenders can apply for Eximbank's Guarantee?

Any bank or provider of private credit is eligible for the program as long as Eximbank determines that the lender has the ability and resources to service the loans.

3. Does the guarantee apply to revolving lines of credit?

Yes, the program guaranties loans for revolving credit lines as well as loans for specific transactions.

4. What are acceptable uses of the loan proceeds?

Loan funds may be used to purchase materials, products, services, and labor for production of goods or services for current or future export sales. Loan funds may also be used for foreign business development such as marketing activities, trade fair participation, or other promotional activities. The guarantee is meant to foster additional export sales and will not cover loans used to pay existing debts.

5. What are the terms and conditions of the loan?

The term of the loan is generally up to 12 months and may be extended. Because Eximbank's intent is to facilitate exports that would not have occurred otherwise, the lender must certify that the loan would not be made without Eximbank's guarantee. Eximbank does not impose any interest rate ceilings or limits on fees the lender may charge. It expects, however, that pricing will reflect the fact that most risks are covered by an agency of the U.S. government.

6. *How much of the loan is covered by the guarantee?*
Eximbank guaranties 90 percent of the principal amount of the loan as well as interest, up to the date of claim payment. Interest covered is at the stated rate on the loan or 1 percent above the U.S. Treasury borrowing rate for comparable maturities, whichever is lower. The lender retains the risk on the remaining 10 percent of the loan and any interest above the guarantied rate.

7. *What are the collateral requirements?*
Eximbank requires that the loan balance not exceed 90 percent of the collateral value. Acceptable collateral includes goods and services purchased with the proceeds of the guarantied loan as well as accounts receivable resulting from transactions generated by the loan. Other types of collateral will also be considered.

8. *What fees does Eximbank charge for the guarantee?*
The fee depends on the length and amount of the loan. If the guarantee period is six months or less, the fee is 1.0 percent of the loan amount. For periods of over six months to one year, the fee is 1.5 percent of the loan amount. For loans with longer maturities, 0.5 percent is added for each additional six-month period or portion thereof.

9. *Who is protected by the Working Capital Guarantee?*
The program protects the lender against default by the exporter. It does not protect the exporter against default by foreign customers. For this reason, exporters and their lenders should determine whether they need credit risk protection on foreign receivables.

Export Credit Insurance. This policy's coverage is very similar to the coverage under various policies mentioned above in that the policies are not limited to only large exporters. It covers 90 percent or more of commercial risks and 100 percent of political risks. To cover these risks, export credit insurance policies are sold and serviced by the FCIA.

How it works: If the foreign customer defaults for political or commercial reasons, FCIA will repay most or all of the outstanding debt. Policies are available to cover a single buyer for medium-term sales. Multibuyer policies cover numerous short-term transactions during a 12-month policy period. Master policies can be designed to cover short- and medium-term sales. Special cover is available for sales through dealers and distributors, sales on consignment, costs incurred prior to shipment, or nonacceptance of the shipped product.

FCIA policies offer considerable protection, but they do not make exporting completely risk free. The exporter is expected to exercise good credit judgment and to assume a portion of the commercial risk.

Eligible exports: FCIA policies can support credit sales of goods and services sold on short term (up to 180 days) or medium term (181 days to 5 years). Typically short-term sales include consumables, raw materials, commodities, spare parts, and small manufactured items. Medium-term insurance covers goods such as automobiles, trucks, and equipment for aviation, construction, agriculture, processing, and communications. Credit sales of contract services, planning, and feasibility studies are eligible for FCIA policies.

The New-to-Export Policy. Companies just beginning to export, or with only limited volume, can take advantage of FCIA's New-to-Export Policy. Although patterned after the Master Policy, the New-to-Export Policy gives added commercial risk protection of 95 percent, with no deductible, in order to further cushion any potential losses during the first two years of a policy's life. The regular Master Policy commercial loss percentages and deductible provisions are added to the New-to-Export Policy in the third, fourth, and fifth years of coverage.

To be eligible for a New-to-Export Policy, companies should meet the following criteria:

- Satisfactory references from Dun & Bradstreet, two suppliers, and a commercial bank.
- Signed financial statements or annual report for at least the latest fiscal year, or start-up statements which reveal a positive net worth.
- Average annual export sales (together with affiliates) during the preceding two fiscal years not exceeding $750,000 exclusive of sales made on terms of confirmed irrevocable letters

of credit or cash in advance. If the preceding fiscal year was the firm's first year of exporting, sales may not exceed $1,000,000.

• No prior direct FCIA average for two years preceding date of application.

Umbrella Policy.   As already previously mentioned, the Umbrella Policy is available to small- to medium-size exporters. To qualify, any business with export sales averaging no more than $2.0 million a year in the preceding two years (not including goods sold for cash or with a confirmed irrevocable letter of credit) and that has had no direct FCIA insurance during that time is eligible for coverage.

Commercial Bank Guarantees.   Commercial banks are sometimes unwilling to make loans to foreign purchasers of U.S. products because of the risks of nonpayment. Eximbank's Commercial Bank Guarantee encourages commercial banks to make these loans by reducing the banks' risks.

How they work: Eximbank guarantees repayment of the outstanding loan if the buyer defaults. Eximbank's guarantee covers 100 percent of the political risks of nonpayment on the financed portion. The exporter and applicant bank each retain at least 5 percent of the commercial risk of the financed portion with Eximbank guaranteeing the balance. In cases where the applicant bank uses its discretionary authority to commit Eximbank, it must assume 15 percent of the commercial risk.

Eligible exports: This program can be used to guarantee sales of U.S. capital equipment and services such as automobiles, trucks, general aviation equipment, construction equipment, agricultural equipment, processing and communications equipment, and planning and feasibility studies.

Requirements: The buyer and the buyer's country must be acceptable to the financial institution and to Eximbank. Coverage is currently available for more than 140 countries.

Eximbank does not specify the rate of interest to be charged, but does guarantee interest up to the lower of either the rate on the note or 1 percent above the rate of interest for U.S. Treasury borrowings with comparable maturities. In the event of a claim, Eximbank pays interest accrued to the date of claim payment.

Eximbank has entered into master guarantee agreements with hundreds of U.S. banks. As the bank prepares an export loan that it wishes Eximbank to guarantee, it files a supplementary application to Eximbank under the master guarantee agreement. When a bank has completed a number of satisfactory guarantied export transactions, Eximbank will consider extending delegated authority, subject to prescribed conditions, enabling the bank to commit Eximbank to guarantee specific transactions without prior Eximbank approval.

Small Business Credit Program. In addition to the risks that the foreign obligor will not repay an export loan, a commercial bank providing export financing faces the risk that its cost of money will rise before the loan is repaid. For this reason, banks generally prefer to extend floating rate loans. Foreign purchasers, however, are frequently unwilling to accept fluctuating interest rate risk in addition to a foreign exchange risk they bear on foreign currency loans.

Eximbank's small business credit program enables U.S. banks to offer medium-term, fixed-rate export loans to finance sales of small U.S. businesses' products. Interest rates are fixed at the lowest rate permitted under the export credit guidelines followed by members of the Organization for Economic Cooperation and Development (OECD). The OECD rates are reviewed every six months and adjusted as necessary to reflect changes in prevailing interest rates.

How it works: This program enables the commercial bank to borrow from Eximbank at 1 percent below the rate on the export loan. The bank must receive an advance commitment from Eximbank for coverage of an individual loan under this program. Once the commitment is received, the bank can request disbursement from Eximbank and will probably do so when its alternative cost of funds exceeds Eximbank's committed discount loan rate. The bank may draw on the discount loan only once for each commitment and only after shipment has gone forward. Multiple disbursements may be made to accommodate multiple shipments. The loan may be repaid at any time without penalty.

Eligible exports: This program is used to support sales of goods and services customarily sold on credit terms of one to five years, such as automobiles, trucks, construction equipment, and feasibility studies. The maximum value of any single contract is $2.5 million and the aggregate limit per buyer is $10 million.

Requirements: The exporter must be a small business as defined by the Small Business Administration. Eximbank requires that the purchaser make a minimum 15 percent cash payment. The bank loan covers up to 85 percent of the export contract, on terms ranging from 365 days to five years. At the time of commitment, the interest rate is fixed according to the classification of the country to which the export is shipped.

EXIMBANK'S PROGRAMS AND GUARANTEES

Direct Loan Program
Eximbank enables U.S. exporters to compete for multi-million dollar export contracts for heavy capital equipment exports and major construction by offering long-term direct credits to foreign purchasers and financial guaranties providing repayment protection for commercial lenders (previously mentioned). As a point of clarification, normally the direct loan program applies only to project type financing, while the financing of goods is done through the medium-term program.

The bank's long-term financing can be either a direct credit to a public or private foreign customer. Or, it can be a financial guaranty assuring repayment of a private credit. These two forms of support are often combined into a single financing package.

Terms and costs: The bank's loans are issued in U.S. dollars, and principal plus interest must be repaid in dollars. It combines its lending with that of funds from private sources to meet a borrower's needs. It often finances the later maturities of the total package. This enables the private lender to repay sooner. This is of particular benefit to the borrower because it can repay at the market rate of the loan to the bank first, and it has a fixed-rate loan from Eximbank for the long term.

- Terms—the exact term is usually determined by the nature of the project, the dollar volume of the deal, the life of the goods, the OECD arrangements governing maximum interest rates, duration, and the terms, if any, offered by other government-sponsored and supported export credit schemes. Repayment is usually made in semiannual installments beginning six months after delivery of the goods or start-up of operation for project-related facilities. Repayment terms normally range between five to ten years. However, Eximbank will grant longer terms to enable U.S. exporters to meet foreign government-supported export credit schemes.

* Amounts financed—Eximbank has no set limit on the minimum size of a direct loan. It does however prefer transactions of $5 million or more. Smaller deals are usually relegated to other programs (i.e., Medium-Term Credit, guaranties, or FCIA insurance). The amount loaned by the bank is determined by the cost of the U.S. exporter's goods and services being exported, the extent of private participation in the loan, and the buyer's cash payment or downpayment. Other factors are Eximbank's credit exposure in the country of the foreign customer and project, commercial credit exposure with the foreign customer, and overall experience.

The bank will issue loans in fixed amounts and deals with price-escalation provisions.

* Percentage covered—The bank limits its direct loans to 65 percent of the U.S. export value and requires the foreign customer to make a cash down payment of at least 15 percent. The remaining 20 percent of the financing is usually provided by the exporter or by commercial banks directly to the borrower. However, the bank will increase its cover to 75 percent if the U.S. exporter agrees to finance 10 percent at a rate no higher than Eximbank's.

* Interest—The bank's interest rates are fixed for the life of a loan at the time of authorization, determined by the category of the country where the export will be shipped. Repayment periods must be in line with the OECD International Arrangement on Officially Supported Export Credits. (Appendix 6–A is a listing of OECD country categories.)

* Fees—The bank's loans are subject to a one-time, 2 percent fee for the credit application, payable up front, no later than 60 days after authorization. It can be amortized over three

years with repayment in semiannual installments at the same fixed rate as the Eximbank loan. In addition, the bank has a semiannual commitment fee of 0.5 percent on the undisbursed balances of direct loans, which accrues 60 days from either the date of the loan's authorization or from the date on which the loan agreement is signed, whichever comes first.

Eximbank direct loans, regardless of size, and loans to intermediaries where the loan amount is more than $10 million or the term is more than seven years will carry the lowest interest rate permitted under the OECD arrangement for the market and term. Where the loan amount is less than $10 million and less than seven years, the loans may be structured as "standby" loan commitments. The intermediary may elect to borrow against this commitment once at any time during the amortization period of its underlying foreign debt obligation. For medium-term intermediary loans, the rate at which financial institutions unrelated to the exporter may borrow from Eximbank is as follows:

Loan Commitment Value	Eximbank's Interest Rate
Less than $1 million	OECD rate minus 150 basis points
$1–5 million	OECD rate minus 100 basis points
Over $5–$10 million	OECD rate minus 50 basis points

Other responsible parties, including exporters, may borrow from Eximbank at the OECD rate. The intermediary must "onlend" to the foreign borrower at the minimum OECD fixed rate, but may charge appropriate fees.

Financial Guarantee Program

As already previously mentioned under direct loans, Eximbank financing packages include financial guarantees to cover part of the privately supplied portion of the total credit. This program of financial guarantees can be used by U.S. and foreign financial institutions. It can also be used independently of the bank's direct loan program to make commercial credits easier to obtain from financial institutions who are reluctant to extend export trade financing to certain countries, especially Third World countries.

Eximbank's guarantee is available for fixed or floating interest rate export loans. Although most Eximbank guarantees are in U.S. dollars, they have been willing in recent years to guaranty foreign currency borrowings to be more competitive.

Eximbank's guarantee is unconditional and freely transferable, subject to a minimum note denomination. In the event of a default, the guarantied lender must file a claim promptly, but not sooner than 30 days after the default. Eximbank will pay the claim within five business days after receipt. In the event of default, interest will be guarantied at the following rates:

1. For fixed rate: the lesser of the rate on the note minus 50 basis points or the U.S. Treasury rate at the time of loan pricing for a comparable term plus 50 basis points.

2. For floating rate: the lessor of the rate on the note minus 50 basis points or a rate determined on the basis of one of the following options, such option to be selected by the guaranteed party at the time of entering into the transaction:

   a. Prime less 200 basis points.

   b. LIBOR less 50 basis points.

   c. U.S. Treasury plus 50 basis points.

Actual rates under each option listed in No. 2 above will be computed as of the first day of the interest period of default.

Eximbank guarantees 100 percent of the principal amount, after a 15 percent cash payment. However, the exporter, or the guarantied lender, must provide Eximbank with a counter-guaranty of 2 percent of the commercial risk on all loans of $10 million or less and a repayment term of seven years or less, unless there is a sovereign buyer or sovereign guarantor.

Repayment Terms: Eximbank-supported financing must follow the repayment term guidelines customary in international trade (i.e., those established by the OECD arrangement):

Contract Value	Maximum Term
Up to $50,000	Two years
$50,001–$100,000	Three years
$100,001–$200,000	Four years
Above $200,000	Five to ten years, depending on the nature of the project and the OECD classification of the buyer's country

A processing fee of $100 must accompany each Preliminary Commitment application and each application for a Final Commitment not preceded by a Preliminary Commitment. The bank charges the obligor a commitment fee of 1/2 of 1 percent per annum on the undisbursed balance of an Eximbank loan and 1/8 of 1 percent on the undisbursed balance of a guaranteed loan. If an intermediary loan is combined with a guarantee, only a loan commitment fee is charged on undisbursed balances of Eximbank's loan to the intermediary.

There are three borrower/guarantor classifications:

Class I	Sovereign borrowers or guarantors, or for political-only cover.
Class II	Creditworthy nonsovereign public institutions or banks, or highly creditworthy private buyers.
Class III	Other.

There are five country classifications, from Class A for countries with the lowest risk to Class E for the highest risk countries in which Eximbank is open. Country classifications and exposure fees are reviewed and adjusted periodically.

The following is an example of the aforementioned:

In the early part of August 1986, Eximbank said it would guarantee a commercial bank loan to the Turkish government for the purchase of locomotive parts from General Motors Corporation. The Eximbank said its loan guaranty, covering a credit to be provided by Irving Trust Co., totals $25.5 million. The diesel engines, generators, and other equipment, costing $30 million, will be assembled at a Turkish factory that is jointly owned by GM and the Turkish state railways.[4]

Mixed Credit Program

The Eximbank mixed credit facility, which combines commercial rate or Export Credit Agency (ECA) financing with a grant component from The Agency for International Developments' (AID) development assistance funds, was created at the discretion of Congress in its Eximbank charter, passed in November 1983. In its reauthorization, Congress specifically directed Eximbank to support U.S. exports at rates and on terms which are fully competitive with those of foreign ECAs. This policy is best understood in the context of the following background information:

> Mixed credit programs have arisen as a direct result of fierce competition among ECAs. In the 1970s this competition led to the creation of an informal agreement among 22 OECD countries on the parameters of export subsidies. This International Arrangement on Export Credits, better known as the Consensus, sets minimum rates for ECA financing. The rates, which are reset every six months, vary according to the relative wealth of the country to which the export will be shipped and the repayment period of the loan. For example, in July 1983, these rates ranged from 13.6 percent for loans over five years to wealthier countries, to 10.7 percent for the poorest countries.

Increasingly, however, ECAs have used mixed credits to circumvent the constraints imposed by the Consensus. The rise of mixed credits has led to a phenomenon known as *undermatching,* by which governments attempt to underbid each other by offering more attractive credit packages. The U.S. government has traditionally eschewed these practices, but under its new mandate, in February 1984, Eximbank approved its first mixed credits. This action was part of a dual strategy designed to eventually curtail the use of mixed credit financing. Eximbank will now use mixed credits to counter undermatching by foreign ECAs. At the same time, the United States is pursuing two objectives in OECD negotiations:

- Increasing the minimum permissible amount of grant element in a mixed credit, thus making it more expensive for the lending country and discouraging its use.
- Strengthening the rules requiring prior notice of the use of mixed credits. Timely disclosure would presumably permit competition in matching aggressive offers, thereby neutralizing their benefit.

How U.S. Mixed Credits Work.   A U.S. exporter requests a grant aid equivalent of mixed credits directly from U.S. AID after having arranged preliminary Eximbank export credits. These requests as of this writing are to be sent to:

Mr. Richard Derham
Deputy Assistant Administrator
Bureau of Program & Policy Coordination
U.S. Agency for International Development
320 21st St. S.W.
Washington, D.C. 20523

This bureau oversees U.S. AID participation tied to aid credits, and must include a detailed description of the exports, the country involved, the competition, their financing terms, and the U.S. exporter's proposed financing package, including Eximbank's participation.

Once U.S. AID is assured that Eximbank or a private source intends to participate, it will consider providing the grant equivalent. Final approvals of all mixed credit packages require the unanimous consent of the seven-member National Advisory Council on International Monetary and Financial Policies (NAC), which includes the U.S. AID Administrator, Eximbank and Federal Reserve Board chairman; the Secretaries of Commerce, State, and Treasury; and the U.S. Trade Representative. With NAC approval, U.S. AID will disburse a single, up-front payment (to minimize its dollar cost) in conjunction with the Eximbank- or privately-financed portion of the credit.

The following are U.S. AID's guidelines for its mixed credit program:

1. Financing must only be defensive.
2. To satisfy the defensiveness criterion, the U.S. exporter must be the "low responsible bidder," and demonstrate that it will lose a contract because of financing offered by another country in support of a foreign contractor.
3. The U.S. exports to be financed must contribute to development objectives of the importing LDC, as determined by U.S. AID.
4. Mixed credits will be available for exports to any country eligible for economic funds (ESF). U.S. AID is authorized to use funds originally allocated to commodity import programs (CIP) for mixed credits to an ESF-recipient country, whether or not that country currently receives CIP funds.

The following are ESF-eligible countries (subject to change by U.S. AID who should be contacted for an up-to-date listing): Africa—Botswana, Chad, Djibouti, Kenya, Niger, Senegal, Somalia, Sudan, Zaire, Zambia, Zimbabwe; Asia—Pakistan, Thailand; Middle East—Jordan, Lebanon, Morocco, Tunisia, Turkey; Latin America and the Caribbean—Belize (1985), Costa Rica, Dominican Republic, El Salvador, Haiti, Honduras, Jamaica, Panama (1985).

The following are examples of approved mixed credit facilities granted to U.S. exporters:

On November 12, 1985, the bank said it had approved "aggressive" export credit offers in six cases, involving competitive mixed-credit financing from other governments, for the sale of U.S.-manufactured equipment valued at about $280 million to Algeria, Tunisia, Brazil, India, and Malaysia.[5]

In the latter part of November 1985, Eximbank stepped up its export-credit battle with France by offering to subsidize the sale to Brazil of hospital equipment valued at about $35 million. The bank said U.S. companies, including Johnson & Johnson of New Brunswick, New Jersey, are bidding for the contract to supply U.S.-manufactured diagnostic and patient-care equipment for use in three hospitals in the state of Minas Gerais, Brazil. The agency said Cie Generale de Radiologie, or CGR of France also is trying to win this contract with the help of subsidized French government "mixed-credit" export financing. To combat the French credit offer, the bank said it is prepared to provide either an outright grant to Brazil to cover one fourth of the cost of the U.S. equipment, or a long-term, low-interest Eximbank loan.[6]

In the early part of September 1986, Eximbank cleared two loans totaling U.S. $35 million to finance the Brazilian government's purchases of hospital equipment from U.S. companies—one at a heavily subsidized 2 percent interest rate. The agency explained that it put together the unusually generous credit package, which will finance sales of diagnostic and laboratory equipment, to prevent French companies from winning the business with "unfair export-credit offers" from their government. John Bohn, the export credit agency's president, said the Eximbank intends to approve such heavily subsidized export-credit financing in other cases as well, as part of a U.S. effort to pressure France and other industrial countries to agree to new restrictions on the practice of combining foreign aid with cut-rate financing to subsidize exports.[7]

Interest Matching Program (I-MATCH)

This program is a way to ensure the availability of loans at International Arrangement rates in support of U.S. exports which are facing officially subsidized foreign financing competition. I-MATCH is a substitute for Eximbank's lending programs (including long-term direct loans and small business and medium-term credits).

How does I-MATCH differ from Eximbank's direct lending programs?

I-MATCH will be no different from the viewpoint of the U.S. exporter or the foreign purchaser of U.S. goods or services being assisted by Eximbank. The only result of substituting I-MATCH should be budgetary. Under current budgetary accounting principles, disbursements under Eximbank's direct loans constitute outlays which increase the overall federal budget deficit. Since loan guaranties do not constitute outlays, I-MATCH will help reduce the overall federal budget deficit.

How will I-MATCH work?

Where necessary to counter officially subsidized foreign competition, a commercial lender will make a fixed rate loan for the term customary in international practice at the lowest interest rate allowed under the International Arrangement at the time the loan is authorized. The same commitment and application fees as are currently charged under Eximbank's direct lending program will be charged under I-MATCH. These fees are 1/2 percent and 2 percent respectively.

Eximbank will fully guarantee repayment of the principal and interest on the loan. In addition, because the International Arrangement interest rate may be below the market rate for the guarantied credit, Eximbank will pay the commercial lender an additional amount of interest so as to enable that lender to earn a market rate of return on the loan. I-MATCH's overall costs should be kept at acceptable levels, since International Arrangement's official export credit lending rates have become linked closely to market rates.

Example

Differential to be paid by Eximbank on commercial loan guaranteed by Eximbank under I-MATCH in support of exports to Category II country

Market rate for transaction	13.7 percent
Arrangement rate for transactions	11.2 percent
Differential to be paid by Eximbank	2.5 percent

How much fixed rate financing will be available under I-MATCH?
The total amount of guarantied loans that Eximbank will be able to cover in FY 1986 under I-MATCH will not exceed $1.8 billion. In addition, at the time of authorization of each loan to be guarantied under I-MATCH, Eximbank will estimate the subsidy cost adjusted for the application fee on a present value basis. The total estimated interest subsidy cost on a present value basis for all loans guarantied under I-MATCH will not exceed $136 million in FY 1986, and when adjusted for Eximbank's application fee, will be limited to $100 million.

How many U.S. exports will be able to be supported under I-MATCH?
As much as $3 billion in U.S. exports can be assisted under I-MATCH depending on the amount of subsidized fixed rate financing necessary to enable a particular export transaction to go forward.

How will I-MATCH be funded?
No appropriations are requested for this program. Eximbank will make use of its borrowing authority and usual sources of funding.

Will Eximbank's authority be sufficient to meet the needs of the U.S. exporting community in FY 1989?
In addition to I-MATCH, Eximbank will continue to provide its support under its regular insurance and guarantee programs. Because International Arrangement rates are so closely tied to market rates, significant amounts of support for transactions involving nuclear power plants and aircraft can be provided under the financing guaranty program.

Engineering Multiplier Program
This program provides enhanced financing benefits to help U.S. architectural and engineering firms win foreign contracts for project-related feasibility studies and preconstruction engineering services. Under the program Eximbank offers medium-term loans directly to the foreign purchasers of those services. It also offers to guarantee private financing for a portion of the local costs of the

project. To qualify for the program, the contract must involve a project with the potential to generate additional U.S. exports worth $10 million or twice the amount of the initial contract, whichever is greater.

The following are some typical questions posed to Eximbank regarding this program:

Why was this program developed?
The program was developed by Eximbank in order to generate additional export sales of American goods and services. The proportion of U.S. equipment and services ordered for a major foreign construction project tends to be much higher when a U.S. company performs the preconstruction feasibility studies, design, and engineering work.

What U.S. companies can be supported by the program?
Any U.S. architectural or engineering firm that plans to perform preconstruction studies or engineering services for a specific project is eligible.

What kinds of contracts qualify for the program?
The program will finance services with a U.S. export value of up to $10 million. These services must involve projects which have the potential of generating subsequent U.S. export orders valued at $10 million or double the original export contract, whichever is greater.
The nature of the potential project must be acceptable to Eximbank. Eximbank must be convinced that the foreign borrower will be able to pay for the final project, whether or not that project is financed by the Bank. In cases where preconstruction services are sold on a negotiated basis, the U.S. supplier does not need to present evidence of foreign competition. However, Eximbank must be satisfied that qualified foreign competition would be encountered if the buyer chose to open the contract to bids.

What support does Eximbank provide under this program?
Eximbank will extend a medium-term (up to five years) direct loan to the foreign purchaser for 85 percent of the U.S. export value. Eximbank will also guarantee commercial financing for the U.S. company's local costs in the host country of up to 15 percent of the U.S. export value. The buyer must make a 15

percent cash payment to the U.S. company prior to or concurrently with the loan disbursement by Eximbank.

Why is the local cost guarantee limited to 15 percent of the U.S. export value?

This is the limit imposed under the Export Credit Arrangement among 22 member nations of the Organization for Economic Cooperation and Development (OECD).

What if the U.S. content of the preconstruction engineering services is estimated to cost more than $10 million?

The costs up to $10 million may be financed under the program. The remaining costs may be financed under Eximbank's regular Direct Loan Program.

If a U.S. company performs architectural and engineering services under this program and Eximbank later extends long-term financing to the foreign client for the resulting project, what happens to the original financing?

If Eximbank approves long-term financing for the resulting project, the remaining balance from the medium-term financing for preconstruction services can be rolled over into the project financing. Eximbank's decision to finance preconstruction services does not represent a commitment to finance the subsequent project. Eximbank will examine requests for long-term project financing in light of all the available information and may or may not approve further financing.

Special Coverages.   The exporter can also obtain a number of special coverages. Preshipment coverage, for example, insures against specified risks from the date of execution of a sales contract instead of from the date of shipment. Exporters find this coverage desirable when their products are specially fabricated or require a long factory lead time (up to a maximum of 18 months). In addition, FCIA will insure political risks for goods on consignment where the exporter retains title until the products are sold.

Should an exporter consummate a sale requiring payment in the currency of the buyer rather than in U.S. dollars, FCIA will, by endorsement, cover such transactions under all policies. No exchange or transfer risk is insurable under this endorsement.

PART B
ADDITIONAL U.S. PROGRAMS

In addition to the programs offered by FCIA and Eximbank, there are a number of non-U.S. government entities and the private sector who offer a wide array of programs to assist exporters.

Many of these entities can offer political risk protection through investment assistance and guarantee programs for overseas project financing such as those offered by the Overseas Private Investment Corporation. In addition, there are a number of state governments offering assistance to exporters, especially small exporters, for the promotion of exports from their own states.

Their programs and guarantees can enhance U.S. exports by reducing the risks inherent in selling to certain countries and can assist the exporter in obtaining export trade financing.

STATE EXPORT TRADE FINANCING PROGRAMS

Since the middle of the 1970s, a number of states have developed their own export development programs to promote U.S. exports. Many other states seem to be working on similar programs because they feel better situated to give specific assistance to companies located within their borders than federal programs. Many states offer export trade financing assistance with the support of FCIA/Eximbank or similar programs. U.S. exporters should contact their states for information. The following briefly summarizes assistance offered by some states:

Washington. The State's Export Assistance Center (EAC) was established in 1983 to provide export counseling and loan packaging for Washington businesses with annual revenue under $100 million. In January 1986, the EAC obtained a $750 million revolving guarantee from Eximbank for the Bank of Gray's Harbor, the smallest bank ever to receive this guarantee. EAC expects the bank to then increase the loan limit to 50–40 percent, supporting $5–6 million in exports from the state. In 1985–86, the EAC arranged some $3 million in loans to support $10 million in exports.

Tennessee. Winner of the President's "E" award for outstanding export efforts, the state was the first to pass legislation establishing an export finance authority called the Tennessee Competitive Export Corporation (TCEC) to help the state's businesses finance overseas sales. The state passed legislation enabling it to issue working capital loans or loan guarantees, as do most state programs. However, Tennessee's program is unique in that it looks at long-term financial needs and tries to develop credit packages appropriate to those needs. TCEC has become a financial consulting operation rather than a lending institution and this has certain advantages. Local companies feel they can be more candid about finances. A more rounded picture of the situation becomes available. Companies learn to think like bankers, to look at the risks and the possibility of loss—not just the profit to be gained. TCEC can establish a seasonal line of credit for the exporter by looking long term, rather than arranging several single-purpose loans. TCEC can work on behalf of banks hesitant to enter into an export loan agreement.

California. With the support of Eximbank, the state has undertaken a strong city and state export finance effort. Initially set up as a pilot program in 1987, it will provide a single center in Los Angeles for information, technical assistance, and direct financing of Los Angeles businesses who are expanding in or just entering the international market. It was anticipated that this program would become a model for providing export trade assistance at the local level in anticipation of financing $100 million in the first year. The goal is to deliver services to smaller businesses since the state estimate is that 85 percent of their export transactions are less than $50,000. The state also has an FCIA policy. California exporters can now go to the state office, and based on the individual transaction, obtain export finance. The state export office looks at the particular transaction, guaranties performance by the exporter, and based on either a strong L/C or FCIA insurance, will be able to finance an individual transaction.

THE INTERNATIONAL COOPERATION AND DEVELOPMENT AGENCY

Operating under the administrative umbrella of the U.S. International Cooperation and Development Agency (IDCA) are three institutions, namely:

The Overseas Private Investment Corporation (OPIC).

The Agency for International Development (AID).

The U.S. Trade and Development Program (TDP).

Their operations can significantly help U.S. exporters establish and expand their overseas markets.

Overseas Private Investment Corporation (OPIC)

OPIC is the largest of the three institutions. Its primary purpose is to insure and guarantee large, long-term U.S. investments abroad. The United States has long recognized that business investment overseas can assist in the economic development of foreign countries, as well as create jobs at home and new markets for American exports. This is especially true of private investment in the world's developing countries, which absorb nearly $100 billion in U.S. exports annually and are today's fastest growing markets.

For more than a decade, the Overseas Private Investment Corporation (OPIC) has served as the federal agency for encouraging mutually-beneficial American business investment in the world's developing nations.

To do this, OPIC provides qualified investors with insurance against certain political risks; loan guaranties; direct loans to small businesses and cooperatives, and a variety of pre-investment and investment encouragement programs. All are designed to reduce the perceived stumbling blocks and risks associated with overseas investment.

OPIC's primary business is providing politial risk insurance, a concept that dates back to 1948 when it was first initiated under the Marshall Plan. At the time, insurance was offered against the risk of currency inconvertibility in order to generate capital formation for rebuilding war-torn Europe.

By the 1950s, when the European recovery was well under way, the political risk insurance aspects of the Marshall Plan were restructured to supplement direct aid programs to the world's developing countries. The program's scope was also broadened to include coverage against the risks of expropriation and war.

In 1961, this insurance program was shifted to the newly formed Agency for International Development (AID), and again broadened to include insurance coverage for revolution and insurrection, as well as a lending authority for loan guaranties and feasibility study assistance. Because AID's primary purpose was, and still remains, the administration of government-to-government assistance, Congress decided in 1969 that a separate, business-oriented agency should be established to provide more effective support for American investors entering the international marketplace.

The result was OPIC, which began operation in 1971. Organized as a corporation and structured to be responsive to private business, the agency's mandate is to "mobilize and facilitate the participation of United States private capital and skills in the economic and social development of less developed, friendly countries and areas."

Currently OPIC programs are available for new business enterprises or expansions in approximately 100 developing countries or areas around the world. Assistance is not available for projects that adversely affect U.S. employment, are financially unsound, or do not promise significant benefits to the social and economic development of the host country or area. Appendix 6–B is a list of OPIC insured investors as of its fiscal year ending 1986.

As a self-sustaining agency, OPIC has received no public funds beyond its original start-up appropriations. Moreover, it has recorded a positive net income for every year in operation, with reserves currently standing in excess of $800 million.

The following is a general overview of OPIC and the many programs and services it offers.

Insurance. While private investors generally have the capability to assess the commercial aspects of doing business overseas, they may be hesitant to undertake long-term investments abroad, given the political uncertainties of many developing nations. To alleviate these uncertainties, OPIC insures U.S. investments against three types of political risks (Figure 6–7 is a summary of funds available for claims payments):

Inconvertibility. This coverage protects an investor against the inability to convert into U.S. dollars the local currency received as profits, earnings, or return of capital on an investment. OPIC's inconvertibility coverage also protects against adverse discriminatory exchange rates. Conversion of local currency into dollars is assured only to the extent that such currency could have been exchanged for dollars at the time the insurance was issued. The coverage does not protect against the devaluation of a country's currency (Figure 6–8 is a summary of inconvertibility exposures by country).

Expropriation. This coverage protects an investor against confiscation or nationalization of an investment without fair com-

FIGURE 6–7
Summary of Funds Available for Claims Payments

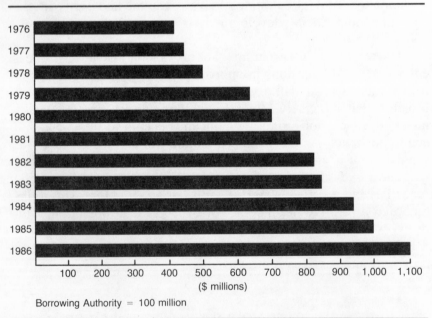

Borrowing Authority = 100 million

Source: Overseas Private Investment Corporation, 1986 Annual Report (Washington, D.C.: 1986), p. 12.

FIGURE 6–8
Inconvertibility Exposure

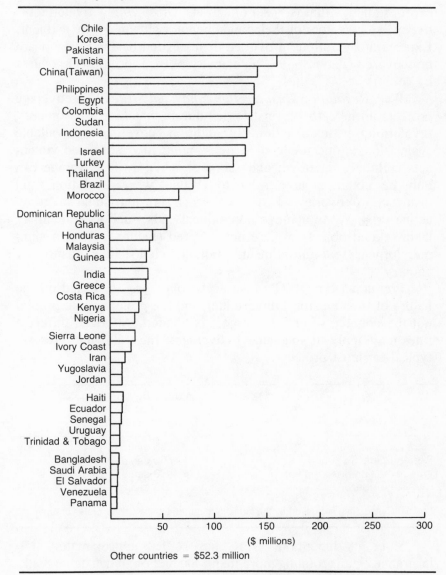

Other countries = $52.3 million

Source: Overseas Private Investment Corporation, 1986 Annual Report (Washington, D.C.: 1986), p. 20.

pensation. Expropriation coverage also protects U.S. investors against losses due to a variety of situations described as "creeping expropriation," that is, a set of actions whose cumulative effect is to deprive investors of their fundamental rights in the investment. Expropriatory actions provoked or instigated by the investor are not covered (Figure 6–9 is a summary of expropriation exposures by country).

War, Revolution, Insurrection, and Civil Strife. This coverage protects an investor against losses due to war (declared or not), revolution, or insurrection. In addition, coverage is available against losses due to "civil strife"—politically motivated violent acts including terrorism and sabotage. Civil strife coverage can only be obtained as a rider to OPIC's war, revolution, and insurrection coverage. Losses caused by an individual or group acting primarily to achieve nonpolitical ends, such as student- or labor-related objectives, are not covered (Figure 6–10 is a summary of war, revolution, insurrection and civil strife exposures by country).

Premiums for OPIC's insurance coverages are based on the nature of the investor's undertaking and the project's risk profile, not the country where the project is located. Although different rates may apply to specialized coverages, the following rates are typical for most projects.

Coverage*	Annual Base Rate per $100 of Coverage
Inconvertibility	30 cents
Expropriation	60 cents
War, revolution, insurrection	60 cents
Civil strife rider	15 cents

* All OPIC insurance is backed by the full faith and credit of the United States of America.

Since its inception, OPIC has settled approximately 150 insurance claims totaling more than $400 million; it has denied only 8 percent of the claims received.

Finance. U.S. investors planning to share significantly in the equity and management of an overseas venture can often utilize OPIC's finance programs for medium- to long-term financing.

FIGURE 6–9
Expropriation Exposure

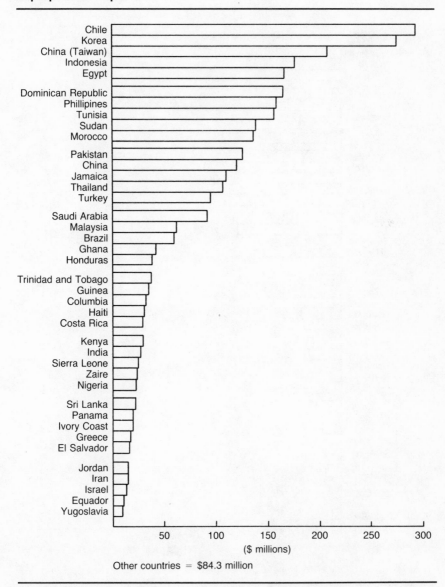

Other countries = $84.3 million

Source: Overseas Private Investment Corporation, 1986 Annual Report (Washington, D.C.: 1986), p. 21.

FIGURE 6–10
War, Revolution, Insurrection, and Civil Strife Exposure

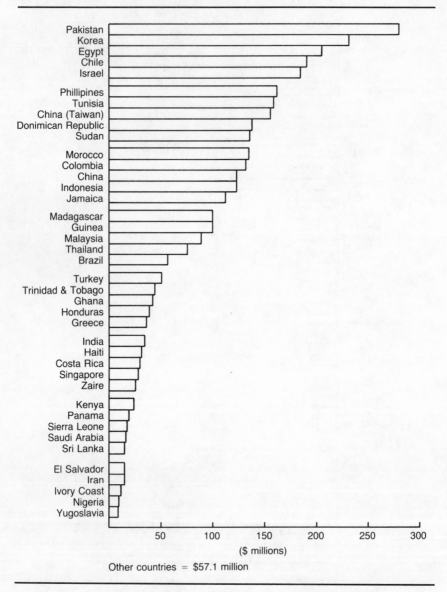

Other countries = $57.1 million

Source: Overseas Private Investment Corporation, 1986 Annual Report (Washington, D.C.: 1986), p. 21.

To obtain OPIC financing, the venture must be commercially and financially sound, within the demonstrated competence of the proposed management, and sponsored by an investor having a proven record of success in the same or closely related business.

OPIC's financing commitment to a new venture may extend to, but not exceed, 50 percent of the total project cost. A larger participation may be considered for an expansion of a successful, existing enterprise. Investors must be willing to establish a sound debt/equity relationship—typically a ratio of 60 percent debt to 40 percent equity.

Currently, OPIC provides financing to investors through two major programs—direct loans and loan guarantees. *Direct Loans,* which usually range from $100,000 to $4 million, are available only for ventures sponsored by, or significantly involving, U.S. small businesses or cooperatives. A small business is generally defined as a firm having revenues or net worth less than that of the smallest firm listed on the Fortune 500. Interest rates vary according to a project's financial and political risk.

Under the *loan guarantee* program, which is available to all businesses regardless of size, OPIC will issue a guarantee under which funding can be obtained from a variety of U.S. financial institutions. The guarantee covers both commercial and political risks. Typical OPIC loan guaranties range from $1 million to $25 million, but can be as large as $50 million. Interest rates on guarantied loans are comparable to those of other U.S. government-guaranteed issues of similar maturity. In addition, OPIC charges the borrower a guaranty fee that ranges from 1½ to 3 percent, depending on a project's commercial and political risk, not its country of location.

Repayment of direct and guarantied loans is normally made in equal, semiannual principal payments following a suitable grace period. Final maturity ranges from 5 to 12 years.

OPIC Finance Services	Rate	Maturity
Direct loans	Commercial equivalent	5–12 years
Loan guaranties*	1½ to 3 percent	5–12 years

* All OPIC guaranties are backed by the full faith and credit of the United States of America.

Special Programs

In addition to its general insurance and finance programs, OPIC has developed special programs to meet the specific needs of investors involved in contracting and exporting, energy exploration and development, and leasing arrangements.

Contractor's and Exporter's Program.   To improve the competitive position of U.S. contractors and exporters seeking to do business in the developing nations, OPIC offers specialized insurance and financing services.

Many developing countries require foreign firms to post bid, performance, or advance payment guaranties in the form of standby letters of credit (discussed in Chapter 4, Part C) when bidding on or performing overseas contracts. OPIC's political risk insurance for contractors and exporters protects against the arbitrary or unfair drawing of such letters of credit.

In addition, contractors and exporters may also obtain insurance against the risks of currency inconvertibility; confiscation of tangible assets and bank accounts; war, revolution, insurrection, and civil strife; and losses sustained when a government power fails to settle a dispute in accordance with the provisions of the underlying contract.

Premium rates are assessed on a semiannual basis, according to the risk profile of the particular project, based on the following guidelines:

Semiannual Costs per $100 of Coverage	
Bid bonds, advance payment and performance guaranties	30 cents
Disputes	40 cents

Costs for inconvertibility; expropriation; and war, revolution, insurrection, and civil strife are comparable to those under OPIC's general insurance programs (mentioned above).

OPIC also offers a special loan guaranty program for small business contractors to assist with their credit needs. This plan provides an OPIC guaranty of up to 75 percent of a standby letter of credit that is issued to a financial institution on behalf of a small business contractor.

Energy Programs. OPIC offers special insurance and finance programs for U.S. investors involved in oil and gas, oil shale, geothermal, mineral, solar, and other energy projects, as well as for investors supplying support services or goods for such commercial projects.

Political risk insurance coverage is available to energy investors for currency inconvertibility; expropriation; war, revolution, insurrection, and civil strife. In addition, coverage against "interference with operations" (cessation of operations due to war, revolution, insurrection or civil strife) is also available. As with other OPIC programs, premium costs are determined by the risk profile of the particular project. However, the following base rates are typical for most projects:

Coverage	Annual Rates per $100 of Coverage	
	Exploration	Development/ Production
Inconvertibility	10 cents	30 cents
Expropriation	40 cents	$1.50
War, revolution, insurrection*	60 cents	60 cents
Interference with operations*	40 cents	40 cents

* Civil strife coverage available for an additional 15 cents per $100 coverage.

Once a commercially feasible energy project is established, OPIC can provide a loan guarantee of up to $50 million to finance as much as 50 percent of the cost of a new project, or 75 percent of an expansion of an existing project. Loan maturities and guarantee fees typically parallel those of OPIC's general finance program.

OPIC's insurance and financial services are not available for oil and gas projects in the member nations of the Organization of Petroleum Exporting Countries (OPEC). OPIC services may be available, however, for other types of energy projects in those countries, and for investors providing goods and services to oil and gas projects.

Leasing.   For U.S. investors in international leasing, OPIC provides specialized insurance and finance services.

Under this program, political risk insurance is available for cross-border operating and capital leases running for at least 36 months. Coverage is available for the lease transaction itself; equity investments in, and loans to, off-shore leasing companies; consigned inventory; and management/maintenance agreements involving leasing firms.

OPIC's loan guaranty program is also available to foreign leasing companies in which there is a significant U.S. private business interest. Loan guaranties to leasing companies generally range in size from $500,000 to $20 million. Guarantee terms are usually from four to seven years, with appropriate grace periods before principal repayment begins. Guarantee fees parallel that of OPIC's general finance program.

Direct loans are available to foreign leasing companies or projects in which a U.S. small business has a significant interest. Terms are similar to those of OPIC's general finance program.

Investment Encouragement Programs

To further foster private investment in world development, OPIC offers two major investment encouragement programs.

Feasibility Studies.   An investor's decision to do business in a developing country frequently hinges on the ability to investigate and analyze the potential of a specific enterprise. To meet this need, OPIC can provide funding assistance for feasibility studies.

Under the program, OPIC will reimburse an investor for up to 50 percent of the study's costs (60 percent for a small business-sponsored study). In all cases, maximum OPIC participation is $100,000.

For small businesses, funding for feasibility studies is provided through an interest-free, reimbursable grant. Repayment (over two years) is required only if the investor moves forward with the study-related project; repayment can be reduced if the investor insures or finances the project through OPIC. In addition, small businesses may apply for a grant up to $5,000 to cover travel costs and per diem expenses associated with visiting a country for the first time to assess its investment climate.

For larger firms, feasibility financing assistance is provided through a two-year loan at a rate generally equivalent to two thirds of the prime rate. Repayment may be reduced if the investment moves forward and the investor elects to obtain OPIC insurance or financing. However, this program is only available to larger firms contemplating investments in the poorest developing countries.

To obtain feasibility study funding, an investor must have a project that would be eligible for insurance or financing from OPIC. The feasibility study itself must be substantially carried out by the investor, rather than a third party.

Special Project Grants and Loans. OPIC also offers grants and loans to support the training and education of host-country nations involved in OPIC-supported projects. Funding is generally provided to businesses on a concessional-loan basis in amounts not exceeding $50,000. The actual amounts and terms of funding depend entirely on the nature of the undertaking.

Financing is made available to cover the foreign exchange costs of these projects, such as the international travel and living expenses of U.S. experts sent abroad to provide training, or the expenses of host-country individuals sent to the United States to acquire new skills. In all cases, the project sponsor must contribute at least 25 percent of the cost of the training.

OPIC also offers grants and loans to nonprofit entities, such as private voluntary organizations or foundations, to initiate imaginative programs for assisting in the transfer of technology to the developing countries or facilitating U.S. investment in those nations. Such projects are generally multi-year undertakings of approximately $100,000 annually.

Pre-Investment Assistance

For most U.S. businesses, especially those with little or no international investment experience, access to information on specific investment opportunities and the business environment in the developing nations is critical to making an investment decision. To aid U.S. firms in this area, OPIC offers two special programs.

Investment Missions. Each year, dozens of U.S. business executives participate in OPIC's investment missions to various developing nations. On these missions, participants can obtain first-hand information about investment opportunities through personal meetings with business leaders and key government officials of the host country.

Countries are selected for investment missions after careful study of their investment needs, the investment climate, and the potential for profitable U.S. projects. Participants are selected on the basis of their financial and management capability to undertake an overseas venture, as well as their experience in those industry sectors having high priority in the host country. Investment mission participants pay all travel and accommodation costs.

Opportunity Bank.   For investors seeking business opportunities in Third World countries, OPIC offers a computer data system that can match an investor's interest with specific overseas opportunities.

This service, known as the Opportunity Bank, allows U.S. firms to submit a description of their business, the type of investment sought, and the developing country or countries of interest. On request, the information can be matched against similar information submitted by foreign businesses seeking U.S. investors.

Any domestic firm or foreign entity can register itself with the Opportunity Bank at no charge; a modest fee is charged for match requests. The Opportunity Bank is designed to foster the exchange of investment information. No determination is made by OPIC as to the accuracy or reliability of information submitted.

Overall Eligibility
OPIC programs are available only if:
- The investor's project is a new venture or an expansion of an existing enterprise.
- The project is located in a developing country where OPIC operates.
- The project will assist in the social and economic development of the host country.
- The project is approved by the host government.
- The project is consistent with the economic interests of the

United States and will not have a significant adverse effect on the U.S. economy or U.S. employment.

OPIC will not support a "runaway plant" project (i.e., the closing down of a U.S. facility to open a foreign facility where the same products or services will be produced for the same markets as before). OPIC cannot support certain other types of projects, including gambling facilities, distilleries, military projects, and projects posing serious environmental hazards.

Specific Program Eligibility.   In addition, the following general restrictions and guidelines should be kept in mind when considering specific OPIC programs.

Insurance—OPIC can only issue insurance to "eligible investors," who are defined as:

- Citizens of the United States.
- U.S. corporations, partnerships, or other business organizations of at least 50 percent U.S. ownership.
- Foreign corporations, partnerships, or other business organizations at least 95 percent owned by investors eligible under the above.

OPIC generally will cover no more than 90 percent of an investment plus attributable earnings. Therefore, the investor typically must bear the risk of loss of at least 10 percent of any investment insured by OPIC.

OPIC insurance is not available retroactively. Investors must obtain an OPIC insurance registration letter before the investment or an irrevocable commitment has been made. Investors are encouraged to contact OPIC in the early stages of investment planning.

There is no fixed form which an investment must take in order to be eligible for OPIC insurance coverage. Conventional equity investments and loans, investment or exposure of funds, goods or services under contractual arrangements, and production-sharing agreements are among the investment forms commonly insured.

Finance—Direct loans are issued only for investment projects sponsored by, or significantly involving, U.S. small businesses or cooperatives.

Loan guaranties are issued to:

- U.S. lenders having over 50 percent U.S. ownership.
- Foreign lending institutions that are at least 95 percent U.S. owned.

OPIC will not purchase equity in a project, but may purchase convertible notes and debt instruments with equity participation features.

For further information about OPIC, its programs and services, write:

Information Officer
Overseas Private Investment Corporation
1129 20th Street, N.W.
Washington, D.C. 20527

The Agency for International Development (AID)

The Agency for International Development (AID) is responsible for all official U.S. bilateral development assistance. Currently, AID provides funds primarily for health, agricultural, and educational programs, and it occasionally funds large-scale infastructural projects.

On large-scale projects, AID either conducts the bidding and contract negotiations, or it follows host country contracting regulations. In the latter case, the contract is awarded by the host government after reviewing competitive bids and consulting AID officials. To qualify, the recipient of the contract must be a business whose ownership is at least 51 percent owned by a U.S. business. All machinery and components ultimately used in the final project must be of U.S. origin or have a certain stipulated percentage of U.S. content. Exceptions to this rule can be arranged under certain circumstances.

For example, a central African country proposed a large water project and requested AID assistance. Following initial consultation and analysis with AID officials, the host government issued a request for technical expenses, as well as a complete cost analysis for the entire project. The host government, assisted by AID, analyzed the competitive bids and selected an engineering firm.

AID has considerable flexibility in all its programs to negotiate terms and conditions for financing, depending on the nature, risk level, and development impact of any project. Some general guidelines issued by AID are:

- Amount of financing: Up to $2.5 million with emphasis on the range of $250,000 to $1 million, but not more than 25 percent of total project cost. AID is particularly interested in solving intermediate and long-term fixed rate, local capital market deficiencies.
- Terms: 15-year maximum term, with grace period on principal negotiable. There are no fixed or minimum collateral requirements. Fixed interest rates will be established to emphasize that the project can achieve market-competitive profitability. The repayment schedule is negotiable, but is generally on a quarterly or semi-annual basis.
- Procurement of loan proceeds: While no absolute U.S. content requirement is specified, the intended sources of goods and services will be a consideration in determining eligibility for AID loans. Loans may be used to capitalize a new enterprise or to expand an existing one.

The Trade and Development Program

The Trade and Development Program (TDP) was established in 1980 to assist in providing project planning services leading to the sale of U.S. technology (both goods and services) for project implementation. In addition, it serves as the coordinating and authorizing agency for the provision of government-to-government technical assistance provided by about two dozen federal agencies on a reimbursable basis. These agencies range from the Army Corps of Engineers to the Veterans Administration. The TDP finances (by extending grants) a variety of project planning services directly including definitional studies, prefeasibility studies, feasibility studies, technology workshops, and technology-oriented missions.

As of this writing, approximately 40 countries are using the services of TDP, including Nigeria, Thailand, China, Zimbabwe, Brazil, Saudi Arabia, Uruguay, Peru, and Venezuela.

Funding for project implementation can come from the host country's own foreign exchange reserves or from international financial institutions, such as the World Bank, regional development banks, Eximbank, commercial borrowings, foreign investments, or even countertrade (explained in Chapter 9).

It is important to note that when a U.S. firm performs an initial feasibility study under TDP, it does not necessarily mean it won the final bid. However, the country that finances and performs the initial feasibility study has a better chance of securing the final engineering and project contract for its exporters.

According to information provided by the agency, for example, two companies that have benefited from TDP's program in the past few years are Fluor Corporation and Land O'Lakes Inc. In 1979, Fluor was awarded the advance engineering contract for Thailand's offshore natural gas project. More recently, Land O'Lakes was awarded a contract to provide livestock, cattle semen, and dairy equipment to Tunisia. In 1982, Bechtel, a leading construction engineering company, won a $5.5 million order it was bidding on in Indonesia to supply management services for a nuclear science and engineering center. The company got the business because it applied and got a grant for the TDP of $350,000 which it gave to the customer in Indonesia.

THE PRIVATE EXPORT FUNDING CORPORATION (PEFCO)

The Private Export Funding Corporation (PEFCO) was established in 1970 and commenced operations in 1971. It is not a government entity, but a private corporation owned by 46 commercial banks, seven manufacturing companies, and one investment banking firm. A majority of PEFCO's shares must be owned or controlled by U.S. citizens.

The principal purpose of PEFCO is to make U.S. dollar loans to public and private borrowers (foreign importers) located outside the United States who require medium- and long-term financing for the purchase of U.S. goods and services. Principal and interest on all of PEFCO's loans must be covered by an unconditional guarantee of the Export-Import Bank of the United States (Eximbank).

PEFCO raises its funds by selling its own debt obligations in the public markets through major securities underwriters or via the private placement route. To assure the lowest possible cost of funds for its debt, the principal portion of the company's publicly sold intermediate-term obligations are secured through a pledge of its Eximbank guaranteed loans to a bank trustee for the benefit of the noteholders. Interest on the secured PEFCO obligations is guaranteed directly by Eximbank.

PEFCO is a supplemental lender, making loans only when the necessary funds are not available from traditional private sector sources on normal credit terms and at competitive rates of interest. Its principal value to the export community has been its ability to make loans during periods of tight money at fixed rates of interest with long commitment periods and for maturities going beyond the normal range acceptable to commercial banks. PEFCO also has made some loans at floating rates of interest. Because commercial banks in today's marketplace are faced with large portfolios of debts owing from less developed countries, they have become reluctant to give long-term loans, even at fixed rates, despite an Eximbank guarantee covering political and commercial risks. PEFCO can help U.S. exporters deal with this problem.

PEFCO's loans have financed a wide variety of capital goods including power plants, aircraft, mining projects, industrial plants, communications facilities, and railroad equipment. Original maturities of PEFCO's loans have in the past extended out to 15 years, but there is no upper limit. PEFCO will not make loans below $1 million except in special cases. There is no maximum amount. Individual loan commitments have ranged from approximately $1 million to $116 million.

A U.S. exporter or potential foreign borrower will usually find it practical to approach PEFCO through one of the 46 commercial banks (see Appendix 6–C for a complete listing). The initial contact generally occurs when the borrower and his bank have agreed on the various components of proposed financing and when there is at least an informal indication of the amount which Eximbank is willing to guarantee and of the portion which the commercial bank does not want to provide. At that time, the commercial bank will contact PEFCO which can then give a prompt indication of its willingness to become part of the lending group. Before it can indicate the interest rate on the proposed loan, the following minimum information must be provided:

- Amount of loan.
- Approximate schedule of disbursements and final availability date.
- Repayment schedule.
- What part of the loan PEFCO is asked to provide.

With this information on hand PEFCO can promptly give an informal indication of the lending rate. If a firm commitment is requested later, some additional information about the loan must be provided, including the status of Eximbank's commitment. PEFCO can make a definitive offer at a fixed interest rate to the borrower through and in cooperation with the commercial bank. This offer is subject only to Eximbank's approval of PEFCO's participation and is generally valid for acceptance by the borrower for up to 45 days (45-day option pricing) pending acceptance of the related offer by the foreign borrower. PEFCO will establish a fixed differential or spread over a specific U.S. Treasury note and hold that differential for up to 90 days pending acceptance of the offer by the foreign importer.

PEFCO's lending rates for fixed rate loans are generally computed in accordance with a standard formula. This rate is based on the estimated cost of money to PEFCO at the time of the offer plus a nominal spread for profit, administrative costs, and a factor reflecting the rate risk exposure during the projected disbursement period. Eximbank's fee and a 3/8 percent per annum commitment fee on the undisbursed and uncancelled amount of the loan commitment for which PEFCO's fixed interest lending rate has been determined, and 1/8 percent per annum on amounts for which such rate has not yet been determined.

PEFCO's interest rate for floating rate loans is set at a spread over the prime rate of the sponsoring commercial bank.

PEFCO's New Note Purchase Facility

PEFCO has implemented a Note Purchase Facility (NPF) designed to provide assured liquidity for Eximbank guaranteed medium-term promissory notes. Through the NPF, PEFCO will make an offer to a lender or noteholder to purchase, without recourse to the seller, any promissory note, newly created or existing, which is secured by Eximbank's new guarantee and which has the following characteristics:

1. Eximbank's guarantee of commercial and political risk.
2. Principal amounts of $10 million or less.
3. Repayment terms of 7 years or less.
4. An interest rate, either fixed or floating, with the Eximbank guarantee on the same basis, net of any withholding tax.
5. Prepayment terms which require noteholder's consent and provide for indemnification under certain circumstances.

PEFCO will extend a variety of offers including an offer for two business days under which, if accepted by the lender/noteholder, the promissory note and related documents are to be delivered to PEFCO, or its agent, for settlement within five business days of acceptance against payment by PEFCO in immediately available funds.

After PEFCO's offer has been accepted by the potential borrower PEFCO becomes a party to the final negotiations on loan agreements and other required documentation. Generally, PEFCO is a party to the same loan agreement as Eximbank. If Eximbank is not a lender, PEFCO may be a party to the commercial bank's agreement, or it may produce its own. Since PEFCO relies on Eximbank's guarantee, most of the loan convenants are generally identical to those required by that bank. Consequently, it is not a significant contributor to the formulation of convenants.

When all conditions precedent to the final utilization of a loan have been fulfilled, PEFCO is ready to receive requests for disbursements. Under the terms of a normal loan agreement, the borrower sends the documents relating to a specific disbursement to either the co-lending commercial bank or Eximbank, as appropriate, for review and approval prior to the first drawing under the credit. On approval, the examining party notifies PEFCO of the amount and the date on which a disbursement is to be made. On the disbursement date, PEFCO makes payment in immediately available funds.

The actual disbursement may take the form of funds paid to the account of the borrower to reimburse him for payments made to the U.S. supplier for the purchase and exportation of approved items. Alternatively, the U.S. suppliers may draw against letters of credit issued or confirmed by pre-authorized agent banks in their favor. Under this procedure, PEFCO normally issued an undertaking to reimburse the agent bank to PEFCO's pro rata share of the payments made under the letters of credit.

THE AGRICULTURAL DEPARTMENT'S COMMODITY CREDIT CORPORATION (CCC)

The Commodity Credit Corporation (CCC) is the fiscal shell corporation used by the United States Department of Agriculture to finance all of its payments to and receipts from the public. This includes price support programs (the principal activity of the CCC), storage programs, export programs, and other activities. Public law 480 (PL 480), Export Credit Sales Program (GSM 5), Noncommercial Risk Assurance Program (GSM 101) and Export Credit Guaranty Program (GSM 102) are among the export programs offered over the past decade under the CCC.

The largest program in terms of sheer volume and frequency of use by U.S. exporters is the Export Credit Guarantee Program (GSM 102). Within the past few years, the Export Credit Sales Program (GSM 5) was used to play a large role in providing credit to foreign countries for the purchase of U.S. agricultural commodities. However, the program did not receive funding in 1982 and again in 1983. The following briefly describes the Export Guaranty Program.

The CCC Export Guarantee Program

This program was designed specifically to expand U.S. agricultural exports by stimulating U.S. bank financing of foreign purchases.

The program can assist U.S. exporters of agricultural goods to increase or maintain their goods to a foreign market and meet competition by guaranteeing commercial banks unwilling to provide financing without a guarantee. The guarantee provided by the CCC can take several forms.

1. An irrevocable foreign bank letter of credit issued in favor of the exporter who may draw drafts for the deferred payments to be presented to the foreign bank as such payments become due.
2. An irrevocable foreign bank letter of credit which authorizes the exporter to draw drafts on a U.S. correspondent bank of the foreign bank.

In addition, the U.S. exporter may assign the accounts receivable to a U.S. bank or financial institution so that the exporter may realize the proceeds of the sale prior to the deferred payment dates, as called for in the export credit sale.

GSM 102 guaranties payment for a variety of agricultural commodities, ranging anywhere from breeding animals to vegetable oils. It covers both commercial and political risks, most of the port (FOB) value of the commodity, and a portion of the accrued interest.

Because of country risk, even with a CCC guarantee, banks are still reluctant to take on additional risk exposures. Therefore, it is recommended that you locate a bank willing to finance the transaction before making any offers to a foreign customer.

CCC will issue guaranties up to three years to eligible countries when the issuance of a guarantee is necessary to secure financing of the respective U.S. export and where there is sufficient foreign exchange to make the scheduled payments.

Guaranty Rates and Fees. The payment guarantee rates are based on the length of the payment terms provided by the export credit sale contract, the degree of risk that CCC assumes as determined by CCC, and any other factors which CCC believes should be considered. Although rates are subject to change, the following will give the reader an idea of what rates are charged:

- For a semiannual repayment of principal, the fee rate per $100 is $0.156 for six months.

- With an annual repayment of the principal, the fee rate is $0.692 for three years.

A typical CCC Export Credit Guarantee involves a foreign government who will indicate in its bid invitation that it reserves the right to use GSM 102 financing guaranties. The bidder will want answers to the following questions:

- What is the letter of credit fee?
- Who will pay for the coverage (usually the exporter)?
- What bank will the bidder be working with? (The importer should have already arranged financing with a bank in the U.S. through its opening bank.)
- What rules and regulations apply to the transaction?

For the export guaranty to be valid, it must be arranged before shipment of the respective agricultural commodity and the shipment must occur usually before the end of the government's fiscal year, September 30.

Those U.S. exporters who are unfamiliar with the CCC and GSM-102, should contact their commercial banker (who should be familiar with the CCC's programs) or:

> The Assistant General Sales Manager
> Export Credits
> Foreign Agricultural Service
> U.S. Department of Agriculture
> The Mall
> 12th & 14th Streets
> Washington, D.C. 20250

THE CREDIT INSURANCE BROKER

Insurance brokers can act in many capacities for exporters—as consultants, contractors, or investors throughout the world. They mainly specialize in assisting exporters obtain credit and political risk insurance to protect their export receivables or investments overseas. Although many large insurers have separate departments or groups who specialize in insurance matters related to export trade, many lack the experience and expertise to reduce costs and obtain the best insurance policies for exporting companies. Therefore, it would be beneficial if the credit manager, working in close coordination with his or her risk management department, to select the best credit insurance broker to meet the exporter's needs and purposes. Although the selection of the right broker can be difficult, it can be narrowed down by answering the following questions:

Experience: How experienced is the staff of the broker as it relates to international trade? Where did they get their experience? Does this staff understand international credit, its problems, needs, and circumstances?

Staffing: Is the broker adequately staffed to service your needs? Who will handle your needs? One person, two people, or more?

Clients Serviced: Is the broker willing to supply you with a list of present or past clients? Will the broker supply a contact person at each client? Does the broker represent some major or minor exporting companies and financial institutions?

Relationships: Does the broker have close working relationships with public and private-sector insurers (i.e., FCIA/ Eximbank, OPIC, or AIG)? Does it have good contacts with the insurers? How familiar is it with their policies and programs?

Credit insurance brokers can be extremely helpful to credit managers and exporters in sifting through the many policies and programs of both public and private sector insurers in an effort to get them the best coverage possible at the lowest premium costs. In this regard, I would like to give the reader a profile of what a professional broker is all about as it relates to credit and international trade.

A professional broker can give exporters insight into the insurance alternatives available, including an up-to-the-minute awareness of the attitudes and actions of the various insurance companies and underwriters involved in writing coverage for these specialized types of risks.

Many specialize in bordering different types of insurance products including:

1. Export credit insurance.
2. Political contingency risks.
3. Foreign investment insurance.
4. Domestic credit insurance.
5. Residual value insurance.

For example, the brokering services offered by The Credit International Associates, Inc. (CIA), New York, can be segmented into the following categories:

- Helping identify the risk and develop an appropriate risk transfer strategy.
- Assembling data to effect a comprehensive underwriting submission.
- Negotiating with underwriters for the best possible quotation (i.e., lowest premium rate, highest discretionary credit limits, lowest deductible in the case of export credit insurance).
- Obtaining buyer credit limit approvals from underwriter's (generally applicable to credit insurance policies only).
- Binding the desired coverage.
- Making certain the policy is issued in proper format (with all necessary endorsements).
- Effecting policy renewal, if applicable, under the most favorable terms and conditions.
- Maintaining an ongoing interface with an insured's administrative personnel to ensure proper coverage interpretation and maintenance of coverage eligibility.
- Rendering counsel and assistance on claim preparation, conduct, and direct negotiations with insurers to effect a settlement.
- Acting as liaison with insureds to keep them abreast of changes in coverage availability and changing policy terms and conditions.

The Credit International Associates (CIA), Alexander & Alexander (A&A), Intercredit (part of Frank B. Hall and Company, New York), and many other brokers endeavor to help clients remain within the insuring parameters of their policy. They can remind you (in advance) of policy expiration dates, when shipment/exposure reports and overdue account forms are due, and, on credit policies, when the final shipment dates expire for special buyer credit approvals. It is important for insureds to keep abreast of these matters so coverage will remain in full force and effect. Staying current in these areas is essential to the maintenance of a trustful relationship between yourself and the underwriter.

Many brokers maintain close relationships with such public and private-sector insurers and their programs as OPIC, FCIA/ Eximbank, Lloyds, AIG, CIGNA, Pan Financial, UIC/Xerox, and others.

Their experience in both public and private sector credit/ political risk programs provide the background and ability to consult on political risk management with companies involved in export activities. They can help with risk evaluation and quantification, claims problems, or other related political risk/export credit insurance concerns. For example, in 1984 CIA was commissioned by the World Bank to do an in-depth study of the Mexican FCIA and Export-Import Bank equivalent (i.e., FOMEX and COMESEC).

When applying for credit insurance coverage, insurers will normally require certain prerequisites before an underwriter will even quote a proposal, such as:

- The credit controls and credit history of the applicant must be impeccable.
- The insured must be willing to assume some significant deductible which will easily cover bad debts written off during the normal course of business. The underwriter assumes that it will never, save for a true catastrophic loss situation, pay a claim under the policy. Most multinationals are willing to assume these normal writeoffs—it is the "big hit(s)" which occur once every 10, 20, 30 years which are being insured.
- The applicant must be prepared to work with brokers and pull together key supporting information which would be required to obtain a favorable quotation from the underwriters.
- A large diversified pool of receivables and a sophisticated global approach towards this insurance coverage is necessary to allow the underwriter to simplify the administrative requirements. This "law of large numbers" will insulate the

underwriter from most of the risks ordinarily seen in a credit policy.

• The credit expertise, keen risk management, co-insurance acceptance, and the knowledge that the future catastrophic risk is what is being insured (not the past, usually exemplary, credit experience) gives brokers the ability to obtain a cost-effective risk transfer mechanism and a financial tool as well.

It is always important for credit managers to remember that credit insurance coverage is often more accurately characterized as a "financial product" rather than a credit insurance policy. Catastrophic commercial credit and/or political risk cover does play an important role, but it is not a substitute for superb credit judgement.

APPENDIX 6–A   COUNTRY CATEGORIES FOR OECD ARRANGEMENT ON OFFICIALLY SUPPORTED EXPORT CREDITS

Rich Countries	Intermediate Countries	Poor Countries
Andorra	Albania	Angola
Australia	Algeria	Bangladesh
Austria	Antigua	Benin
Bahrain	Argentina	Bolivia
Belgium	Bahamas	Burkina
Bermuda	Barbados	Burma
Brunei	Belize	Burundi
Canada	Botswana	Cameroon
Czechoslovakia	Brazil	Central African Rep.
Denmark	Bulgaria	Chad
Finland	Colombia	China, People's Rep. of
France	Chile	Congo, People's Rep.
Germany, D.R.	Costa Rica	Egypt
Germany, F.R.	Cuba	El Salvador
Greece	Cyprus	Ethiopia
Iceland	Dominican Republic	Gambia
Ireland	Ecuador	Ghana

Source: The Export-Import Bank of the United States (Washington, D.C., 1986).

Rich Countries	Intermediate Countries	Poor Countries
Israel	Fiji	Guinea-Bissau
Italy	Gabon	Guyana
Japan	Gilbraltar	Haiti
Kuwait	Guatemala	Honduras
Liechtenstein	Hong Kong	India
Luxembourg	Hungary	Indonesia
Libya	Iran	Kenya
Monaco	Iraq	Lesotho
Netherlands	Ivory Coast	Liberia
New Zealand	Jamaica	Madagascar
Norway	Jordan	Malawi
Qatar	Kiribati	Mauritania
San Marino	N. Korea	Mozambique
Saudi Arabia	S. Korea	Nepal
Spain	Lebanon	Nicaragua
Sweden	Macao	Niger
Switzerland	Malaysia	Pakistan
United Arab Emirates	Malta	Philippines
United Kingdom	Mauritius	Rwanda
United States	Mexico	Senegal
U.S.S.R.	Montserrat	Sierra Leone
Vatican City	Morocco	Somalia
	Namibia	Sri Lanka
	Nauru	Sudan
	Netherlands Antilles	Tanzania
	Nigeria	Thailand
	Oman	Togo
	Panama	Uganda
	Papua New Guinea	Yemen Arab Rep.
	Paraguay	Yemen, P.D.R.
	Peru	Zaire
	Poland	Zambia
	Portugal	Zimbabwe
	Romania	
	St. Kitts-Nevis	
	St. Lucia	
	Seychelles	
	Singapore	
	South Africa	
	Suriname	
	Syria	
	Taiwan	
	Trinidad and Tobago	
	Tunisia	
	Turkey	
	Uruguay	
	Venezuela	
	Yugoslavia	

Note: Not all countries listed are eligible for Eximbank financing. Also, the list is subject to change by the OECD and Eximbank at any one time. Exporters are recommended to contact Eximbank for the latest country categories.

APPENDIX 6—B OPIC INSURED INVESTORS FISCAL YEAR 1986

Investor	Country	Project	Insured Investment	Largest Single Cover
A. K. Robins & Co., Inc.	Egypt	Canning Equipment	$ 31,500	$ 31,500
A. K. Robins & Co., Inc.	Egypt	Food processing	14,400	14,400
A. K. Robins & Co., Inc.	Egypt	Packaging machinery	20,700	20,700
Abbott Laboratories	Indonesia	Pharmaceuticals	3,150,000	3,496,500
Abbott Laboratories	Philippines	Pharmaceuticals	5,625,000	5,625,000
Abbott Laboratories	Thailand	Pharmaceuticals	2,137,500	3,600,000
Admiral International Corp.	Honduras	Household appliances	961,500	1,266,000
American Center of Oriental Research	Jordan	Research center	1,350,000	1,350,000
American Express Bank Ltd.	Bangladesh	Banking	1,165,000	6,993,000
American Standard, Inc.	China	Sanitary wares	2,740,000	2,740,000
Anglo-Suisse (Pakistan), Inc.	Pakistan	Oil and gas	50,000,000	50,000,000
Applied Magnetics Corp.	Korea	Magnetic recording heads	5,992,323	10,210,652
Autodynamics, Inc.	Bangladesh	Training systems	245,588	245,588
Axxon Corp.	Egypt	Incinerators	158,575	158,575
Bank of America, N.T. & S.A.	Egypt	Banking	2,656,827	2,656,827
Bell Helicopter Textron, Inc.	Turkey	Helicopters	45,000	45,000
Cargill, Inc.	Korea	Animal feed	2,700,000	8,100,000
Carrier Corp.	Korea	Air conditioners	20,340,000	20,340,000
Chase Manhattan Bank, N.A.	Dominican Republic	Banking	3,150,000	6,300,000
Chemical International Finance, Ltd.	Turkey	Banking	2,911,050	8,733,150
Chew International Group	Egypt	Canning equipment	36,000	36,000
Citibank Overseas Investment Corp.	Chile	Credit/collections agency	89,910	90,000
Citibank, N.A.	Jordan	Banking	5,070,423	10,211,268
Citibank, N.A.	Pakistan	Banking	1,080,000	2,000,000
Citibank, N.A.	Portugal	Banking	7,706,886	11,988,490
Citibank, N.A.	Thailand	Banking	5,670,000	11,340,000

Company	Country	Business		
Citibank, N.A.	Thailand	Banking	9,000,000	18,000,000
Citibank, N.A.	Uruguay	Banking	1,800,000	2,000,000
Citicorp	Taiwan	Banking	4,646,700	8,809,700
Citicorp	Taiwan	Banking	5,276,529	1,889,487
Citicorp International Trading Co., Inc.	Chile	Trade finance	405,000	1,215,000
Coiltronics, Inc.	St. Christopher-Nevis	Electronics assembly	90,000	35,100
Del Marez, Archie	St. Lucia	Marina	3,570,522	3,570,522
Dravo Engineers, Inc.	Thailand	Olefins plant	1,350,000	1,350,000
Edlow Resources Ltd.	Central African Republic	Gold mining	$ 427,500	$ 855,000
Electronic Devices, Inc.	Haiti	Instrumentation devices	1,350,000	1,350,000
Equicom International, Inc.	Philippines	Data preparation and entry	450,000	450,000
Firestone Tire & Rubber Co.	Costa Rica	Tires	2,000,000	2,000,000
Fuller International, Inc.	Egypt	Calcination plant	441,000	441,000
General Electric Co.	Pakistan	Turbine generators	4,620,030	4,620,030
General Electric Co.	Saudi Arabia	Turbine generators	3,204,630	3,204,630
General Electric Co.	Saudi Arabia	Turbine generators	3,580,804	3,580,804
General Foods Corp.	India	Food processing	3,690,000	11,070,000
General Foods Corp.	China	Food processing	873,000	2,619,000
General Foods Corp.	China	Food processing	1,800,000	1,800,000
General Railway Signal Co.	China	Railway signal equipment	9,900,000	8,925,000
General Resistance, Inc.	Haiti	Electronics assembly	522,000	510,000
Gilbert/Commonwealth International, Inc.	Saudi Arabia	Transmission lines	168,750	168,750
The Gillette Company	Egypt	Razor blades	984,750	1,994,119

Source: Overseas Private Investment Corporation, 1986 Annual Report (Washington, D.C., 1986), pp. 28–30.

557

Investor	Country	Project	Insured Investment	Largest Single Cover
The Gillette Company	Indonesia	Writing instruments	1,248,750	3,746,250
Gilley & Associates, Inc.	India	Petroleum drilling	108,000	108,000
Global EX-IM & Manufacturing, Ltd.	Haiti	Toys and garments	876,150	876,150
H. J. Heinz Co.	Korea	Food processing	11,340,000	8,640,000
Henry R. Jahn & Son, Inc.	Syria	Bucket excavators	45,416	45,416
Holiday Inns (Costa Rica), Inc.	Costa Rica	Hotel	1,350,000	4,750,000
Hybritex Automotive Controls, Inc.	Costa Rica	Automotive parts	837,000	2,000,000
Inn of the Sun, Ltd.	Honduras	Resort	600,000	600,000
Intel Corp.	Israel	Semiconductors	53,460,000	93,960,000
ITEC International, Inc.	India	Telephone switching equipment	155,700	155,700
Kimberly-Clark Corp.	Korea	Tissue paper products	3,903,282	3,903,282
Kyndyl International, Ltd.	Malawi	Woodburning cookstoves	135,000	405,000
La Selva, Inc.	Ecuador	Jungle tourist lodge	17,024	51,073
Lawmaster, Bruce A.	Honduras	Resort	67,500	75,000
Lobell, Donald Travis, Jr.	Bahamas	Poultry farm	360,000	443,500
Mallon Minerals Corp.	Costa Rica	Precious minerals mining	$ 990,000	$ 2,000,000
Marx, Edgar B.	Malaysia	Coconut dessicating	623,700	1,683,990
McKinnon Corp.	Costa Rica	Coffee and tropical fruit	50,067	50,067
North Hills Electronics, Inc.	Israel	Power supply equipment	360,000	2,624,400
Nyle International Corp.	Chile	Lumber drying and grading	517,500	517,500
O. F. Jensen International, Inc.	Pakistan	Water treatment plant	4,710	4,710
Overseas Bechtel, Inc.	Colombia	Pump station	886,561	886,561

Company	Country	Description		
Pacific Queen Seafood Distributors	Costa Rica	Shrimp farm	139,950	135,000
Parfet, Courtland E.	Kenya	Cattle ranch	90,000	121,500
Parsons Brinckerhoff International, Inc.	Turkey	Motorway construction	184,658	184,658
Pennzoil Co. et al.	Morocco	Oil and gas	125,000,000	125,000,000
Phelps Dodge International Corp.	Thailand	Telephone cables	1,500,000	1,500,000
Phelps Dodge International Corp.	India	Telephone cables	1,000,000	1,000,000
Pilgrim Food Companies, Inc.	Belize	Cocoa, timber	945,000	945,000
PPG Industries, Inc.	Korea	Paint coatings	4,196,000	2,196,000
Quanta Corp.	Turkey	Television graphics equipment	35,870	35,870
Republic Importing & Exporting Co., Inc.	Costa Rica	Banana plantation	6,750,000	7,350,000
Rhodes, William M., Jr.	Costa Rica	Leatherleaf fern farm	135,000	135,000
Seaview Villas, Inc.	Jamaica	Tourist villas	596,700	400,000
Secuador Ltd.	Ecuador	Flour mill	1,155,958	3,467,874
Sewer Rodding Equipment Co.	Pakistan	Sewage equipment	3,772	3,772
Slater Electric, Inc.	Jamaica	Electrical wiring devices	292,680	742,680
Smith, Barry L.	Jamaica	Tourist villa	450,000	450,000
Squibb Middle East, S.A.	Egypt	Pharmaceuticals	7,002,000	7,002,000
Taylor/Cross International, Inc.	Jamaica	Rice growing and milling	713,400	713,400
TII Industries, Inc.	Dominican Republic	Telecommunications components	2,700,000	2,700,000
TII Industries, Inc.	Haiti	Telecommunications components	3,690,000	3,690,000
Uppers Manufacturing Co., Inc.	Costa Rica	Shoe components	270,000	270,000
Victaulic Company of America	Chile	Iron foundry	1,113,750	1,113,750
Warner Lambert Co.	China	Gelatin capsules	6,300,000	6,300,000
Wood Industries International, Ltd.	Congo	Wood treatment	891,000	1,782,000

APPENDIX 6–C
PEFCO COMMERCIAL
BANK LISTING

East

The Bank of New York
Bankers Trust Company, New York
Brown Brothers Harriman & Co., New York
The Chase Manhattan Bank, N.A., New York
Chemical Bank, New York
Citibank, N.A., New York
The Connecticut Bank and Trust Company, Hartford
Connecticut National Bank, Hartford
Equitable Bank, N.A., Baltimore
European-American Banking Corporation, New York
Fleet National Bank, Providence
Irving Trust Company, New York
Manufacturers Hanover Trust Company, New York
Marine Midland Bank, N.A., Buffalo and New York
Mellon Bank, Philadelphia
Morgan Guaranty Trust Company of New York
National Westminster Bank USA, New York
The Riggs National Bank of Washington, New York
IBJ Schroder Bank & Trust Company, New York
Sterling National Bank & Trust Company of New York

Middle West

Continental Illinois National Bank and Trust Company of Chicago
First of American Bank-Detroit, N.A.
The First National Bank of Chicago
First National Bank of Minneapolis
First National Bank of Saint Paul
First Wisconsin National Bank of Milwaukee
Harris Trust and Savings Bank, Chicago
The Indiana National Bank, Indianapolis
Mercantile Trust Company, N.A., St. Louis
The Northern Trust Company, Chicago
PNC Financial Corp., Pittsburgh
Society Corporation, Cleveland

West
Bank of America, N.T. & S.A., San Francisco
The Bank of California, San Francisco
First Interstate Bank of California, Los Angeles
Lloyds Bank California, Los Angeles
Security Pacific Corporation, Los Angeles
United States National Bank of Oregon, Portland
Wells Fargo Bank, N.A., San Francisco

Southwest
First City National Bank of Houston
First Republic Bank, Dallas

South
Commerce Union Bank, Nashville
First National Bank of Commerce, New Orleans
First Alabama Bank, Mobile
North Carolina National Bank, Charlotte
Southeast Bank, N.A., Miami

REFERENCES

1. Louis J. Celi and I. James Czechowicz, *Export Financing: Handbook of Sources & Techniques* (Morristown, N.J.: Financial Executive Research Foundation, 1985), p. 15.
2. Ibid., p. 15.
3. Ibid., pp. 15–16.
4. "Ex-Im Bank to Back Loan of $25.5 Million to Turkey for Parts," *The Wall Street Journal,* August 5, 1986, p. 35.
5. "Export-Import Bank Offers to Subsidize Sale to Brazil," *The Wall Street Journal,* November 22, 1985, p. 18.
6. Ibid., p. 18.
7. "Ex-Im Bank Clears Loans to Brazil for $35 Million," *The Wall Street Journal,* September 10, 1986, p. 36.

CHAPTER 7

PRIVATE SOURCES OF EXPORT FINANCE

Before the recent international debt crisis, banks, finance companies, and credit insurance organizations were standing in line to offer companies export trade credit financing and risk insurance. With the rapid increase in external debts overseas, however, easy export credit is almost a thing of the past. Many regional banks have pulled out of international business, and money center banks are increasingly leary of added credit exposure with debtor nations.

Exports to less developed countries (LDCs) have been hardest hit. Despite the less hospitable environment for export trade, there are still a number of private sources of financing to which an exporter can turn. These include money center banks, regional banks, branches of foreign banks, investment banks, export finance companies, factoring houses, forfait houses, leasing companies, export trading companies, and private insurance companies. The point is that credit managers must shop around to see who is offering what type of financing assistance and to which countries. It must be an on-going process.

Many successful exporters use several different commercial banks and turn to other types of financial institutions as well, to fill their various financing needs. For example, a number of exporters have found U.S. branches of foreign banks that are willing to provide financing at better rates or to countries that many U.S. commercial banks considered too risky. Others are discovering forfait houses as sources of nonrecourse, medium-term financing. Exporters that seek overseas markets or that must fulfill countertrade commitments are turning to export trading companies.

This chapter describes the private sources of export finance, including private insurance programs, and examines the strategies that successful exporters employ to tap them.

COMMERCIAL BANKS

There are generally four types of commercial banks to choose from as sources for export trade finance:

1. Money center banks.
2. Regional banks.
3. Foreign branch banks.
4. Investment banks.

The large money center banks usually cater to large businesses. They have sophisticated knowledge of virtually all facets of export financing needed by major multinational companies (MNC). Unfortunately, they are virtually closed to smaller exporters because their export sales volume is small in comparison to MNCs. Therefore, smaller firms have traditionally turned to regional banks for export financing assistance. These banks generally have far less knowledge and weaker commitments to export trade finance than do the money center banks, but some can be very helpful to business. Foreign bank branches on the other hand, located in major U.S. cities and throughout the world, can be particularly useful for financing exports to their home countries or to countries with which their governments have historical relationships (e.g., former colonies; France—Morocco, Algeria, Sierra Leone, such as Credit Lyonnais and Societe Generale; England—Hong Kong, India, South Africa, such as Barclays Bank and Lloyds Bank.

It is, however, far more important to pick the "right" bank than the "leading" bank when it comes to export trade finance. The search process starts by first seeking answers to the following questions:

- How sophisticated, experienced, and creative is it in export trade finance? Does it have an export trade finance department? Are the individuals you are dealing with knowledgeable? Discuss your business needs with a representative from the export trade financing group. Don't speak or rely solely on an account officer or a banking generalist.

- What types of products and services do you need? It doesn't matter how sophisticated or knowledgeable a bank is if its products and services do not match your needs. For example, if your company is frequently faced with countertrade requirements, look for a bank or banks with an export trading company.
- Is export trade financing available in the markets needed? Shop around for the bank most willing and able to finance deals for extended periods of time for a particular country or group of countries. Do they have branches, correspondent bank relationships, or representative offices in the countries you want to do business in? Do these banks have long-standing business relations with your markets?

A list of bank contacts to call or visit will help minimize the problem of finding trade finance when business comes your way. Just because one bank's financing package is uncompetitive doesn't necessarily mean that another bank will not offer a good package.

A bank's willingness and ability to do export trade financing deals to a particular country or countries, particularly to the riskier ones, will vary based on each bank's credit exposure in each country and current perception of country risk. While some banks are willing to take risks, others are not. This includes banks who are willing to confirm letters of credit. This is why it is important to try several banks and financial institutions. A particular bank that is unwilling to finance or confirm a deal today, may be willing to do business three to six months from now. With all of the Third World debt refinancing taking place constantly, bank credit exposures and attitudes towards risk markets might change from negative to positive.

If a business does find a bank willing to commit to provide financing to a risk market, it is always a good idea to get the bank to hold the financing for a period of time, preferably in writing. This will probably involve a commitment fee. Further questions to seek answers to include:

- Are there any restrictions on your exports? Some banks, as a matter of policy, will not finance sales of military goods. Some will finance "defense" goods, but not "offensive" goods.
- How responsive is the bank? Look for banks that will give you a financing decision quickly and execute the deal promptly. A bank's inefficiency can be costly.
- How much risk will it take? Seek banks that do not demand that the exporter provide guaranties or insurance on riskier exports. Some will want insurance, others won't, and some will refuse financing even with insurance.

The following are some of the more important export-related services a bank can offer:

Foreign exchange

Export collections

Multisourcing information

Marketing trade data

Requirement for insurance

Cost of financing

Ease of obtaining export financing

In order to get bank financing to meet your exporting and international needs at a reasonable cost the right bank must be selected. This can be painstaking and frustrating—especially when an order is in hand, needs to be shipped shortly, needs credit approval, but must be financed. The criteria for choosing a bank or banks is difficult for small exporters. To make the task easier, it is wise to have a checklist to discern the complexities of bank selection.

The inexperienced businessperson will find contacting a bank an endless process of referral from one person to another and one phone number after another. Because of banking regulations, both state and federal, and because banks seek to concentrate and operate in different geographic areas allowed under such regulations, a number of different banking "forms" are found.

More than likely, contacting the main office of the bank is a good starting point. Many banks have international divisions—

departments or international trade companies established specifically to handle international trade. In smaller or medium-size cities there is usually no great problem. The smaller regional banking centers are more centralized and involve international personnel at an early stage.

While many banks have internationalized themselves by building and developing relationships with banks abroad, referred to as correspondent banks, others don't have large networks of correspondent banks or may not have the right correspondents to match your needs. The following is a listing of the key ingredients of selecting a bank or banks:

The Overall Relationship. Most export transactions in excess of $1 million are economically feasible and attractive to commercial banks. In effect, the larger the export transaction, the better. However, even large exporters will occasionally have to fill small export orders, whether profitable or unprofitable for the bank. Stressing the relationship value of the financing to the bank, the exporter may be able to consummate a small trade credit. This is done by the business maintaining large balances with the bank plus the other overall business it gets from the account.

Evaluation. Many experienced credit managers and their treasury departments evaluate their banks' performance in export financing and other related services by establishing lists. The decision from a credit managers' perspective is based on how supportive they are or have been in financing exports, how automated their export documentary collection services are, and if the automation meets the needs of the credit manager.

Information. A number of banks are familiar with many overseas businesses who buy and sell goods and services on a continuous basis or are capable of buying an exporter's goods and using its services. Banks should be knowledgeable with the major international traders, such as, the major Japanese and South Korean export trading companies (i.e., Mitsui, Mitsubishi, Samsung, Hyundai, or the Daewoo Group) or such government owned entities as Mexico's Pemex, Brazil's Petrobras, and IRI or ENI of Italy, including major competitors in U.S. industry.

Programs. Finance, insurance, guaranties—banks should be totally familiar with the government and nongovernment sponsored credit insurance policies and guaranty programs, such as those offered by Eximbank. A bank that has a good network of overseas subsidiaries or correspondent banks can inform U.S. exporters of a host country's credit insurance and guarantee schemes. The smart exporter, depending on its worldwide structure, should continuously look at a myriad of possibilities for marketing, selling, and financing goods internationally. A bank willing and able to finance goods and services, no matter where domiciled in the world, should never be disregarded if the exporter has the ability to use those services.

Questions to Ask.
1. Can the bank pay irrevocable letters of credit (predicated on correspondent network)?
2. Can it confirm letters of credit in risk countries?
3. Can it do buyer, forfait, or bankers' acceptance financing in Third World markets?
4. Is the bank innovative and creative in its financing schemes?

Relationships. Businesses who develop good working relationships with bank account officers are more likely to get favorable treatment and assurances of prompt service. From the perspective of both the businessperson and banker, it is important to cultivate this relationship in order to foster a mutual understanding of what the businessperson wants to accomplish and how the bank fits in.

Negotiate. The terms and conditions, rates and fee structure of a bank are almost always negotiable. This is why it is important for the credit manager to obtain quotes from several banks interested in the same deal to seek out the best rates and terms and conditions. In turn, the credit manager may have to increase his business activity with the bank as an incentive for the bank to offer attractive rates. The increase of business from the credit manager assists the banker in justifying the low rates.

Full or Partial Recourse. In order to get the business for marketing/sales, a credit manager must be prepared to accept full or partial recourse, subject to his management's policies to accept such recourse. At this point, the credit manager must weigh the pros and cons or risks/rewards of financing the business deal under this scenario. From the bank's point of view, the deal is risky, and even with credit insurance in place, it still has a retention factor to consider. Is it worth losing the business to competition or accepting full or partial recourse?

Money Center Banks

U.S. Money Center banks are usually capable of handling a wide range of international trade related facilities and services. In other words, they are "full-service" financial institutions. They can meet almost all of the needs of an exporter.

Many large multinational businesses prefer to work with Money Center banks because they can service many or all of their needs. In turn, large multinational customers of the banks represent important customers. They can give the banks plenty of business, such as large deposits, short- and long-term borrowing, and lock box receipts. The banks are more than willing to service their needs and not do anything to jeopardize the loss of any or all of their business. Therefore, it is important to note that the larger the company's business to a Money Center Bank, the more "clout" it can exercise over the bank.

The products and services of these banks fall into three broad categories. Many of these products and services are also available at regional banks and U.S. branches of foreign banks. The products and services are:

1. Trade financing products.
2. Nontraditional products.
3. Trade related services.

Trade Financing Products. The services associated with export trade financing include: Advising, paying and confirming export letters of credit, opening import letters of credit, Bankers' Acceptance financing, forfait financing, purchasing export related accounts and notes receivables, refinancing sight drafts, and purchasing foreign currency drafts.

Banks vary in their ability and willingness to offer these products and services. Some see it as opportunities to get loans and funds on their books; others see it as part of their overall products and services or an avenue of approach to get business from customers.

Nontraditional Products. Money Center Banks can offer export trade financing in two areas: Official export credit insured programs and financing related to countertrade, leasing, and factoring.

The banks can offer export trade financing in conjunction with different types of U.S. and foreign export credit programs. For example: The FCIA Bank Letter of Credit policy encourages insured banks to support U.S. exports by protecting them against loss on their confirmations or negotiations of irrevocable letters of credit issued by foreign banks in favor of U.S. exporters; the banks can assist exporters in securing direct loans from Eximbank for their foreign customers and can participate in the financing deal by offering loans for the amount not guarantied by Eximbank; foreign subsidiaries of the U.S. Money Center banks can assist a U.S. based parent company's foreign subsidiary by providing financing using export credit programs of the host country. It can prove very beneficial for businesses who are sourcing goods from more than one country to fill a foreign customer's order in a risk market (country).

Bank export trade finance specialists can assist exporters in structuring complicated deals, not only for exporters, but for the foreign customer as well. However, many experienced exporters prefer to deal with Eximbank and FCIA directly.

Complex deals requiring the use of foreign export credit programs can be structured by the U.S. exporter using its Money Center Bank as lead coordinator and structurer of the deal with the bank's foreign subsidiary banks.

Many banks have formed export trading companies (ETCs), discussed later in this chapter. ETCs can be particularly useful for exporters faced with countertrade requirements. Other banks, in addition to their ETCs, may be actively involved in international leasing (discussed in Chapter 8), another benefit to exporters of capital goods. Banks may even provide factoring services to smaller exporters.

Trade Related Services. One very important trade related service that is directly related to a credit managers' cash management of export related receivables is the documentary collection services (discussed in Chapter 5) that is provided by banks. Money Center banks' branches and correspondent banks can improve an exporter's cash mobilization techniques with the right people, systems, procedures, and network in place (i.e., The Philadelphia National Bank, The Chase Manhattan Bank, N.A., and Security Pacific).

These banks can assist exporters in managing their foreign currency exposures. Small- to medium-size businesses that lack expertise in these areas will find the banks' services and advice very beneficial. Because exporters are faced with having to invoice their export transactions in currencies other than U.S. dollars, mainly for competitive reasons, they are not always aware of the pros and cons of foreign currency (F/X) billings. Banks can hedge F/X exposures when an exporter invoices in a foreign currency and give advice on which currencies to use.

Other major Money Center banks have established broad-based advisory services related to international trade, such as Chase Manhattan's World Information Corporation, Chemical Bank's World Trade Group, or Citibank's International Trade Services Group. These additional services can include: market research, computerized global intelligence, automated letter of credit and documentary collection services, information about country regulations, identification of markets for an exporter's goods, and location of distributors, foreign agents, brokers, and joint-venture partners, or offer seminars and workshops on trade finance or specific trade issues.

Money Center banks for the most part are structured to support businesses with large exports. They are particularly interested in repeat business which smaller exporters don't often have. However, if the banks have an Edge Act bank (explained next), at or near the smaller exporter, there is a better chance it can handle its export business.

It is also important to point out that Money Center banks vary in their approach to U.S. business. They might be willing to make exceptions for "relationship" reasons on smaller business. Although the exports of a business may be small in relation to its size, the potential to lock in a new customer or to strengthen an existing relationship might be the motivating factor for these banks to handle smaller export volumes.

Edge Act and Agreement Corporations

Edge Act and Agreement Corporations are subsidiaries of U.S. banks, incorporated in the United States under Section 25 of the Federal Reserve Act to engage in international banking and financing operations. Not only may such subsidiaries engage in general international banking, they may also finance commercial, industrial, or financial projects in foreign countries through long-term loans or equity participation. Such participation, however, is subject to the day-to-day practices and policies of the Federal Reserve System.

Edge Act and Agreement Corporations are physically located in the United States. Because U.S. banks cannot have branches outside their own state, Edge Act and Agreement Corporations are usually located in other states in order to conduct international banking activities. Growth in Edge Act banking was greatly facilitated in June 1979 when the Federal Reserve Board issued new guidelines that permitted interstate branching by Edge Act corporations. Previously an Edge Act corporation had to be separately incorporated in each state. By increasing their interstate penetration through Edge Act corporations, the large money center banks are establishing a physical presence in most of the important regional financial centers in order to prepare for the day when interstate branching will be permitted for domestic business.

The Interstate Banking Act of 1978 extended the Edge Act privilege to foreign banks operating in the United States. In return, the previous ability of foreign banks to conduct a retail banking business in more than one state was severely limited. They must pick a single state as home base. In that state they can conduct full-service banking. In all other states they must limit their activities to Edge Act banking in the same manner as U.S. banks.

The origin of Edge Act corporations comes from Section 25 of the Federal Reserve Act as amended in 1916 to allow national banks and state banks belonging to the Federal Reserve System and having capital and surplus of $1 million (since increased to $2 million) or more to invest up to 10 percent of that capital and surplus in a subsidiary incorporated under state or federal law to conduct international or foreign banking. A bank forming such a subsidiary would enter into an "agreement" with the board of governors of the Federal Reserve System as to the type of activities in which they would engage—hence the name *Agreement Corporation*.

In 1919 Congress passed an amendment, proposed by Senator Walter E. Edge of New Jersey, that expanded the original provisions of the Act to allow such subsidiaries to be chartered "for the purpose of engaging in international or foreign banking or other international or foreign financial operation . . . either directly or through the agency, ownership, or control of local institutions in foreign countries."[1] Subsidiaries chartered under this amendment, known as Edge Act corporations, can make equity investments abroad, an operation barred to domestic banks.

Edge Act corporations are federally chartered and not subject to the banking laws of the various states. They may accept demand and time (but not savings) deposits from outside the United States (as well as from within, if such deposits are incidental to or for the purpose of transactions in foreign countries). Each corporation can:

1. Make loans, although commitments to any one borrower cannot exceed 10 percent of capital and surplus.
2. Issue or confirm letters of credit.
3. Make loans or advances to finance foreign trade, including production loans.
4. Create bankers' acceptances.
5. Receive items for collection (i.e., documentary collections).
6. Offer services such as remittance of funds abroad, or buying, selling, or holding securities for safekeeping.

7. Issue guarantees. . . .
8. Act as paying agent for securities issued by foreign governments or foreign corporations.
9. Engage in spot and forward foreign exchange transactions.

Branches

Branches of U.S. domestic banks are not only located domestically, but internationally. The Federal Reserve Board's Regulation K permits foreign branches of U.S. banks to engage in certain activities internationally other than the ones they are permitted domestically. They include such activities as:

1. Issuing guaranties within certain limitations (domestic branches cannot).
2. Investing in foreign governments or private entities.
3. Underwriting, distributing, and selling the obligations of foreign governments.
4. Acting as an insurance agency or broker.
5. Engaging in repurchase arrangements involving commodities and securities that may be considered extensions of credit.
6. Lending to officers of the bank and paying employees a greater rate of interest than the depositors.

Branches of foreign banks are commonly located in U.S. cities where they have identified certain markets.

Regional Banks

Regional banks have been an important source of export financing, for small- and medium-sized exporters—even large exporters. However, their activity in international trade has been hampered by the international debt crisis. Many regional banks have dramatically reduced their involvement in international trade. The impact of this reduced participation has been severe for small- and medium-sized exporters, because they have limited access to money center banks.

Some regional banks are still good sources of export trade finance. There are some regional banks still willing to finance sales without recourse to countries considered high risks in Latin America and other countries throughout the world. Although they are selective, they find opportunities from voids created by money center and other regional banks that are sometimes unable and unwilling to assume risks in certain high risk countries. The void this unwillingness causes can often be filled by a regional bank.

Export trade financing can be developed over time by the local business and banker fostering a close working relationship. The bank is more apt to do a financing deal because it knows the local business, understands its goals and objectives, and knows management. Exporters should seek out those regional banks that remain committed to export trade financing, even though some regional banks' are withdrawing from financing international trade. When one regional bank closes its doors to international trade, this can open doors to other banks who see it as an opportunity to gain a foothold with local businesses and thus gain customer loyalty, the booking of loans, the financing of international trade, handling the exporter's documentary collections, and increasing cash flow. Regional banks who remain wholly or partially committed to financing international trade are still potential sources for exporters.

Characteristics of Regional Banks.   The following are some basic fundamental characteristics to look for in regional banks:

Correspondent relationships: Regional banks do not normally have their own overseas networks of subsidiaries or branches like the money center banks. They do have entry to foreign banks through a correspondent relationship. The relationships with overseas banks vary in number, quality, and services agreed on (i.e., handling a letter of credit, ability to confirm a letter of credit, amount of credit extended). The exporters should ask for a listing of the bank's correspondent relationships to compare them with other regional bank listings and to determine who these overseas banks are in relation to services. It is important to remember that the overseas bank because of its size might have limited capabilities or be financially unsound. A number of overseas banks primarily in Third World countries, such as Argentina and Kenya have gone bankrupt.

People and officers: Are the people involved in international trade experienced? Are there many officers of the bank with international trade experience? If not, the bank may not be attuned to international trade, and might consider it a secondary product and a minor part of the bank. Its services and products will more than likely be poor or inadequate.

Experience: Where did the officers get their experience and education? Where did they come from? Were they trained at a major money center bank? Have they spent considerable time abroad? A bank person who has spent time abroad will more than likely have considerable insight and practical knowledge about certain overseas markets and customs, habits, and traditions.

Staff size: How large is the trade finance department? What kind of support do they receive from senior management? Will certain personnel be assigned to handle your documentary collection business and export trade financing needs? Are the staffs well organized and properly structured to provide the service you need to do your job?

Products and services: What services does the bank offer? Will it do only letters of credit and can it confirm credits where and when needed? How sophisticated is it in handling bankers' acceptances? Does the staff know about, and have they worked with, the various U.S. and foreign export credit insurance and guarantee programs? Who are the people in the bank that are totally familiar with the products and services offered by government sponsored and private insurers and guarantors?

Foreign Banks in the United States

Foreign banks in the United States are another source of finance, simply because many U.S. commercial banks are no longer in a position to offer financing of U.S. export sales because of their Third World debt problems. Many exporters are finding that foreign banks are more aggressive, take risks, and will offer financing at attractive rates to gain a niche or increase market share in the United States.

Subsidiary banks of foreign-based banks can be found operating in financial centers throughout the world. In the United States, they operate under state or federal charters. This type of banking operation is an entity legally separate from the foreign parent bank that owns its stock. If the domestic company requires a concentration of expertise in doing business in a particular foreign country, the foreign subsidiary bank's contacts and relationship with its parent can provide specialization, expertise, and knowledge about the foreign country where that parent is based.

These foreign banks operating in the United States are well experienced in export trade finance simply because their parent countries have long been involved in international trade. For example, during the colonialization period of the United Kingdom and France, exporters of goods and services were very dependent on the banks to help them find customers, finance their sales, and obtain the necessary foreign government approvals. They tend to take a long-term perspective towards international trade. It is important to remember that many countries are very much dependent on international trade for export earnings needed to retire import bills. Their exports represent a higher percentage of GDP (gross domestic product) than in the United States. This is one of the principal reasons why they take an aggressive stance toward exports.

There are 325 to 350 foreign banks from 50 or 60 countries with branches or offices in New York alone. The following are some guidelines for choosing the right foreign bank. Select a bank of the country to which you are exporting. They are more likely to be familiar with your foreign customer, more willing and able to assume political and commercial risk, and finance your goods and services. They can be especially useful and helpful in countries where they have traditionally had a strong involvement—such as those with long established colonial ties. European banks have colonial ties in Asia and Africa; the Japanese banks traditionally have had strong ties in Asia or the Pacific Rim area; while the Austrian, German, and Swiss banks are positioned to handle deals in Eastern Europe. Likewise, Arab banks operating in the United States can help with trade to the Middle East. The French banks have strong colonial ties with Morocco, Algeria, and Sierre Leone; the English banks with India, South Africa, and Hong Kong. They can offer favorable export trade financing in particular countries within those geographic areas where other banks cannot. Exporters who have found it impossible to get a confirmed L/C on an export for Nigeria may want to consider a U.K. bank or for

Argentina a German bank. Particular attention should be paid to new bank openings in the United States and abroad. They will be hungry for business. (*The Banker's Almanac* is a good source of reference.)

It is important to look at the commercial and country risks of the parent company bank and its country when seeking confirmation or doing an export trade financing deal with a foreign bank in the United States. The foreign bank is only as good as its parent and country. These banks can be an excellent source of information regarding their home country's export credit programs. They may not necessarily be totally familiar with U.S. credit programs, but can certainly act as an intermediary for working out a complex deal involving the subsidiary of a United States based company in the home country of the foreign bank.

Investment Banks

Investment banks are mainly involved in project financing. In most cases they work only with the host country or a foreign government agency. These banks can act for exporters as financial advisor, to orchestrate a whole deal (including bonds [the structuring of a bid or performance bond], commercial paper, or stock issues), evaluate financing alternatives, assist project engineers, and, from prior experience in certain countries, provide high-level contacts.

The primary way investment banks can be helpful to exporters is by providing information on projects they are presently handling or have handled in the past.

EXPORT FINANCE COMPANIES

Export finance companies can be particularly helpful to small- and medium-sized exporters, especially those who do not have their own FCIA or other insurance coverage. Also, those who are dealing with foreign customers that do not want to open letters of credit or who are having difficulty arranging financing by commercial banks can be assisted by export finance companies.

Finance houses in the United States were primarily formed by former executives of British finance or confirming houses. Many of them have long-term working relationships with certain foreign customers or countries. In many cases, certain foreign customers use export finance companies not only as sources of supply (i.e., the finance company will find reliable suppliers) but to arrange better financing deals for them. In effect, the credit evaluation process is substituted for that of the exporter. However, it is still prudent management for the credit manager to check out the creditworthiness of its foreign customer. It is conceivable the finance company may want full or partial recourse back to the exporter in the event of nonpayment due to commercial reasons.

For example, a U.S. exporter selling on sight draft terms to an overseas distributor in the Philippines now wants 180 day payment terms due to competition. Since the foreign distributor has an established working relationship with a finance company in the United States, they were willing to extend 180 days to the Philippine distributor. In turn, the U.S. exporter can get paid "at sight" by the finance company on its receipt of documents from the exporter. The finance company will charge a fee which the exporter can wholly or partially build into its price to the distributor and still be competitive. A vast majority of finance companies can extend longer terms and take on greater risks primarily because they are insured by FCIA.

Like any financing arranged through a third or intermediary party, the exporter needs to compare the charges of the finance company with that of other finance companies, commercial bank financing packages, and others for the best deal possible, not only for itself, but for the foreign customer as well. In most competitive situations, foreign customers can only absorb so much from suppliers before the per unit cost of the imported goods becomes uncompetitive. To maintain or increase its market share, the exporter may have to absorb a portion of the charges and fees for financing the exported goods.

A number of export finance companies are either foreign or locally owned. If foreign owned, the exporter needs to not only consider the creditworthiness of the local company, but the overseas parent as well. There are a number of export finance companies located in the United States that an exporter can choose from. Appendix 7–A is a listing of many of the major players operating in the United States.

Companies seeking an export finance company should ask the following questions: How much experience does it have? The more experience the company's people have, the better. Is the company financed and backed by financial institutions? Is it highly leveraged which will limit its capability to finance large transactions over extended period of time? Does it have adequate lines of credit to draw from in order to do large volume export trade financing transactions? What does the company look like financially? In other words, you need assurances about the company's financial capability to repay you. Based on the above, is it prepared to do short- and medium-term financing? If yes, under what terms and conditions? How quickly is the company prepared to give you an answer on whether or not it is prepared to undertake a financing deal on your behalf? In other words, how long will it take to make a credit decision? Is it prepared to give you its answer in writing? If yes, what are the terms and conditions? Exporters should insist on getting a commitment in writing so there are no misunderstandings. What are the rates or its fee structure? How frequently does it change its rates and fees? Will you get sufficient advance notification of these changes? Exporters should shop around for favorable rates and then negotiate to try to get even lower rates.

Trafco: Fixed-Interest Loans from the Private Sector[2]
U.S. exporters stymied by less-than-favorable government export credit and by the increasing reluctance of U.S. banks to finance trade because of glaring international debt, may have another vehicle for their borrowing needs. The Trade Finance Corporation (Trafco) is now providing substantial medium-term financing. It draws its own funding from a relatively untapped market. Entering areas of finance served only by governments. Trafco's programs were originally implemented in cooperation with AIG Political Risk Inc., which acts as a credit insurer, and Salomon Brothers Inc., which serves as a placement agent. It now uses other types of insurance schemes.

The conduit financing program involves aggregating many loans into a large pool in which principal and interest loans are "passed through" to investors in the form of payments of principal and interest on a bond. Trafco simultaneously sells bonds to investors and purchases export receivables for exporters. The basic idea is to use the methods of finance employed in the domestic property market and in the public sector, and to apply them to international trade. In effect, it takes a package in international trade debt, enhances it with some form of wrap-around credit insurance, and places it in the capital markets at triple A rates.[3]

In 1987, Trafco was in the process of developing a short-term facility for 30, 60, 90, and up to 270 day receivables.

The financing being offered ranges between two and five years with the following benefits:

- Fixed interest rate funding for the life of the loan. A borrower will know up front what his interest costs will be.
- Low cost of export financing. Trafco sees its rates in the nonsubsidized market as "more than competitive."
- Ability to finance trade between all "acceptable nations" without restriction regarding the national content of the goods shipped. Trafco will cover countries that Eximbank does, and some that it does not.
- Flexible terms and conditions that are not governed by traditional restraints in government-based loans.

FACTORING HOUSES

Another intermediary source of export trade finance that is particularly suited for small- and medium-sized exporters are export factoring houses. These organizations not only provide nonrecourse financing, but can perform credit investigations, guarantee commercial and political risks, assume collection responsibilities, and finance accounts receivable. In addition, the factoring house can perform such auxiliary services as computer generated management reports, letters of credit, term loans, ledgering (accounting), and marketing assistance. These are important, time-consuming functions that the small- to medium-size exporter may not be capable administratively to perform. They can provide all the necessary services a small- to medium-sized exporter cannot afford or put together and run successfully. Although smaller firms are typical customers, exporters of all sizes and levels of sophistication can benefit from their services.

Many factors have established credit departments specifically for handling U.S. exports that make credit investigations and decisions. Others have established offices overseas. These offices are staffed with local credit personnel who are knowledgeable about local customs, habits, and practices. Still others have allied themselves with a network of independent foreign factoring companies that are primarily bank owned. The network of factors throughout the world operate under the terms and conditions of an agreement among all members. The overseas factors are ideal for a United States factor to use since they also conduct their own domestic factoring business in their own country.

Factoring is practical to exporters that meet the following criteria: They must have a broad client base that is located throughout the world, payment terms range from sight or time draft and open account up to 180 days in each type of payment term transaction, the markets for the business's goods are highly competitive making it essential to offer favorable credit terms to foreign customers, repetitive sales are the norm (rather than one-shot deals), and there is a need for trade financing.

However, factoring is not practical for exporters with the following characteristics: A seller of heavy capital equipment or commodities, one who has numerous financial resources and sources of export trade finance, and with a large percentage of its foreign customers in countries with a high degree of commercial or political risk.

A factor typically wants to learn all it can about an exporter. It will ask: What is the present and projected annual sales volume, product line or lines, and type of customers? Who is the distributor, manufacturer, processor, miller, miner, retailer, or end-user? What is the total number of foreign customers? Total number of active customers? What is their payment experience, percentage of exports to total sales, average monthly accounts receivable balance of countries sold to, and average currency value of each invoice per product line? What is the name, address, and bank reference listing of the exporters' major foreign customers, payment terms by product line or country, and credit limit requirements by foreign customer?

The factor will perform a credit investigation on each foreign customer based on the criteria provided and its sources of information to determine creditworthiness of each customer and to establish credit limits and payment terms for each customer.

Sources of Export Factoring.   The world's four major international factoring organizations are the following:

Walter Heller Overseas Corp. is presently the largest international factoring company. Its subsidiaries range from wholly owned firms to joint ventures with major banking partners. In the joint ventures, Heller's equity position ranges from 20 percent to 95 percent. The Heller Overseas Network has affiliates in 22 countries.

International Factors, the oldest international factoring organization, is an association of local companies organized by First Bank of Boston. First Bank of Boston has a minority equity position in the companies ranging from 10 to 20 percent. International Factors also has affiliates in 22 countries. The joint venture partners are major commercial banks in the host countries.

Credit Factoring International is part of the National Westminister Bank in the United Kingdom. National Westminster currently has subsidiaries in seven countries, five of which are wholly owned and two of which are joint ventures. The bank holds a minority interest in the joint ventures, and the partners are major commercial banks in the host countries.

Factors Chain International is a group of independent factoring companies in 22 countries around the world. There is no common ownership in Factors Chain, but the members follow standard procedures. Some of the members of Factors Chain in the United States are William Iselin & Co., Chemical Business Credit, Rosenthal & Rosenthal, and C&S Financial.

There are a few companies that offer export factoring without aligning themselves with one of the four existing international factoring organizations. Such firms usually reinsure their exposures through some type of insurance program.

  Evaluating Export Factors. Exporters should evaluate export factors using the following criteria: Is the company flexible? Can it adapt its service to your specific needs? Does it have local subsidiaries or affiliates in your overseas markets? Exporters should seek out those factors with operations in the countries to which they export currently or plan to export. Will the export factor provide export credit protection? How much and in countries where it doesn't have a local presence? Is the factor committed to export trade finance? Is its export factoring service merely an adjunct to its domestic business? Is it staffed with competent full-time personnel to handle international business? How experienced and knowledgeable is the staff? Can they provide advice and guidance on country import restrictions, exchange regulations, and payment terms in countries where the exporter has not had previous experience? What will its service cost? The exporter should evaluate both the commission rate and, if funding is involved, the interest rate against the services offered. Are there any local partners? Who are they? Does your foreign customer or distributor have any prior dealings with one or both organizations. What is their experience? Will the export factor cover political risk? Will the export factor cover the foreign exchange risk if the exporter sells in a foreign currency? How good are the export factor's systems, and what information is made available to the exporter? Will it be sufficient? Will the service rendered by the export factor reduce the exporter's workload? Will the export factor advance payment against foreign receivables? Is it willing to enter into a tripartite arrangement that will allow the exporter to fund at attractive rates from a second lending institution? What about terminating the contract with the factor? Will it be easy? Is the factor considered creditworthy?

FORFAIT HOUSES

For those exporters selling capital equipment who are faced with competition quoting fixed-rate financing over a medium-term (five to seven years) period or want to be more competitive, can turn to forfait financing. The mechanics or modus operandi of this export financing mechanism are explained in Chapter 8.

It is a well-known export trade finance technique that has existed in Western Europe for over 25 years. It is principally conducted by forfait houses who are based in Zurich, Geneva, Vienna, and London and are subsidiaries of Swiss, Austrian, and East European banks. Most recently, a few U.S. banks have entered the forfait market in New York where it is principally conducted in the United States.

Exporters should look for a forfait house that best suits their needs by shopping around for the best financing package possible. Since not all forfait houses are alike, the prudent exporter should seek answers to the following questions.

Experience: How experienced is it in doing forfait financing? How long has it been in the market? Where did its personnel get the experience?

Countries: Which countries is it open to do business with? Why is it not open to doing business with a particular country? Did it have poor experience with a guarantor or the country in general? Is it simply at its credit limit with the guarantor or country? When will it open its door to your country of interest? Or, is it simply not interested in financing certain particular countries?

Creditworthiness: How creditworthy is the forfait house? The exporter should ask for and perform a financial statement analysis on the forfait house. Ask for and investigate a listing of its clients.

Service: How fast and efficient is the house in delivering and conducting a deal? Is the deal well structured?

Rates: What are its rates per country? Are the rates competitive with that of other houses? How long is it willing to hold a quote? What about commitment fees? How long will it hold a commitment? Does it change its rates frequently and by how much?

Amounts: What are the minimum and maximum amounts it is willing to undertake per country or guarantor?

Currency: What currencies is it willing to finance and to which countries?

Term: What term periods is it willing to accept (two, three, five years, or longer) and to which countries?

INTERNATIONAL LEASING COMPANIES

Exporters of large capital goods can turn to an international leasing company as an alternative source of financing from both the perspective of the exporter and foreign importer.

The following are some sources of information for International Leasing Companies:

> The membership roster of the American Association of Equipment Lessors (AAEL) who represent a vast majority of U.S. leasing companies. Those involved in international leasing are primarily affiliates of the larger U.S. multinational banks.

> Examine the World Leasing Yearbook, published by Hawkins Publishers Ltd., London. The book briefly describes the leasing industry in each of approximately 40 countries and a classified list of leasing companies operating in approximately 60 countries.

> Contact the larger multinational financial institutions in the United States, Europe, and Asia. In the case of Europe and Asia, contact their foreign owned banks operating in the United States. They can be the wholly or partial owner entity of major leasing companies in their countries.

Once again, the exporter should shop around for the best deal. The exporter should seek answers to the following questions:

Experience: How much experience does the lessor have? How long has it been operating in leasing? Where did its personnel get leasing experience?

Countries: Not all leasing companies have experience in certain countries nor are they entering into leasing arrangements with certain countries. The Third World debt crisis also effects leasing companies. Where will the lessor do leasing?

Recourse/Nonrecourse: To do the leasing arrangement, the exporter may have to assume a percentage of the risk. Find out whether or not the export related sale to a particular country and foreign customer can be financed on a nonrecourse or recourse basis? What percentage of the risk will you have to assume if necessary?

Rates: What are its rates per country? In most cases, the rates will depend on tax benefits and accelerated depreciation to the lessor, in addition to other criteria for determining rates.

Term: What term periods is it willing to accept and to which countries?

Amounts: How large a deal is it willing to accept? Is there a minimum and maximum?

Service: How quickly can a leasing deal be put together? How will it be structured?

IN-HOUSE FINANCE COMPANIES

A business can establish an in-house finance company to perform a variety of functions, such as:

- Purchasing or financing accounts receivable.
- Raising capital.
- Making loans.
- Shifting and investing excess liquidity.
- Managing foreign exchange exposures.

In-house finance companies, often set up as subsidiaries, frequently finance sales that are not "bankable"—that is, sales that a commercial bank will not accept.

A vast major advantage of in-house finance companies have access to international capital markets and the ability to use loans to manage liquidity and foreign exchange exposure.

By using loans and accounts receivable purchases as management techniques, captive finance companies present fewer administrative and legal problems than do reinvoicing centers. Since finance companies do not reinvoice, they do not have to generate and trace duplicate invoices, and there are fewer government restrictions on the purchase of accounts receivable (on an arm's length basis) than on reinvoicing. Reinvoicing is discussed in Chapter 8.

Finance companies can be particularly useful for supplementing a business's export trade financing capabilities both for intercompany and foreign customer (third-party) receivables.

PRIVATE INSURANCE

The traditional entity for export insurance in the United States has always been the Foreign Credit Insurance Association (FCIA), discussed in Chapter 6, Part A. However, over the last 10 years a market of private insurers has developed. Although it consists of several companies, the most important one in the United States is the American Insurance Group (AIG) New York. It offers comprehensive export credit insurance (CECI) policies covering commercial and political risks on sales and credit to both public and private foreign customers.

Other U.S. based private insurers include Chubb, Continental, and INA. They only offer coverage for political risk on sales to public sector buyers.

SPECIALIZED IN-HOUSE COMPANIES

Many companies have set up in-house wholly owned companies to improve their export trade financing. There are a number of entities a company can implement, namely Export Trading Companies (ETCs), reinvoicing centers, export factoring units, finance companies, Foreign Sales Corporations (FSCs) and Domestic International Sales Corporations (DISCs). To function, most companies centralize their export trade finance expertise for the purposes of reducing financing costs by managing or coordinating bank relations, to increase liquidity through leading and lagging, to centralize the management of export trade credit risk and insurance, the setting of payment terms, and the discounting of receivables.

These specialized units can be given an almost limitless number of capabilities beyond the normal scope of decentralized operations. They can move beyond export trade financing into other export related activities, such as managing currency exposure, marketing, tax planning, improving operating efficiency, strengthening cash management, handling countertrade requests or just plain being creative because of the centralization of their expertise.

The two main reasons or advantages companies cite for their

interest in wholly owned, independent trading subsidiaries are the following:

1. To provide an in-house centralized gathering of expertise in international trade to service the needs of customers and their companies on a whole.
2. To minimize duplication of efforts such as selling to the same customers on different terms and financing techniques, centralize export documentation to improve efficiency, and to take full advantage of the tax advantages offered by FSCs and DISCs.

APPENDIX 7–A   EXPORT FINANCE COMPANIES

Balfour Williamson, London (previously Lloyds Bank, now LONRHO).

Barclays International Finance, London (formerly UDT International Finance).

Brandts Finance, London (now part of Citibank, London).

Bremar Holdings, London, New York, Turkey.

Creditcorp International, New York (Banco Urquijo, Spain).

Greyhound Financial, London (Greyhound Corp.).

Intercontinental Credit, New York.

Manufacturers Hanover Export Finance Ltd., London.

Merban (Associated Metals and Minerals), New York.

Midland International Trade Services, New York (formerly Export Credit Corp. and London American Finance).

Philadelphia Overseas Credit Corp., San Francisco (formerly part of Philadelphia National Bank and now owned by Crocker Bank, which in turn is owned by Midland).

Rosenthal Overseas Funding Corp. (ROFCO).

Tennant Guaranty/Mercator (Royal Bank of Canada), London, New York.

Tozer Kelmsley Milbourn (TKM), New York and London (now part of Hong Kong & Shanghai Banking Corp.).

Trade and Industry Group, New York, London, and South Africa.

Trade Finance Corporation (Trafco), Florida.

Trend Export Funding, Connecticut.

Trade Finance International, London (TFI-Valgos) and New York, owned by Bankinvest Zurich and SIB.

REFERENCES

1. David K. Eiteman and Arthur I. Stonehill, *Multinational Business Finance,* 3rd ed. (Reading, Mass: Addison-Wesley Publishing Company, 1982), p. 500.
2. Louis J. Celi and I. James Czechowicz, *Export Financing: Handbook of Sources & Techniques* (Morristown, N.J.: Business International, Financial Executive Research Foundation, 1985), chapter 6.
3. L. Stroh, "TRAFCO, CAM FINANCE Package Credit Enhanced Trade Debt for Capital Markets," *The Exporter,* Trade Data Reports Inc., New York, April 1987, p. 8.
4. Louis J. Celi and Czechowicz, *Export Financing,* chapter 4.

CHAPTER 8

EXPORT TRADE FINANCING

Export trade financing is one area where the credit manager needs to coordinate his or her activity with their treasury finance department, controller, president, or general manager of their company, depending on its size and structure. In this capacity, the credit manager mainly assumes the role of a finance manager. The financing that backs up the sales deal is a vital link that could make or break the sale because of the costs of extended credit, the norm in international trade, and the financing offered by competition, especially foreign competition. It is an area where the credit manager can excel by finding a dynamic and flexible way to finance the sale of goods by looking for the financing technique that satisfies the interests of both the exporter and importer.

This chapter discusses in detail the different types of export trade financing available to finance the sale of goods between exporters and importers.

GUARANTEES

In most contexts related to international trade, the word *guarantee* can mean the guaranteeing of a transaction to commit to and/or perform something, or a guarantee for the repayment of a debt obligation from someone. The common factor in all these transactions is that the guarantor agrees to guaranty the repayment of the debt obligation of another party or the fulfillment of an obligation in case the primary party defaults. In most export trade transactions, if a guarantee is used, it is often a bank guarantee. However, there are circumstances when a credit person might ask for the guarantee of a company or "corporate guarantee."

Corporate Guarantee

A corporate guarantee is where one company undertakes to pay if the principal debtor does not pay a matured debt obligation to a creditor. Typically, creditors will ask the corporate or parent company to guarantee one or more of its subsidiaries or affiliates who in the opinion of the credit person is not considered credit-worthy for the export related sales transaction, a specific line of credit or credit limit.

It is important to note that corporate guaranties from companies based in countries outside the United States are subject to varying local laws, regulations, and the guarantor's own by-laws. They are not subject to the Uniform Commercial Code (UCC) of the United States. Therefore, the guarantee should state which country law the guarantee will be governed by. If the guarantee is to be governed by the laws of a country other than the exporter, local counsel should be sought for proper language to make it an enforceable instrument. Based on the experience of most credit managers, corporate guaranties tend to be of little value when applied locally (country of the guarantor) because of prior existing priority claims and insufficient assets to back up the guarantee. Any corporate guarantee from a company in another country is only as good as the creditworthiness and trust of the issuer to honor the guarantee. Does it have any assets that are not encumbered in a worse case scenario. On the other hand, corporate guarantees issued by companies based in the United States who guarantee debts of their overseas subsidiaries or affiliates are subject to the UCC.

Bank Guarantee

A bank guarantee is only a financial instrument. It has no obligation or interest to supply goods or services. Its duty as guarantor is limited to the payment of a certain sum of money in the event of nonperformance or nonpayment by an exporter/supplier (i.e., performance bonds) or by a foreign importer in the event of a payment default for goods purchased from a foreign supplier.

In the case of performance, the bank guarantee provides security in three ways:[1]

Attestation: A bank guarantee testifies to the exporter's ability to perform a contract. Since the issue of a guarantee constitutes an irrevocable undertaking of payment, a bank will not enter into such a commitment without first making a thorough examination of the financial capability and technical capability of the exporter.

Motivation: The principal stands to lose the guarantee amount if it fails to fulfill the contract terms. This gives it a strong motive to perform the contract, even if the transaction has become unattractive to it.

Compensation: If the principal fails to fulfill its contractual obligations, the foreign customer has the right to demand payment of the guarantee amount, which will compensate it wholly or in part for the financial consequences of the breach of contract.

There are many different types of guarantees issued by banks for different types of transactions between exporters and foreign customers. In today's international climate, more and more guarantees are being not only requested, but required by foreign customers and their countries for export trade related to bids on contracts and the performance of an exporter's goods in the country of the foreign customer. Bank guarantees in this regard are issued in lieu of bid (tender) and performance bonds. Both of these were discussed in Chapter 4, Part C.

Other Types of Guarantees

Bill of Lading Guarantee: Individual bills of lading or the full set may be lost or delayed in the mail. The carrier will be reluctant to hand over the goods to the consignee without the requisite bill of lading because it makes itself liable for damages. It will be prepared to do so, however, if a bank will issue a guarantee in its favor for 100–200 percent of the value of the goods. This way the carrier covers itself in the event of a claim when it releases the goods without the original.

Customs Guarantee: Customs guarantees provide cover against possible customs duties. They are frequently used when goods are imported temporarily into a country. The beneficiary can then claim under the guarantee if the goods are not re-exported within a prescribed time frame.

Sole of Exchange Guarantee (Aval): The bank, as guarantor in favor of the drawer, drawee, or endorser, undertakes to make punctual payment of the bill of exchange. The usual condition is that the bill must be payable at the guarantor bank. Furthermore, the principal must authorize the bank in writing to debit the amount of the bill and commissions and expenses to its account.

Loan Guarantee: The granting of a loan is often made conditional on security provided by the borrower or a third party. A bank guarantee is one of the means whereby a creditor can ensure that the loan will be repaid.

Contract Payment Guarantee: This type of guarantee covers payments under all sorts of contracts.

Distraint Guarantee: If a debtor's assets are distrained, it can recover control over them by getting a bank to issue an appropriate guarantee (i.e., a joint and several guarantee).

BANK LINE OF CREDIT

In order to finance international trade, banks can provide an exporter with a line of credit. It is a sum of money allocated to the exporter by a bank or banks that the exporter can draw from in order to finance its imports or exports. It could also be structured to finance an export transaction from the foreign customer's side.

In effect, the bank line of credit allows the exporter to extend credit terms to foreign customers to be competitive, thus creating an export or foreign accounts receivable. Extending credit terms actually represents working capital (current assets minus current liabilities) tied up in receivables. For the exporter to finance its business by extending credit terms, the exporter must borrow funds or obtain loans from someone in order to maintain its liquidity ratios. In most cases, these funds will come from a bank or banks if the exporter has obtained lines of credit from them. Depending on the size of the business borrower, the bank may want the receivables or some other form of security pledged as collateral (perfected liens on equipment, inventory, personal guarantees of the principals), to provide the line of credit facility. As mentioned in Chapter 6, one of the best means of obtaining bank lines of credit, especially for small- to medium-size exporters, are the programs and guarantees offered by FCIA/Eximbank (i.e., the Working Capital Guarantee Program, Expanded Programs for Banks). An assignment of proceeds from an export credit insurance policy is another technique used by banks to extend lines of credit to an exporter.

The extent of the lines of credit vary in size according to its assessment of the creditworthiness of the exporter. Simply because an exporter needs a $150,000 line of credit does not necessarily mean it will get all or part of it. Once extended, the line of credit is customarily granted for a one-year period. At the end of the one-year period the bank again determines the creditworthiness of the exporter to determine if the line of credit can be renewed or increased, assuming the exporter wants it continued or increased.

The general rule of thumb is that the smaller the size of the business, the less financial resources the business has to sell its goods and services on extended or deferred payment terms. Thus, they need to borrow from someone to finance or bridge the credit period. It is advisable for exporters to arrange bank lines of credit before the actual export transaction takes place so it knows exactly under what terms and conditions the bank is extending a line of credit to the exporter. In some cases, the bank line of credit may be insufficient to bridge the gap if the export transaction is unusually large. In this case, the exporter may need the line of credit increased by the bank or need to obtain additional lines of credit from other financial institutions. In some cases, obtaining additional lines of credit might be difficult if the original lender has all of the security and collateral of the exporter (all of the assets of the exporter have been pledged as security for the line of credit).

The process of obtaining a bank line of credit for export business is similar to obtaining a domestic line of credit. However, it is not uncommon for banks to provide a line of credit for the domestic and export transactions of a business. The bank evaluates the creditworthiness of an exporter in a manner similar to that of a business credit manager. It will evaluate the traditional criteria of the exporter's financial condition, management character and capabilities, its business, the industry it is in, and its overseas markets to determine the extent of its country risks, whether export credit insured or uninsured.

One of the most positive advantages of obtaining a bank line of credit is that it provides the exporter with continuous liquidity. It eliminates the problem of the exporter having to obtain a separate loan each and every time funds are needed to finance an export related sale transaction on extended terms.

EXPORTER-SUPPLIER LINE OF CREDIT

There may be certain instances when the foreign customer is unable in whole or in part to obtain sufficient lines of credit from a local bank or banks to finance its annual purchases of goods and services from export suppliers around the globe. This might occur in the event an importer cannot obtain trade related financing (i.e., buyer credits, forfait facilities, letters of credit) in sufficient amounts to transact the amount of business they wish to transact among each other.

Under these circumstances, it is not unlikely for some exporters to extend loans direct to selected foreign customers or issue its own partial corporate guarantee to domestic or foreign banks or finance houses. The purpose of the guarantee is to encourage the bank or finance house to provide term financing to the guarantor's foreign customer which minimizes the risk of the bank or finance house from both commercial and political risks. In the event of nonpayment either from commercial or political risk, the bank or finance house will look to the amount of the guarantor's guarantee first for payment. It will look to the foreign customer or country secondly for the remainder of the balance outstanding. This is normally done under the following circumstances:

- The exporter has an indirect vested interest in the foreign customer because of its strong market position in a particular country or geographic area.
- The exporter wants to maintain or increase its market share in a country or geographic area.
- The foreign customer purchases a large portion of goods from an exporter's plant. The purchases affect plant capacity and production.
- The exporter wants to maintain or increase its return on investment.

- Long-term strategy dictates supporting the foreign customer.

   In certain instances, the issuance of an exporter's guaranty to a lender or consortium of lenders might prompt them to provide short- or long-term financing to foreign customers which is directly tied in to purchasing the goods and services of the export guarantor.

BUYER CREDIT

A buyer credit trade financing arrangement is one in which one or more financial institutions in an exporter's country extend credit to a foreign customer of an exporter. Although most buyer credit financing is done to finance capital equipment purchases, other goods with payment terms up to one year can be financed by buyer credits. Buyer credits are normally provided by a bank or banks not involved in the underlying export commercial transaction. A vast majority of buyer credit financing is done under an export credit insurance program or guarantee of an Eximbank program of the financial institution or the exporter itself (discussed later). It is done to minimize a bank's credit exposure to a given foreign customer and/or its country.

   Buyer credits are normally arranged with exporters on a nonrecourse or partial recourse basis. Therefore, without the added feature of credit insurance or guaranties of Eximbank, the bank would look to the creditworthiness of the exporter on a recourse basis in the event of nonpayment from the foreign customer.

   One of the most logical sources for buyer credit financing are the financial institutions themselves, especially Edge Act banks, the exporters primary or lead banks, and trade finance houses. Exporters should not limit themselves to their primary or lead banks alone because many of them have reached their country credit limitations with many countries, especially Third World debtor nations.

When to Arrange a Buyer Credit

In many cases, export sales are won or lost to competition not only on price, quantity, and quality of goods, but by the financing arrangement initially offered at the negotiating table by the prudent exporter. The quicker the credit manager knows about potential business, the better off he or she is in obtaining the best buyer credit deal available for all parties to the export transaction. Therefore, it is important to arrange and offer a buyer credit when the foreign customer's financing facilities are limited. It is also important when local or external bank financing is scarce, insufficient to finance the amount of the import or imports, too expensive or contains too many restrictive loan convenants (minimum net worth, working capital, debt-to-equity), or if local government restrictions or regulations prohibit local banks from financing all or part of an import related deal. If competition is offering attractive financing packages, it may be advantageous for the exporter to offer a financing package that will finance a foreign company's inventory of your goods, especially when it concerns distributors.

Initial Steps Leading to a Buyer Credit

There are essentially four agreements that need to be consumated by the parties to the buyer credit financing:[2]

1. A terms and conditions of sale contract between the exporter and foreign customer.
2. A bank (or banks) provides a letter of intent to the exporter which sets forth the terms and conditions of the financing to the foreign customer and the financing charges to the exporter. The bank or banks may or may not charge an option fee which holds the financing in place as set forth in the letter of intent until the exporter knows whether or not it has won the business.
3. Once the exporter obtains the business, a contract or letter of agreement is executed between the bank or banks and the foreign customer, and the bank or banks and exporter.
4. An agreement is executed between the exporter or bank/banks and the export credit insurer, whoever holds the

policy. The agreement obligates the insurer to cover the proposed export transaction to a specific foreign customer. Usually a Special Buyer Credit Limit (SBCL) with FCIA (discussed in Chapter 6, Part A).

There are circumstances when the bank or banks does not consider the export credit insurance policy or guarantee of Exim-bank, provided by the exporter, as sufficient coverage. This occurs when the policy or guarantee does not cover the risk of nonacceptance of the goods by the foreign customer in case the exporter does not have a nonacceptance clause; nonpayment of interest that accrues between the maturity dates of unpaid export bills and the dates on which claims are paid by the export credit insurer; the policy or guarantee does not provide for sufficient coverage in the event FCIA or Eximbank implements restrictive country limitations on the percentages it is willing to cover (i.e., less than 90 or 95 percent commercial risk coverage; less than 100 percent political risk coverage).

Under these scenarios, the bank or banks will either look to the creditworthiness of the exporter for the shortfall or for additional security/collateral (i.e., an overseas bank aval or guarantee in the buyer's country).

Putting the Deal Together

Banks and specialized trade finance houses all compete against one another for trade finance business. Each can offer different terms and conditions. Therefore, exporters and foreign customers need to take the following factors into consideration:

Will one or more lenders or financers be needed to fund the export trade deal?

Will a guarantee be needed? If yes, will it come from the exporter, the exporter's parent company, the importer's bank, the importer's parent company, or the importer's government?

How long is the term of the credit?

What is competition offering?

Is there a grace period and how long is it? (From date of signing, six months to six years is typical.)

What is the commitment fee on the unused portion of the loan? (Could be 0.25 percent to 0.75 percent per annum.)

What is the interest rate charged by the bank to the foreign customer? (Sometimes it is a small percentage over LIBOR, BAs or prime, such as 0.25–2 percent per annum over.)

How much is charged for setting up the credit facility? Is it a flat or annual fee?

What loan documents are required by the lenders or financers? Are there many or just a few?

Is there an additional fee or rate charged by the lenders or financers for discounting the trade paper for the exporter? What is it and how will it be assessed?

Are the rates competitive?

If discounted, can the charges be passed on to the foreign customer in lieu of longer payment terms—or at least shared?

When banks or finance houses quote, they should offer alternative means of financing the buyer credit such as, quoting a spread over LIBOR, bankers' acceptances, prime rate, treasury bills, federal funds rate or money market rates. The pricing or interest rate will reflect the lender's or financer's assessment of the credit risk related to the loan's maturity, credit facilities, and the amount. In addition, it will reflect a spread or profit margin for the lender or financer, its administrative fees, and its assessment of the country conditions of the foreign customer.

Advantages and Disadvantages of a Buyer Credit

There are both advantages and disadvantages of a buyer credit to an exporter and foreign customer.

Advantages—Exporter:
1. Provides nonrecourse or limited recourse financing to exporters because of the backing of the full faith and credit of FCIA/Eximbank to the debt instruments created from the sale of goods or services.
2. Increases the cash flow of the exporter when the added feature of discounting is included in the financing.

3. Minimizes the potential risk of default by the foreign customer to the exporter if done on a full nonrecourse basis.
4. Reduces the exporter's cost of capital in carrying the foreign receivable for the term of the financing.
5. The debt instruments should make it attractive for the exporter to obtain cheaper financing.
6. The exporter's credit facilities are not usually affected because the financing is between the lenders and the foreign customer.

Disadvantages—Exporter:

1. Documentation can be complex, if the buyer credit is syndicated by several banks.
2. Where it is needed most, in Third World markets, buyer credit financing is very limited from financial institutions.
3. FCIA/Eximbank's country limitations with certain countries might be too restrictive to be competitive.
4. Banks might require the exporter to share more of the risk because of their debt exposure with certain countries, irrespective of the export credit insurance coverage.

Advantages—Importer:

1. The financing is cheaper than local borrowing rates.
2. Credits are generally available on a floating rate basis versus fixed rate financing from forfait financing (discussed next).
3. Buyer credits are available in a number of different currencies. It does not have to be financed in the currency of the contract between the exporter and foreign customer. Mixed credits can spread the currency risk.
4. As an incentive to increase sales revenue, credit terms are lengthened, especially if the foreign customer agrees to absorb all or part of the discount charges.

Disadvantages—Importer:

1. Documentation can be complex, if the buyer credit is syndicated by several banks.
2. FCIA/Eximbank's country limitations might make the financing too restrictive and expensive.
3. Exporters may not be able to offer extended credit terms to foreign customers when buyer credit financing is difficult to find or is too restrictive from financial institutions.

FORFAITING

Forfaiting, also referred to as *a forfait,* is an alternative method to traditional export trade financing techniques that protects an exporter from certain risks—commercial or political. The term *forfaiting* comes from the French term *a forfait,* which connotes the surrendering of rights, a basic significance involved in forfaiting. In German it is known as *Fortaitierung,* in French *le forfaitage,* in Italian *la forfetizzazione,* and in Spanish *la forfetizacion.*

This means of financing export related sales of goods and services is relatively unknown in the United States. It is a well known export trade finance technique that has been used in Europe for over 25 years, mainly starting out to finance exports from Western Europe (Germany, Austria, and Switzerland) into Eastern Europe. It is, however, available for financing exports to Latin America, Canada, and the Far East, especially Third World countries. Actual forfaiting transactions are largely conducted in Zurich and London, but it is taking hold in New York. The forfait market consists of a primary and secondary market. The primary market consists of banks and forfait houses who buy properly executed and documented debt obligations direct from exporters. They can also assist exporters with the financial calculations and arrangements. The secondary market consists of trading these forfait debt obligations among themselves.

It is a transaction in which an exporter transfers responsibility of commercial and political risks for the collection of a trade related debt to a third party (the forfaiter), such as a financial institution, and in turn, receives immediate cash after the deduction of its interest charge (the discount). These proceeds or funds represent the net present value of a series of future payment obligations made by the importer over the life or repayment schedule of the forfait transaction. More specifically, the term is used to denote the purchase of obligations falling due at some future date, arising mostly from the export delivery of goods and services without recourse to any previous holder of the obligation. The discount used by the forfaiter is based on its cost of funds plus a premium. The premium can range anywhere from ½ to 5 percent depending on the country of importation. Every forfait financing transaction involves at least four parties to the transaction: an exporter, the forfaiter, the importer, and the importer's guarantor.

It is generally used when:

- Exporters are unable themselves to provide medium-term financing (shorter term financing is available).
- Direct bank financing to the foreign customer is too complex.
- The exporter wants to offer fixed rate financing to be competitive.
- Competition offers a forfait financing.
- Export credit insurance coverage is unavailable.

The financial instruments in forfaiting are usually time drafts or bills of exchange and promissory notes. Other less common ones are specific accounts receivable or booked debts, and deferred payment letters of credit.

Forfaiting is basically used to finance the export of capital equipment where transactions are usually medium term (i.e., three to eight years) at fixed rate financing. Shorter term financing, from 90 days up to one year, is possible on a floating interest rate basis. Even transactions up to 10 years have been financed. The typical transaction sizes range between U.S. $100,000 and U.S. $5,000,000. Although U.S. dollars are mentioned, forfaiting is possible in any currency in which the forfaiter can obtain congruent refinancing over the credit period. The main currencies used, besides U.S. dollars, are those of the Euromoney market, accompanied by the respective national currency of the forfaiter. If the export transaction is up to one year in term, the possibility of including other foreign currencies is possible.

Even though bank and forfait houses prefer the larger dollar volume exports with extended terms, the forfait market is available for smaller exporters whose exports are traditionally small. One of the most active markets for small exporters is Italy where forfaiting is used extensively.

One of the most significant features in forfaiting is the undertaking of a financial institution in the form of an aval or an unconditional irrevocable guarantee which is freely transferable and acceptable to the forfaiter. The unconditional feature is very important because the guarantor agrees to pay the importer's maturing debt obligations in the event of nonpayment irrespective of a contract dispute (i.e., pricing of the goods, defective goods). The guarantee of a reputable financial institution is preferable since in all likelihood the importer or debtor of the claim is not known to the exporter nor is the importer's country considered a good risk. In the event of nonpayment either by the importer or because of some sort of political risk, the only security the exporter has under the forfaiting arrangement is the guarantee of a financial institution and the nonrecourse feature of the forfait transaction. Likewise, the forfaiter looks to the guarantor in the event of nonpayment by the obligor. The nonrecourse feature comes into effect by the exporter simply endorsing such obligation with the words *without recourse* in each endorsement. This endorsement transfers ownership of the debtor's repayment obligation to a new beneficiary, the forfaiter.

The guarantee may take the form of an express guarantee whose format is similar to a U.S. commercial bank standby letter of credit. A more preferred form of the guarantee is an *aval* which is simply the guarantor's duly-signed acceptance stamp on each promissory note. Avalized promissory notes may be unbundled and sold separately to different secondary forfaiters.[3]

Under this type of trade financing the sole responsibility of the exporter is to manufacture and deliver the goods, plus the correct drawing up of the debt instrument. It is basically up to the financial institution to impose its own limits on the guaranteeing bank, the country of the debtor or importer, and how much of a portfolio of forfaiting obligations it wishes to hold. It assesses the risks (commercial in the event of nonpayment of the debtor; the political or country risks as it pertains to war, riot, revolution, insurrection, confiscation of import permits; and foreign exchange or currency risk) involved and for selling the claim to possible investors. With banks owned in whole or in part by governments, the guarantees issued by these financial institutions are identical to those associated with country or political risks.

Figure 8–1 depicts the flow and illustrates the various stages of an a forfait transaction.

Notes:
1. Commitment letter including the fixed discount rate given by the forfaiting bank to the exporter.
2. Sales contract agreed on between the supplier and the foreign customer.

FIGURE 8–1
Forfaiting Transaction

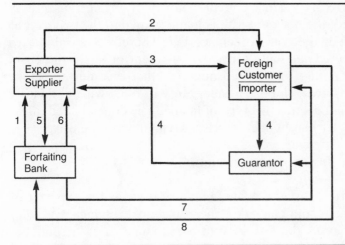

3. Goods manufactured and delivered.
4. In exchange for title to the goods a series of promissory notes/bills of exchange are delivered to the exporter.
5. Exporter endorses the promissory notes/bills of exchange to the forfaiting bank on a without recourse basis.
6. Forfaiting bank deducts interest at the discount rate agreed at from the face value of the promissory notes/bills of exchange and pays the discounted proceeds to the exporter.
7. At maturity, the forfaiting bank presents each promissory note/bill of exchange for payment.
8. The forfaiting bank receives payment.

Forfaiting possesses three significant features—simplicity, speed, and financing costs.

Simplicity: Because the implementation of forfait deals uses highly standardized and basic documentation, they are more straightforward deals than other forms of export trade financing. It can reduce legal and other costs versus other forms of financing.

Speed: Exporters can receive a firm commitment and price from the forfait market within a very short period of time—usually within 48 hours. The commitment will specify the amount, maturity, discount rate and fees.

Financing Costs: Since a great majority of forfait transactions are discounted, the discount rate is made known to the exporter at the beginning of the commitment period. Therefore, the exporter has the ability to negotiate a price adjustment or share the costs associated with the forfait transaction with the importer before shipment transpires. Importer uncertainty of borrowing at floating rates is eliminated since this type of financing is done at fixed rates, and the importer can budget interest payments more easily.

Characteristics for the Exporter and Importer

For the exporter, the nonrecourse feature relieves the exporter of commercial and political risks, including no exchange risks because it eliminates the risk of future exchange rate fluctuations. Because rates are fixed, the exporter runs no risks from interest rate fluctuations. The exporter's balance sheet is clean of receivables owed from importers and/or countries considered risks while reducing the balance sheet of contingent liabilities because of the nonrecourse feature. It improves the cash flow of the exporter by increasing cash receipts when promissory notes are discounted with the forfaiter. Banking facilities such as lines of credit are not affected and administration and collection procedures are reduced, plus all related costs pertaining thereto. In addition, individual export orders can be financed, financing costs are known in advance, credit decisions are done expeditiously and delays are not incurred for reimbursement in whole or in part from insurance claims or under the uninsured portion of an export credit insurers policy. Any proportion of foreign goods can be included in the export sale transaction. Export credit insurance programs require that a certain percentage of the goods be of home country origin, and these are bound by rigid country limitations and payment terms.

For the importer, 100 percent financing of the import transaction can be obtained for goods sourced from any country at fixed rate financing which enables the importer to know in advance the exact cost of the financing deal. There is lack of a cross-default clause which shields the importer's other borrowings and if one note is defaulted, all other notes are not accelerated. In addition, there are no restrictive loan covenants and the loan agreement increases the importer's flexibility and reduces legal expenses. Documentation is simplified, financing deals are put together quickly and transactions are handled confidentially, involving no publicity. Different currencies can be handled in separate financial instruments of payment and the financing offers flexible repayment programs. The maturity schedule is often longer than most other types of trade financing.

Technical Aspects

The following lists the major technical aspects of a forfait transaction:

The instrument of payment (drafts or bills of exchange and promissory notes) normally carries a bank aval or guarantee.

The discount rate is based on the LIBOR (London Interbank Offer Rate) for the average life and currency of the payment instrument to cover the commercial, political and transfer risks, the risks related to fluctuations in exchange and interest rates, the administration costs of holding and collecting the instrument of payment and the profit element.

Rates and availability are dictated by market conditions (i.e., the forfaiting house can buy the instrument of payment from a customer which they can either hold or on-sell immediately).

Days of grace are included in the discount calculations to cover delays in receipt of payment.

A commitment fee on a per annum or per month (not points) is normally payable between the signing of a contract between the exporter and the bank and the delivery to the bank of the guarantied instrument of payment.

The instruments of payment are normally in a series of six monthly maturities with a maximum of five to seven years.

The currency can be any freely transferable one, but typically are Deutsche marks, Swiss francs, and U.S. dollars.

The amounts involved are normally $100,000 to $2 million, but can be higher. Syndications are possible.

The discount calculations can be based on interest on the reducing balance or interest on each instrument of payment amount separately. Instruments of payment of equal amounts (covering both capital and interest) can be arranged.

Down payments can be taken into account, as can an interest rate which the importer has agreed to bear and which differs from market rates.

The Process Leading to a Forfait Transaction

Buyer and Seller Agreement.   Before approaching a bank or forfait house, the buyer and seller should have a general idea of what credit terms will be given, the interest rate the buyer is prepared or permitted (country regulations might establish a maximum permissible interest rate an external or overseas supplier can charge) to pay and the repayment period. It is always possible that the buyer might be prepared to bear all of the finance costs. However, this depends on competition bidding for the same business. It is important to remember that in forfaiting, it may be possible to show one rate of interest to the buyer, with the price adjusted to cover another rate of interest in the actual forfaiting transaction.

Forfaiter Selection.   The exporter should shop around for potential forfaiters that first of all can accept the risks of the buyer, its country, and especially the guarantor. Are any or all of these acceptable risks to the forfaiter? If the guarantor is unacceptable to the forfaiter, can an alternative acceptable guarantor be offered? What type of financing are forfaiters quoting? The exporter should shop for the best deal in terms of itself and especially the buyer when competitive situations arise.

Option or Preliminary Offer Period.   When an exporter is involved in a competitive bidding situation, it will want to know the potential costs associated with financing under forfait. It will ask a forfaiter for a financing commitment although it does not know if it will be awarded the order. The commitment period runs from the date of commitment to the time that shipment of goods would be made if the order is won. This is done because not all of the details of the export transaction are known or fixed to enable the forfaiter to issue a binding offer.

The time between the start of the commitment and the anticipated date of award of contracts by the importer is designated as the *option period*. From the perspective of the exporter, the pricing of the option period is an integral part of the commitment period, except that it carries an option fee rather than a commitment fee. This option period can last up to three months, and the charge is on a flat rate or a per annum basis.

Procedures for Forfaiting.   Before making a firm commitment, the forfaiting house needs to know:

- The currency, amount, and period to be financed.
- The country of export (if one is not dealing directly with the exporter).
- The name and country of the importer.
- The name and country of the guarantor.
- Whether drafts, bills of exchange, or promissory notes will be provided.
- Whether an aval or separate guarantee is available.
- The amounts and maturities of the paper or repayment schedule.
- The nature of the goods involved (to be exported).
- The delivery date of the goods.
- The date the documents will be delivered to the forfaiter.
- The necessary authorization and licenses.
- The domicile for payment of the instruments of payment.

The Commitment Period.   The commitment period is the time between when an agreement to purchase is signed and when the actual discounting by the forfaiter occurs. This period can take up to 18 months, but is usually shorter. This period of time is of significant importance since many exporters will want to fix the financing terms a considerable time before actual shipment of the goods to be exported. The commitment fee charged by the forfaiter is usually a per annum fee charged to cover the lost opportunity costs of holding funds available for the exporter and to cover the risks of interest rate fluctuations. Remember forfaiting involves fixed rate financing. The fee is usually 1 percent per annum, but it can vary slightly depending on the country of import.

Endorsement and Delivery.   Once the exporter fulfills its portion of the contract, it will typically present debt instruments (bills or notes) to the importer for its signature, and the importer, in turn, will deliver them to the guarantor.

When the documents are returned to the exporter, they are endorsed over to the forfaiter, who then deducts the financing costs for the entire period from the face value of the debt instruments, paying the net proceeds at once to wherever the exporter designates. Since the endorsement always includes a "without recourse" clause or endorsement, the exporter at this point can be removed from the transaction, provided all other appropriate conditions have been fulfilled.

It is the responsibility of the forfaiter to verify the documents and signatures on each debt instrument. Valid and enforceable signatures are usually accomplished by the execution of signature cards executed by the exporter on behalf of the forfaiter. The signature cards contain the signatures of only those authorized by the exporter to sign the debt instruments.

Discount and Payout.   The next and last stage of the forfait process is the discounting of the individual debt obligation amounts. This will produce the payout and the amount which will be credited to the exporter. Interest for the whole life of the claims are deducted in advance. The basis, from which this interest is deducted, is the total amount which becomes due in the future (100 percent):

- Export of equipment.
- Amount of the goods to be exported: U.S. $500,000.
- Credit period: 5 years.
- Repayment schedule: 10 semiannual installments (principal and interest); first installment six months after delivery.
- Interest agreed on between importer and exporter (internal rate) 10 ½ percent per annum, calculated on the open credit

balance, i.e., to each maturity interest is added on the outstanding balance, thus making: Invoice amount (credit amount): U.S. $644,375.
- Days grace: five.
- Payout: U.S. $487,132.

Settlement. The net payout is usually transferred to the exporter's bank account by wire transfer, and the details of the forfait transaction are sent to the exporter or the presenter of the documents.

BANKERS' ACCEPTANCES

Bankers' acceptances (BAs) originated in Europe, around the 12th Century. In Europe, banks advanced credit to buyers of goods for trade transactions by countersigning ("accepting") the bill of exchange for a fee. In London, the banks that specialized in this form of lending funds to traders became known as *accepting houses*.

With the added support of reputable banking houses who guarantied future payments, traders could enter into commercial transactions by an extension of credit. These traders, on obtaining the acceptance of banking houses on a bill of exchange discounted these bills in the marketplace.

Bankers' acceptances are different from most forms of bank lending. One unique attribute of this type of financing is that a bankers' acceptance is a discountable instrument. When discounted, the number of dollars extended to the drawer of an accepted draft is less than the face amount of the draft, usually by the market discount rate plus the bank's acceptance commission. Specific examples of the cost of financing under bankers' acceptances will be discussed later.

Another unique aspect of bankers' acceptance financing is that in all cases, with the exception of dollar exchange acceptances, the nature of the financing is self-liquidating. This means that the transaction being financed will, in and of itself, generate funds which will liquidate the acceptance liability.

The first significant use of U.S. dollar bankers' acceptances occurred in the United States after the passage of the Federal Reserve Act of 1913. The most common use of BAs has traditionally been the financing of import and export transactions. Unlike a conventional bank loan, an acceptance is a negotiable and marketable instrument for which a well-established and active secondary market exists.

There are many dealers in this secondary market to handle BAs, many with nationwide branches. The BA market is an over-the-counter market, and many of the firms dealing in these instruments also deal in a variety of other marketable instruments. Acceptance trading often constitutes only one part of their overall activities. Participants in the market, in addition to these dealers, are the accepting banks, Edge Act corporations (see Chapter 7), investors of all types—from individuals to foreign central banks— and the Federal Reserve System. Trading in this market is done on a negotiated basis, with bid and ask rates normally published for informational purposes only.

By definition a bankers' acceptance is a time draft (30, 60, 90, up to 180 days after sight or date) drawn on and accepted by a bank. It may arise as a result of the following principal categories of transactions which may give rise to "eligible" acceptance financing:

1. A commercial letter of credit (import or export).
2. A documentary or clean collection (import or export).
3. Drafts drawn on banks from a domestic shipment of goods.
4. Storage of readily marketable staples.
5. A refinancing acceptance, arising from the shipment of goods between third countries or storage of readily marketable staples in third countries.
6. Dollar exchange acceptances.
7. A financing instrument for "off-balance sheet" financing.

In export trade, BAs are usually derived from time or usance commercial letters of credit based on payment terms mutually agreed on between the exporter and foreign customer (i.e., 90 days date draft from B/L date). In effect, the exporter is granting terms to the foreign customer through a letter of credit. When the credit is confirmed by a U.S. bank, the beneficiary draws its draft on the confirming bank (provided the credit instrument stipulates to draw

FIGURE 8–2
Example of Bankers' Acceptance

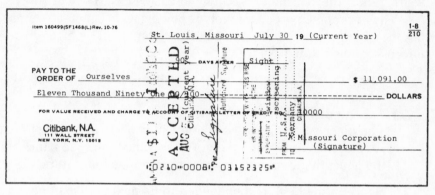

Source: Leonard A. Back, *Introduction to Commercial Letters of Credit*, (New York: Citibank, N.A., 1977), p. 23.

drafts on the confirming bank), the bank will "accept" the draft drawn on it, thus creating a Bankers' Acceptance. Similarily, if the credit instrument is advised by a U.S. bank, the beneficiary, when permitted, draws its draft on the advising bank which "accepts" the draft, creating a BA. In most cases, BAs will not be created by a bank unless it has confirmed the credit. Therefore, the draft is payable 90 days from date of the draft. This assumes the beneficiary has complied with the terms and conditions of the credit instrument.

The creation of a BA by the acceptor or creator (usually a bank or Edge Act banking corporation) is a negotiable instrument and unconditional promise of the acceptor to pay the draft at its maturity to whoever holds the BA. When the draft is "accepted," this means an officer of the advising/confirming bank writes crosswise on the face of the draft *accepted,* its signature and date of the transaction, creating a BA. (See Figure 8–2 for a sample BA.) The obligor may be another bank (on behalf of its customer) or a corporation. It may or may not be the drawer of the draft. The beneficiary can sell the instrument immediately in the Bankers' Acceptance market at the current discount rate, discount the instrument at a later date when the rates are more attractive, or hold the instrument until maturity. The beneficiary can obtain funds immediately at a discount by selling the BA, instead of waiting until the BA matures, thus increasing cash flow.

The acceptance process involves placing an acceptance stamp on the face of the draft by the accepting bank which gives information as follows:

- The type of transaction underlying the draft (export, import, storage).
- The goods involved.
- The place of shipment from and to (or place of storage).
- A reference number, a date of acceptance, and the name of the accepting bank along with an authorized signature.

The accepting bank is then guided to its next course of action by the letter of credit instrument (if any); the drawer, or by other prearranged arrangements. Banks that create BAs from time or usance letters of credit are not obligated to discount the BA. In most cases, banks are willing to do so because they can earn an acceptance fee. However, the reason a bank would not want to discount the BA it created are mostly circumstances that involve the U.S. agency bank of a foreign based bank that is encountering foreign exchange unavailability.

When extended or usance payment terms are granted by the exporter to a foreign customer under a letter of credit, it must be determined who will pay the discount charges when the BA is discounted. This must be determined up front between the credit department and the marketing/sales department before the sales contract is negotiated between the buyer and seller (costs are discussed later). The credit person should determine the estimated cost of acceptance financing based on the extended or usance payment terms to be granted, if any, to the foreign customer for whatever the reasons. Marketing/sales should take these financing costs into context with the profit margins and sales to be gained or lost as a result of absorbing or passing on the costs of acceptance financing to the foreign customer.

If the discount charges are for the account of the foreign customer, the credit instrument should state that "all bank discount and/or acceptance costs are for the account of the opener/buyer." The costs, at the time the BA is discounted, will be passed on to the opener/buyer of the credit instrument.

If the discount charges are for the account of the drawer, the drawer may choose to discount with another bank if the rates are more favorable. Absent instructions to the contrary, the accepting bank has only one decision; to accept and hold the draft to maturity. No money changes hands at this time. At maturity the funds change hands between buyer and seller through the accepting bank.

If the drawer wishes to discount the draft, if not specified otherwise in the letter of credit, the drawer receives its funds, less the discount charges. The discounting bank then has two options: hold the BA in its portfolio until maturity, funded from its common pool of funds, or sell it into the secondary market through specialized dealers. The latter can occur at any time period during the life of the BA. When an acceptance is sold by a bank to an acceptance dealer, who in turn sells the instrument to an investor, the investor becomes the party financing the original transaction.

If any exporter discounts a BA drawn and created under a usance credit, in the majority of cases, it can do so without recourse as the credit of the issuing bank substitutes for that of the exporter.

Bankers' acceptance financing offers exporters (and importers) an alternative means to finance goods on extended terms which might otherwise be prohibitive without the use of a letter of credit. The use of this financing facility might be as or more competitive with other forms of financing and borrowing for the buyer and seller.

The Federal Reserve's Open Market Committee (FOMC) is the single largest investor in the U.S. bankers' acceptance market. The FOMC may make purchases for its own account as well as for the account of its customers, mainly foreign central banks. Other private investors may also participate in the bankers' acceptance secondary market. While the acceptance market is "thin" in comparison with the government securities market and concentrated with relatively few dealers, quality acceptances are considered liquid, and thus readily marketable instruments.

Banks that place their "acceptance" on drafts are subject to Federal Reserve Bank regulations governing the creation and use of BA instruments because BA financing involves the use of bank credit. The U.S. bankers' acceptance market as it exists today is based on governing regulations of the Federal Reserve Board as well as the Federal Reserve Bank's willingness to support the market through its collateral, purchase, and rediscount programs. Federal Reserve member banks may pledge eligible bankers' acceptances as security to meet their reserve obligations at the Federal Reserve. It is the policy of the Fed to purchase only acceptances established as "prime" bankers' acceptances. Prior to November 1974, the Federal Reserve guarantied acceptances it purchased for the account of its foreign correspondent bank customers. This was done to encourage the develpment of the U.S. bankers' acceptances market. As the volume of acceptance financing increased, the justification of extending a guarantee favoring this money market instrument and group of investors no longer existed. This resulted in the establishment of a two-tier market structure. The designation of a particular instrument as a *prime bankers' acceptance* depends largely on the familiarity of the accepting bank in the marketplace and the financial soundness of the accepting bank as well as the eligibility of the acceptance instrument itself.

The U.S. bankers' acceptance market as it operates today is based on tenets established by the Federal Reserve Board. Specifically, U.S. banks that are members of the Federal Reserve System are authorized to create acceptances under Section 13, Regulation A of the Federal Reserve Act. This regulation limits Federal Reserve member banks in acceptance creation per the following criteria:

- Types of acceptance transactions allowable.
- Maturity of acceptance transactions.
- Volume of acceptances outstanding.

A pertinent portion of paragraph seven of Section 13 follows:

Any member bank may accept drafts or bills of exchange drawn upon it having not more than six months' sight to run, exclusive of days of grace, which grow out of transactions involving the importation or exportation of goods; or which grow out of transactions involving the domestic shipment of goods provided shipping documents conveying or securing title are attached at the time of acceptance; or which are secured at the time of acceptance by a warehouse receipt or other such document conveying or securing title covering readily marketable staples.

Additionally, paragraph 12 of Section 13 provided for the creation of dollar exchange acceptances:

> Any member bank may accept drafts or bills of exchange drawn upon it having not more than three months' sight to run, exclusive of days of grace, drawn under regulations to be prescribed by the Board of Governors of the Federal Reserve System by banks or bankers in foreign countries or dependencies or insular possessions of the United States for the purpose of furnishing dollar exchange as required by the usages of trade in the respective countries, dependencies, or insular possessions.

The word *eligible,* when used to describe bankers' acceptances, means that a particular bankers' acceptance meets the requirements of Regulation A and the Federal Reserve Act as "eligible for discount." All acceptances which are not eligible for discount are considered *ineligible* acceptances. There is nothing improper or illegal about an ineligible acceptance; however, if the Federal Reserve does purchase an ineligible instrument, it does so at a deeper discount rate when compared to the rate at which it purchases eligible bankers' acceptances.

Additionally, ineligible acceptances are subject to requirements. This means that if a bank sells an acceptance which is not eligible under Regulation A, it must deposit a certain percentage of the proceeds with its local federal reserve bank in an interest-free account as a reserve deposit. Consequently, an ineligible acceptance is lower, when compared to that of an eligible acceptance, by a percentage corresponding to the amount of the required reserve deposit. Banks will generally pass this additional cost on to their customers in the form of a higher discount rate.

As previously discussed, drafts drawn and accepted in accordance with the Federal Reserve Act's criteria are classified as eligible. The marketability and pricing advantages of eligible bankers' acceptances vis-à-vis those declared ineligible have caused customers, investors, and bankers to deal primarily with this form of acceptance paper.

To qualify as eligible for discount by a Federal Reserve bank, a bankers' acceptance must meet certain specific requirements relating to the transaction being financed and to the maturity of the draft. The following is a brief description of these requirements, outlined in Regulation A of the Federal Reserve Act:

1. The tenor or maturity of the draft must not be more than 180 days from date of acceptance. The terms of the acceptance must not be greater than the period during which the related goods will remain in the channels of trade and in no instance for more than six months.
2. The draft must be drawn on a U.S. bank.
3. The exportation or importation (shipment) of goods between the United States and any foreign country or between foreign countries.*
4. The shipment of goods within the United States must provide shipping documents conveying or securing title that are attached or are in the physical possession of the accepting bank or its agent at time of acceptance.
5. The storage of readily marketable staples is in the United States or in any foreign country provided the draft or bill of exchange is secured at the time of acceptance by a warehouse receipt or other document conveying or securing title covering such readily marketable staples.

Within each of the principal categories mentioned above there are different rules as to what characteristics the draft and the transaction must have in order to be considered eligible. There are some general requirements that apply to all of the above categories. The following represents the general attributes which an acceptance transaction must possess in order to be considered "eligible."

a. An eligible acceptance draft must show a bank as drawee on the draft and that bank must be a member of the Federal Reserve System.

For example, a draft which is drawn on ABC Bank of New York must meet the test of a bank as drawee, and the Federal Reserve member test as well. A draft drawn by a foreign importer on his U.S. exporter would not be eligible since a bank is not the drawee on the draft; similarly, a draft drawn by a foreign importer

---

* Bills or drafts created and accepted to finance trade between foreign countries stored abroad are known as "third country bills."

on his local bank would not meet the test for eligibility because the overseas bank is not a member of the U.S. Federal Reserve System.

  b. An eligible acceptance draft must be "two-party" paper.

This means that the drawer's liability must remain on the draft after the member bank has accepted it. In order to qualify as an eligible acceptance, the instrument must display the acceptance stamp of the bank in addition to the simple unlimited endorsement of the drawer/payee. The drawer/payee may not, therefore, endorse the draft "without recourse" in an attempt to limit its liability. Two parties have to retain liability on the draft for it to be considered eligible. For example, if the accepting bank is not able to satisfy its obligation to repay the holder of the acceptance instrument at maturity, the investor also has the contingent liability of the drawer of the draft to obtain repayment. This is one of the primary reasons that bankers' acceptances are considered safe financial instruments for investment purposes.

  c. The maturity of the draft cannot exceed a period of six months.

The basic principle guiding this maturity requirement is that the repayment of a bankers' acceptance should come from the proceeds of the trade transaction being financed. Therefore, the terms extended in the underlying transaction, the so-called channels of trade sequence, will have a bearing on the permitted maturity of the acceptance. For example, the permitted acceptance financing period would include the period of shipment as well as normal payment terms. In addition, the financing period may include a limited time for pre-export storage and assembly of goods for shipment. If those periods, taken as a whole, equal approximately 90 days, an eligible acceptance cannot be created for 180 days. To summarize this important requirement, the term to maturity of the accepted draft must bear a reasonable relationship to the length of time required to complete the underlying trade transaction. In any event, financing outside of normal trade terms or for a period longer than six months may not be considered eligible.

One exception to the six-month maximum maturity guideline

relates to the creation of dollar exchange acceptances. Acceptance financing for the creation of dollar exchange is limited to a maximum maturity of 90 days. Dollar exchange acceptances are unique in that they are designed to alleviate seasonal shortages of dollars for payment of external obligations of certain nations, particularly those in Latin America, that typically rely on a limited number of crops for their foreign exchange earnings. These instruments anticipate proceeds from exports forthcoming within 90 days from the creation of the BA and usually apply for the use of foreign central banks. The creation of dollar exchange acceptances has been restricted by the Federal Reserve Act, since only certain countries are eligible for this form of credit.

  d. No other means of financing the underlying transaction may be employed.

  The document which a bank receives from the drawer of a draft must contain a representation to this effect. This usually appears in a bank's acceptance agreement with a customer which sets out the terms included in the drawing of individual drafts. This requirement is understandable when one considers that one of the primary reasons acceptances have proven to be relatively secure and liquid instruments with an active secondary market is that, from a credit standpoint, this financing is self-liquidating in nature (as discussed earlier). It is essential to attract prospective investors by the assurance that no third party has provided financing and may be looking to the goods underlying the trade transaction as collateral for its loan.

  The final general requirement pertaining to all eligible acceptances created to finance trade transactions is that the accepting bank must have the relevant transaction information before the bankers' acceptance is created. This includes, at a minimum, a description of the goods, the value of the goods in U.S. dollars, points of shipment, maturity of the draft and, additionally, in creating acceptances covering domestic storage transactions, the exact location of the goods must be known.

  There are several specific requirements for creating eligible bankers' acceptances that depend on the particular category of acceptances be created. A brief description of these other requirements by category follows.

For international shipments there must be a firm contract for sale before a draft can be accepted and discounted. This contract may take several forms. In the normal trade transaction where a buyer and seller don't know each other and are operating under a letter of credit, the letter of credit suffices as evidence of a firm contract for sale. If there is no letter of credit, a bank must nonetheless receive evidence of a firm contract for sale. A simple purchase order signed by the prospective buyer is sufficient to satisfy this requirement.

The acceptance must be created to support a specific import or export transaction. Banks may also extend acceptance financing to cover the accumulation of goods prior to shipment in an import/export transaction as long as there is evidence of a firm contract for sale of the merchandise being financed. Bankers' acceptances may be used to finance the import/export of goods between any two countries. This type of financing is available to either the importer or the exporter in a trade transaction. However, the financing should be obtained within a reasonable period of time after the merchandise has been shipped.

For domestic shipments of goods (within the United States), there must be a firm contract for sale before a draft can be accepted. This requirement is the same as that which applies in the international shipment context explained above.

The accepting bank, or its agent, must have physical possession of the documents securing title to the goods being financed before a draft can be accepted. For domestic shipment transactions, the accepting bank must have control of the documents conveying title to the merchandise in transit. These title documents must be issued by authorized common carriers, relevant to the mode of transportation used, such as bills of lading or barge receipts, etc. If different modes of transportation are used for the same merchandise (i.e., from train to barge to truck, a title document must be controlled by the accepting bank during each phase of the shipment).

As a result of this requirement, eligible acceptance financing of domestic shipments is often impractical, particularly when short hauls are involved. This is because it may be difficult to deliver the title documents to the location of the accepting bank quickly enough for it to provide the funds for a significant period of time.

This is particularly true in the case of our earlier example where a single transaction employs successive modes of transportation. This requirement is considered to be the principal reason why the volume of domestic shipment acceptances outstanding usually represent only a very minor portion of total acceptances outstanding in any one period.

For the storage of goods (international or domestic), the accepting bank, or its agent, must have physical possession of the documents securing title to the goods being financed before a draft can be accepted. This requirement is the same as that which applies in the domestic shipment context explained above.

Additionally, to satisfy Federal Reserve Board requirements regarding title documents in this context, the accepting bank must hold a warehouse receipt issued by a party independent of the borrower. In some cases, field warehouse receipts may suffice, but you are advised to consult a bank to discuss how you may best satisfy these title requirements.

The goods under storage must be readily marketable staples. This requirement might be considered to parallel the reasoning behind the "firm contract for sale" requirement for acceptances covering international and domestic shipments. A ready market for the goods in storage offers evidence of the value of the goods and, therefore, makes it possible for the accepting bank to determine the reasonable value of the draft which a drawer is presenting. One is not required to have a firm contract for sale in the domestic storage context, because it is the "storage while awaiting sale" period that is being financed.

While there is no precise definition of readily marketable staples as it relates to Regulation A, a number of published Federal Reserve interpretations are available on this subject. A good basic rule of thumb is: if there is a market in a commodity and a published list of prices so that an independent party could reasonably determine the value of the goods on any given day, then the goods would probably qualify as readily marketable staples.

Clean Acceptance Financing

U.S. exporters can finance the sale of goods to foreign customers by the creation of a clean bankers' acceptance which is created independently of a letter or credit for the underlying export of goods. A clean acceptance is created when the bank accepts a time draft drawn on it by an exporter under a separate agreement wih the accepting bank called an Acceptance Agreement (see Appendix 8–A). The agreement may cover one specific export related transaction or a series of transactions over a period of time. The draft drawn on the bank is still eligible for all of the terms and conditions set forth by the Federal Reserve Bank for eligible acceptances as previously mentioned. The drafts are usually accompanied by a statement that includes the following information:

- The value of the goods shipped and to be financed.
- A general description of the merchandise.
- The country of exportation and the country of importation.
- The date of shipment.
- A certificate attesting that the shipment is not being financed by any other means.

By signing the Acceptance Agreement the exporter agrees to pay the bank the face value of the acceptance plus charges, no later than one business day preceding the maturity date of the acceptance. The bank will consider:

- The customer's credit line and rating.
- The extent to which the bank wishes to engage in acceptance financing.
- Compliance of the transaction with Federal Reserve regulations for BAs.

U.S. exporters can enter into acceptance financing for shipments abroad without a covering letter of credit instrument under two methods or scenarios: Pre-Export Financing and Export Financing for D/P or D/A and open account export shipments.

Pre-Export Financing.   Acceptance financing can be used if the exporter has a firm sales contract with a foreign customer, but needs financing to acquire and prepare its goods for shipment provided the goods will not be altered or transformed in any way. The goods to be financed are usually readily marketable staples, but can also be manufactured or processed goods. BA financing cannot be used to acquire raw materials and cover manufacturing costs. Once the goods are finished and available for export, they can be financed with an eligible BA. One excellent use of pre-export financing with clean acceptances are goods which are manufactured to the specifications of a foreign customer.

Under this arrangement, the exporter draws a U.S. dollar *time* draft on the bank up to six months prior to shipment, with the maturity coinciding with the expected payment date (tenor not to exceed six months) covering the value of the shipment. The bank accepts the draft, creating a bankers' acceptance, and discounts the BA. The exporter uses the proceeds to acquire the goods and prepare them for shipment. The proceeds may not be used to acquire goods which will be altered prior to shipment. Once the goods are available for export, it ships the goods to the foreign customer. At maturity, the exporter reimburses the accepting bank under the acceptance agreement with the proceeds collected from the sale of the goods from the foreign customer and the bank applies the funds to the BA.

Export Financing: D/P or D/A, and Open Account.   Under a D/P or D/A transaction, acceptance financing can be used to finance (for exporters) the period between shipment of the goods and receipt of payment from foreign customers on a documents against acceptance (D/A) or documents against payment (D/P) basis (both are discussed in Chapter 4, Part A).

Under this type of transaction, the exporter ships the goods and submits its title documents and draft drawn on the foreign customer, not its bank, for collection. At the same time, the exporter draws a time draft on its bank with the maturity date coinciding with the date it expects to collect payment from the foreign customer of the sight or time draft. Again, the tenor must not exceed six months. On receipt of the draft, the bank accepts it, thus creating a BA, and immediately discounts it based on its "all-in" rate (discussed later). This provides immediate cash flow to the exporter. On receipt of funds by the exporter from the foreign collecting bank, it applies the funds from the collection to reimburse the accepting bank at the maturity of the BA. If funds are not received at the maturity of the BA, it will debit the exporter's account to reimburse itself.

Under an open account transaction, the exporter ships the goods and invoices the foreign customer. The exporter in turn, draws a time draft on its bank, with the tenor equivalent to the expected collection period, not to exceed six months. The bank accepts the draft, thus creating a BA, and discounts the BA for immediate funds to the exporter based on its "all-in" rate, providing immediate cash flow to the exporter. The exporter reimburses the accepting bank with the proceeds of its collection from the foreign customer at the maturity of the BA. If funds are not received at the maturity of the BA, it will debit the exporter's account to reimburse itself.

Advantages versus Disadvantages

Advantages:
1. Increases cash inflow and reduces days sales outstanding (DSO) if the BA is discounted.
2. The customer/country risk is substituted for that of the U.S. bank.
3. The financing usually requires no compensating balance. Commercial bank loans usually do.
4. The financing may be cost advantageous to the borrower. This assumes a company has difficulty borrowing at prime rate or other rates.
5. During tight credit conditions, the financing may be advantageous because commercial bank liquidity may not meet demand.

Disadvantages:
1. Can be more expensive than other types of export trade financing.
2. Banks may not be willing to have drafts drawn on themselves (i.e., in the case of banks with problems country loan portfolios).
3. Discount charges can be expensive, making the export sale less profitable.

Costs. When a bank accepts a draft, the bank also charges an acceptance commission. This is its compensation for its assumption of credit risk and administrative costs to cover the associated transaction. When a bank discounts a BA, thus advancing funds against the BA, it provides funds at a rate determined by conditions present in the money markets at the time of discounting. While interest and other fees are most often collected in arrears under other forms of financing, the acceptance commission and discount charges on bankers' acceptances are collected from the borrower at the time of acceptance and disbursement, or the charges are deducted from the proceeds. This assumes that the same bank is used; otherwise, if another bank is used for discounting, the acceptance commission is collected by the bank which created the BA and the discount charges are collected from the discounting bank. These fees are generally combined and quoted as an "all-in" rate if the same bank is used for acceptance and discounting. The effective cost of acceptance financing can be calculated as follows:

$$\frac{\text{"All-in" rate}}{1 - \dfrac{\text{Tenor}}{360} \times \text{"All-in" rate}} \times 100 = \text{Effective annual interest rate}$$

Example

Draft amount:	$50,000
Payment terms:	90 days date
"All-in" rate:	7.75 percent

$$\frac{0.0775}{1 - \dfrac{90}{360} \times 0.0775} \times 100 = \frac{0.0775}{1 - 0.019375} = 7.90\%$$

Therefore, the net proceed after deducting the discount charges for the BA is $49,031.25.

OFF-BALANCE SHEET FINANCING

Another means of financing export related transactions is the selling on a nonrecourse or recourse basis of an exporter's drafts, promissory notes, or invoices to a bank or banks. They in turn will impose a finance charge or discount fee on the obligations.

Most U.S. banks will not do this type of financing on a nonrecourse basis to exporters because of administrative costs and procedures. They will normally only do it with their own customers who have broad knowledge and years of experience in international trade. To minimize the commercial and political risk, banks often require that the exporter obtain comprehensive export credit insurance (see Chapter 6, Part A for more information on export credit insurance schemes).

One of the most significant advantages to the exporter, if it is properly structured, is the increase of cash flow when its liquidity is tight. The exporter's bank lines of credit are not materially affected by the financing and can be used for other purposes.

Structure of the Deal

An off-balance sheet financing of receivables can be arranged if the bank is willing to structure the deal without getting involved in complex legal binding agreements that require a lot of documentation and constraints. It can be put together quite simply by a letter agreement between an exporter and bank (groups or consortium of banks is not recommended). The letter agreement should spell out some specifics, but for the most part is broad and simplistic in structure. The letter agreement should basically consist of the following major parts:

1. Foreign receivables to be financed.
2. Credit insurance and assignment of receivables.
3. The percentage financed.
4. Discount rate.
5. Funding.
6. Collections.
7. Repayment terms.

The Foreign Receivables to Be Financed. Since the bank is only willing to finance foreign receivables insured by an export credit insurer (i.e., FCIA, AIG, or AFIA), the only receivables financed are those eligible for export credit insurance coverage as specified by the insurer. The bank and exporter should both be cognizant of what defines an eligible export sales/receivable as per the insurer's policy to eliminate any doubts. Normally confirmed irrevocable letters of credit, consignment receivables, sales to U.S.

exporters (sales billed to a company in the United States, but goods are shipped direct overseas), and intercompany sales are excluded.

Receivables financed under different schemes should be excluded from the overall pool or portfolio of receivables to be financed by the bank. These would include, but are not limited to clean or documentary bankers' acceptances, buyer credits, and forfaited items.

Credit Insurance and Assignment of Proceeds.   The exporter is responsible for keeping an export credit insurance policy in force and in compliance with its terms and conditions throughout the term of the financing. The bank or finance house may request a copy of the policy and any endorsements, exclusions, or special buyer credit limits. Normally an Assignment of Proceeds, obtained from the insurer, is executed between the exporter and bank or finance house.

Throughout the financing, the exporter is responsible for the administration and servicing of the policy. This means the exporter is responsible for meeting all of the terms and conditions of the insurer's policy. It is only logical the exporter be responsible for policy compliance because of its basic strategies, policies, and objectives in marketing and financing of the sale of goods and services overseas.

The Percentage Financed.   Since not all receivables are 100 percent insured for commercial and political risks, which takes into consideration any country limitation percentages, restrictions or conditions imposed by the insurer, the bank or finance house and exporter will have to agree on what percentage of the receivables will be financed. Most policies extend 100 percent political risk coverage but from time-to-time the percentage might decrease on a country case-by-case basis due to severe country risks.

This element of the deal is important because it determines whether the exporter will get anywhere between 80 to 100 percent of receivables financed or funded. Because most credit insurers are only willing to insure anywhere between 90 to 95 percent of commercial risk, depending on the policy, it is much easier for both parties to agree that in the event of nonpayment from a foreign customer due to commercial risks, the exporter be responsible for the uninsured portion, including the deductible. This will eliminate any doubts or disputes.

Discount Rate. The exporter should look for a bank or finance house that is willing to offer alternative means of financing the sale of its receivables. The alternatives could include a spread over LIBOR (London Interbank Offered Rate), bankers' acceptance discount rates, the prime rate, a CD rate, or even the federal funds rate. Of course, the spread quoted by the bank will mainly be based on the spread of risk contained in the receivables, and the creditworthiness of the exporter and its years of experience in international trade. The bank will also take into consideration the performance of the credit department in managing its foreign receivables over a period of time.

The exporter must assess and weigh all of the bank's fees (bank may incur costs related to reserves, special deposits, taxes, and other charges) and discount charges in comparison to its internal cost of capital or discounted net present value to determine if off-balance sheet financing is an attractive or alternative means for financing its business. However, if the exporter's other alternative means of financing itself have dried-up or become too expensive, off-balance sheet financing might prove to be beneficial.

The finance or discount charge agreed on is calculated on the face value or amount of the pool of eligible export receivables from the period of the date of funding until the maturity or term of the financing.

Funding. The exporter needs to develop the internal capability of automating its accounts receivable with the capability of identifying those receivables eligible for export credit insurance protection and financing under the deal. Alternatively, the exporter will have to identify these eligible receivables for sale to the bank or finance house manually.

Funding should occur at the beginning of each month by phoning or telexing an appropriate or designated individual at the bank or finance house of the amount of receivables eligible for financing that month. The bank wire transfers the funds to wherever designated by the exporter. The amount should only include new eligible export credit insured sales that occurred the prior month, not any previous month's sales. All of this is followed shortly by an aged accounts receivable listing by foreign customer. This receivable listing will verify and justify for the bank or finance house the amount given to the bank and the condition of the receivables by foreign customer.

When funding is done over the telephone or by telex, usually the exporter leaves presigned drafts with the bank or finance house to expedite financing.

Collections. One of the most important features of off-balance financing of receivables is the collection aspect of the eligible receivables financed by the bank or finance house. In this case, it is advantageous for the bank to assign the exporter as its "agent" to collect the receivables financed. It only stands to reason that the exporter knows the foreign customers better than the bank or finance house. It will always be the responsibility of the exporter to be cognizant of and resolve any foreign customer disputes pertaining to such things as product quality or quantity claims, pricing problems, freight rate problems, or goods returned. Since the exporter will always know its foreign customers better than anyone else, it is in a better position to collect past due obligations.

Repayment Terms. The parties to the financing deal will have to agree on when the bank or finance house is to be repaid by the exporter for each monthly pool of receivables financed. This can easily be accomplished by the exporter and financer analyzing several months of receivables to determine the average payment term maturity or by the parties simply agreeing on a repayment term. The average payment terms can be determined by adding the term or maturity date of each sale and dividing it by the total number of transactions. Several months of receivables need to be studied because of sales fluctuations or seasonality periods.

Whatever is agreed on, the responsibility for collecting the amount of receivables financed (funded) by the bank or finance house will obviously be the responsibility of the exporter's credit department. Shortfalls between the amount funded and collected will have to come from the coffers of the exporter.

It is also conceivable that the bank or finance house may want to file a financing statement (lien) on the accounts receivable of the exporter under the UCC (Uniform Commercial Code) within the county and state of the exporter's headquarters. Most bank or finance houses may want to file a blank lien on all of an exporter's accounts receivable, which means including domestic and ineligible export receivables of the exporter. However, it may be more advantageous for the exporter to permit only a lien on those accounts receivable eligible for funding under the program. This will free up all other receivables which the exporter may need to provide as collateral to other creditors to obtain financing (short or long term).

EXPORT FACTORING

Factoring has been used to finance domestic sales in the United States for over 50 years, but was not used to finance international sales until the 1960s. In the United States, it is normally associated with such industries as textiles, furniture, apparel, and consumer electronics.

Export factoring of receivables can include not only the function of finance, but service as well—all for a fee. The services can be a combination of credit investigation, credit approval, collections, bookkeeping, and the compiling of statistics. The finance side can include the obtaining of bank loans, discounting receivables, and a tripartite arrangement.

For the benefit of the reader, it is important to note there are differences or distinctions between off-balance sheet versus export factoring of receivables.

Off-Balance Sheet versus Export Factoring

Off-Balance Sheet	Export Factoring
Accounts receivable are sold and assigned to bank as collateral.	Accounts receivable are sold to factor.
Funds can be advanced up to 100 percent.	Purchase of 70 to 90 percent of invoice value, funded now or later.
Often confidential.	Only confidential in some cases.

Off-Balance Sheet	Export Factoring
The bank's debtor is the exporter.	The factor's debtor is the foreign customer of the exporter.
Commercial and political (country) risks are exporters. Must adhere to terms and conditions of export credit insurer.	Commercial and political (country) risks are factors. Credit insurance is not applicable.
Collections performed by exporter.	Collections performed by factor.
No services done by bank.	The factor supplies a wide range of services.
Funding is for large receivables.	Funding can be from small to large funding of accounts receivable.
Sole purpose: Financing	Purpose—According to interest: financing, collections, bookkeeping.
Costs: Discount facility only.	Costs: Cost of finance plus a charge for the services desired.

By eliminating the administrative aspects for an exporter, the exporter is saving money by reducing overhead costs. By reducing these costs, the exporter might be placed in a position to lower its price and be more competitive. Of course, these administrative cost savings to an exporter (i.e., credit and collection personnel, accounting and cash application personnel, automated system), must be weighed against the fees from the factor. Unlike other trade financing programs which are directly tied to export credit insurance schemes, factoring an exporter's receivables means its goods do not have to be of U.S. origin, there is no deductible, nor is there a commercial first loss provision. In addition, factoring provides the exporter with a hedge against foreign exchange risks if it invoices in currencies other than its own. Factors will frequently assume the foreign exchange risk by buying a futures contract to sell the foreign exchange from the export sales. The currencies however must be agreed on in advance.

In a nonbinding application for factoring, the exporter will give a brief description of the business and industry, information about the international marketplace of the exporter (i.e., type of customers sold, markets, distribution), the composition of the export portfolio of receivables which includes such things as: number of active accounts with addresses and bank references, size of an average export shipment as invoiced, number of invoices per month, average turnover of receivables, and collection history. The application will be accompanied by the exporter's latest detailed aging of accounts receivable. The factor will evaluate this information to determine what services it can provide and at what fee. It will reserve the right to decline an individual foreign customer, probably because of commercial risks and billing currencies.

Services Performed

Credit Investigation. The exporter, prior to a reasonable time before shipment of the goods, must submit credit information on each foreign customer for approval by the factor. The information must include:

- Name and address of the foreign customer.
- Payment terms.
- Billing currency.
- Amount of the export order.
- Anticipated credit exposure with the foreign customer.
- The shipping date.

Based on this credit information, the factor will perform a credit investigation on the foreign customer, but on behalf of the exporter. The factor may use its subsidiary or affiliate office in the foreign customer's country, if it has an office, to do the credit check.

Credit information overseas leaves much to be desired, especially as it pertains to the quality and quantity of the information. But, by the factor using its overseas affiliate or subsidiary, it stands a better chance of getting credit information on foreign customers because many of these overseas offices are in partnership with major financial institutions, especially commercial banks. Overseas commercial banks have access to better sources of information than do many other types of financial institutions. In countries where the U.S. factor does not have an overseas office, it will perform the credit investigation using its own sources of information. In general, a credit investigation performed by an overseas office is usually quicker than one performed by the U.S. factor itself. The difference timewise between the two in getting credit approval can be approximately three weeks.

If the local credit investigation is positive, meaning the foreign customer is creditworthy for the export sale, the factor's overseas office may guarantee the debt to the U.S. factor. The U.S. factor will in turn guarantee both the commercial and political risk to the exporter. The guarantee to the exporter is 100 percent without recourse and without a first loss or deductible. If the overseas office of the U.S. factor did a poor job in its credit investigation, but was credit approved anyway and the debtor defaults, either because of commercial or political risks, the U.S. factor will suffer the bad debt loss.

Based on the anticipated volume of sales and number of shipments, the U.S. factor can assign one of two credit limits: an order limit or a revolving credit limit. If the factor assigns an order limit, it means the exporter must obtain prior approval from the factor before each shipment. Under a revolving credit limit, the exporter can make shipments up to a specified credit limit without receiving the prior approval of the factor.

For example: If the factor assigns a revolving credit limit on a foreign customer of $75,000 and each order is for $25,000, the exporter can make three shipments. Another example with a different twist would be a revolving credit limit of $150,000. The exporter will make four shipments, each for $50,000 to a foreign customer. If all of the shipments are made before the first shipment is due for payment, the highest credit exposure will be $200,000 or $50,000 higher than the credit limit. Until the first $50,000 shipment is paid, the exporter will be at risk. Once the first $50,000 is paid, the last shipment will automatically be the responsibility of the factor, not the exporter.

Collection. Under a factoring arrangement with an exporter, it is usual for the foreign customers of the exporter to be notified of the sale of its receivables to a factor. The foreign customer is directed to pay its maturing debt obligations directly to wherever the factor so designates. In most cases, if the factor has an overseas office in the country of the foreign customer, it will be instructed to pay the factor's local office. If the factor does not have an office in the country of the foreign customer, it will pay the U.S. factor in the country of the exporter.

It is the sole responsibility of the factor to collect each maturing debt obligation because it now owns the receivables of the exporter. In cases where the U.S. factor has an overseas office, that office will use the customary collection practices of the country which in all probability are more effective than collecting from the United States.

Bookkeeping. The factor must keep accurate and timely accounting information to monitor its accounts receivable performance and provide information to the exporter. The information includes the following.

Monthly Statement: A record of all open invoices with balances, a daily running balance, and a closing balance for month-end purposes. It will include, but is not limited to, such things as commissions paid, expenses, debits and credits, and the sales assigned by the exporter to the factor.

Aging of Accounts Receivable: A report which is usually generated at month-end which lists all of the foreign customers assigned to the factor. If the factor is automated with an on-line system, it can monitor the performance daily of any one foreign customer assigned to it.

Credit Managers' Activity Report: Gives the exporter a report daily, weekly or monthly status on foreign customers regarding such information as availability under revolving lines of credit, date they expire, past due buyers, high credit balance outstanding, year-to-date sales, and buyers near their credit limit.

Credit Approval: The factor will use a form for completion by the exporter. Although the exporter can obtain its approval verbally, it is always backed up by the form, signed by an authorized individual at the factor. The form includes the foreign customer's name, address, bank, credit and payment terms requested, and the date the credit limit was assigned and expires.

Daily Cash Report: Indicates by foreign customer—closed items by invoices paid, the amount received, date received, date of remittance, and any deductions.

Payment. The exporter can be paid by the factor by either one of three methods:
1. Based on collections.
2. Average collections.
3. At maturity.

Based on collections, the exporter is paid by the factor when funds are received by the factor from an importer; nonpayment is determined due to commercial risks (i.e., default of payment, bankruptcy, liquidation of the business); nonpayment is determined due to political or country risks (i.e., war, riot, revolution, confiscation or import licenses, confiscation of goods, foreign exchange delays); and under a bankruptcy, the proceeds from any distributions.

In cases which are not covered above, it may be agreed that the past due debts will be paid by the factor within a specified period of time (i.e., 90 or 120 days from due date). Such cases might include billing currency unavailability, dock strikes, or congestion at the port of importation.

For average collections the factor pays the exporter based on historical payment trends of each foreign customer. For example, if a foreign customer has been paying on average every 95 days based on 90 day payment terms, the factor would pay the exporter on the 95th day the next time a payment comes due from the foreign customer. The average payments are adjusted by foreign customer based on the factor's payment experience with each foreign customer. In most cases the factors' automated system tracks and calculates these averages by foreign customer.

At maturity payment is remitted to the exporter based on a fixed date once a month for all payments maturing within that month. The fixed date is based on the weighted average maturity date of the receivables with a preset number of additional collection days included in the calculation.

For example, two invoices are generated in June on net 90 day terms. One invoice is for $10,000 and matures August 1. The second invoice is for $5,000 and matures August 30. The weighted average maturity date would be March 8, but if 10 additional collection days are added, the date the exporter would be paid is March 18.

The daily cash report is important for the exporter because it assists in verifying the calculations of the factor to pay the exporter at specified maturity dates.

The use of a factor can provide much needed funds to exporters who are in cash flow binds or desire to minimize administrative expenses associated with credit and accounting. The exporter can obtain loans or funding by either one of the following methods: Bank loans, discounting receivables, or entering into a tripartite agreement.

Bank Loans. By utilizing the services of a factor (credit approval, collections, bookkeeping), with 100 percent guaranteed nonrecourse protection against most risks, an exporter can get bank loan financing. This is accomplished by the exporter assigning the receipt of funds or credit balances due from the factor to a bank. Because the bank collects its funds from a factor, the bank views the entire deal as more favorable to provide loans to the exporter. The charges will consist of a commission from the factor of 1.5 to 2.0 percent and the bank might charge interest at 1.0 to 2.0 percent over the prime rate or other rates.

An exporter might need to arrange this type of financing after it encounters poor prior experience with an export credit insurance agency and/or it experiences increasing bad debt losses. For example, some exporters might find it difficult to comply with all of the terms and conditions of an export credit insurer. It may find it difficult to get paid on claims filed with the insurer if it failed to comply with its conditions (i.e., lack of sufficient and up-to-date credit information on foreign customers insured under discretionary credit limits, goods were shipped over the insured discretionary credit limits, or the exporter shipped a foreign customer on credit terms not authorized by the insurer). Because of this poor prior experience with the insurer, the whole purpose of the policy might be considered self-defeating and is dropped by the exporter. Without the credit insurance in place, bank loan financing could be discontinued or the amount of financing is reduced.

Discounting Receivables. Factors will discount purchased receivables of exporters based on an agreed on discount rate. The factor will advance funds to an exporter based on a monthly pool or portfolio of receivables to be factored, up to a specified percentage of the exporter's receivables.

To provide this facility, the factor may look for additional collateral of the exporter (i.e., assignment of inventory, assignment of domestic receivables, pledge of stock, lien on certain fixed assets). The entire financing package is primarily based on an assessment of the discounted receivables and the factors' collection experience or probability or timely repayments based on the countries and even foreign customers if it has prior experience. Therefore, most factors will discount and advance funds to exporters anywhere between 70 to 90 percent of the total receivables purchased. This is done because the factor may wind up with something less than the total amount of receivables purchased and discounted. For example, if the factor purchased $800,000 in export related receivables from an exporter and discounted 80 percent, the exporter would receive proceeds of $640,000. But, if the factor only collected 70 percent of these receivable or $448,000, it will come up short for a remainder of $192,000 ($640,000 − $448,000 = $192,000).

Charges from the factor to provide this type of financing are usually higher than a commercial bank. Exporters should carefully weigh all of the charges and fees plus the amount of funds being made available from a bank and factor. They may find one slightly cheaper and more flexible than the other or basically the same.

Tripartite Agreements. A significant portion of U.S. export financing using factors is done with tripartite agreements. This is done when a factor provides the services and the exporter assigns the proceeds or credit balances due from the factor to a second financial institution, which does the funding.

This system is particularly effective for a business able to borrow from a commercial bank at rates close to the prime rate, but that has used most of its existing bank lines of credit for domestic business or for other uses.

Considerations and Costs

Exporters should carefully weigh all of the pros and cons of using factors. Many people will argue that the services of a factor are quite expensive. However, this may not necessarily hold true if the following points are considered:

1. Can the factor improve an exporter's accounts receivable turnover thus reducing the amount of working capital tied up in receivables and its cost of capital? How will the increase in receipts or funds be invested or utilized (will it generate interest income)?
2. Will the reduction in administrative costs versus the factor's commission and/or additional fees increase operating profit?
3. Can the factor improve receivable turnover without loss of an exporters foreign customers due to tighter or more lenient credit controls (i.e., criteria of credit approval and collecting could be tighter or looser; their credit decisions might prove better than an inexperienced exporter who might ask for letter of credit payment terms which may not be necessary)? Can the losses be offset by improved receivable turnover?
4. Will export credit sales increase as a result of utilizing the services of a factor?
5. What about bad debt losses? Will they be reduced? If yes, the exporter's reserve for doubtful accounts should be reduced, thus increasing profits.

A factor's service charges are quoted on a commission basis. Their commissions can range anywhere between 1 to 2.5 percent or even 3.0 percent.

LEASING

Leasing as a means of export trade finance is being increasingly stressed by leasing companies operating internationally. It has come about because producers of capital goods find that the financing assistance they can offer exporters helps in the marketing of their goods and the financing of a customer's operations (i.e., it has balance sheet and income statement implications, pro and con). However, businesses with a high technical know-how frequently do not have staffs with sufficient financial knowledge in these matters. It would, therefore, be a difficult and risky undertaking for them to offer their foreign customers.

What Is It?

Leasing is an arrangement whereby, an investor (the user), in this case the foreign customer, does not want to purchase the goods itself. Instead, it buys the use of the goods against payment of a monthly rental (lease) fee to a leasing company (the lessor), which owns the goods by holding title. Leasing substitutes an actual investment by a simple rental relationship over a fixed period of time.

The supplier of the goods (i.e., the producer or exporter), can be the lessor. There are basically two types of leasing: operating leasing and capital or finance leasing. In operating leasing, normally the producer itself offers its goods for lease, together with technical services and continuous replacement of updated goods. In capital or finance leasing, a triangular relationship is set up between the producer of the goods, the buyer who becomes the lessor, and the leasing party known as the lessee, which in this case is the foreign customer. It is this kind of leasing which is most commonly discussed and used in export trade financing. It is solely a financial arrangement with no technical obligations on the part of the lessor towards the lessee, as in operating leasing.

For example, under a triangular arrangement, ABC Co. is the producer of capital goods and XYZ Inc. wants its products. Instead of ABC selling the capital goods to XYZ, who has cash flow problems, on credit terms (usually three to five years), ABC Co. will sell the capital goods to a leasing company on a cash basis. The leasing company in turn will lease the capital goods to XYZ Inc. and be repaid a rental or lease payment, including amortization, interest, and a leasing contract fee.

Leasing internationally creates many legal and tax problems.

In most cases, at the end of a leasing period, the capital goods are bought by the lessor at a reasonably low price (depreciated price).

The leasing of certain capital goods could involve containers, trucks, railway carriages, or ships and aircraft, but could also occur with construction machinery or, more important currently, oil prospect drilling rigs and platforms. For leasing companies going across national boundaries or leasing goods internationally, this poses an additional risk. They may find it more difficult to establish rights of ownership in the case of nonfulfillment of the leasing contract by the lessee. In the United States, collateral is secured by perfected liens with states who adhere to the Uniform Commercial Code (UCC), excluding Louisiana who follows the French code or Code Napoleon. Internationally, there is no UCC. Goods can be registered in the country of the foreign customer, but the means of determining whether any prior existing liens exist on the lessee that would encumber your goods is difficult or nearly impossible to determine.

Cross-Border Leasing

Cross-border leasing takes the place of an export transaction. The goods are shipped to the foreign country, but remain the property of the domestic leasing company. This creates many legal and tax problems. In most cases, at the end of a leasing period, the goods are bought by the lessee at a low price. The item is thus finally exported and title transfer takes place, although it has been in possession of the lessee for some time.

As already previously mentioned, there are certain legal and tax problems. The question of when custom duties have to be paid, and on what value, is one of the inherent problems of cross-border leasing. Another problem is taxes. If there are tax agreements between the two countries of the lessor and the lessee, the lessor can probably avoid double taxation. Further complications arise in connection with value-added taxes (applicable to EEC countries, Argentina, Mexico, and others) which are deductible within the national tax system, but not across borders. Other problems could arise, for instance, out of fiscal schemes for permitted depreciations. The leasing company has to take into consideration all such foreign regulations when calculating its rental fee.

In addition to all these fiscal problems, cross-border leasing may be hampered by legal uncertainties. Will the rights of ownership of the leasing company be honored in the case of the lessee's default or bankruptcy. Some countries still consider leasing as a special way of purchasing on credit. The leasing company, therefore, would have only the same legal status as other lenders to the business. Moreover, cross-border leasing to Socialist countries founders on the regulations governing ownership of the means of production.

Currency problems still remain despite the aforementioned. In which currency should the rental payments be effected? If the leasing contract provides for payment in the foreign currency, it is the leasing company which has to cover the currency risk by equivalent refinancing. There is also the risk of interest fluctuations. If the leasing payments are made in the lessor's domestic currency, the lessee runs the risk that its leasing payments might become more expensive following a devaluation of its national currency against the foreign billing currency.

Cross-border leasing can incur large costs and encounters strong competition for local leasing companies, which can operate with all the advantages of the simpler domestic leasing. The following is a simpler way to lease goods internationally.

International Leasing

In international leasing the problems of differences between national fiscal and legal systems for lessor and lessee can be avoided. This is true if the international leasing company is a member of an association of leasing companies, or has its own subsidiaries abroad.

An international leasing arrangement can be initiated by an exporter and foreign customer. This is accomplished by the foreign customer contacting its leasing company which finds, on behalf of its foreign associate, an exporter willing to supply the capital goods. The exporter might sell the goods directly to the foreign leasing company, or it might sell them to his national leasing company which would then sell them to its partner company in the lessee's country. Associates in an international chain of leasing companies may arrange with their partners for a commission to be paid for their assistance, but some do cooperate for free.

The first step towards setting up an international leasing arrangement will be the application followed by a contract. Four parties are involved in the arrangement:

The *supplier* wishes to sell its' goods, and looks to leasing as a means of achieving cash flow, speed, and certainty.

The *lessee* wants to buy goods, but cannot due to cash flow problems.

The *bank of the lessee* is interested in the commercial success of its customer, and can assist the lessee find a leasing company.

The *leasing company* knows the requirements of its customers and keeps in close contact with them.

The leasing company will assess the creditworthiness of the lessee, the reliability of the supplier, and the risk of the leased goods. The lessee will be asked to fill out a leasing application. It will certainly want to know if the leased goods will help increase the cash flow of the lessee.

In the process of the leasing company performing an assessment of the creditworthiness of the lessee to determine if it can make rental payments now and in the future, the leasing company will require certain financial information. In this regard, it will require a balance sheet and income statement for the last three years, budget plans plus cash flow projections for the next three to five years. The lessee may also be asked if it has leasing arrangements with other leasing companies. In some countries, leasing obligations do not show up in the balance sheet or income statement.

In finance leasing, the lessee will be asked to insure the leased goods and to cede all rights to the lessor. It is the rule in finance leasing that the lessee pays for service, maintenance, and repairs. The actual leasing costs consist of:

1. A small fee due when signing the contract, calculated as a percentage of the purchase value.
2. The monthly lease installments.

From the point of view of the lessee, leasing is a medium- to long-term means of financing itself. It is an alternative to financing out of equity. Rather than outlaying the cash purchase now, the foreign customer can spread out its cash flow over extended periods of time. Although it is somewhat more expensive than a simple purchase, it has the advantage that payments are due only with the return on the investment. Leasing can be tailored to the needs of the lessee, by making the rental or lease payments progressive or declining, by adjusting the leasing period, and by agreeing on full or only partial amortization leasing. The producer/exporter of the goods should negotiate with the leasing company and lessee for the best possible deal for the lessee, its customer.

In many countries, since the leased goods are not capitalized in the balance sheet, and corresponding rental obligations do not appear on the liabilities side, the balance sheet of a foreign customer obtaining the goods through leasing looks very different from that of a business that purchases the goods and takes up corresponding financing.

Since the balance sheet of a lessee is lighter than that of a business which has purchased the goods with borrowed funds, the lessee has a higher borrowing capacity. Leasing is therefore different than equipment purchased on credit (supplier credit) or to drawing a bank loan.

Leasing helps to conserve liquidity which can be put to other uses (i.e., into research and development, marketing, or product development). It also has tax advantages, depending on the country's national tax system. When the investor buys the equipment, it will be allowed, in most cases, to deduct the interest on loans and the depreciation for taxable income in accordance with tax allowance schemes. When leasing, it may be allowed to deduct the total rental or lease payments.

CONSIGNMENT

Another means of financing purchases of goods for foreign customers is to enter into a consignment contract with the foreign customer. Under a consignment arrangement, the goods are only "consigned," but not sold to the foreign customer. Also discussed in Chapter 4, Part A. In this case, the exporter (consignor) retains title (holds the original bill of lading) to the goods until the foreign customer (consignee) has sold them to a third party or purchased the goods themselves as distributor, end-user, manufacturer, or processor.

The risks of the consignment arrangement to the exporter are extremely high. It is normally only done by exporters with their own branches or subsidiaries abroad. The following are just a few of the many risks. The consignor has little evidence of the foreign customer's obligation to pay for the goods shipped on consignment. Where will the goods be stored? In a government or private bonded warehouse, warehouse of the consignee, or a warehouse managed by a financial institution? Clearly, establishing a consignment stock at a warehouse of the consignee is the riskiest. The exporter may ship too many goods into the consignment stock and the consignee may not withdraw as many goods as planned. Accounting for the goods held in consignment could prove to be a nightmare. How will you be notified of withdrawals (i.e., which goods, the quantity, and value)? Goods held in and in-transit to a consignment stock are accounted for as inventory until title transfer takes place. The consignee may default when payment is due. What if the consignee withdrew a lot of goods, but couldn't pay for the first withdrawal because of a major devaluation or adverse competitive pricing situation? The laws in some countries are difficult to understand and interpret when it concerns ownership of the goods, duties and taxes, and rights to return goods to the country of origin. How will the goods enter the country without an original negotiable bill of lading? Availability of the exporter's billing currency is a major concern. Foreign exchange that is initially available for import payments may be difficult to obtain by the time the consignee has sold the goods and wanted to remit payment abroad. Who will pay for the warehousing charges, fire and theft insurance, administrative fees, and transportation charges from the exporter's location until the goods are placed in the consignment stock? If the exporter is under the auspices of an export credit insurer, can the goods still be insured or what will be the insurer's attitude regarding a consignment arrangement?

Clearly the only benefits to such an arrangement are from a marketing point of view, especially in the face of similar arrangements offered by competition, and from the point of view of the consignee. The consignee benefits because it has readily available on-site goods to draw from in its country and it does not have to carry large amounts of goods on its balance sheet in the form of inventory, especially from the point of view of distributors. However, it loses the capability of offering more inventory as collateral to obtain additional bank financing.

Exporters electing to enter into a consignment arrangement must first have a tremendous amount of trust and faith in the consignee. Undoubtedly the area of creditworthiness must be unquestionable. Secondly, the exporter must seek the advice of retained counsel in the country of the consignment arrangement. Lastly, all parties to the arrangement, that is, the exporter, importer and bonded warehouse company, must clearly spell out each party's duties, responsibilities, and liabilities in a legal binding contract or contracts.

PROJECT FINANCING

Project financing relates to the obtaining of long-term loans and export credit financing for the development of local government sponsored, capital-intensive projects that are related to such industries as mining, energy, and hydroelectric and chemical plants. Most of the funds are channeled to developing countries who need the assistance of foreign exporters with sources of long-term debt financing, such as Eximbank. Many of the project financing packages are directly linked to export development. Repayment of the projects mostly stems from cash flows generated out of the completed operating investment project.

To entice exporters to their projects, host governments provide support to finance projects ranging from unlimited, limited, or conditional guarantees to contractual arrangements with purchasers of the project's output. The projects are financed with long-term debt rather than equity participation. Therefore, debt service depends greatly on the cash flows anticipated from the project after completion.

Project financing mainly stems from three principal sources:

national export credit programs, development banks, and commercial banks.

The second source comes from development banks who assist developing countries by channeling funds to them from developed countries. The principal development banks for this type of financing are the World Bank (also known as the Bank for Reconstruction and Development or IBRD), and its interrelated entities, the International Development Association (IDA), the International Finance Corporation (IFC) and the Inter-American Development Bank (IDB). Their financing basically consists of two programs—regular and concessionary. Based on regular programs, these sources can run up to 20 years in the case of the World Bank and 15 to 30 years in the case of the Inter-American Development Bank. In the case of concessionary programs, the IDB can give the borrower up to 50 year term financing at low interest rates. In November 1986, the IDB approved $459 million in loans to Argentina to help construction of a major hydroelectric-power project on the Parana River, to help farmers and ranchers increase output, and to expand public water-supply systems in the western part of Buenos Aires.

The third source of project financing can come from commercial banks. In today's marketplace, because of their Third World debt problems, these banks find it extremely difficult to get involved in project financing. Many are at their country credit limits and directly involved in the on-going process of refinancing their debt positions with many of these debtor nations. Still, the exporter should not totally eliminate these banks as potential sources of finance. As already previously mentioned in other chapters, the smart exporter will shop around in an effort to evolve multiple sources of financing from commercial banks. This is otherwise known as multisourced financing, joint financing, parallel financing, mixed credits, and complementary financing.

Exporters who contemplate getting involved in a project financing deal either as a vendor or sponsor should be aware of the criteria lenders use to evaluate project financing risks. Because the payback is tied to the project itself, analysis will focus on the specifics of the project's operating cycle from the start of construction to the potential for sales of the finished goods. There are five major risks that they use.

Supply Risk: Are the required raw materials in abundant supply? How likely is a price increase for factors of production such as minerals or energy sources?

Production Risk: Will the project be run efficiently? How experienced are the managers? How likely is technological obsolescence? Will the project be completed on time? Has the government given the necessary approvals? Are the participating firms financially healthy?

Market Risk: Will there be sufficient demand for the end-product to create the cash flow to pay off the debt financing? Can the product be maintained at the price levels necessary to take care of the payback?

Foreign Exchange Risk: How strong is the currency of sales or revenues from the project? Are exchange controls or devaluation likely?

Political Risk: How stable is the government where the project is located? Is there a threat of expropriation?

REINVOICING COMPANIES

A reinvoicing company is one of the commonly used vehicles for administering, managing, and financing intercompany and third-party (foreign customer) sales and receivables. They are usually formed as wholly owned subsidiaries of a parent company, established in a low-tax haven location. It acts as an intermediary party between a company's manufacturing locations and marketing/sales offices throughout the world.

It principally is a paper operation, buying goods from its manufacturing locations and rebilling the export related transaction to other company related companies or directly to foreign customers. Companies are forming these reinvoicing companies due in part to ever increasing commercial and country risks, to obtain optimum efficiency and control of their export trade credit related transactions, centralize export trade finance expertise, improve cash flow, and increase financial flexibility.

A reinvoicing company can provide a wide spectrum of export trade related financing benefits: As it relates to foreign customers, it can invoice the third party in a competitive currency. By doing so, this method centralizes the currency risk at one location and removes the F/X risk from the income statement of the manufacturing location. It can centralize the management of currency, receivable, payable, and multicustomer/intercompany transactions. For businesses that organize themselves under a decentralized organizational structure with different operating units sourcing and marketing their goods around the world, they create multiple currency, receivable, payable and multicustomer/intercompany transactions. The obvious question is how does business under this scenario manage its exposures, especially when multi-operating units are selling and marketing goods and services to the same commercial and country risks? The answer could lie in a reinvoicing company. By concentrating its management of these areas previously mentioned, the company can centralize its financing needs with the various sources of finance. Since the sum is greater than the whole of its parts, it can exercise clout over international commercial banks by offering high-volume business. The banks in turn are more adept at offering lower financing costs on extended terms for riskier exports. By centralizing intercompany receivables and payables, the company can create its own multicurrency netting system and shift liquidity between subsidiaries by leading and lagging intercompany payments. Thus, it can offer a concentrated management effort of corporate liquidity positions. The benefits obtained from such a company should be reduced financing costs, better credit terms, and improved export trade financing packages, thus reducing cost per unit prices and an improved competitive position. Reinvoicing can improve cash management practices and techniques by controlling cash flows, information, and forecasting to ultimately minimize currency and commercial risks. It can enhance bank relations, provide tax advantages, act as a respository of credit information, and centralize all credit approvals and collections.

Centralizing a company's activities into a reinvoicing company does not necessarily mean only one company is established. Many businesses have set up numerous reinvoicing companies throughout the world. Therefore, it is conceivable for a decentralized business with multi-operating units to each have their own reinvoicing company.

For example, a typical reinvoicing company is usually invoiced by a manufacturing location in its own currency, but it in turn, rebills in the currency of the exporter. However, there are

FIGURE 8–3
Reinvoice Transaction

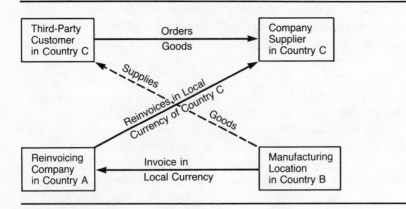

exceptions in the case of Eastern Europe and Nigeria which do not have freely convertible traded currencies and/or they lack a forward market. Under these exceptions, the reinvoicing company would either invoice in U.S. dollars or another strong currency.

Figure 8–3 illustrates the flow of a typical reinvoicing transaction.

Reinvoice Transaction

A third-party customer in Country C places an order for some goods with the local marketing/sales office of a reinvoicing company located in Country C. The local marketing/sales office does not have an inventory of the goods so it places an order with one of its company's manufacturing locations located in Country B. It delivers the goods direct to the marketing/sales office or to the third-party customer, whichever is permissible by the local authorities, and invoices the reinvoicing company located in Country A in the local currency of Country B. The reinvoicing company in turn, reinvoices the marketing/sales office in Country C in the local currency of Country C.

Many businesses find reinvoicing companies especially attractive when dealing with exotic countries such as in the Middle East, Africa, Eastern Europe, and Latin America. It is better than developing the expertise to deal with these market in every exporting subsidiary.

The costs to cover the services provided by the reinvoicing company are usually covered in the transfer price. However, it must be pointed out that many businesses are leery of establishing reinvoicing companies because they come under heavy scrutiny of tax authorities.

DEBT SWAPPING

Debt swapping refers to a debt-to-equity swap where debt, primarily debt which is owed to commercial banks, is exchanged at a discount for equity in pre-agreed categories of investment in a debtor's country. However, it is not solely limited to commercial banks. It can and does in fact include debts owed to private exporters.

Most debt swapping occurs with Third World debtor nations, primarily those in Central and Latin America. The extent of this debt swapping for equity in foreign companies by commercial banks is quite extensive. One bank reported at an FCIB meeting owing a chunk of a hotel in Cancun, Mexico.

Debt swapping is being done as one way to reduce debt exposures to banks and private exporters owned by debtor nations and foreign customers who cannot repay their external obligations. The short- and long-term advantages and disadvantages to banks and exporters are extremely difficult to evaluate. Each will have to evaluate the extent of the payback (how long will it take and at what cost). In many circumstances, taking an equity position in a foreign company means you are not allowed to take your equity out within a certain period of time. You may have to retain your equity for a minimum period of time (i.e., five years) and you may not be able to sell your investment to another party. Most countries will more than likely encourage or regulate by local law, long-term investments rather than a quick arbitage on the difference between the debt that you can buy at a discount.

Converting debt to equity means, in most cases, taking a minority share interest in a local company and accounting for your investment. It means your investment will be subject to all of the foreign company's country regulations pertaining to foreign investments such as, exchange rates, dividend repatriation, and local management decisions.

APPENDIX 8–A SAMPLE ACCEPTANCE AGREEMENT

**Continuing Acceptance Agreement
For Domestic/International Shipments
Presigned Drafts**

◆ CHASE

Date _____

The Chase Manhattan Bank, N.A.
1 Chase Manhattan Plaza
New York, New York 10081

Gentlemen:

From time to time the undersigned may request you (the "Bank") to accept or accept and discount drafts drawn on the Bank by or on behalf of the undersigned. In the event that the Bank agrees to make such acceptance or acceptance and discount, the undersigned in consideration thereof agrees with the Bank as follows:

1. The Bank will hold as custodian upon the terms herein set forth such presigned drafts, substantially in the form of Exhibit A hereto, as shall be received by the Bank for the undersigned's account. Each such draft shall be drawn on the Bank by or on behalf of the undersigned but shall be blank as to amount, date of issue, maturity date and details of the underlying transaction. The Bank shall use the same care with respect to the safekeeping of such drafts as the Bank uses in respect of its own similar property but shall not be obligated to maintain any insurance for the undersigned's benefit.

2. Upon receipt of telephoned or written instructions on behalf of the undersigned from anyone purporting to be an authorized representative of the undersigned, the Bank shall complete each such draft in accordance with such instructions. The Bank may rely and act upon any such instructions which the Bank in good faith and in the exercise of ordinary care believes to have been given on the undersigned's behalf by an authorized representative of the undersigned. The Bank may complete and accept or complete, accept and discount drafts hereunder even though the authorized representative of the undersigned who signed the drafts thereafter ceased to be a representative of the undersigned.

3. Written confirmation of telephoned instructions hereunder shall be mailed, telexed, or transmitted by telefacsimile to the Bank on the same day such telephoned instructions were given, but the Bank shall have no responsibility for any lack of conformity between such instructions and such confirmation, or otherwise. All written instructions, which may be by letter, tested telex, or telefacsimile, and written confirmations of telephoned instructions, shall be substantially in the form of Exhibit B hereto. Each transmission of telephoned or written instructions hereunder shall constitute a representation and warranty that on and as of the date of such transmission (a) the representations and warranties in Paragraph 4 hereof are true with respect to the subject transaction(s) and (b) no event of default specified in Paragraph 8 hereof has occurred and is continuing.

4. The undersigned represents and warrants that (a) each such draft will grow out of one or more transactions involving the domestic shipment of goods within the United States or the importation or exportation of goods between two countries pursuant to a contract in existence at the time of presentation of the draft for acceptance, (b) each such draft will finance a current shipment of goods; (c) each such draft drawn by or on behalf of the undersigned as seller/exporter will have a tenor reasonably commensurate with the anticipated time required for shipment plus usual credit terms extended to the purchaser/importer or six months, whichever is shorter, (d) each such draft drawn by or on behalf of the undersigned as purchaser/importer will have a tenor reasonably commensurate with the anticipated time required for receipt of the goods plus preparing the goods for distribution into the channels of trade or six months, whichever is shorter, (e) the aggregate face amount of such drafts will not exceed the c.i.f. value of the shipment(s) financed thereby plus the lesser of (i) customs duties, taxes and other incidental costs related thereto or (ii) such additional amount as is permitted by the current policies of the Board of Governors of the Federal Reserve System, (f) no other financing is or will be outstanding in respect of such transaction during the period from the date of such draft until the maturity thereof, (g) all necessary licenses for the exportation, importation and payment of the purchase price and related costs of shipment will have been obtained, (h) upon the Bank's request the undersigned will promptly furnish additional information about each such transaction, including, without limitation, any documents or copies thereof required to establish that any drafts accepted hereunder are or were eligible for discount with a Federal Reserve Bank or that all taxes or charges incurred by the undersigned in connection with any draft accepted hereunder, or in connection with any payment to the Bank hereunder, have been paid, and (i) the undersigned has the corporate power and legal right to enter into this agreement and to execute and deliver drafts and to incur and perform its obligations hereunder and thereunder, and the execution, delivery and performance by the undersigned of this agreement and the drafts have been duly authorized by all necessary corporate action and will not violate any provision of law or of the undersigned's organizational documents.

5. Each acceptance or acceptance and discount of a draft hereunder will take place on a day on which the principal office of the Bank at 1 Chase Manhattan Plaza, New York, New York 10081 (the "Principal Office") is open for business in compliance with the laws of the State of New York. The Bank's charge for accepting or accepting and discounting any draft hereunder may be deducted by the Bank before crediting the proceeds of the acceptance to the undersigned's account.

6. The undersigned will pay to the Bank at its Principal Office, in United States dollars in immediately available funds, the face amount of each draft accepted or accepted and discounted by the Bank hereunder not later than the maturity date thereof or upon demand at any time prior thereto after the happening of any one or more of the events of default listed in Paragraph 8 hereof, together with all unpaid charges or other sums owing to the Bank hereunder, free and clear of and without deduction by reason of any taxes or charges whatsoever and without any set-off or adjustment on account of any counterclaim. In any case the undersigned agrees that (a) the Bank, without being so obligated, may debit any deposit account of the undersigned at any office of the Bank for obligations and liabilities then due and owing hereunder and (b) the undersigned shall pay interest on any of the obligations and liabilities of the undersigned hereunder which are not paid at maturity at a rate equal to _____% plus the prime commercial lending rate announced by the Bank at its Principal Office, as from time to time in effect.

7. The term "Obligations" as used herein shall mean all obligations and liabilities of the undersigned hereunder and all other obligations and liabilities of the undersigned owing to the Bank however arising, whether absolute or contingent, due or not due, and whether now existing or hereafter arising.

8. In the event of the happening of any one or more of the following events of default: (a) the nonpayment of any of the Obligations when due; or (b) the breach of any agreement, representation or warranty of the undersigned to the Bank in connection herewith, or (c) the application for the appointment of a receiver, trustee or similar official for the undersigned or any of its property, the making of any assignment for the benefit of creditors of the undersigned, the commencement of a case under bankruptcy or similar laws by or against the undersigned, or any other act indicating to the Bank probable insolvency of the undersigned, or (d) any seizure, vesting or intervention by or under authority of a government by which the management of the undersigned is displaced or its authority is curtailed; THEN, the Bank may, by notice to the undersigned, declare all of the Obligations immediately due and payable by the undersigned, whereupon such Obligations shall be immediately due and payable without demand or other formalities of any kind, all of which are hereby expressly waived by the undersigned.

9. No delay on the part of the Bank in exercising any rights or options hereunder shall operate as a waiver thereof or prejudice the Bank's rights against the undersigned. The Bank shall not be deemed to have waived any of its rights hereunder except by means of a duly executed waiver in writing and no such waiver shall be effective as to any transaction which occurs after the date of such waiver. Any notice to or demand on the undersigned shall be deemed effective (if not already given) when forwarded by mail, telex, telephone or otherwise to the last address or telephone number of the undersigned appearing on the Bank's books.

10. This is a continuing agreement and shall apply to any draft or drafts which may be accepted or accepted and discounted by the Bank hereafter at the request of the undersigned and shall remain in full force and effect until written notice is actually received by the Bank that it has been terminated by the undersigned, but any such termination shall not release the undersigned from any obligations incurred hereunder prior to receipt by the Bank of such notice. Except for the Bank's gross negligence or willful misconduct, the undersigned hereby agrees to indemnify the Bank and hold it harmless from and against any loss, liability, expense or claim of any kind in any way relating to (a) this agreement or the acts contemplated hereby, and (b) the imposition of reserve requirements on the Bank because of a determination by a court, the Board of Governors of the Federal Reserve System or any Federal Reserve Bank that any draft accepted hereunder was not eligible for discount by a Federal Reserve Bank.

11. This Agreement shall be deemed to be made under and shall be governed by and construed in accordance with the law of the State of New York.

Source: *Dynamics of Trade Finance,* copyright 1984, The Chase Manhattan Bank, printed with permission of the publisher, Global Business Communications, Inc., P.O. Box 99, Gillette, N.J. 07933, p. 113.

12. For the purpose of any action or proceeding relating to its agreements set forth or referred to herein and its undertakings with respect to any drafts drawn as contemplated hereby, the undersigned agrees that the courts in and of the State of New York shall be a proper forum, submits to the non-exclusive jurisdiction of such courts, irrevocably waives any immunity the undersigned or any of its property may now or hereafter have from suit, jurisdiction, attachment (whether prior to judgment or in aid of execution), execution or other legal process, and if the undersigned is organized or incorporated in a jurisdiction outside the United States of America, designates the Consul General in New York City of the country of incorporation of the undersigned (or, if there is no such Consul General, _____) as the true and lawful agent and attorney-in-fact of the undersigned for receipt of all summons, writs and notices in connection with any such action or proceeding.

Very truly yours,

_____
(Name of Obligor)

_____
(Address)

F100 C 12-83

By: _____
(Title)

REFERENCES

1. L. Stroh, "Bank Guarantees as Additional Security in International Business," *The EXPORTER* (New York: Trade Data Reports, Inc., April 1987), p. 10.
2. Louis J. Celi and I. James Czechowicz, *Export Financing: Handbook of Sources & Techniques* (Morristown, N.J.: Business International, Financial Executive Research Foundation, 1985), p. 196.
3. L. G., Lindsay, "Forfaiting, An Alternative Approach to Export Trade Finance," *The EXPORTER* (New York: Trade Data Reports Inc., March 1987), p. 3.

CHAPTER 9

COUNTERTRADE

You're negotiating an export sales arrangement with a foreign customer. The potential for breaking into a new or old market was lost to competition several years ago, and the possibility of future sales looks quite promising and substantial. Soon you'll be meeting with the foreign customer to discuss contract terms and conditions, credit terms and delivery.

During the meeting, the foreign customer indicates a willingness to purchase your goods only if you are willing to buy something from them in return. In other words, they are asking you to agree to a *countertrade arrangement*. You may be familiar with the term, but are not sure exactly what it means or how it differs from a regular export sale of goods and services.

Countertrade is a subject of growing importance to businesses interested in expanding their international trade. It concerns new ways of doing business. It is not the preferred method of transacting international trade, but, given the changing and highly competitive economic conditions and challenges prevailing now and in the future, U.S. business must be able to respond to new demands that are being made on them if they wish to sell goods abroad. They must be flexible. Otherwise, they will lose potential markets and sales to competition—not only to other companies from the United States, but to those in Western Europe, Japan, and other parts of the world where businesses are prepared to respond to the new rules of international trade.

Businesses that are seeking to enter the Peoples Republic of China (PRC), Eastern Europe, the USSR and Third World countries are increasingly finding that doing business there requires a willingness to receive payment in forms other than cash, drafts or bills of exchange, promissory notes, and letters of credit.

These new forms of payment or financing an export transaction abroad are generally referred to as *countertrade*. The term covers a variety of business arrangements where payment is made by means other than just a cash-for-goods basis. These methods include barter, one of the oldest forms of trade. When nations first traded, they bartered—the Portuguese traded cloth for Indian tea and spices.

Why do exporters become involved in any of the different forms or types of countertrade? Probably the main reason is because many socialist and Third World countries lack foreign exchange to pay for imported goods and services. The inconvertibility of their currencies to your billing currency and their need to preserve valuable and precious foreign exchange, combined with sluggish economies, adverse international economic conditions, lack of demand for their basic commodities, and depressed prices, increases their demands for countertrade.

This last chapter of the book will discuss many of the different forms of countertrade used in international trade.

UNDERLYING REASONS FOR COUNTERTRADE

What are the other basic underlying reasons why a country or foreign customer will want to impose countertrade requirements on overseas suppliers? Economists generally agree on some underlying reasons, starting with:

1. The increase of energy prices in the 1970s. Beginning with the 1973 OPEC oil price hike, rising energy costs have thrown the international economic order into chaos and disarray by straining Western economies and nearly bankrupting many developing Third World countries.
2. The decline in the confidence in the U.S. dollar and other currencies in the 1970s and early-to-mid-1980s. Looking back, many businesses can probably remember when the price of gold was estimated to go above U.S. $1,000. Lack of confidence in the U.S. dollar sent it spiraling upward, making it more expensive for foreign customers to purchase U.S. goods billed in U.S. dollars. It is important to

remember that oil is billed in U.S. dollars which helps drain the coffers or foreign exchange reserves of oil importing nations, especially those of developing nations.

3. Third World countries will push for countertrade. Third World countries, rich in natural resources, but short of foreign exchange coupled with ambitious industrialization programs, will want to do business in countertrade. It will be a way to market their commodities and raw materials and gain foreign exchange and valuable technology to stabilize their economies. Chinese Premier Deng Xiaping has specifically cited countertrade as an important means of paying for China's industrialization and economic development program.

4. Foreign companies in developing and socialist countries will have to comply with their local government guidelines or import regulations. Local governments in these countries are imposing countertrade requirements on their local importers to preserve their foreign exchange. In addition, foreign investors who want to build factories in their countries are being required to export a portion of their plant's production in order to assist the host country in improving or maintaining their balance of payments.

5. Developing and socialist nations need to build the means for exporting their goods and services. Because of their poor marketing channels and expertise in developing overseas markets for their goods and services, these nations will demand countertrade to assist them in building their own export markets.

6. Third World and socialist countries are heavy in debt. Countries such as Poland, Turkey, and Zaire are faced with enormous problems, not only because new lines of credit are generally not available, but because of the enormous debt service charges on loans they already have. Poland spends approximately one fourth of its foreign exchange annually to service its debts.

Countertrade can be a powerful device for businesses that want to expand their sales, increase productivity and profits, and tap into a low-cost supply of goods. It is even conceivable that a measured assertive approach to this technique could be a key to increasing exports for U.S. businesses and the country in the coming years.

As a rule of thumb, any business with annual sales in excess of $5 million and exports over $1 million can successfully countertrade. Yet, many U.S. companies view countertrade as merely a nuisance of doing business because of its complications with some countries, including these in the Eastern Bloc and much of the Third World.[1] Businesses that overlook countertrade business are missing an opportunity to promote their exports and to motivate potential foreign companies to buy goods.

Historically, countertrade was utilized by Eastern European countries that had limited reserves of hard currency. Currently more than 88 developing countries have imposed or are involved in some sort of countertrade deals.[2]

The U.S. government defines countertrade as a "transaction in which export sales are conditioned on the seller purchasing something from the foreign buyer." In other words, the basic agreement says, "I'll buy something from you, if you'll buy something from me." Countertrade is any arrangement in which a business agrees to accept products of the importing country. It is important to note that no two countertrade transactions are exactly alike.

Countertrade can be categorized or divided into a number of terms or arrangements:

Barter
Counterpurchase
Compensation
Switch trade
Evidence accounts
Offset

WHAT'S INVOLVED?

Whether you're involved or familiar with countertrade or not, to complete a successful transaction you must first define your objectives and assess your capabilities to meet those objectives. Let's consider some of the steps involved.

Define Your Objectives and Assess Your Capabilities

Businesses do not initially consider countertrade as a means of furthering their export trading objectives. Most U.S. businesses prefer conventional trading arrangements instead of counter-trade—commercial letters of credit, drafts, and open account. One reason is that there are substantial risks in purchasing quantities of goods which may not meet a business's quality specifications and performance standards. Also, countertrade transactions are usu-ally costly and time consuming.

However, businesses may accept the risk and inconvenience of countertrade to enhance the prospects of current and future sales, rather than lose the overseas market or customer to compe-tition.

Before thinking about your potential sales prospects, assess your product and marketing expertise, and your ability to under-take overseas operations in markets which may be unfamiliar to you. Few businesses possess the capability to handle countertrade internally.

You should also determine if you need to countertrade in order to preserve, increase, or initiate an overseas sales opportunity. Find out if countertrade is used as a financial tool by the markets to which you sell or by the markets to which you hope to sell.

Two of the most important questions countertraders face are:

1. Can countertrade goods be used internally, or will outside services be needed to dispose of them?
2. Should an in-house countertrade unit be developed, or should the expertise be hired as needed?

Risks generally increase as you accept goods further removed from your area of expertise. If you do not wish to accept countertrade goods for internal use you may market the goods through an existing department of your business or set up a new department to purchase and market the goods or employ an outside trading service to dispose of the goods.

Countertrading requires trading expertise, extensive networks and contacts, and a great deal of coordination throughout your operation. Marketing the goods through existing channels or setting up a new department may give rise to such problems as product liability and after-sales service.

A few exporters who regularly encounter countertrade maintain an in-house capability. In general, exporters are strongly advised to obtain the assistance of outside specialists.

Specialist services are offered by trading companies, brokers, consultants, bankers, and suppliers of market intelligence, usually for a fixed fee and/or a commission. The fee charged will depend on the volume of goods, their marketability, the trader's market position, and the time span over which the deliveries occur. For any of these services, you should shop around.

Know the Process

Don't be put off or intimidated by seemingly impossible demands. Initial harsh countertrade requirements can be negotiated. A country may at first insist on firm commitments backed by penalties for nonperformance, a high ratio of export sales to countertrade goods, or an unreasonable deadline. You can improve these terms with persistent and confident negotiations, and by ensuring that the provisions of your contract are well defined.

Many countertrade transactions require three separate agreements. They are the primary, the counterpurchase, and the protocol or "bridging" agreements. The primary and counterpurchase agreements are similar to regular export contracts, indicating such items as price, delivery dates, inspection provisions, and dispute clauses. The protocol agreement defines the terms of relationship between the primary and the counterpurchase agreements.

Be sure that the counterpurchase agreement allows for the widest range of goods to be purchased and does not limit the geographic area to which you can sell the goods. In addition, provisions for nonperformance should allow you to void the counterpurchase agreement if the primary agreement is cancelled.

Know the Country You Are Dealing With

To enhance your market opportunities, know the country's commercial, economic, and political objectives, the means being used to achieve them, and the organizational structure overseeing the process.

Countries generally use countertrade as a means to stabilize prices, create new markets, decrease debt, increase long-term investment, and/or help develop the overall economy.

Know the Laws and Regulations

All imports into and all exports from the United States, countertraded or not, are subject to U.S. trade laws. Likewise, there are laws and regulations of the foreign customer in its country.

If you choose to import countertraded products into the United States, assess the effects your goods may have on domestic producers. The anti-dumping, countervailing duty, and customs valuation laws serve to protect domestic producers from the sale of imported products at prices considered "less than fair value," or from sources of unfair competition.

Countertrade laws and regulations of overseas countries differ in both approach and purpose. Methods of approach range from mandating countertrade for government procurements, as in Indonesia, to evaluating transactions on a case-by-case basis, as in Brazil. Purposes range from boosting traditional exports, as in Jordan, to emphasizing nontraditional exports, as in Ecuador.

Know Your Finance and Insurance Options

Countertrade arrangements, except for barter, are financed like non-countertrade arrangements. Exports and imports are usually financed by a letter of credit issued by an international bank, merchant bank, or brokerage firm. However, since countertrade is a conditional contract, you get paid for your export only if you import something. Many international banks will not finance countertrade transactions.

You should also insure your countertrade arrangement against financial and political risks. In addition, because countertrade transactions are performance contracts, you need to have insurance to cover nonperformance. There are several private insurance companies that offer performance insurance for countertraders.

TYPES OR FORMS OF COUNTERTRADE

Barter

This type of transaction involves the direct exchange of goods having offsetting values, without any monetary payments taking place. It is a one-time transaction effected under one contract covering the offsetting deliveries of goods between two parties. Typically, the exchange takes place over a relatively short period of time (under two years). The goods exchanged have no relation to each other.

During the period following World War II barter was widespread. For example, Austrian shipments of timber were used to pay for badly needed food from Hungary.

Barter arrangements are much less common than counterpurchase or compensation transactions. They are only performed in the rarest cases today.

For example, in 1982, New Zealand swapped lamb for Iranian oil. In the same year, the United States helped out the recently elected, friendly but cash-strapped government of Jamaica by taking about U.S. $47 million worth of bauxite for America's strategic stockpile. In return it sent Jamaica some surplus dairy products held in storage by the U.S. Department of Agriculture.

The following are the basic characteristics of barter transactions:[3]

1. The exchange of goods is set out in a single contract.
2. The goods to be exchanged are specified in quantity and quality, without any value being given to them, either in total or individually, in any unit of currency.
3. Payment is made exclusively by the counter-supply of the agreed goods. There is no financing in money.
4. The exchange of goods takes place between two trading partners. No provision is made for the intervention of a third.
5. The exchange of goods usually happens simultaneously. Between delivery and counterdelivery there is seldom a delay of more than one year.

Counterpurchase

Counterpurchase is the most frequently practiced form of countertrade. It involves two parallel agreements: a sales contract and a counterpurchase obligation to buy products or services from the foreign customer's country. As a condition of the sale, the exporter is required to buy products or services from the buyer's country over an agreed period of time. These obligations can range from 25 percent to several times the sales volume. The exchanged goods are technically independent of one another.

Counterpurchase has the following characteristics:

1. Delivery and counterdelivery represent two legally self-contained contracts.
2. Each delivery is paid independently of each other.
3. The transactions are invoiced in agreed on currencies.
4. The goods often derive from different industries.
5. The goods can originate through the same foreign trade organization.
6. The intervention of a third party is possible as a result of separate supply contracts.
7. Delivery and counterdelivery can extend over an extended period of time, such as a medium-term period, but in most cases takes place within five years of each other.

Under a counterpurchase there can be two special forms: Parallel and Linked deals.

Parallel Deals. These involve two trade transactions for which separate contracts are drawn up. Each delivery results in a commitment to pay, which must be satisfied irrespective of the performance of the counterdeal. These two trading agreements are linked by a skeleton contract, which sets out the commitment of the Western supplier to make a counterpurchase or arrange for one to be made within a certain fixed time. A further link exists on the East European side, where the currency proceeds of the counterdelivery are credited to the importing company. Such internal clearing between two East European companies, which do not always belong to the same foreign trade organization, may involve a payment of an acknowledgement premium by the foreign customer to the exporter for the release of its foreign exchange holdings.[4]

As a rule, the two trade agreements are no different from any other export or import deal. The Western supplier, in granting credit terms to its foreign customer, is using available financing, be it credit insurance and financing, or commercial bank financing.[5]

Linked Deals. The linked deal, often known by its name Junctim, is like a reversed parallel deal. A Western importer demands from an East European or Third World exporter the right to link subsequent Western sales with his purchase, to connect them contractually and have them set off as counterpurchases. This right may be conceded to him if, during negotiations, he does not bargain for too low a price. He will then look for Western exporters who are committed to counterpurchase, and are prepared to pay him a subsidy for taking over the commitment. He will thus achieve the desired price reduction in arrears for his import, but must meanwhile put up with a degree of uncertainty.[6]

Example

Several years ago, Fried. Krupp of West Germany won a large order for big capacity hydraulic truck cranes from the USSR by agreeing to buy back 15 percent of the total contract value in Soviet machine tools and other equipment. The tools and equipment were either resold or used at Krupp's West German plants. Krupp's competitors in the deal, such as Grove Manufacturing and Harnischfeger Corp. of the United States and Coles Crane of the United Kingdom were not prepared to accept the countertrade requirement. Thus Krupp won a U.S. $9 million contract. In this particular deal, the vendors who were unable to absorb the countertraded machine tools and equipment internally would have had to dispose of them on the open market at a discount of up to 40 percent, making the entire deal unattractive.

McDonnell Douglas Corporation has had certain successes over the years with counterpurchases. In Yugoslavia, the company bought back canned hams, tools, and other products and services in exchange for a major Yugoslavia purchase of DC-9 passenger jets. The corporation also encouraged its employees to fly on JAT-Yugoslav airlines and to vacation at that Adriatic country's seashore. This kind of arrangement helped McDonnell Douglas gain an edge over competitors such as Boeing and Airbus of France.

In yet another McDonnell Douglas transaction, they exported F-18 aircraft to Canada. This U.S. $2.4 billion sale was offset by some McDonnell Douglas production in Canada, together with a commitment to help Canada find customers for C. $2.9 billion of Canadian goods and services. The deal included an agreement by McDonnell Douglas to shift U.S. $350 million worth of subcontracts to Montreal's Canadair and McDonnell's own Toronto subsidiary. McDonnell Douglas's partner, General Electric, agreed to build a U.S. $60 million plant in Quebec for the export of C. $600 million worth of propeller and turbine blades.[7]

Compensation

This type of arrangement, also known as buyback, involves repayment in resultant or related products. Compensation arrangements also involve two separate, but linked, contracts covering the sale by a Western business of technology, plant or equipment, and the purchase by the Western supplier of products derived directly from or produced by the Western-supplied technology, plant, or equipment. This form of countertrade is often a part of an industrial cooperation agreement or a joint venture without equity.

Compensation transactions generally involve long-term arrangements over a period of 10 to 20 years, and there is often a much greater time lag between reciprocal deliveries than in counterpurchase arrangements. The cumulative value of Western purchases over the life of the long-term compensation contract is often equal to or greater than the value of the Western export contract.

Unlike barter deals, compensation transactions need not provide for 100 percent counterdelivery. There are basically two options: partial or full compensation. In a partial compensation a specified fraction of the Western export must be compensated by the purchase of goods, the balance being exempt from counterpurchase commitments. In a full compensation deal, the agreed on compensation purchases make up 100 percent or even more of the Western export.

Example

International Harvester Company, now called Navistar, sold technology for making crawler tractors to the Polish foreign trade organization Bumar. International Harvester agreed to buy back a percentage of the components made at the Polish plant for use at its plant in Western Europe.

In a similar example, Clark Equipment of Buchanan, Michigan, provided to Bumar, technology to manufacture construction equipment axles and received a percentage of the finished axles as payment. Bumar has had similar deals with Jones Crane and Coles Crane of England, and Koehring Co. of Milwaukee, Wisconsin.

Levi-Strauss & Company of San Francisco, California sold a turnkey plant and the design of its famous blue jeans to Hungary. In turn, Levi-Strauss is receiving part payment in the form of the plant's production.

Dunbee-Combex-Marx Limited, a British toy manufacturer, agreed to furnish $50 million worth of toy machinery and molds to the People's Republic of China (PRC). The Chinese agreed to pay for half the costs in hard currency and half in finished toys. In addition, the British firm will also have sole rights to sell the toys in Great Britain for 10 years and for three years in the United States. A similar deal was completed by the toy manufacturer with the USSR.

Evidence Accounts

Evidence accounts are also known as an offset or contra account. These are agreements for a certain amount of exchange of currency between a business and the local foreign trade organization that is monitored by the country's bank of foreign trade where the business maintains an account.

In an evidence account agreement, the business is selling goods or services to one local foreign trade organization while at the same time it is buying certain products from another foreign trade organization over a specified period, usually one year, to balance the account.

Switch Trading

This type of countertrade involves the equalization of trade imbalances or sluggish international currency flows between trading partners engaged in clearing, or bilateral, trade, and payment agreements. It means that one country that is a party to a bilateral trade agreement can transfer an imbalance it has developed to a third nation or party.

A clearing transaction is an exchange of goods in which payment is made through an existing arrangement between governments. The overall objective of switch trading is to achieve an agreed on value of trade which is tabulated in nonconvertible clearing account units.

Example

A Western business wants to sell a plastic manufacturing plant to the USSR, which did not have the cash or currency allocated to pay for it. However, the USSR does have a clearing agreement with the country of Austria which was buying Russian natural gas. Instead of Austria paying the USSR for the gas, the country simply pays the Western firm an amount correspondent to the price of the factory.

Another example is the use by 3M Company of a clearing agreement between Hungary and Brazil. The company's European office used the Hungarian position of the agreement to ship industrial adhesives to Brazil. The company benefited because it was able to work within Brazilian import restrictions and sell its goods while Hungary benefited by a commission on the sale, and the two countries could continue to say their bilateral agreement was adhered to.

BLOCKED CURRENCIES

Blocked currencies occurs when a business or individual cannot repatriate its holdings or funds from a country because of foreign exchange restrictions or regulations. Countries implement these restrictions or regulations mainly out of economic necessity. Hard currency investments of business or individuals are "blocked" by the local government for extended periods of time (i.e., a few years). In other currencies with "soft" or devalued currencies, the business or individual might be able to convert funds into a hard currency or currencies, but only at a substantial discount from the official exchange rate, making it economically infeasible.

There are a few solutions to this problem. One is to purchase local products with local currencies that cannot be easily converted and then export them. Another solution involves motion pictures and television productions which can provide a vehicle for utilizing soft currency funds in the creation of a product that can earn U.S. dollars or another hard currency through royalties from worldwide distribution. By producing films in soft currency countries, benefits can be obtained for both the hard and soft currency investor, the host country, and the independent producer. Let's look at how it works.

The Soft Currency Investor: About 50 percent of the total production cost of a project could be incurred while on location and will be paid for in the soft currency of the host country. The soft currency investor will be entitled to receive a royalty equal to the U.S. dollar or other hard currency value of his investment, determined at the time of his investment, and paid in U.S. dollars or other hard currency. While not participating in further revenues from the project, the soft currency investor enjoys a highly attractive benefit by receiving a repatriated 100 percent return on investment, generally within 12–18 months. In addition, any devaluation of the soft currency against the U.S. dollar or other hard currency during the intervening 12–18 month period is, in effect, a gain on the soft currency investor. In many cases this could quite possibly be the only transfer option available for years to come.

The Hard Currency Investor: The other half of a film's production cost will be paid in U.S. dollars. A significant portion of the soft currency investor's equity is shifted to the hard dollar investor once the payout limitation is reached. A dual benefit will accrue to the investor who funds both the hard and soft currency requirements of a project—desirable currency conversion coupled with favorable upside potential.

The Country: Local currency is utilized for location costs; funds that otherwise may be dormant. Because they stimulate the economy, American film projects are welcomed by most foreign governments. Futhermore, the resulting film is not subject to export quotas or tariffs that restrict most other investment vehicles.

The Independent Producer: It is estimated that cost savings of

10 to 20 percent can be realized during the principal photography phase of a film shot in a foreign location, with no sacrifice in production values or quality. In fact, exotic foreign locations often enhance a film's appeal, as the James Bond series and many other successful movies attest.

Example

A project which began as an effort to spend blocked currencies became successful as a result of using blocked currencies, then made money from royalties when the movie was shown outside the country where it was made was the production of the movie *The Ninth Configuration* in Hungary. Pepsico, Inc., which has an agreement with the Hungarians to provide syrup for Pepsi, made plans to pay for the film's production costs as a way to spend blocked currencies. When the project got underway, Pepsico's blocked currency reserve had been used up. However, the Hungarian government accepted the spending of the funds for the movie's production in lieu of countertrade requirements usually made when the Hungarians bought the soft drink syrup. Pepsico owns half the movie rights and will receive royalties from box office receipts.

CONTRACT CONSIDERATIONS

Drafting contracts for countertrade deals usually involves three parties (excluding barter which only involves two parties). The contracts must be carefully negotiated and prepared. Any omission or the attitude that small details are unnecessary could be devastating to the exporter. It is highly advisable for all parties to the countertrade deal to participate with your legal department, outside counsel, or outside specialists to assist in the drafting of the contracts.

The three contracts, although each a separate legal instrument, must somehow interrelate to each other. The three documents are:

1. The original contract for a sale by a Western export supplier. In effect, it is a standard sales contract or agreement.
2. The countertrade contract which sets forth the terms and

conditions of the original seller's obligation to purchase goods from the buyer in the first contract. The contract also calls for payment in hard currency for deliveries. It sets the terms for the seller to purchase goods at a later date, or over specified periods of time.

3. The protocol that serves to link the two contracts. This contract is under most circumstances, drafted last. It is in effect an "agreement to agree" under which both parties commit themselves to enter into their respective contract to purchase the other party's goods.[8]

The need for the first two contracts to be independent legally binding instruments is important because it permits each to obtain financing and credit risk guarantees or coverage from commercial banks or insurers. Banks and even insurers are usually reluctant to provide credit when the debtor's ability to repay the loan is contingent on the contractural performance of a third party (foreign). Two contracts actually provide more flexibility in regard to contract performance stipulations. For example, if one contract calls for delivery of goods within two to three years, the second contract should allow for counterdelivery of goods within five to ten years.

FINANCING

Contradictory as it may sound, parties to the countertrade deal, exclusive of barter, must still finance themselves until the contracts are fulfilled or completed. In this case, credit is used to enhance the countertrade deal, in conjunction with the ability of the buyer to pay for the goods purchased. In the case of compensation and production sharing joint ventures, credit arrangements are a must because the importer usually waits a number of years before the purchased equipment goes on stream, produces sales or revenues, and earns cash-flow or receives payment from the sale of goods to service its debt.

With the exception of compensation deals, most other countertrade deals usually only require short-term financing. The financing of countertrade involves such standard methods as government-supported credit programs, bank-to-bank credit lines, and buyer and supplier credit facilities. These were discussed in Chapters 6, 7, and 8. What type of financing to select depends on such things as the financial status or condition and needs of the supplier and buyer, the costs associated with the contracts, the tenure of the contracts, and the credit policies of the parties to the countertrade deal.

Large compensation countertrade deals usually involve government or private-supported credit facilities. It is not uncommon for government and private export credit facilities to be used in association with each other. Banks can provide cash flow loans which are usually secured by the resultant products by taking title to the goods as collateral or consignment of the bills of lading. As the goods are sold, the proceeds are collected by the bank and applied to the loan. This type of financing lends itself to project financing.

Guarantees

In cases of barter trade deals, both parties can protect themselves. It is done through the normal transfer of shipping documents for each set of goods being bartered in conjunction with a standby bank guarantee. Under this arrangement, the Western supplier requests that the second party's bank issue a standby letter of credit in the event the second party fails to meet its obligation under the deal, such as, failing to ship the goods as its part of the deal to the Western party. The standby letter of credit, in the event of default by the second party would entitle the Western party to draw against the credit for payment in the hard currency of the goods. In cases of uncertainty with the political or country condition of the second party's country, it is advisable for the Western party to have the letter of credit confirmed by a bank in its country.

It is conceivably possible for the second party to the barter deal to request the same protection from the Western party. In this case, it simply requests a standby letter of credit issued in its favor from the first party.

An alternative form of guarantee might be a performance bond. Since confirmed letters of credit are difficult to obtain from the People's Republic of China (PRC), performance bonds are a means for overcoming this problem. Since U.S. banks are not permitted by U.S. banking law to issue guarantees, a foreign branch of a U.S. bank can issue guarantees to secure the performance bond of the second party.

Supplier Credits

Western banks can make credit facilities available to suppliers by providing the refinancing necessary under most countertrade deals. In most cases, banks will link a line of credit to a supplier for specific deals because the supplier is short of cash flow until the countertrade deal is complete—meaning payment is deferred by the Western supplier to a foreign second party. Therefore, before the Western supplier enters into an actual countertrade deal by supplier goods or services, it should arrange or secure an extension of credit from its bank in the form of a supplier credit line facility. Usually, suppliers will supplement the banks facility by simultaneously arranging for its government-sponsored export credit guarantee to be assigned to the bank to reduce the bank's downside risks. Remember, banks and insurers are likely to provide financing and insurance coverage for countertrade deals that are composed of separate contacts.

Repayment by the supplier to its bank depends on the credit term arrangements agreed on by the parties to the deal. Although documentary letters of credit can be used, the element of trust is diminished and countertrade deals are predicated on a lot of trust for each to fulfill its agreed on commitment. The element of a documentary letter of credit, although a necessity in certain circumstances, is rather self-defeating and may destroy a countertrade deal under negotiation.

A more popular method where trading partners have a well-established relationship, each party feels comfortable with each other, or good reputation is established, is to settle payment by means of Documents against Payment.

Letters of Credit

Letters of credit are another means for settling certain countertrade deals. It not only reduces the element of commercial risk in the event the creditworthiness of trading partners is not well established, but also reduces the important element of country risk.

Letters of credit are more common in East European and Third World country deals than in the Soviet Union or China. Soviet trade officials consider a request by a Western trade partner for a letter of credit an insult to their creditworthiness. Letters of credit from China are difficult to get confirmed, if at all, and are untransferable through the Bank of China.

Buyer Credits

Supplier credits are normally supplemented by buyer credits under most countertrade deals which lets the borrower use the funds to finance deals with any country. Both supplier and buyer credits are eligible for official support in varying degrees through refinancing facilities, subsidized interest, and insurance against political risks. When credits are guaranteed by governments, however, use of the funds is normally tied to purchases in the country providing the credit. The countries belonging to the Council for Mutual Economic Assistance as well as the People's Republic of China urge their commercial enterprises and foreign trade organizations to use buyer credits as much as possible.[9]

REFERENCES

1. Charles H. Miller, "Centralized Approach to Countertrade Keys U.S. Export Growth", *CASHFLOW*, September 1985, pp. 35–38.
2. C. R. Cline, "Countertrade—An Age-Old Business in the 20th Century," *Quarterly Statistical Reports, The Chase World Guide for Exporters* (New York: World Information Corp., The Chase Manhattan Bank, Fall 1979), p. 1–3.
3. Charles J. Gmur, *Trade Financing* (London, England: Euromoney Publications Limited, 1981), p. 17.

4. Ibid., p. 23.
5. Ibid., p. 23.
6. Ibid., p. 23.
7. Louis J. Celi and I. James Czechowicz, *Export Financing: A Handbook of Sources & Techniques* (New York: Financial Executive Research Foundation, 1985), p. 301.
8. Leo G. B. Welt, *Trade Without Money: Barter and Countertrade* (New York: Harcourt Brace Jovanovich, 1984), p. 40.
9. Ibid., p. 66.

CONCLUSION

INTERNATIONAL BUSINESS CREDIT MANAGEMENT IN THE 1990s

In order to develop a successful export trade financing approach for the 1990s, U.S. companies will first have to believe and recognize one very important fact: the world is truly headed into a "New World Economy" where countries are dependent on each other's goods and services. Consequently, companies from around the globe will be more heavily dependent on the vagaries of the international marketplace than they have ever been before. While exporting can be profitable, a company's reliance on global trade does expose it to unexpected risks and severe competition both from within its home market and especially from abroad.

U.S. companies and our educational system must take international trade seriously. If not, foreign competition will gobble up all of the opportunities and position themselves to the point where nothing but a carcass is left for U.S. companies. For those companies who will be dependent on the U.S. marketplace for business, what will happen when you are faced with sagging domestic demand for your goods and services? Ever since the post World War II era began, foreign competition has been positioning itself in the international arena. Why do you think foreign competition today is swallowing up one U.S. company after another? U.S. companies must look abroad now to the enormous opportunities not only in the industralized markets of Western Europe and Japan, but to the faster growing economies in Asia/Pacific, and potentially strong economies in Latin America, the Middle East, and Africa.

What should U.S. companies be doing in order to compete in the 90s? Here are some thoughts that might work for your company:

Staff Yourself with Professional Credit People. Like any other department in your company, you should have the best people employed in your credit department—people who have the skills, experience, and expertise to finance export sales.

Develop Continuous Training Programs. Your company should devote the time and money to continually train not only credit people to develop better skills and ideas to finance international trade, but others in your company as well (i.e., accounting, marketing, and sales). It means not only developing internal training programs, but sending your people to external workshops, seminars, lectures and courses on international trade finance and international trade in general. Organizations such as the Finance Credit and International Business (FCIB), the American Management Association (AMA), the World Trade Institute, private consultants and banks all offer some excellent subject matter related to the aforementioned.

Better Integration of the Sales, Credit and Finance Functions. The conflicting and misunderstood objectives of sales, credit, and finance should be reduced by effective communication and integration between the functions. It can best be accomplished by the two functions clearly understanding the goals and strategies of each function. Does anyone in your company clearly understand what a credit department does and what it is all about? What about establishing objectives and projections jointly? Sales must be under a better credit and financial framework in which credit and finance policy is set and implemented while credit and finance must understand and support the export marketing objectives of sales.

Consider Establishing International Divisions or Departments. It permits centralized direction of a company's international operations and expertise under one umbrella. It concentrates international know-how and skills in a separate unit detached from domestic responsibilities. It makes it possible for a company's personnel to devote and concentrate their thoughts and efforts solely on international trade, expansion, and investment. Under a decentralized structure, personnel are constantly trapped between making domestic versus international decisions. Companies with a small percentage of exports versus domestic business usually treat exports with low priority, don't understand it, and lack the experience and expertise to handle it efficiently and effectively.

Invoice in Foreign Currencies. To meet or beat competition, you should be willing to invoice your exports to foreign customers in currencies other than your own. If foreign customers will accept invoices and drafts in currencies which are selling at a premium to the U.S. dollar, your products may be more competitively priced.

Risk Sharing between You as an Exporter and Financial Institutions. Due to the Third World debt situation, many financial institutions are unwilling to take additional risks or assume more debt in these nations. So don't expect them to. They might be willing to if you don't always look for 100 percent nonrecourse financing. You must be willing to share the risks (i.e., 70 percent for the bank, 30 percent for you). Or, it could take the form of a directly subsidized interest rate as a means to induce the making of a fixed rate loan. An exporter agreeing to hold a bank harmless from certain risks in the export transaction when the bank purchases export paper is another alternative. There are many different scenarios to risk sharing.

Reexamine Your Intercompany Payment Terms—Must They Always Be on Open Account? Problems of country risk and slow payment of intercompany receivables are often a difficult problem. A shift to D/A or D/P payment terms permits access to export trade finance. Banks might be more willing to finance an exporter's wholly-owned subsidiary or affiliate than a nonrelated foreign customer. The use of a negotiable draft better protects assests and might even spur an action by the subsidiary or affiliate (i.e., to pay or accept drafts before it gets goods). For example, the drafts may be used to access financing by selling the draft with or without recourse to a bank and telling the subsidiary or affiliate it must be paid on a timely basis because it has been sold to a third party. Such action might even encourage or inspire subsidiaries or affiliates to collect or clean up its own delinquent receivables.

You Should Consider the Following Export Trade Financing Alternatives.

1. Transactional financing—banks prefer it over other types of trade financing. There may be a cost savings by doing it. For example, discounting accepted documentary drafts with the accepting bank and/or using clean bankers' acceptance financing for your trade transactions.
2. Shift from sight to time letters of credit—it can prove to be more attractive to your foreign customers and you will gain access to documentary bankers' acceptance financing which is often cheaper than other alternatives. It is even off-balance sheet when discounted.
3. Shift from letters of credit to 90, 120, 150, or 180-day documents against acceptance (D/A)—accepted drafts may be sold to banks without recourse (if banks are willing to accept the risk); alternatively, they may be sold with recourse or on a limited recourse basis. You will still have the balance sheet advantage of exchanging a direct liability for a contingent one.

Colleges and Universities Should Develop Courses on Export Trade Finance and International Trade in General. Our institutions of higher learning must start offering full-time courses on the practical aspects of export trade finance and international trade in general. The time is now and it is vitally important to our economic and social future! Theory is fine and a necessity, but the practical side of international trade makes all the difference in the world on whether a sale and foreign customer is won or lost to foreign competition.

GLOSSARY

GENERAL TERMS

accept   To agree to pay at some future date a draft drawn on the accepting party.

acceptance   A draft which a drawee has agreed to pay at a future date.

account party   The party instructing a bank to open a letter of credit and on whose behalf the bank agrees to make payment. In most cases, the account party is a foreign customer or buyer, but alternatively, may be a construction contractor or a supplier bidding on a contract.

acquisition   A transaction in which any one company entity acquires a majority or minority ownership in another company. The same applies to financial institutions.

ad valorem   Method of levying duty which expresses charges as a percent of value of goods.

advice of fate   Notice given by the collecting bank to the remitting bank as to payment, acceptance, nonpayment, or nonacceptance of a draft presented at the remittings bank's request.

advised (in letters of credit)   A letter of credit whose authenticity has been verified by a bank, generally in the beneficiary's location. This bank then advises the beneficiary of the authenticity of the letter of credit, but does not take on any payment obligation unless otherwise so instructed on its letterhead.

advising bank   An exporter's domestic bank which handles letters of credit for a foreign (opening) bank by notifying the exporter (beneficiary) of an L/C opened in its favor.

affiliate   A company which directly or indirectly through one or more intermediaries controls, is controlled by, or is under common control with another company.

arbitrage   An operation in which foreign exchange, stocks, bonds, silver, gold, and other commodities are purchased in one market and sold in another market at a profit.

authority to pay   Similar to authority to purchase.

authority to purchase   One of the less commonly used methods of making payment for goods in international trade.

balance of payments (BOP)   A double-entry bookkeeping record of every transaction between a country and its trading partners during a particular period of time.

bank draft   A check, drawn by a bank on another bank.

bank guarantee   See guarantee.

bankers' acceptance (BA)   A draft drawn on a bank and bearing the bank's promise to pay at a future date. In the United States it is a BA which meets the requirements of the Federal Reserve Bank for discounting.

beneficiary   The party in whose favor a letter of credit is established or a draft is drawn.

bid   The quoted buying rate for a currency.

bid bonds   A financial guarantee given in support of the obligation of a bidder to sign a contract if it is successful in its bid.

bill of exchange (B/E)   Another name for a draft used in European trade transactions.

bill of lading   A document evidencing receipt of goods by a carrier and when properly drawn and endorsed gives title of the respective goods to the holder.

blocked account   An account that cannot be transferred freely into convertible currencies.

bond   A certificate of debt or debt instrument due to be paid by a government or company (usually corporations) to an individual holder and usually bearing a fixed rate of interest.

bonded warehouse   A warehouse in which goods subject to excise taxes and customs duties are temporarily stored without the taxes or duties being assessed until the goods are withdrawn from the warehouse.

branch   A separate banking unit that is part of a United States or foreign bank.

broker   An agent who arranges for the purchase or sale of foreign exchange between banks and companies, but who is not a principal in the transaction.

cable transfer   A type of remittance. Funds are transfered from one bank or company to a named party at another bank or company, using electronic transmission.

call money   Money, placed on deposit or loaned, which has no fixed term and no fixed rate of interest.

call rates   Interest rates at which call money can be deposited or loaned.

case-of-need   Name given to the party designated to act for a beneficiary of a draft if a drawee refuses to pay or accept a draft.

central bank swaps   The exchange between government central banks of deposits of each other's currency, usually to provide foreign exchange and enable each government to protect its own rates of exchange.

certificate of deposit (CD)   A negotiable form of a time deposit on which a bank pays principal at maturity. Interest may be paid at intervals or at maturity.

certificate of origin   Document attesting to the country of origin (manufacture) of an article in trade, or of one or more of its components.

chips   An acronym for the *C*learinghouse *I*nterbank *P*ayments *S*ystem, is a computer system operated by New York banks to settle international payments. Using CHIPS, checks are cleared, other instruments are exchanged, and net balances are settled among banks.

C & F   Term of sale denoting *c*ost and *f*reight.

CFF   *C*ooperative *f*inancing *f*acility (Export-Import Bank).

CIF   Term of sale denoting *c*ost, *i*nsurance, *f*reight.

clean draft (collection)   A draft without accompanying documents payable in dollars or in a foreign currency.

collateral   Assets or securities pledged as security for the repayment of a loan or line of credit such as, equipment, land, common stock, or buildings.

collection (item)   Items (i.e., drafts, notes, acceptances) that are received by a bank, subject to collection before being credited to the depositor's (exporter's) bank account.

collecting bank   Bank to which a remitting bank sends the draft and documents for collection (see remitting bank).

commercial bank   A bank that both accepts deposits and grants loans and, under certain stipulations in some countries like the United States, pays interest on checking accounts.

commercial invoice   Bill rendered by an exporter for goods shipped; it is one of the documents normally accompanying an export draft.

commercial paper   In international trade (as distinguished from customary usage in domestic finance), any draft or other item to be presented for collection.

commercial risk   In export financing/trade, the risk of the foreign customer's ability and willingness to repay.

commission   A bank charge for creating a bankers' acceptance expressed as a percent per annum (per year). A percentage paid by exporters to agents, distributors, and others for services rendered based on sales of goods and services.

common carrier   An individual, partnership, or corporation such as a railroad or steamship line, which undertakes for hire to transport persons or commodities from place to place. Governed by special business offered them within their regulations.

compensating balances   A banking practice in the United States whereby the lending bank requires the borrower to maintain deposit balances equal to a specified percentage of the loan amount and/or the commitment.

competitive devaluation   A devaluation greater than the extent required to bring equilibrium to the balance of payments in an effort to make exports more competitively priced.

compound (duty)   Method of charging duty combining specific and ad valorem duties.

confirm (a letter of credit)   To assume an obligation to pay under a letter of credit.

consignment   Method of payment for exports by which title of goods does not pass to an importer, and goods are not paid for, until they are sold to a third party.

consular invoice   Document, issued by consul of country of destination, covering a shipment of goods.

contract   A business agreement, particularly the written evidence of the agreement. A standby letter of credit is based on, but distinct from, the business agreement outlined in the contract.

contract limit   A limit established between a bank and a customer which sets forth the amount of foreign exchange contracts the bank will have outstanding (open) at any one time for a customer.

convertibility   The ability of a company or individual owner of a currency to exchange its currency for other foreign currencies or gold in the open or black markets.

convertible currency   A currency that can be freely exchanged for other main currencies.

conversion exposure   The exposure inherent in the conversion or translation of a foreign subsidiary's balance sheet into the consolidated corporate balance sheet.

convertible   A feature of certain bonds, debentures, or preferred stocks which allows them to be exchanged by the owner for another class of securities, in accordance with the terms of the issue.

cooperative financing facility (CFF)   A program of the Export-Import Bank providing funds to banks abroad for lending to foreign buyers of U.S. goods.

corporate or company guarantee   See guarantee.

correspondent bank   A bank which is a depository for another bank and which performs various banking services for its depositor throughout the world.

correspondent relationships   The agreement which governs transactions between two banks.

country credit limit   The limit established by a bank on a particular country which is the maximum amount of credit the bank will expose itself to regarding that country. Conversely, the same can apply with companies who wish to limit their credit exposures to particular countries.

country risk   Refers to the acceptance of a country's political, economic, social, foreign exchange, and internal/external risk conditions when accepting the risk of a foreign customer.

covering   The purchase or sale of a foreign currency spot or forward to reduce the risk of rate fluctuations.

credit   A term used interchangeably with letters of credit.

credit limit   The limit established by a bank on a customer which is the maximum amount of credit the bank will expose itself to on that customer. Conversely, it is the limit established by a company on a foreign customer which is the maximum amount of credit the company will expose itself to on that foreign customer.

cross rates   The rates of two currencies calculated from the rates of a common currency (Canada/U.S. rate and U.S. dollar/Pound Rate, to obtain Canada/G.B. Pound [Sterling Rate]).

customs invoice   A document that contains a declaration by the seller, the shipper, or the agent of either as to the value of the goods covered.

D/A   *D*ocument against *a*cceptance, an instruction given for presentation of time drafts, denoting that the accompanying documents are to be released on acceptance of a draft by the drawee.

debenture   An obligation secured by the general credit of the issuer rather than being backed by a specific lien on property.

debt service   The payment of principal and interest on a loan.

deferred payment credit   A type of export letter of credit providing for payment some time after presentation of the shipping document by the exporter.

del credere agent   Sales agent who, for a certain percentage over and above its sales commission, will guarantee payment to the person for whom it is selling, on shipment made to the seller's customers.

demand deposit   A bank deposit that may be withdrawn by the depositor at any time without prior notice of intended withdrawal.

depletion   An income tax deduction figured as a percent of the gross income received from the sale of natural resources, computed property-by-property. Formulas for depletion vary from country to country.

devaluation   A downward change in the value of a currency in relation to another currency.

development bank   A lending agency that provides assistance to encourage the establishment of productive facilities in different countries.

disc   See *D*omestic *I*nternational *S*ales *C*orporation.

direct collection   A service offered to a company with export collection activity in order to expedite the processing of export collections and accelerate payments. The remitting bank provides the collection forms which the company, rather than the bank, prepares and mails with any accompanying documentation to the overseas collecting bank. Copies of the collection form are sent to the remitting bank for control and for followup if payment and/or acceptance is not received.

discount   The difference between the spot rate and the forward rate, resulting in a lower forward rate in foreign exchange. An amount equivalent to a rate of interest which is deducted from the face value of a bankers' acceptance at the time of the sale. An amount which a foreign customer can deduct from its payment if payment is made within a specified period of time as stated in a company's payment terms.

dishonor (a draft)   To refuse to pay or accept a draft on presentation.

documents   Refers to items presented to foreign customers and/or banks for collection in accordance with stipulated payment terms mutually agreed on by all parties to the export transaction. These items could include, but are not limited to, bills of lading, commercial invoices, customs invoices, a marine insurance policy or certificate, a certificate of origin, and packing lists.

documentary Refers to drafts on other items for collection, denotes that documents are attached for delivery to a specified party on specified terms and conditions; opposite of clean drafts (see drafts).

documentary collection An export collection in which a draft is accompanied by shipping or other documents.

documentary credit A credit that requires export documents to accompany the draft or demand for payment.

domestic international sales corporation (DISC) Type of company authorized by the U.S. Revenue Act of 1971 to remove tax disadvantage suffered by U.S. exporters in competition with those in other countries. In 1984 Congress passed the Deficit Reduction Act of 1984, which authorized the creation of foreign sales corporations (FSC), replacing DISC. Small exporters may continue to use DISC under revised and less favorable rules.

D/P *D*ocuments against *p*ayment, an instruction given for presentation of sight drafts, denoting that accompanying documents are to be released on payment of the draft.

draft Instrument by which one party directs another party to make payment and/or acceptance.

drawee The party named on a check or draft from whom payment of the draft is expected.

drawer The party who orders, in a bill or draft, that money be paid over to a third party by the drawee.

drawing The presentation of drafts and/or documents required by the terms of a letter of credit.

Edge Act (bank) A subsidiary of a U.S. bank, established under section 25(a) of the U.S. Federal Reserve Act passed on December 24, 1919 with the title, "Banking Corporations Authorized to do Foreign Banking Business." Regulation K governs operations of Edge Act Corporations. Their purpose is to aid in financing and stimulating international trade.

equity The ownership interest of preferred and common stockholders in a company.

Eurocurrency Deposits of foreign currencies placed with a bank outside the monetary control of those currencies.

Eurodollars Deposits of U.S. dollars in foreign banks, or U.S. banks outside U.S. Federal Reserve jurisdiction.

Eurodollar market   The markets which deal in Eurodollars and Eurocurrencies for lending and borrowing.

European Economic Community (EEC)   An organization composed of Belgium, Denmark, France, W. Germany, Great Britain, Ireland, Italy, Luxembourg, The Netherlands, and most recently Spain and Greece. The intent of the integration of these member countries is to promote the economic efficient regional development of the member countries and to enhance Europe's economic power in the world, via negotiated management of exchange rates, a common external tariff, and free internal trade. Ultimate objectives include a common monetary and fiscal policy, free movement of factors of production, and common currency (i.e., the idea behind the European Monetary System).

exchange exposure   The risk occurring whenever an asset or liability resulting from a transaction is expressed in a currency other than that in which the corporate books are kept.

exchange rate   The price of one currency in terms of another at a given moment in time.

exchange rate risk   The risk due to fluctuations in foreign exchange transactions.

exchange spread   The difference between the buying and selling rates for a given currency.

ex dock   Term of sale denoting that the seller bears all costs of transporting the goods to dock at port of importation.

Eximbank   The Export-Import Bank of the United States is an independent corporate agency of the United States. The bank's purpose is to aid in financing and to facilitate exports.

export credit insurance   A system to underwrite the collection of credits extended by exporters against various contingencies (commercial and political risks). In some countries only noncommercial risks can be insured. This type of insurance is usually underwritten by either public or private organizations or insurance companies, or both, in different countries.

export management company (EMC)   This is a company that performs export functions for companies, manufacturers, or producers usually on an exclusive basis. They handle all details to an export transaction such as, sales, shipments, documentation, collections and payments.

export trading company (ETC)   These are companies that purchase U.S. goods from companies for resale in foreign countries. ETCs usually have large and efficient sales, distribution, and service networks throughout the world.

FAS   Term of sale denoting *free along side*.

FCIA   *F*oreign *C*redit *I*nsurance *A*ssociation is an association of leading insurance companies, operating in cooperation with and as agent of the Export-Import Bank of the United States (Eximbank). It offers insurance policies protecting U.S. exporters against the risks of nonpayment by foreign debtors.

federal funds   The U.S. dollar balances of a member bank with a Federal Reserve Bank. They are equivalent to fully cleared balances on deposit and these may also be referred to as *good funds, available funds* and *cleared funds*.

fiduciary   An individual, company, or association, such as a bank or trust company, to whom certain property is given to hold in trust, according to the trust agreement or its by-laws.

financial guarantee   Form of guarantee issued by the Export-Import Bank in connection with large export transactions.

first of exchange   Phrase appearing on the original of a draft when a duplicate also is being presented (this practice, common when mail went by steamer and was subject to long delays, has largely been discountinued with use of air mail).

fixed foreign exchange rate   A rate that is based on a fixed parity whose fluctuation is confined to a specified spread above and below that parity.

floating foreign exchange rate   A rate which is either not based on a parity or the parity is not enforced, leaving the rate to fluctuate freely.

foreign draft   A draft drawn by any bank or other drawer in one country on a bank or other drawee in another country.

foreign exchange   Refers to the buying and selling of foreign currencies, for immediate or future delivery.

forward/future exchange   Foreign currencies bought or sold for delivery at a specified future date.

free port   Port where merchandise may be stored duty free while awaiting reshipment or while on consignment awaiting sale.

free trade zone (FTZ)   Specific area, in or near a port, offering duty-free storage on the same basis as a free port.

GATT   The *G*eneral *A*greement on *T*ariffs and *T*rade was established in 1947. It is a framework of rules for countries to manage their trade policies. It also provides a forum in which disputes can be negotiated.

general partnership   See limited partnership.

guarantee An undertaking or contract to give assurance that a thing will be done, or an obligation will be fulfilled, as promised. In business transactions, a formal assurance given as security that another's debt or obligation will be fulfilled. Guarantees can be issued by banks, companies, and individuals.

hard currency Convertible currency likely to appreciate in value.

hedging Fixing the local currency value of exposures in a foreign currency by entering into forward exchange contracts.

honor (a draft) To pay or accept, as the case may be, on presentation.

inland shipping document Bill of lading or other receipt evidencing shipment from point of origin to port or other intermediate point, rather than to final destination.

interest The price or compensation paid for use of money over a period of time. It is expressed as a percentage of the amount of money borrowed or used for a period of time.

intervention The process by which governments buy and sell currencies in an effort to affect exchange rates according to a predetermined policy.

investment bank A type of financial institution whose main function is to locate and collect funds for clients so they can finance new investment projects. Investment banks engage in buying and selling securities, such as stocks, bonds, and mortgages. They also act as intermediaries between companies, who want funds for such improvements as new equipment, new buildings, or plant expansions, and the investor, who wants to invest its savings. Investment banks may promote a new industry, handle the finances of a companys' expansion purposes, or act as brokers with other investment banking firms in the flotation of stocks and bonds.

irrevocable credit A letter of credit that cannot be changed or cancelled without the consent of all parties involved.

joint venture A term used to describe any jointly owned company or partnership which owns, operates, or constructs a project. More specifically, an arrangement between two or more entities for the joint management or operation of a project under an Operating Agreement which is not a partnership. Tax consequences are different than a partnership or business firm corporation in that income and costs are flowed through to the entities to the joint venture who can make independent tax elections. Tax treatment for joint ventures vary from country to country. A new commonly used term for joint venture is a strategic alliance.

leading and lagging   Premature or delayed payments in anticipation of a more favorable exchange rate.

legal lending limit   A limit under the U.S. National Banking Act which states the total obligations to any national banking association of any person, co-partnership, association, or company shall at no time exceed 10 percent of the amount of the capital stock of such association actually paid in and unimpaired, and 10 percent of its unimpaved surplus fund. There are numerous qualifications and exceptions to the limit.

legal reserves   The portion of its deposits which a bank is required by law to maintain in the form of cash or readily available balances to meet the demands of depositors.

letter of credit   A bank's commitment to a designated beneficiary to pay drafts drawn by the beneficiary up to a stated amount and within a stated time provided specified conditions are met by the beneficiary.

letter of instruction   Directions given by an exporter, to be followed by a bank presenting a draft and/or accompanying documents for acceptance or payment.

LIBOR   An acronym for the *L*ondon *I*nter*b*ank *O*ffered *R*ate. The interest rate at which banks in London place Eurocurrency/ Eurodollar deposits with each other for a specific period of time.

limited partnership   In the United States, a partnership consisting of one or more general partners, jointly and severally responsible as ordinary partners, by whom the business is conducted; and one or more limited partners, contributing in cash payments a specific sum as capital and who are not liable for the debts of the partnership beyond the funds so contributed. Basically, there are two classes of partnerships. General Partnerships manage the business and are liable for debts and obligations of the partnership over and above their investment. Limited Partnerships contribute capital, are not active in management, and are not liable beyond their investments in the partnership. A Limited Partnership must have at least one general partner. Some of the legal aspects between the two types of partnerships vary from country to country.

line of credit   A commitment of a bank to a borrower (company, foreign bank, foreign customer, or country) to extend a series of credits to the borrower under certain terms and conditions up to an agreed maximum amount. A line of credit may include issuance of a succession of letters of credit, acceptances and/or of multiple loans or advances, and other forms of credit. Conversely, a company can have lines of credit established for its foreign customer and even countries. Usually lines of credit are established as credit control guidelines.

liquidity The ability to convert a security into cash promptly with minimum risk to principal. Current assets which can readily be converted into cash (liquid assets).

loan collection Method of financing by which an exporter borrows on basis of drafts turned over to a bank for collection.

maturity The date on which any obligation to pay money becomes due and payable, such as, the maturity of drafts, open account invoices, or bank or company notes.

merchant bank A European form of an investment bank.

merger The business combination of two or more companies or financial institution entities. Company mergers involve the exchange of securities, assets, exchange of stock, or even the issuance of new securities or both.

money market The market for shorter-term securities, generally those with one year or less remaining to maturity, handled by such financial institutions as commercial banks, savings, banks, trust companies, insurance companies, stock brokerage firms, investment banks, investors, or mortgage banks.

multi-currency term loan A loan made by a bank to a company for a stipulated period of time and in one or more of several currencies.

multilateral netting A system generally offered by financial institutions to multinational companies to cut down the number of transactions necessary to complete international payments.

multinational corporation (MNC) A company having divisions, subsidiaries, branches, or joint ventures—operations in more than one foreign country.

multiple exchange rates A condition in which several different rates of exchange exist relative to the different types of foreign exchange transactions or instruments being used, such as exports/imports, or tourist rates.

negotiable instrument Any written evidence of a payment obligation which may be transferred by endorsement or by delivery, such as checks, bills of exchange, drafts, promissory notes, and some types of bonds or securities, and of which the transferee may become a holder in due course.

negotiation To verify that the documents presented under a letter of credit conform to the requirements and then, if the documents are in order, to pay the seller of goods (beneficiary).

negotiation credit   A credit that permits any bank that is willing to do so, to negotiate (usually in the locality of the beneficiary) on or before the expiration date; the engagement clause to honor drafts is in favor of drawers, endorsers, or bona fide holders.

net worth   See shareholders equity.

nostro accounts   Current accounts of banks with their correspondents.

note (promissory note)   An instrument recognized as legal evidence of debt that is signed by the maker, promising to pay a certain sum of money, on a specified date, at a certain place of business, to the payee or other holder of the note.

offer   A quoted selling rate or price of a currency.

open (a letter of credit)   To establish or issue a letter of credit.

open account   A method of settling an export transaction without the use of negotiable instruments evidencing obligations to pay, typically the exporter presents a commercial invoice for payment to a foreign customer with stated payment terms, terms of sale and payment conditions.

opening bank   A bank which establishes or issues a letter of credit.

option future contracts   Commercial forward exchange contracts that have a flexible delivery date, between two specific periods of time, normally one calendar month.

par value (parity)   The official per unit worth of a currency based on a determined value content, such as gold.

participation financing   A program of the Export-Import Bank for financing large projects in foreign countries utilizing U.S. exports.

payee   The party named on a check or draft as recipient of the payment.

PEFCO   The *P*rivate *E*xport *F*unding *C*orporation; lends to foreign customers to finance exports from the United States.

pegged rate   An exchange rate which is connected to another currency by an official fixed value.

performance bond   A bond supplied by one entity to protect another against loss in the event of default of an existing contract.

personal guarantee   See guarantee.

political risk   In export trade and financing, the risk of loss due to such causes as currency inconvertibility, government action preventing entry of goods, expropriation or confiscation, war, riot, or revolution.

por aval   It is a promise to pay, written directly by using the words *por aval* plus an authorized signature onto the document, representing an unconditional and irrevocable guarantee of payment. When it is stated on drafts (bills of exchange), it is necessary to stipulate that the aval is given on behalf of the drawee.

premium   The difference between spot and forward rates which results in a higher forward rate.

presentation   Presentation of an incoming collection to the drawee, the named payer. Under a letter of credit it is the time the draft and/or documents are presented to the appropriate bank, usually the negotiating or paying bank.

protest   The formal legal process of demanding payment of a negotiable item from the maker or drawee who has refused to pay or accept the instrument.

quota   A physical limit, mandatory or voluntary, set on the import of a product. It is a common form of nontariff barrier. GATT rules are more permissive on quotas than on tariffs.

recourse   A term which defines the rights of the holder in due course of a negotiable instrument to force prior endorsers to meet their legal obligations by making payment on the instrument should it be dishonored by the maker or acceptor.

remittance   A transfer of funds from one place to another. A remittance may or may not be payment of an obligation.

remitting bank   A bank which sends a draft to an overseas bank for collection (see collecting bank).

revaluation   An upward change in the value of a currency against another.

revocable credit   A letter of credit that can be changed or cancelled by the issuing bank, up until the time payment is made.

shareholders equity   The book value of the net assest (total assets minus total liabilities) is called shareholder's equity, or net worth. Accounts which comprise net worth in the United States are preferred stock, common stock, paid-in surplus, and retained earnings. Deferred accounts and reserve accounts such as reserves for pensions, while generally not thought of as true equity, are not considered equity, except in certain countries (i.e., countries in Latin America).

short   Refers to the situation of being oversold, or having a deficit of foreign exchange.

sight draft   A draft payable immediately on presentation or on demand, pursuant to the instructions of the drawer, by the drawee.

soft or weak currency   A currency which at a given moment is prone to devaluation.

sole of exchange Phrase appearing on a draft to indicate no duplicate is being presented (this usage dates from times when it was customary to send duplicate drafts because of possible delays due to steamer mail).

special drawing rights (SDRs) An International Monetary Fund created medium of exchange for transactions between central banks and the IMF SDRs constitute part of the monetary reserves of a country.

spot transactions A foreign exchange transaction with a settlement date for within the next one or two business days. In trading terminology, spot means a specific date which depends on the currency under discussion and the geographic area in which the discussion takes place.

stale dated (documents) Documents dated or not presented within reasonable time after issuance.

straight credit A letter of credit in which the opening bank limits its promise to pay to the beneficiary.

subordinated debt All debt (short and long term) which, by agreement, is subordinate to senior debt. It does not include reserve accounts or deferred credits.

swap transactions The simultaneous purchase or sale on a near date against a sale or purchase on a far date of the same amount of foreign currency.

SWIFT An acronym for *S*ociety for *W*orldwide *I*nformation and *F*unds *T*ransfer. This international system and organization has been established to move funds and information among member banks.

term loan A loan with an original maturity beyond one year. Loans with maturities of one year or less are classed as "short-term" credits.

tariff A duty or tax on imports that can be either a percentage of cost or a specific amount per unit of import.

time draft A draft payable in a specified number of days "after sight" (after presentation) or "after date" (date draft is drawn).

trade acceptance A time draft drawn by the exporter of goods on the buyer and accepted by the buyer for payment at a specified future date.

trust receipt An instrument by which an accredited importer may obtain possession of goods (but not title to them) before paying or accepting a draft.

UCP An acronym for the *U*niform *C*ustoms and *P*ractices for Documentary Credits. It is a publication issued by the International

Chamber of Commerce, Publication No. 400, 1983 revision, which outlines the rules and guidelines involved in letter of credit transactions. Their provisions are followed by a vast majority of banks and exporters throughout the world.

unclean bill of lading   Also known as a foul bill of lading, this is a lading that has written across its face, stating exceptions to the receipt of merchandise "in apparent poor order" are noted, exceptions such as, bursted bales, rusted goods, or external packing damage.

usance (time)   A term used to denote a period of time between presentation of a draft and its maturity.

value date   The day or date on which foreign exchange transactions are to be settled.

warehouse receipt   An instrument which lists, and is a receipt for goods or commodities, deposited in the warehouse which issues the receipt. These receipts may be negotiable or nonnegotiable. A negotiable warehouse receipt is made to the "bearer," while a nonnegotiable warehouse receipt specifies to whom the goods shall be delivered.

BIBLIOGRAPHY

CHAPTER 1

A Basic Guide to Exporting. Washington, D.C.: U.S. Department of Commerce, 1981.

Brooke, Michael Z., and H. Lee Remmers. *The Strategy of Multinational Enterprise: Organization and Finance.* New York: American Elsevier, 1970.

Christie, George N., and Albert E. Bracuti. *Credit Management Handbook.* Lake Success, New York: The Credit Research Foundation, 1981.

The Export Trading Company Guidebook. Washington, D.C.: U.S. Department of Commerce, International Trade Administration, March 1984.

International Credit Executives Minutes. New York: N.Y.: FCIB–NACM Corporation, 1973–1988.

Robock, Stefan H., and Kenneth Simmonds. *International Business and Multinational Enterprises,* 4th ed. Homewood, Ill.: Richard D. Irwin, 1989.

Sweeny, Allen, and Robert Rachlin. *Handbook of International Financial Management.* New York: McGraw-Hill Book Company, 1984.

Walker, Allen J. *Credit and Financial Management.* New York: National Association of Credit Management, May 1967.

CHAPTER 2

Aabel-Malek, Talaat. "Managing Exchange Risks Under Floating Rates: The Canadian Experience." *Columbia Journal of World Business,* Fall 1976.

Aggarwal, Ray. *Financial Policies for the Multinational Company: The Management of Foreign Exchange*. New York: Praeger, 1976.

Aliber, Robert Z. *Exchange Risk and Corporate International Finance*. New York: Wiley, 1979.

Antl, Boris, and Albert G. Henry. "The Case for a Coordinated Hedge." *Euromoney*, May 1980.

Ensor, Richard. *Assessing Country Risk*. London, U.K.: Euromoney Publications, 1981.

Aubey, R. T., and R. H. Cramer. "Use of International Currency Cocktails in the Reduction of Exchange Rate Risk." *Journal of Economics and Business*, Winter 1977.

Biger, Nahum. "Exchange Risk Implications of International Portfolio Diversification." *Journal of International Business Studies*, Fall 1979.

Calderon-Rossel, Jorge R. "Covering Foreign Exchange Risks of Single Transactions: A Framework for Analysis." *Financial Management*, Autumn 1979.

Christie, George N., and Albert E.Bracuti. *Credit Management Handbook*. Lake Success, New York: The Credit Research Foundation, 1981.

Christofides, N., R. D. Hewins, and G. R. Salkin. "Graph Theoretic Approaches to Foreign Exchange Operations." *Journal of Financial and Quantitative Analysis*, September 1979.

Donaldson, J. A. *Corporate Currency Risk*. London: Financial Times Business Information, Ltd., 1980.

Dukes, Ronald. *An Empirical Investigation of the Effects of Statement of Financial Accounting Standards No. 8 on Security Return Behavior*. Stamford, Conn.: Financial Accounting Standards Board, 1978.

Dynamics of Trade Finance. Gillette, N.J.: Global Business Communications, Inc., 1984.

Eaker, Mark, R. "Denomination Decision for Multinational Transactions." *Financial Management*, Autumn 1980.

Eiteman, David K., and Arthur P. Stonehill. *Multinational Business Finance*. Reading, Mass., Addison-Wesley, 1982.

Evans, Thomas G., William R. Folks, Jr., and Michael Jilling. *The Impact of Statement of Financial Accounting Standards No. 8 on the Foreign Exchange Risk Management Practices of American Multinationals: An Economic Impact Study*. Stamford, Conn.: Financial Accounting Standards Board, 1978.

"FASB No. 8 and Reported Results of Multinational Operations: Hazard for Managers and Investors." *Journal of Accounting, Auditing and Finance*, Spring 1978.

Fitzsimons, Robert B. "Exposure Management Is Too Important to be Left to the Treasurer." *Euromoney,* March 1979.

Folks, William R., Jr. "Decision Analysis for Exchange Risk Management." *Financial Management,* Winter 1978.

Giddy, Ian H. "Why It Doesn't Pay to Make a Habit of Forward Hedging." *Euromoney,* December 1976.

George, Abraham M. *Foreign Exchange Management and the Multinational Corporation.* New York: Praeger, 1978.

George, Abraham M., and Barry L. Klein. "Hedging Foreign Currency Exposure on an After-Tax Basis." *University of Michigan Business Review,* November 1976.

Global Business Communications, Inc. *The Chase World Guide for Exporters.* Gillette, N.J.

Hagemann, Helmut. "Anticipate Your Long-Term Foreign Exchange Risks." *Harvard Business Review,* March/April 1977.

Hollis, Martha. "A Decentralized Foreign Exchange Risk Model." *Management International Review,* Vol. 3, 1980.

Howlett, Keith. "Forward Hedging Does Pay, Because the Long Run is Too Long." *Euromoney,* April 1977.

Kenyon, Alfred. *Currency Risk Management,* New York: Wiley, 1981.

Lever, Harold, and Christopher Hukne. "*Debt and Danger.*" Boston and *The Atlantic Monthly Press,* 1986.

Mattlin, Everett. "How Corporations Are Playing the Currency Game." *Institutional Investor,* May 1976.

"Some Aspects of Exchange Risk Policies Under Floating Rates." *Journal of International Business Studies,* Fall/Winter 1976.

Sweeny, Allen, and Robert Rachlin. *Handbook of International Financial Management.* New York: McGraw-Hill Book Company, 1984.

CHAPTER 3

A Basic Guide to Exporting. Washington, D.C.: U.S. Department of Commerce, Nov. 1981.

Boyalic, Arthur E. *The Documentation Dilemna in International Trade.* New York: Columbia Journal of World Business, Fall 1982.

Clean Bills of Lading. The International Chamber of Commerce, Pub. No. 283, 1963.

Combined Transport Documents. The International Chamber of Commerce, Pub. No. 298, 1975.

Dynamics of Trade Finance. Gillette, N.J.: Global Business Communications, Inc., 1984.

Eiteman, David K., and Arthur P. Stonehill. *Multinational Business Finance*. Reading, Mass: Addison-Wesley, 1982.

Guide to Incoterms. The International Chamber of Commerce, Pub. No. 354, 1980.

Manring, A. B. *Exporting From The U.S.A*. Vancouver, Canada: International Self-Counsel Press Ltd., 1981.

CHAPTER 4

A Basic Guide to Exporting. Washington, D.C.: U.S. Department of Commerce, Nov. 1981.

Documentary Credits: Standard Documentary Credit Forms, Guidance Notes—Recommendations. The International Chamber of Commerce, Pub. No. 416, 1986.

Documentary Credits: Standard Documentary Credit Application, Guidance Notes for Credit Applicants. The International Chamber of Commerce, Pub. No. 416 A, 1986.

Documentary Credits: UCP 1974/1983 Revisions, Compared and Explained. The International Chamber of Commerce, Pub. No. 411, 1984.

Guide to Documentary Credit Operations. The International Chamber of Commerce, Pub. No. 415, 1985.

Dynamics of Trade Finance. Gillette, N.J.: Global Business Communications, Inc., 1984.

Manring, A. B. *Exporting From the U.S.A*. Vancouver, Canada: International Self-Counsel Press Ltd., 1981.

Trade Financing. London, U.K.: Euromoney Publications, 1981.

CHAPTER 5

Beehler, Paul J. *Contemporary Cash Management: Principles, Practices and Perspectives*. New York: Wiley, 1983.

Documentary Credits: UCP 1974/1983 Revisions, Compared and Explained. The International Chamber of Commerce, Pub. No. 411, 1984.

Dynamics of Trade Finance. New York, N.Y.: The Chase Manhattan Bank, N.A., 1984.

Morgan Guaranty Trust Co. of New York. *The Financing of Exports and Imports*. New York: Morgan Guaranty Trust Co., 1980.

Trade Financing. London, U.K.: Euromoney Publications, 1981.

CHAPTER 6

First National Bank of Chicago. *National Export Credit Programs.* Chicago: The First National Bank of Chicago, 1983.

Manring, A. B. *Exporting From the U.S.A.* Vancouver, Canada: International Self-Counsel Press Ltd., 1981.

Sweeny, Allen, and Robert Rachlin. *Handbook of International Financial Management.* New York: McGraw-Hill Book Company, 1984.

CHAPTER 7

Bruce, J., and J. Pierce. "Understanding the Export Trading Company Act and Using (or Avoiding) Its Antitrust Exemptions." 38 *Bus. Law* 975 (1983).

Figate, W. "The Export Trade Exception to the Antitrust Laws: The Old Webb-Pomerene Act and the New Export Trading Company Act." 15 *Vand. J. of Transnat'l Law* 673, 1982.

Golden, C., and C. Kolb. "The Export Trading Company Act of 1982: An American Response to Foreign Competition." 58 *Notre Dame Law Rev.* 743, 1983.

Griffin, J., ed. *The Export Trading Company Act of 1982.* International Law Institute, Georgetown University Law Center, 1982.

LaMont, N., and D. Unkovic. "The Export Trading Company Act of 1982: Invitation to Aggressive Export Expansion." 87 *Dick L. Rev.* 205, 1983.

New Opportunities under the Export Trading Company Act of 1982. Law & Business, Inc., 1983.

Sweeny, Allen, and Robert Rachlin. *Handbook of International Financial Management.* New York: McGraw-Hill Book Company, 1984.

The Export Trading Company Act. Practicing Law Institute, 1983.

Zarin, D. "The Export Trading Company Act: Reducing Antitrust Uncertainity in Export Trade." 17 *Geo. Wash. J. Int'l & Econ.* 29, 1983.

CHAPTER 8

Curtin, Donald. "The Unchartered $4 Billion World of Forfaiting." *Fortune,* August 1980.

Duffield, Jeremy G., and B. J. Summers. "Bankers' Acceptances."

Instruments of the Money Market. Federal Reserve Bank of Richmond, 1981.

Forfaiting: An Alternative Approach to Export Trade Finance. The International Chamber of Commerce, Pub. No. 900, 1984.

Gershman, Michael. *Smarter Barter*. New York: Viking Penguin Inc., 1986.

Guild, Ian, and Rhodri Harris. *Forfaiting, An Alternative Approach To Export Trade Finance*. New York: Universe Books Publications, 1986.

Hartfield, Henry. *Bank Credits and Acceptances*. New York: Wiley, 1974.

Eli, Louis J., and James I. Czechowicz. *Export Financing: A Handbook of Sources & Techniques*. Business International, N.J.: Financial Executives Research Foundation, 1985.

Trade Financing. London, U.K.: Euromoney Publications, 1981.

CHAPTER 9

Gmur, Charles J. *Trade Financing*. London, U.K.: Euromoney Publications, 1981.

U.S. Department of Commerce. *International Countertrade—A Guide for Managers and Executives*, 1983.

Verzariu, Pompiliu. *Countertrader, Barter, Offsets: New Strategies for Profit in International Trade*. New York: McGraw Hill, 1986.

Welt, Leo G. B. *Trade Without Money: Barter and Countertrade*. New York: Law & Business, Inc. (Harcourt Brace Jovanovich), 1984.

INDEX